MW00993942

Conversational
Latin
for Oral Proficiency

—— THIRD EDITION ——

PHRASE BOOK AND DICTIONARY

—— JOHN C. TRAUPMAN ——

Bolchazy-Carducci Publishers, Inc.
Wauconda, Illinois USA

Conversational Latin
for Oral Proficiency

General editors:
Laurie Haight Keenan
Georgine Cooper

Bolchazy-Carducci Publishers, Inc.
1000 Brown Street
Wauconda, IL 60084 U.S.A.

http://www.bolchazy.com

International Standard Book Number:
Softbound 0-86516-438-X

Printed in the United States of America
2003
by Bang Printing

Enlarged 2003 edition (2nd edition 1999; 1st edition 1997)

Library of Congress Cataloging-in-Publication Data

Traupman, John C.
  Conversational Latin for oral proficiency / John C. Traupman ; general editors, Laurie Haight Keenan, Georgine Cooper.— 3rd ed.
      p. cm.
   ISBN 0-86516-438-X
  1. Latin language—Conversation and phrase books. 2. Latin language, Colloquial. I. Keenan, Laurie Haight. II. Cooper, Georgine. III. Title.

  PA2107.T74 2003
  478.3'421—dc21

                                          2003012183

Other Publications by the Author

The New College Latin & English Dictionary, Second Edition, 1994. Amsco School Publications, Inc., 315 Hudson Street, New York, NY 10013-1085. ISBN 0-87720-561-2. Second Edition, 1995.
Simultaneously published by Bantam Books, Inc., 1540 Broadway, New York, NY 10036. ISBN 0-553-57301-2.

Latin is Fun: Book I: Lively Lessons for Beginners. Amsco, 1989. ISBN 0-87720-550-7. *Teacher's Manual and Key.* Amsco, 1989. ISBN 0-87720-554-X.

Latin is Fun: Book II: Lively Lessons for Beginners. Amsco, 1995. ISBN 0-87720-565-5. *Teacher's Manual with Answers.* Amsco, 1995. ISBN 0-87720-567-1.

The New College German & English Dictionary. Amsco, 1981. ISBN 0-87720-584-1. Bantam, 1981. ISBN 0-533-14155-4.

German Fundamentals: Basic Grammar and Vocabulary. 1992. Barron's Educational Series, Inc., Hauppauge, NY 11788.

Lingua Latina: Book I Latin First Year. Amsco, 1999, ISBN 1-56765-426-6 (Hardbound); ISBN 1-56765-425-8 (Softbound).
Teacher's Manual and Key, 1999, ISBN 1-56765-428-2.

Lingua Latina: Book II: Latin Second Year. Amsco, 2001, ISBN 1-56765-429-0 (Softbound);
Teacher's Manual and Key, Amsco, 2001, ISBN 1-56765-431-2.

Also Available from Bolchazy-Carducci Publishers

Conversational Latin for Oral Proficiency
Audio Cassette

(2000) Cassette, ISBN 0-86516-475-4

Contents

Boy meets girl.
Mario runs into his friend Julia.
Tullia introduces her friend to Luke.

The censor asks the father some questions.
A son learns about his family tree from his
    father.
Two friends discuss their family circumstances.

Cynthia tries to persuade her friend Gloria to
    come to her house to play.
A potential buyer wants to purchase a home
    through a real estate agent.
Sabina tries to impress her friend Silvia with the
    big home her parents own.

Contents

Acknowledgements

A debt of gratitude is due to Professor Jeffrey Wills of the Ukranian Catholic University, to Professors Terence O. Tunberg and Christopher Gerard Brown of the University of Kentucky, and to Professor David W. Morgan Of Furman University, SC, for their many suggestions for improvement in both form and substance and for sharing their resources with me. Dr. Dominic M. Roberti, chemistry professor turned desktop publisher, gave much helpful advice; he is responsible for the page design and typesetting of this book. The author gratefully acknowledges the kind support of Dr. Ladislaus J. Bolchazy of Bolchazy-Carducci Publishers, Inc.

How to Use This Book

Unlike your usual textbook, this book allows you to start at any chapter that interests you. Why? Because the chapters are *not* arranged in the order of difficulty. On the other hand, the model conversations in each chapter are arranged in order of difficulty. That is, the grammatical structures of the conversations at Level 1 are simpler than those at Levels 2 and 3. Therefore it is quite possible to go through the entire book using only the conversations at Level 1 and then go through the book again, using Levels 2 and 3.

In the conversations you may run across grammatical forms that you have not covered in class as yet. For instance, you may come across the subjunctive form **eāmus** (let's go). It happened to be called for in that conversation. So what if you haven't learned the entire subjunctive system as yet? You now know what it means, and so you can use it.

You may be used to working your way through a Latin sentence in order to come up with a translation. In this book you are provided with an English translation of all the Latin. (And you'll notice that the translations are not the stiff, literal versions that are sometimes found in textbooks.) So the idea is to practice the model conversations until you have pretty well mastered them. One way to do this is for you to switch roles with your partner and repeat the dialogue again. Then you can proceed to the next stage. This is most easily done by drawing on the topical vocabulary in the chapter to form new Latin conversations of your own choosing on the topic at hand. Because the book is arranged with its facing Latin and English texts, it lends itself to your covering one side, whether the Latin or the English, and then speaking the part in the language that is covered; you could then uncover the concealed text to see how you have done.

The topical vocabulary of each chapter contains not only the words that have occurred in the model conversations but also additional words on that topic that will make it possible for you to have new conversations. The general vocabulary that occurred in the conversations of each chapter is assembled at the end of the book, together with additional useful words. But that general vocabulary will not meet all your needs. You will then have to consult a Latin-English dictionary. Be sure to make full use of the topical vocabulary of the various chapters, no matter what topic you are dealing with. For instance, Chapter XI contains hundreds of everyday expressions that will come in handy in any conversation. Furthermore, whenever you need some expression of time, you will probably find the expression you want in Chapters IX and X. You should use both the topical and general vocabularies to look for the words you need.

To make it easier for you to find what you are looking for, the phrases are arranged alphabetically according to the key word in each phrase. For example, you want to say that someone is "feeding a person a line." In Chapter XI you will find it under the word "line," like this: **line: that fellow is feeding you a line** *iste tibi verba dat.* Sometimes there could be two possible key words in a phrase. If you do not find the phrase under the one key word, check under the other. For instance, in the phrase quoted above, either "feed" or "line" can be considered key words. In this case, the phrase is listed under "line"; it could have been listed under "feed" as well. Such double entries would have made the book too bulky.

In conversational Latin, meaningful and realistic communication is the aim and goal. Accuracy comes with practice.

Pronunciation

VOWELS

CLASSICAL METHOD	LATE LATIN METHOD
ă *a* in *a*go: **cómpărō**	
ā *a* in f*a*ther: **imā́gō**	
e *e* in p*e*t: **próperō**	
ē *a* in l*a*te: **lēnis**	Generally the same as in the
ĭ *i* in h*i*t: **ĭdem**	Classical Method. However, in
ī *ee* in k*ee*n: **amī́cus**	practice the different values of the
ŏ *o* in *o*ften: **mŏdus**	vowels are frequently not rigidly
ō *o* in h*o*pe: **nōmen**	adhered to.
ŭ *u* in p*u*t: **ŭt**	
ū *u* in r*u*de: **ūtor**	
ў *ü* in German H*ü*tte: **mўrta**	
ȳ *ü* in German *ü*ber: **Tȳdeus**	

Note—The length of a long vowel is about one and one half that of a short vowel.

DIPHTHONGS

CLASSICAL METHOD	LATE LATIN METHOD
ae *y* in b*y*: **caecus**	**ae** *a* in l*a*te: **caecus**
au *ow* in n*ow*: **nauta**	**au** as in Classical Method
eî *ey* in th*ey*: **heî**	**ei** as in Classical Method
eû *eu* in h*ey you* (without the h and y): **Orpheûs**	**eu** as in Classical Method
oê *oi* in *oi*l: **coêpit**	**oe** *a* in l*a*te: **coepit**
uî *uey* in gl*uey*: **cuî;** after **q,** *wee* in w*ee*k: **qui**	**ui** same as in Classical Method

CONSONANTS

	CLASSICAL METHOD		LATE LATIN METHOD
b	English *b*	**b**	English *b*
c	always *c* in *c*an: **cīvis, cantō, cēdō**	**c**	before **e, i, ae,** or **oe** = *ch* in *ch*erry: **celsus, cīvis, caelum, coepit,** but before other letters, *c* in *c*an: **cantō, actus**
d	English *d*	**d**	English *d*
f	English *f*	**f**	English *f*
g	always *g* in *g*o: **gallína, genus, grātus, gula**	**g**	before **e** or **i** = *g* in *g*entle: **genus, regína,** but before other letters except **g** and **n** (see under Consonant Groups) = *g* in *g*o: **gallína, grātus, gula, rogō**
h	English *h*	**h**	English *h*
i	*y* in *y*es: **iam, iungō**	**i**	as in Classical Method, sometimes written **j**
k	English *k*, but unaspirated	**k**	English *k*
l	English *l*	**l**	English *l*
m	English *m*, but in verse final **m** before an initial vowel or **h** in the following word was presumably not pronounced	**m**	English *m*
n	English *n*	**n**	English *n*
p	English *p*, but unaspirated	**p**	English *p*
q	English *q*	**q**	English *q*
r	trilled *r* as in the Romance languages	**r**	as in Classical Method
s	always *s* in *s*ing: **miser, mors**	**s**	*s* in *s*ing: **salūs,** but when standing between two vowels or when final and preceded by a voiced consonant = *z* in do*z*en: **miser, mors**
t	English *t*, but unaspirated, as *t* in water	**t**	as in Classical Method
u	*w* in *w*ine, when unaccented, preceded by **q**, sometimes by **s**, and sometimes by **g**, and followed by a vowel: **qui·a, suá·vis** (but **su·ó·rum**), **dis·tín·guō** (but **ex·í·gŭ·us**)	**u**	as in Classical Method

CONSONANTS

v	*w* in *w*ine: **vīvō**

x	*x* in si*x*: **extrā**	**v**	English *v*
		x	*x* (as **ks**) in si*x*: **pāx;** but in words beginning with **ex** and followed by a vowel, **h,** or **s,** = *x* (as **gz**) in e*x*haust: **exaúdī, exhálō,**
z	*dz* in a*dz*e: **zōna**		**exsólvō**
		z	as in Classical Method

CONSONANT GROUPS

	CLASSICAL METHOD		**LATE LATIN METHOD**
bs	*ps* in a*ps*e: **obsídō, ur*bs***	**bs**	*bs* in o*bs*ession: **obsídō,** but in the final position = *bs* (as **bz**) in o*bs*erve: **ur*bs***
bt	*pt* in ca*pt*ain: **ob*t*inére**	**bt**	*bt* in o*bt*ain: **ob*t*inére**
cc	*kk* in boo*kk*eeper: **ecce, occído, occásum, occlúdō**	**cc**	before **e** or **i** = *tch* in ca*tch*: **ecce, occído;** but before other letters = *kk* in boo*kk*eeper; **occásum, occlúdō**
ch	*ch* in *ch*aotic: **pul*ch*er**	**ch**	as in Classical Method
gg	*gg* in le*g g*uard: **agger**	**gg**	before **e** or **i** = *dj* in a*dj*ourn: **agger;** but before other letters = *gg* in le*g* guard: **ággregō**
gn	*ngn* in ha*ngn*ail: **di*gn*us**	**gn**	*ny* in ca*ny*on: **di*gn*us**
gu	see consonant **u**	**gu**	as in Classical Method
ph	*p-h* in to*p-h*eavy: **phōca**	**ph**	*ph* in *ph*oenix: **phōca**
qu	see consonant **u**	**qu**	as in Classical Method
sc	*sc* in *sc*ope: **scíō, scūtum**	**sc**	before **e** or **i** = *sh* in *sh*in: **ascéndō, scíō;** but before other letters = *sc* in *sc*ope: **scandō, scūtum**
su	see consonant **u**	**su**	as in Classical Method

Note—Double consonants are to be pronounced in such a way that each consonant is heard. For example, in the word **agger** (embankment), each **g** should be heard, in contrast to **ager** (field) with only one **g**.

th *t* in *t*ake: *th*eátrum

ti *ti* in English pa*ti*o: **nắ*ti*ō**

th as in Classical Method

ti when preceded by **s, t,** or **x,** or when followed by a consonant = *ti* in English pa*ti*o: **hós*ti*a, admíx*ti*ō, fór*ti*ter;** but when unaccented, followed by a vowel, and preceded by any letter except **s, t,** or **x** = *tzy* in ri*tzy*: **nắ*ti*ō, pré*ti*um**

Abbreviations

abbr	abbreviation	*med*	medical
abl	ablative	*mf*	masculine or feminine noun
acc	accusative		
adj	adjective	*mil*	military
adjs	adjectives	*mpl*	masculine plural noun
adv	adverb	*mus*	music
advs	adverbs	*n*	neuter noun
anat	anatomy	*neut*	neuter
cf	compare	*nom*	nominative
coll	colloquial	*npl*	neuter plural nouns
comp	comparative	*opp*	opposite
comput	computer	*part*	participle
conj	conjunction	*pass*	passive
dat	dative	*pej*	pejorative
defect	defective	*perf*	perfect
dim	diminutive	*pl*	plural
eccl	ecclesiastical	*poet*	poetry
esp	especially	*pol*	politics
f	feminine noun	*pp*	past participle
fem	feminine	*pref*	prefix
fig	figurative	*prep*	preposition
fin	finance	*pres*	present
fpl	feminine plural noun	*print*	printing
fut	future	*pron*	pronoun
gen	fenitive	*refl*	reflexive
imperf	imperfect	*rel*	relative
impers	impersonal verb	*relig*	religion
indecl	indeclinable	*rhet*	rhetoric
indef	indefinite	*s*	substantive
indic	indicative	*singl*	singular
inf	infinitive	*s.o.*	someone
interj	interjection	*s.th.*	something
interrog	interrogative	*subj*	subjunctive
intr	intransitive	*suf*	suffix
leg	legal	*superl*	superlative
ling	linguistics	*topog*	topography
lit	literal	*tr*	transitive
loc	locative	*usu*	usually
m	masculine noun	*v*	verb
masc	masculine	*vulg*	vulgar
math	mathematics	*w*	with

Chapter I: Greetings

CONVERSATIONS _____

┌────────── LEVEL I   **Boy meets girl.**

Paulus	Salvē! Quid est nōmen tibi?	***Paul:*** *Hello! What is your name?*
Glória	Salvē et tū! Mihi nōmen est Glória. Quid est nōmen tibi?	***Gloria:*** *Hello yourself! My name is Gloria. What's your name?*
Paulus	Nōmen mihi est Paulus. Quid agis?	*My name is Paul. How are you doing?*
Glória	Váleō, grátiās. Quid agis tū?	*I'm fine, thanks. How are you doing?*
Paulus	Váleō. Hui, ego tē nōvī! Nōnne in próximō vīcō hábitās?	*I'm fine. Hey, I know you. You live in the next block, don't you?*
Glória	Étiam, hábitō.	*Yes, I do.*
Paulus	Quid novī ibi?	*What's new there?*
Glória	Nihil novī. Valē, Paule.	*Nothing new. Goodbye, Paul.*
Paulus	Valē, Glória.	*Goodbye, Gloria.*

┌────────── LEVEL II   **Mario runs into his friend Julia.**

Marius	Salvē, Iúlia! Ut valēs?	***Mario:*** *Hello! How are you?*
Iúlia	Nōn male. Et tū, Marī?	***Julia:*** *Not bad. And you, Mario?*
Márius	Égone? Bene mihi est. Ut frāter tuus valet? Salvus est?	*I? I'm doing fine. How's your brother doing? How is he?*
Iúlia	Sīc valet ut numquam mélius.	*He's doing as well as ever.*
Márius	Ut valet família tua?	*How is your family doing?*
Iúlia	Omnēs domī bene sē habent.	*All are doing fine.*

15

| **Márius** | Et amícus tuus, quid agit? | *And your friend, how is he doing?* |
| **Iúlia** | Rēctē valet. | *He's doing right well.* |

| **Márius** | Unde venīs? | *Where are you coming from?* |
| **Iúlia** | Dē bibliothḗcā. | *From the library.* |

| **Márius** | Quō tē agis? | *Where are you going?* |
| **Iúlia** | Domum. | *Home.* |

| **Márius** | Quīn nunc abeúndum mihi est. Valē. | *Well, I must go now. Goodbye.* |
| **Iúlia** | Bene valē. Cūrā ut vál"eās. | *Goodbye. Take care of yourself.* |

LEVEL III   **Tullia introduces her friend to Luke.**

| **Lúcius** | Salva sīs, Túllia. Quid agis? | *Luke: Hello, Tullia. How are you doing?* |
| **Túllia** | Salvē, Lūcī. Quid agis tū? | *Tullia: Hello, Luke. How are you doing?* |

| **Lúcius** | Nōstī mē. Mē semper bellē hábeō. Quis est haec puélla quae tēcum est? | *You know me. I'm always fine. Who is this girl that you have with you?* |
| **Túllia** | Lūcī, velim trádere tibi cōnsōbrínam meam, Prīscíllam. | *Luke, I'd like to introduce you to my cousin Priscilla.* |

| **Lúcius** | Prīscílla, mihi pergrátum est tē conveníre. Habitásne in hāc vīcíniā? Ego ipse hábitō duōs sōlum vīcōs hinc. | *Priscilla, I'm glad to meet you. Do you live in this neighborhood? I live only two blocks from here.* |
| **Prīscílla** | Mínimē vērō. Hábitō in oppídulō Árdeā. | *No. I live in the little town of Ardea.* |

| **Lúcius** | Árdea? Estne in Campániā an in Látiō? | *Ardea? Is Ardea in Campania or in Latium?* |
| **Prīscílla** | In Látiō, nōn procul ab urbe. | *In Latium, not far from the city.* |

| **Lúcius** | Dīc mihi, quótiēs Rōmam venīs? | *Tell me, how often do you come to Rome?* |
| **Prīscílla** | Quotiēscúmque cōnsōbrína mea mē invítat. | *As often as my cousin invites me.* |

Túllia	Haec háctenus! Mē paénitet, Lūcī, sed nōbīs nunc eúndum est. Frāter meus nōs in gymnásiō iamdúdum exspéctat.	*Enough of this. I'm sorry, Luke, but we have to go now. My brother has been waiting a long time for us in the gym.*
Lúcius	Túllia, amábō tē, iubē frātrem tuum Túllium salvére. Prīscílla, cūrā ut váleās. Mox, ut spērō, tē íterum vidébō.	*Tullia, please say hello to your brother Tullius. Priscilla, take care of yourself. I hope to see you again soon.*
Túllia	Valē. Cūrā ut váleās.	*Goodbye. Take care of yourself.*
Príscílla	Bene valē, Lūcī.	*Bye-bye, Luke.*

TOPICAL VOCABULARY

be fine bene sē habére; vál·eō -ére -uī

be very well rēctē valére

goodbye valē *(pl:* valéte); bene valē *(pl:* bene valéte)

hello! salvē *(pl:* salvéte); salvus (-a) sīs

how are you? (how are you doing?) quid agis? *(pl:* quid ágitis?); ut valēs? *(pl:* ut valétis?)

I am fine bene mihi est

introduce *(to)* trā·dō -dere -didī -ditus (+ *dat*)

know *defective v* nōvī nōvísse (**you know** nōvístī *or* nōstī)

meet *tr & intr* con·véniō -veníre -vénī -véntus

name nōm·en -inis *n*

not bad nōn male

pleased to meet you! mihi pergrátum est tē conveníre

say hello to s.o. iubē *(pl:* iubéte) áliquem salvére

thanks! grátiās!

thanks a lot! grátiās máximās!

thanks a million! sescéntās grátiās!

ADDITIONAL GREETINGS AND RESPONSES

Where are you from?	*Unde es?*
Where are you coming from?	*Unde venīs?*
How are you?	*Quī valēs?*
Fine.	*Rēctē.*
—	*Bellē.*
Very well.	*Perbéllē.*
—	*Bellíssimē.*

I'm fine.	*Mē bene hábeō.*
I'm doing quite well.	*Haud male quidem váleō.*
How are you?	*Ut tē habēs?*
So-so.	*Váriē.*
Fairly well.	*Mediócriter quidem váleō.*
Not bad.	*Haud male.*
Not too well.	*Nōn óptimē sānē.*
As usual.	*Ut sóleō.*
Lousy.	*Plānē īnfēlíciter.*
Everything O.K.?	*Satīn' salvē?*
Everything is O.K.	*Ómnia sunt pulchrē.*
—	*Ómnia sunt fēlíciter.*
—	*Ómnia sunt fēstíviter.*
Hello. How've you been?	*Salvē. Valuistíne?*
Fine! Great!	*Probē! Euge!*
Well, I'm still alive.	*Em, vīvō.*
Hello.	*Salvē.*
Same to you.	*Salvē et tū.*
Hello. Pleasure to meet you.	*Salvē. Tē convēnísse volup est.*
Hello. The pleasure is mine.	*Salvē. Mihi quidem volup est.*
How are things with you? Everything all right?	*Quō pactō rēs sē tibi habent? Rēcténe sunt ómnia?*
In fair shape.	*In medíocrī statū.*
In great shape.	*In óptimō statū.*
Glad to hear that.	*Laetus (-a) istud aúdiō.*
Glad to hear that.	*Haud invítus (-a) aúdiō.*
I'm delighted to hear that.	*Est mihi istud audítū perquam iūcúndum.*
I'm glad for you.	*Gaúdeō tuā causā.*
I'm sincerely glad to hear that.	*Audíre istud ex ánimō gaúdeō.*
Thank heavens.	*Laus súperīs.*

Goodbye for now.	*Nunc valē.*
God bless you.	*Dī tē ament.*
Take care (of yourself).	*Tē cūrā.*
Take it easy.	*Ōtiōsus (-a) estō.*
Goodbye and good luck.	*Váleās béneque tibi sit.*

SUGGESTED CLASSROOM ACTIVITY _____

First, let pairs of students repeat the conversation of each level. After you have greeted several individual students with a question or two, pair off the students and have them ask each other similar questions. Questions and answers can easily be gleaned from the dialogues, Topical Vocabulary, and Additional Greetings and Responses.

It is important to repeat this activity from time to time so that the questions and answers become spontaneous.

Chapter II: Family

CONVERSATIONS

┌──────────── LEVEL I **The censor asks the father some questions.**

Cēnsor	Quid nōmen tibi est?	*Censor: What is your name?*
Aulus	Nōmen mihi est Aulus Gabínius Macer.	*Aulus: My name is Aulus Gabinius Macer.*
Cēnsor	Esne tū marítus an caelebs?	*Are you married or single?*
Aulus	Marítus sum. Hábeō uxốrem.	*I am married. I have a wife.*
Cēnsor	Esne tū paterfamíliās?	*Are you the head of a family?*
Aulus	Ita.	*Yes.*
Cēnsor	Quod nōmen est uxốrī?	*What's your wife's name?*
Aulus	Nōmen uxốrī est Sulpícia.	*Her name is Sulpicia.*
Cēnsor	Habḗsne lítberōs?	*Do you have (any) children?*
Aulus	Hábeō.	*I do.*
Cēnsor	Quot lítberōs habēs?	*How many children do you have?*
Aulus	Duōs fílliōs et ūnam fílliam.	*I have two sons and one daughter.*
Cēnsor	Habḗsne frātrēs sorōrḗsve?	*Do you have (any) brothers or sisters?*
Aulus	Ūnum frātrem et ūnam sorốrem hábeō.	*I have one brother and one sister.*
Cēnsor	Habḗsne áliōs cognātốs?	*Do you have other relatives?*
Aulus	Ūnum avúnculum et trēs ámitās.	*One uncle and three aunts.*
Cēnsor	Vivúntne adhūc paréntēs tuī?	*Are your parents still alive?*
Aulus	Sānē.	*Yes.*
Cēnsor	Quis domī tuae hábitat?	*Who lives at your home?*
Aulus	Uxor et lítberī et eốrum avus avíaque.	*My wife, my children, and their grandfather and grandmother.*

| **Cēnsor** | Meā senténtiā, habēs famíliam admīrắbilem. | *In my opinion, you have a wonderful family.* |
| **Aulus** | Sīc ego quoque putō. | *I think so too.* |

┌──────── LEVEL II   **A son learns about his family tree from his father.**

Fílius	Pater, velim cognṓscere plūra dē famíliā nostrā.	*Son: Father, I'd like to know more about our family.*
Pater	Bene, mī fīlī. Quid velīs cognṓscere dē stirpe nostrā?	*Father: Fine, my boy. What would you like to know about our family tree?*
Fílius	Quandō tū Mámmam in mātrimṓnium dūxístī?	*When did you marry Mom?*
Pater	Abhinc vīgíntī annōs.	*Twenty years ago.*
Fílius	Quot annōs nātus es tū?	*How old are you?*
Pater	Quadrāgíntā annōs nātus sum.	*I am forty years old.*
Fílius	Quot annōs nāta est Mamma?	*How old is Mom?*
Pater	Duodēquadrāgíntā annōs nāta est.	*She is thirty-eight years old.*
Fílius	Quot sorṓrēs habēs?	*How many sisters do you have?*
Pater	Trēs hábeō.	*I have three.*
Fílius	Quae est máxima nātū?	*Which one is the oldest?*
Pater	Paulína est máxima nātū.	*Pauline is the oldest.*
Fílius	Quot frātrēs habēs?	*How many brothers do you have?*
Pater	Duōs hábeō, Stéphanum et Michaḗlem, pátruōs tuōs.	*I have two, your uncles Stephen and Michael.*
Fílius	Quis est māior nātū, tū an Stéphanus pátruus?	*Who is older, you or uncle Stephen?*
Pater	Ego sum duṓbus annīs māior nātū quam Stéphanus pátruus sed duṓbus annīs minor quam Michaḗlis pátruus.	*I am two years older than uncle Stephen, but two years younger than uncle Michael.*
Fílius	Habitāvērúntne avus et ávia semper in hāc urbe?	*Did grandfather and grandmother always live in this city?*
Pater	Ita. Étiam eṓrum átavī.	*Yes, and also their forefathers.*

Fílius	Dīc mihi, amábō tē, patérne tuus et avus tuus in rē públicā versā́tī sunt?	*Tell me please, were your father and grandfather involved in politics?*
Pater	Immō próavus tuus ōlim erat praeféctus urbī.	*Well, your great-grandfather was once mayor of the city.*
Fílius	Quid dē avō meō?	*What about my grandfather?*
Pater	Avus tuus vērō erat multōs annōs sócius cōnsíliī. Tūne vīs versā́rī aliquándō in rē públicā?	*In fact, your grandfather was a cabinet member for many years. Do you wish someday to be involved in politics?*
Fílius	Mínimē vērō hercle! Spērō mē aliquándō futū́rum esse āthlḗtam praeclā́rum!	*Heck no! I hope to be a famous athlete someday.*

LEVEL III   **Two friends discuss their family circumstances.**

Mārcélla	Anna, fortūnā́ta es. Habēs paréntēs bonōs, marítum amántem, socrum benígnam. Tibi quidem invídeō.	*Marcella: Anna, you are fortunate. You have good parents, a loving husband, and a kind mother-in-law. I really envy you.*
Anna	Ita. Ego hábeō étiam admīrā́bilem marítum soróris et uxórem frātris. Sed cūr tū mihi ínvidēs?	*Anna: Yes. I also have a wonderful brother-in-law and sister-in-law. But why do you envy me?*
Mārcélla	Abhinc duōs annōs mātrem meam āmī́sī, et nunc novércam hábeō.	*I lost my mother two years ago, and now I have a stepmother.*
Anna	Mē paénitet haec cognóscere. Estne novérca crūdḗlis?	*I'm sorry to hear that. Is your stepmother cruel?*
Mārcélla	Novérca quidem neque crūdḗlis neque amábilis est, sed locum mātris meae numquam ūsurpā́re potest.	*Well, my stepmother is neither cruel nor lovable. But she can never take the place of my mother.*
Anna	Suntne frāter et soror tua aequē īnfēlī́cēs?	*Are your brother and sister equally unhappy?*
Mārcélla	Vidéntur īnfēlī́cēs, sed pauca dē hīs rēbus dīcunt.	*They seem unhappy, but they say little about these matters.*
Anna	Temptā́sne ánimōs eórum ērígere?	*Do you try to cheer them up?*

Mārcélla	Ánimōs eōrum ērígere temptō, sed nihil prōdest.	*I try to cheer them up, but it does no good.*
Anna	Míseram Mārcéllam! Quid dīcit pater tuus?	*Poor Marcella! What does your father say?*
Mārcélla	Est ádmodum sollícitus. Dīcit: "Patiéntia, patiéntia. Tempus ómnia sānat."	*He is quite concerned. He says: "Patience, patience. Time heals everything."*

SUGGESTED CLASSROOM ACTIVITY

Ask a few students:

Quot annōs nātus *(or* nāta) es tū?	*How old are you?*
Quot annōs nātus est pater?	*How old is your father?*
Quot annōs nāta est māter?	*How old is your mother?*
Quot frātrēs habēs?	*How may brothers do you have?*
Quot sorōrēs habēs?	*How many sisters do you have?*
Quī frāter est máximus nātū?	*Which brother is the oldest?*
Quī frāter est mínimus nātū?	*Which brother is the youngest?*
Quae soror est máxima nātū?	*Which sister is the oldest?*
Quae soror est mínima nātū?	*Which sister is the youngest?*
Quod nōmen est frātrī?	*What is your brother's name?*
Quod nōmen est sorórī?	*What is your sister's name?*

Then pair off the students and have them ask each other these questions. From the dialogues of the chapter, many other such simple questions can be generated. Or have the students bring family photographs into the classroom and explain who the members of the family (or extended family) are, e.g.:

Hic est pater meus.

Haec est māter mea.

Hic est avus meus.

Haec est avia mea.

Hic est frāter meus.

Haec est soror mea.

TOPICAL VOCABULARY

adoptive daughter fīli•a -ae *f* adoptīva

adoptive son fīli•us -ī *m* adoptīvus

aunt *(mother's side)* mātérter•a -ae *f*

aunt *(father's side)* ámit•a -ae *f*

baby īnf•āns -ántis *mf*

brother frā•ter -tris *m*

brother-in-law *(husband of sister)* marít•us -ī *m* soróris

children líber•ī -órum *mpl*

cousin *(sister's daughter)* cōnsōbrín•a -ae *f*

cousin *(brother's child)* patruél•is -is *mf*

cousin *(sister's son)* cōnsōbrín•us -ī *m*

dad, daddy tat•a -ae *m*

daughter fīli•a -ae *f*

daughter-in-law nur•us -ūs *f*

family famíli•a -ae *f*

family tree stirp•s -is *f*

father pa•ter -tris *m*

father-in-law soc•er -erī *m*

father of the family paterfamíliās *(gen:* patrisfamíliās) *m*

forefathers átav•ī -órum *mpl*

granddaughter nept•is -is *f*

granddad tat•a -ae *m*

grandfather av•us -ī *m*

grandma mamm•a -ae *f*

grandmother ávi•a -ae *f*

grandson nep•ōs -ótis *m*

great-aunt *(on father's side)* ámit•a -ae *f* magna; *(on the mother's side)* matérter•a -ae *f* magna

great-grandfather próav•us -ī *m*

great-grandmother proávi•a -ae *f*

great-uncle *(on the father's side)* pátru•us -ī *m* magnus; *(on the mother's side)* avúncul•us -ī *m*

husband marít•us -ī *m*

in-law affín•is -is *mf*

little brother frātércul•us -ī *m*

little sister sorórcul•a -ae *f*

Mom Mamm•a -ae *f*

mother mā•ter -tris *f*

mother-in-law socr•us -ūs *f*

nephew fīli•us -ī *m* soróris; fīli•us -ī *m* frātris

niece fīli•a -ae *f* soróris; fīli•a -ae *f* frātris

parent párēns -éntis *mf*

relative cognát•us -ī *m*, cognát•a -ae *f*

sister-in-law *(sister of husband)* glōs glōris *f*

sister-in-law *(wife of brother)* ux•or -óris *f* frātris

son fīli•us -ī *m*

son-in-law gener, génerī *m*

spouse con•iūnx -iugis *mf*

stepdaughter prīvígn•a -ae *f*

stepfather vítric•us -ī *m*

stepmother novérc•a -ae *f*

stepson prīvígn•us -ī *m*

uncle *(mother's brother)* avúncul•us -ī *m*

uncle *(father's brother)* pátru•us -ī *m*

wife ux•or -óris *f*

young daughter fīlíol•a -ae *f*

young son fīlíol•us -ī *m*

Chapter III: House and Furniture

CONVERSATIONS

┌─────── LEVEL I   **Cynthia tries to persuade her friend Gloria to come to her house to play.**

Cýnthia   Glória, potésne veníre domum meam?   *Cynthia: Gloria, can you come to my house?*

Glória   Quid potérimus fácere ibi?   *Gloria: What can we do there?*

Cýnthia   Potérimus librōs légere in cubículō meō.   *We can read books in my bedroom.*

Glória   Benígnē. Ego multōs librōs domī hábeō.   *No, thank you. I have many books at home.*

Cýnthia   Fortásse potérimus cóquere crústula in culínā nostrā.   *Maybe we can bake cookies in our kitchen.*

Glória   Benígnē. Ego saepe coquō crústula in culínā meā.   *No, thank you. I often bake cookies in my kitchen.*

Cýnthia   Recēns ego comparávī novum cátulum. Vīsne lúdere cum meō novō cátulō in peristýliō nostrō?   *Recently I got a new puppy. Do you want to play with my new puppy in our courtyard?*

Glória   O, ego prōrsus adórō cátulōs! Eámus illūc currículō!   *Oh, I absolutely adore puppies! Let's go there on the double!*

┌─────── LEVEL II   **A potential buyer wants to purchase a home through a real estate agent.**

Ēmptor   Mónstrā mihi, quaesō, partem interiórem huius domūs.   *Buyer: Please, show me the interior of this home.*

Praediátor   Libénter. Est vērō domus élegāns. Sunt pictúrae in quōque paríete.   *Real Estate Dealer: Gladly. It is really an elegant home. There are pictures on every wall.*

Ēmptor   Quot cubícula sunt in hāc domō?   *How many bedrooms are there in this house?*

Praediátor   Omnínō quáttuor cubícula.   *Four bedrooms in all.*

Ēmptor	Quid est in quōque cubículō?	*What is in each bedroom?*
Praediátor	Bīnī lēctī et bīnae cáthedrae et vestiárium.	*Each bedroom has two beds and two chairs and a clothes closet.*
Ēmptor	Estne tablínum huic dómuī?	*Does this house have a study?*
Praediátor	Étiam. Est profécto magna mēnsa scrīptória rōbórea ibi; atque sunt plúteī circā paríetēs omnēs.	*Yes. There is, in fact, a large oak desk there; and there are bookshelves around all the walls.*
Ēmptor	Habétne domus amplam culínam?	*Does the house have a spacious kitchen?*
Praediátor	Ita; est magnus camínus in culínā atque fūsórium.	*Yes; there is a big stove in the kitchen as well as a sink.*
Ēmptor	Ubi est trīclínium?	*Where is the dining room?*
Praediátor	Trīclínium situm est inter culínam et bálneum. Prope bálneum est lātrína. In bálneō est sólium magnum.	*The dining room is located between the kitchen and the bathroom. Near the bathroom is a toilet. There is a large bathtub in the bathroom.*
Ēmptor	Quantī cōnstat haec domus?	*How much does this house cost?*
Praediátor	Cōnstat centum mílibus dollarórum.	*It costs $100,000.*
Ēmptor	Fortásse potes mihi mōnstráre domum minórem?	*Perhaps you can show me some smaller home?*
Praediátor	Possum, sed nōn in hāc regióne urbis.	*I can, but not in this section of the city.*

┌─────── LEVEL III **Sabina tries to impress her friend Silvia with the big home her parents own.**

| **Sílvia** | Sabína, habitásne in aédibus an in ínsulā? | *Silvia: Sabina, do you live in a house or in an apartment building?* |
| **Sabína** | In aédibus hábitō. Magnam vērō domum hábeō. | *Sabina: I live in a house. In fact, I have a large home.* |

Sílvia	Ítane? Quot conclávia domus habet?	*Is that so? How many rooms does your home have?*
Sabína	Átrium, tablínum, tríclínium, culínam, bálneum, sex cubícula, peristýlium cum bellō hortō.	*An atrium, study, dining room, kitchen, bathroom, six bedrooms, and a courtyard with a nice garden.*
Sílvia	Suntne cubícula ómnia in pedeplánīs?	*Are all the bedrooms on the ground floor?*
Sabína	Quáttuor cubícula in pedeplánīs sunt; cétera in tabulátō secúndō sunt. Servī et ancíllae in tabulátō secúndō dórmiunt.	*There are four bedrooms on the ground floor; the rest are on the second floor. The servants and maids sleep on the second floor.*
Sílvia	Sīquidem marítus tuus cōnsul est, conveniúntne multī cliéntēs domī tuae ad offícium?	*Since your husband is a consul, do many clients gather at your home for the courtesy call?*
Sabína	Ita, nam sīc est mōs. Bene māne cliéntēs frequéntant nōn sōlum vēstíbulum sed étiam átrium. Deínde cliéntēs marítum meum in forum dēdúcunt.	*Yes, for that is the custom. Early in the morning the clients pack not only the vestibule but also the atrium. Then they accompany my husband to the forum.*
Sílvia	Manésne in átriō inter offícium?	*Do you stay in the atrium during the courtesy call?*
Sabína	Mínimē vērō, eō témpore ego sátagō in culínā aut in peristýliō.	*Not at all. At that time I am busy in the kitchen or in the courtyard.*
Sílvia	Quid facis in peristýliō?	*What do you do in the courtyard?*
Sabína	Ego cūrō rosās et áliās plantās in hortō.	*I look after the roses and the other plants in the garden.*
Sílvia	Quid facis in culínā?	*What do you do in the kitchen?*
Sabína	Cēnam coquō, quia marítus meus saepe vocat cliéntēs ad cēnam. Ego ipsa cibum adpónō in tríclíniō.	*I cook dinner, since my husband often invites clients to dinner. I myself serve the food in the dining room.*
Sílvia	Sit dīs grátia, ego in víllulā rūrī hábitō! Vīta est tam simplex ibi!	*Thank heaven I live in a little farmhouse in the country! Life is so simple there!*

TOPICAL VOCABULARY

See also the General Vocabulary for additional items.

air conditioner īnstrūmént·um -ī *n* áërī temperándō

alarm suscitábul·um -ī *n;* **the alarm went off** suscitábulum sónuit; **to set the alarm for (seven o'clock)** óbicem īnfīg·ō -ere īnfīxī īnfīxus ad (séptimam hōram)

alarm clock hōrológi·um -ī *n* suscitātórium

apartment diaét·a -ae *f;* **furnished apartment** diaéta omnī supelléctile īnstrúcta

apartment building ínsul·a -ae *f*

armchair sell·a -ae *f* bracchiáta

atrium átri·um -ī *n*

attic subtēguláne·um -ī *n*

back door postíc·um -ī *n*

balcony maenián·um -ī *n*

banister adminíul·um -ī *n*

barrel dóli·um -ī *n,* cup·a -ae *f; (wooden barrel)* lígneum vās, vāsis *n*

basement hypogé·um -ī *n,* cellári·um -ī *n* subterráneum

bathroom bálne·um -ī *n*

bath towel gausápin·a -ae *f*

bathtub sóli·um -ī *n,* lābr·um -ī *n*

bay window prōiectúr·a -ae *f*

bed lect·us -ī *m; (small)* léctul·us -ī *m;* **to go to bed** cúbitum īre; **to make the bed** lectum stern·ō -ere strāvī strātus

bed covers strágul·a -órum *npl*

bedding strágul·a -órum *npl*

bed frame spond·a -ae *f*

bedroom dormītórium cubícul·um -ī *n*

bedspread opertóri·um -ī *n,* peristróm·a -atis *n*

bench scabéll·um -ī *n*

blanket lōd·īx -ícis *f*

blinds *see* **Venetian blinds**

bolt *(on door)* péssul·us -ī *m;* **to bolt the door** óstium obseráre

bookcase bibliothéc·a -ae *f* paríetī īnsérta

bookshelf plúte·us -ī *m*

bowl catín·us -ī *m*

broom scōp·ae -árum *fpl*

bucket sítul·a -ae *f*

carpet tapét·um -ī *n*

casette casét·a -ae *f; (for video)* caséta magnētoscópica

casette recorder casētophón·um -ī *n*

ceiling tēct·um -ī *n; (arched or vaulted)* cámer·a -ae *f; (paneled)* lacún·ar -áris *n*

cellar cellári·um -ī *n* (subterráneum)

central heating calefácti·ō -ónis *f* centrális

chair *(normally without back or arm-rests)* sell·a -ae *f; (w. rounded back)* arisélli·um -ī *n;* **back of the chair** arc·us -ūs *m* sellae

chandelier lámpadum corýmb·us -ī *m*

chimney fūmári·um -ī *n*

China fictília Sinénsium vās·a -órum *npl*

clock hōrológi·um -ī *n;* **the clock keeps good time** hōrológium rēctē métitur; **to look at the clock** hōrológium īnspíc·iō -ere īnspéxī; **to set the clock** hōrológium temperáre; **to wind the clock** hōrológium intén·dō -dere -dī inténsus

closet armári·um -ī *n* paríetī īnsértum

clothes closet vestiári•um -ī *n* paríetī īnsértum

clothes hook unc•us -ī *m* vestiárius

clothes rack, coat rack sustentácul•lum -ī *n* véstium

couch tor•us -ī *m* tōméntō fartus

courtyard peristýli•um -ī *n*

cup pócul•um -ī *n,* pōcíll•um -ī *n*

curtains aulaé•a -ōrum *npl,* cortín•ae -árum *fpl*

desk mēns•a -ae *f* scrīptória

dining couch lect•us -ī *m*

dining room trīclíni•um -ī *n; (informal)* cēnáti•ō -ónis *f*

dish catíll•us -ī *m; (open and flat)* pátin•a -ae *f; (large)* lān•x -cis *f;* **dishes** *(including pots and pans)* vās•a -ōrum *npl*

dishwasher máchin•a -ae *f* ēlūtória

door iánu•a -ae *f,* ósti•um -ī *n;* **folding doors** valv•ae -árum *fpl*

doorknob iánuae manúbri•um -ī *n*

doorstep līm•en -inis *n*

doorway ósti•um -ī *n*

double home dom•us -ūs *f* duárum familiárum

downstairs: he is downstairs in īmō tabulátō est; **to go downstairs** scālās dēscénd•ō -ere -ī

drawer lócul•us -ī *m*

dressing table mēns•a -ae *f* cōmātória

dryer *(for hair; for clothes)* īnstrūmént•um -ī *n* siccātórium (capillórum; véstium)

easy chair arcisélli•um -ī *n* tōméntō fartum

electrical appliance ēléctricum īnstrūmént•um -ī *n* [**īnstrūméntum** *can be used for a single appliance or collectively for all the appliances*]

electrical outlet cápsul•a -ae *f* contáctūs ēléctricī

electric fan máchin•a -ae *f* ventígena

electric shaver rāsóri•um -ī *n* ēléctricum

faucet epitóni•um -ī *n;* **to turn on (off) the faucet** epitónium versáre (reversáre)

fireplace foc•us -ī *m*

floor *(paved)* pavīmént•um -ī *n,* sol•um -ī *n;* **ground floor** pedeplān•a -ōrum *npl;* **marble floor** pavīméntum *(or* solum) marmóreum; **mosaic floor** pavīméntum *(or* solum) teselátum; **wooden floor** tabulát•um -ī *n*

fluorescent light túbul•us -ī *m* lūcífluus

food processor máchin•a -ae *f* coquīnária

freezer caps•a -ae *f* frīgorífica

front door antíc•um -ī *n*

front hall vēstíbul•um -ī *n*

furnish a home domum supelléctile ínstru•ō -ere īnstrúxī īnstrúctus

furnish an apartment diaétam supelléctile īnstrúere

furniture suppéll•ex -éctilis *f;* **piece of furniture** supelléctilis par•s -tis *f*

garden hort•us -ī *m;* **vegetable garden** hortus (h)olitórius

ground floor pedeplán•a -ōrum *npl*

guest room hospíti•um -ī *n*

hall *(large room)* oec•us -ī *m*

hallway andr•ōn -ónis *m*

home dom•us -ūs *f*

home appliance īnstrūmént•um -ī *n* domésticum ēléctricum; **home appliances** ēléctrica domūs ūtēnsíl•ia -ium *npl*

hopper lābéll•um -ī *n* íntimum, sell•a -ae *f* familiárica

house dom•us -ūs *f,* aed•ēs -ium *fpl*

kitchen culín·a -ae *f*

kitchen knife cult·er -rī *m* coquīnáris

kitchen utensils īnstrūmént·a -órum *npl* coquinātória

ladle trūll·a -ae *f*

lamp lucérn·a -ae *f*

landing *(on stairs)* scālári·um -ī *n*

laundry lāvātóri·um -ī *n*

light lūm·en -inis (ēléctricum) *n;* **to turn on (off) the light** lūmen accénd·ō -ere -ī accénsus (expéd·iō -íre -ívī *or* -iī -ítus)

light bulb glóbul·us -i *m* ēléctricus

linen closet armári·um -ī *n* lineárium (paríetī īnsértum)

living room sessóri·um -ī *n,* synoeci·um -ī *n*

mattress cúlcit·a -ae *f;* **air mattress** cúlcita īnflátilis

microwave oven furn·us -ī *m* undárum brévium

night table ménsul·a -ae *f* cubiculáris

oven furn·us -ī *m*

pantry cell·a -ae *f* pēnária

peristyle peristýli·um -ī *n*

pillow cervíc·al -ális *n*

pillow case cervīcális tégim·en -inis *n*

pipe fístul·a -ae *f* aquária

pitcher úrce·us -ī *m*

plate pátin·a -ae *f*

plug spin·a -ae *f* contáctūs ēléctricī

plug in adnéct·ō -ere adnéxuī adnéxus

porch pérgul·a -ae *f*

portico pórtic·us -ūs *f*

pot *(ceramic)* oll·a -ae *f; (of metal)* a(h)én·um -ī *n;* **pots and pans** vās·a -órum *npl* coquīnária

radiator calóris radiá·trum -trī *n*

radio radiophón·um -ī *n;* **to turn on (turn off) the radio** radiophónum excitáre *or* accénd·ō -ere -ī (expéd·iō -íre -iī -ītus); **to turn down (turn up) the radio** vim radiophónī remítt·ō -ere remísī (amplificáre)

radio broadcast ēmíssi·ō -ónis *f* radiophónica

rain basin *(in the atrium)* implúvi·um -ī *n*

reading lamp lampas, lámpadis *f* lēctória

receiver *(of telephone)* auscultábul·um -ī *n*

record player discophón·um -ī *n*

refrigerator frīgidár·ium -ī *n*

roof tile tégul·a -ae *f*

roof tēct·um -ī *n*

room cubícul·um -ī *n,* conclav·e -is *n; (small room)* cell·a -ae *f*

room with bath (shower) cubícul·um -ī *n* bálneō (bálneō pluviō) īnstrúctum

row home aed·ēs -ium *fpl* seriálēs

rug tapét·e -is *n*

salt shaker salín·um -ī *n*

saucer páter·a -ae *f*

section *(of a city)* régi·ō -ónis *f*

sew su·ō -ere -ī sūtus

sewing machine máchin·a -ae *f* sūtória

sheet strágul·um -ī *n* línteum

shower balnéol·um -ī *n* plúvium; **to take a shower** balnéolō plúviō ūtor ūtī ūsus sum

shower curtain aulaé·um -ī *n* balnéolī plúviī

shower door for·ēs -um *fpl* balnéolī plúviī

shrine sacrári·um -ī *n*

shutter forícul·a -ae *f*

silverware argénte·a -órum *npl* escária

sink *(in a bathroom)* lābéll·um -ī *n; (in a kitchen)* fusṓri·um -ī *n*

sitting room exédr·a -ae *f,* sessṓri·um -ī *n*

skylight complúvi·um -ī *n*

sofa tor·us -ī *m* tōméntō fartus

stairs scāl·ae -árum *fpl*

steps grad·ūs -uum *mpl*

stereo stereophṓn·um -ī *n*

stool scabéll·um -ī *n; (for sitting or mounting)* scamn·um -ī *n*

storeroom cell·a -ae *f*

story tabulát·um -ī *n*

stove fócul·us -ī *m;* **electric (gas) stove** fóculus ēléctricus (gáseus)

study *(room)* studíol·um -ī *n; (in a Roman home)* tablín·um -ī *n*

sugar bowl váscul·um -ī *n* sáccharī

suite *(of rooms)* diaét·a -ae *f*

table mēns·a -ae *f;* **to set the table** mēnsam pōn·ō -ere pósuī pósitus

tablecloth mantél·e -is *n*

tableware īnstrūmént·a -órum *npl* escária

tape recorder magnētophṓn·um -ī *n,* casētophṓn·um -ī *n*

telephone tēlephṓn·um -ī *n (see Chapter IV on Daily Activities)*

television (set) tēlevīsṓri·um -ī *n (see Chapter V on Sports and Other Leisure Activities)*

television screen quadr·um -ī *n* tēlevīsíficum

toaster tostr·um -ī *n*

toilet latrín·a -ae *f*

toilet bowl lābéll·um -ī *n* íntimum, lásan·um -ī *n*

towel gausápin·a -ae *f;* **bath towel** gausápina balneária; **hand towel** manutérgi·um -ī *n*

tray fércul·um -ī *n*

TV room conclắv·e -is *n* tēlevīsṓriō īnstrúctum

upstairs: the upstairs dom·us -ūs *f* supérior; **to go upstairs** scālās ascénd·ō -ere -ī

upstairs bedroom cubícul·um -ī *n* supérius

vacuum cleaner púlveris haurītóri·um -ī *n*

VCR videoexceptóri·um -ī *n*

vegetable garden hort·us -ī *m* holitórius

Venetian blinds trānsénn·a -ae *f* volúbilis; **to close (open, let down, raise) the blinds** trānsénnam clau·d·ō -dere -sī -sus (apér·iō -íre -uī, dēmítt·ō -ere dēmísī dēmíssus, subvólv·ō -ere -ī)

[NOTE 1. The most common Latin word for "room" is **cubículum,** or, for a smaller room, **cella. Cubículum** very frequently means "bedroom." To avoid ambiguity where the context did not make it clear, the Romans used **dormītórium cubículum** or simply **dormītórium** to designate a "bedroom."

NOTE 2. **Iānua** and **óstium** both mean "door" and are often used interchangeably, but **óstium** also means "doorway." A **iánua** often had two panels, called **forēs** or **valvae.**

NOTE 3. The common Latin word for "house" is **aed·ēs -ium** *fpl;* **domus** is normally used to designate an upscale home. The declension of **domus** is partly of the fourth and partly of the second declension. In the following paradigm, the more common form is given first:

	SINGULAR	PLURAL
NOM	**domus**	**domūs**
GEN	**domūs**	**domṓrum** (**dómuum**)
DAT	**domō** (**dómuī**)	**dómibus**
ACC	**domum**	**domōs** (**domūs**)
ABL	**domō**	**dómibus**
LOC	**domī**	

Prepositions are used with **domum** when modified by an adjective, e.g., **domum meam** or **in domum meam.** The preposition **apud** *(w. acc of the pronoun)* is often used in place of the locative, e.g., **apud mē** at my home, **apud eum** at his house; **ad mē** "to my house" is used at times in place of **domum** as the accusative. The locative **domī** "at home" takes the possessive pronominal adjective in the genitive, e.g., **domī suae** "at his own home," **meae domī** "at my home."]

Chapter IV: Daily Activities

CONVERSATIONS

LEVEL I **Mother calling from downstairs.**

[NOTE—Time of day can be computed according to the Roman system, beginning at 6:00 A.M., or according to the modern system, beginning the day at midnight. See page 78 on the Roman hours.]

Māter	Victŏria, surge. Tempus est súrgere.	***Mother:*** *Victoria, get up. It's time to get up.*
Victŏria	O māter, ego tam fessa sum. Librum meum ad multam noctem lēgī. Quota hōra est?	***Victoria:*** *Oh mother, I'm so tired. I read my book till late at night. What time is it?*
Māter	Iam hōra diḗ tértia est. Vigilắsne?	*It's already eight o'clock. Are you awake?*
Victŏria	Vígilō. Ubi sunt cálceī meī?	*Yes, I am. Where are my shoes?*
Māter	Quŏmodo sciam? Ubi, ut opŕnor, tū eōs dētraxístī herī vésperī. Victŏria, éxcitā ē somnō tuam sorŏrculam Olŕviam.	*How should I know? I suppose, where you took them off last night. Wake up your little sister Olivia.*
Victŏria	Māter, Olŕvia nōn vult súrgere. Sub strắgulīs adhūc iacet et sē nōn movet.	*Mother, Olivia doesn't want to wake up. She's still lying under the covers and doesn't move.*
Māter	Vigilátne nunc Olŕvia?	*Is Olivia awake now?*
Victŏria	Mínimē édepol! Ista pigra nē óculōs quidem áperit. Quid fáciam nésciō.	*Heck no! That lazy thing doesn't even open her eyes. I don't know what to do.*
Māter	Éxcitā eam íterum.	*Wake her again.*
Victŏria	Excitắvī. Nōn prōdest. Díctitat: "Omnŕnō ōdī súrgere tam bene māne."	*I have. It doesn't do any good. She keeps on saying: "I absolutely hate to get up so early in the morning."*

| **Māter** | Éxtrahe eam ē léctulō. Aliṓquīn ego ipsa sūrsum véniam et eam excitā́bō. | *Drag her out of bed. Otherwise I'll come upstairs myself and wake her up.* |
| **Victṓria** | Bene est, Mamma; Olī́via tandem ē léctulō rḗpsit. | *It's O.K., Mom. Olivia has finally crawled out of bed.* |

┌─────────── LEVEL II   **Two sisters bicker as they get ready for the day.**

Victṓria	Olī́via, ágedum, tē lavā et dentēs pū́rgā.	*Victoria: Olivia, come on, wash yourself and brush your teeth. [lit: "clean" your teeth]*
Olī́via	Cūr omnēs in hāc famíliā mē carpunt? Quṓmodo possum mē lavā́re sī aquā́lem nōn hábeō?	*Olivia: Why does everyone in this family pick on me? How can I wash myself if I don't have a basin?*
Victṓria	Postquam tū tē lāvístī, meméntō purgā́re dentēs. Et meméntō stérnere léctulum tuum.	*After you have washed, remember to brush your teeth. And remember to make your bed.*
Olī́via	Quṓmodo dentēs purgā́re possum, sī tū dentifrícium tōtum habēs?	*How can I brush my teeth if you have all the tooth powder?*
Victṓria	Et meméntō péctere capíllōs, sī nōn vīs vidḗrī símilis Medū́sae.	*And remember to comb your hair if you don't want to look like Medusa.*
Olī́via	Quṓmodo capíllōs péctere possum, sī quis péctinem meum sústulit?	*How can I comb my hair if someone swiped my comb?*
Victṓria	Et meméntō, mea cāra sorṓrcula, crīspā́re capíllōs.	*And remember, my dear little sister, to curl your hair.*
Olī́via	Quṓmodo capíllōs crīspā́re possum, sī neque calamístrum neque spéculum invenī́re possum?	*How can I curl my hair if I can't find the curler or the mirror?*
Victṓria	Mísera Olī́via, tōtus mundus tibi adversā́tur!	*Poor Olivia, the whole world is against you!*
Māter	Puéllae, dēsínite rīxā́rī. Venī́te deórsum. Ientā́culum est parā́tum.	*Girls, stop bickering. Come downstairs. Breakfast is ready.*

L<small>EVEL</small> III   **Mother and daughters do the daily chores.**

Māter	Victória et Olívia, dēsíderō auxílium vestrum hódīē. Ego iam lectōs omnēs strāvī et pavīméntum lāvī.	*Victoria and Olivia, I need your help today. I have already made all the beds and have washed the floor.*
Victória	Promptae sumus. Dīc quid velīs ut nōs faciámus.	*We are ready. Tell us what you want us to do.*
Māter	Victória, prīmum ómnium, lavā pátinās et vāsa quibus in prándiō ūsī sumus.	*Victoria, first of all, wash the dishes and the pots and pans which we used at lunch.*
Victória	Vísne étiam mē mēnsam pónere ad cēnam?	*Do you also want me to set the table for dinner?*
Māter	Ita. Deínde prōme áliquid vīnī ē cellā vīnáriā.	*Yes. Then get out some wine from the wine cellar.*
Olívia	Quid ego fáciam?	*What should I do?*
Māter	Fortásse tū potes hauríre aquam ē cistérnā. Ecce sítulam.	*Perhaps you can draw some water from the cistern. Here's the bucket.*
Olívia	Quid aquā fáciam?	*What should I do with the water?*
Māter	Implē sólium in balnéolō.	*Fill the bathtub in the bathroom.*
Olívia	Quicquam áliud?	*Anything else?*
Māter	Implē aquálēs in ómnibus cubículīs.	*Fill the wash basins in all the bedrooms.*
Olívia	Postquam ego ómnia fécerō, licēbítne forās éxeam lūsum? Amícae meae mē exspéctant.	*After I have done everything, may I go outside to play? My friends are waiting for me.*
Mater	Certē, exī forās et lūde cum amícīs tuīs usque ad hōram cēnándī.	*Certainly, go outside and play with your friends until dinner time.*

TOPICAL VOCABULARY

answering machine respõnsr•um -ī *n*

awake: to be awake vigilā́re

basin aquā́l•is -is *m (f)*

breakfast ientácul•um -ī *n;* **to eat breakfast** ientā́re; ientáculum sū́m•ō -ere sū́mpsī sū́mptus

brush the teeth dentēs purgā́re [*lit: to clean the teeth*]

cell phone telephṍnul•um -ī *n* portā́bile

clean purgā́re, mundā́re; **to clean out the kitchen** culī́nám mundándam cūrā́re

comb *tr* pect•ō -ere pexī pectus; **to comb the hair** capíllum (*or* capíllōs *or* crīnēs *or* comam) péctere; **to comb out** expéctere; **to comb back** repéctere

comb *s* pect•en -inis *m*

curl crīspā́re

curler calamístr•um -ī *n*

dine cēnā́re

dish pátin•a -ae *f;* **to wash the dishes** pátinās lavā́re

draw water aquam haúr•iō -íre hausī haustus

dust the furniture supelléctilem dētér•geō -gére -sī -sus

eat edō ḗsse ḗdī ḗsus; (*breakfast, lunch, dinner*) sū́m•ō -ere sū́mpsī sū́mptus

fill ímpl•eō -ére -évī -étus; **to fill the water basins** aquā́lēs -ium implére

floor pavīmént•um -ī *n*

get up surg•ō -ere surréxī surréctum

go to bed dormítum (*or* cúbitum) [*supine*] eō íre iī *or* ívī itum

go shopping obsōnā́re

iron clothes vestīménta prem•ō -ere pressī pressus

layer the hair comam in gradūs frang•ō -ere frḗgī frāctus

make the bed lectum (*or* léctulum) stern•ō -ere strāvī strātus

mirror spécul•um -ī *n*

mow the lawn grām•en -inis *n* résecō -ā́re -uī -tus

nap brevis somn•us ī *m;* **to take a nap** brevem somnum cáp•iō -ere cḗpī captus

polish shoes cálceōs pól•iō -íre -ívī -ítus

pots and pans vās•a -órum *npl*

put on (*clothes*) índu•ō -ere -ī -útus (*opp:* exúere)

set the table cibā́ria (vā́scula) in mēnsam appón•ō -ere appósuī appósitus

snack merénd•a -ae *f;* **to have a snack** meréndam cáp•iō -ere cḗpī captus

soap sap•ō -ṓnis *m;* **bar of soap** sapṍnis quádrul•a -ae *f*

sweep the floor pavīméntum verr•ō -ere -ī versus

take off (*clothes*) détrah•ō -ere dētrā́xī dētráctus; éxu•ō -ere -ī -útus

telephone *s* tēlephṍn•um -ī *n;* **by telephone** tēlephṍnicē; **to call s.o. on the telephone** aliquem tēlephṍnicē compellā́re; **to dial a (telephone) (area code) number** númerum (tēlephṍnicum) (númerum praesēlēctṍrium) sélig•ō -ere sēlḗgī sēléctus; **to speak with s.o. on the telephone** cum áliquō tēlephṍnicē cólloquor cólloquī collocútus sum; **to use a pay phone** tēlephṍnō monētálī ūtor ū́tī ū́sus sum

telephone *adj* tēlephṍnic•us -a -um; **telephone call (local, long-distance)** tēlephṍnicum collóqui•um -ī *n* (locā́le, longínquum)

telephone *tr* per tēlephṓnum vocā́re

telephone book catálog•us -ī *m* tēlephṓnicus

telephone booth cell•a -ae *f* tēlephṓnica

telephone number númer•us -ī *m* tēlephṓnicus

television *s* tēlevīsṓri•um -ī *n; (see* **television,** ChapterIV) **to watch television** tēlevīsṓri•um spectā́re

tidy up ōrdinā́re

tired fess•us -a -um

toothbrush pēnícul•us -ī *m* dentā́rius

toothpaste past•a -ae *f* dentā́ria

vacuum *tr* púlveris haurītṓriō purgā́re

vacuum cleaner púlveris haurītṓri•um -ī *n*

wake up *tr* (ē somnṓ) excitā́re **‖** *intr* expergísc•or -ī experréctus sum

wash *tr* lav•ō -ā́re lāvī lautus **‖** *intr* lavā́rī, sē lavā́re

water the flowers flōrēs irrigā́re

Chapter V: Sports and Other Leisure Activities

CONVERSATIONS

LEVEL I **Her teacher asks Dorothy how she spends her free time.**

Magístra	Quómodo cōnsúmis ótium diébus prōféstīs?	*Teacher: How do you spend your leisure time on weekdays?*
Dorothéa	Postquam stúdia cōnfécī, cum amícīs meīs lūdō.	*Dorothy: After I have finished my studies, I play with my friends.*
Magístra	Quid facis fíne hebdómadis?	*What do you do on the weekend?*
Dorothéa	Prīmum, dórmiō quam diū mihi libet.	*First, I sleep as long as I please.*
Magístra	Quid facis pósteā?	*What do you do after that?*
Dorothéa	Deínde ego et amícae dēambulámus.	*Then I and my friends go for a walk.*
Magístra	Quid facis diē Sātúrnī vésperī?	*What do you do on Saturday evening?*
Dorothéa	Intérdum eō in cīnēmatéum.	*Sometimes I go to the movie theater.*
Magístra	Quid ámplius facis?	*What else do you do?*
Dorothéa	Intérdum amāns meus mē ad saltātiónem dūcit.	*Sometimes my boyfriend takes me to a dance.*
Magístra	Quid áliud facis?	*What else do you do?*
Dorothéa	Saepe tēlevīsórium spectō.	*I often watch television.*
Magístra	Quómodo vacātiónem aestívam cōnsúmis?	*How do you spend your summer vacation?*
Dorothéa	Scílicet áliquot pēnsa domī fáciō; multum autem tempus líberum hábeō.	*Of course I do some chores at home; still, I have a lot of free time.*

Magístra	Quid ergō facis?	*So, what do you do?*
Dorothéa	Multa quidem. Intérdum vísitō cognátōs meōs. Intérdum ōram marítimam petō.	*A lot of things, really. At times I visit my relatives. Sometimes I head for the shore.*
Magístra	Quibúscum?	*With whom?*
Dorothéa	Aut cum famíliā aut cum amánte meō.	*Either with my family or with my boyfriend.*
Magístra	Quid áliud facis?	*What else do you do?*
Dorothéa	Per occāsiṓnem ad concéntum eō.	*Occasionally I go to a concert.*

┌──────── LEVEL II **His teacher asks Theodore how he spends his free time.**

Magíster	Quṓmodo tempus líberum tuum cōnsū́mis?	***Teacher:*** *How do you spend your free time?*
Theodórus	Diébus prōfḗstīs plérúmque in āthlética versor.	***Theodore:*** *On weekdays I am generally involved in sports.*
Magíster	Quid facis fīne hebdómadis?	*What do you do on the weekend?*
Theodórus	Multa. Pilā lūdō. Latrúnculīs lūdō. Atque músicam amō.	*A lot of things. I play ball. I play checkers. And I also love music.*
Magíster	Potesne cánere īnstrūméntō músicō?	*Can you play a musical instrument?*
Theodórus	Possum pulsā́re týmpanum atque cánere tūbā.	*Yes, I can play the drum as well play the trumpet.*
Magíster	Potésne cánere órganō?	*Can you play the organ?*
Theodórus	Nōn.	*No.*
Magíster	Quid facis fīne hebdómadis?	*What do you do on the weekend?*
Theodórus	Diē Sātúrnī ego et amícī meī ad forum ī́mus et īnspícimus multās tabérnās.	*On Saturday I and my friends go to the mall and look at many shops.*
Magíster	Vōsne umquam in bibliothḗcam ī́tis?	*Do you ever go to the library?*
Theodórus	Rārō. Sed saepe ī́mus ad áream lūsṓriam extrā bibliothḗcam. Patinā́mus aut corbípilā ibi lū́dimus.	*Rarely. But we often go to the playground outside the library. We skate there or play basketball.*

Magíster	Quid facis inter fériās aestívās?	*What do you do during the summer holidays?*
Theodórus	Saepe piscátum eō cum patre meō.	*I often go fishing with my father.*
Magíster	Habēsne īnstrūméntum piscātórium?	*Do you have fishing tackle?*
Theodórus	Nūper pater īnstrūméntum piscātórium mihi ēmit: cálamum, líneam, rēte.	*Recently my father bought me fishing tackle: a rod, line, and a net.*
Magíster	Scīsne piscārī?	*Do you know how to fish?*
Theodórus	Ut tibi vērum dīcam, pater pōnit éscam in hāmō prō mē.	*To tell you the truth, my father puts the bait on the hook for me.*

LEVEL III   **Paula and Robert discuss sports**

Paula	Robértē, quibus āthléticīs lūdis?	*Paula: Robert, what sports do you play?*
Robértus	Vernō témpore plērúmque pillamálleō lūdō, sed intérdum étiam tenísiā lūdō.	*Robert: In the springtime I usually play golf, but at times I also play tennis.*
Paula	Euge! Quibus āthléticīs aestáte lūdis?	*Great! What sports do you play in summer?*
Robértus	Ut vērum dīcam, aestáte in pilamálleī campō saepe sum; egō prōrsus amō pilamálleō lúdere. Postíllāc in nostrā piscínā novā aliquámdiū natō. Sed étiam mē dēléctat basípilā lúdere.	*To tell you the truth, in summer I am often on the golf course; I just love to play golf. After that I swim in our new pool for a while. But I also like to play baseball.*
Paula	Quō locō lūdis?	*What position do you play?*
Robértus	Ad prīmam basim lūdō, sed intérdum intermédius basiárius lūdō. Nempe audíre clāmórēs fautórum mihi placet, quandōcúmque pilam extrā campum lūsórium pulsō.	*Mostly I play first base, but at times I play shortstop. Naturally, I like to hear the cheers of the fans in the stands whenever I hit the ball out of the ball park.*

Paula	Macte virtúte estō, Robérte! Et quid dē autúmnō?	*Good for you! And what about the fall?*
Robértus	Au! Nōlī dē autúmnō mentiónem mihi fácere, quia eō témpore in scholam íterum mihi redeúndum est.	*Ouch! Don't mention fall to me. That's when I have to go back to school.*
Paula	At nōn semper in scholā es. Ágedum, áliquid temporis subsicívi āthlēticīs habēs	*But you are not always in school. You certainly have some spare time for sports.*
Robértus	Rēctē dīcis. Ineúnte autúmnō adhūc basípilā lūdō. Sed deínde cum forīs frīgéscit, corbifólle intus lūdō.	*You're right. At the beginning of fall I still play baseball. But when it gets cold, I prefer to play basketball inside.*
Paula	Qūo locō in turmā lūdis?	*What position do you play on the team?*
Robértus	Quod ego statúrā prōcérā sum, ego centrális sum. Annō superióre turma nostra invicta erat.	*Because I am tall, I am the center. Last year our team was undefeated.*
Paula	Quibus āthléticīs híeme lūdis?	*What sports do you play in winter?*
Robertus	Híeme amō per gláciem patináre in stagnō nōn procul ā mē. Postquam nivis cāsum, saepe nartō in cóllibus in próximō.	*Well, in winter I love to skate on the pond not far from my home. After a snowfall, I often ski on the hills nearby.*
Paula	Édepol, tū quidem magnus āthléta es. Vīsne nunc audíre quibus āthléticīs ego stúdeam? Ego . . .	*Gee, you are a great athlete. Now do you want to hear what sports I go in for? I . . .*
Robértus	Benígnē, Paula. Enimvérō occupātíssimus sum. Gymnásium petō. Amícī meī mē iam dudum exspéctant. Nunc bene valē.	*No, thank you, Paula. You see, I'm really very busy. I am heading for the gym. My friends have been waiting there for me for a long time. Bye-bye for now.*

TOPICAL VOCABULARY_____

Sports

GENERAL TERMS *The following terms can be applied to several sports:*

athlete āthlḗt·a -ae *m,* āthlḗtri·a -ae *f*

athletic āthlḗtic·us -a -um

athletics āthlḗtic·a -ae *f*

ball pil·a -ae *f; (inflated)* fol·lis -is *m;* **catch the ball** pilam *or* follem excíp·iō -ere excḗpī excéptus; **kick the ball** follem pede pulsáre *or* īcō ícere ícī ictus; **play ball** pilā *or* folle lū́dere; **throw the ball** pilam *or* follem coníc·iō -ere coniḗcī coniéctus

ball field camp·us -ī *m* lūsṓrius

ball game lū́s·us -ūs *m* pilae (*or* follis)

ball park camp·us -ī *m* lūsṓrius

bench *s (wooden seat)* scamn·um -ī *n; (ballplayers)* cṓpi·ae -árum *fpl* subsidiáriae

bench *tr* ad scamnum relegáre

bleachers for·ī -ṓrum *mpl*

block ob·stō -stáre -stitī (+ *dat),* obsíst·ō -ere óbstitī (+ *dat),* óbstru·ō -ere obstrúxī obstrúctus

coach *s* exercitā́·tor -tṓris *m* (·trīx -trícis *f)*

coach *tr & intr* exercitáre

compete against conténd·ō -ere -ī contrā (+ *acc)*

competition conténti·ō -ṓnis *f; (event)* certám·en -inis *n*

competitor competī́·tor -tṓris *m* (·trīx -trícis *f)*

equipment apparát·us -ūs *m,* īnstrūmént·um -ī *n*

fan fau·tor -tṓris *m* (·trīx -trícis *f)*

foul offḗns·a -ae *f;* **commit a foul** offḗnsam commítt·ō -ere commísī commíssus, poenáliter agō ágere ḗgī áctus

game lū́d·us -ī *m,* lū́s·us -ūs *m; (contest)* certám·en -inis *n*

half: first half prior pars *f* certáminis; **second half** áltera pars certáminis

half-time dīmídium temp·us -oris *n*

lose *tr* **lose a game** lūdō superárī, lúdum per·dō -dere -didī -ditus ‖ *intr* vinc·or -ī victus sum

losing team turm·a -ae *f* victa

match certám·en -inis *n*

net rēt·e -is *n*

offside: be offside seórsum esse *or* stāre

opponent adversári·us -ī *m* (·a -ae *f)*

overtime additícium temp·us -oris *n*

place: be in first place prīmári·us -a -um esse; **be in second place** secundári·us -a -um esse; **be in third place** térti·us -a -um esse; **hold first (second, third) place** statum prīmárium (secundárium, tertium) habḗre

play lū́d·ō -ere lū́sī lū́sum; **play a game** lū́dum lū́dere; **play ball** pilā lū́dere

player lū́s·or -ṓris *m,* lūstr·īx -ícis *f*

playing field camp·us -ī *m* lūsṓrius

position loc·us -ī *m;* **what position do you play?** quō locō lūdis?

referee árbi·ter -trī *m* (·tra -trae *f)*

point pūnct·um -ī *n;* **score a point** pūnctum ferō ferre tulī lātus

score summ·a -ae *f* pūnctórum, status -ūs *m; (in golf)* summa íctuum; **final score** status fīnális; **keep score** ratiṓnem pūnctṓrum notáre; **the**

score is tied summae pūnctórum sunt parēs

scoreboard tábul·a -ae *f* pūnctórum

sport dīspórt·us -ūs *m*, āthlétic·a -ae *f;* **go in for sports** dīspórtibus *(or* āthléticāe) stúd·eō -ére -uī; **play sports** in dīspórtibus *(or* āthléticā) vers·or -ári -átus sum, dīspórtibus *(or* āthléticā) lúdere

sport shirt camísi·a -ae *f* campéstris

sportswear vest·is -is *f* campéstris

squad turm·a -ae *f*

stadium stádi·um -ī *n*

stands *(for seating)* for·ī -órum *mpl*

sub, substitute succēdáne·us -ī *m* (·a -ae *f),* supposítíci·us -ī *m* (-a -ae *f)*

team turm·a -ae *f*

throw s.o. out of the game áliquem ā campō (lūsório) relegáre

umpire árbit·er -rī *m* (·tra -trae *f)*

warm-up exercitáti·ō -ónis *f*

whistle síbil·us -ī *m;* **blow the whistle** síbilum ēmítt·ō -ere ēmísī ēmíssus; **final whistle** síbilus fīnális; **starting whistle** síbilus initiális

win victóri·a -ae *f*

win a game lūdō vinc·ō -ere vícī

winning team turm·a -ae *f* victrīx

win on points praevalénti·a -ae *f* pūnctórum

win on points praevál·eō -ére -uī per pūncta

SPECIFIC SPORTS

archery sagittáti·ō -ónis *f*

arrow sagítt·a -ae *f*

bow arc·us -ūs *m*

hit fér·iō -íre

bull's eye médius scop·us -ī *m*

target scop·us -ī *m*

badminton lūd·us -ī *m* pilae pinnátae; **play badminton** pilā pinnátā lúdere

net rēt·e -is *n*

net ball pil·a -ae *f* rēte perstríngēns

racket rētícul·um -ī *n* (manubriátum)

baseball *(the ball itself)* basípil·a -ae *f; (the sport)* lūd·us -ī *m* basípilae; **play baseball** basípilā lúdere

base (first, second, third, home) bas·is -is *(acc:* -im) (príma, secúnda, tértia, summa *or* doméstica)

baseball game basípilae lūs·us -ūs *m,* basípilae certámen -inis *n*

baseman (first, second, third) (prímus, secúndus, tértius) basiári·us -ī *m* (·a -ae *f)*

bat clav·a -ae *f* (lūsória)

batter clavá·tor -tóris *m* (·trīx -trícis *f),* pulsá·tor -tóris *m* (·trīx -trícis *f*

catch excíp·iō -ere excépī excéptus

catcher excépt·or -óris *m,* excéptr·īx -ícis *f*

fly pil·a -ae *f* volāns

glove digitábul·um -ī *n*

hit *s* puls·us -ūs *m*

hit *tr* pulsáre; **hit the ball out of the park** pilam extrā campum lūsórium pulsáre

home plate bas·is -is *f* summa, basis doméstica

home run circúit·us -ūs *m* básium; **hit a home run** circúitum básium fácere

inning miss·us -ūs *m*

outfielder extérnus (-a) cust·ōs -ódis *mf*

pitcher coniéct·or -ốris *m,* coniéctr·īx -ícis *f*

pitcher's mound coniectốris (coniectrícis) grūm·us -ī *m*

shortstop intermédius (-a) basiắri·us -ī *m* (·a -ae *f*)

basketball *(ball)* corbifốll·is -is *m; (game)* corbifốllis lūd·us -ī *m;* **play basketball** corbifốlle lúdere

    basket corb·is -is *m;* **make a basket** corbifốllem per corbem iníciō inícere iniḗcī iniéctus

    center centrắl·is -is *mf*

    court aul·a -ae *f* lūsốria

    dribble *tr & intr* repercutitáre

    dribbling repercúti·ō -ốnis *f*

    forward oppugnắ·tor -tốris *m* (·trīx -trícis *f*)

    foul offḗns·a -ae *f;* **commit a foul** offḗnsam commítt·ō -ere commísī commíssus, poenắliter agō ágere ēgī

    foul line líne·a -ae *f* poenắlis

    foul shot iact·us -ūs *m* ā líneā poenắlī

    guard cust·ōs -ốdis *mf*

    pass *(the act)* corbifốllis trānsiécti·ō -ốnis *f; (the passed ball)* corbifốllis *m* trānsiéctus

    pass the ball corbifốllem trāns·íciō -ícere -iḗcī -iéctus

    slam dunk tuxtax (per corbem) iniéct·us -ūs *m*

boxing pugilắt·us -ūs *m,* pugilắti·ō -ốnis *f*

    box *intr* pugi(l)láre

    boxer pugil -is *mf*

    boxing champion púgilum rēx, rēgis *m;* **heavy-weight champion** púgilum rēx máximī pónderis

boxing glove caest·us -ūs *m*

boxing match certắm·en -inis *n* pugilātốrium

knock down stern·ō -ere strāvī strātus

knock out s.o. cérebrum álicui dīmínu·ō -ere -ī

punch *s* pugn·us -ī *m;* **land a punch on s.o.** pugnum álicui dúcere

punch *tr* pugnō *(or* pugnīs) caed·ō -ere cecídī

punching bag córyc·us -ī *m,* foll·is -is *m* pugilātốrius

ring suggést·us -ūs *m* pugilātốrius

round congréss·us -ūs *m;* **lose a round** congréssū vinc·or -ī victus sum; **win a round** congréssū vinc·ō -ere vícī

bowling cōnốrum lūd·us -ī *m,* cōnilúdi·um -ī *n*

    bowl *intr* globum volutắre, cōnīs lúdere

    bowling alley *(single lane)* cōnốrum āréol·a -ae *f; (building of bowling alleys)* aed·ēs -is *f* ad cōnilúdium

    bowling ball glob·us -ī *m* lūsốrius, glob·us -ī *m* cōnốrum

    bowling lane cōnốrum āréol·a -ae *f*

    bowling pin cōn·us -ī *m* lūsốrius

    make a strike omnēs cōnōs (lūsốriōs) simul dēcút·iō -ere dēcússī dēcússus

discus throwing discī iact·us -ūs *m*

fishing piscắt·us -ūs *m*

    bait esc·a -ae *f*

    catch, haul piscắt·us -ūs *m*

    catch fish pīscēs captáre

fish *intr* (hamō) pisc·or -ā́rī -ā́tus sum; **go fishing** piscā́tum eō īre īvī *or* -iī

fish *s* pisc·is -is *m*

fisherman piscā́t·or -ṓris *m*

fish hook hām·us -ī *m;* **put the bait on the hook** escam hāmō im·pṓnō -pṓnere -pṓsuī -pṓsitus

fishing line līne·a -ae *f* (piscātṓria)

fishing net rēt·e -is *n* (piscātṓrium)

fishing rod cálam·us -ī *m* piscātṓrius, harúnd·ō -inis *f*

fishing tackle īnstrūmént·um -ī *n* piscātṓrium

net rēt·e -is *n*

football *(game)* pedifṓlli·um -ī *n,* pedilū́di·um -ī *n* (mṓre Americā́nō) *(ball)* pedifṓll·is -is *m;* **play football** pedifṓlle lū́dere

center centrā́l·is -is *m*

end (left, right) (siníster, dexter) ālā́ri·us -ī *m or* ext·er -erī *m*

extra point pūnct·um -ī *n* additī́cium; **kick an extra point** prō pūnctō additī́ciō pede pulsā́re

football player pedilū́s·or -ṓris *m*

football shoes calceāmént·a -ṓrum *npl* pedifṓliī

fullback póster·us -ī *m*

goal line calx, calcis *f,* crḗt·a -ae *f*

goal post pāl·us -ī *m* portae

guard *s* custōs, custṓdis *m*

halfback sēmipóster·us -ī *m*

intercept inter·cípiō -cípere -cḗpī -céptus

interception intercépti·ō -ṓnis *f*

interceptor intercépt·or -ṓris *m*

kick pede pulsā́re, pede īc·ō ī́cere īcī ictus

kickoff pede puls·us -ūs *m* initiā́lis

linesman iūd·ex -icis *m* līneā́rius

pass pedifṓllis trāiéct·us -ūs *m*

pass the ball to pedifṓllem trā·íciō -ícere -iḗcī -iéctus ad (+ *acc)*

play in the first (second) half in parte priṓre (ā́lterā) certā́minis lū́dere

quarterback cardinā́l·is -is *m*

punt pedifṓllem pede pulsā́re

sideline līne·a -ae *f* laterā́lis

tackle *s* assultā́t·or -ṓris *m*

tackle *tr* stern·ō -ere strāvī strātus

touchdown: make *or* **score a touchdown** calcem *(or* crḗtam) attíngō -ere áttigī attáctus

golf pilamā́lle·us -ī *m;* **play golf** pilamā́lleō lū́dere

bunker obstrā́cul·um -ī *n*

caddy clā́vig·er -erī *m*

fairway prāt·um -ī *n* perlóngum

golf club clāv·a -ae *f; (driver)* clāva agitātṓria; *(iron)* clāva férrea

golf course pilamā́lleī camp·us -ī *m*

golfer pilamā́lleī lūs·or -ṓris *m* (lūstr·īx -ī́cis *f*)

green ā́re·a -ae *f* víridis

hit īcō ī́cere ī́cī ictus

hole fovéol·a -ae *f*

miniature golf course loc·us -ī *m* pilamā́lleī minū́tī

sand trap harēnā́ri·a -ae *f*

score summ·a -ae *f* íctuum

stroke ict·us -ūs *m*

tee grū́mul·us -ī *m*

tee off prīmum īc·ō -ere īcī

gymnastics gymnástic·a -ae *f*

  balance beam tīgn·um -ī *n* aequilíbriī

  gym, gymnasium gymnási·um -ī *n*

  gym shoes cálce·ī -órum *mpl* gýmnicī

  horizontal bar ferr·um -ī *n* trānsvérsum

  horse ecúle·us -ī *m*

high jump salt·us -ūs *m* in altum

hockey lūd·us -ī *m* hoccéius, alsūlégi·a -ae *f;* **play hockey** hoccéiō lūdere

  blue line líne·a -e *f* caerúlea

  center centrál·is -is *mf*

  defenseman dēféns·or -óris *m*

  field hockey pedilús·us -ūs *m* campéstris

  goal port·a -ae *f;* **score a goal** dísculum in portam immítt·ō -ere immísī

  goalie portári·us -ī *m*

  hockey stick ped·um -ī *n,* férul·a -ae *f* repánda

  left defenseman dēféns·or -óris *m* siníster

  left wing ālári·us -ī *m* siníster

  puck díscul·us -ī *m;* **pass the puck to** dísculum trā·íciō -ícere -iéci -iectus ad (+ *acc*)

  red line líne·a -ae *f* rubra

  right defenseman dēféns·or -óris *m* dexter

  right wing ālári·us -ī *m* dexter

  rink stádi·um -ī *n* glaciále

  wing āl·a -ae *f*

hunting vēnáti·ō -ónis *f; (the practice of hunting)* vēnātúr·a -ae *f*

  hunt *s* vēnát·us -ūs *m*

hunt *tr & intr* vēn·or -árī -átus sum

  hunting dog can·is -is *m* vēnáticus

  hunting gear īnstrumént·um -ī *n* vēnātórium

  hunting gun sclopétum -ī *n* vēnātórium

  game *(prey)* vēnáti·ō -ónis *f*

  shotgun focíl·e -is *n* bifistulátum

ice-skating (per gláciem) patináti·ō -ónis *f*

  figure skating patináti·ō -ónis *f* artificiósa

  ice-skate *s* pátin·us -ī *m*

  ice-skate *intr* (per gláciem) patináre

  speed skating patináti·ō -ónis *f* vēlōx

judo luctáti·ō -ónis *f* Iūdóica *(or* Iapónica)

karate luctáti·ō -ónis *f* carática

lacrosse lūd·us -ī *m* lacrossénsis

  crosse *or* **lacrosse stick** cróci·a -ae *f;* **cradle the crosse** cróciam agitáre

long jump salt·us -ūs *m* in longum

mountain climbing ascénsi·ō -ónis *f* móntium

  climb ascénd·ō -ere -ī ascénsus

  mountain climber ascéns·or -óris *m* (ascénstr·īx -ícis *f*) móntium

  repel fūne dēscénd·ō -ere -ī

  rope fūn·is -is *m* scēnsórius

pentathlon pentáthl·um -ī *n;* **win the pentathlon** pentáthlō vinc·ō -ere vīcī

Ping-Pong mēnsuális pilae lūd·us -ī *m;* **play Ping-Pong** mēnsálī pilā lúdere

  net rēt·e -is *n*

  net ball pil·a -ae *f* rēte perstríngēns

  paddle pálul·a -ae *f*

pole vaulting salt·us -ūs *m* perticárius

pole-vault *intr* pérticā sál·iō -íre -uī

bar repágul·um -ī *n;* **to clear the bar** repágulum trāsíl·iō -íre -uī

pole pértic·a -ae *f*

polo alsūlégi·a -ae *f* equéstris

rollerskating patináti·ō -ónis *f* rotális

rollerblade pedirótīs lābor lābī lāpsus sum

rollerblades pedirót·ae -árum *fpl*

rollerskate rotéllīs patináre

rollerskates pátin·ī -órum *mpl* rotálēs

skating *s* patináti·ō -ónis *f*

skate patináre

skate board tábul·a -ae *f* subrotáta

skater patiná·tor -tóris *m* (·trīx -trícis *f*)

rowing rēmigáti·ō -ónis *f*

crew rēmígi·um -ī *n*

oar rēm·us -ī *m*

regatta certám·en -inis *f* rēmígiī

row rēmigáre

rowboat cumb·a -ae *f or* scaph·a -ae *f* rēmígera

rower rēm·ex -igis *m*

rugby harpást·um -ī *n;* **play rugby** harpástō lúdere

sailing vēlificáti·ō -ónis *f*

mast māl·us -ī *m*

sail vēl·um -ī *n*

sail vēlificáre

sailboat scaph·a -ae *f* vēlífica

tack *intr* scapham flect·ō -ere flexī

topsail súppar·um -ī *n*

skiing *s* nartáti·ō -ónis *f*

ski *s* nart·a -ae *f;* **put on skis** nartās pédibus aptáre, nartās adstrín·gō -gere -xī; **take off the skis** nartās dēstríngere; **wax the skis** nartās incerāre

ski *intr* nartáre

ski boot cálig·a -ae *f* nartātória

skier nartát·or -óris *m,* nartátr·īx -ícis *f*

ski instructor nartándī magís·ter -trī *m* (·tra -trae *f*)

ski jump suggést·us -ūs *m* dēsultórius

ski jump(ing) dēsultúr·a -ae *f* nartātória

ski lift anabáthr·um -ī *n* nartātórium

ski lodge cas·a -ae *f* nartātórum

ski pole bácul·um -ī *n* nartātórium

ski run currícul·um -ī *n* nivále

ski slope clīv·us -ī *m* nartātōrius

slalom *(slope)* dēcúrsi·ō -ónis *f* flexuōsa; *(contest)* certám·en -inis *n* dēcursiónis flexuósae

snow nix, nivis *f;* **powdery snow** nix pulvérea

soccer pedifólli·um -ī *n,* pedilúdi·um -ī *n;* **play soccer** pedifólle lúdere

card: show the red (yellow) card chártulam rubram (flāvam) mōnstráre

corner kick pede puls·us -ūs *m* anguláris

fullback (left, right) (siníster, dexter) dēféns·or -óris *m,* (sinístra, dextra) dēfénstr·īx -ícis *f*

get possession of the ball pedifólle pót·ior -írī -ítus sum

goal port·a -ae *f;* **score a goal** follem per portam pede pulsáre

goal! Hei, follis per portam!

goalie portári·us -ī *m* (·a -ae *f)*

goal area áre·a -ae *f* portária

goal line líne·a -ae *f* portária

half-time score stat·us -us *m* dīmídiī témporis

header cápite puls·us -ūs *m*

head the ball pedifóllem cápite pulsáre

heel kick calce puls·us -ūs *m*

kick pede pulsáre

linesman iūd·ex -icis *m* līneárius

midfield (center, left, right) (centrális, siníster, dexter) lūs·or -óris *m* médius, (centrális, sinístra, dextra) lūst·rīx -rícis *f*

pass the ball to pedifóllem trānspulsáre ad

pass trānspuls·us -ūs *m*

penalty area áre·a -ae *f* poenális

penalty kick pede puls·us -ūs *m* poenális; *(from 11 meters)* pede puls·us -ūs *m* úndecim metrórum; *(from 7 meters)* pede puls·us -ūs *m* septem metrórum

period: play in the first (second, third) period in parte prióre (álterā, tértiā) certáminis lúdere

soccer player pedilús·or -óris *m* (·tr·īx -trícis) *f*

soccer shoes calceámént·a -órum *npl* pedifólliī

soccer stadium stádi·um -ī *n* pedifóliī

striker oppugná·tor -tóris *m* (·trīx -trícis *f*)

sweeper lūs·or -óris *m* líber, lūstr·īx -ícis *f* líbera

wing (left, right) (siníster, dexter) ālári·us -ī *m,* (sinístra, dextra) ālári·a -ae *f*

surf *intr* tábulā flūctívagā per summās undās prōláb·or -ī prōlápsus sum

surfboard tábul·a -ae *f* flūctívaga

swimming *s* natáti·ō -ónis *f*

  back stroke natátiō *f* resupína

  dive *s* praeceps salt·us -ūs *m*

  dive praeceps sál·iō -íre -iī *(or* -uī)

  diving board tábul·a -ae *f* dēsultória

  free-style natátiō *f* líbera

  breast stroke natátiō *f* pectorális *(or* prōna)

  swim natáre

  swimming instructor natándī magist·er -rī *m* (·ra -rae *f)*

  swimming meet certám·en -inis *n* natātórium

  swimming pool piscín·a -ae *f,* natábul·um -ī *n*

tennis tenilúdi·um -ī *n,* tenísi·a -ae *f;* **play tennis** tenísiā lúdere

  backhand drive puls·us -ūs *m* invérsus

  doubles tenilúdi·um -ī *n* bis binórum

  drive *s* pila *f* vī prōpúlsa

  drive *tr* **drive the ball** pilam vī prōpéll·ō -ere prōpúlsī prōpúlsus

  fault víti·um -ī *n*

  hit pulsáre; **to hit out of bounds** ultrā líneam pulsáre

  net rēt·e -is *n*

  net ball pil·a -ae *f* rēte prestríngēns

  racket rētícul·um -ī *n* (manubriátum)

  serve *s* dēiéct·us -ūs *m*

  serve *intr* déíc·iō -ere dēiécī

  set áct·us -ūs *m*

  singles tenilúdi·um -ī *n* singuláre

  tennis ball pil·a -ae *f* tenísiae

tennis court camp·us -ī *m* tenísiae

tennis match certám·en -inis *n* tenísiae

tennis player tenilús·or -óris *m* (·trīx -trícis *f*), lenilúdi·us -ī *m* (·a -ae *f*)

track *(the sport)* cursúr·a -ae *f; (course laid out for running)* currícul·um -ī *n*

  finish line calx, calcis *f,* crēt·a -ae *f;* **reach the finish line** calcem *(or* crētam) attíng·ō -ere áttigī attáctus

  hundred meter dash curs·us -ūs *m* centum metrórum

  lap currícul·um -ī *n,* spáti·um -ī *n*

  long-distance running curs·us -ūs *m* spátiī longī

  runner curs·or -óris *m,* curstr·īx -ícis *f*

  start iníti·um -ī *n* cursūs

volleyball foll·is -is *m* volátilis; *(game)* lūd·us -ī *m* follis volátili

  net rēt·e -is *n*

  play volleyball folle volátilī lúdere

  spike the ball follem magnā vī prōpéll·ō -ere prōpúlsī prōpúlsus

water-skiing per summās undās nartáti·ō -ónis *f*

  water-ski *intr* per summās undās nartáre

  water-ski *s* nart·a -ae *f* aquática

weight-lifting subláti·ō -ónis *f* pónderis

wrestling luctáti·ō -ónis *f*

  wrestle luct·or -árī luctátus sum

  wrestler luctát·or -óris *m*

  wrestling match certámen -inis *n* luctātiónis

OTHER LEISURE ACTIVITIES

admission ticket tésser·a -ae *f* aditiális

amplifier amplificátr·um -ī *n*

amusement park hort·ī -órum *mpl* públicī oblectáriī

band symphóni·a -ae *f*

camera phōtomáchin·a -ae *f,* máchínul·a -ae *f* phōtográphica; **digital camera** phōtomáchin·a digitális

card chártul·a -ae *f* lūsória; **(ace** bíni·ō - ónis *m;* **card game** chártulárum (lūsóriárum) lūd·us -ī *m;* **club** crux, crucis *(gen pl:* crucum) *f;* **diamond** rūt·a -ae *f;* **heart** cor, cordis *n;* **jack** pedísequ·us -ī *m;* **joker** chártul·a -ae *f* fortúnāns; **king** rēx, rēgis *m;* **queen** rēgín·a -ae *f;* **spade** pāl·a -ae *f)*

  play cards chártulīs (lūsóriīs) lúdere

  pass céterīs cēd·ō -ere cessī

  shuffle (cut, deal) the cards chártulās mísc·eō -ére -uī mixtus (sēpón·ō -ere sēpósuī sēpósitus, distríbu·ō -ere -uī)

  suit col·or -óris *m*

  trick vicēs *fpl* (síngulae, bīnae, trīnae, quatérnae)

  trump *s* col·or -óris *m* praelátus

  trump *intr* (chártulās) fér·iō -íre

cartoon *(on television)* spectácul·um -ī *n* animátum

checker latrúncul·us -ī *m;* **checkers** *(game)* latrúnculórum lūd·us -ī *m;* **play checkers** latrúnculīs lúdere

  crown corōnáre

  king rēx, rēgis *m*

chess lūd·us -ī *m* scācórum, scācilúdium -ī *n;* **castle** *s* turr·is -is *f; tr* adroccáre; **checkmate** rēgem tén·eō -ére -uī; **checkmate!** cavē rēgī!; **chessboard** scācári·um -ī *n;* **chess piece** scāc·us -ī *m;* **king** rēx, rēgis *m;* **knight** equ·es -itis *m;* **pawn** ped·es -itis *m;* **queen** rēgín·a -ae *f;* **rook**

roch·us -ī *m;* **square** *(on chessboard)* cas·a -ae *f;* **play chess** scācīs lúdere

chore pēns·um -ī *n;* **do chores** pēnsa fác·iō -ere fēcī factus

CD compáctus disc·us -ī *m*

CD player discophóni·um -ī *n*

comedy cōmoédi·a -ae *f*

concert concént·us -ūs *m*

dance *intr* saltāre

dance *s* saltắti·ō -ốnis *f*

dancer saltắt·or -ốris *m,* saltắtr·īx -ícis *f*

discotheque discothếc·a -ae *f*

documentary documentắri·um -ī *n*

evening vésper·a -ae *f;* **in the evening** vésperī; **on Saturday evening** diē Sātúrnī vésperī

film pellícul·a -ae *f,* taeníol·a -ae *f;* **documentary film** pellícul·a -ae *f* documentária; **educational film** pellícula didascálica; **movie film** pellícula cīnēmatográphica; **photographic film** taeníola phōtográphica; **show a film** pellículam (cīnēmatográphicam) exhíb·eō -ếre -uī -itus

free time tempus *n* líberum

gamble áleā lūd·ō -ere lūsī

game *(prey)* praed·a -ae *f,* vēnắti·ō -ốnis *f; (play)* lūd·us -ī *m*

game show spectácul·um -ī *n* lūsốrium

gun sclopết·um -ī *n*

hide and seek: play hide and seek per lūsum latitắre et quaeritắre

holidays fếri·ae -árum *fpl*

library bibliothếc·a -ae *f*

monopoly monopóli·um -ī *n;* **play monopoly** monopóliō lúdere

motor boat nāvícul·a -ae *f* automatária

movie *adj* cīnēmatográphic·us -a -um, cīnēmátic·us -a -um

movie pellícul·a -ae *f* cīnēmatográphica; **go to see (watch) a movie** pellículam cīnēmatográphicam vīs·ō -ere -ī (spectắre); **horror movie** pellícula horrífera; **show a movie** pellículam cīnēmatográphicam exhíb·eō -ếre -uī -itus

movie camera māchínul·a -ae *f* cīnēmatográphica

movie film pellícul·a -ae *f (or* taeníol·a -ae *f)* cīnēmatográphica

movies imágin·ēs -um *fpl* movéntes

movie screen línte·um -ī *n* lātē exténtum

movie theater cīnēmatế·um -ī *n;* **go the movie theater** *(or* **to the movies) in** cīnēmatếum eō īre īvī

music músic·a -ae *f*

musical *adj* músic·us -a -um

musical *s* melodrāmáti·um -ī *n*

musician músic·us -ī *m,* músic·a -ae *f*

nightclub discothếc·a -ae *f*

opera melodrắm·a -atis *n;* **go to see an opera** melodráma vīs·ō -ere -ī

operetta melodramáti·um -ī *n*

organ órgan·um -ī *n*

overture exốrdi·um -ī *n* (melodrámatis)

paint *s* pigmént·um -ī *n,* col·or -ốris *m*

paint *tr & intr* ping·ō -ere pīnxī pīctus

paint brush pēnicíll·us -ī *m*

painting *(the art; picture)* pīctűr·a -ae *f*

pheasant phāsiắn·a -ae *f*

photograph imág·ō -inis *f* phōtográphica

photograph *tr* phōtográphicē rédd·ō -ere réddidī rédditus

photographer phōtógraph·us -ī *m* (·a -ae *f*)

photographic film taeníol·a -ae *f* phōtográphica

piano clāvicórdi·um -ī *n*

picnic cénul·a -ae *f* subdiális; **go on a picnic** excursiónem ad cénulam subdiálem sūméndam fáci·ō -ere fēcī

picnic basket pānári·um -ī *n*

Ping-Pong mēnsuális pilae lūs·us -ūs *m;* **play Ping-Pong** mēnsálī pilā lūd·ō -ere lūsī

play *(in a theater)* fábul·a -ae *f*

play lūd·ō -ere lūsī lūsum; *(an instrument)* can·ō -ere cécinī cantus *(+ abl of the instrument); (records, tape recorder, tapes)* impéll·ō -ere ímpulī impúlsus; **play a game** lūdum lúdere; **play ball** pilā lúdere; **play chess** scācīs lúdere; **play the drum** týmpanum pulsáre;

playground áre·a -ae *f* lūsória

polka saltáti·ō -ónis *f* Bohémica; **dance the polka** Bohémicē saltáre

radio radiophón·um -ī *n;* **by** *(or* **on the) radio** radiophónicē; **listen to the radio** radiophónum audíre; **turn down the radio** vim radiophónī remítt·ō -ere remísī remíssus; **turn on (off) the radio** radiophónum excitáre *or* impéd·iō -íre -ívi -ítus (expedíre)

radio broadcast ēmíssi·ō -ónis *f* radiophónica

radio station státi·ō -ónis *f* radiophónica

record orb·is -is *m* phōnográphicus; **play (listen to) records** orbēs phōnográphicōs impéll·ō -ere ímpulī impúlsus (aúdi·ō -íre -ívī)

record player māchínul·a -ae *f* phōnográphica

remote control moderátr·um -ī *n* remótum

sneakers cálce·ī -órum *mpl* gýmnicī

stage play fábul·a -ae *f* theatrális *(or* scaénica)

stereo system systéma -atis *n* stereophónicum

summer *s* aest·ās -átis *f*

summer vacation fériae aestívae; **spend the vacation** fériās agō ágere ēgī āctus

swing *intr* oscilláre

swing *s* oscíll·um -ī *n*

talk show spectácul·um -ī *n* disputātívum

tape *s (audiotape)* phōnotaeníol·a -ae *f; (audiocasette)* phōnocasét·a -ae *f*

tape *tr* in phōnotaeníolā ímprim·ō -ere impréssī impréssus

tape recorder magnētophón·um -ī *n*

television tēlevísi·ō -ónis *f;* **television set** tēlevísóri·um -ī *n;* **run on (turn off) the television** tēlevísórium excitáre (impéd·iō -íre -ívī -ítus) (expedíre); **turn down (turn up) the television** vim tēlevísórii remítt·ō -ere remísī remíssus (aúg·eō -ére auxī auctus); **watch television** tēlevīsiónem spectáre, tēlespectáre

television audience tēlevísór·ēs -um *mpl*

television broadcast ēmíssi·ō -ónis *f* tēlevīsífica

television channel canál·is -is *m* tēlevīsíficus

television commercial praecóni·um -ī *n* tēlevīsíficum

television news tēlediúrn·a -órum *npl*

television program prográmm·a -atis *n*
tēlevīsíficum, ēmíssi·ō -ốnis *f*
tēlevīsífica

television screen quadr·um -ī *n*
tēlevīsíficum

television series séri·ēs -éī *f* tēlevisífica

television set tēlevīsốri·um -ī *n*

television show spectácul·um -ī *n*
tēlevīsíficum

telvision station státi·ō -ốnis *f*
tēlevīsífica

television viewer tēlevís·or -ốris (·trīx
-trícis *f)*

tragedy tragoédi·a -ae *f*

TV room conclắve -is *n* tēlevīsốriō
īnstrúctum

vacation vacắti·ō -ốnis *f,* fếri·ae -ắrum
fpl; **at the end of vacation** fếriīs
peráctīs; **spend the vacation** férias

agō ágere ēgī āctus; **summer
vacation** fếriae aestívae, vacắtiō
aestíva

video cassette casết·a -ae *f*
magnētoscópia; **listen to (play) a
video cassette** aúd·iō -íre -ívī *or* -iī
-ítus (ēvólv·o -ere -ī) casétam
magnētoscópiam

video cassette recorder (VCR)
magnētoscópi·um -ī *n*

video game lūs·us -ūs *m*
magnētoscópicus; **play video games**
lūdōs magnētoscópicōs lúdere

walk: go for a walk dēambulắre

week hébdom·as -adis *f,* septimắn·a -ae *f*

weekday di·ēs -éī *m* prōfếstus

weekend fīn·is -is *m* hebdómadis; **on
the weekend** hebdómade exeúnte,
fīne hebdómadis

Chapter VI: The Human Body

CONVERSATIONS _____

> LEVEL I **The teacher notices that Linda looks sick. She asks Linda what is wrong with her.**

Magístra	Linda, esne tū aegrṓta?	*Teacher: Linda, are you sick?*
Linda	Ita, magístra.	*Linda: Yes, teacher.*
Magístra	Pállida es. Quid est tibi?	*You are pale. What's the matter with you?*
Linda	Stómachus meus dolet.	*My stomach hurts.*
Magístra	Dolétne quicquam áliud?	*Does anything else hurt?*
Linda	Caput meum dolet.	*My head hurts.*
Magístra	Habḗsne febrem?	*Do you have a fever?*
Linda	Fortásse. Frōns et genae sunt cálidae.	*Maybe. My forehead and my cheeks are hot.*
Magístra	Vīse médicum quam prīmum.	*Go see a doctor as soon as possible.*
Linda	Grắtiās tibi, magístra.	*Thank you, teacher.*

> LEVEL II **A doctor is called in for the sick little girl, Scintilla.**

Scintílla	Salvē, médice. Mē male hábeō hódiē.	*Scintilla: Hello, doctor. I'm not feeling good today.*
Médicus	Salvē, Scintílla. Quid est?	*Doctor: Hello, Scintilla. What's the trouble?*
Scintílla	Mē male hábeō. Aegrṓta enim sum.	*I don't feel good. You see, I'm sick.*
Médicus	Quid dolet? Habḗsne dolṓrem stómachī?	*What hurts? Do you have a stomach ache?*

Scintílla	Vae mihi, caput dolet; stómachus dolet; faucēs dolent.	*Oh my, my head hurts; my stomach hurts; my throat hurts.*
Médicus	Frōns vidḗtur cálida. Febrem magnam habēs. Habḗsne cibī appeténtiam bonam?	*Your forehead seems hot. You are running a high fever. Do you have a good appetite?*
Scintílla	Mínimē. Ego nullam omnī́nō appeténtiam hábeō.	*No. I have no appetite at all.*
Médicus	Potḗsne noctū dormī́re?	*Are you able to sleep at night?*
Scintílla	Noctem pervigilā́bam.	*I was awake all night long.*
Médicus	Gravḗdine labṓrās. Ecce, medicī́nam tibi hábeō. Et necésse est tibi manḗre in lectō duōs trēsve diēs.	*You're suffering from a cold. Look, I have medicine for you. And it is necessary for you to stay in bed for two or three days.*
Scintílla	Num in scholam īre possum?	*I can't go to school, can I?*
Médicus	Mínimē vērō!	*Definitely not.*
Scintílla	Ō, grā́tiās, médice; multās grā́tiās! Iam mē mélius hábeō.	*Oh, thanks, doctor; thanks a lot. I already feel better.*

┌──────── LEVEL III   **A doctor arrives at the scene of a fire to treat one of the victims, a young man.**

Médicus	Quid nōmen est tibi? Et quid tibi cóntigit?	***Doctor:*** *What is your name? And what happened to you?*
Aduléscēns	Nōmen mihi est Domínicus. Fuit incéndium in cēnā́culō meō.	***Young man:*** *My name is Dominic. There was a fire in my apartment.*
Médicus	Incendiúmne? Quṓmodo effūgístī?	*A fire? How did you escape?*
Aduléscēns	Flammae capíllōs et fáciem et brácchia cremā́bant. Deínde dē fenéstrā in terram dēsíluī.	*The flames burned my hair and my face and my arms. Then I jumped from the window to the ground.*

Médicus	Licet vídeam num ūlla ossa frḗgeris. Genū dextrum et tālus dexter sunt tumidíssima; fortásse crūs frēgístī.	*Let me see whether you have broken any bones. Your right knee and ankle are very swollen; maybe you broke your leg.*
Aduléscēns	Cḗnseō mē étiam áliquās costās frēgísse. Latus dextrum valdē dolet.	*I think that I also broke some ribs. My right side hurts a lot.*
Médicus	Potésne pedem dextrum movḗre?	*Can you move your right foot?*
Aduléscēns	Possum. Sed dextrō pede stāre nōn possum. Ego quidem nōn omnī́nō cōnsúrgere possum.	*I can. But I can't stand on my right foot. In fact, I can't get up at all.*
Médicus	Nōlī temptā́re cōnsúrgere! Crḗdíbile est tē áliqua ossa frēgísse.	*Don't try to get up. It is possible that you broke some bones.*
Aduléscēns	Quid fáciam?	*What should I do?*
Médicus	Prīmum dābō tibi pílulam quae dolṓrem levábit. Deínde púerī meī tē in lectī́cā domum meam gerent. Possum cūrā́re tē mélius ibi.	*First, I will give you a pill which will relieve your pain. Then my boys will carry you in a litter to my home. I can take care of you better there.*
Aduléscēns	Tibi hábeō magnam grā́tiam ob benefícium tuum.	*I am very grateful to you for your kindness.*

Topical Vocabulary_____

ankle tāl·us -ī *m*

appendix appénd·ix -icis *f*

arm brácchi·um -ī *n; (upper)* lacért·us -ī *m*

armpit āl·a -ae *f,* axíll·a -ae *f*

artery artḗri·a -ae *f*

back terg·um -ī *n*

backside postī́c·um -ī *n*

beard barb·a -ae *f*

belly alv·us -ī *f*

belly button umbilī́c·us -ī *m*

bile bīl·is -is *f*

bladder vēsī́c·a -ae *f*

blood sangu·is -inis *m; (outside the body)* cru·or -ṓris *m*

bone os, ossis *n*

bosom sin·us -ūs *m*

bowels alv·us -ī *f*

brain cérebr·um -ī *n*

breast pect·us -oris *n; (female)* mamm·a -ae *f,* mammī́ll·a -ae *f*

buttocks nat·ēs -ium *fpl*

calf sūr·a -ae *f*

cartilage cartilā́g·ō -inis *f*

cheek gen·a -ae *f*

chin ment·um -ī *n*

colon cōl·on -ī *n*

curl cirr·us -ī *m,* cincínnul·us -ī *m*

curly cirrắt·us -a -um, cincínnul·us -a -um; **to have curly hair** cincínnulō capíllō esse

diaphragm praecórdi·a -ốrum *npl*

ear aur·is -is *f; (outer)* aurícul·a -ae *f*

elbow cúbit·um -ī *n,* uln·a -ae *f*

esophagus gul·a -ae *f*

eye ócul·us -ī *m*

eyeball orb·is -is *m* óculī

eyebrow supercíli·um -ī *n*

eyelashes cíli·um -ī *n*

eyelid pálpebr·a -ae *f*

face fáci·ēs -ếī *f*

finger dígit·us -ī *m*

   finger tip dígitus *m* extrḗmus

   index finger ind·ex -icis *m*

   little finger dígitus *m* mínimus

   middle finger dígitus *m* médius

   ring finger dígitus *m* ānulắris

   thumb poll·ex -icis *m*

fingernail ungu·is -is *m*

fist pugn·us -ī *m*

flesh car·ō -nis *f*

foot pēs, pedis *m*

forehead frōns, frontis *f*

genitals genitắl·ia -ium *npl; (female)* muliébr·ia -ium *npl; (male)* viríl·ia -ium *npl*

groin ingu·en -inis *n*

gum gingív·a -ae *f*

hair *(a single hair or hair collectively)* capíll·us -ī *m,* crīn·is -is *m*

hair of the head capíll·ī -ốrum *mpl;* com·a ae *f;* caesári·ēs -ếī *f*

hamstring popl·es -itis *m*

hand man·us -ūs *f*

head cap·ut -itis *n*

   back of the head occipíti·um -ī *n*

   top of the head vert·ex -icis *m*

hearing *(sense)* audīt·us -ūs *m*

heart cor, cordis *n*

heel cal·x -cis *f*

hip cox·a -ae *f,* coxénd·ix -icis *f*

intestines intestín·a -ốrum *npl*

jaw maxíll·a -ae *f*

joint artícul·us -ī *m*

kidneys rēn·ēs -ium *mpl*

knee gen·u -ūs *n*

kneecap patéll·a -ae *f*

knuckle artícul·us -ī *m* dígitī

lap grémi·um -ī *n*

leg crūs, crūris *n*

ligament ligắm·en -inis *n*

lip labr·um -ī *n*

   lower lip labrum *n* īnférius

   upper lip labrum *n* supérius

liver iec·ur -oris *n*

lung pulm·ō -ốnis *m*

marrow medúll·a -ae *f*

mouth ōs, ōris *n*

muscle mắscul·us -ī *m*

mustache súbi·um -ī *n*

mucus mūc·us -ī *m*

nail ungu·is -is *m;* **to cut the nails** unguēs résec·ō -ắre -uī -tus

navel umbilíc·us -ī *m*

neck coll·um -ī *n,* cerv·īx -ícis *f*

nipple papíll·a -ae *f*

nose nās·us -ī *m*

nostrils nār·ēs -ium *fpl*

organ vīsc·us -eris *n*

palate palắt·um -ī *n*

pancreas páncre·as -atis *n*

pelvis pelv·is -is *f*

penis pēn·is -is *m*

phlegm pītuǐt·a -ae *f*

pill pílul·a -ae *f*

pupil pūpíll·a -ae *f*

rectum ān·us -ī *m*

rib cost·a -ae *f*

saliva salív·a -ae *f*

shinbone tíbi·a -ae *f*

shoulder húmer·us -ī *m*

shoulder blade scápul·a -ae *f*

side lat·us -eris *n,* íli·a -órum *npl*

sight *(sense)* vīs·us -ūs *m*

skull calvắri·a -ae *f*

smell *(sense)* odōrắt·us -ūs *m*

sole sol·um -ī *n,* plant·a -ae *f*

spine spīn·a -ae *f*

spit spūt·um -ī *n*

stomach stómach·us -ī *m,* ven·ter -tris *m*

sweat sūd·or -óris *m*

taste *(sense)* gustắt·us -ūs *m*

tear lácrim·a -ae *f*

temple temp·us -oris *n*

tendon tend·ó -inis *m*

testicle testícul·us -ī *m*

thigh fem·ur -oris *n*

thumb poll·ex -cis *m*

throat fauc·ēs -ium *fpl*

toe dígit·us -ī *m* (pedis)

　big toe poll·ex -icis *m*

toenail ungu·is -is *m* pedis

tongue lingu·a -ae *f*

tonsils tonsíll·ae -árum *fpl*

tooth dēns, dentis *m*

　incisors dentēs *mpl* prīmórēs

　molars dentēs *mpl* māxillárēs

touch *(sense)* tact·us -ūs *m*

vagina vāgín·a -ae *f*

vein vēn·a -ae *f*

vertebra vértebr·a -ae *f*

windpipe artéri·a -ae *f*

womb úter·us -ī *m*

waist média pars *f* córporis

wrist prīmóris man·us -ūs *f*

wrist bone carp·us -ī *m*

Chapter VII: Health and Physical Fitness

CONVERSATIONS

LEVEL I **A trainer interviews a young athlete.**

Exercitátor	Claudī, vīsne esse āthlḗta?	*Trainer: Claude, do you want to be an athlete?*
Claúdius	Ita. Ego cōtī́diē mē exérceō.	*Claude: Yes. I exercise every day.*
Exercitátor	Quid facis?	*What do you do?*
Claúdius	Ego cōtī́diē tolū́tim cúrsitō.	*I jog daily.*
Exercitátor	Euge! Quam longē tolū́tim cúrsitās?	*Terrific! How far do you jog?*
Claúdius	Duo mī́lia póssuum tolū́tim cúrsitō.	*I jog two miles.*
Exercitátor	Quid áliud facis?	*What else do you do?*
Claúdius	Sī tempus mihi est, lībrāmḗnta tollō.	*If I have time, I lift weights.*
Exercitátor	Euge! Quid áliud facis?	*Terrific! What else do you do?*
Claúdius	Ego natō in piscī́nā nostrā.	*I swim in our swimming pool.*
Exercitátor	Sī tū haec assíduē fáciēs, tū quidem eris āthlḗta summus.	*If you do this regularly, you'll surely become a top athlete.*

LEVEL II **The trainer attends to an injured athlete.**

Exercitátor	Paule, quid tibi est?	*Trainer: Paul, what's wrong with you?*
Paulus	Ego mihi nócuī in gymnásiō.	*Paul: I hurt myself in the gym.*
Exercitátor	Quid áccidit? Vídeō contūsiṓnēs in crū́ribus.	*What happened? I see bruises on your legs.*
Paulus	Ego et amī́cus currēbā́mus; ego cāsū cécidī et mē cóntudī.	*My friend and I were running; I accidentally fell and bruised myself.*

58

Exercitátor	Habḗsne dolṓrem ingéntem?	*Do you have a lot of pain?*
Paulus	Sānḗ. Ecce genū sinístrum tumḗscit.	*Yes. Look, my left knee is swelling up.*
Exercitátor	Vídeō genū esse tumidíssimum.	*I see that your knee is very swollen.*
Paulus	Quid fáciam?	*What should I do?*
Exercitátor	Prīmum ómnium, fovḗ illud genū in aquā frígidā bis in diē.	*First of all, soak that knee in cold water twice a day.*
Paulus	Id hódiē ter iam fōvī, sed nihil prōdest.	*I've already soaked it three times today, but it doesn't do any good.*
Exercitátor	Potḗsne ambulā́re?	*Are you able to walk?*
Paulus	Aegrḗ. Cum ambulā́re temptō, genū veheménter dolet. Quid fáciam nésciō.	*Hardly. When I try to walk, my knee hurts terribly. I don't know what to do.*
Exercitátor	Cum prīmum fíerī potest, ī in valētūdinā́rium. Nōn possum id cūrā́re hīc. Médicus genū sānā́bit.	*As soon as it is possible, go to the infirmary. I can't treat it here. The doctor will heal your knee.*

───── LEVEL III   **A mother checks her daughter's health.**

Māter	Amā́nda, quid est tibi? Nōn salva vidḗris. Óculī rubent et vidḗris febricitā́re.	***Mother:** Amanda, what's wrong with you? You don't look well. Your eyes are red and you seem to be running a fever.*
Amā́nda	Vídeor labōrā́re gravḗdine. Faucēs meae sunt raucae et ego contínuē álgeō et cōnstánter tússiō.	***Amanda:** I seem to be suffering from a cold. My throat is hoarse, and I am continually cold, and constantly coughing.*
Māter	Mīrum est, nam valētū́dine bonā úteris.	*That's strange, since you enjoy good health.*
Amā́nda	Vḗra dīcis, māter. Valētū́dinem semper cūrā́vī. Assíduē mē exérceō.	*You're right, mother. I have always taken care of my health. I exercise constantly.*

Māter	Id sciō. Tū es córporis hábitūs excelléntis. Fortásse tū hanc gravédinem contraxístī apud scholam.	*I know that. You are in excellent shape. Maybe you caught this cold at school.*
Amánda	Id fíerī potest, Mamma. Pleraéque ex amícīs meīs gravédine labórant.	*That's possible, Mom. Most of my friends are suffering from colds.*
Māter	Vídeō. Fortásse áliquis puer, gravédine labórāns, tē bāsiávit.	*I see. Perhaps some boy with a cold kissed you.*
Amánda	Rēs omnínō nōn ita est. Ego iam tussiébam ántequam mē bāsiávit!	*That's not at all the case. I already had a cough before he kissed me.*

TOPICAL VOCABULARY

ache *s* dol•or -ōris *m*

ache *intr* dol•eō -ēre -uī; **my muscle aches** músculus mihi dolet

aching dol•ēns -entis

acne acn•ē -ēs *f*

acupuncture acūpūnctúr•a -ae *f*

acute *(illness)* acút•us -a -um

adrenaline adrēnālín•um -ī *n;* **the adrenaline flows** adrēnālínum fluit

agile ágil•is -is -e

ail: what ails you? quid est tibi?

ailment mal•um -ī *n*

appetite (cibī) appeténti•a -ae *f;* **lack of appetite** inédi•a -ae *f;* **to give s.o. a good appetite** álicui (cibī) appeténtiam excitáre *or* fác•iō -ere fēcī factus

apply *(a remedy)* adhíb•eō -ére -uī -itus

arthritis arthrít•is -idis *f*

aspirin aspirín•um -ī *n*

asthma asthm•a -atis *n*

athlete āthlét•a -ae *mf;* **like an athlete** āthléticē

athletic āthlétic•us -a -um; **athletic competition** āthlētárum certám•en -inis *n*

athletics āthlétic•a -ae *f*

attack *s (of illness)* ímpet•us -ūs *m,* accéssi•ō -ónis *f*

attack *tr (of a disease)* occupáre

bad aliénus -a -um; **wine is bad for you** vīnum est aliénum tibi

bad breath foet•or -óris *m*

bald calv•us -a -um

baldness calvíti•um -ī *n*

bandage *s* fásci•a -ae *f*

bandage *tr* ligáre

bathe *(a sore limb)* fóv•eō -ére fōvī

bed lect•us -ī *m;* **to be confined to bed** lectō tén•eor -érī tentus sum; **to get out of bed** ē lectō sur•gō -gere -réxī

bed-ridden valētūdinári•us -a -um

biopsy biópsi•a -ae *f*

black and blue lívid•us -a -um; **black and blue mark** lív•or -óris *m*

blood pressure préssi•ō -ónis *f* sánguinis

bloodshot: he has bloodshot eyes óculī eius sánguine suffū́sī sunt

boil fūrúncul·us -ī *m*

bowlegged valg·us -a -um

breathe spīrā́re; **to breathe in** īnspīrā́re; **to breathe out** exspīrā́re

bruise *s* contū́si·ō -ṓnis *f*

bruise *tr* contúnd·ō -ere cóntudī contū́sus

bundle up sē bene opér·iō -íre -uī

cancer can·cer -crī *m*

capsule cápsul·a -ae *f*

cardiac arrest stas·is -eōs *f* cardíaca

carcinoma carcinṓm·a -atis *n*

care cūr·a -ae *f; **take good care of your health!** cūrā dīligénter valētū́dinem tuam!

catarracts catarráct·ae -ā́rum *fpl* oculā́rēs

cause *(pain, swelling)* móveō movḗre mōvī mōtus

chicken pox varicéll·ae -ā́rum *fpl*

chronic long·us -a -um, diūtúrnus -a -um

coach *(of gymnastic training)* exercitā́t·or -ṓris *m*, (·rīx -rī́cis *f*)

cold *s* gravéd·ō -inis *f;* **to catch a cold** gravḗdinem cón·trahō -tráhere -tráxī -tráctus; **to have a cold** gravḗdine labōrā́re

cold *adj* frī́gid·us -a -um; **to feel cold** álg·eō -ḗre alsī

complexion col·or -ṓris *m*; **having a healthy complexion** colōrā́t·us -a -um

condition stat·us -ūs *m*; **physical condition** córporis hábit·us -ūs *m*

confined to bed lectō tenḗrī

contract cóntrah·ō -ere contráxī contráctus; **to contract an illness**

morbum *or* advérsam valētū́dinem contráhere

convalesce convalḗsc·ō -ere

cool off *tr* refrīgerā́re ‖ *intr* refrīgerā́rī

cough *intr* túss·iō -íre

cough *s* tuss·is -is *m;* **to have a cough** túss·iō -íre

cough drop pastíll·us -ī *m* tussiculā́ris

cramp convúlsi·ō -ṓnis *f*

curable sānábil·is -is -e

cure sānā́re

dentist médic·us -ī *m* dentā́rius; médic·a -ae *f* dentā́ria

dermatologist dermatólog·us -ī *m* (·a -ae *f*)

diabetes diabḗt·ēs -is *m* mellī́tus

diaphragm praecórdi·a -ṓrum *npl*

diet *s* victūs rát·iō -ṓnis *f*

diet *intr* victūs ratiṓnem observā́re

digest cón·coquō -cóquere -cóxī -cóctus

digestion concócti·ō -ṓnis *f*

disease morb·us -ī *m*

dizziness vertī́g·ō -inis *f*

dizzy vertīginṓs·us -a -um

doctor médic·us -ī *m*, médic·a -ae *f*

doctor's office medicī́n·a -ae *f*

dose pórti·ō -ṓnis *f*; **small dose** portiúncul·a -ae *f*

drug *(as remedy, medicine)* medicāmént·um -ī *n*, medicắm·en -inis *n*; *(as hallucinogen)* medicāment·um -ī *n* psychotrópicum

enjoy *(good health)* ūtor ūtī ūsus sum (valētū́dine prṓsperā)

exercise *s* exercitā́ti·ō -ṓnis *f*

exercise *intr* sē exérc·eō -ḗre -uī

exhale spíritum ēmítt·ō -ere ēmī́sī ēmíssus

fart *s* pēdit·um -ī *n*

fart *intr* pēd·ō -ere pepēdī

fat obés·us -a -um *(opp:* grácil·is -is -e)

fatigue fatigáti·ō -ónis *f*

fever febr·is -is *f;* **constant fever** contínua febris; **high fever** magna *or* ardēns febris; **slight fever** febrécul·a -ae *f;* **to run a fever** febricitáre

fracture fractúr·a -ae *f*

germ germ·en -inis *n*

glaucoma glaucóm·a -atis *n*

go down *(fever)* conquiésc·ō -ere conquiévī; *(swelling)* sē summítt·ō -ere summísī

gym gymnási·um -ī *n*

gym instructor exercitát·or -óris *m;* exercitátr·īx -ícis *f*

gymnastic gymnástic·us -a -um

gymnastics ars, artis *f* gymnástica

hale and hardy salv·us et válid·us -a -um

hard on inimíc·us -a -um (+ *dat*)

have *or* **suffer from** *(an illness, a disease)* affíc·ior affícī afféctus sum (+ *abl) or* labōráre (+ *abl,* ab + *abl,* ex + *abl);* **that man has cancer** ille cancrō afficitur *or* cancrō labórat

heal *tr* sānáre ‖ *intr* sānésc·ō -ere

health *(good or bad)* valētúd·ō -inis *f;* **bad health** advérsa *(or* mala, gravis, infírma) valētúdō; **bad health suddenly hit me** mala valētúdō mē repéntē invásit; **good health** bona, *(or* firma, cómmoda, próspera) valētúdō; **in sound health** válid·us -a -um

health food alimént·um -ī *n* salúbre

healthy sān·us -a -um, salv·us -a -um

heart attack ímpet·us -ūs *m* cardíacus

heart failure dēfécti·ō -ónis *f* cardíaca

heart transplant cordis trānsplantáti·ō -ónis *f*

hernia hérni·a -ae *f*

heroin heroín·um -ī *n* **to use heroin** heroínō ūtor ūtī ūsus sum

high blood pressure hypertóni·a -ae *f*

hoarse rauc·us -a -um

hormone hormón·um -ī *n*

hospital valētūdinári·um -ī *n*

hygiene hygiéni·ē -ēs *f;* **practice hygiene** hygiēniēn exercére

hygienic hygiēnic·us -a -um

illness morb·us -ī *m,* (mala) valētúd·ō -inis *f;* **serious illness** gravis valētúdō

ills mal·a -órum *npl*

indigestion crúdit·ās -átis *f*

infirmary valētūdinári·um -ī *n*

inflame īnflammáre

inflammation īnflammáti·ō -ónis *f*

irritate exasperáre

kidney stones cálcul·ī -órum *mpl* rēnálēs

jog tolútim cursitáre

lack of appetite inédi·a -ae *f*

laxative medicám·en -inis *n* laxatívum

lift weights librāmént·a -órum *npl* toll·ō -ere sústulī sublátus

ligament ligám·en -inis *n*

lotion linimént·um -ī *n*

lump tubércul·um -ī *n*

medical practice medicín·a -ae *f*

medication medicámént·um -ī *n*

medicine medicín·a -ae *f;* **to practice medicine** medicínam exérc·eō -ére -uī

mouthwash collūtóri·um -ī *n*

mumps parōtít·is -idis *f*

muscle múscul·us -ī *m;* **pull a muscle** músculum distórqu·eō -ére distórsī distórtus

musclebound músculīs nimis cōnstríct·us -a

muscle cramp músculī convulsi·ō -ōnis *f*

muscle spasm músculī spasm·us -ī *m*

muscular mūsculós·us -a -um

muscular distrophy dystróphi·a -ae *f* mūsculáris

nearsighted my·ops -ópis

nearsightedness myópi·a -ae *f*

nerve nerv·us -ī *m*

nourishment alimént·um -ī *n*

nurse nosócom·a -ae *f;* nosócom·us -ī *m*

nursing home gerontocómi·um -ī *n*

obese obés·us -a -um

obesity obésit·ās -átis *f*

ophthalmologist ophthalmólog·us -ī *m* (·a -ae *f*)

pacemaker impulsóri·um -ī *n* cardíacum

pain dol·or -óris *m;* **severe pain** ingēns *or* véhemēns dolor

patient *s* ae·ger -grī *m*, ae·gra -grae *f*

physical condition córporis hábit·us -ūs *m*

pill pílul·a -ae *f*

pimple pústul·a -ae *f*

pulse vēnárum puls·us -ūs *m;* **(fast** vegétior; **weak** languídior); **to feel s.o.'s pulse** vēnās *or* pulsum vēnárum alicújus tentáre

psychiatrist psȳchíátr·ter -trī *m* (·tra -trae *f*)

psychologist psȳchológic·us -ī *m* (·a -ae *f*)

radiation treatment cūráti·ō -ónis *f* radiális

recover recíp·iō -ere recépī suam valētúdinem bonam; **to recover from a serious illness** ē gravī morbō recreárī

relieve leváre

remedy for remédi·um -ī *n* (+ *gen*)

run curr·ō -ere cucúrrī cursum

running cursúr·a -ae *f*

runny nose distillātión·ēs -um *fpl*

shape: to be in bad (good) shape malī (bonī) hábitūs esse, in malō (bonō) hábitū esse

shiver trem·or -óris *m; (severe)* membrórum quassáti·ō -ónis *f*

shiver trem·ō -ere -uī

shortness of breath anhēláti·ō -ónis *f*

sick ae·ger -gra -grum, aegrót·us -a -um; **to get sick** in morbum íncid·ō -ere -ī

sickly male válid·us -a -um

sickness morb·us -ī *m*

situps: to do situps idéntidem resíd·eō -ére resédī

skin cut·is -is *f* **(pale** pállida; **dry** árida; **soft** mollis; **tough** dūra; **wrinkled** rūgós·us -a -um)

skinny macilent·us -a -um

slim grácil·is -is -e *(opp:* obésus)

smallpox varíol·ae -árum *fpl* **smallpox vaccination** vaccīnáti·ō -ónis *f* variolárum

sneeze stérn·uō -úere -uī

sneezing sternūmént·um -ī *n*

sore dol·ēns -entis; **my back is sore** tergum mihi dolet

sound ínte·ger -gra -grum

spasm spasm·us -ī *m*

sprain *s* luxātúr·a -ae *f*

sprain *tr* luxáre

stroke apopléxi·a -ae *f* cérebrī

strong válid·us -a -um *(opp:* imbecíll·us -a -um)

sun tan adústus col·or -óris *m;* **to get a sun tan** coloráre

suntanned adústus

surgeon chīrúrg·us -ī *m* (·a -ae *f)*

sweat *s* sūd·or -óris *m;* **to break a sweat** īnsūdáre

sweat *intr* sūdáre

swell sē attóll·ō -ere *(opp:* sē summíttere)

swell up *(of limbs)* túrg·eō -ére tursī

swollen túmid·us -a -um

symptom not·a -ae *f,* sign·um -ī *n*

tablet pastíll·us -ī *m*

tendonitis tendovāgīnít·is -idis *f*

throat fauc·ēs -ium *fpl*

toothache dol·or -óris *m* déntium

toothbrush pēnícul·us -ī *m* dentárius

toothpaste past·a -ae *f* dentária

train *tr (for physical proficiency)* exercitáre **‖** *intr* sē exercitáre

trainer *(of athletes)* exercitát·or -óris *m,* exercitátr·īx -ícis *f*

treat cūráre

treatment (for) cūráti·ō -ónis *f (+ gen of illness)*

trouble: to have stomach trouble stómachō labōráre

tuberculosis phthís·is is *f*

turn for the worse in dētérius inclīnárī

virus vīr·us -ī *n;* **there is a virus going around** vīrus percrēbréscit

vitamin vītamín·um -ī *n*

well salv·us -a -um

wrinkle rūg·a -ae *f*

wrinkled rūgós·us -a -um

Chapter VIII: Food and Drink

CONVERSATIONS

┌──────── LEVEL I   **A waitress waits on a senator.**

Minístra	Salvē, senåtor. Possúmne tibi ministråre?	*Waitress: Hello, senator. Can I help you?*
Senåtor	Étiam.	*Senator: Yes.*
Minístra	Vīsne súmere ientåculum an prándium?	*Do you want to eat breakfast or lunch?*
Senåtor	Quīn bene māne est. Ítaque ientåculum sūmam, quaesō.	*Why, it's early in the morning. And so I'll have breakfast, please.*
Minístra	Vīsne ōva frīcta an ōva mīxta an ōva dūra an ápala?	*Do you want fried eggs or scrambled eggs or hard-boiled eggs or soft-boiled?*
Senåtor	Volō habére láganum ex ōvīs.	*I want to have an omelet.*
Minístra	Vīsne lardum cum láganō?	*Do you want bacon with your omelet?*
Senåtor	Étiam, at tantúmmodo pauca segménta.	*Yes, but just a few strips.*
Minístra	Vīsne pānem tostum an pānículōs?	*Do you want toast or rolls?*
Senåtor	Affer ad mē áliquid pānis tostī.	*Bring me some toast.*
Minístra	Et quid vīs potáre? Cáffeam?	*And what do you want to drink? Coffee?*
Senåtor	Ita, pocíllum cáffeae cum crēmō. Et própéra! Fame mórior.	*Yes, a cup of coffee with cream. And hurry! I'm dying of hunger.*
Minístra	Ientåculum tuum mox hīc erit.	*Your breakfast will soon be here.*

LᴇᴠᴇL II   **A waiter serves dinner.**

Miníster	Salvē. Possúmne tibi nunc servíre, bone vir?	*Waiter: Hello. Can I serve you now, sir?*
Philíppus	Sānē potes.	*Philip: Yes, indeed, you can.*
Miníster	Quid in cēnā sūmēs?	*What will you have for supper?*
Philíppus	Búbulam assam velim, quaesō.	*I'd like roast beef, please.*
Miníster	Utrum sēmicóctam an percóctam?	*Rare or well done?*
Philíppus	Percóctam, quaesō. Et solána frīcta.	*Well done, please. And fried potatoes.*
Miníster	Vīsne iūs an acētária?	*Do you want soup or a salad?*
Philíppus	Quod iūs habēs hódiē?	*What kind of soup do you have today?*
Miníster	Iūs collýricum suāve ex búbulā.	*Delicious beef noodle soup.*
Philíppus	Accípiam acētária.	*I'll take the salad.*
Miníster	Vīsne pocíllum cáffeae an pocíllum theae?	*Do you want a cup of coffee or a cup of tea?*
Philíppus	Neutrum vērō. Praéferō vīnum.	*Actually, neither. I prefer wine.*
Miníster	Utrum vīnum album an sanguíneum?	*White wine or red?*
Philíppus	Accípiam vīnum sanguíneum. Praéferō vīnum austérum vīnō dulcī.	*I'll take the red wine. I prefer dry wine to sweet wine.*
Miníster	Vīsne bellária?	*Do you want dessert?*
Philíppus	Estne in promptū placénta ex socolátā?	*Is chocolate cake available?*
Miníster	Sānē quidem. Vīsne áliquid ámplius?	*Yes, indeed. Do you want anything else?*
Philíppus	Nihil ámplius, grátiās.	*Nothing else, thanks.*
Miníster	Appōnam cibum quam prīmum.	*I'll serve your meal as soon as I can.*

┌─────────── LEVEL III   **Planning a shopping trip.**

Māter	Phyllis, nōbīs obsōnándum est hódiē māne. Esne prompta?	*Mother: Phyllis, we have to go shopping this morning. Are you ready?*
Phyllis	Bene, Mamma. Dīc mihi quid velīs et ego ómnia in hāc tábulā dēnotábō.	*Phyllis: Fine, Mom. Tell me what you want and I'll jot down everything on this tablet.*
Māter	Prīmum ómnium, ad laniénam íbimus.	*First of all, we will go to the butcher shop.*
Phyllis	Quibus cárnibus egḗmus?	*What meats do we need?*
Māter	Velim émere offās porcínās et búbulam assam, et fortásse áliquot hillās caléntēs.	*I'd like to buy pork chops and roast beef and some hot dogs.*
Phyllis	Áliquid ámplius?	*Anything else?*
Māter	Nihil ámplius apud laniénam. Cārō hódiē tam pretiósa est! Deínde íbimus in forum holitórium.	*Nothing more at the butcher shop. Meat is so expensive nowadays. Next we will go to the vegetable market.*
Phyllis	Quae hólera vīs émere ibi?	*What vegetables do you want to buy there?*
Māter	Lactúcam, cucúmerēs, carótās, brássicam. Adhūc hábeō satis aliórum hólerum.	*Lettuce, cucumbers, carrots, and cabbage. I still have enough of the other vegetables.*
Phyllis	Vīsne īre étiam in forum piscárium?	*Do you also want to go to the fish market?*
Māter	Tantúmmodo sī passer recēns est vēnális hódiē.	*Only if fresh flounder is for sale today.*
Phyllis	Egēmúsne áliquō dē pīstrínā?	*Do we need anything from the bakery?*
Māter	Ita, trēs pānēs et decem pānículōs atque áliquot crústula.	*Yes, three loaves of bread and ten rolls, as well as some cookies.*
Phyllis	Cūr tot obsónia nōbīs eménda sunt?	*Why do we have to buy so many groceries?*

Māter	Pater pátruum suum et ámitam et eórum líberōs ad cēnam vocávit. Spērō eōs canem suum nōn allātúrōs.	*Because father invited his uncle and aunt and their children to dinner. I hope they don't bring their dog along.*
Phyllis	Sīc ego ipsa spērō.	*I hope so too.*

TOPICAL VOCABULARY

alcohol álcohol -is *n*

alcoholic alcohólic·us -a -um

almond amýgdal·um -ī *n*

appetizer gustáti·ō -ónis *f*

apple māl·um -ī *n*

apple pie crūst·um -ī *n* ex mālīs

apricot armeníac·um -ī *n*

artichoke cínar·a -ae *f*

asparagus aspárag·us -ī *m*

bacon lard·um -ī *n*

baker pīst·or -óris *m*, pīst·rīx -rícis *f*

bakery pīstrín·a -ae *f*

banana arién·a -ae *f*, banán·a -ae *f*

bean fab·a -ae *f*

beef búbul·a -ae *f*

beer cervísi·a -ae *f*

berry bacc·a -ae *f*

birthday cake līb·um -ī *n* nātále

bland lēn·is -is -e

boiled ēlíx·us -a -um

booze tēmét·um -ī *n*

bread pān·is -is *m*

breaded salígne·us -a -um

breakfast ientácul·um -ī *n*

broil tórr·eō -ére -uī tostus

broth iūs, iūris *n*, iúscul·um -ī *n*

bun collýr·is -idis *f*

butcher láni·us -ī *m*

butcher shop lanién·a -ae *f*

butter *s* butýr·um -ī *n*

butter *tr* butýrum adhib·eō -ére -uī -itus ad (+ *acc*)

cabbage brássic·a -ae *f*, cramb·ē -ēs *f*

cake placént·a -ae *f*

candy cuppédi·ae -árum *fpl*

carrot carót·a -ae *f*

catsup *see* **ketchup**

cauliflower brássic·a -ae *f* Pompēiána

celery helēoselín·um -ī *n*

cereal cereál·ia -ium *npl*

cheese cake savíll·um -ī *n*

cheese cáse·us -ī *m*

cherry céras·um -ī *n*

cherry pie crūst·um -ī *n* ex cérasīs

chestnut castáne·a -ae *f*

chicken (*as food*) gallīnáce·a -ae *f*

chocolate socolát·a -ae *f*

clam my·ax -acis *m*

clear the table mundáre mēnsam

cocktail própom·a -atis *n*, cinn·is -is *m*

coffee cáffe·a -ae *f*

coffee cup pocíll·um -ī *n* caffeárium

coffee pot oll·a -ae *f* cáffeae

coffee set sýnthes·is -is *f* caffeária

cook coqu·ō -ere coxī coctus

cookie crústul·um -ī *n*

corkscrew extrácul·um -ī *n*

corn maízi·um -ī *n;* **corn on the cob**
maízium -ī *n* in spīcā

course fércul·um -ī *n*

cream crēm·um -ī *n*

cucumber cúcum·is -eris *m*

cup of coffee (of tea) pocíll·um -ī *n*
cáffeae (theae)

dessert bellári·a -órum *npl*

dine cēnáre; **to dine out** forīs cēnáre

dinner cēn·a -ae *f;* **to eat dinner** cēnáre,
cēnam sūm·ō -ere -psī -ptus; **to have
a roast for dinner** assum in cēnā
háb·eō -ére -uī -itus

dressing embámm·a -atis *n*

drink *s* póti·ō -ónis *f;* **drinks** pōtión·ēs
-um *fpl,* pōtulént·a -órum *npl*

drink *tr* pōtáre

duck *(as food)* anatín·a -ae *f*

eat edō ēsse ēdī ēsus; *(a meal)* sūm·ō
-ere -psī -ptus

egg ōv·um -ī *n;* **fried** frīctum; **hard-
boiled** dūrum; **soft-boiled** ápalum;
scrambled permíxtum

fish *(as food)* piscát·us -ūs *m*

flounder pass·er -eris *m*

food cib·us -ī *m*

fork furcíll·a -ae *f,* fuscínul·a -ae *f*

fresh rec·ēns -éntis

fruit pōm·a -órum *npl*

frozen congelāt·us -a -um; **frozen
dinner** cēn·a -ae *f* congelāta; **frozen
food(s)** cib·ī -órum *mpl* congelātī

fry fríg·ō -ere frīxī frīctus

frying pan sartág·ō -inis *f*

garlic áli·um -ī *n*

grape ūv·a -ae *f*

green pepper piperít·is -idis *f*

grill *s* crátícul·a -ae *f*

grill *tr* super crātículam assáre

ham pern·a -ae *f;* **smoked ham** perna
fūmósa

hamburger búbul·a -ae *f* concísa

have *(e.g., dinner)* sūm·ō -ere -psī -ptus

hazelnut avellán·a -ae *f*

honey mel, mellis *n*

hot dog hill·a -ae calēns *(gen:* hillae
caléntis) *f*

hunger fam·ēs -is *f*

ice cream congélidum crēm·um -ī *n*

jelly quil·on -ī *n*

juice succ·us -ī *m*

ketchup kétsup·um -ī *n*

kidney bean phasél·us -ī *m*

ladle trūll·a -ae *f*

lamb *(as food)* agnín·a -ae *f*

lemon cítre·um -ī *n*

lemonade līmonát·a -ae *f*

lentil lēn·s -tis *f*

lettuce lactúc·a -ae *f*

loaf of bread pān·is -is *m*

lobster locúst·a -ae *f*

macaroni past·a -ae *f* tubuláta

margarine margarín·um -ī *n*

market macéll·um -ī *n*

mashed potatoes pultícul·a -ae *f* ex
solánīs

mayonnaise liquám·en -inis *n*
Magónicum

meal cib·us -ī *m*

meat car·ō -nis *f*

meat tray carnári·um -ī *n*

menu ind·ex -icis *m (or* tabéll·a -ae *f)*
cibórum

milk lāc lactis *n*

mineral water aqu·a -ae *f* minerális

mixed salad commíxta acētắri·a -ŏrum *npl*

muffin scriblít·a -ae *f*

mulberry mōr·um -ī *n*

mushroom fung·us -ī *m*

mustard sináp·i *(or* sináp·e) -is *n*

napkin mapp·a -ae *f*

noodle soup iū·s -ris *n* collýric·um

nut nux, nucis *f*

olive oil óle·um -ī *n*

olive olív·a -ae *f*

omelet lágan·um -ī *n* ex ōvīs

onion caep·a -ae *f*

orange māl·um -ī *n* aurántium

orangeade mālī aurántiī pŏti·ō -ŏnis *f*

orange juice aurántiī succ·us -ī *m*

oyster óstre·a -ae *f*

pancake artolágan·um -ī *n*

parsley ápi·um -ī *n*, petroselín·um -ī *n*

pasta collýr·a -ae *f*

pea pīs·um -ī *n*

peach pérsic·um -ī *n*

peanut árach·is -idis *f* (hypogéa)

peanut butter būtýr·um -ī *n* ex arachídibus

pear pir·um -ī *n*

peel *s* cut·is -is *f*

peel *tr* resecắre cutem (+ *gen)*

pepper pip·er -eris *n*

pepper shaker piperín·um -ī *n*

pickle sálgam·um -ī *n*

pie crūst·um -ī *n*

piece frūst·um -ī *n*

pineapple píne·a -ae *f* (Americána)

pitcher úrce·us -ī *m*

plate patéll·a -ae *f*

plum prūn·um -ī *n*

pork porcín·a -ae *f*

pork chop off·a -ae *f* porcína

potato solán·um -ī *n*

potato chips lámin·ae *fpl* solānŏrum

powder sugar sácchar·um -ī *n* pulvéreum

pretzel pretíol·a -ae *f;* **soft pretzel** mollis pretíola

prune prūn·um -ī *n* condítum

radish rādícul·a -ae *f*

raisin (ūva) pass·a -ae *f*

rare sēmicóct·us -a -um *(opp:* percóctus)

raspberry mōr·um -ī *n* Īdaéum

restaurant caupŏn·a -ae *f*

rice orýz·a -ae *f*

roast *tr* assắre

roast *s* ass·um -ī *n*

roast beef būbul·a -ae *f* assa

roast pork porcín·a -ae *f* assa

roll pānícul·us -ī *m*

salad acētắri·a -ŏrum *npl*

salt shaker salín·um -ī *n*

salt sāl, salis *n*

sandwich pastíll·um -ī *n* fartum; **ham sandwich** pastíllum pernā fartum

sardine sard·a -ae *f*

sauce iūs, iūris *n*

sausage farcím·en -inis *n,* bótul·us -ī *m*

seasoning condīmént·um -ī *n*

serve *(a person)* sérv·iō -íre -iī; *(food)* appón·ō -ere appósuī appósitus

shell putám·en -inis *n*

shrimp squill·a -ae *f*

silverware argénte·a -ŏrum *npl*

sip sorbillắre

slice segmént·um -ī *n*

soup iūs, iūris *n,* iúscul·um -ī *n;* **hot soup** iūs férvēns

spicy ācer ācris ācre

spoon cóchle·ār -áris *n*

steak frūst·um -ī *n* búbulae

stove foc·us -ī *m*

straw *(for drinking)* sīph·ō -ónis *m*

strawberry frāg·um -ī *n*

strip segmént·um -ī *n*

sugar sácchar·um -ī *n*

sugar bowl vāscul·um -ī *n* sáccharī

sugar cube sácchar·um -ī *n* cúbicum

table mēns·a -ae *f*

taste sáp·iō -ere -ívī *or* -iī; **to taste like** sápere (+ *acc*)

tea the·a -ae *f*

tip corollári·um -ī *n;* stips, stipis *f*

toast pān·is -is *m* tostus

tomato lycopérsic·um -ī *n*

tray fércul·um -ī *n*

veal vitulín·a -ae *f*

vegetable hol·us -eris *n*

venison vēnáti·ō -ónis *f*

vinegar acét·um -ī *n*

waiter minís·ter -trī *m*

waitress minístr·a -ae *f*

walnut jūgl·āns -ándis *f*

water aqu·a -ae *f*

watermelon pep·ō -onis *f,* mēl·ō -ōnis *m* aquōsus

white bread pān·is -is *m* cándidus

whole-wheat bread autopýr·us ī *m*

wine vīn·um -ī *n;* **dry** austérum; **sweet** dulce; **red** sanguíneum; **light** ténue; **white** album

[NOTE—The Romans did not have candy, chocolate, coffee, corn, ice cream, peanuts, potatoes, popcorn, tea, tomatoes, or turkey. They knew of butter and sugar, but used them only for medicinal purposes. Some of these items came into use in the Middle Ages, when Latin was still a widely spoken language.]

Chapter IX: Days, Weeks, Months, Years

CONVERSATIONS

LEVEL I   **Two friends discuss their birthdays.**

Patrícius	Mắrcia, quārē tū hódiē tam exōrnắta es?	*Patrick: Marcia, why are you so decked out today?*
Mắrcia	Quod hódiē est meus diēs nātắlis.	*Marcia: Because today is my birthday.*
Patrícius	Quot annōs nāta es?	*How old are you?*
Mắrcia	Duodēvīgíntī annōs nāta sum. Quot annōs nātus es tū?	*I am eighteen years old. How old are you?*
Patrícius	Ūndēvīgíntī annōs.	*I'm nineteen.*
Mắrcia	Quō mēnse nātus es?	*In what month were you born?*
Patrícius	Ego mēnse Augústō nātus sum. Quō diē nāta es?	*I was born in August. On what day were you born?*
Mắrcia	Quīntō diē mēnsis Māiī scílicet.	*On the fifth of May, of course.*
Patrícius	At enim quō diē hebdómadis nāta es?	*What I mean is, on what day of the week were you born?*
Mắrcia	Ut vēra dīcam, certum nōn sciō. Diē Véneris, crēdō.	*To tell you the truth, I don't know for sure. On Friday, I believe.*
Patrícius	Quốmodo nātắlem celebrắbis?	*How are you going to celebrate your birthday?*
Mắrcia	Māter agitắbit nātālíciam hódiē vésperī. Et tū invītắris.	*My mother is throwing me a birthday party this evening. And you are invited.*
Patrícius	Grắtiās. Ắfferam tibi bellum nātālícium.	*Thanks. I'll bring you a nice birthday present.*

LEVEL II   **Two friends discuss their favorite seasons.**

Glória	Robérte, quod tempus annī tibi máximē placet?	*Gloria: Robert, which season do you like best?*
Robértus	Aestátem praecípuē amō, quia in piscínā nostrā aut in stāgnō natáre possum. Pilā porrō lúdere possum.	*Robert: I especially love summer because I can swim in our swimming pool or in the pond. Besides, I can play ball.*
Glória	Quod tempus annī tibi mínimē placet?	*Which season do you like least?*
Robértus	Hiems, opínor. Nivem amō, sed frígoris impátiēns sum. Inter Decémbrem et Februárium ego semper gravédinem terríbilem cóntrahō.	*Winter, I suppose. I love the snow, but I can't take the cold. I always catch a terrible cold between December and February.*
Glória	Sed híeme nartáre et patináre et pilās níveās conícere póssumus. Et tráheā vehī póssumus.	*But in winter we can ski and skate and throw snowballs. And we can go sleigh riding.*
Robértus	Probē dīcis, at, illō témpore annī, viae nōnnúmquam sunt lúbricae et perīculósae.	*You're right, but at that time of the year the roads are often slippery and dangerous.*
Glória	Placétne tibi vēr?	*Do you like spring?*
Robértus	Placet. Post sevéram híemem, amoénum est íterum forīs lúdere. Quid tū dē vēre putās?	*Yes, I do. After a harsh winter, it is pleasant to play outside again. What do you think of spring?*
Glória	Ō, amō vidére flōrēs flōréscere. Quid autem dē autúmnō?	*O, I love to see the flowers begin to blossom. Now, what about the fall?*
Robértus	Cum dē autúmnō putō, statim dē scholā putō. Saepe mīror num magístrī sint vērō tam cúpidī ad scholam redeúndī post férias aestívās.	*When I think about autumn, I immediately think about school. I often wonder whether teachers are really all that eager to return to school after summer vacation.*
Glória	Nésciō, sed id dúbitō.	*I don't know, but I doubt it.*

┌──────────── LEVEL III   **A father gives his son some family history.**

Marcus	Pater, quandō nātus es?	***Mark:*** *Father, when were you born?*
Cícerō	Tértiō diē (mēnsis) Iānuáriī.	***Cicero:*** *On the third of January.*
Marcus	Ubi adulēscébās?	*Where did you grow up?*
Cícerō	Adulēscéntiam omnem in oppídulō Arpínō trānségī.	*I spent my entire youth in the small town of Arpinum.*
Marcus	Ubi lūdum frequentábās ut adulēscéntulus?	*Where did you attend school as a youngster?*
Cícerō	Prīmō lūdum Arpínī frequentábam. Ante autem décimum quārtum annum meum, pater meus Rōmam migráre cōnstítuit.	*First I attended school in Arpinum. But before my fourteenth year, my father decided to move to Rome.*
Marcus	Rediístī umquam Arpínum?	*Did you ever return to Arpinum?*
Cícerō	Nōn per multōs annōs. Décimum quíntum agēns, ego togam virílem sūmpsī. Nōn diútius eram adulēscéntulus sed aduléscēns.	*Not for many years. At the age of fifteen, I received the toga of manhood. I was no longer a youngster, but a young man.*
Marcus	Quandō tū cōnsul creátus es?	*When were you elected consul?*
Cícerō	Quadrāgésimum quārtum annum agēns, cōnsul creátus sum. Tum vix eram vir médiae aetátis.	*I was elected consul in my forty-fourth year. At that time I was barely a middle-aged man.*
Marcus	Senténtiā tuā, tē nunc senēscénte, quae aetās erat óptima ómnium?	*In your opinion, now that you are growing old, what age was the best of all?*
Cícerō	Est difficile dictū. Quaeque enim aetās—īnfántia, puerítia, adulēscéntia, juvénta, média aetās, étiam senéctūs—habet et gaúdia et incómmoda.	*It is hard to say. For each age— infancy, boyhood, adolescence, youth, middle age, even old age—has its joys and disappointments.*
Marcus	Quod est gaúdium máximum senectútis?	*What is the greatest joy of old age?*
Cícerō	Quamquam iam aetáte prōvéctus sum, tamen conténtus sum, quod mihi est mēns sāna in córpore sānō. Sed gaúdium máximum est família amāns et amícī fidélēs.	*Although I am now up in years, I am content, because I have a sound mind in a sound body. But the greatest joy is a loving family and loyal friends.*

TOPICAL VOCABULARY

adult *adj* adúlt·us -a -um

age aet·ās -átis *f; **at age fifteen**
décimum quīntum annum ag·ēns
-éntis; **he was ten years of age** erat
decem annōs nātus

aged longaév·us -a -um

be up in years aetáte prōvéct·us -a -um
esse

birth nātívit·ās -átis *f*

born: to be born nāsc·or -ī nātus (-a)
sum

boyhood pueríti·a -ae *f*, aet·ās -átis *f*
puerílis; **from boyhood on** ā púerō

calendar fāst·ī -órum *mpl*, calendári·um
-ī *n*

century saécul·um -ī *n*

death mor·s -tis *f*

die mór·ior -ī mórtuus (-a) sum

grow old senésc·ō -ere sénuī

grow up iuvenésc·ō -ere iúvenī

growing up adulésc·ēns -éntis

grown-up *adj* adúlt·us -a -um

infancy īnfánti·a -ae *f*

month mēns·is -is *m*

    January Iānuári·us -ī *m*

    February Februári·us -ī *m*

    March Márti·us -ī *m*

    April Apríl·is -is *m*

    May Māi·us -ī *m*

    June Iúni·us -ī *m*

    July Iúli·us -ī *m*

    August Augúst·us -ī *m*

    September Septém·ber -bris *m*

    October Octó·ber -bris *m*

    November Novém·ber -bris *m*

    December Decém·ber -bris *m*

more (less) than ... years old māior
(minor) quam ... annōs nāt·us -a -um

old vétul·us -a -um; **older** māi·or -or -us
nātū; **oldest** máxim·us -a -um nātū;
to be ... years old ... annōs nāt·us
-a -um esse

old age senéct·ūs -útis *f*, senéct·a -ae *f*

old lady an·us -ūs *f;* **little old lady**
anícul·a -ae *f*

old man sen·ex -is *m*

old woman an·us -ūs *f*

oldster sen·ex -is *m*

over sixty years old māior (quam)
annōs sexāgíntā nāt·us -a -um

period of life aet·ās -átis *f* vītae

season temp·us -oris *n* annī

    spring vēr, vēris *n*

    summer aest·ās -átis *f*

    fall autúmn·us -ī *m*

    winter hi·ems -emis *f*

week hébdom·as -adis *f*, septimán·a -ae *f*

weekday di·ēs -éī *m* prōféstus

    Sunday di·ēs -éī *m* Sōlis; domínic·a
-ae *f*

    Monday di·ēs -éī *m* Lūnae

    Tuesday di·ēs -éī *m* Mārtis

    Wednesday di·ēs -éī *m* Mercúriī

    Thursday di·ēs -éī *m* Iovis

    Friday di·ēs -éī *m* Véneris

    Saturday di·ēs -éī *m* Sātúrnī,
Sábbat·a -órum *npl*

year ann·us -ī *m;* **in my twenty-first
year** annum prīmum et vīcésimum
ag·ēns -éntis ego ...

young parv·us -a -um, párvul·us -a -um;
younger iúni·or -or -us; min·or -or
-us (nātū); **youngest** mínim·us -a
-um (nātū)

young lady adulḗsc·ēns -éntis *f,*
  muliércul·a -ae *f*

young man adulḗsc·ēns -éntis *m,*
  iūven·is -is *m*

youngster adulēscéntul·us -ī *m,*
  adulēscéntul·a -ae *f*

youth *(age)* adulēscénti·a -ae *f (between*
  puer *and* júvenis, *between 15 and 30*
  years and even beyond); (young men
  collectively) iuvént·ūs -ū́tis *f; (young*
  person) iúven·is -is *mf*

youthful iuvenī́l·is -is -e; iúven·is -is -e

THE JULIAN CALENDAR

◆ The names of the Roman months are:
**Iānuárius, Februárius, Mártius,
Aprílis, Māius, Iúnius, Iúlius,
Augústus, Septémber, Octóber,
Novémber, Decémber.** The name of
the month functions as an adjective
in agreement with **Kaléndae, Nōnae,
Ídūs.** Before Augustus, the months
July and August were called
Quīntílis and **Sextílis.** *(Originally
the Roman calendar began with
March. This explains the names
Septémber, Octóber, etc. In the year
153 B.C., in order to give the new
consuls time to organize their armies
and reach the latest frontier, the year
was made to begin with January.)*

◆ The Romans counted backward from
three points in the month, Calends
(Kaléndae), Nones **(Nōnae),** and
Ides **(Ídūs),** to which the names of
the months are added as adjectives:
**Kaléndae Iānuáriae, Nōnae
Ianuáriae, Ídūs Iānuáriae.** The
Calends are the first day, the Nones
the fifth, and the Ides the thirteen. In
March, May, July, and October the
Nones and the Ides are two days
later.

◆ In counting backward, the Romans
used **prídiē** (+ acc) for "the day
before": **prídiē Kaléndas Iānuáriās**
(= December 31), **prídiē Nōnās
Iānuáriās** (= January 4); **prídiē Ídūs
Iānuáriās** (= January 12).

◆ Because the Romans, in counting
backward, counted both ends of the
series, the second day before (by our
system of reckoning) was designated
as **diē tértiō ante Kaléndās, Nōnās,
Ídūs.** Similarly, the third day before
(by our system of reckoning) was
designated as **diē quārtō,** and so on.

◆ To complicate matters further, the
Romans generally did not say, for
example, "the third day before the
Calends of January" but "before the
third day Calends January," **ante
diem tértiam Kaléndās Iānuáriās,**
often abbreviated **a. d. III Kal. Iān.**
This was the most common form for
indicating dates. Others were:

diē tértiō ante Kaléndās Iānuáriās

tértiō ante Kaléndās Iānuáriās

tértiō (III) Kaléndās Iānuáriās

◆ These phrases are treated as nouns
and combined with the prepositions
ex (from), **ad** or **in** (up to), e.g.:

**ex ante diem tértium Kaléndās
Iānuáriās** (from December 30)

ad *(or* **in) ante diem tértium
Kaléndās Iānuáriās** (up to
December 30)

◆ In leap years, the 25th was reckoned
as the extra day in February. The
24th was called **ante diem VI
Kaléndās Mártiās** and the 25th as
**ante diem bis VI Kaléndās
Mártiās.**

day of the month	March, May, July, October	January, August, December	April, June, September, November	February	February (leap year)
1	Kaléndīs	Kaléndīs	Kaléndīs	Kaléndīs	Kaléndīs
2	VI Nōnās	IV Nōnās	IV Nōnās	IV Nōnās	IV Nōnās
3	V Nōnās	III Nōnās	III Nōnās	III Nōnās	III Nōnās
4	IV Nōnās	Prídiē Nōnās	Prídiē Nōnās	Prídiē Nōnās	Prídiē Nōnās
5	III Nōnās	Nōnīs	Nōnīs	Nōnīs	Nōnīs
6	Prídiē Nōnās	VIII Īdūs	VIII Īdūs	VIII Īdūs	VIII Īdūs
7	Nōnīs	VII Īdūs	VII Īdūs	VII Īdūs	VII Īdūs
8	VIII Īdūs	VI Īdūs	VI Īdūs	VI Īdūs	VI Īdūs
9	VII Īdūs	V Īdūs	V Īdūs	V Īdūs	V Īdūs
10	VI Īdūs	IV Īdūs	IV Īdūs	IV Īdūs	IV Īdūs
11	V Īdūs	III Īdūs	III Īdūs	III Īdūs	III Īdūs
12	IV Īdūs	Prídiē Īdūs	Prídiē Īdūs	Prídiē Īdūs	Prídiē Īdūs
13	III Īdūs	Ídibus	Ídibus	Ídibus	Ídibus
14	Prídiē Īdūs	XIX Kal.	XVIII Kal.	XVI Kal.	XVI Kal.
15	Ídibus	XVIII Kal.	XVII Kal.	XV Kal.	XV Kal.
16	XVII Kal.	XVII Kal.	XVI Kal.	XIV Kal.	XIV Kal.
17	XVI Kal.	XVI Kal.	XV Kal.	XIII Kal.	XIII Kal.
18	XV Kal.	XV Kal.	XIV Kal.	XII Kal.	XII Kal.
19	XIV Kal.	XIV Kal.	XIII Kal.	XI Kal.	XI Kal.
20	XIII Kal.	XIII Kal.	XII Kal.	X Kal.	X Kal.
21	XII Kal.	XII Kal.	XI Kal.	IX Kal.	IX Kal.
22	XI Kal.	XI Kal.	X Kal.	VIII Kal.	VIII Kal.
23	X Kal.	X Kal.	IX Kal.	VII Kal.	VII Kal.
24	IX Kal.	IX Kal.	VIII Kal.	VI Kal.	VI Kal.
25	VIII Kal.	VIII Kal.	VII Kal.	V Kal.	bis VI Kal.
26	VII Kal.	VII Kal.	VI Kal.	IV Kal.	V Kal.
27	VI Kal.	VI Kal.	V Kal.	III Kal.	IV Kal.
28	V Kal.	V Kal.	IV Kal.	Prídiē Kal.	III Kal.
29	IV Kal.	IV Kal.	III Kal.		Prídiē Kal.
30	III Kal.	III Kal.	Prídiē Kal.		
31	Prídiē Kal.	Prídiē Kal.			

Hours of the Day and Watches of the Night _____

Table of Hours of the Day and Watches of the Night Among the Romans
Tabula Hōrārum Diēī Vigiliārumque Noctis Apud Rōmānōs

DAY			DIES	
Morning	6	o'clock	Mātūtī́num	hōra prīma
	7	o'clock	tempus	hōra secúnda
	8	o'clock		hōra tértia
	9	o'clock		hōra quārta
	10	o'clock		hōra quīnta
	11	o'clock		hōra sexta
Midday	**12**	**o'clock**	**Merī́diēs**	**hōra séptima**
	1	o'clock		hōra octáva
	2	o'clock		hōra nōna
	3	o'clock		hōra décima
	4	o'clock		hōra ūndécima
	5	o'clock		hōra duodécima
NIGHT			**NOX**	
Evening	6	o'clock	Vespertī́num	hōra prīma
	7	o'clock	tempus	hōra secúnda
	8	o'clock		hōra tértia
	9	o'clock		hōra quārta (vigília secúnda)
	10	o'clock		hōra quīnta
	11	o'clock		hōra sexta
Midnight	**12**	**o'clock**	**Média nox**	**hōra séptima (vigília tértia)**
	1	o'clock		hōra octáva
	2	o'clock		hōra nōna
	3	o'clock		hōra décima (vigília quārta)
	4	o'clock		hōra ūndécima
	5	o'clock		hōra duodécima

Note—The Romans considered a day as extending from midnight to the next midnight, just as we do. However, they counted the hours from 6:00 a.m. When the Romans wished to distinguish day-time hours from night hours, they said, for example **prīma diḗī hōra** and **prīma noctis hōra**.

Chapter X: Expressions of Time

CONVERSATIONS

┌──────── LEVEL I   **Marie asks her friend how he spends his days.**

María   Joséphe, quómodo diem ágitās?   *Marie: Joseph, how do you spend your day?*

Ioséphus   Bene māne surgō et mē lavō.   *Joseph: I get up early in the morning and wash (myself).*

María   Quotā hōrā ientáculum sūmis?   *At what time do you eat breakfast?*

Ioséphus   Ad tértiam hōram aut mox deínde ientáculum sūmō.   *I eat breakfast at the third hour (8:00 A.M.) or soon thereafter.*

María   Lūdísne deínde in aédibus an forīs?   *Do you then play in your house or outdoors?*

Ioséphus   Intérdum in aédibus lūdō, áliās lūdō forīs.   *Sometimes I play in my house, at other times I play outdoors.*

María   Lūdísne semper domī?   *Do you always play at home?*

Ioséphus   Nōnnúmquam tempus mātūtínum apud amícum ágitō. Nōn idem cōtídiē fáciō.   *Sometimes I spend the morning at my friend's house. I don't do the same thing every day.*

María   Quotā hōrā prándium sūmis?   *At what time do you eat lunch?*

Ioséphus   Plerúmque sextā aut séptimā hōrā. Váriat in diēs.   *Generally at the sixth or seventh hour (i.e., noon or 1:00 P.M.). It varies from day to day.*

María   Quid facis postmerídiē? Pater tē adhūc in forum dūcit?   *What do you do in the afternoon? Does your father still take you to the forum?*

Ioséphus   Utcúmque tempus patrī est, mē in forum dūcit.   *Whenever my father has time, he takes me to the forum.*

María	Quidnam in forō fácitis?	*Just what do you do in the forum?*
Ioséphus	Cum prīmum in forum pervénimus, tabérnās novās ibi vīsitámus.	*As soon as we get to the forum, we visit the new shops there.*
María	Quid in tabérnīs fácitis?	*What do you do in the shops?*
Ioséphus	Obsōnámus. Pater mihi mūnúsculum saepe emit.	*We shop. My father often buys me a little gift.*
María	Pater tē in forum cōtídiē dūcit?	*Does your father take you to the forum every day?*
Ioséphus	Nōn cōtídiē. Praetéreā, hīs tempóribus pater est occupātíssimus.	*Not every day. Besides, these days my father is very busy.*
María	Eō cāsū, quómodo tempus postmerīdiánum ágitās	*In that case, how do you spend the afternoon?*
Ioséphus	Ego plērúmque tempus postmerīdiánum cum amícīs ágitō.	*I generally spend the afternoon with my friends.*
María	Quid vésperī post cēnam facis?	*What do you do in the evening after dinner?*
Ioséphus	Áliqua pēnsa fáciō. Deínde, sī tempus mihi est, librum legō, dōnec dormítum eō.	*I do some chores. Then, if I have time, I read a book till I go to sleep.*

⌐————— LEVEL II   **A coach interviews a new athlete.**

Exercitátor	Salvē. Tūne āthlḗta novus es?	*Coach: Hello. Are you the new athlete?*
Āthlḗta	Sum.	*Athlete: Yes, I am.*
Exercitátor	Quandō ad gymnásium pervēnístī?	*When did you arrive at the gym?*
Āthlḗta	Paulō ante. Sērōne vēnī?	*A little while ago. Am I late? [lit: have I come late?]*
Exercitátor	Nōn. Vēnístī quidem témperī. Sed áliī āthlḗtae omnēs iam adsunt. Quótiēns tē exércēs?	*No. Indeed, you're on time. But all the other athletes are already here. How often do you exercise?*
Āthlḗta	Ut vēra dīcam, cōtídiē: māne, merídiē, noctū.	*To tell you the truth, daily: morning, noon, and night.*

Exercitátor   Quótiēns ad fūnem salīs?   *How often do you jump rope?*

Āthlḗta   Saltem bis in diē.   *At least twice a day.*

Exercitátor   Ante merídiem an post merídiem?   *Before noon or in the afternoon?*

Āthlḗta   Modo ante merídiem, modo post merídiem. Váriat.   *Sometimes before noon, sometimes in the afternoon. It varies.*

Exercitátor   Quam diū ad fūnem salīs?   *How long do you jump rope?*

Āthlḗta   Saltem sēmihóram.   *At least for half an hour.*

Exercitátor   Quandō novíssimē tolútim cursitāvístī?   *When did you last jog?*

Āthlḗta   Núdius tértius et herī.   *The day before yesterday and yesterday.*

Exercitátor   Hodiḗne tolútim cursitábis?   *Are you going to jog today?*

Āthlḗta   Ita. Mihi in ánimō est tolútim cursitáre pósteā aliquántō.   *Yes. I intend to jog a little later.*

Exercitátor   Senténtiā meā, tū eris āthlḗta praestāns.   *In my opinion, you will be an outstanding athlete.*

LEVEL III   **A traveler is about to take a bus trip to Florida.**

Viátor   Velim iter fácere ā Septentriōnálī Cārolī́nā in Flóridam.   ***Traveler:*** *I'd like to travel from North Carolina to Florida.*

Amícus   Quī est tibi locus dēstinátus?   ***Friend:*** *What is your destination?*

Viátor   Locus dēstinátus mihi est Miámī.   *My destination is Miami.*

Amícus   Habḗsne vectúram in promptū?   *Do you have your fare ready?*

Viátor   Ecce vectúram. Quandō raeda longa discḗdet?   *Here's the fare. When does the bus depart?*

Amícus   Mox. Proféctō secúndā hōrā.   *Soon. In fact, at seven o'clock.*

Viátor   Bene! Intérdiū magis quam noctū iter fácere praéferō.   *Fine. I prefer to travel by day rather than at night.*

Amícus   Quōúsque vīs īre prīmō diē?   *How far do you want to go on the first day?*

Viátor	Velim perveníre in Merīdiōnálem Cārolínam crās sub noctem, sī fíerī potest.	*I'd like to arrive in South Carolina tomorrow by nightfall, if possible.*
Amícus	Ubi pernoctábis?	*Where will you spend the night?*
Viátor	Probābíliter in nésciō quō dēversóriō vehiculáriō.	*Probably in some motel or other.*
Amícus	Quam diū ibi manébis?	*How long will you stay there?*
Viátor	Nōlō équidem multum témporis ibi pérdere.	*I don't want to waste a lot of time there.*
Amícus	Quómodo vésperam agēs?	*How will you spend the evening?*
Viátor	Statim post cēnam, bálneō plúviō ūtar et deínde rēctē íbō dormítum.	*Immediately after dinner, I'll take a shower and then I will go right to sleep.*
Amícus	Quotā hōrā illinc discédere cupis?	*At what time do you want to leave from there?*
Viátor	Statim post ientáculum. Ad próximam noctem spērō nōs in merīdiōnálī Geórgiā futúrōs esse.	*Immediately after breakfast. By the following night, I hope that we will be in southern Georgia.*
Amícus	Istud mehércle est spátium longíssimum!	*Gee, that's a very long stretch!*
Viátor	Sī illūc ante tempus pervēnérimus, póterō mē remíttere paulísper.	*If we arrive there before time, I'll be able to relax a bit.*
Amícus	Quam diū vīs ibi manére?	*How long do you want to stay there?*
Viátor	Mihi in ánimō est bene māne postrídiē discédere. Sī merídiē in septentriōnálī Flóridā pránderō, locum dēstinátum sub noctem pervéniam.	*I intend to leave early in the morning on the next day. If I eat lunch in northern Florida, I will arrive at our destination by nightfall.*

Topical Vocabulary

ago *(prepositive)* abhinc, *e.g.*, **ten years ago** abhinc decem annōs; **a short while ago** paulō ante; **how long ago?** quam prīdem?; **long ago** iamdū́dum, iamprī́dem; **not so long ago** haud ita prīdem; **sometime ago** prīdem dūdum

after *conj* postquam (+ *indic*); *prep* post (+ *acc*); **after this** post hāc

afternoon temp·us -oris *n* postmerīdiā́num; **in the afternoon** postmerī́diē, post merī́diem

afterwards posthāc

again and again étiam atque étiam, idéntidem

always semper

around circā, círciter (+ *acc*), dē (+ *abl*); **around midnight** dē médiā nocte; **around noon** círciter merī́diem

as long as quámdiū (+ *indic*); **as soon as possible** quam prīmum; **as yet** adhūc

at: at least útique; **at most** summum; **at once** contínuō, moméntō

before *conj* ántequam, priúsquam (+ *indic*); *adv* ántea; *prep* ante (+ *acc*); **before daylight** ante lūcem; **before long** propédiem; **before now** ántehāc

beginning prīncípi·um -ī *n;* **at the beginning of the year** prīncípiō annī

briefly summátim

by *(not later than)* ad (+ *acc*); **by January** ad mēnsem Iānuárium; **by now:** iam; **by the sixth hour** ad sextam hōram

calendar fāst·ī -órum *mpl;* calendári·um -ī *n*

century saécul·um -ī *n*

clock hōrológi·um -ī *n* (*see also* **clock,** Chapter III)

dark: after dark dē nocte; **in the dark** dē nocte

darkness ténebr·ae -árum *fpl*

date: di·ēs -éī *f;* **by what date?** quam ad diem?

day: di·ēs -éī *mf;* **a day,** *e.g.,* **twice a day** bis (in) diē; **any day now** propédiem; **by day** intérdiū; **day and night** et diēs et noctēs; **every day** cōtī́diē, in síngulōs diēs; **from day to day** in diēs; **from that day on** ex eō diē; **just the other day** nūper quidem; **one day** *(on a certain day in the past)* quōdam diē; **on the day before he departed** prī́diē quam abíret; **on the day before the Ides** prī́diē Ī́dūs; **(on) the following day** pósterō diē; **on the third day before the Calends of March** ante diem quārtum Kaléndās Mártiās; **the day after** postrī́diē; **the day after that** postrī́diē eius diḗī; **the day after tomorrow** peréndiē; **the day before** prī́diē; **till late in the day** ad multum diem; **two days after that** post diem tértium eius diḗī; **these days** hīs tempóribus

dawn: at dawn prīmā lūce; **before dawn** antelū́culō

daybreak: at daybreak prīmā lūce, dīlū́culō; **till daybreak** in prīmam lūcem, ūsque dīlū́culum

during inter (+ *acc*)

end: in the end ab extrémō; **toward the end of his life** témpore extrémō

evening vesp·er -erī *m,* vésper·a -ae *f;* **in the early evening** prīmā vésperā; **in the evening** vésperī; **last evening** herī vésperī; **this evening** hodiē vésperī; **very late in the evening** pervésperī

ever umquam

every day cōtī́diē

finally ad extrḗmum, tandem

first *(at first)* prīmō; *(in a series, followed by* deínde, postrḗmō*)* prīmum; **at first** inítiō; **first of all** prīmum ómnium; **for the first time** prīmō

for *(during a certain period, expressed by acc),* e.g., **for ten days** decem diēs; *(to denote the appointment of definite time)* in *(+ acc),* e.g., **he invited her to dinner for the following day** eam ad cēnam vocávit in pósterum diem

from *prep* ab *or* dē *or* ex *(+ abl);* **from day to day** diem dē diē; diem ex diē; in síngulōs diēs; **from sunrise till late in the day** ab sōle ortō in multum diḗī; **from that day to this** ex eā diē ad hanc diem; **from the time when** ex quō; **from the very beginning** iam inde ā prīncípiō; **from this (that) time forward** ex hōc (illō) témpore

future futū́r·a -ṓrum *npl;* **in the future** in pósterum

hereafter posthāc

here and now dēpraesentiárum *(adv)*

hour hōr·a -ae *f;* **a half hour** sēmihōŕ·a -ae *f;* **an hour and a half** sēsquihōŕ·a -ae *f;* **a quarter of an hour** quadr·āns -ántis *m* hōrae; **every hour** síngulīs hōrīs; **from hour to hour** in hōrās; **three quarters of an hour** dōdr·āns -ántis *m* hōrae; **to last a few hours** in paucās hōrās dūrā́re

hourly in hōrās

how long? quam diū?

how long ago? quam prīdem?; quam dūdum?

how often? quótiēns?

how soon? quam mox?

immediately statim, contínuō

just *adv* modo; **just as** cum máximē; **just as I was writing** cum haec máximē scríberem; **just before** *(an event)* sub *(+ acc);* **just in time** témporī; **just then** tunc máxime; **just the other day** modo; **just when** cum máximē

last *(adj used where English uses an adv)* novíssim·us -a -um, e.g., **Cicero spoke last** Cícerō novíssimus locútus est; **last night** próximā nocte

late *adj* sēr·us -a -um

late *adv* sērō; **all too late** immō iam sērō; **too late** sḗrius; **very late** sēríssimē

lately nūper

later pósteā; **a little later** pósteā aliquántō; **to postpone till later** díf·ferō -férre dístulī dīlā́tus in áliud tempus

latest: perhaps tomorrow, at latest the day after that fortásse crās, summum peréndiē

least: at least saltem

long diū; **how long** quam diū; **how much longer** quámdiū étiam; **long ago** prīdem; **long after (before)** multō post (ante); **longer** diū́tius; **too long** diū́tius, nímium diū

meanwhile ínterim

midnight média no·x, -ctis *f;* **around midnight** médiā círciter nocte; **at midnight** médiā nocte

minute minū́t·a -ae *f;* **in a minute** mōméntō témporis; **the minute I saw you** extémplō ubi ego tē vīdī; **this minute** *(right now)* iam; **wait a minute** exspéctā paulum, manē dum, manē paulísper

morning temp·us -oris *n* mātūtī́num; **early in the morning** bene māne, multō māne; **from morning till evening** ā māne ūsque ad vésperam; **in the morning** māne; **the next**

morning māne postrídiē; **this morning** hódiē māne

night nox, noctis *f;* **at night** noctū; **at this time of night** hōc noctis; **by night** noctū; **every night** per síngulās noctēs; **last night** próximā nocte, hāc nocte; **night after night** per síngulās noctēs; **on the following night** próximā nocte; **on the night before last** superiốre nocte; **till late at night** ad multam noctem

nightfall: just before nightfall sub noctem; **till nightfall** ūsque ad noctem

never numquam; **never yet** nōndum

no longer nōn diútius

noon merídi·ēs -ḗī *m;* **at noon** merídiē

not yet nōndum

now nunc; *(denoting emphasis and urgency)* iam; **even now** iam nunc; **just now** *(a moment ago)* modo; **now and then** subínde, nōnnúmquam, aliquándō; **now at last** nunc tandem; **now ... now** modo ... modo; **now that** posteáquam (+ *indic*); **right now** *(immediately)* iam; **ten years from now** ad decem annōs

nowadays hódiē, nunc

occasion: for the occasion in tempus

occasionally subínde

o'clock: at two o'clock *(7:00 A.M.)* hōrā diḗī secúndā *(see p. 78)*

once *(on a certain occasion)* quōdam diḗ; *(one time)* semel; **at once** flícō, statim; *(simultaneously)* simul; **once or twice** semel atque íterum; **once upon a time** ōlim

past: in the past ántehāc

period spáti·um -ī *n*

point: at this point (in time) hōc locō

previously ántehāc, prius

rarely rārō

right from the start in prīncípiō flícō; **right now** nunc iam

second secúnd·a -ae *f*

since *(temporal)* ut (+ *indic*)

someday *(in indef. fut.)* aliquándō, áliquā diḗ

sometime aliquándō

sometimes nōnnúmquam; intérdum; **sometimes ... sometimes** áliās ... áliās, modo ... modo, intérdum ... intérdum

soon mox; *(in a minute)* iam; **as soon as** cum prīmum; **as soon as possible** quam prīmum; **soon thereafter** mox deínde; **too soon** nímium cito

sooner or later sḗrius ócius, sḗrius aut cítius

then *(at that time)* tum; *(next)* deínde; **just then** tunc máximē; **then and there** flícō

till ūsque ad (+ *acc*), in (+ *acc*); **till the month of July** in mēnsem Iúlium

time temp·us -oris *n;* **ahead of time** ante tempus; **a long time already** (+ *present tense*) iam dūdum, e.g., **I've been here a long time already** iam dūdum adsum; **around the time of** sub tempus (+ *gen*); **at about the same time** sub idem tempus; **at another time** áliās; **at one time ... at another** áliās ... áliās; **at that time** ad id témporis; **at the right time** tempestívē; **at the time when** quā tempestáte; **at the wrong time** intempestívē; **at times** intérdum; **a very short time ago** modo; **before time** *(prematurely)* ante tempus; **for a long time** iam diū; **for a short time** brevī témpore; **for the first time** prīmum; **for the last time** extrḗmum; **for the time being** in tempus; **from time to time** subínde; **I have no time** tempus nōn est mihi; **in a short time** in brevī spátiō; **in**

good time, in plenty of time mātū́rē; **in (the course of) time** témpore; **it is high time for you to** tempus máximē est ut tū (+ *subj*); **long ago** iam dūdum; **make up for lost time** cessā́ta témpora córrig·ō -ere corrḗxī; **not to have the time to** ṓtium nōn habḗre *(w. dat ger);* **once upon a time** ṓlim; **on time** témperī; **some time ago** dūdum, prīdem; **there was a time when** (tempus) fuit cum; **to ask what time it is** hōrās inquī́rere; **to postpone to another time** différre in áliud tempus; **to ask the time** quaérere hōrās; **to see what time it is** hōrās īnspícere; **to spend time** tempus sū́mere (ágere, agitā́re); **to waste time** tempus pérdere; **what time is it?** quota hōra est?; **quot hōrae sunt?; to while away the time** tempus fall·ō -ere feféllī

times *(use numeral adverbs) e.g.,* **ten times** déciēs; **no more than three times** ter nec ámplius

today hódiē; **before today** ante hunc diem; **starting today** ex hōc diē

tomorrow crās; **day after tomorrow** peréndiē; **tomorrow morning** crās mā́ne; **until tomorrow** in crā́stinum

tonight hāc nocte

twilight crepúscul·um -ī *n;* **at twilight** crepúsculō

until *conj* dōnec; *prep* ūsque ad (+ *acc*)

up till now ántehāc

when cum, ubi, ut; *(interrog)* quandō

whenever quandōcúmque, utcúmque, quótiēns

while *s* **a little while before** paulō ante; **after a little while** paulō post; **a short while ago** paulō ante

while *conj* dum

while *tr* **to while away the time** tempus fall·ō -ere feféllī

year: annus -ī *m;* **every year** quotánnīs; **the following year** próximus annus; **the previous year** supérior annus; **at the beginning of the year** ineúnte annō, prīncípiō annī; **at the end of the year** exeúnte annō; **a hundred years from now** ad centum annōs

yesterday herī; **the day before yesterday** núdius tértius *(adv, also written as one word);* **yesterday morning** herī mā́ne

Chapter XI: Useful Colloquial Expressions

CONVERSATIONS

LEVEL I **Brian finds Jeffrey to be in a hurry.**

Bríanus	Astā, Gálfride; manē dum, quaesō.	*Brian: Hold it, Jeffrey. Wait a minute, please.*
Gálfridus	Quid reī est, Bríane? Mē paénitet, vērum enim própero.	*Jeffrey: What's up, Brian? I'm sorry but I'm really in a hurry.*
Bríanus	Quid festínās? Quō tē agis?	*What's your hurry. Where are you going?*
Gálfridus	Ego bibliothécam petō.	*I'm heading for the library.*
Bríanus	Quam ob rem?	*Why?*
Gálfridus	Certē nōn ánimī causā.	*Certainly not for my amusement.*
Bríanus	Cūr ígitur?	*Why then?*
Gálfridus	Rogās? Scílicet óperis árduī amóre.	*What a question! Of course, out of love for hard work.*
Bríanus	Quid tibi in ánimō est ibi fácere?	*What do you intend to do there?*
Gálfridus	Ut sóleō, indāgātiónem āctúrus sum.	*As usual, I am going to do research.*
Bríanus	Em, eō cāsū tē nōn dētinébō.	*Well, in that case I'll not hold you up.*
Gálfridus	Nunc valē. Ōtiósus estō.	*So long for now. Take it easy.*

LEVEL II **Phyllis wants to discuss a problem with Marie.**

Phyllis	Heus María. Velísne mēcum forīs cēnáre?	*Phyllis: Hey Marie, would you like to go out to dinner with me?*
María	Quíppinī? Sed quid tibi in ánimō est?	*Marie: Why not? But what's on your mind?*

Phyllis	Ut vēra dīcam, ego in angústiīs versor.	*To tell you the truth, I'm in a tight spot.*
María	Nōn téneō. Quid est negṓtiī?	*I don't get it. What's the problem?*
Phyllis	Ego équidem ádmodum sollícitor.	*I'm really quite worried.*
María	Quid id est? Quā causā ádeō perturbā́ris?	*What is it? Why are you so upset?*
Phyllis	Ūnō verbō, sollícitor dē rē pecūniā́rī.	*In a word, I'm worried about my personal finances.*
María	Perge porrō. Quid dē rē pecūniā́rī?	*Go on. What about your personal finances?*
Phyllis	Mālim tēcum dē eā in prīvā́tō loquī. Rem enim tōtam per cēnam per síngula iníbō.	*I'd rather talk to you about that in private. You see, I'll go into the whole matter in detail over dinner.*
María	Eā́mus ígitur. Nempe tibi succúrram quoad possim. Nōlī sollicitā́rī.	*Let's go then. Naturally, I'll help you as far as I can.* [lit: as far as I may be able] *Don't worry.*

LEVEL III   **Annette turns to her sister for advice.**

Annétta	Christína, cāra soror, rēcta cōnsília semper dās. Nunc velim ā tē cōnsílium pétere.	***Annette:*** *Christine, my dear sister, you always give good advice. Now I'd like to ask you for advice.*
Christína	Cedo, Annétta. Cōnsílium dē quō?	***Christine:*** *Out with it, Annette. Advice about what?*
Annétta	Ut bréviter dīcam, iam dūdum géstiō iter in Ítáliam fácere.	*To make a long story short, I have been itching for a long time to take a trip to Italy.*
Christína	Euge! Rōma vērō hōc annī témpore est bellíssima. At quid est negṓtiī?	*Splendid! Rome, in fact, is very pretty at this time of the year. But what's the trouble?*
Annétta	Em, argéntum mihi, ut ita dīcam, paúlulum déficit.	*Well, I am, so to speak, a little short of money.* [lit: money is running a little low for me]
Christína	Quam mox prōficíscī tibi in ánimō est?	*How soon do you intend to leave?*

Annétta	Cum prīmum argéntum conrádere póterō.	*As soon as I can scrape the money together.*
Christína	Nōnne ades fréquēns ūnā cum áliquot amícīs dīvítibus? Quidnī eās argéntō mútuō ferīs?	*You hang out with rich friends, don't you? Why don't you hit them for a loan?*
Annétta	In grátiā quidem cum eīs sum, sed eās numquam possim argéntum rogáre.	*I'm on good terms with them all right, but I could never ask them up for money.*
Christína	Iam téneō. Ex verbīs tuīs cólligō tē pecúniam magis quam cōnsílium ā mē pétere. Nōnne ita est?	*Now I get it. I infer from what you say that you are asking me for money rather than advice. Right? [lit: isn't it so?]*
Annétta	Bene putās, Christína! Quid fáciam sine tē? Et benévola et benéfica es. Ut aiunt, ea amíca est quae in rē dúbiā rē iuvat.	*Good thinking, Christine! What would I do without you? You're both kind and generous. As they say, a friend in need is a friend indeed.*

TOPICAL VOCABULARY

Additional colloquial expressions will be found in the General Vocabulary.

ability: to the best of my ability prō meā parte

above: to be above *(e.g., bribery)* indígn•or -árī -átus sum (+ *acc*)

absence: in my absence mē absénte

absolutely nothing nihil prōrsus

active: to be active in vers•or -árī -átus sum in (+ *abl*)

addition: in addition accédit quod (+ *indic*)

advantage: to be of advantage prōsum prōdésse prófuī

advantage: to take advantage of the opportunity occāsiónem nancísc•or -ī nānctus sum

advice: I will take your advice on the matter cōnsílium tuum illíus reī cápiam

advice: on your advice tē auctóre

afraid: what are you afraid of? quid est quod métuis?

after all rē vērā

aha! attát!

ahead: go ahead, tell me! ágedum, dīc mihi!

ail: what ails you? quid tibi est?

all along: I knew all along ūsque ab inítiō scīvī

all but propémodum; **I have all but given up hope** propémodum spem dēmísī

all over: it's all over! Āctum est!

all the same *(anyhow)* níhilō sétius

all there: are you quite all there? satísne sānus (-a) es?

all's well salva rēs est

amount: it amounts to the same thing tantúndem est

amusement: for one's amusement ánimī causā

and so forth et perínde

angry: he did nothing for you to be angry at nihil fēcit quod suscḗnseās

answer: I'll answer you point by point tibi respondḗbō *(in writing:* rescrī́bam) ad síngula

answer: now I'll answer your questions nunc respondḗbō ad ea quae rogāvístī

answer: that's not an answer to my question áliud tē rogō

answer: to give s.o. an answer álicui respṓnsum rédd•ō -ere -idī -itus

anyhow *(just the same)* nec eō sḗtius; *(in any event)* útique

anything else I can do for you? num quid áliud mē vīs?

apologize: I apologize to you mē tibi excū́sō

apology: please accept my apologies quaesō, áccipe excūsātiṓnēs

apparently ut vidḗtur

applecart: to upset the applecart plaustrum percéll•ō -ere pérculī

appointment: to have an appointment with cōnstitū́tum háb•eō -ēre -uī cum (+ *abl)*

appointment: to keep an appointment ad cōnstitū́tum vén•iō -íre vénī

appreciate: I appreciate your kindness benefícium tuum túeor

argue: stop arguing! dḗsine *(pl:* dēsínite) argūmentā́rī!

argument: to get into an argument in lítem ambíguam dēscénd•ō -ere -ī

argument: to put up an argument recūsā́re

ashamed: I'm ashamed of it mē pudet eius

ashamed: I'm ashamed to say mē pudet dī́cere

ask further questions quaer•ō -ere quaesī́vī ultrā

ask: he asked me whether quaesī́vit ā mē *(or* dē mē *or* ex mē) num

ask: he asked you a question ille tē interrogā́vit

ask: I want to ask you this hoc tē rogā́re volō

ask: to ask s.o. for s.th. áliquem áliquid rogā́re

ask: why do you ask me that? quid mē istud rogās?

at all prōrsum, omnī́nō; **you have no common sense at all** nōn cor omnī́nō habēs

attend: I'll certainly attend to it dabō équidem óperam

available: to be available praestō esse

average: on the average médiā hábitā ratiṓne

aw, keep quiet! au, tacē!

aye yai yai! heu heu!

back: to back s.o. álicui fáveō -ḗre fāvī fautū́rus

bad: wine is bad for you aliḗnum tibi vīnum est

baloney! fā́bulae!

bamboozle: you bamboozled me mihi dēdístī verba

beat around the bush circumitiṓne ū́t•or -ī ū́sus sum

begin: to begin with prī́mum enim

best: to do one's best prō virī́lī parte

best: to make the best of it aequō ánimō ferō ferre tulī lātus

bet: I bet he has taken off pṓnō eum abī́vísse

bet: I bet you he doesn't win tē spōnsiṓne próvocō illum nōn esse victū́rum

better half: where is your better half? Úbinam est tua áltera?

better: it's better to commódius est (+ *inf*)

better: it's for the better in mélius est

better late than never pótius sērō quam numquam

better: there, that's better! em istuc rḗctius!

big-mouth! ōs dūrum!

big-mouth: he was always a big-mouth semper dūrae buccae fuit

blame: I don't blame you tibi nōn impróperō

blame: to push the blame on culpam in (+ *acc*) cónferō conférre cóntulī collātus

blame: you are to blame tū peccās *or* tū in culpā es

bless you dī tē ament; *(after a sneeze)* salvē *or* salū́tem!

bore: don't be a bore nē sīs odiṓsus (-a)

bother: don't bother me nē mihi moléstus (-a) sīs

bother: don't bother nōlī tē *(pl:* nōlī́te vōs) movḗre

brag: he brags too much about his money pecū́niam nimis iactat

brains: she's got brains corcíllum habet

brief: make it brief! in pauca cōnfer!

briefly: to put it briefly ut bréviter dīcam

brilliant! sophos!

bring oneself to *(do s.th.)* ánimum indū́c·ō -ere indū́xī ut (+ *subj*)

broke: to be broke solvéndō nōn esse

bump into s.o. álicui occúrrere *(or* álicui óbviam fíerī)*

burst out laughing rīsum effúnd·ō -ere effū́dī

bury the hatchet simultā́tem dēpṓn·ō -ere dēpósuī

bush: don't beat around the bush nōlī *(pl:* nōlī́te) schēmās loquī

bush: he didn't beat around the bush nīl circumitiṓne ūsus est

business: I always mind my own business negṓtium agō semper meum

business: it's my (your, *etc.*) business to see what's going on meum (tuum, *etc.*) est vidḗre quid agā́tur

business: that's none of my business nihil ad mē áttinet

business: to put s.o. out of business áliquem dē negṓtiō dēíc·iō -ere dēiḗcī dēiéctus

business: what business is it of yours? quid id ad tē áttinet?

busy: I'm busy labōriṓsus (-a) *or* occupā́t·us -a sum

busybody: ardḗli·ō -ṓnis *mf*

buttonhole s.o. áliquem prehēnsā́re

cahoots: to be in cahoots with s.o. cum áliquō collū́·dō -dere -sī

care: for all I care meā causā

care: I don't care about such things Ista nōn cūrō

care: I don't care for *(don't like)* nīl mor·or -ā́rī -ā́tus sum (+ *acc*)

care: I don't care to say more nōn libet plūra dícere

care: I don't really care as long as … meā nīl rēfert dum (+ *indic*)

care: take care of yourself cūrā ut váleās *(pl:* cūrā́te ut valeā́tis)

care: what do I care! quid meā!

carry away: don't get carried away with enthusiasm nōlī *(pl:* nōlī́te) stúdiō efférrī

case: get off my case! nē mihi moléstus (-a) sīs!

case: if that's the case, sī rēs sīc habet,

case: in any case utcúmque

case: in case you have not … sī minus …

case: in no case haudquā́quam

case: in that case ígitur; eō cāsū

case: since that's the case, quae cum ita sint,

case: that's not the case nōn ita rēs est

case: that's the case sunt ista *or* sīc rēs habet

catch breath: let me catch my breath, please sine respī́rem, quaesō

catch red-handed flagrántī dēlíctō dēprehén·dō -dere -dī -sus

catch sight of cōnspíc·iō -ere cōnspéxī

catch: I didn't catch what you're saying nōn satis exaudiḗbam quae lóqueris

catch: there's a catch to it enim istaec cáptiō est

certain: I don't know for certain nōn certō *(or* certum) sciō **I take it as certain** prō certō hábeō

chance: he didn't give me a chance to answer mihi nōn potestátem dedit respondéndī

change: for a change varietátis causā

chat: to have a chat with cōnfābulā́rī cum (+ *abl)*

chew out: why did the instructor chew you out? quā dē causā docēns tē pilā́vit?

clear out of here! hinc ápage!

clear: to clear $1000 in the first year prīmō annō mille dóllarōs dētérg·eō -ére dētérsī dētérsus

clever: very clever! *(well said!)* facéte dictum!

come here this minute! concéde hūc āctū́tum!

come about ēvén·iō -íre ēvḗnī ēvéntum

come: come back soon redī *(pl:* redī́te) cito

come down with an illness morbō corríp·ior -ī corréptus sum

come: come what may, we'll take it philosophically quod fors feret, ferḗmus aequō ánimō

comfortable: make yourselves comfortable rogō ut vōbīs suā́viter sit

coming: he's got what's coming to him habet quod sibi dēbēbátur

common sense: to have common sense cor háb·eō -ére -uī

company: to keep each other company inter sē cólere

concern: as far as I'm concerned per mē

concern: how does that concern you? quid id ad tē áttinet?

concerned: I'm not terribly concerned about … labṓrō nōn valdē dē (+ *abl)*

condition: in excellent condition habitíssim·us -a -um

condition: in good (bad) condition bene (male) hábit·us -a -um

condition: on condition that eā lḗge ut (+ *subj)*

congratulations! macte virtū́te estō!

consent: without my consent mē invī́tō

contradict oneself pugnántia loqu·or -ī locū́tus sum

control yourself tē cóntinē

convenience: do it at your convenience id fac cómmodō tuō

convenience: write me at your earliest convenience scrībe ad mē cum commodíssimē póteris

convenient: when it will be convenient for you cum erit tuum cómmodum

conversation: to engage in conversation with sermốnēs cum (+ *abl*) cốnferō cōnférre cóntulī

cook up (*fig*) excōgitắre

count: you can count on it that ... erit tibi perspéctum (+ *acc & inf*)

count: you can count on me potes nītī mē [*abl*]

count: you don't count extrā númerum es mihi

crazy: he's crazy about her déperit eam

crazy: he's crazy about sports morbốsus est in lūdōs

creep: it makes my skin creep facit ut hórream

cut it out dēsinās! (*pl:* dēsinátis!); dēsíste! (*pl:* dēsístite!)

cut that out right now supérsedē istīs rēbus iam

cut the talk! it's boring sēgregā sermốnem! taedet

damned: I'll be damned if I know dī mē perdant, sī sciō

darn: I don't give a darn about that (him, them) id (eum, eōs) nōn fáciō floccī

darned: I'll be darned if ... male mī sit, sī ...

darned: Well, I'll be darned if I ever male mī sit, sī umquam (+ *fut indic*)

dead: I'm dead! intériī! *or* périī!

deaf: you're preaching to deaf ears ad surdās aurēs cantās

deal: a good deal of aliquántum (+ *gen*)

deal: it's a deal pactam rem habḗtō (*pl:* habētốte)

decked out: why are you all decked out? quámobrem sīc subōrnátus (-a) es?

deliver: the mailman delivered the letter yesterday tabellắrius lítterās herī réddidit

deny: I do not deny that ... nōn īnfíti·or -ắrī (+ *acc & inf*)

depend: it depends a lot on whether ... plúrimum rēfert num ...

depend: it (all) depends on you tōtum in tē pósitum est

detail: to go into a matter in detail rem per síngula ín·eō -íre -iī *or* -ívī

difference of opinion dissénti·ō -ốnis *f*

difference: it makes no difference nīl ínterest

difference: it makes no difference to me (you, etc.) whether ... or nīl meā (tuā, *etc*) ínterest (*or* rēfert) utrum ... an (+ *subj*)

difference: what's the difference anyhow! quid útique ínterest! *or* quid útique rēfert?

dig up s.th. about quicquam erúere dē (+ *abl*)

dirt cheap prō lutō

dirty look: to give s.o. a dirty look respíc·iō -ere respéxī áliquem minus familiắrī vultū

disagree: I strongly disagree with you veheménter ā tē disséntiō

disappear: to disappear from sight ē cōnspéctū aúferor auférrī ablắtus sum

disappoint: I'll not disappoint you nōn fallam opīniốnem tuam

do good: it will do you (a lot of, no) good próderit (multum, nihil) tibi

do in: he has done me in pérdidit mē

do one's best óperam dō dare dedī

do: I don't know what to do quid fáciam nésciō

do: it won't do to (+ *inf*) nōn satis est (+ *inf*)

do: what else can I do? quid áliud fáciam?

do: what more can I do? quid fáciam ámplius?

do: will this do? sátin(e) est?

dogs: they're going to the dogs pessum eunt

doing: what's doing? quid ágitur?

done for: I'm done for! nullus sum *or* Périī

doubt: I have no doubt that ... nōn mihi dúbium est quīn (+ *subj*)

down pat: you have the whole thing down pat órdine omnem rem tenēs

downhill: it was all downhill after that proclívia ómnia erant postílla

downhill: things are going downhill inclīnáta rēs est

drive s.o. mad: áliquem dēméntem fác•iō -ere fēcī factus

drop it! (*no more of that!*) missa istaec fac!

drop it, please! mitte, amábō!

drop in on (*to visit*) invís•ō -ere -ī

drop: let's drop the subject missa haec faciámus

duck the issue rem ēvītáre

duped: you've been duped good and proper tibi ōs est súblitum plānē et probē

dying to know: I am dying to know how you are doing valdē áveō scīre, quid agās

eat out forīs cēnáre

effort: make an effort to be on time dā óperam ut tempestívē adsīs

effort: you've wasted all your effort omnem óperam perdidístī

else: who else is more deserving? quis alter est dígnior homō?

embarrassed: I am embarrassed by sum perturbátus cum (+ *abl*)

end: put an end to fīnem impón•ō -ere impósuī (+ *dat*)

end: that's the end of me Āctum est dē mē

enough of this! haec quidem háctenus!

evidently vidélicet

excuse: excuse me ignósce mihi

excuse: please excuse me óbsecrō, mihi ignóscās

expect: what do you expect? quid vīs fíerī?

expression: to change one's expression vultum flect•ō -ere flexī flexus

eye: keep an eye on that guy adsérvā (*pl:* adserváte) istum

eye: look me in the eye aspícedum contrā mē

eyes: keep your eyes open cavē circumspíciās

face to face: to be face to face with you praesēns praeséntī tibi esse

face to face: we can discuss that face to face cōram id ágere possumus

face: make a face ōs dūc•ō -ere dūxī

fact: as a matter of fact enimvérō

fact: in fact vērō; quidem

fact: the facts speak for themselves rēs ipsa índicat *or* rēs prō sē lóquitur

fact: the fact that ... quod (+ *indic*)

fail: words fail me quid dīcam nōn invéniō

fair: fair and square sine fūcō ac fallắciīs

fair: I think that's fair id aequī fác•iō -ere -fēcī

fair: that's not fair of you nōn aequum facis

fall flat *(of a speech, etc.)* frĭgeō frīgḗre

fall for *(a trick)* fall•or -ī *(+ abl)*

fall sick in morbum íncid•ō -ere -ī

far from it! mínimē!

far-fetched idea conquisĭtum cōnsíli•um -ī *n*

far: as far as I'm concerned per mē

fault: to be at fault in culpā esse

favor: ask s.o. for a favor grắtiam ab áliquō pet•ō -ere petĭvī

favor: do s.o. a favor grātum álicui fác•iō -ere fēcī factus

favor: please do me this favor amắbō tē, fac *(or for a previous favor,* refer) hanc grắtiam mihi

fear of God: he put the fear of God into them cūrắvit ut illīs iúpiter īrắtus esset

feel bad (good) sē male (bene) habḗre; **to feel really bad about** valdē dól•eō -ēre -uī dē *(+ abl)*

feel better *(physically)* mélius vál•eō -ēre -uī

feel well: not feel quite well minus vál•eō -ēre -uī

feel: because I felt like it quia mihi líbitum est

feel: I felt like it líbuit

feel: you'll feel bad tibi cordólium erit

feelers: put out feelers to tentắre

feeling: I wasn't feeling well ego mē nōn bellē habḗbam

figure on *(rely on)* nĭt•or -ī nĭxus sum *or* nĭsus sum

figure out excōgitắre

fine! probē!

fine: you did fine fēcístī probē

fine: everything's fine rēctē est

fine: that's fine bene hoc habet

finger: not lift a finger pressīs mánibus séd•eō -ēre sēdī

finger: to point the finger at s.o. dígitum ad áliquem inténd•ō -ere -ī

fingers: to snap the fingers dígitīs cóncrep•ō -ắre -uī

fix: to be in a fix in angústiīs vers•or -ắrī -ắtus sum

flabbergast conturbắre

flabbergasted: we were absolutely flabbergasted nōs omnĭnō conturbābắmur

fly: to fly off the handle cito férv•eō -ḗre -ī

fond: to be fond of díligo -ere dīléxī dīléctus

for all that nec eō sḗtius *or* níhilō sḗtius

for that matter ádeō

forget about it! iécte id ex ánimō!

free: if you are free sī vacắbis

friend: she's my best friend amĭca summa mea est

from a to z: he explained everything to me from a to z ab áciā et acū mihi ómnia expósuit

fun: he always makes fun of me *(or* **pokes fun at me)** iste mē semper ēlúdit *(or* inrĭdet)

fun: it was pure fun hilária mera erat

fun: it's no fun if you ... nōn iūcúndum est sī tū ...

geez eu édepol *or* eu hercle

general: in general ferē, vulgō

get out of my way! dē viā meā dēcéde *(pl:* dēcédite)!

get (the business) over and done with (negótium) absólv•ō -ere -ī absolútus

get along: they get along well with each other *(or* **one another)** concórditer inter sē cóngruunt

get carried away by *or* **with** éfferor efférrī ēlátus sum (+ *abl*)

get: do you get it now? iam tenēs? **I get it** téneō

get: don't you get it? nōn tū tenēs? **now I get it!** iam téneō!

get even with s.o. for ulcísc•or -ī ultus sum áliquem quod (+ *indic*)

get even: if only I could get even with him for what he did Útinam istum ulcíscī possem prō factīs eius

get: I can't get him to talk nōn queō ōráre ut loquátur

get: I get it all right satis ea téneō

get: now get this nunc cognósce rem

get rid of: I want to get rid of that pest istum moléstum āmolírī volō

gist: the gist of what he said was this: hanc in senténtiam dīxit:

give it here cedo *(pl:* cette) *(an old imperative; can take a direct object)*

give it to 'em! ádhibē! *(pl:* adhíbite!)

glued: I'm glued to my books in librīs haér•eō -ére haesī

glum: why so glum? quid tū es tam tristis?

go and see whether he has come home or not abī, vīse redierítne an nōndum domum

go on! perge *(pl:* pérgite) porrō

go on: what's going on here? quid reī hīc est?

go well: things are going fairly well ágitur satis

go: I don't go for *(don't like)* nīl mor•or -árī -átus sum (+ *acc*)

go: I don't go in for sports lūdīs [*dat*] nōn stúdeō

go: please let me go mitte mē sīs

go: what's going on? quid negótī est? *or* quid ágitur?

go: where are you going? quō tē agis?

god bless you! tibi dī bene fáciant; *(after a sneeze)* salvē *or* salútem

going: good going! bene factum!

goner: geez, I'm a goner périī hercle

good for you! macte virtúte estō! *(said in praise)*

good job! bene factum!

good lord! o dī bonī!

good thinking! bene putās!

good for: how long is that good for? quam diū valébit?

good, good! euge, euge!

good-for-nothing *adj* nēquam *(indecl)*

good-for-nothing *s:* **to be a good-for-nothing** nihil hóminis esse

good: to do a lot of good multum prōsum prōdésse prófuī

good: you're a good fellow frūgī es

grateful: I am deeply grateful to you tibi grátiam hábeō máximam *(or* grátiās máximās)

great! eu!

great: that's great! bene hercle factum!

ha, ha, ha! hahahaé!

hand over: hand it over! cedo *(pl:* cette)! *(an old imperative; can take a direct object)*

hand: hand me that food pórrige mihi illum cibum

hands: to have one's hands full sátag•ō -ere satégī

hands: to sit on one's hands *(doing nothing)* compréssīs mánibus séd•eō -ére sēdī

hang around with frequēns adésse ūnā cum (+ *abl*)

hang: you can just go and hang yourself! ī dīrḗcte in máximam malam crūcem!

happen: what happened? quid factum est?

hard: he was hard on me in mē dūrus erat

hard: it's hard to do, but I'll try just the same difficile factū est, sed conábor níhilō sḗtius

hard: to take this hard hoc dūrum accíp·iō -ere accḗpī

harp on the same theme cantilḗnam eándem can·ō -ere cécinī

have it your way! estō ut lubet!

have a tough time of it valdē labōrāre

have it in for s.o. álicui perículum dēnuntiáre

have to do: what do you have to do with him? quid reī tibi est cum illō?

have to say: this I have to say haec hábeō dícere

head: come into one's head in buccam vén·iō -íre vēnī [*lit: come into one's cheek*]

head: from head to foot ā cápite ūsque ad calcem

head: to put heads together cápita cónferō cōnférre cóntulī

headway: we are making some headway, I hope ut spḗrō, prōfícimus aliquántum

health: for reasons of (bad) health valētúdinis causā

heart: from the heart ex ánimō; **heart and soul** tōtō péctore

heart: my heart was in my throat ánima mihi in nāsō erat [*lit: my breath was in my nose*]

heart: to take to heart familiáriter ferō ferre tulī lātus

heaven: for heaven's sake óbsecrō [*lit: I pray*]

heaven: I'm in seventh heaven dígitō caelum attíngō

heavens above! o dī immortálēs!

heck: who the heck are they? quī, malum, istī sunt?

heels: to take to his heels sē conícere in pedēs

hell: I'm going to catch hell habḗbō convícium

hello: Terentia says hello to you Teréntia tibi salútem dīcit

here I am Ecce mē

here with it! cedo! (*pl:* cette!) (*can take an accusative object, e.g.:* **here with that book!** cedo istum librum!)

hey you, I'm talking to you! heus tū, tibi ego dīcō!

hide: to be after s.o.'s hide córium alicúius pet·ō -ere petívī

hide: to risk his own hide córiō suō lúdere

hide: to save his own hide córium serváre

hit it off: did you hit it off with them? concordābásne cum illīs?

hit: hit s.o. for a loan feríre áliquem mútuō argéntō

hmmmmm hem

hogwash: that's hogwash! quisquíliae!

hold it! I won't let you leave astā! abíre hinc nōn sinam

honest to god médius fídius

honestly: tell me honestly dīc bonā fide

hoot: I don't give a hoot about him eum floccī nōn fáciō

how come? quī istuc?

how so? quīdum? *or* quid ita?

how's that? *(what did you say?)* quīdum? *or* quid iam?

humor: to humor s.o. álicui mōrem gerō gérere gessī

hurray! euax!

hurry! mātū́rā! *(pl:* mātūráte!)

hurry: but I'm in a hurry at próperō

hurry: what's your hurry? quid festī́nās?

I'll be right there iam áderō

idea: you're full of ideas plēnus (-a) cōnsíliī es

importance: it is of the greatest importance to me that ... permágnī meā ínterest (+ *acc & inf*)

important: it is (very) important to me (you) that magnī (máximē) meā (tuā) ínterest (+ *acc & inf*)

important: it's not all that important tantī nōn est

impression: to make a deep impression on máximē commóv•eō -ére commṓvī (+ *acc*)

in: is your father in? estne pater intus?

infer: I infer from what you say that ... ex verbīs tuīs cólligō (+ *acc & inf*)

influence: to have a lot of influence with multum posse in (+ *abl*)

inform: to inform s.o. about áliquem certiṓrem facere dē (+ *abl*)

initiative: on my own initiative meā sponte

inside: go inside! ī *(pl:* īte) intus!

intend: I intended to set out straight for home erat mihi in ánimō rēctā proficī́scī domum

intentions: with the best intentions óptimō ánimō ū́tēns

interested: I am interested in music mū́sicae [*dat*] stúdeō

interested: I am interested in that id mihi cūrae est

interesting: that book is interesting ille liber mē tenet

interrupt: don't interrupt me! nōlī *(pl:* nōlī́te) mihi óbloquī!

is that so? ítane?

itch: I'm just itching to gést•iō -íre quidem (+ *inf*)

jam: to be in a jam in angústiīs vers•or -ā́rī -ā́tus sum

job: good job! rēctē factum!

job: it's a big job but ... magnum opus est sed tamen ...

joke: all joking aside iocō remṓtō

joke: as a joke per iocum

joke: now you're joking iocáris nunc tū

jokingly per iocum *or* inter iocum

judgment: against my better judgment advérsum ingénium meum

just about *(pretty well, virtually)* propémodum

just the same *(anyhow)* tamen *or* níhilō sḗtius

keep this to yourself haec tū tēcum habḗtō

keep your cool! compésce mentem!

keep a stiff upper lip! fac ut ánimō fortī sīs!

keep: am I keeping you? num dētíneō tē?

kept: what kept you? quid ténuit quō minus venī́rēs?

kick the bucket ánimam bullíre

kid: don't kid me nē mē lūdās

kidding: you're kidding lūdis mē

kill time tempus fall•ō -ere feféllī

knock it off! parce! *(pl:* párcite!)

know better: he thinks he knows better than I do cēnset sē plūs sápere quam mē

know for sure certum *(or* certō) sciō scīre scīvī

know: get to know nōsc•ō -ere nōvī nōtus

know: let me know what you are doing tū mē velim certiórem fáciās, quid agās

know: let me know where you are fácitō ut sciam ubi sīs

latest: today, at latest tomorrow hódiē, summum crās

laugh: I laughed till I cried rīsī ūsque ad lácrimās

lay a finger on s.o. áliquem ūnō dígitō attíng•ō -ere áttigī

lay off! dēsine *(pl:* dēsínite) tandem!

leave me alone! omítte *(pl:* omíttite) mē

leave it up to s.o. to ... álicui mandáre (+ *subj*)

leave no stone unturned nullō locō dēsum dēésse dēfuī

let down: to let s.o. down álicui dēsum dēésse dēfuī

let fall: dēmítt•ō -ere dēmī́sī dēmíssus

let me go! mítte *(pl:* míttite) mē!

let me know fácitō *(pl:* facitóte) ut sciam

life and death: it's not a question of life or death nōn cápitis rēs ágitur

life: but such is life sed vīta fert; **to lead the life of riley** vītam chiam ger•ō -ere gessī

life: on my life! ita vīvam!

light: to make light of in levī háb•eō -ére -uī

like: he said something like this haec ferē dīxit

like: I like this hoc mihi placet

like: I like to do this mē iuvat hoc fácere

like: I'd like you to come velim (ut) véniās

like: that's more like it propémodum est

likely: it is more likely that facílius est ut (+ *subj*)

likely: most likely he will come próximum est ut véniat

line: drop me a line when you have time scrībe áliquid litterárum quandō vacās

line: he's feeding you a line verba tibi iste dat

line: to form a long line longum agmen fác•iō -ere fēcī factus

line: to lay it on the line dīréctum loquor loquī locútus sum

lip: keep a stiff upper lip fac, ut ánimō fortī sīs

live it up fériās ag•ō -ere ēgī āctus

living: to make a living quaestum fácere *or* vīctum quaeritáre

living: you're living on borrowed time dē lucrō vīvis *(pl:* vívitis)

loaded with money cōpiós•us -a -um

loaf cessáre

loan: may I hit you for a loan? licet tē mútuō feríre?

long: it would take too long to ... longum erat (+ *inf*)

look like: I don't know what he *(or* **she) looks like** quā sit fácie, néscio

look: aha, the very person I was looking for Attát, quem quaerébam!

look: it looks that way to me ita mihi vidétur

low: I am low on *(e.g.,* **paper)** (charta) mihi dēest

luck: good luck! fēlíciter!

lump s.o. together with áliquem accúd·ō -ere (+ *dat*)

mad: I'm mad at you tibi suscénseō *or* ego tibi īrátus sum

mad: to be mad about *(be madly in love with)* dēpér·iō -íre -iī (+ *acc*)

mad: to go mad mente aliēnárī

mail: I mailed the letter yesterday lítterās herī dedī

matter: for that matter ádeō

matter: it doesn't matter to me nihil ad mē pértinet

matter: no matter how... quamvīs (+ *subj*)

matter: what does that matter to me (you, us)? quid id meā (tuā, nōbīs) rēfert?

matter: what on earth's the matter? quidnam est?

matter: what's the matter? quid est? *or* quid istuc est reī?

mean: do you know whom I mean? scīsne quem dīcam?

mean: do you mean me? mēne vīs? **yes, you** tē

mean: do you really mean it? ain vērō? **yes, I do** aiō

mean: how do you mean that? quī istuc vīs?

mean: now you know what I mean scīs iam quid loquar

mean: what do you mean? quid tibi vīs?

mean: what do you mean by that? quid istuc est verbī?

mean: what does this mean? quid hoc sibi vult?

mean: what I mean is *(in correcting a misunderstanding)* at enim

means: by all means! máximē!

memory: if my memory serves me right, sī ego satis comméminī,

memory: in memory of in memóriam (+ *gen*)

memory: to commit to memory memóriae committ·o -ere commísī

mention: I don't want to mention him by name eum nōlō nōmináre

mention: not to mention ut nōn (*or* nihil) dīcam dē (+ *abl*)

mention: not to mention the fact that ... ut mittam quod (+ *indic*)

mention: since mention has been made of money, quóniam nummórum méntiō facta est,

mess: geez, what a mess! eu édepol rēs turbuléntās!

mince: without mincing words sine fūcō ac falláciīs

mind: he's out of his mind aliēnátus est ā sē

mind: I don't mind if you stay, provided you're quiet nōn labórō sī manēs, modo táceās

mind: I don't mind that ... nōn cūrō quod (+ *indic*)

mind: I made up my mind not to hurry erat in ánimō nihil festīnáre

mind: I made up my mind to leave cōnstítuī hinc abíre *or* certum est mihi hinc abíre

mind: I really don't mind that istuc quidem nōn moléstē ferō ferre tulī

mind: I was out of my mind when ... dēsipiébam mentis cum ...

mind: I've made up my mind mihi certum est

mind: if you don't mind sī tibi moléstum nōn est *or* sī tibi vidétur

mind: it had not entered my mind mihi in mentem nōn vénerat

mind: it slipped my mind to write to you fūgit mē ad tē scrſbere

mind: never mind! *(let is pass)* sine! *(pl:* sſnite)

mind: never mind what he says mitte id quod dīcit

mind: set your mind at ease habē ánimum lēnem et tranquíllum

mind: to change one's mind mentem mūtáre

mind: to have in mind to in ánimō habére (+ *inf*)

mind: to mind s.o. else's (one's own) business aliéna (sua) negótia cūráre

mind: what's on your mind? quid tibi in ánimō est?

misquote: you are misquoting me mē áliīs verbīs pōnis

mistake: by mistake imprúdēns, pérperam

mistake: you're making a big mistake errās pervérsē *or* veheménter errās

mood: to be in a good mood bonum ánimum háb·eō -ére -uī

more of this another time sed dē hōc áliās plúribus

mouth: I had better keep my mouth shut táceam óptimum est

mouth: shut your mouth óbserá ōs tuum!

my oh my! vae mſserō (-ae) mihi!

naturally *(of course)* nempe

necessary: if it is necessary for you to stay on sī opus est tē commorárī

necessary: if it is necessary for your health sī opus est ad valētúdinem

need: I (you, we) need money opus est mihi (tibi, nōbīs) argéntō [*abl*]

needless to say quid quaeris?

neither: that's neither here nor there *(a matter of indifference)* susque dēque est

nerve: what nerve! Ō audáciam!

news: if you happen to have any news about ... sī quid forte novī habēs dē (+ *abl*); **if you have no news about ...** sī nihil novī habēs dē (+ *abl*); **I'll tell you when I have any news** narrábō, cum áliquid habébō novī **is there any news?** num quid novī? **no other news** nihil praetéreā novī

nice: it was nice of you to invite me, but no, thank you bene vocās, sed tam grátia est

nice: it wasn't nice of you to say that nōn bellē fēcſstī quī id dſxeris

nick: you've come in the nick of time in ipsō artículo témporis ádvenis

no way! mínimē! *or* nullō modō!

no, thanks tam grátia est *or* benígnē

nonsense! nūgās!

nonsense: cut out the nonsense omítte nūgās

nonsense: that's a lot of nonsense nūgae sunt istae magnae

nonsense: you are talking nonsense nūgās garris

nose: to have a good nose for these things haec fēstſvē odōrárī

nose: under one's very nose ante óculōs

nosey: I don't want to be nosey but ... nōn libet cūriósus (-a) esse sed ...

now here's the point nunc cognósce rem

now what? quid nunc?

nuts: he's nuts aliēnátus est ā sē

nuts: you're nuts dēlſrās

O.K. fiat *or* licet

O.K.: if it's O.K. with you, sī tibi vidétur

O.K.: we're O.K. bene habémus

objection: I have no objection per mē licet

obliged: I'm much obliged to you for sending me your book fēcístī mihi pergrátum quod librum ad mē mīsístī

occasion: if occasion should arise, sī fúerit occásiō,

occur: that had never occurred to me mihi istuc numquam in mentem vénerat

of course scílicet, proféctō

off: I'm off to the forum ego hinc mē ad forum (agō)

off: where are you off to? quō tē agis?

oh boy! eu!

once I get started, I can't stop quandō incípiō, dēsínere nequēo

one on one: we can discuss that one on one id cōram ágere póssumus

ouch! oieí!

out with it! *(tell me!)* cedo! *(pl:* cette!) *(an old imperative)*

out of place: if it is not out of place, nisi aliénum est,

over: it's all over! Āctum est! *or* Ílicet!

overwhelmed: to be overwhelmed with work óbruī, tamquam fluctū, sīc ópere

pain : stop being a pain in the neck moléstus (-a) nē sīs

pain: feel pain dolóre affíc·ior -ī afféctus sum

pardon: pardon me for what I said ignósce mihi, quod díxerō

particular: in particular potíssimum

pass for *(appear to be)* probáre prō (+ *abl)*

pave: to pave the way to viam fác·iō -ere fēcī factus ad (+ *acc)*

pay: it pays to listen prétium óperae est auscultáre

pay s.o. a visit áliquem invís·ō -ere -ī

period: I'll not give in period nōn concédam dīxī

pickle: to be in a pickle in angústiīs vers·or -árī -átus sum

pinch: in a pinch in rē dúbiā

pity: I pity you miséreor tuī *(pl:* vestrī)

place: this is not the place to ... nōn est hic locus ut (+ *subj)*

plans: to make plans for the trip cōnsílium cáp·iō -ere cēpī dē itínere

play up to s.o. áliquem col·ō -ere cóluī

play: stop playing games dēsíste lūdōs fácere

please sōdēs (= sī audēs); quaesō; *(very informal)* amábō tē

pleasure: with pleasure libénter

plus: consider it a plus id députā esse in lucrō

point: at this point hīc

point: beside the point nihil ad rem; **get the point?** tenésne *(pl:* tenētísne) rem? **get to the point!** venī ad rem! **it got to the point where** eō dēcúrsum est ut (+ *subj);* **that's the main point** id caput est **up to this point** háctenus; **what was the point of your writing to me?** quid rétulit tē míttere ad mē lítterās? **what's the point of that?** quam ad rem istud réfert? **what's your point?** *(what are you driving at?)* quō ēvádis? **you miss the point** nihil ad rem pértinet

point: but to return to the point ... sed ad prōpósitum ...

point: on that point hāc dē rē

point: the point is that I no longer care about such things quod caput est, iam ista nōn cūrō

possible: is it really possible that ... numquid; **is it really possible that you are telling the truth?** numquid vēra dīcis?

pretend: I'll pretend I don't know him dissimulábō mē eum nōvísse

pretend: I'll pretend I'm leaving assimulábō quasi ábeam

pretext: he left under the pretext that ... hinc ábiit quasi (+ *subj*)

pretty well (*just about*) propémodum

privately: I want to speak with you privately velim tēcum loquī in prīváto *or* in secrétō

problem: what's the problem? quid est negótī?

promise: I am not making any definite promise nihil certī pollíceor

promises: to break promises prōmíssa frang·ō -ere frḗgī frāctus

promises: to keep promises prōmíssa serváre

promises: to make many promises multa pollíc·eor -érī pollícitus sum

prove: this proves that ... documéntō est (+ *acc & inf*)

public: in public forīs

pull a fast one on verba dare (+ *dat*)

pull oneself together sē cóllig·ō -ere collḗgī

put off: let's put this off to another time hanc rem in áliud tempus differámus

put up with with s.o. áliquem perpét·ior -ī perpéssus sum

put yourself in my place fac quī ego sum, esse tē

put: you're putting it on a little thick es pūtidiúculus

question: many questions are raised multa quaerúntur

question: no question, he's at fault nempe in culpā est

question: that's a loaded question captiósum interrogátum est

question: to answer the question ad rogátum (*or* interrogátum) respónd·eō -ére -ī

question: to ask a loaded question captiósē interrogáre

question: why do you ask such questions? cūr ista quaeris?

quiet: why don't you keep quiet? quīn tū tacēs?

racket: to raise a racket clāmórem toll·ō -ere sústulī sublátus

rat: I smell a rat áliquid mihi súbolet

rate: at any rate útique

rather: do you know this fellow? hunc nōvístī? **rather!** fácile!

reason: for various reasons multīs dē causīs

reason: what's the reason why ... quid est enim, cūr ...

recall: as I recall ut mea memória est

red cent: I don't owe anyone a red cent assem aerárium némini débeō

red cent: I haven't a red cent assem aerárium hábeō nūllum

regards: give him (her) my best regards dícitō eī multam meīs verbīs salútem

remember: if I remember right, sī bene méminī,

reminder: as a reminder memóriae causā

retire in ótium vén·iō -íre vēnī ventúrus

right away contínuō

right from the start in prīncípiō ílicō

right now nunciam

right: that's right sīc est

right: you have every right to ...
omne fās tibi est (+ *inf*)

right: you're right bene dīxístī *or* vēra
dīcis

risk: at your own risk tuō perículō

rough guess īnformáta cogitátiō

round up cōg•ō -ere coégī coáctus

rubbish! quisquíliae!

**ruckus: why are you raising such a
ruckus?** quid istum clāmórem tollis
(*pl:* tóllitis)?

run into s.o. on the street áliquem
offénd•ō -ere -ī in platéā

sake: for the sake of causā (+ *gen*); **for
heaven's sake** óbsecrō (*lit: i pray*);
for your sake tuā (*pl:* vestrā) causā

same: it's all the same to me meā nihil
ínterest

satisfaction: to your satisfaction ex tuā
senténtiā

satisfy: you can't satisfy everyone nōn
potes ómnibus satis fácere

say: so they say ita aiunt

scared: I am scared to death
exanimátus (-a) metū sum

**score: he doesn't know what the score
is** nescit quid agátur

scram! ápage

**scrape: I'll try to scrape together the
money** cōnábor argéntum conrádere

see that you do it fácitō ut fáciās

see: now I see (*I understand*) iam téneō

see: I'll see to it that ... cūrábō ut (+
subj) ...

self: he was not his usual self nōn fuit
cuius modī solet

serious: are you serious? sērióne dīcis
tū?

service: to be at s.o.'s service praestō
(+ *dat*) esse

**seventh heaven: to be in seventh
heaven** in caelō esse

shake hands dextrae iúngere dextram *or*
dextram iúngere cum áliquō

shame on you! prō pudor!

shame: that's a darn shame édepol
fácinus ímprobum

shame: what a shame! fácinus
indígnum! *or* Ō rem indígnam!

shoes: please put yourself in my shoes
fac, quaesō, quī ego sum, tē esse

shook: all shook up veheménter
perturbátus

short: in short in summā, ad summam

show: this shows that ... indíciō est (+
acc & inf)

shut up! óbserā ōs tuum!

shut: why don't you just shut up?
quīn tū tacē modo?

**sick and tired: I am sick and tired of
hearing the same thing over and
over** (mē) pertaédet iam audíre
éadem idéntidem

**sick and tired: I am sick and tired of
the business** mē negótī pertaédet

silly: don't be silly nōlī ineptíre

**simply: I simply don't know what he
is thinking of** iam plānē quid cógitet
nésciō

**situation: that's the situation here in
Rome** hīc Rōmae rēs sē sīc habent

situation: you see what the situation is
vidēs quō in locō haec rēs sit

skull: I'll break your skull dīmínuam
ego tibi caput

slip: a slip of the tongue laps•us -ūs *m*
linguae

slip: it has slipped my mind memóriā
éxcidit

slip: it slipped my mind to ... fūgit mē (+ *inf*)

smart: don't talk smart to me nōlī male dícere mihi

smart: she is smart ingeniósa est

snowed: to be snowed under with óbruī, tamquam fluctū, sīc (+ *abl*)

so far so good bellē adhūc

so to speak ut ita dīcam

so help me god! médius fídius!

so: that's not so! haud ita est

sooner: no sooner said than done dictō cítius *or* dictum factum

speak of the devil lupus in fábulā

speak I'm listening lóquere aúdiō

speak: well, speak up! quīn tū ēlóquere

spirit: that's the right spirit now nunc tū frūgī bonae es

splendid! euge!

splendid: absolutely splendid! nimis factum bene!

split one's sides laughing ília sua rīsū dissólv•ō -ere -ī

square: this simply doesn't square nōn sānē quadrat

stand: I can't stand him istum ferre nequeō

stand: I'd like to know how matters stand velim scīre quō modō rēs sē hábeat

standing ovation: to give s.o. a standing ovation álicui stantēs plau•dō -dere -sī

start: you've made a good start bene habent tibi prīncípia

starters: for starters prīncípiō

step on it! mātū́rā! (*pl:* mātūrā́te!)

stick to one's guns in senténtiā stō stāre stetī

stick to the truth in vēritáte mán•eō -ére mānsī

stone: I will leave no stone unturned nihil praetermíttam

stop right there! stā ī́licō!

stop off at dēversā́rī apud (+ *acc*)

stop off at s.o.'s house dēvért•ō -ere -ī ad áliquem

stop! astā!

stop: he finally stopped talking fīnem loquéndī dēmum fēcit

story: to make a long story short nē longus sim *or* nē longam fáciam

straighten out a matter rem explicáre

strictly speaking própriē

stroll: would you like to take a stroll? velísne spatiárī?

stuck: he is stuck on some girl or other in amórem haeret apud nésciō quam vírginem

stuck: I'm stuck (*out of ideas*) haéreō

suggestion: at your suggestion tē auctóre

sum: to sum up ad summam *or* in summam *or* in summā

suppose: I suppose (*parenthetical*) ut opínor

sure: be sure to come fácitō (*or* fac) modo ut véniās

sure: I am sure that certus (-a) sum (+ *acc & inf*)

sure: to know for sure certum (*or* certō) scīre

suspense: not to keep you any longer in suspense nē diútius péndeās

suspense: to be in suspense ánimī péndeō pendére pepéndī

sweat: no sweat nōn labórō

take it easy! parce! (*pl:* párcite!)

take into consideration respíc·iō -ere respéxī

take it hard that gráviter ferō ferre tulī (+ *acc & inf*)

take pains to in magnō negótiō háb·eō -ére -uī (+ *inf*)

take place fīō fíerī factus sum

take upon oneself (to) in sē cōnférre (+ *inf*)

take: here, take it áccipe, em

take: I can't take it anymore patī néqueō ámplius

take: I take it (*parenthetical*) ut opínor

taken in: they know that they were taken in sciunt sibi data esse verba

talk: that's mere talk verba istaec sunt

tear: I can't tear myself away from writing (from my books) in scrībéndō (in librīs) haér·eō -ére haesī

tenterhooks: to be on tenterhooks ánimī pénd·eō -ére pepéndī

terms: I'm on good terms with in grátiā sum cum (+ *abl*); mihi cum (+ *abl*) magna necessitúdō est

thank you (*for a future favor*) amábō tē; (*for a favor done*) amō tē

thank you for (+ *gerund*) tibi grátiās agō ágere ēgī quod (+ *indic*)

thank: I thank you for helping me grátiās tibi agō quod mē iūvístī

thankful: I am thankful to you grátiam tibi hábeō

thankful: you ought to be thankful to me grátiam hábeās mihi

thanks a lot multum tē amō

thanks for your gifts grátiās tibi dē dōnīs tuīs

thanks to me (you, *etc.*) meā (tuā, *etc*) óperā

that'll do sat est

that's it! (*enough!*) tantum est!

that's right (*in response to a question*) sīc est

that's so ita est

then and there ibi contínuō; ílicō

think over reputáre

think s.th. over áliquid sēcum reputáre

think: I don't think so ego nōn putō

think: I think so sīc opínor

think: that is exactly what I think ita prōrsus exístimō

think: what do you think? quid cēnsēs?

tie up impéd·iō -íre -ívī -ítus

tie: to be tied up (*e.g., with business*) impéd·ior -írī -ítus sum

time: for the time being prō témpore

time: he's having a good time by himself eī bene est sōlī

time: I haven't the time haud mihi ótium est

time: I'm having a good (lousy) time mihi bene (male) est

time: in my spare time cum tempus subsicívum mihi est

time: there is no time to study nōn vacat studére

tip: it was on the tip of the tongue erat in labrīs prīmóribus

to each his own cuique suum

too bad about male (mehércule) dē (+ *abl*)

too bad about Marcus! male dē Márcō!

tooth and nail tōtō córpore et ómnibus úngulīs

top (*surpass*) superáre

top banana: he wants to be top banana vult sē esse prīmum ómnium rērum

top: at the top of one's voice summā vōce

topsy-turvy: everything was topsy-turvy ómnia erant sūrsum deórsum

track down s.th. áliquid indagā́re

trick: is this a trick? num hoc est cáptiō?

tricks: to be up to some tricks lascī́v‧us -a -um esse

trouble: I'm expecting some big trouble nésciō quod magnum malum exspéctō

trouble: if it is no trouble sī grave nōn erit

trouble: more trouble ámplius negṓtī

trouble: to be in trouble labōrā́re

trouble: to make big trouble for s.o. dare magnum malum álicui

trouble: what's the trouble? quid illuc malī est? *or* quid est negṓtī?

true: that's true rēs ita est *or* ita profḗctō est

truth: to tell you the truth ut vērum loquar *or* nē quid méntiar

try one's best to (not to) óperam dō dare dedī ut (nē) (+ *subj*)

turkey: to talk turkey with latī́nē loqu‧or -ī locū́tus sum cum (+ *abl*)

turn out fine bellē cádō -ere cécidī cāsū́rus

turn up: something will turn up, I hope fiet áliquid, spḗrō

uh-uh (*seeing s.o. unexpectedly*) attát

understand: do you understand now? iam tenēs?

understand: I don't quite understand nōn satis intéllegō

up in the air (*in uncertainty*) in médiō relíct‧us -a -um; **to be up in the air** (*to be undecided*) péndeō pendḗre pepéndī

ups and downs: there are ups and downs modo sīc, modo sīc

upset: don't be upset nōlī (*pl:* nōlī́te) perturbā́rī

upset: that upset me istuc mē ipsum commovḗbat

upsetting: that was more upsetting to me than to you illud mihi maiṓrī stómachō erat quam tibi

upside down: everything was upside down ómnia erant sūrsum deórsum

use: it's no use ī́licet

use: what's the use! quid opus est?

utter: she never uttered a word nullum verbum ēmī́sit

vein: in a similar vein ad símilem senténtiam

very well (*in agreement*) fiat

virtually propḗmodum

visit: to go to visit, pay a visit to vīs‧ō -ere -ī -ū́rus

wait a minute, please manē dum, quaesō

wait: wait a minute if you don't mind manē dum nisi piget

want: now what do you want? quid nunc tibi vīs?

waste one's breath óperam per‧dō -dere -didī

waste: I'm wasting my time frustrā tempus cónterō

watch out: hey you, watch out! heus tū, cavē!

way: by the way óbiter

way: he must always have his own way semper faciéndum est quod vult

way: I'm in a bad way mihi male est

way: if it's not too much out of the way for you sī tibi nōn sānē dḗvium erit

way: is that the way you help me? istṓcine pactō mē ádiuvās?

way: on one's way inter viās

way: to be on the way to iter habḗre ad (+ *acc*)

well done! factum óptimē!

well said! facḗtē dictum!

well immō *or* em *or* quīn

well, well enim vērō

what (is the trouble) now? quid iam?

what about me? quid ego?

what about the dough (money)? quid dē argéntō?

what do you take me for? for a fool? prō quō mē habēs? prō stultō?

what else can I do for you? quid est quod tibi effícere possum ámplius?

what for? quam ob rem?; quā causā?

what is it? *(what's the probem?)* quid est negṓtī?

what is it? out with it! quid est? cedo!

what next? quid deínde?

what's it to me how you ... quid istuc ad mē áttinet, quṓmodo tū (+ *subj*)

what's that? *(what did you say?)* quid est?

what's that to you? quid ad tē áttinet?

what's the reason why ... quid est quod (+ *indic*)

what's up? quid reī est?

while away the time fall•ō -ere feféllī tempus

who are you? quis tū homō es?

who is he (she)? quis homō est?

who is it? it's me quis homō est? ego sum

who says so? quis hoc dīcit factum?

whole: taken as a whole in summam

why is it that ... quid est quod (+ *indic*)

why not? *(challenging what has been said)* quid ita nōn?; *(as an expression of assent: of course)* quíppinī? *or* quidnī?

why say more? quid plūra?

why so? quid ita? *or* quāprópter?

why so? because ... quid ita? quia ...

why, this very day quīn hódiē

willy-nilly nōlens volēns

wise guy! ímpudēns!

wise guy: don't be a wise guy nē sīs ímpudēns

wonder: and no wonder nec mīrum

wonder: I wonder what's up mīror, quid hoc sit negṓtī

wonder: I wonder where he is ubi sit cṓgitō

word: I want a word with you paucīs tē volō *or* volō tē verbīs paúculīs

word: to give (break, keep) one's word fidem dare (frángere, servắre)

word: why should I take your word for it? cūr tibi crēdam?

words fail me mihi verba dēsunt

worry: don't you worry! tū nōlī sollicitắrī!

worse: to get worse ingravḗsc•ō -ere; **to turn out for the worse** in pēiṓrem partem vertor vertī versus sum

worth: he's worth a lot of money dīvítiās máximās habet

worth: he's worth nothing nihil est

worth: it isn't worth it nōn est óperae prétium **it's not worth all that** tantī nōn est

worthwhile: it is worthwhile óperae prétium est

wow! *(in shocked surprise)* papaé!

wrong: if I have done anything wrong, I'm sorry sī quid pérperam fēcī, mē paénitet

wrong: what's wrong with you? quid est tibi? *or* quid est tēcum?

yes: I say yes you say no ego aiō tū negās

Chapter XII: Clothing and Jewelry

CONVERSATIONS _____

┌──────────── LEVEL I   **Priscilla buys clothes.**

Vestiária	Salvē. Quómodo tibi ministráre possum?	*Saleslady: Hello. How can I help you?*
Prīscílla	Salvē. Ego stolam émere volō.	*Priscilla: Hello. I want to buy a gown.*
Vestiária	Quem colórem cupis?	*What color do you want?*
Prīscílla	Stolam caerúleam cúpiō.	*I want a blue gown.*
Vestiária	Cupísne quicquam áliud?	*Do you want anything else?*
Prīscílla	Ita, pār soccórum cúpiō.	*Yes, I want a pair of shoes.*
Vestiária	Cupísne émere sandália?	*Do you want to buy sandals?*
Prīscílla	Mínimē. Soccōs albōs cúpiō.	*No. I want white shoes.*
Vestiária	Habémus hódiē vestēs séricās vīlēs.	*We have inexpensive silk dresses today.*
Prīscílla	Benígnē. Quantī haec cōnstant?	*No, thank you. How much do these (items) cost?*
Vestiária	Decem dēnáriīs ex tōtō.	*Ten denarii in all.*
Prīscílla	Ecce tibi decem dēnáriōs.	*Here are your ten denarii.*

┌──────────── LEVEL II   **Peter buys some winter clothes..**

Vestiárius	Salvē. Quómodo tibi ministráre possum?	*Salesman: Hello. How can I help you?*
Petrus	Salvē. Velim émere mihi áliquot vestīménta hībérna.	*Peter: Hello. I'd like to buy myself some winter clothes.*

110

Vestiárius	Em, habémus paénulās scórteās ex Hispániā.	*Well, we have leather raincoats from Spain.*
Petrus	Bene. Cúpiō paénulam manicátam. Vēnditásne digitália?	*Fine. I want a long-sleeved raincoat. Do you sell gloves?*
Vestiárius	Hábeō digitália scórtea et lānáta.	*I have leather and woolen gloves.*
Petrus	Dā mihi duo pária digitálium lānātórum. Égeō étiam pílleō lānátō.	*Give me two pairs of woolen gloves. I also need a woolen cap.*
Vestiárius	Vīsne émere tībiália lānáta?	*Do you want to buy (some) woolen stockings?*
Petrus	Sānē, égeō duóbus páribus.	*Yes, I need two pairs.*
Vestiárius	Vīsne quicquam áliud?	*Do you want anything else?*
Petrus	Cíngulum scórteum, sī praestō est.	*A leather belt if it's available.*
Vestiárius	Cíngula semper in hāc tabérnā vestiáriā praestō sunt. Quot cíngula cupis?	*Belts are always available in this clothing store. How many belts do you want?*
Petrus	Ūnum, opínor, satis est.	*I suppose one is enough.*
Vestiárius	Quámobrem egēs hīs vestīméntīs hībérnīs?	*Why do you need these winter clothes?*
Petrus	Quia ego iter factúrus sum trāns Alpēs in Germániam.	*Because I'm going to take a trip across the Alps to Germany.*

LEVEL III **Two daughters get dressed for a party.**

Māter	Lēda et Vanéssa, vōsne parátae estis ad convívium quod María ágitat?	*Mother: Leda and Vanessa, are you ready for the party that Maria is throwing?*
Lēda	Māter, ego hábeō nihil prōrsus quod geram.	*Leda: Mother, I have absolutely nothing to wear.*
Māter	Nūgās! Habēs vērō cēnātória bellíssima. Habēs enim tālárem vestem róseam et tālárem vestem violáceam et tālárem vestem caerúleam.	*Nonsense! In fact, you have very pretty party clothes. You have, you know, a pink gown, a violet gown, and a blue gown.*
Lēda	Ita rēs est. At ego eās omnēs abhinc trēs diēs ad fullónicam áttulī.	*That's true. But I took all of them to the laundry three days ago.*

Māter	Vanéssa, tū útique sat supérque vestēs habēs. Quoad ego sciō, tū habēs pulchrās túnicās manicátās et túnicās sine mánicīs. Dā Lēdae ūnam ex tuīs túnicīs.	*Vanessa, you at least have more than enough clothes. As far as I know, you have beautiful long-sleeved and sleeveless dresses. Give Leda one of your dresses*
Vanéssa	Māter, Lēda semper vestēs meās mūtuátur. Praetéreā, mea túnica coccínea et túnica víridis sunt véterēs et trītae.	*Mother, Leda is always borrowing my clothes. Besides, my deep red dress and my green dress are old and worn out.*
Māter	Lēda!	*Leda!*
Lēda	Quid est?	*What is it?*
Māter	Cūrā ut ábeās currículō ad fullónicam et petās vestēs tuās.	*See to it that you take off on the double for the laundry and fetch your clothes.*
Lēda	Eī óperam dābō extémplō, māter.	*I'll attend to that immediately, mother.*
Māter	Et tū, Vanéssa ...	*And you, Vanessa ...*
Vanéssa	Quid?	*What?*
Māter	Sī vīs īre exōrnáta ad convívium, tibi licet gerās meās inaúrēs et moníle gemmátum.	*If you want to go to the party all decked out, you may wear my earrings and my necklace of precious stones.*
Vanéssa	Grátiās, māter.	*Thank you, mother.*
Māter	Lēda, tibi licet gérās meam armíllam et moníle baccátum.	*Leda, you may wear my bracelet and my pearl necklace.*
Lēda	Papaé! Quāle convívium id erit!	*Great! What a party that will be!*

Topical Vocabulary

ankle-length tālár·is -is -e

apron súblig·ar -áris *n*

belt cíngul·um -ī *n;* zōn·a -ae *f (wide belt, usu. of cloth, used by men and women with a tunic; often used as money belt)*

blouse pēlúsi·a -ae *f*

boot pēr·ō -ónis *m (of rawhide, reaching up to the calf, worn by peasants, shepherds, soldiers);* cálig·a -ae *f (worn by soldiers of lower rank)*

bra stróphi·um -ī *n,* mamillár·e -is *n*

bracelet armíll·a -ae *f (worn on the upper arm)*

brocade séric·um -ī *n* aurō (*or* argéntō) intéxtum (*or* intertéxtum)

bundle up *(against the cold)* sē bene opér·iō -íre -uī

button *s* glóbul·us -ī *m*

button *tr* glóbulīs string·ō -ere strīnxī strictus

cap pílle·us -ī *m*

cape lacérn·a -ae *f*

chain catéll·a -ae *f*

change mūtáre

charm amulét·um -ī *n*

clasp fíbul·a -ae *f*

cloak pálli·um -ī *n (Greek item)*

clogs sóle·ae -árum *fpl* lígneae

cloth *(as a fabric)* text·um -ī *n; (a piece of cloth)* pann·us -ī *m*

clothe vést·iō -íre -ívī *or* -iī ítus

clothes vestīmént·a -órum *npl;* hábit·us -ūs *m (outfit of a particular class or occasion)*

clothier *(sales person in a clothing store)* vestiári·us -ī *m,* vestiári·a -ae *f*

clothing store tabérn·a -ae *f* vestiária

clothing vest·is -is *f,* vestít·us -ūs *m,* vestīmént·um -ī *n*

coat paénul·a -ae *f,* amícul·um -ī *n*

collar collár·e -is *n*

deep red coccíne·us -a -um

dinner clothes cēnātóri·a -órum *npl,* sýnthes·is -is *f*

dress *s* vest·is -is *f* mulíebris; *(ankle-length)* vestis tāláris; *(Roman)* stol·a -ae *f*

dress *tr* índuō indúere índuī indútus, vést·iō -íre -ívī *or* -iī -ítus; amíc·iō -íre amícuī *or* amíxī amíctus; **to dress oneself, get dressed** sē indúere, sē vestíre, sē amicíre; **to dress up** sē exōrnáre

dress shoes socc·ī -órum *mpl,* sóccul·ī -órum *mpl (for women, of different colors and often decorated with gems)*

earrings inaúr·ēs -ium *fpl*

embroidered *(with colors)* pīct·us -a -um

emerald smarágd·us -ī *m*

evening wear cēnātóri·a -órum *npl*

fabric *(pattern of weaving)* text·us -ūs *m* (**coarse** crassus; **sheer, thin** ténuis; **thick** pinguis)

fashion cultūs mod·us -ī *m*

fringe fímbri·a -ae *f*

fur coat amícul·um -ī *n* pellícium

fur jacket iacc·a -ae *f* pellícia

garter períscelis, periscélidis *f*

girdle stropp·ī -órum *mpl*

gloves digitál·ia -ium *npl*

gown tāláris vest·is -is *f; (Roman)* stol·a -ae *f*

green vírid·is -is -e

handbag *(of leather)* pérul•a -ae *f* coriácea

hat pétas•us -ī *m (with broad brim)*

hem limb•us -ī *m*

housecoat vest•is -is *f* mātūtína

jacket iacc•a -ae *f; (of leather)* iacc•a -ae *f* scórtea; **fur jacket** iacca pellícea

jeans brāc•ae -árum *fpl* Genuénsēs

jewel gemm•a -ae *f*

laundry fullónic•a -ae *f; (dirty clothes)* lavandári•a -órum *npl*

leather *adj* ex córiō; *(for weatherproofing)* scórte•us -a -um

leather *s* córi•um -ī *n*

leather raincoat scórte•a paénul•a -ae *f (waterproof)*

linen *adj* líne•us -a -um

linen *s* línteum -ī *n*, līn•um -ī *n*

linen cloth sában•um -ī *n*

locket *(worn by boys, of leather, silver or gold)* bull•a -ae *f;* **wearing a locket** bullát•us -a -um

long-sleeved manicát•us -a -um

miniskirt cástul•a -ae *f* brevíssima

money belt ventrál•e -is *n, (of cloth)* zōn•a -ae *f*

necklace torqu•ēs -is *m*, moníl•e -is *n; (of precious stones)* moníle gemmátum

necktie focál•e -is *n*

nightgown camísi•a -ae *f* noctúrna

outfit hábit•us -ūs *m*, sýnthes•is -is *f*

overcoat superindūment•um -ī *n*

pajamas sýnthes•is -is *f* dormītória

palla *(female "toga," worn over the stola)* pall•a -ae *f*

pallium *(Greek "toga," made of wool)* pálli•um -ī *n;* **wearing a pallium** palliát•us -a -um

pants brāc•ae -árum *fpl*

pattern *(of weaving)* text•us -ūs *m*

pearl earrings margarítae -árum *fpl* dēpendéntēs

pearl necklace moníl•e -is *n* baccátum

pink róse•us -a -um

pleated undulát•us -a -um

pocket lócul•us -ī *m*

print vest•is -is *f* imāgínibus impréssa

purse pérul•a -ae *f*

put on índuō indúere índuī indútus

raincoat scórte•a -ae *f; (hooded)* paénul•a -ae *f; (open mantle, fastened at shoulder)* lacérn•a -ae *f*

ribbon taéni•a -ae *f*

ring ánul•us -ī *m*

robe vest•is -is *f*

safety pin fíbul•a -ae *f*

saleslady *(in a clothing store)* vestiári•a -ae *f*

sandal *(w. covered toes)* sandáli•um -ī *n; (simplest form of sandal, with the sole fastened to feet with thongs)* sóle•a -ae *f; (with thick leather sole, tied with straps, characteristically worn by Greeks)* crépid•a -ae *f*

sash zōn•a -ae *f*

scarf amictóri•um -ī *n*

sheer *(fabrics)* rall•us -a -um

shirt indǔsi•um -ī *n*

shoe *(worn with toga)* cálce•us -ī *m; (oxfords)* cálceī subtālárēs; *(fancy low shoe, of different colors, gold, yellow, decorated with pearls, etc.)* socc•us -ī *m*, sóccul•us -ī *m; (red shoes of senator)* cálceus múlleus *m*

shoelace corrígi•a -ae *f*

shorts subligácul·um -ī *n; (street wear)* breviốrēs brāc·ae -árum *fpl*

ski boot cálig·a -ae *f* nartātória

ski jacket iacc·a -ae *f* nartātória

silk *adj* séric·us -a -um; **silk clothes** séric·a -ốrum *npl*

silk *s* séric·um -ī *n*

skirt cástul·a -ae *f*

skirt indúcul·a -ae *f*; gunn·a -ae *f*

sleeve mánic·a -ae *f*

sleeveless sine mánicīs

slip hypozốni·um -ī *n*

slipper sóle·a -ae *f,* socc·us -ī *m; (of felt)* ūd·ō -ốnis *m*

sneakers cálce·ī -ốrum *mpl* gýmnicī

sole *(of shoe or foot)* sol·um -ī *n*

stocking tībiál·e -is *n; (of felt and covering part of the legs)* impíli·um -ī *n*

strap *(for shoe or sandal, sometimes decorated with gems)* obstrágul·um -ī *n*

street clothes forếns·ia -ium *npl*

style modus -ī *m; to go out of style* ex(s)olếsc·ō -ere ex(s)óluī ex(s)olétus

suit sýnthes·is -is *f*

sweater thōr·āx -ácis *m* lánius

swimsuit vest·is -is *f* balneáris

swim trunks súblig·ar -áris *n* balneáre

take off *(clothes)* éxuō exúere éxuī exútus; *(clothes, shoes, ring)* détrahō dētráhere dētráxī dētráctus

toga tog·a -ae *f; (bright-white toga, worn by candidates)* toga cándida; *(worn by men and boys after the age of about fifteen)* toga virílis *or* pūra; *(toga with purple border, worn by curule magistrates, by boys up to the age of manhood, and by girls until marriage)* toga praetéxta; *(toga embroidered with silver stars)* toga pícta; *(toga of smooth cloth)* toga rāsa

topcoat amícul·um -ī *n*

trousers brāc·ae -árum *fpl*

try on *(clothes)* induéndō probáre

undershirt *(worn by both sexes)* subúcul·a -ae *f*

undress éxuō exúere éxuī exútus; **to get undressed** sē exúere

uniform hábit·us -ūs *m;* **in uniform** subōrnát·us -a -um

veil vēl·um -ī *n*

wear ger·ō -ere gessī gestus, gest·ō -áre -ávī -átus; **wearing a belt** zōnā incínctus

women's winter shoes calceátus -ūs *m* fēminárum hībérnus

wool lān·a -ae *f*

woolen lānát·us -a -um, láni·us -a -um

wrap amíct·us -ūs *m*

wrist watch hōrológi·um -ī bracchiále

zipper clausúr·a -ae *f* tráctilis

Chapter XIII: School

CONVERSATIONS

┌──────── LEVEL I   **Checking on homework.**

Magístra	Siléntium, quaesō! Andréa!	*Teacher: Silence, please! Andrea!*
Andréa	Adsum.	*Andrea: Present.*
Magístra	Cōnfēcistíne tuum praescríptum domésticum?	*Did you finish your homework?*
Andréa	Cōnfécī.	*I have.*
Magístra	Quid fēcístī?	*What did you do?*
Andréa	Vocábula Latína ēdídicī.	*I memorized the Latin vocabulary.*
Magístra	Quid ámplius?	*What else?*
Andréa	Scrīptúram compósuī.	*I wrote a composition.*
Magístra	Dē quō?	*About what?*
Andréa	Dē monuméntīs in forō.	*About the monuments in the forum.*
Magístra	Quae monuménta dēscrīpsístī?	*Which monuments did you describe?*
Andréa	Basílicās et cúriam et vária templa et cétera.	*The courthouses and the senate building and the various temples, and so forth.*
Magístra	Trāde mihi.	*Hand it in.*
Andréa	Ecce.	*Here it is.*
Magístra	Christína!	*Christine!*
Christína	Adsum.	*Present.*
Magístra	Dē quō in compositiṓne scrīpsístī?	*What did you write about in your composition?*
Christína	Dē stātū mulíerum.	*About the status of women.*

Magístra	Bene. Trāde mihi.	*Fine. Hand it in.*
Christína	Ecce.	*Here it is.*

LEVEL II   **Getting the lesson straight.**

Cárolus	Magíster, quid dīcās ego nōn intéllegō.	*Carl: Teacher, I don't understand what you are saying*
Magíster	Cómparō rem públicam Rōmánam cum rē públicā nostrā.	*Teacher: I am comparing the Roman government with our government.*

Cárolus	At ego sciō nihil ferē dē rē públicā Rōmánā.	*But I know practically nothing about the Roman government.*
Magíster	Lēgistíne caput quārtum tuae *História Rōmána?*	*Have you read the fourth chapter of your Roman History?*

Cárolus	Adhūc ego lēgī sōlum ūsque ad caput tértium.	*So far I have read only up to chapter three.*
Magíster	At ego caput quārtum assignávī in diem hodiérnum.	*But I assigned chapter four for today.*

Cárolus	Éxplicā, quaesō, quid in cápite quārtō sit.	*Please explain what is in the fourth chapter.*
Magíster	Em, áperī librum tuum ad páginam sexāgésimam séptimam.	*Well, open your book to page sixty-seven.*

Cárolus	Apéruī eum.	*I've opened it.*
Magíster	Quid est scrīptum in summā páginā?	*What is written at the top of the page?*

Cárolus	"Dē Rē Públicā Rōmánā."	*"The Roman Government."*
Magíster	Lege ídeō illud caput in diem crástīnum. Disputábimus dē illā rē crās.	*Then read that chapter for tomorrow. We'll discuss that topic tomorrow.*

Cárolus	Certē illud legam.	*Sure, I'll read it.*
Magíster	Nisi illud légeris, cadēs prō certō in próximā probātióne.	*If you don't read it, you'll flunk the next test for sure.*

LEVEL III   **A teacher conducts her class efficiently.**

Magístra	In manūs cápite libéllōs vestrōs. Corrigḗmus exercítium quod modo cōnfēcístis.	*Teacher: Get out your notebooks. We're going to correct the exercise that you just completed.*
Iásōn	Ignṓsce mihi, magístra; nōn hábeō cálamum.	*Jason: Excuse me, teacher; I don't have a pen.*
Magístra	Ubi est cálamus tuus, Iásōn?	*Where is your pen, Jason?*
Iásōn	Domī relíquī, ut vidḗtur. Quid fáciam?	*I left it at home, it seems. What should I do?*
Magístra	Fortásse potes mūtuárī cálamum ā próximō tuō.	*Perhaps you can borrow a pen from your neighbor.*
Iásōn	Estne haec probátiō?	*Is this a test?*
Magístra	Nōlī sollicitárī. Ut prius dīxī, corrigḗmus tantúmmodo exercítia vestra.	*Don't worry. As I said earlier, we're only going to correct your exercises.*
Iásōn	Īnsunt multa menda meō exercítiō.	*There are lots of mistakes in my exercise.*
Magístra	Per ignōrātiṓnem an incúriam?	*Through lack of knowledge or through carelessness?*
Iásōn	Per utrámque, ut vidḗtur.	*Through both, it seems.*
Magístra	Récitā clārē exercítium tuum et ego menda indicábō.	*Read your exercise aloud and I will point out the mistakes.*
Iásōn	Legámne statim cunctum exercítium an per síngulās senténtiās?	*Should I read the whole exercise at one time or sentence by sentence?*
Magístra	Per síngulās senténtiās. Eō modō ego quóque mendum indicábō corrigámque et tū póteris annotáre figúram corréctam.	*Sentence by sentence. In that way I can point out and correct each mistake, and you can jot down the correct form.*

TOPICAL VOCABULARY

abbreviate immínu•ō -ere -uī imminútus

abbreviation not•a -ae *f* compendiária

ability facúlt•ās -átis *f;* **ability to read and write** legéndī scrībendíque facúltās; **natural ability** ingéni•um -ī *n*

absent abs•ēns -éntis; **to be absent** absum abésse áfuī āfutúrus

absentee ábsēns, abséntis *mf*

academy académi•a -ae *f*

add adíc•iō -ere adiécī adiéctus

aloud clārē

answer *s* respóns•um -ī *n;* **to give an answer to s.o.** álicui respónsum red•dō -dere -didī -ditus

answer *tr (in both speaking and writing: with dat of person and* ad + *acc of the thing)* respón•deō -dére -dī -sum; **to answer a question** ad interrogátum respondére

ask rogáre; *(for information)* quaerō quaérere quaesívī quaesítus; **to ask about (someone, something)** dē (áliquō) rogáre; **to ask a few questions** pauca quaérere; **to ask s.o. s.th.** áliquem áliquid rogáre; **to ask s.o. for s.th.** ab áliquō áliquid rogáre; **to ask the teacher (student) a question** docéntem (discéntem) interrogáre; **to ask this question** hoc quaérere

assign assignáre

assignment pēns•um -ī *n; (written)* praescrípt•um -ī *n*

audiovisual aid audīvīsíficum subsídi•um -ā -um

ballpoint pen stil•us -ī *m* sphaerátus

basics elemént•a -órum *npl*

bathroom *(toilet)* latrín•a -ae *f;* **may I go to the bathroom?** licetne mihi in latrínam īre? **yes, OK** licet

blackboard tábul•a -ae *f* ātra

book li•ber -brī *m*

book bag cápsul•a -ae *f* scholáris

cafeteria refectóri•um -ī *n*

calculator māchínul•a -ae *f* calculātória

call roll nómina citáre

capital letter lítter•a -ae *f* māiúscula

carbon copy exémpl•um -ī *n* trānscúsum, antígraph•um -ī *n*

chalk crēt•a -ae *f*

chapter cap•ut -itis *n*

chemistry chémic•ē -ēs *f*

class classis -is *f;* **to be at the head of the class** classem dūc•ō -ere dūxī

classroom concláv•e -is *n* scholáre

college collégi•um -ī *n*

composition scrīptúr•a -ae *f,* compositi•ō -ónis *f*

copy *s* exémpl•um -ī *n*

copy *tr* exscríb•ō -ere exscrípsī **(from** ex + *abl) (by cheating* clandēstínō)

correct *adj* rēct•us -a -um *(opp:* prāvus), ēmendát•us -a -um *(free from faults),* corréct•us -a -um *(in the sense of "corrected")*

correct *tr (esp. mistakes in writing)* ēmendáre; *(a person or mistake)* córrig•ō -ere corréxī corréctus

correction corrécti•ō -ónis *f,* ēmendáti•ō -ónis *f*

correctly rēctē *(opp:* prāvē), ēmendátē; **to speak (spell) correctly** rēctē loquī (scríbere)

corridor ambulácr·um -ī *n,* andr·ōn -ṓnis *m*

deal with *(topic, person)* tractắre

dean decắn·us -ī *m;* decắn·a -ae *f*

desk mēns·a -ae *f* scrīptṓria

dictionary dictiōnắr·ium -ī *n,* léxic·on -ī *n*

discuss disputắre dē (+ *abl*)

discussion disputắti·ō -ṓnis *f*

door iắnu·a -ae *f*

drive, enthusiasm stúdi·um -ī *n,* vīs *(acc: vim) f*

educate īnstít·uō -úere -uī -útus

education īnstitúti·ō -ṓnis *f (Note that ēdūcắtiō refers to "raising, bringing up" and can apply to the raising of children as well as livestock, the training of the body, etc.)*

elementary school litterắrius lūd·us -ī *m*

eraser *(for a blackboard)* dētersṓri·um -ī *n; (on a pencil)* gumm·is -is *f*

erasure litǘr·a -ae *f*

error *(in writing)* mend·um -ī *n,* mend·a -ae *f,* víti·um -ī *n;* **to commit (make) an error** mendum admítt·ō -ere admī́sī admíssus

essay tractắt·us -ūs *m*

examination exāmināti·ō -ṓnis *f*

examine exāminắre

exercise *(written)* exercíti·um -ī *n; (practice)* exercitắti·ō -ṓnis *f*

explain explānắre, explicắre

explanation explānắti·ō -ṓnis *f,* explicắti·ō -ṓnis *f*

express éxprim·ō -ere expréssī expréssus

faculty magistéri·um -ī *n*

flunk: to flunk a test cad·ō -ere cécidī cāsǘrus in probātiṓne

form *(grammatical)* figǘr·a -ae *f*

freshman tīr·ō -ṓnis *mf*

front of the room prior par·s -tis *f* scholae

get *(to understand)* tén·eō -ére -uī tentus; **I get it** téneō; **now I get it** iam téneō

globe glob·us -ī *m* terrắrum

grade *s* grad·us -ūs *m; (for performance)* not·a -ae *f*

grade *tr (papers)* notắre; *(to evaluate)* aestimắre

graduate gradūs suscíp·iō -ere suscḗpī

hallway ambulắcr·um -ī *n,* andr·ōn -ṓnis *m*

hand in *tr* trā·dō -dere -didī -ditus

handwriting chīrógraph·um -ī *n*

heading cap·ut -itis *n,* ind·ex -icis *m* cápitis

high school schol·a -ae *f* supérior

history histṓri·a -ae *f*

home room conclắve -is *n* scholắre próprium

homework pēns·um -ī *n* dométicum; *(written)* praescrī́pt·um -ī *n* dométicum

hooky: to play hooky ínsciīs paréntibus ā scholā abesse

illiterate analphabét·us -a -um

improve *(to get better in study)* prṓfíc·iō -ere prṓfḗcī prṓféctum

improvement prōféct·us -ūs *m*

ink ātrāmént·um -ī *n*

instruct s.o. in s.th. ínstru·ō -ere īnstrúxī īnstrúctus áliquem áliquō

instruction *(teaching)* īnstitúti·ō -ṓnis *f;* **instructions** praecépt·a -ṓrum *npl*

instructor praecépt·or -ṓris *m* (·rīx -rícis *f*), doc·ēns -éntis *mf*

jot down annotắre

junior iúni·or -ṓris *mf*

key clāv·is -is *m*

know sciō scīre scīvī scītus; **know how to** scīre (+ *inf*); **not know** nésc·iō -íre -ívī *or* -iī

Latin *(to know, read, teach, speak, understand, write)* Latínē; **Are you learning Latin?** Discísne Latínē?; **Did you forget Latin?** Esne oblítus (-a) Latínē?; **Do you know Latin?** Nōstíne Latínē?; **Do you know how to speak Latin?** Scīsne Latínē loquī?; **Do you read Latin easily?** Legísne Latínē fácile?; **Do you speak Latin (fluently)?** Loquerísne Latínē (prōfluénter)?; **Do you teach Latin?** Docésne Latínē?; **Do you understand Latin?** Intellegísne Latínē?; **Since when have you been learning Latin?** Ex quō témpore Latínē didicístī?; **Where did you study Latin?** Ubi Latíne studuistī?; **Who is able to write Latin?** Quis Latíne scríbere potest?

Latin teacher Latinitātis magis·ter -trī *m* (·tra -trae *f*)

learn disc·ō -ere dídicī; **to learn by heart** ēdíscere

learner disc·ēns -éntis *mf*

line vers·us -ūs *m* (*of prose or poetry*)

map tábul·a -ae *f* geográphica

manuscript manuscrípt·um -ī *n*

memorize ēdísc·ō -ere ēdídicī

meter númer·us -ī *m*

mistake mend·um -ī *n*, víti·um -ī *n*

note not·a -ae *f;* **to take notes** commentáriōs cōnfíc·iō -ere cōnfécī cōnfectus

note pad pugillár·ēs -um *mpl*

notebook libéll·us -ī *m*

page págin·a -ae *f;* **at the bottom (top) of the page** in īmā (summā) páginā

paper chart·a -ae *f*

paper clip fībícul·a -ae *f* chartárum

paragraph parágraph·us -ī *m*

pass: to pass a test probātiónem sustín·eō -ére -uī

passage *(in a text)* loc·us -ī *(pl:* locī) *m*

pen penn·a -ae *f,* cálam·us -ī *m* scrīptórius

pencil gráphi·um -ī *n*

poem poém·a -atis *n*

point out indicáre

poster fóli·um -ī *n* mūrále

practice *s* exercitáti·ō -ónis *f;* **extensive and continous practice** multa et contínua exercitátiō

practice *tr* exérc·eō -ére -uī -itus

prepare paráre; (*in advance*) praeparáre

present: to be present adsum adésse ádfuī adfutúrus

progress prōféct·us -ūs *m; to make progress* prōfíc·iō -ere prōfécī prōféctum

promote ad superiórem classem prōmóv·eō -ére prōmóvī prōmótus

pronounce prōnūntiáre

prose prōs·a -ae *f*

pupil discípul·us -ī *m,* discípul·a -ae *f*

question rogát·um -ī *n;* interrogát·um -ī *n;* quaésti·ō -ónis *f;* **to raise a question** quaestiónem pōn·ō -ere pósuī

question mark sign·um -ī *n* interrogātiónis

quiz quaestiúncul·a -ae *f*

read leg·ō légere lēgī lēctus

reading lécti·ō -ónis *f*

recitation recitáti·ō -ónis *f*

recite recitáre

repeat répet·ō -ere -ívī -ítus

repetition repetíti·ō -ónis *f*

research *s* investīgắti•ō -ṓnis *f*

research *tr* investīgắre

restroom loc•us -ī *m* sēcrḗtus; **may I go to the restroom** licetne mihi in locum sēcrḗtum inī́re? **Yes, OK** licet

review *s* retractắti•ō -ṓnis *f*

review *tr* retractắre

roll call nṓminum recitắti•ō -ṓnis *f;* **to take roll call** nṓmina recitắre

scan (poetry) *tr* scand•ō -ere -ī scānsus

school building aed•ēs -is *f* scholắris

school lūd•us -ī *m; (advanced)* schol•a -ae *f;* **to attend school** scholam frequentắre; **to go to school** scholam óbeō obī́re obiī *or* obī́vī; **to skip school** īnsciīs parḗntibus ā scholā absum abḗsse

school supplies īnstrūmḗnt•um -ī *n* scholắre

scribble exarắre, cōnscrībillắre

seat subsélli•um -ī *n* (scholắre)

senior séni•or -ṓris *mf*

sheet schid•a -ae *f*

silence silénti•um -ī *n*

slide imắg•ō -inis *f* phōtogrắphica trānslū́cida; **to show slides** imắginēs phōtogrắphicās exhíb•eō -ére -uī -itus

slow to learn segn•is -is -e

small letter lítter•a -ae *f* minúscula

sophomore sophomṓr•us -ī *m,* sophomṓr•a -ae *f*

spell scrīb•ō -ere scrīpsī scrīptus

spelling orthogrắphi•a -ae *f*

staple *s* uncī́nul•us -ī *m* metállicus

staple *tr* cṓnsu•ō -ere -ī -ū́tus

stapler cōnsūtṓri•um -ī *n* (chartắrum), uncīnātṓri•um -ī *n*

student stud•ēns -éntis *mf,* discípul•us -ī *m,* discípul•a -ae *f*

studies stúdi•a -ṓrum *npl;* (stúdium *in the singular means "drive, enthusiasm")*

study period spáti•um -ī *n* studiṓsum

stumble over new words nova verba offénd•ō -ere -ī

subject disciplī́n•a -ae *f; (topic)* argūmḗnt•um -ī *n*

subject matter mātéri•a -ae *f*

subtract détrah•ō -ere dētráxī dētráctus

take down *(notes, lecture)* excíp•iō -ere excḗpī excéptus

talent ingéni•um -ī *n*

talented ingeniṓs•us -a -um

teach *(w. double acc)* dóc•eō -ére -uī -tus

teacher magís•ter -trī *m,* magístr•a -ae *f; (in elementary school)* litterắt•or -ṓris *m,* litterắtr•īx -ī́cis *f*

teaching method docéndī rắti•ō -ṓnis *f*

test probắti•ō -ṓnis *f*

textbook lib•er -rī *m* scholắris

theme *(topic)* mātéri•a -ae *f,* argūmḗnt•um -ī *n; (essay)* tractắt•us -ūs *m*

toilet latrī́n•a -ae *f;* **may I go to the toilet** licétne mihi in latrī́nam īre? **Yes, OK** licet

topic mātéri•a -ae *f,* rēs, reī *f*

translate (con)vért•ō -ere -ī (con)vérsus; **to translate from Latin to English** ex Latī́nō in Ánglicum (con)vértere

transparency pắgin•a -ae *f* pellū́cida

tutor domésticus (-a) praecépt•or -ṓris *m* (•rīx -rī́cis *f*)

type māchínulā scrīptṓriā scrīb•ō -ere scrīpsī scrīptus, dactylographắre

typewriter māchínul•a -ae *f* scrīptṓria, dactylṓgraph•um -ī *n*

typewriter key plēctr•um -ī *n* (dactylogrắphicum) malléol•us -i *m*

typewriter ribbon taeni·a -ae *f* dactylográphica

understand intélleg·ō -ere intelléxī intelléctus

verse vers·us -ūs *m*

vocabulary vocábul·a -órum *npl*

white board tábul·a -ae *f* alba

window fenéstr·a -ae *f*

write scrīb·ō -ere scrīpsī scrīptus

writing scrīptúr·a -ae *f;* **writings** scrīpt·a -órum *npl*

COMMANDS FOR THE CLASSROOM

N.B. *For all commands dealing with Latin grammar see Chapter 25.*

answer me respóndē mihi; **answer my question** respóndē (respondéte) ad meum rogátum

be on time, please venī (veníte) témperī (*or* ad tempus), quaesō

be quiet (silent) tacē (tacéte); siléntium tenē (tenéte)

close the door claude (claúdite) iánuam

come here venī *(pl:* veníte) hūc

come in intrā *(pl:* intráte)

come on, try to remember ágedum, temptā (temptáte) meminísse

continue (reading, writing, speaking, translating) perge (pérgite) (légere, scríbere, dícere, vértere)

cut it out désine (désínite); désíste (désístite)

cut out the chatter, please ōmítte (ōmíttite) garrulitátem, quaesō

cut out the noise, please omítte (omíttite) strépitum, quaesō

cut out the nonsense omítte (omíttite) nūgās

don't cheat nōlī (nōlíte) exscríbere ex próximō

don't forget to do your homework nōlíte oblīvíscī perfícere pēnsum vestrum

don't interrupt, please nōlī (nōlíte) interpelláre

don't laugh at him (her) nōlī (nōlíte) rīdére eum (eam)

don't speak English nōlī (nōlíte) loquī Ánglicē

don't tease him (her) nōlī (nōlíte) eum (eam) taxáre

explain this construction éxplicā (explicáte) hanc cōnstructiónem

form a single (double) line fac (fácite) agmen únicum (duplex)

get out your book(s) librum in manum cape, librōs in manūs cápite; librum prōme, librōs prómité

go on *(continue)* perge (pérgite)

go to the blackboard accéde (accédite) ad tábulam ātram

hand me the book librum cedo (cette) [*an old imperative*]

hand in the papers chartās redde (réddite), chartās trāde (trádite)

hand out the papers distríbue (distribúite) chartās *or* prōmptā (prōmptáte) chartās

hurry up matúrā (matūráte)

I want a word with you after class paucīs tē volō post classem

knock it off, please parce (párcite), quaesō

listen carefully audī (audíte) dīligénter

listen to me mē auscúlt·a (auscultáte)

look at me convérte (convértite) óculōs in mē

look it up in the dictionary id inquī́re (inquī́rite) in dictiōnā́riō

lower your voice remítte (remíttite) vōcem

make it brief in pauca cónfer (cōnférte)

never mind sine (sínite)

open your book(s) to page … áperī librum (aperī́te librōs) ad pắginam …

outline the story (the essay) dēlínea (dēlineā́te) fābulam (tractā́tum)

pay attention atténde (atténdite); **pay attention to what I am saying** atténde (atténdite) dicta mea

put your book(s) away sēpṓne librum (sēpṓnite librōs)

raise your hand(s) attólle manum (attóllite manūs)

read the next sentence lege (légite) senténtiam próximam; *(read aloud)* récitā (recitā́te) senténtiam próximam

read aloud (slower, faster, louder, with inflection of the voice) lege (légite) clārē (léntius, celérius, clárius, flexā vōce)

repeat after me eī́sdem verbīs mihi redde (réddite)

repeat the passage répete (repétite) locum

repeat what you just said répete (repétite) quid modo dī́xerīs (dīxerī́tis)

review: let's review the pronouns prōnṓmina rectractḗmus

show me your homework osténde (osténdite) mihi pēnsum *(or* praescrī́ptum)

silence, please! siléntium, quaesō!

sit down, please cōnsī́de (cōnsī́dite), quaesō

sit up straight rēctē sedē (sedḗte)

speak slowly (louder), please lóquere (loquíminī) lentē (clárius), quaesō

speak up ēlóquere (ēloquíminī)

stop arguing dḗsine (dēsinite) argūmentā́rī *(squabbling)* rīxā́rī

stop talking dḗsine (dēsínite) loquī

stand up surge (cōnsúrgite); (esp. as a mark of respect) assúrge (assúrgite)

stop writing dḗsine (dēsínite) scrī́bere

take notes ánnotā (annotā́te)

take your seats revértite ad subséllia

translate this sentence from English to Latin convérte hanc senténtiam ex Ánglicō in Latī́num

translate this sentence from Latin to English convérte (convértite) hanc senténtiam ex Latī́nō in Ánglicum

turn around tē verte *(pl:* vōs vértite)

turn to page __ ēvólve librum (ēvólvite librōs) ad pắginam __

use your dictionary útere (ūtíminī) dictiōnā́riō

whoa! not so fast! eho, nōn tam cito!

write out the sentences senténtiās perscrī́be (perscrī́bite)

write that on the board scrī́be (scrī́bite) id in tábulā ātrā *(or* albā)

write the following words scrībe (scrī́bite) haec verba

Chapter XIV: Buying and Selling

CONVERSATIONS

LEVEL I **Lydia explains to Diane why she bought new clothes.**

Diána	Lýdia, ubī terrárum illam stolam bellam ēmístī?	*Diane: Lydia, where on earth did you buy that pretty gown?*
Lýdia	In tabérnā vestiáriā in Viā Lātā.	*Lydia: In the clothing store on Broad Street.*
Diána	Quantī cōnstábat?	*How much did it cost?*
Lýdia	Percára erat. Trīgíntā dóllarīs cōnstábat.	*It was very expensive. It cost thirty dollars.*
Diána	Et habēs novōs soccōs.	*And you have new dress shoes.*
Lýdia	Ita. Étiam inaúrēs et moníle aúreum.	*Yes. Also earrings and a gold necklace.*
Diána	Dīc mihi, cūr haec vestīménta nova ēmístī?	*Tell me, why did you buy these new clothes?*
Lýdia	Quia meus amáns novus mē ad saltātiónem scholárem invītávit.	*Because my new boyfriend invited me to the school dance.*
Diána	Ego quoque saltātiónī intérerō. Ítaque dēsīderábō novam stolam.	*I, too, will attend the dance. And so I'll need a new gown.*
Lýdia	Vidébō tē apud saltātiónem, ut spērō. Bene valē!	*I'll see you at the dance, I hope. Bye-bye!*
Diána	Bene valē! Ábeō currículō ad Viam Lātam.	*Bye-bye! I'm taking off on the double for Broad Street.*

```
┌──────────┐ LEVEL II     Sulpicia explains why she is going shopping.
```

Aulus	Quō hinc abīs, Sulpícia?	*Aulus: Where are you off to, Sulpicia?*
Sulpícia	Ad macéllum in Subúram.	*Sulpicia: To the market in the Subura.*
Aulus	Obsōnātúra es íterum?	*You're going shopping again?*
Sulpícia	Quidnī? Placet mihi obsōnáre.	*Why not? I like to shop.*
Aulus	Quid cupis émere?	*What do you want to buy?*
Sulpícia	Multa, sī annóna in macéllō nōn nímia est.	*Many things, if the price of food at the market is not too high.*
Aulus	Et sī annóna nōn cāra est?	*And if the price of food is not high?*
Sulpícia	Obsōnábō pōma, hólera, cáseum, búbulam, cuppédia.	*I'll shop for fruit, vegetables, cheese, beef, and pastries.*
Aulus	Cūr, malum, tot mercēs obsōnábis?	*Why the devil are you going to buy so many items?*
Sulpícia	Quia crās est nātális diēs amántis meī. Agitábō convívium prō eō.	*Because tomorrow is my boyfriend's birthday. I'm going to throw him a party.*
Aulus	Emésne étiam novam stolam ad convívium?	*Will you also buy a new gown for the party?*
Sulpícia	Certē. Sed nōn in macéllō. Tabérna vestiária autem nōn procul illinc est.	*Certainly. But not in the market. The clothing store, however, is not far from there.*
Aulus	Quīn, ego quoque novam togam emam, sī tū mē invītábis.	*Well, I, too, am going to buy a new toga, if you invite me.*
Sulpícia	Invītábō, proféctō, tē. Valē in crástinum.	*Of course I'll invite you. So long till tomorrow.*

```
┌──────────┐ LEVEL III    A storekeeper makes a sale.
```

Tabernárius	Quómodo possum tē iuváre?	*Storekeeper: How can I help you?*
Ēmptor	Numquam ánteā fuī in Subúra. Subúra vidétur esse plēna praestántium tabernárum.	*Customer: I've never been in the Subura before. The Subura seems to be full of fine shops.*

Tabernárius	Ut vidēs, sunt quidem multae tabérnae in hōc locō: tabérna vestiária, tabérna chartária, tabérna librária, medicāmentária. Quid vīs īnspícere?	*As you see, there indeed are many stores around here: a clothing store, a stationery store, a bookstore, a drugstore. What do you wish to look at?*
Ēmptor	Estne quoque tabérna ferrária? Et tabérna vīnária?	*Is there also a hardware store? And a wine shop?*
Tabernárius	Sānē; étiam laniéna et cuppédō et pīstrína. Quidquid cupis, id in hōc locō émere potes.	*Yes. Also a butcher shop and a pastry shop and a bakery. You can buy whatever you wish around here.*
Ēmptor	Suntne mercēs in hīs tabérnīs cārae?	*Is the merchandise expensive in these shops?*
Tabernárius	Ut álibī, áliae mercēs sunt cārae, áliae sunt vīlēs. In hāc tabérnā ego vénditō státuās extrínsecās.	*As elsewhere, some items are expensive, others are cheap. In this shop I sell statues from abroad.*
Ēmptor	Quantī cōnstat haec imágō Véneris?	*How much does this bust of Venus cost?*
Tabernárius	Est cāríssima. Ut vidére potes, ūsque ē Graéciā vēnit. Quadrāgíntā dēnáriīs cōnstat.	*It's very expensive. As you can see, it came all the way from Greece. It costs forty denarii.*
Ēmptor	Nōn possum dēnumeráre tibi argéntum praesentárium.	*I cannot pay you the money in cash.*
Tabernárius	Nōlī sollicitárī. Bonā fidē es. Potes dare mihi hódiē vīgíntī dēnáriōs arrabónī.	*Don't worry. Your credit is good. You can give me twenty denarii today as a down payment.*
Ēmptor	Bene. Céterōs nummōs ad diem dictam solvam.	*Fine. I'll pay you the rest of the money on time.*
Tabernárius	Quot dēnáriōs potes mihi sólvere hódiē?	*How may denarii can you pay me today?*
Ēmptor	Ego vīgíntī sōlum dēnáriōs mēcum hábeō.	*I have only twenty denarii with me.*
Tabernárius	Id mihi placet. Quómodo solvēs quod réliquum est?	*That's fine with me. How will you pay the rest?*
Ēmptor	Sī licébit, duábus pēnsiónibus persólvam.	*If I may, I'll pay it off in two installments.*

Tabernárius	Probē! Mihi crēde, bene emis hanc imáginem. Ecquid placet?	*Fine! Believe me, you are buying this statue at a bargain. Do you like it?*
Ēmptor	Immō édepol vērō pérplacet.	*Heavens, yes. I really like it a lot.*
Tabernárius	Grátiās! Et nunc, sīs, potes vísere álterās tabérnās in Subū́rā.	*Thanks. And now, if you wish, you can go to see the other shops in the Subura.*
Ēmptor	Vīsam proféctō. Valē!	*I will indeed. Goodbye!*

TOPICAL VOCABULARY

advertise prōscríb•ō -ere prōscrípsī prōscríptus

ask the price of an item mercis prétium inquír•ō -ere inquīsívī inquīsítus

bargain préti•um -ī *n* speciále

be sold, be up for sale vḗn•eō -íre -iī

bookstore librári•a -ae *f*

business district empóri•um -ī *n*

butcher láni•us -ī *m*

butcher shop laniéna -ae *f*

buy paráre; em•ō -ere ḗmī ḗmptus **(from s.o.** dē áliquō); **to buy at a bargain** bene émere

buyer ēmpt•or -óris *m,* ēmptr•íx -ícis *f*

cash argént•um -ī *n* presentárium; **to pay $10 in cash for** dēnumeráre decem dóllarōs praesentáriōs prō (+ *abl*)

cent centésim•a -ae *f*

cheap vīl•is -is -e

cheaply parvō *or* vīlī prétiō; **more cheaply** minóris prétiī

check sýngraph•a -ae *f;* **to write a check for** sýngrapham (+ *gen*) perscríb•ō -ere perscrípsī perscríptus

clerk tabernári•us -ī *m,* tabernári•a -ae *f*

clothing store tabérn•a -ae *f* vestiária

cost *intr* cōnst•ō -áre -itī; **to cost a lot (little, nothing, more, less)** multī

(parvī, grátīs, plūris, minóris) cōnstáre

cost *s* impéns•a -ae *f*

credit *(com)* fid•ēs -eī *f;* **to buy on credit** fidē suā émere; pecúniā haud praesentáriā emere; **to have good credit** bonā fidē esse

customer ēmpt•or -óris *m,* ēmptr•íx -ícis *f*

deal mercimóni•um -ī *n*

dealer merc•āns -ántis *mf,* mercát•or -óris *m,* mercátr•íx -ícis *f*

debt aes, aeris *n* aliénum; **this has put me in debt** hoc mihi aes aliénum áttulit

denarius dēnári•us -ī *m (worth about one dollar)*

discount remíssi•ō -ónis *f;* **five- (ten- twenty-) percent discount** quinárum (dēnárum, vicēsimárum) centēsimárum remíssiō

dollar dóllar•us -ī *m*

down payment árrab•ō -ónis *f;* **to make a down payment of $20** *(or* **to pay $20 down)** vīgíntī dóllarōs arrabṓnī dare

drugstore medicāmentári•a -ae *f*

expensive cār•us -a -um; **very expensive** percárus

flea market for•um -ī *n* rērum vēnálium

go for: at what price do these items go for? quibus prétiīs hae mercēs vēneunt?

groceries obsṓni·a -ṓrum *npl*

grocery store macéll·um -ī *n*

hardware store tabérn·a -ae *f* ferrária

how much did you sell it for? quantī hoc vēnit?; **how much is this?** quantī hoc cōnstat?

installment pénsi·ō -ṓnis *f;* **to pay in five installments** quīnque pēnsiṓnibus solv·ō -ere -ī solū́tus

item of merchandise merx, mercis *f*

mall for·um -ī *n* subtēgulā́neum

market mercā́t·us -ūs *m*, macéll·um -ī *n*

marketable vēndíbil·is -is -e

marketplace mercā́t·us -ūs *m*, for·um -ī *n*

merchandise vēnālíci·a -ṓrum *npl*, merc·ēs -ium *fpl*

money pecū́ni·a -ae *f*, argént·um -ī *n*, numm·ī -ṓrum *mpl*

pastries cuppḗdi·a -ṓrum *npl*

pastry baker cuppēdinā́ri·us -ī *m* (·a -ae *f*)

pastry shop cuppḗd·ō -inis *f*

pay solv·ō -ere -ī solū́tus; **to pay s.o. $20 for** dēnumerā́re álicuī vīgíntī dóllarōs prō (+ *abl*); **to pay off a debt** débitum persólvere; **to pay on time** ad tempus *or* ad diem dictam sólvere; **to pay out (money) to** dēnumerā́re (nummōs) (+ *dat*)

percent centésim·a -ae *f*

pound lībr·a -ae *f;* **per pound** in lībrās

price préti·um -ī *n;* **at a high (low, very low, exorbitant) price** magnō (parvō, mínimō, nímiō); **higher price** prétium ámplius; **to set a price** prétium fácere; **the price for it is 10 denarii per pound** prétium eī in lībrās est decem dēnáriīs; **the price of food** annṓn·a -ae *f*

purchase *s* ēmpt·um -ī *n*

purchase *tr* merc·or -ā́rī -ā́tus sum

purchasing ḗmpti·ō -ṓnis *f*

receipt ápoch·a -ae *f*

run a business negótium exérc·eō -ére -uī -itus; **to run a shop** tabérnam exercére

sale vēndíti·ō -ṓnis *f;* **for sale, on sale** vēnālíci·us -a -um, vēnā́l·is -is -e; **to put up for sale** vēnum dō dare dḗdī datus

sell vēnd·ō -ere véndidī vénditus; *(of a merchant)* vēnditā́re

seller vḗndit·or -ṓris *m*, véndetr·īx -ícis *f*

set a price prétium fác·iō -ere fēcī factus *or* státu·ō -ere -ī statū́tus

shoe store tabérn·a -ae *f* sūtrína

shop, store tabérn·a -ae *f*

shop *intr (at a grocery store)* obsōnā́re; **to shop for** emō emere ēmī ēmptus; obsōnā́re *(groceries)*

shopkeeper tabernā́ri·us -ī *m* (·a -ae *f*)

shopping ḗmpti·ō -ṓnis *f; (for groceries)* obsōnā́t·us -ūs *m;* **to go shopping** ēmptum īre; *(for groceries)* obsōnā́tum īre

shopper ēmpt·or -ṓris *m; (for groceries)* obsōnā́t·or -ṓris *m*, obsōnā́tr·īx -ícis *f*

small change nummul·ī -ṓrum *mpl*

stationery rēs, rērum *fpl* chartáriae

stationery store tabérn·a -ae *f* chartária

store tabérn·a -ae *f*

supermarket superīnstitṓri·um -i *n*

trade mercātū́r·a -ae *f*

valuable: to be valuable prétium háb·eō -ére -uī -itus

wares merc·ēs -ium *fpl*

wholesale magnā́ri·us -a -um

wholesaler negōtiā́t·or -ṓris *m* magnárius

Chapter XV: The Weather

CONVERSATIONS

LEVEL I **A boy and a girl in Rome contrast the weather of Rome with that of Switzerland.**

Puer Rōmánus	Est frígidum hódiē.	*Roman Boy: It's cold today.*
Puélla Helvétia	Frīgidúmne? Quómodo id dícere potes?	*Swiss Girl: Cold? How can you say that?*
Puer	Quia ego álgeō.	*Because I feel cold.*
Puélla	At sōl lūcet et véntulus mītis flat. Prōrsus, est diēs bellus et tépidus.	*But the sun is shining and a gentle breeze is blowing. All in all, it is a nice warm day.*
Puer	Haec dícis, quia tempéstās in Helvétiā semper frígida est. Nihil habēs in Álpibus praeter nivem et gláciem.	*You say that because the weather is always cold in Switzerland. You have nothing in the Alps but snow and ice.*
Puélla	Parum vērum est! Estō; híemēs in Álpibus sunt longae. Sed tempéstās ibi aestáte est bellíssima.	*That's not quite true. Granted, the winters are long in the Alps. But the weather there in summer is very nice.*
Puer	Hīc hiems est plúvia, et diēs aestáte sunt calidíssimī.	*Here the winter is rainy and the days in summer are very hot.*
Puélla	Sed hīc Rōmae neque grándinat neque ningit. Ágedum, eámus forās lūsum. Mox tū nōn iam algébis.	*But here in Rome it neither hails nor snows. Come on, then, let's go play outside. Soon you will no longer be cold.*
Puer	Vēra dícis. Iam disserénat.	*You're right. The weather is already clearing up.*

LEVEL II — **Martha explains to her teacher how the weather kept her from going to school.**

Magístra	Cūr nōn in scholam herī vēnístī?	*Teacher: Why didn't you come to school yesterday?*
Martha	Propter procéllam.	*Martha: Because of the storm.*
Magístra	Quid áccidit?	*What happened?*
Martha	Mātūtínum quidem erat serénum, sed súbitō Áquilō perfláre incépit. Imber cádere incépit.	*The early morning was fair all right, but suddenly the north wind began to blow hard. Rain began to fall.*
Magístra	Erásne adhūc domī eō témpore?	*Were you still at home at that time?*
Martha	Modo discēdébam domō. Mox vehementíssimē pluit. Imber vērō urceátim cadébat.	*I was just leaving home. Soon it rained very hard. In fact, the rain came down in buckets.*
Magístra	Erásne formīdolósa?	*Were you afraid?*
Martha	Ita. Ictūs fúlminis et tónitrus mē terrébant. Ventī árborēs dēiēcérunt trāns viās. Vix póteram vidére quō īrem.	*Yes. The bolts of lightning and thunder frightened me. The winds knocked down trees across the streets. I could scarcely see where I was going.*
Magístra	Quid deínceps fēcístī?	*What did you do then?*
Martha	Cōnstítuī flicō domum redíre, ubi māter mē ánxia exspectábat.	*I decided on the spot to return home where my mother was waiting anxiously for me.*
Magístra	Sapiénter dēcrēvístī.	*You made a wise decision.*

LEVEL III — **The weather of Rome and Switzerland is again debated.**

Caecílius	Quālis tempéstās tibi potíssimum placet?	*Cecil: What kind of weather do you like best?*
Sonja	Caelum tépidum mihi potíssimum placet. In Álpibus nix per māiórem partem annī perdúrat.	*Sonja: I like warm weather best. In the Alps the snow lasts through most of the year.*

Caecílius Quid ibi facis cum ningit?   *What do you do there when it*
                                                           snows?

Sonja Postquam nīnxit, in nive lū́dimus.   *After it has snowed, we play in*
           Intérdum pilās nívis inter nōs   *the snow. Sometimes we throw*
           conícimus. Intérdum virum   *snowballs at one another.*
           nívis fácimus. Intérdum dē colle   *Sometimes we build a*
           tráheā lā́bimur.   *snowman. Sometimes we slide*
                                                           down the hill on a sled.

Caecílius Quam tibi invídeō! Ego numquam   *How I envy you! I have never*
               nivem vīdī. Māter tamen mihi   *seen snow. However, my*
               dē nive et grándine et glácie   *Mother told me about snow and*
               nārrā́bat.   *hail and ice.*

Sonja Numquam vīdístī stī́riās dē tēctīs   *You never saw icicles hanging*
           dēpendéntēs?   *from a roof?*

Caecílius Ego tantúmmodo imāginā́rī   *I can only imagine icicles hanging*
               possum stī́riās dē tēctīs   *from the roofs and the roofs of*
               dēpendéntēs et tēcta dómuum   *houses covered with soft snow.*
               nive mollī obdúcta.

Sonja At cum Áquilō perflat et ningit et   *But in the Alps, when the north*
           grándinat in Álpibus, vīta potest   *wind blows and it snows and*
           esse dūra in Helvḗtiā. Ítaque   *hails, life can be tough in*
           prǽferō tempestā́tem tépidam   *Switzerland. And so I prefer the*
           Rṓmae. Ibi saltem numquam   *warm climate of Rome. At least*
           álgeam.   *there I would never feel cold.*

Caecílius Mihi crēde, vī́vere sub aestuṓsō   *Believe me, living in a sultry*
               caelō nullō modō rosā́rium est!   *climate is by no means a bed of*
               Habḗmus aestā́tēs aestuṓsās.   *roses! We have sweltering*
                                                           summers.

Sonja Tū saltem nōn gelā́ris. Potes   *You at least do not freeze. You*
           lū́dere forīs síngulīs diḗbus.   *can play outdoors every day.*

Caecílius At quis, malum, potest lū́dere in   *But who the devil can play in such*
               tam aestuṓsā tempestā́te?   *weather? We sweat and sweat.*
               Sūdā́mus et sūdā́mus. Et   *And the flies and mosquitoes*
               muscae culicḗsque sunt   *are a big pain in the neck.*
               molestíssimī.

Sonja Pactiṓnem faciā́mus. Tū in   *Let's make a deal. You move to*
           Helvḗtiam migrā et ego Rṓmam   *Switzerland, and I'll move to*
           migrā́bō. Ítaque utérque   *Rome. Then both of us will be*
           nostrum conténtus erit.   *satisfied.*

Topical Vocabulary

Note: *Expressions such as* it is hot, *etc., can be expressed as* **cálidum est** *(used impersonally, or with* caelum *= weather understood).*

bad *(weather)* advérs·us -a -um, grav·is -is -e

barometer barómetr·um -ī *n*

blast flāt·us -ūs *m*

blow flấre; **to blow hard** perflấre

bolt of lightning ict·us -ūs *m* fúlminis

breeze véntul·us -ī *m*, aur·a -ae *f*

bright serḗn·us -a -um

bucket: to come down in buckets ūrceấtim cad·ō -ere cécidī cāsū́rus; **to rain buckets** ūrceấtim plúere

changing *(weather)* vári·us -a -um

chilly frīgídul·us -a -um

clear serḗn·us -a -um, sū́d·us -a -um

clear up disserēnấre

climate cael·um -ī *n*

cloud nūb·ēs -is *f*

cloudless sū́d·us -a -um

cloudy nūbilós·us -a -um; **to become cloudy** nūbilấre

cold *s* frīg·us -oris *n*, gel·ū -ūs *n;* **to catch a cold** gravḗdinem cón·trahō -tráhere tráxī tráctus; **to have a cold** gravḗdine laborấre

cold *adj (the most general word, applied to all degrees from pleasant coolness to severe cold)* frígid·us -a -um; gelid·us -a -um; **liable to get cold** alsiós·us -a -um; **to feel cold** álgeō algḗre alsī; **to get cold** algḗsc·ō -ere; **to turn cold** frīgḗsc·ō -ere frīxī

cold spell frígor·a -um *npl*

cold weather gel·u -ūs *n*

cover up *(against the cold)* opér·iō -íre -uī -tus

dark *adj* obscū́r·us -a -um; **as soon as it got dark** prīmīs ténebrīs

dark *s:* **after dark** dē nocte; **in the dark** per obscū́rum; sine lū́mine

darkness ténebr·ae -árum *fpl;* **darkness had suddenly come** ténebrae factae sunt repéntē

degree grad·us -ūs *m*

dew rōs, rōris *m*

drizzle *s* plúvi·a -ae *f* rāra et minū́ta

drizzle *intr* lḗniter pluit plúere pluit

drop *(e.g., of rain)* gutt·a -ae *f*

east wind Eur·us -ī *m*

fair serḗn·us -a -um

fall *s* autúmn·us -ī *m*

favorable *(wind)* secúnd·us -a -um

fine *(weather)* serḗn·us -a -um; **fine weather** serḗnit·ās -átis *f*

flash of lightning fulg·ur -uris *n*

fog nébul·a -ae *f*

foggy nebulós·us -a -um

freeze *tr* gelấre ‖ *intr* gelấrī

freezing gélid·us -a -um

frost pruín·a -ae *f*

frosty pruīnós·us -a -um

frozen rig·ēns -entis

gale procéll·a -ae *f*

glisten nít·eō -ḗre -uī

good *(weather)* serḗn·us -a -um

hail *s* grand·ō -inis *f*

hail *impers v* grándin·at -ấre

hailstorms grándin·ēs -um *fpl*

hot *(of a person, sun, water, bath, day)* cálid·us -a -um *(opp:* frígid·us -a

-um); **it is hot** cálidum est; **to become hot** calésc·ō -ere; **to be hot** cál·eō -ḗre -uī; **to be uncomfortably hot** aéstuáre

hot weather aest·us -ūs *m*

hurricane tȳph·ōn -ṓnis *m*

ice gláci·ēs -éī *f;* **to turn to ice** glaciā́rī

icicle stī́ri·a -ae *f*

icy glaciā́l·is -is -e

lightning *s* fulm·en -inis *n*

lightning: it is lightning fulget fulgḗre fulsit, fúlgur·at -ā́re -ā́vit

lousy *(weather)* spurc·us -a -um

melt *tr* dissól·vō -vere -vī -ū́tus **‖** *intr* liquḗsc·ō -ere

mild mīt·is -is -e

mist nébul·a -ae *f*

misty nebulṓs·us -a -um

muggy aestuṓs·us -a -um

nice bell·us -a -um

north wind Áquil·ō -ṓnis *m*

open: in the open (air) sub dī́vō

overcast nūbilṓs·us -a -um, nū́bil·us -a -um; **to become overcast** nūbilā́re

rain *impers v* pluit pluere pluit; **to rain hard** veheménter *(or* multum) plúere

rain *s* plúvi·a -ae *f,* im·ber -bris *m;* **heavy, steady rain** magnī et adsíduī imbrēs; **the rain is letting up** imber dētūmḗscit; **it looks like rain** vidḗtur quasi pluat

rainbow arc·us -ūs *m* caeléstis, plúvius arcus

rain cloud nimb·us -ī *m*

rainy plúvi·us -a -um

shifting *(wind, weather)* vári·us -a -um

shine lū́c·eō -ḗre lūxī; **to shine on** illū́c·eō -ḗre illū́xī (+ *dat)*

shower im·ber -bris *m*

sky cael·um -ī *n*

sleet im·ber -bris *m* grándine mīxtus

slippery lū́bric·us -a -um

sloppy *(weather)* spurc·us -a -um

snow nix, nivis *f* **covered with snow** níve·us -a -um

snow *impers v* ningit níngere nīnxit

snowball pil·a -ae *f* nivis

snowdrift ningu·is -is *f*

snowfall nivis cās·us -ūs *m*

snowstorm ning·or -ṓris *m*

snowy nivṓs·us -a -um, nivā́l·is -is -e

south wind Aus·ter -trī *m*

spring vēr, vēris *n*

storm tempést·ās -ā́tis *f;* procéll·a -ae *f;* **a storm arose** tempéstās coórta est

stormy procellṓs·us -a -um, turbulént·us -a -um

summer aest·ās -ā́tis *f*

sun sōl, sōlis *m;* **full sun** plū́rimus sōl

sunny aprī́c·us -a -um

sunshine sōl, sōlis *m*

sultry aestuṓs·us -a -um

sweltering aestuṓs·us -a -um

temperature temperātū́r·a -ae *f;* **the temperature fell below thirty-two degrees** temperātū́ra lāpsa est subter duōs et trīgintā gradūs; **what is the temperature?** quō gradū stat temperātū́ra?

thermometer thermómetr·um -ī *n*

thunder *s* tónitr·us -ūs *m*

thunder *impers v* tonat tonā́re tónuit

thunderbolt fulm·en -inis *n*

tide aest·us -ūs *m;* **high tide** aestūs accéss·us -ūs *m;* **low tide** aestūs recéss·us -ūs *m*

tornado turb·ō -inis *m*

warm tépid·us -a -um; **it is getting warm** tepéscit

weather *(good or bad)* tempést·ās -átis *f,* cael·um -ī *n;* **depending on the weather** ut diēs suādet; **kinds of weather** tempestátēs; **owing to changes in the weather** propter caelī varietátēs

weather conditions tempestát·ēs -um *fpl*

west wind Zéphyr·us -ī *m*

wind vent·us -ī *m;* **head wind** ventus advérsus; **tail wind** ventus secúndus; **the wind is dying down** ventus dētuméscit; **the wind is picking up** ventus increbréscit

wind storm procéll·a -ae *f*

windy ventós·us -a -um

winter hiem·s -is *f;* **at the end of winter** híeme exeúnte; **because of the severity of the winter** propter híemis magnitúdinem

zero zer·um -ī *n*

Chapter XVI: Animals

CONVERSATIONS

┌────────── LEVEL I   **A visit to the zoo.**

Bárbara	Salvē, David. Unde venīs?	*Barbara: Hello, David. Where are you coming from?*
David	Modo vīvárium vīsébam.	*David: I was just visiting the zoo.*
Bárbara	Quās ferās ibi vīdístī?	*What wild animals did you see there?*
David	Panthérās et leónēs et elephántōs et tigrēs et zebrās.	*Panthers, lions, elephants, tigers, and zebras.*
Bárbara	Nōnne frémitūs ferárum tē terruérunt?	*The roars of the wild animals scared you, didn't they?*
David	Mínimē, hercle. Omnēs enim ferae in claustrīs cohibéntur.	*Heavens, no! You see, all the wild animals are kept in cages.*
Bárbara	Quod ánimal tē potíssimum dēlectávit?	*What animal did you like best?*
David	Símiī.	*The monkeys.*
Bárbara	Quam ob rem?	*Why?*
David	Tam iocósī sunt, quod sē gerunt paene quasi hómines.	*They are so funny because they behave almost like human beings.*
Bárbara	Vīdistíne étiam crocodílōs et strūthiocamélōs et rhīnocerótēs?	*Did you also see the crocodiles and giraffes and rhinoceroses?*
David	Eī quidem in vīvário sunt, sed eōs nōn vīdī.	*They're in the zoo all right, but I didn't see them.*
Bárbara	Ítaque cūr eōs nōn vīsístī?	*Then why didn't you go see them?*
David	Ótium mihi nōn erat ad omnēs ferās vīséndās.	*I didn't have the time to visit all the wild animals.*
Bárbara	Vīdistíne dinosaúrōs?	*Did you see (any) dinosaurs?*
David	Tū sānē iocáris!	*You must be kidding!*

┌──────── LEVEL II   **A visit to a pet shop.**

Grátia	Salvē. Velim dēlíciās émere.	*Grace: Hello. I'd like to buy a pet.*
Cốciō	Euge! Hábeō omnis géneris dēlíciās vēnắlēs.	*Dealer: Great! I have every kind of pet for sale.*
Grátia	Ita vídeō.	*So I see.*
Cốciō	Vīsne émere catéllum vel fēlem vel cunículum?	*Do you want to buy a puppy or a cat or a rabbit?*
Grátia	Mínimē, iam mihi est catéllus et fēlis et cunículus. Quantī cōnstat ille psíttacus?	*No, I already have a puppy, cat, and rabbit. How much does that parrot cost?*
Cốciō	Cōnstat trīgíntā dóllarīs. Ūsque enim ex Áfricā dēvectus est.	*It costs thirty dollars. You see, it was shipped all the way from Africa.*
Grátia	Et quantī cōnstant fringíllae Canáriae?	*And how much do canaries cost?*
Cốciō	Tantúmmodo decem dóllarīs.	*Only ten dollars.*
Grátia	Vāh, nimis cārae mihi sunt. Habḗsne híppurōs vēnắlēs?	*Wow, they are too expensive for me. Do you have goldfish for sale?*
Cốciō	Scílicet hábeō. Meī híppurī sunt vīlēs. Quísque cōnstat ūnō dóllarō. Et dōnắbō tibi áliquid ēscae piscáriae grātīs.	*Of course I have. My goldfish are inexpensive. They are one dollar apiece. And I'll give you some fish food gratis.*
Grátia	Nunc Latīnē lóqueris! Duōs emam. Ecce duōs dóllarōs.	*Now you're talking turkey! I'll buy two. Here are the two dollars.*
Cốciō	Grátiās tibi. Bene valē.	*Thank you. Goodbye.*

┌──────── LEVEL III   **Young Mark visits old Cato's farm.**

| **Marcus** | Catō, quam ob rem mávīs rūrī habitắre quam in urbe? | *Marcus: Cato, why do you prefer to live in the country rather than in the city?* |
| **Catō** | Quia vīta in fundō ācta longē iūcúndior est quam in urbe. | *Cato: Because life spent on the farm is far more pleasant than in the city.* |

Marcus	Quid ita?	*How so?*
Catō	Quī vīctum in fundō quaéritat, quamvīs dīves numquam fiat, līber tamen est.	*One who makes his living on a farm, although he may never get rich, is nevertheless free.*
Marcus	Osténde mihi pecus, quaesō, sī ótium tibi est.	*Please show me your livestock, if you have the time.*
Catō	Libénter. Ecce vaccās ovésque in prātō ac equōs in páscuō.	*Gladly. See the cows and sheep in the meadow and the horses in the pasture.*
Marcus	Ēducásne pullōs gallīnáceōs et ánserēs?	*Do you raise chickens and geese?*
Catō	Ita. Éducō étiam porcōs et caprōs. Eī sunt ultrā hórreum.	*Yes. I also raise pigs and goats. They are on the other side of the barn.*
Marcus	Exstántne piscēs in illō rívulō quī per prātum fluit?	*Are there fish in that brook that flows through the meadow?*
Catō	Ut vēra dīcam, piscósus est ille rívulus. Tructōs captáre queō, quotiēscúmque libet.	*To tell you the truth, that brook is teeming with fish. I can catch trout whenever I please.*
Marcus	Óbiter, forte notávī fundum silvam continére. Illícne umquam vēnáris?	*By the way, I happened to notice that your farm includes a forest. Do you ever go hunting there?*
Catō	Étiam. Vēnor cunículōs, phāsiánās, cervōs.	*Yes. I hunt rabbits, pheasants, and deer.*
Marcus	Habēsne canem vēnáticum?	*Do you have a hunting hound?*
Catō	Hábeō quidem sagācíssimum canem; sine eō numquam vēnor.	*I do have a very keen-scented hound; I never go hunting without him.*
Marcus	Valdē fortūnátus es, Catō. Aliquándō ego fundum mihi parábō.	*You are very fortunate, Cato. Someday I will get myself a farm.*
Catō	Probum cōnsílium, aduléscēns!	*Good idea, young man!*

Topical Vocabulary

animal ánim·al -ális *n*; **wild animal**
fer·a -ae *f*

ant formíc·a -ae *f*

ape sími·us -ī *m*, sími·a -ae *f*

    chatter stríd·eō -ére -uī

bat vespertíli·ō -ónis *m*

bear urs·us -ī *m*, urs·a -ae *f*

    cub ursae cátul·us -ī *m*

    grunt *intr* grunn·iō -íre -ívī *or* -iī
-ítum

    grunt *s* grunnít·us -ūs *m*

beaver fi·ber -brī *m*

bedbug sciníph·is -is *m*

bee ap·is -is *f*

    beehive álve·us -ī *m*

    buzz bombiláre

    hum murmuráre

    sting *tr* īc·ō -ere īcī ictus

    sting *s (on the bee)* acúle·us -ī *m;*
(bite) ict·us -ūs *m*

    swarm of bees ápium exám·en
-inis *n*

bird av·is -is *f*

    beak rōstr·um -ī *n*

    cage cáve·a -ae *f*

    chirp pīpáre, pípiláre

    egg ōv·um -ī *n*

    feather penn·a -ae *f*

    flap the wings ālīs plaud·ō -ere
plausī plausum

    flight volát·us -ūs *m*

    fly voláre; **to fly away** āvoláre

    land (on) īnsíd·ō -ere īnsédī *(+ dat)*

    nest nīd·us -ī *m;* **to build a nest**
nīdificáre

    sing can·ō -ere cécinī cantum

    song cant·us -ūs *m*

    tail caud·a -ae *f*

    wing āl·a -ae *f*

blackbird mérul·a -ae *f (see* **bird**)

boar ap·er -rī *m*

    grunt grúnn·iō -íre -ívī *or* -iī -ítum

buffalo ūr·us -ī *m*

bug cīm·ex -icis *m*

bull taur·us -ī *m* (*see* **cattle**)

butterfly pāpíli·ō -ónis *m*

cage claustr·a -órum *npl*, cáve·a -ae *f*

calf vítul·us -ī *m*, vítul·a -ae *f (see*
cattle)

camel camél·us -ī *m*

    hump gibb·er -eris *m*

canary fringíll·a -ae *f* Canária (*see* **bird**)

cat fēl·is *or* fēl·ēs -is *f*; catt·a -ae *f*,
catt·us -ī *m*

    meow fél·iō -íre

    purr *intr* murmuráre

    purr *s* murm·ur -uris *n*

caterpillar erúc·a -ae *f*

cattle bov·ēs -um *mpl (dat & abl pl:*
bōbus *or* būbus)

    bellow (*or* **low**) múg·iō -íre -ívī *or* -iī
-ítum

    graze pāsc·or -ī pāstus sum

    head of cattle pec·us -oris *n*

chick pull·us -ī *m (see* **bird**)

    peep pīpiláre

chicken (gallīnáceus) pull·us -ī *m (see*
bird)

    chicken coop gallīnári·um -ī *n*

    cluck glóc·iō -íre

    egg ōv·um -ī *n*

    eggshell (ōvī) putám·en -inis *n*

egg white (ōvī) alb•um -ī *n*

lay *(eggs)* pár•iō -ere péperī partus

yolk vitéll•us -ī *m*

cockroach blatt•a -ae *f*

colt équol•us -ī *m* (*see* **horse**)

cow vacc•a -ae *f*

  milk *s* lac lactis *n*

  milk *tr* múl•geō -gḗre -sī -ctum

  moo mū́g•iō -íre -ívī *or* -iī -ítum

  udder ūb•er -eris *n*

crane grūs, gruis *mf* (*see* **bird**)

  crunkle gru•ō -ere

cricket gryll•us -ī *m*

  chirp fritínn•iō -íre

crocodile crocodíl•us -ī *m*

crow corn•īx -ícis *f* (*see* **bird**)

  caw crōcitā́re

deer cerv•us -ī *m*, cerv•a -ae *f*

  bray rud•ō -ere -ívī -ítum

dinosaur dinosaúr•us -ī *m*

dog can•is -is *mf*

  bark *intr* latrā́re; **bark at** allatrā́re

  bark *s* latrā́t•us -ūs *m*

  collar collár•e -is *n*

  growl ring•or -ī rictus sum

  leash cíngul•um -ī *n*

  leash a dog canem cíngulō alligā́re

  pet *(stroke)* permúlc•eō -ḗre -sī

  snarl gánn•iō -íre

  tail caud•a -ae *f;* **wag the tail** caudam movēre

  take for a walk dūc•ō -ere dūxī ductus

dolphin delphín•us -ī *m*

donkey ásin•us -ī *m*

  heehaw *intr* rud•ō -ere -ívī -ítum

heehaw *s* rudít•us -ūs *m*

dove palumb•ēs -is *f* (*see* **bird**)

  coo gem•ō -ere -uī

duck an•as -atis *f* (*see* **bird**)

  quack tetrínn•iō -íre

eagle áquil•a -ae *f* (*see* **bird**)

  screech stríd•eō -ḗre -uī

eel anguíll•a -ae *f*

elephant elephánt•us -ī *m*

  trumpet bárr•iō -íre

  trunk man•us -ūs *f*

falcon falc•ō -ónis *m* (*see* **bird**)

  screech stríd•eō -ḗre -uī

farm animals pec•us -oris *n or* pécor•a -um *npl*

fish pisc•is -is *m*

  fin pinn•a -ae *f*

  fish food ēsc•a -ae *f* piscária

  fish pond piscín•a -ae *f*

  gills bránchi•ae -árum *fpl*

  scale *s* squām•a -ae *f*

  scale *tr* dēsquāmā́re

  scaly squāmṓs•us -a -um

  swim natā́re

flea pūl•ex -icis *m*

flounder pass•er -eris *m* (*see* **fish**)

fly musc•a -ae *f*

  buzz bombilā́re

flock *(of birds, sheep, goats)* grex, gregis *m*

fox vulp•ēs -is *f*

  yelp gánn•iō -íre

frog rān•a -ae *f*

  croak coaxā́re

game preserve thērotrophí•um -ī *n*

giraffe camēlopárdal•is -is *f*

gnat cul·ex -icis *m*

goat cap·er -rī *m*, capr·a -ae *f*

    bleat bālā́re

goldfish híppur·us -ī *m* (*see* **fish**)

goose ans·er -eris *m* (*see* **bird**)

    cackle gíngr·iō -ī́re

grasshopper grill·us -ī *m*

    chirp fritínn·iō -ī́re

haddock gad·us -ī *m* (*see* **fish**)

hawk accípi·ter -tris *m* (*see* **bird**)

    caw plīpiā́re

    shriek clāmā́re

heifer iuvénc·a -ae *f* (*see* **cattle**)

hen gallī́n·a -ae *f*

    cluck glóc·iō -ī́re

herd armént·um -ī *n*

hippopotamus hippopótam·us -ī *m*

hog sū·s -is *mf*

    oink grúnn·iō -ī́re

hornet crābr·ō -ṓnis *m* (*see* **bee**)

horse equ·us -ī *m*

    hoof úngul·a -ae *f*

    mane iūb·a -ae *f*

    neigh *intr* hínn·iō -ī́re -iī́; **neigh at** adhinnī́re

    neigh(ing) hinnī́t·us -ūs *m*

    tail caud·a -ae *f*

horsefly tabā́n·us -ī *m*

    buzz bombilā́re

insect īnséct·um -ī *n*

lamb agn·us -ī *m* (·a -ae *f*)

    bleat bālā́re

lark alaúd·a -ae *f* (*see* **bird**)

leopard pard·us -ī *m*

    mew rictā́re

lion le·ō -ṓnis *m*, leaén·a -ae *f*

mane iūb·a -ae *f*

    roar rū́g·iō -ī́re

livestock pec·us -oris *n*

lizard lacért·us -ī *m*, lacért·a -ae *f*

lobster ástac·us -ī *m*

locust locúst·a -ae *f*

    chirp strī́d·eō -ére -uī

louse pēdícul·us -ī *m*

mackerel scomb·er -rī *m* (*see* **fish**)

mole talp·a -ae *f*

monkey sī́mi·us -ī *m*, sī́mi·a -ae *f*

    chatter strī́d·eō -ére -uī

moth blatt·a -ae *f*

mouse mū·s -ris *m*

    squeak míntr·iō -ī́re

mule mūl·us -ī *m*, mūl·a -ae *f*

    bray rud·ō -ere -ī́vī -ī́tum

ostrich strūthiocamḗl·us -ī *m* (*see* **bird**)

owl būb·ō -ṓnis *m* (*see* **bird**)

    hoot būbilā́re

ox bōs, bovis *m* (*dat & abl pl:* bōbus *or* būbus)

    bellow boā́re

oyster óstre·a -ae *f*

    oyster bed ostreā́ri·um -ī *n*

    shell conch·a -ae *f*

panther panthḗr·a -ae *f*

parakeet melopsittac·us -ī *m*

parrot psíttac·us -ī *m*

partridge perd·īx -ī́cis *mf* (*see* **bird**)

peacock pāv·ō -ṓnis *m*, pāv·a -ae *f* (*see* **bird**)

pelican onocrótal·us -ī *m* (*see* **bird**)

perch (*fish*) perc·a -ae *f* (*see* **fish**)

pet dēlíci·ae -ā́rum *fpl*

pheasant phāsiā́n·a -ae *f* (*see* **bird**)

pig porc·us -ī *m*
   oink grúnn·iō -íre
   pigsty suíl·e -is *n*
pigeon colúmb·a -ae *f,* colúmb·us -ī *m*
   (*see* **bird**)
   coo gem·ō -ere -uī -itum
   pigeon coop columbári·um -ī *n*
pony mann·us -ī *m* (*see* **horse**)
porcupine hystr·ix -icis *f*
poultry av·ēs -ium *fpl* cohortálēs
pup cátul·us -ī *m*
   whimper gánn·iō -íre
   puppy catéll·us -ī *m*
quail cotúrn·īx -ícis *f* (*see* **bird**)
rabbit cuníul·us -ī *m*
   squeal vág·iō -íre
ram ári·ēs -etis *m*
   bleat bāláre
rat mū·s -ris *m*
   squeak míntr·iō -íre
raven corv·us -ī *m* (*see* **bird**)
   croak crōcitáre
reindeer tarándr·us -ī *m*
rhinoceros rhīnócer·ōs -ótis *m*
robin rubécul·a -ae *f* (*see* **bird**)
   chirp pīpáre
rooster gall·us -ī *m* (*see* **bird**)
   crow cūcúr·iō -íre; can·ō -ere cécinī cantum
salmon salm·ō -ónis *m* (*see* **fish**)
sardine sardín·a -ae *f* (*see* **fish**)
scorpion scórpi·ō -ónis *m*
   sting *tr* īc·ō -ere īcī ictus
   sting *s* ict·us -ūs *m*
seal vítul·us -ī *m* marínus
serpent serp·ēns -éntis *m*

bite *tr* īc·ō -ere īcī ictus
bite *s* ict·us -ūs *m*
crawl serp·ō -ere -sī
hiss sībiláre
shark pistr·is -is *m*
   dorsal fin pinn·a -ae *f* dorsális
sheep ov·is -is *f*
   bleat bāláre
   shepherd pāst·or -óris *m*
   pen (*for sheep*) ovíl·e -is *n*
   wool lān·a -ae *f*
snake angu·is -is *mf* (*see* **serpent**)
snail cóchle·a -ae *f*
sow sū·s -is *f*
   oink grúnn·iō -íre
sparrow pass·er -eris *m* (*see* **bird**)
   chirp pīpáre
spider aráne·us -ī *m*
   cobweb aráne·a -ae *f*
squirrel sciúr·us -ī *m*
stag cerv·us -ī *m*
   bray rud·ō -ere -ívī -ítum
starling sturn·us -ī *m* (*see* **bird**)
   chirp fritínn·iō -íre
steer iuvénc·us -ī *m*
stork cicóni·a -ae *f* (*see* **bird**)
swallow hirúnd·ō -inis *f* (*see* **bird**)
swan cycn·us -ī *m* (*see* **bird**)
thrush turd·us -ī *m* (*see* **bird**)
tiger tigr·is -is *or* -idis *m*
   growl frem·ō -ere -uī
toad būf·ō -ónis *m*
trout truct·us -ī *m,* truct·a -ae *f* (*see* **fish**)
tuna thunn·us -ī *m* (*see* **fish**)
turkey gallopáv·ō -ónis *m*

turtle testū́d·ō -inis *f*
  shell testūd·ō -inis *f*
vulture vult·ur -uris *m*
wasp vesp·a -ae *f (see* **bee***)*
weasel mustḗl·a -ae *f*
whale balaén·a -ae *f*
wolf lup·us -ī *m,* lup·a -ae *f*
  cub lupae cátul·us -ī *m*

howl *intr* ululā́re
howl *s* ululā́t·us -ūs *m*
whelp gánn·iō -íre
woodpecker pī́c·us -ī *m (see* **bird***)*
worm verm·is -is *m*
  earth worm lumbrī́c·us -ī *m*
zoo vīvā́ri·um -ī *n*

Chapter XVII: Emotions and Qualities

CONVERSATIONS

LEVEL I **Diane and Debbie discuss the new teacher.**

Diána: Salvē, Debra. Quō pactō tēcum ágitur? Aúdiō tē novam magístram hōc annō habére.

Diane: Hello, Debbie. How is it going with you? I hear that you have a new teacher this year.

Debra: Salvē, Diána. Bene váleō. Rēctē audīvístī.

Debbie: Hello, Diane. I'm fine. You heard right.

Diána: Estne bona magístra?

Is she a good teacher?

Debra: Sevéra est sed aequa; nam tractat nōs omnēs eódem modō.

She is strict but fair. She treats all alike.

Diána: Quámdiū iam docet?

How long has she been teaching?

Debra: Nésciō. Sed est perītíssima magístra. Nēmō obdormíscit in eius classe.

I don't know. But she's a very experienced teacher. No one falls asleep in her class.

Diána: Quómodo condiscípulī tuī cum eā cóngruunt?

How do your classmates get along with her?

Debra: Amant eam quóniam pátiēns hiláraque est.

They love her because she is patient and cheerful.

Diána: Maniféstō, magístra ipsa bonum exémplum praebet.

Obviously, the teacher herself sets a good example.

Debra: Ita, exémplum admīrábile.

Yes, a wonderful example.

LEVEL II **A new girlfriend is the subject of discussion.**

Valéria: Salvē, Ricárde. Ut valēs? Rūmor per tōtam vīcíniam pervagátur tē novam amículam repperísse.

Valerie: Hello, Richard. How are you? There's a rumor going around the whole neighborhood that you have found a new girlfriend.

Ricárdus: Salvē. Bene váleō. Fāma est vēra; eam nōn īnfítior.

Richard: Hello. I'm fine. The story is true; I'll not deny it.

Valéria:	Quid nōmen eī est? Égone eam nōvī?	*What is her name? Do I know her?*
Ricárdus:	Nōmen eī est Donna. Eam nōn nōvístī.	*Her name is Donna. You do not know her.*
Valéria:	Quālis homō est illa?	*What sort of person is she?*
Ricárdus:	In prīmīs est bella et venústa. Bréviter, mīrífica est.	*First of all, she is pretty and attractive. In a word, she is fantastic.*
Valéria:	Nōn, nōn. Dīcébam dē eius índole.	*No, no. I was talking about her personality.*
Ricárdus:	Iam téneō. Donna est intéllegēns et hílara et hūmána et ténera.	*Now I get it. Donna is intelligent, cheerful, kind, and gentle.*
Valéria:	Estne géneris tacitúrnī?	*Is she the silent type?*
Ricárdus:	Est magis loquāx et sociábilis quam tacitúrna; hāc dē causā, apud familiárēs grātiōsíssima est. Étiam corcíllum habet, sed numquam id iactat.	*She is talkative and sociable rather than quiet; for that reason she is very popular with her close acquaintances. She also has brains, but she doesn't brag about that.*
Valéria:	Donna mihi vidétur speciósa adulēscéntula. Spērō tē eam mihi aliquándō trāditúrum esse.	*Donna seems to be a very interesting young lady. I hope that you will introduce her to me sometime.*
Ricárdus:	Quidnī?	*Why not?*

┌───────── LEVEL III   **Sizing up a political candidate.**

Titus:	Márcia, quid opīnáris dē Bíbulō candidátō quī cōnsulátum petit?	*Titus: Marcia, what is your opinion of the candidate Bibulus, who is running for the consulship?*
Márcia:	Vīsne illum Bíbulum quī Caésaris competítor est? Praédicat sē reī pūblicae prōfutúrum esse.	*Marcia: Do you mean the Bibulus who is Caesar's opponent? He claims that he will be good for the country.*
Titus:	Crēdísne eum esse vērácem sincērúmque?	*Do you believe that he is honest and sincere?*
Márcia:	Multa quidem prōmíttit, sed mīror num fidem servātúrus sit.	*He certainly makes a lot of promises, but I wonder whether he will keep his word.*

Titus:	Mihi vidétur astútus, audāx, ambitiósus.	*He seems to me to be shrewd, bold, and ambitious.*
Márcia:	Dē eā rē tēcum fúnditus cōnséntiō. Porrō audīvistíne eius recéntēs orātiónēs?	*I fully agree with you on that point. Besides, have you heard his recent speeches?*
Titus:	Audívī. Ut candidátī solent, iste competītórēs suōs inpúgnat et idéntidem praédicat eōs omnēs esse arrogántēs et dolósōs.	*I have. As candidates usually do, he attacks his opponents and again and again claims that they are all arrogant and tricky.*
Márcia:	Rūrsus tēcum omnínō cōnséntiō. Cēnsétne sē sōlum esse locuplétem et cándidum et amántem pátriae?	*Again I fully agree with you. Does he think that he alone is trustworthy, candid, and patriotic?*
Titus:	Immō fácile est áliōs candidátōs reprehéndere; sed quid iste habet quod dē suā ratiōne dīcat?	*Well, it's easy to criticize other candidates; but what does he have to say about his own policy?*
Márcia:	Dē suā ratióne interrogátus, ambíguus fit. Dīcit quidquid in buccam vénerit. Quandōcúmque urgétur, fit indignābúndus ac dīcāx.	*When asked about his own policy, he becomes evasive. He says whatever comes into his head [lit: has come into his mouth]. Whenever he is hard pressed, he becomes indignant and sarcastic.*
Titus:	Ut vēra dīcam, nésciō cuī candidátō suffrāgātúrus sim.	*To tell you the truth, I don't know for which candidate I am going to vote.*
Márcia:	Ego ipsa exspectábō diem comitiálem ántequam ego cōnstítuam.	*I myself am going to wait till election day before I make up my mind.*
Titus:	Tē nōn culpō. Ego idem fáciam.	*I don't blame you. I'll do the same.*

Topical Vocabulary

ability facúlt·ās -átis *f*

absurd absúrd·us -a -um

abusive malédic·us -a -um

accomplished ērudítus -a -um

active ála·cer -cris -cre

admirable admīrábil·is -is -e

admiration admīráti·ō -ónis *f*

adult *(mature)* adúlt·us -a -um

affable affábil·is -is -e

affected affectát·us -a -um

affection am·or -óris *m*

affectionate am·āns -ántis

afraid formīdulós·us -a -um; **I am afraid that** vér·eor -érī véritus sum nē; **to be afraid** métu·ō -ere -ī

aged annós·us -a -um

agreeable cómmod·us -a -um, grāt·us -a -um

alert ā·cer -cris -cre

alluring illecebrós·us -a -um

alone sōl·us -a -um

ambition ambíti·ō -ónis *f*

ambitious ambitiós·us -a -um

anger īr·a -ae *f*

angry (at) īrát·us -a -um (+ *dat*); **to get angry with** īrásc·or -árī (+ *dat*)

anguish ang·or -óris *m*

annoyance molésti·a -ae *f*

annoyed: to be annoyed at moléstē ferō ferre tulī

antagonistic īnfést·us -a -um

anxiety (about) cūr·a -ae *f* (+ *gen*)

apathetic dēs·es -idis

appetite cibī appeténti·a -ae *f*, cibī appetíti·ō -ónis *f*

arouse *(feelings)* exagitáre, suscitáre

arrogance arrogánti·a -ae *f*

arrogant árrog·āns -ántis

articulate disért·us -a -um

astute astút·us -a -um

athletic āthlétic·us -a -um

atrocious atr·ōx -ócis

attentive attént·us -a -um, ēréct·us -a -um

attitude gest·us -ūs *m*

attractive amábil·is -is -e; *(in looks)* speciós·us -a -um

austere asp·er -era -erum, austér·us -a -um

awful dīr·us -a -um

awkward inconcínn·us -a -um

backward *(mentally)* lent·us -a -um

bad mal·us -a -um, ímprob·us -a -um

banish *(worries, cares)* éxim·ō -ere exémī exémptus

beautiful pulch·er -ra -rum, formós·us -a -um

beauty pulchritúd·ō -inis *f*

becoming dec·ēns -éntis

big-hearted magnánim·us -a -um

bitter acérb·us -a -um

bitterly: to complain bitterly gráviter queror querī questus sum

bitterness acérbit·ās -átis *f*

blind caec·us -a -um

blindness caécit·ās -átis *f*

blush ērubésc·ō -ere ērúbuī

boastful iact·āns -ántis

bold aud·āx -ácis

boldness audáci·a -ae *f*

bombastic bullát·us -a -um

boorish agrést·is -is -e

bother *(annoy)* exérc·eō -ére -uī -itus

bothered exercitắt·us -a -um

brag about iactáre

brains: have brains corcíll·um -ī *n* háb·eō -ére -uī

bright *(person)* argū́t·us -a -um

callous dū́r·us -a -um

callousness dūríti·a -ae *f*

calm plácid·us -a -um

calmly aequō ánimō

candid cándid·us -a -um, apért·us -a -um

care cū́r·a -ae *f*

care dīligénti·a -ae *f*

careful dī́lig·ēns -éntis

careless incūriós·us -a -um

carelessness incū́ri·a -ae *f*

cause *(stir up)* excitáre

caution caúti·ō -ónis *f;* **to exercise caution** cáv·eō -ére cāvī

cautious caut·us -a -um

character mōr·ēs -um *mpl,* índol·ēs -is *f*

charm amoénit·ās -átis *f,* dec·or -óris *m,* grắti·a -ae *f*

charming amoén·us -a -um, lepid·us -a -um

chaste cast·us -a -um

cheer up *tr* hilaráre, laetificáre; **cheer up!** habē ánimum bonum!

cheerful ála·cer -cris -cre, hílar·us -a -um

cheerfulness alácrit·ās -átis *f,* hilaritū́d·ō -inis *f*

choice exquisī́t·us -a -um

civilized hūmắn·us -a -um

clever cállid·us -a -um

cleverness callídit·ās -átis *f*

clumsy incompósit·us -a -um, inconcínn·us -a -um

cold *(dispassionate)* frī́gid·us -a -um

comfort *s* levắti·ō -ónis *f*

comfort *tr* alleváre

common sense: to have common sense cor háb·eō -ére -uī -itus

compassion clēménti·a -ae *f,* hūmắnit·ās -átis *f*

compassionate clēm·ēns -éntis, hūmắn·us -a -um

concern cū́r·a -ae *f*

concise brev·is -is -e

confide in cōnfī́d·ō -ere (+ *dat*)

confidence fīdū́ci·a -ae *f,* cōnfīdénti·a -ae *f*

confident cōnfī́d·ēns -éntis; **to be confident** cōnfī́d·ō -ere cōnfī́sus sum

consternation cōnsternắti·ō -ónis *f*

contempt contémpt·us -ūs *m,* dēspicắti·ō -ónis *f;* **to feel contempt for** contémn·ō -ere -psī; **to hold s.o. in contempt** áliquem dēspicátum háb·eō -ére -uī -itus

contemptuous (of) dēspíci·ēns -éntis (+ *gen*)

content contént·us -a -um; **to your heart's content** arbitrátū tuō

control coérc·eō -ére -uī -itus, contín·eō -ére -uī

control *(restraint)* continénti·a -ae *f;* *(power)* potést·ās -átis *f;* **out of control** effrēnát·us -a -um

convenience: at your convenience tuō cómmodō

cool (toward) frī́gid·us -a -um (in + *acc*); *(great) (coll)* mīrand·us -a -um; **that's cool!** mīrandum est!

coolness *(indifference)* frī́g·us -oris *n*

cope with pār esse (+ *dat*); **unable to cope with** impār esse (+ *dat*)

courage fortitū́d·ō -inis *f*

courageous animós·us -a -um, fort·is -is -e

courteous cōm·is -is -e

courtesy cōmit·ās -átis *f*

crabbiness morósit·ās -átis *f*

crabby morós·us -a -um

craving for appetíti·ō -ónis *f* (+ *gen*)

crazy dēlír·us -a -um

credible crēdíbil·is -is -e; **to be credible** fídem háb·eō -ére -uī -itus

criminal facinorós·us -a -um

cruel crūdél·is -is -e

cruelty crūdélit·ās -átis *f*

cry fl·eō -ére -évī; **to cry over** flére

culture hūmánit·ās -átis *f*

cunning collubrín·us -a -um

curiosity cūriósit·ās -átis *f*

cute bell·us -a -um, béllul·us -a -um

dainty dēlicát·us -a -um

daring aud·ēns -éntis, aud·āx -ácis

darling anímul·us -ī *m*, anímul·a -ae *f*

dear cār·us -a -um

deceitful fall·āx -ácis

decency decénti·a -ae *f*

decent dec·ēns -éntis; **to do the decent thing** frūgem fác·iō -ere fēcī

deep-seated ínsit·us -a -um

dejected dēmíss·us -a -um

delicate dēlicát·us -a -um

demented dēm·ēns -éntis

depressed abiéct·us -a -um; **to be depressed** abiéctō ánimō sum esse fuī

depression contrácti·ō -ónis *f* ánimī

deranged (*mind*) commót·us -a -um

deserving (of) dign·us -a -um (+ *abl*)

desire cupídit·ās -átis *f*

despair dēspēráti·ō -ónis *f*

despair dēspēráre

desperate dēspērát·us -a -um

desperation dēspēráti·ō -ónis *f*

despicable dēspicát·us -a -um

despise dēspíc·iō -ere dēspéxī dēspéctus

destructive exitiós·us -a -um

develop (*character, mind*) cōnfirmáre

dignified grav·is -is -e

dignity grávit·ās -átis *f*, dígnit·ās -átis *f*

diligence dīligénti·a -ae *f*

diligent dílig·ēns -éntis

disappoint frustr·or -árī -átus sum

disappointment dēstitúti·ō -ónis *f*

disgrace dédec·us -oris *n*, ignōmíni·a -ae *f*; **to be a disgrace to** dēdécorī esse (+ *dat*)

disgraceful dēdecór·us -a -um, ignōminiós·us -a -um

dishonorable dēdecór·us -a -um

dismay cōnsternáti·ō -ónis *f*

disposition afféct·us -ūs *m* (ánimī)

distinguished illústr·is -is -e

distress dol·or -óris *m*

distrust (of) diffīdénti·a -ae *f* (+ *gen*)

distrust diffíd·ō -ere diffísus sum (*semi-deponent*) (+ *gen*)

downcast: to be downcast iác·eō -ére -uī

downhearted dēmíss·us -a -um; **to be downhearted** ánimō percúlsō esse

dread formīdáre

dreadful dīr·us -a -um

drunk ébri·us -a -um

drunkenness ēbríet·ās -átis *f*; **habitual drunkenness** ēbriósit·ās -átis *f*

dull héb·es -etis

eager (for) cúpid·us -a -um (+ *gen*)

eagerly cupiénter

eagerness cupídit·ās -átis *f*

easy-going facil·is -is -e *f*

educated ērudít·us -a -um

effeminate effēmināt·us -a -um

efficiency efficiénti·a -ae *f*

efficient effíci·ēns -éntis

efficiently efficiénter

elegance ēlegánti·a -ae *f*

elegant éleg·āns -ántis

eloquence ēloquénti·a -ae *f*

eloquent éloqu·ēns -éntis

emotion ánimī mōt·us -ūs *m;* **to express emotions** ánimī mōtūs éxprim·ō -ere expréssī expréssus

encourage hort·or -árī -átus sum

encouragement hortát·us -ūs *m*

energetic nāv·us -a -um, ímpig·er -ra -rum

envious ínvid·us -a -um; **to be envious of** invíd·eō -ére invídī (+ *acc or dat*)

envy invídi·a -ae *f*

esteem dílig·ō -ere dīléxī dīléctus

estranged: to become estranged from s.o. áliquem ā sē aliēnáre

evasive ambíguus -a -um

exact accūrát·us -a -um, exáct·us -a -um

excessive (in) immódic·us -a -um (+ *gen or abl*)

excite excitáre

excited commót·us -a -um

excitement ánimī commóti·ō -ónis *f;* **to feel excitement** éxcit·or -árī excitátus sum

experience experiénti·a -ae *f,* experīmént·um -ī *n,* ūs·us -ūs *m*

experienced (in) perít·us -a -um (+ *gen or abl*)

expert in gnār·us -a -um (+ *gen*)

expressive *(eyes)* argút·us -a -um

fair, fair-minded aequ·us -a -um

fairness aéquit·ās -átis *f*

faith fid·ēs -eī *f;* **in bad faith** dē fidē malā; **in good faith** (ex) bonā fidē

faithful fidél·is -is -e

fall (desperately) in love with (pérditē) amáre coep·ī -ísse

false fals·us -a -um

fantastic mīrífic·us -a -um

faultless ēmendát·us -a -um

favor benefíci·um -ī *n;* **to accept and return a favor** benefícium accípere et réddere

fear métu·ō -ere -ī

fear met·us -ūs *m*

fearless impávid·us -a -um

feeble imbēcíll·us -a -um

feebleness imbēcíllit·ās -átis *f*

feel *(hunger, pain, cold, etc.)* sént·iō -tíre -sī -sus; **I don't feel well** míhi nōn bene hábeō; **to feel annoyed** grav·or -árī -átus sum; **to feel down and out** īnfráctum ánimum ger·ō -ere gessī; **to feel good** sē bene háb·eō -ére -uī; **to feel happy** gaúd·eō -ére gāvísus sum; **to feel pain** dolóre afficior áfficī afféctus sum; **to feel sad** maest·us -a -um esse

feeling sēns·us -ūs *m,* afféct·us -ūs *m*

fidelity fidélit·ās -átis *f*

fierce fer·ōx -ócis

firm firm·us -a -um

flame *(sweetheart)* flamm·a -ae *f*

flattering bland·us -a -um

flattery blandíti·a -ae *f*

fluent prófflu·ēns -éntis

fond of cúpid·us -a -um (+ *gen*); **to be fond of** amáre

fondness am·or -óris *m*

foolhardy temerári·us -a -um

foolish dēsípi·ēns -éntis

foolishly: to act foolishly inépt·iō -íre

foolishness dēsipiénti·a -ae *f*

fortunate fortūnắt·us -a -um

frame: of mind ánim·us -ī *m*; **to be in a good frame of mind** bonō ánimō esse

frank apért·us -a -um

friendly amíc·us -a -um; **in a friendly way** amícē

friendship amīcíti·a -ae *f*

frighten térr·eō -ére -uī -itus

frivolous frívol·us -a -um

frustrate frūstr·or -árī -átus sum

frustration frūstráti·ō -ónis *f*

funny iocós·us -a -um

generosity līberálit·ās -átis *f*

generous līberál·is -is -e

gentle clēm·ēns -éntis, mīt·is -is -e

get along with concórditer cóngru·ō -ere -uī cum (+ *abl*)

get over (*grief, anger, etc.*) superáre

glad laet·us -a -um; **to be glad** laet·or -árī -átus sum

gloat over exsultáre (+ *abl*)

gloom maestíti·a -ae *f*

gloomy, glum maest·us -a -um

glutton héllu·ō -ónis *m*; **to be a glutton** héllu·or -árī

gluttonous ed·āx -ácis

gluttony edácit·ās -átis *f*

good (*also morally*) bon·us -a -um

good-natured fácil·is -is -e

goodness (*integrity, good behavior*) bónit·ās -átis *f*

goodwill benevolénti·a -ae *f*

gossip (*person*) fāmigerất·or -óris *m*, fāmigerátr·īx -ícis *f*

grave grav·is -is -e

greed avāríti·a -ae *f*

greedy avárus -a -um; **greedy for** avárus (+ *gen*)

gregarious (*sociable*) congregábil·is -is -e

grief maer·or -óris *m;* **to feel grief** condolésc·ō -ere condóluī

groan gem·ō -ere -uī -itum

groan gémit·us -ūs *m*

gullible crédul·us -a -um

habit cōnsuetúd·ō -inis *f*

handsome formós·us -a -um

happiness beātitúd·ō -inis *f*

happy beát·us -a -um, laet·us -a -um

hard to please diffícil·is -is -e

hard-working labōriós·us -a -um

harsh (toward) dūr·us -a -um (in + *acc*)

harshness dūríti·a -ae *f*

hate *tr* ōdī ōdísse (*defective verb*)

hate *s* ódi·um -ī *n*

hatred (of, toward) ódi·um -ī *n* (in + *acc*)

haughty ēlát·us -a -um

heart: from the heart ex ánimō; **heart and soul** tōtō péctore

heartache cūr·a -ae *f*, cordóli·um -ī *n*

helpless in·ops -opis

helplessness inópi·a -ae *f*

holiness sánctit·ās -átis *f*

holy sānct·us -a -um

homely īnspeciós·us -a -um

homesick: to be homesick ex dēsīdériō labōráre; **I am homesick for** mē dēsīdérium tenet (+ *gen*)

honest prob·us -a -um; *(speaking the truth)* vēr·āx -ácis

honor hon·or -ōris *m*

honor honōráre

honorable honōrábil·is -is -e, honést·us -a -um

honorably honéstē

hope spēs, speī *f*

hope spēráre; **lose hope** dēspēráre

hopeless dēspērát·us -a -um

horrible horríbil·is -is -e

hot-tempered īrācúnd·us -a -um

humane hūmán·us -a -um

humor fēstívit·ās -átis *f*

humorous fēstív·us -a -um

humorously fēstívē

hunger fam·ēs -is *f*

hypocrite simulát·or -óris *m,* simulátr·ix -ícis *f*

hypocritical coáct·us -a -um

idea cogníti·ō -ónis *f*

ideal exémpl·ar -áris *n*

ignorance īnsciénti·a -ae *f*

ignorant īnscít·us -a -um

ill-mannered male mōrát·us -a -um

illogical absúrd·us -a -um

immature immātúr·us -a -um

immaturity immātúrit·ās -átis *f*

immoderate immódic·us -a -um

immodest impudíc·us -a -um

impartial aequ·us -a -um

impatient: to be impatient with iníquō ánimō ferō ferre tulī

impatiently iníquō ánimō

impetuous férvid·us -a -um

impolite inurbán·us -a -um

important magn·us -a -um

impress commóv·eō -ére commóvī commótus

improper índec·ēns -éntis

improve ēmendáre **ǁ** *intr* mél·ior -ior -ius fiō fíerī factus sum; *(in studies)* prōfíc·iō -ere prōfécī

imprudent imprúd·éns -éntis

impulse ánimī ímpet·us -ūs *m*

inappropriate inépt·us -a -um

indecent índec·ēns -éntis

indecisive ambígu·us -a -um

indifference frīg·us -oris *n;* **indifferent (towards)** négleg·ēns -éntis (in + *acc*)

indignant indignābúnd·us -a -um

inept inépt·us -a -um

inexperienced (in) inexpért·us -a -um (ab + *abl or* in + *acc or* advérsus + *acc*)

infamous īnfám·is -is -e

infatuated: to be infatuated with s.o. áliquem efflíctim amáre

influence gráti·a -ae *f*

influential grātióos·us -a -um

ingenious artificióos·us -a -um

injustice iniūstíti·a -ae *f*

innocence innocénti·a -ae *f*

innocent (of) ínnoc·ēns -éntis (+ *gen*)

inquisitive cūrióos·us -a -um

insane īnsán·us -a -um

insanity īnsánit·ās -átis *f*

insensitive dūr·us -a -um

insensitivity dūríti·a -ae *f*

insincere īnsincér·us -a -um

integrity honést·ās -átis *f*

intellect ánim·us -ī *m*

intelligence intellegénti·a -ae *f*

intelligent intélleg·ēns -éntis

intense *(emotions)* grand·is -is -e

interesting speciós·us -a -um

irresponsible inofficiós·us -a -um

irritable īrācúnd·us -a -um

itching, to be itching to gést·iō -íre (+ *inf)*

jealous ínvid·us -a -um; **to be jealous of** invíd·eō -ére invídī (+ *acc or dat*)

jealousy invídi·a -ae *f*

jerk *(coll)* bucc·ō -ōnis *m*

joy gaúdi·um -ī *n;* **to feel joy** gaúd·eō -ére gāvísus sum

jump for joy exsultáre

just iūst·us -a -um

justice iūstíti·a -ae *f*

kind benévol·us -a -um; **to be kind toward** benévolus esse ergā (+ *acc*)

kind: what kind of person is … ? quī homō est …?

kind-hearted benévol·us -a -um, benígn·us -a -um

kindness benevoléntia -ae *f;* **to show kindness to s.o.** benevoléntiam álicui praest·ō -áre praéstitī

knowledge cogníti·ō -ónis *f,* scienti·a -ae *f*

laziness ignávi·a -ae *f*

lazy ignáv·us -a -um

learned doct·us -a -um, ērudít·us -a -um

lecherous sal·āx -ácis, libīdinós·us -a -um

lie fals·um -ī *n*

listless dēs·es -idis

liveliness alácrit·ās -átis *f*

lively ála·cer -cris -cre

loneliness sōlitúd·ō -inis *f*

lonely sōlitári·us -a -um; **to be lonely for** dēsīderáre

long for dēsīderáre

longing for dēsīdéri·um -ī *n* (+ *gen*)

look down on *(despise)* despectáre

loudmouth clāmát·or -óris *m,* clāmátr·īx -ícis *f*

lovable amábil·is -is -e

love amáre

love am·or -óris *m*

loving am·āns -ántis

low-born ignóbil·is -is -e

loyal fidél·is -is -e, fíd·us -a -um; **to remain loyal** in fidē mán·eō -ére mānsī

loyalty fidélit·ās átis *f*

luck fortún·a -ae *f*

lucky fortūnát·us -a -um

lust cupídit·ās -átis *f,* libíd·ō -inis *f*

lying falsíloqu·us -a -um

meticulous accūrát·us -a -um

mild clēm·ēns -éntis

mind ánim·us -ī *m;* **I have made up my mind** dēstinátum mihi est; **of sound mind** comp·os -otis mentis; **to be in one's right mind** apud sē esse

misery miséri·a -ae *f*

miserable mis·er -era -erum

miss dēsīderáre

mistake err·or -óris *m;* **to make a mistake** erráre

mistaken fals·us -a -um

model exémpl·ar -áris *n*

modest modést·us -a -um

modesty modésti·a -ae *f*

mood afféct·us -ūs *m* ánimī, ánim·us -ī *m*; **to get over one's mood** ánimum vinc·ō -ere -vīcī, superáre

motivation for ráti·ō -ṓnis *f* (+ *gen*)

motive caus·a -ae *f*

mourn *tr & intr* lúg·eō -ére lūxī

mourning maer·or -ṓris *m*

narrow-minded angúst·us -a -um

narrow-mindedness angústi·ae -ā́rum *fpl*

natural *(unaffected)* incompósit·us -a -um

nature nātū́r·a -ae *f*

needy in·ops -opis

negligence negligénti·a -ae *f,* incū́ri·a -ae *f*

negligent néglig·ēns -éntis

nervous intént·us -a -um, trépid·us -a -um

nervousness trepidáti·ō -ṓnis *f,* ánim·us -ī *m* trépidus

nice *(courteous)* concínn·us -a -um; *(pleasant)* lépid·us -a -um; *(cute)* bell·us -a -um

noble *(sentiments)* grand·is -is -e

object lesson documént·um -ī *n*

obliging cómmod·us -a -um

obscurity ignōbílit·ās -ā́tis *f*

over-confident cōnfī́d·ēns -éntis

outspoken lībéri·or -ṓris

painstaking operṓs·us -a -um

passion cupídit·ās -ā́tis *f; (lust)* libī́d·ō -inis *f*

passionate ārd·ēns -éntis

passionately efflíctim

pathetic ēlāmentábil·is -is -e

patient páti·ēns -éntis

patiently aequō ánimō

patriotic am·āns -ántis pátriae

persistence assidúit·ās -ā́tis *f*

persistent assídu·us -a -um

personality índol·ēs -is *f*

pessimistic īnfḗl·īx -ī́cis

phoney affectā́t·us -a -um

pitiful flébil·is-is -e

pity misericórdi·a -ae *f;* **to feel pity for** commiserésc·ō -ere (+ *gen*)

pity misér·eō -ére -uī (+ *gen*)

pleasant iūcúnd·us -a -um

pleasantness iūcúndit·ās -ā́tis *f*

pleasing grāt·us -a -um

polite to cōm·is -is -e (+ *dat or* ergā *or* in + *acc*)

politeness cōmit·ās -ā́tis *f*

pompous glōriṓs·us -a -um

poor *(pitiful)* mis·er -era -erum

popular grātiṓs·us -a -um; **to be popular with s.o.** grātiṓsus esse apud áliquem

popularity grā́ti·a -ae *f;* **to enjoy popularity among** grā́tiam háb·eō -ére -uī -itus apud (+ *acc*)

practice *(patience, etc.)* exérc·eō -ére -uī

precise exáct·us -a -um

prestige auctṓrit·ās -ā́tis *f*

presumptuous cōnfī́d·ēns -éntis

pretty bell·us -a -um, béllul·us -a -um

pride glṓri·a -ae *f;* **source of pride** glṓri·a -ae *f;* **to take pride in** glṓri·or -ā́rī dē *or* in (+ *abl*)

proper dec·ēns -éntis, decṓr·us -a -um

proud glōriṓs·us-a -um; **to be proud of** glṓri·or -ā́rī (+ *acc or* dē *or* in + *abl*)

quiet tacitúrn·us -a -um

rage fur·or -ṓris *m;* **to fly into a rage** īrásc·or -ā́rī

refined hūmā́n·us -a -um

reform ēmendā́re

regret paeniténti·a -ae *f*

regret: I regret mē paénitet (+ *gen*)

relentless dīr·us -a -um

relief: to be a relief levāméntō esse

rely on cōnfī́d·ō -ere cōnfī́sus sum (+ *dat*); **relying on** frēt·us -a -um (+ *dat or abl*)

remember commemorā́re

renown fām·a -ae *f*

repress (*emotions*) cohíb·eō -ére -uī -itus

repression continénti·a -ae *f*

reputation fām·a -ae *f*; **bad reputation** īnfā́mi·a -ae *f*; **good reputation** honést·ās -ā́tis *f*

resentful īrācúnd·us -a -um

resentment īrācúndi·a -ae *f*

resolute cōnfirmā́t·us -a -um

respect honōrā́re, observā́re

respectability honést·ās -ā́tis *f*

respectable honést·us -a -um

respected honōrā́t·us -a -um

respectful obsérv·āns -ántis

respectfully honōrífice

responsibility for cūr·a -ae *f* (+ *gen*); **it is my responsibility to** ... est mihi cūrae (+ *inf*)

restless inquiét·us -a -um

rich dīv·es -itis

riches dīvíti·ae -ā́rum *fpl*

rid: get rid of (*worries*) dílu·ō -ere -ī; (*persons*) āmṓl·ior -ī́rī āmōlī́tus sum

ridiculous rīdícul·us -a -um

role model exémpl·ar -āris *n*

rough asp·er -era -erum

rude (*character*) asp·er -era -erum

sad trist·is -is -e, maest·us -a -um

sadness tristíti·a -ae *f*

sarcasm dicácit·ās -ā́tis *f*

sarcastic dicácul·us -a -um, dic·āx -ácis

scandalous flāgitiṓs·us -a -um

scholarly ērudī́t·us -a -um

scorn contémpti·ō -ṓnis *f*

seductive illecebrṓs·us -a -um

self-confidence fīdúci·a -ae *f*

self-confident cōnfíd·ēns -éntis; **to be self-confident** sibi cōnfī́d·ō -ere cōnfī́sus sum

self-control abstinénti·a -ae *f*

self-controlled comp·os -otis suī

self-respect dígnit·ās -ā́tis *f*

sense of duty, of responsibility píet·ās -ā́tis *f*

sensible: to be sensible sáp·iō -ere

serious grav·is -is -e

seriousness grávit·ās -ā́tis *f*

shake up commóv·eō -ére commṓvī commṓtus

shabby sórdid·us -a -um

shame ignōmíni·a -ae *f*

shameful ignōminiṓs·us -a -um

shameless ímprob·us -a -um

shifty mṓbil·is -is -e; **shifty like the wind** ventṓs·us -a -um

show off sē iactā́re

shrewd astū́t·us -a -um

shy tímid·us -a -um

sigh gémit·us -ūs *m*

sigh *intr* gem·ō -ere -uī -itum; **to sigh over** gémere

silliness dēlīrā́ti·ō -ṓnis *f*, inépti·a -ae *f*

silly dēsípi·ēns -éntis, inépt·us -a -um; **to be silly** dēsíp·iō -ere

sincere sincér·us -a -um

skill artifíci•um -ī *n*

skilled cállid•us -a -um

skillful artificiốs•us -a -um

skillfulness callídit•ās -ấtis *f*

slow *(physically, mentally)* lent•us -a -um

sluggish heb•es -etis; **to be sluggish** héb•eō -ếre

sly astū́t•us -a -um

small-mindedness humílit•ās -ấtis *f*

smart cállid•us -a -um; *(impertinent)* ínsol•ēns -éntis

smile subrī́d•eō -ếre subrī́sī

smooth-talking blandíloqu•us -a -um

smug cōnfī́d•ēns -éntis

smugness cōnfīdénti•a -ae *f*

snobbish fastīdiốs•us -a -um

sober abstếmi•us -a -um

sociable sociábil•is -is -e

sorry: I feel sorry for the others mē míseret aliố rum

stability fírmit•ās -ấtis *f*

stable firm•us -a -um

state of mind affectấti•ō -ốnis *f* ánimī

stern asp•er -era -erum

stingy sórdid•us -a -um

strict sevếr•us -a -um; *(person in authority)* acérb•us -a -um

stubborn obstinất•us -a -um

surly diffícil•is -is -e

suspicion suspíci•ō -ốnis *f;* **to come under suspicion** in suspiciốnem vén•iō -ī́re vénī

suspicious súspic•āx -ắcis; *(suspected)* suspéct•us -a -um

sweet dulc•is -is -e

sympathy: to show sympathy for commíser•or -ắrī -ắtus sum

talent artifíci•um -ī *n*, ingéni•um -ī *n*

talented ingeniốs•us -a -um

talkative loqu•āx -ắcis

tall alt•us -a -um, prōcếr•us -a -um

task op•us -eris *n*, cū́r•a -ae *f*

taste: lack of good taste dēfórmit•ās -ấtis *f*

tense intént•us -a -um

tension conténti•ō -ốnis *f*

terrify terrificắre

terror terr•or -ốris *m*

thrifty frūgắl•is -is -e, frūgī́ *(indecl)*

tireless assídu•us -a -um

tough dū́r•us-a -um

tremble trem•ō -ere -uī; **to tremble all over** cóntrem•ō -ere -uī

tricky dolốs•us -a -um

trouble exérc•eō -ếre -uī -itus

troubled exercitất•us -a -um

trust fīd•ō -ere fī́sus sum (+ *dat or abl*)

trust fīd•ēs -eī *f*

trusting cōnfī́d•ēns -éntis

trustworthiness fīdúci•a -ae *f*

trustworthy lócupl•ēs -ếtis

trusty firm•us -a -um

truthful vērídic•us -a -um

trying *(tough)* exercitất•us -a -um

two-faced dup•lex -icis, bilíngu•is -is -e

ugliness dēfórmit•ās -ấtis *f*

ugly dēfórm•is -is -e; turp•is -is -e

unattractive invenúst•us -a -um

uncontrolled effrēnất•us -a -um

uncouth hórrid•us -a -um

uneducated inērudī́t•us -a -um

unfair iníqu•us -a -um

unfairly iníquē

unfaithful īnfidél·is -is -e

unfriendly inimíc·us -a -um

unhappiness īnfēlícit·ās -átis *f*

unhappy īnfél·īx -ícis

unpleasant iniūcúnd·us -a -um

unrestrained effrēnát·us -a -um, effús·us -a -um

unstable īnstábil·is -is -e

unsteady *(tottering)* cādúc·us -a -um

untrustworthy īnfíd·us -a -um

upset *adj* commót·us -a -um

upset *tr* commóv·eō -ére commóvī commótus

urge ánimī ímpet·us -ūs *m*

vigorous álac·er -ris -re

violence violénti·a -ae *f*

violent violént·us -a -um

weak inválid·us -a -um

welcome grāt·us -a -um

well-born honést·us -a -um

well-mannered bene mōrát·us -a -um

well-off bene aerátus -a -um

wicked ímprob·us -a -um

wickedness impróbit·ās -átis *f*

wild efferát·us -a -um

wily dolós·us -a -um, súbdol·us -a -um

wonderful admīrábil·is -is -e

word: to break one's word fidem fall·ō -ere feféllī; **to give one's word** fidem dō dare dedī datus; **to keep one's word** fidem serváre

word of honor fid·ēs -eī *f*

worry cūr·a -ae *f*, sollicitúd·ō -inis *f*

worry *tr* sollicitáre **‖** *intr* sollícit·or -árī -átus sum

worthless inán·is -is -e

worthlessness inánit·ās -átis *f*

worthy (of) dign·us -a -um (+ *abl*)

yearn for dēsīderáre

yearning (for) dēsīderáti·ō -ónis *f* (+ *gen*)

Chapter XVIII: Trades and Professions

CONVERSATIONS

┌──────── LEVEL I   **Donna gets a new hairdo.**

Tōnstrīx	Salvē, Donna. Quid agis?	*Hairdresser: Hello, Donna. How are you?*
Donna	Váleō. Velim tōnsū́ram, quaesō.	***Donna:*** *I'm fine. I'd like a haircut, please.*
Tōnstrīx	Cōnsíde, amábō tē, in hāc sellā tōnsṓriā.	*Sit down in this chair, please.*
Donna	Grátiās! Nōlī nimis dētondḗre comam.	*Thank you. Don't cut my hair too short.*
Tōnstrīx	At hódiē puéllae gerunt comam curtam.	*But nowadays girls are wearing their hair short.*
Donna	Id sciō, sed comam curtam nōn cūrō.	*I know, but I don't care for short hair.*
Tōnstrīx	Quṓmodo ergō cupis mē tondḗre comam?	*How then do you want me to cut your hair?*
Donna	Frange comam in gradūs.	*Cut my hair in layers.*
Tōnstrīx	Vīsne ántiās?	*Do you want bangs?*
Donna	Nōlō. Repécte comam.	*No. Comb my hair back.*
Tōnstrīx	Vīsne étiam cṓmere comam novíssimō modō?	*Do you want me to set your hair in the latest style?*
Donna	Ita. Utrum prius lautū́ra es comam?	*Yes. Are you going to wash my hair first?*
Tōnstrīx	Scílicet ego semper comam lavō ántequam eam cōmō.	*Of course, I always wash the hair before I set it.*
Donna	Sī tū vacās, nōn modo crīspā sed étiam tinge comam.	*If you have time, don't only curl my hair but also color it.*

Tōnstrīx	Vacō. Mihi crēde, amā́bis hunc novum cōmptum.	*I have time. Believe me, you will love this new hairdo.*

― LEVEL II   **Choosing a career.**

Pater	Vīsne, mī fīlī, esse aliquándō ratiōcinā́tor?	**Father:** *Son, would you like to be an accountant someday?*
Fīlius	Nullō modō! Meā senténtiā, mathēmática est doctrína difficíllima. Porrō, taedet mē tabulā́rum accéptī et expḗnsī.	**Son:** *No way! Math, I think, is a very difficult subject. Besides, accounting books bore me.*
Pater	Fortásse velīs medicínam exercḗre. Médicī, ut scīs, magnā auctōritā́te ūtúntur.	*Maybe you'd want to practice medicine. Doctors, as you know, enjoy a lot of prestige.*
Fīlius	At médicī arcessúntur ómnibus hōrīs diḗī et noctis. Numquam tempus subsicívum habent.	*But doctors are on call at all hours of the day and night. They never have time off.*
Pater	Velísne fíerī causídicus? Rē vērā, causídicī ingéntem pecúniam fáciunt.	*Would you like to become a lawyer? After all, lawyers make big money.*
Fīlius	Mihi nōn est ista callíditās quae est causidicórum, sī scīs quid mihi velim.	*I don't have that shrewdness that is typical of lawyers, if you know what I mean.*
Pater	Velísne rempúblicam iníre et aliquándō senā́tor fíerī?	*Would you like to enter politics and eventually become a senator?*
Fīlius	Senātṓrēs quidem multum valent, sed saepe sibi magis quam pópulō cṓnsulunt.	*Senators do have a lot of clout, but often they look after themselves rather than the people.*
Pater	Fortásse mālīs exercḗre ūnum ex artifíciīs.	*Perhaps you would prefer to practice one of the trades.*
Fīlius	Nōlō fíerī neque tōnsor neque pīstor neque lánius neque sūtor neque argentā́rius neque. . . .	*I don't want to become a barber or a baker or a butcher or shoe-maker or a banker or a . . . .*

Pater	At ūnusquísque nostrum debet vīctum quaeritáre quōmodocúmque! Quid dē ártibus ēlegantiÓribus?	*But each and every one of us must earn a living some way or other. What about the fine arts?*
Fílius	PīctÓrēs et sculptÓrēs et scrīptÓrēs habent próprium ingénium quod mihi omnÍnō dēest.	*Painters and sculptors and writers have a special talent which I lack completely.*
Pater	Quod tibi plānē dēest, mī fílī, nōn est ingénium sed ambítiō!	*Son, what you obviously lack is not ability but ambition!*

LEVEL III   **A man plans to build a home.**

Dóminus	In ánimō hábeō domum novam aedificáre.	**Owner:** *I plan to build a new home.*
Condúctor	Quō in locō?	**Contractor:** *Where?*
Dóminus	In Viā Novā in Monte Aventínō.	*On New Street on the Aventine Hill.*
Condúctor	Quandō opus mihi incipiéndum est?	*When do I have to begin the work?*
Dóminus	Scílicet quam prīmum. Quem architéctum comméndās?	*Of course, as soon as possible. Whom do you recommend as architect?*
Condúctor	Vitrúvius potest architectáre tibi domum pulchram.	*Vitruvius can design you a beautiful home.*
Dóminus	Ego eum prótinus arcéssam.	*I'll call him right away.*
Condúctor	Et ego prótinus condúcam caementáriōs, láterum strūctÓrēs, tēctÓrēs, fabrōs tignáriōs atque magnum gregem operāriÓrum.	*And I will immediately hire (some) workers in concrete, bricklayers, plasterers, carpenters and a large crew of laborers.*
Dóminus	Quandō póterunt caementáriī fundāméntum iácere?	*When can the concrete workers pour the foundation?*
Condúctor	Tríduō aut quadríduō summum.	*Within three days or four at most.*
Dóminus	Quid deínde?	*What then?*
Condúctor	Post iactum fundāméntum, strūctÓrēs láterēs strúere póterunt.	*After the foundation has been laid, the bricklayers will be able to lay the bricks.*

Dóminus   Quid fit deínde?   *And what happens then?*

Condúctor   Tēctṓrēs tēctṓrium pariétibus indū́cent.   *The plasterers will plaster the walls.*

Dóminus   Nōlī oblīvī́scī, iubē pictṓrēs paríetēs ā́triī tablī́níque píngere.   *Don't forget, have the painters paint the walls of the atrium and the study.*

Condúctor   Vīsne étiam pictū́rās ūdō tēctṓriō?   *Do you also want frescoes?*

Dóminus   Ita. Volō pictū́rās Mūsā́rum et nymphā́rum.   *Yes. I want pictures of the Muses and nymphs.*

Condúctor   Ubi vīs opus tessellā́tum in pavīméntīs?   *Where do you want mosaics on the floor?*

Dóminus   In ā́triō et trīclī́niō et tablī́nō et ómnibus cubículīs.   *In the atrium, the dining room, the study, and all the bedrooms.*

Condúctor   Cōnfíciam tōtam domum intrā sex mēnsēs.   *I shall finish the entire home within six months.*

Dóminus   Bene sānē. Cūrā́bō ut contráctus cōnscrībā́tur.   *Very good. I shall see to it that the contract is drawn up.*

TOPICAL VOCABULARY

accountant ratiōcinā́t·or -ṓris *m* (·rī́x -rī́cis *f*), ratiōnā́ri·us -ī *m* (·a -ae *f*)

   account ráti·ō -ṓnis *f*; **the account balances** rátiō cōnstat

   account books tábul·ae -ā́rum *fpl* (accéptī et expḗnsī)

   accounting cōnfécti·ō -ṓnis *f* tabulā́rum

   audit accounts ratiṓnēs dispún·gō -gere -xī -ctus

   balance accounts ratiṓnēs cṓnferō cōnférre cóntulī collā́tus

   keep books tábulās cōnfíc·iō -ere cōnfḗcī cōnféctus

acrobat fūnámbul·us -ī *m*

actor hístri·ō -ṓnis *m*, ā́ct·or -ṓris *m*

   act *tr & intr* ag·ō -ere ēgī ā́ctus

actress scḗnic·a -ae *f*, ā́ct·rix -rī́cis *f*

   go on the stage in scaenam prṓdeō prōdī́re prṓdiī

movie fā́bul·a -ae *f* cīnēmatográphica

play fā́bul·a -ae *f*

play the lead role prīmās partēs ag·ō -ere ēgī ā́ctus

play the role of a general imperātṓrem agere

scenery scēn·a -ae *f*

stage scēn·a -ae *f*, proscḗni·um -ī *n*

ambassador legā́t·us -ī *m*

announcer annūntiā́t·or -ṓris *m*, annūntiā́t·rīx -rī́cis *f*

architect archítéct·us -ī *m*

   architecture architectū́r·a -ae *f*

design *(buildings)* architectáre

artist ártif·ex -icis *mf*

athlete āthlḗt·a -ae *mf*

  athletics āthlḗtic·a -ae *f*

baker pīst·or -ṓris *m*, pīstr·ix -ícis *f (see also Chapter VIII)*

  bake cóqu·ō -ere coxī coctus

  bakery pīstrín·a -ae *f*

banker argentári·us -ī *m (·a -ae f)*

  account ráti·ō -ṓnis *f*

  bank argentári·a -ae *f*, tabérn·a -ae *f* argentária

  bank book libéll·us -ī *m* comparsṓrium, argentāriae libéllus

  banking business argentári·a -ae *f;* **to run a (big) banking business** argentáriam (máximam) fác·iō -ere fēcī factus

  bill *(paper money)* numm·us -ī *m* chartáreus; **ten-dollar bill** nummus chartáreus decem dollarṓrum

  borrow money at interest pecúniam faénorī accíp·iō -ere accépī accéptus

  check sýngraph·a -ae *f*, mandát·um -ī *n* nummárium; **to cash a check** arcáriō sýngrapham praéb·eō -ére -uī solvéndam; **to write a check** sýngrapham perscríb·ō -ere perscrípsī

  compound interest anatocísm·us -ī *m*

  deposit money in the bank pecúniam in argentáriā dēpṓn·ō -ere dēpósuī dēpósitus

  interest faen·us -oris *n;* **at interest** faénorī *or* faénore

  lend money at interest pecúniam faénorī dō dare dedī datus

  manage a bank argentáriam móder·or -árī moderátus sum

  passbook argentáriae libéll·us -ī *m*

  principal cap·ut -itis *n*

  simple interest perpétuum faen·us -oris *n*

barber tōns·or -ṓris *m*

  barber chair sell·a -ae *f* tōnsṓria

  barber shop tōnstrín·a -ae *f*

  clippers máchínul·a -ae *f* capíllīs resecándīs

  comb *s* pect·en -inis *m*

  comb *tr* pect·ō -ere pexī pexus

  cut *(hair)* tóndeō tondḗre totóndī tónsus

  hair *(of the head)* capíll·us -ī *m, (or with no distinction)* capíll·ī -ṓrum *mpl*, com·a -ae *f; (in locks or dressed)* crīn·is -is *m*

  hairdo cōmpt·us -ūs *m*

  haircut tōnsū́r·a -ae *f*

  hair style tōns·us -ūs *m*

  razor novácul·a -ae *f*

  scissors forfícul·ae -árum *fpl*

  shave *tr* rād·ō -ere rāsī rāsus; *(regularly)* rāsitáre; **to shave every day** fáciem cōtídiē rāsitáre

  shave *s* rāsū́r·a -ae *f*

bartender ministrát·or -ṓris *m*, ministrátr·ix -ícis *f*

  serve *(drinks, food)* **to** ministráre *(+ dat)*

beautician ōrnátr·ix -ícis *f (see* **hairdresser)**

bookkeeper actuári·us -ī *m (·a -ae f) (see* **accountant)**

bookseller bibliopṓl·a -ae *m*

  bookcase bibliothḗc·a -ae *f*

  book li·ber -brī *m*

  bookshelf plúte·us -ī *m*

  bookstore librári·a -ae *f*

boxer pugil, púgil·is *m (see Chapter V)*

bricklayer láterum struct·or -ṓris *m (see* **mason)**

brick *s* lat·er -eris *m* (coctílis = baked)

brick *adj* lateríci·us -a -um

lay bricks láterēs stru·ō -ere struxī structus

builder strūct·or -ṓris *m,* aedificắt·or -ṓris *m*

build éxstru·ō -ere exstrúxī exstrúctus, aedificáre

building aedifíci·um -ī *n*

erect, put up exstrúere

businessman negōtiắt·or -ṓris *m*

a business negóti·um -ī *n*

be engaged in business in negṓtiō vers·or -ắrī -ắtus sum

business *adj* negōtiắl·is -is -e

business establishment *(with its premises)* negōtiắti·ō -ṓnis *f*

business letter epístul·a -ae *f* negōtiắlis

businesswoman negōtiắtr·īx -ícis *f*

close a business deal negótium *(or* rem) cōnfíc·iō -ere cōnfḗcī cōnféctus

do (carry on) business negóti·or -ắrī -ắtus sum

run a business negótium exérc·eō -ére -uī -itus

transact business with s.o. negótium cum áliquō trắnsig·ō -ere -ḗgī -áctus

butcher láni·us -ī *m (see Chapter VIII)*

butcher shop laniḗn·a -ae *f*

carpenter fá·ber -brī *m* tignắrius

chisel *s* scalpr·um -ī *n*

chisel *tr* scalprō caed·ō -ere cecídī caesus

drill *s* térebr·a -ae *f*

drill *tr* terebrắre

hammer málle·us -ī *m*

nail *s* clāv·us -ī *m*

nail *tr* **(to)** clāvīs cōnfíg·ō -ere cōnfíxī cōnfíxus (+ *dat*); **to nail (boards) together** (tábulās) inter sē clāvīs cōnfígere

plane *s* runcín·a -ae *f*

plane *tr* runcīnắre

pliers for·ceps -cipis *mf*

ruler rḗgul·a -ae *f*

saw *s* serr·a -ae *f*

saw *tr* serrā sec·ō -ắre -uī -tus ‖ *intr* serram dūc·ō -ere dūxī ductus

square nōrm·a -ae *f*

cashier arcắri·us -ī *m,* arcắri·a -ae *f*

chauffeur autoraedắri·us -ī *m*

chef archimagír·us -ī *m* (·a -ae *f*)

chemist chémiae perít·us -ī *m* (·a -ae *f*)

chemical *adj* chémic·us -a -um

chemical *s* chémic·um -ī *n*

chemistry chémi·a -ae *f*

cook *s* coqu·us -ī *m,* coqu·a -ae *f*

bake tórr·eō -ére -uī tostus; in furnō cóquere

boil *tr* fervefác·iō -ere fervefḗcī fervefáctus ‖ *intr* férv·eō -ére férbuī

boiled ēlíx·us -a -um

cook *tr* cóqu·ō -ere coxī coctus ‖ *intr* (*of s.th. cooked in liquid*) īnfervḗsc·ō -ere

fry frīg·ō -ere frīxī frīctus

kitchen culín·a -ae *f*

oven furn·us -ī *m*

stove foc·us -ī *m*

craftsman fa·ber -brī *m*

craft artifíci·um -ī *n*

craftsmanship artifíci·um -ī *n*

doctor médic·us -ī *m*, médic·a -ae *f*
  cure *tr* sanáre
  cure *s* remédi·um -ī *n*
  doctor's office medicín·a -ae *f*
  heal sānáre
  medicine medicín·a -ae *f*
  pill pílul·a -ae *f*
  treat cūráre
  treatment cūr·a -ae *f*
druggist medicāmentári·us -ī *m* (·a -ae *f*)
  drug medicám·en -inis *n*
  drugstore medicāmentári·a -ae *f*
dry cleaner full·ō -ónis *m*
  dry cleaner's *(establishment)* fullónic·a -ae *f*
electrician ēléctridis ártif·ex -icis *m*
  electricity ēléctr·is -idis *f*
  electric(al) ēléctric·us -a -um
  wire fīl·um -ī *n*
engineer machinát·or -óris *m* (·rīx -rícis *f*)
  engineering machinális sciénti·a -ae *f*
farmer agrícol·a -ae *mf*
  barley hórde·um -ī *n*
  barn hórre·um -ī *n*
  barnyard cóh·ors -órtis *f*
  cattle pec·us -oris *n*
  chicken pull·us -ī *m* gallīnáceus, gallín·a -ae *f*
  corn maízi·um -ī *n*
  corncob maíziī spíc·a -ae *f*
  cow vacc·a -ae *f*
  crops *(standing grain)* seg·es -etis *f*; *(field produce)* frūg·ēs -um *fpl*
  farm fund·us -ī *m*

farm house vīll·a -ae *f* rústica
feed pāsc·ō -ere pāvī pāstus
field a·ger -grī *m*; *(untilled)* camp·us -ī *m*
garden hort·us -ī *m* rústicus
grain frūmént·um -ī *n*
harvest *s* mess·is -is *f (m)*
harvest *tr* démetō -ere dēméssuī dēméssus
hay fēn·um -ī *n*; **to make hay** fēnum sec·ō -áre -uī -tus
hayloft fēníl·ia -ium *npl*
herd grex, gregis *m*
horse equ·us -ī *m*
meadow prāt·um -ī *n*
milk lac, lactis *n*
milk *tr* múl·geō -gére -sī -sus *or* -ctus
oats avén·a -ae *f*
orchard pōmári·um -ī *n*
pasture páscu·um -ī *n*
pig porc·us -ī *m*, porc·a -ae *f*
plant ser·ō -ere sēvī sātus; **to plant a field** agrum cōnsérere
plow *s* arátr·um -ī *n*
plow *tr* aráre
raise *(crops, animals)* ēducáre
reap met·ō -ere méssuī messus
reaper mess·or -óris *m*; *(machine)* mestr·um -ī *n* ligātóriūm
sheep ov·is -is *f*
stable stábul·um -ī *n*; *(for horses)* equíl·e -is *n*; *(for cows)* bovíl·e -is *n*; *(for sheep)* ovíl·e -is *n*; *(for pigs)* suíl·e -is *n*
straw strāmént·um -ī *n*
till col·ō -ere -uī cultus
wheat trític·um -ī *n*

fireman vig·il -ilis *m*, sīphōnắri·us -ī *m*

fire incéndi·um -ī *n; to put out a fire* incéndium exstíngu·ō -ere exstínxī exstínctus

fire engine sīph·ō -ốnis *m*

fisherman piscắt·or -ốris *m* (*see Chapter V*)

fortuneteller haríol·us -ī *m*, haríol·a -ae *f*

tell fortunes haríol·or -ắrī -ắtus sum

grocer macellắri·us -ī *m* (·a -ae *f*)

grocery store macéll·um -ī *n*

groceries obsốni·um -ī *n*

guard cust·ōs -ốdis *m*

hairdresser ōrnắtr·īx -ícis *f*, tōnstr·īx -ícis *f* (*see* **barber**)

bangs ánti·ae -ắrum *fpl*

blond *adj* flāv·us -a -um

brunette fusc·us -a -um

color colōrắre, tíng·ō -ere tínxī tínctus

comb *s* pect·en -inis *m*

comb *tr* pec·tō -tere -xī -xus; **to comb back** repéctere; **to comb forward** prōpéctere; **to comb out** expéctere

curl *s* (*natural*) cirr·us -ī *m*; cincínn·us -ī *m*

curl *tr* crīspắre

curler calamístr·um -ī *n*

curly crīsp·us -a -um

cut tónd·eō -ére totóndī tōnsus

do (*the hair*) cōm·ō -ere cōmpsī cōmptus

dye *tr* tíng·ō -ere tínxī tínctus

hair com·a -ae *f*, capíll·us -ī *m, or* capíll·ī -ốrum *mpl*

hairdo cōmpt·us -ūs *m*

hair style tōns·us -ūs *m*

layer the hair comam in gradūs frang·ō -ere frēgī frāctus

mirror spécul·um -ī *n*

part *s* discrím·en -inis *n*

part *tr* (*the hair*) discrīminắre

redhead rútil·a -ae *f*

style mod·us -ī *m*

wavy crīsp·us -a -um

innkeeper caup·ō -ốnis *m*

inn caupốn·a -ae *f*

journalist diurnắri·us -ī *m*, (·a -ae *f*)

journalism diurnắria ar·s -tis *f*

judge jūd·ex -icis *mf*

laborer operắri·us -ī *m* (·a -ae *f*)

lawyer causídic·us -ī *m* (·a -ae *f*); (*for the defense*) advocắt·us -ī *m* (·a -ae *f*)

librarian bibliothēcắri·us *m*, (·a -ae *f*)

library bibliothéc·a -ae *f*

machinist māchinắt·or -ốris *m*

magician mag·us -ī *m* (·a -ae *f*)

do tricks praestígi·or -ắrī

magic mágica ar·s -tis *f;* **practice magic** mágicās artēs exérc·eō -ére -uī -itus

maid ancíll·a -ae *f*, fámul·a -ae *f*

mailman tabellắri·us -ī *m*

deliver red·dō -dere -didī -ditus

forward déferō dēférre détulī dēlắtus

mail epístul·ae -ắrum *fpl*, rēs *fpl* cursuắlēs

mail *tr* dō dare dedī datus

mailbox caps·a -ae *f* tabellắria

packet, package fascícul·us -ī *m*

postage vectúr·a -ae *f* litterắrum

stack of mail multíiugae lítterae

stamp pittắci·um -ī *n* cursuắle

mason fa·ber -brī *m* lapidárius *(see* **bricklayer)**

  concrete concrét·um -ī *n*

  cement cal·x -cis *f*

  level libr·a -ae *f*

  mortar harēnát·um -ī *n*

  plummet perpendícul·um -ī *n*

  square norm·a -ae *f*

  trowel trull·a -ae *f*

mechanic mechánicus ópif·ex -ícis *m*

  repair refíc·iō -ere refécī reféctus

merchant mercát·or -óris *m; (in a market)* macellári·us -ī *m* (·a -ae *f*)

  merchandise merc·ēs -ium *fpl*

metal worker metallórum fab·er -rī *m*

midwife obstétr·īx -ícis *f*

miner metallári·us -ī *m*

  mine *s* fodín·a -ae *f,* metáll·um -ī *n;* **coal mine** fodín·a -ae *f* carbónária; **gold mine** aurifodín·a -ae *f;* **silver mine** argentifodín·a -ae *f;* **iron mine** ferrifodín·a -ae *f;* **salt mine** fodín·a -ae *f* salinária; **to operate a mine** metállum exérc·eō -ēre -uī -itus

  mine *tr* effód·iō -ere effódī effóssus

  mine shaft fodínae púte·us -ī *n*

minister minís·ter -trī *m* (·tra -trae *f*), pāst·or -óris *mf*

musician músic·us -ī *m,* músic·a -ae *f*

  band symphóni·a -ae *f*

  concert concént·us -ūs *m*

  drum týmpan·um -ī *n;* **to play the drum** týmpanum pulsáre

  flute tíbi·a -ae *f*

  guitar cíthar·a -ae *f* Hispánica

  lyre lyr·a -ae *f*

  musical instrument órgan·um -ī *n*

  orchestra symphóni·a -ae *f*

  organ órgan·um -ī *n*

  piano clāvicórdi·um -ī *n*

  play *(an instrument)* cantáre *(+ abl),* can·ō -ere cécinī cantus *(+ abl)*

  trumpet tub·a -ae *f*

  violin fidícul·a -ae *f*

nurse aegrórum minístr·a -ae *f,* nosócom·a -ae *f; (male)* aegrórum miníst·er -rī *m,* nosócom·us -ī *m*

painter píct·or -óris *m* (·rīx -rícis *f*)

  brush pēnicíll·us -ī *m*

  canvas téxtil·e -is *n*

  paint *s* pigmént·um -ī *n*

  paint *tr & intr* ping·ō -ere pīnxī pictus

  painting *(the art; picture)* pictúr·a -ae *f; (painting on a board)* tábul·a -ae *f* (pícta)

perfumer myrapól·a -ae *m*

  perfume od·or -óris *m,* myr·um -ī *n*

  perfume shop myrapóli·um -ī *n*

pharmacist *(see* **druggist)**

photographer phōtógraph·us -ī *m,* phōtógraph·a -ae *f*

  photo shop officín·a -ae *f* phōtográphica

pilot gubernát·or -óris *m* (·rīx -rícis *f*) *(see* **pilot,** Chapter XXIV)

plasterer tēct·or -óris *m*

  plaster *s* tēctóri·um -ī *n*

  plaster *tr* **(a wall)** tēctórium (paríetī) indúc·ō -ere indúxī indúctus

playwright fābulárum scrīpt·or -óris *m* (·rīx -rícis *f*)

plumber ártif·ex -icis *m* plumbárius

  pipe fístul·a -ae *f*

poet poét·a -ae *m*

  poem poém·a -atis *n;* **to write a poem** poéma fác·iō -ere fēcī factus

poetess poétri·a -ae *f*

poetry poés·is -is *f*

police officer vigil, vígilis *mf*

porter báiul·us -ī *m*

potter fígul·us -ī *m*

   potter's clay crēt·a -ae *f* figlína

   potter's wheel rot·a -ae *f* figuláris

   pottery fictíl·ia -ium *npl*

priest sacérd·ōs -ótis *mf*

   priesthood sacerdóti·um -ī *n*

producer chorág·us -ī *m*

prostitute méretr·īx -ícis *f,* prōstitút·a -ae *f;* **to be a prostitute** prōst·ō -áre próstitī

psychiatrist psȳchīát·er -rī *m* (·ria -riae *f*)

psychologist psȳchólog·us -ī *m* (·a -ae *f*)

publisher édit·or -óris *m,* éditr·īx -ícis *f*

retailer propól·a -ae *m*

sailor naut·a -ae *m,* naútri·a -ae *f*

saleslady *(in a shop)* tabernári·a -ae *f*

salesman *(in a shop)* tabernári·us -ī *m*

   traveling salesman ínstit·or -óris *m*

sculptor sculpt·or -óris *m* (·rīx -rícis *f*)

   bust imág·ō -inis *f*

   carve sculp·ō -ere -sī -tus

   chisel scalpr·um -ī *n*

   sculpture sculptúr·a -ae *f*

   statue státu·a -ae *f,* sign·um -ī *n*

seamstress *(making clothes)* vestífic·a -ae *f; (altering clothes)* sarcinátr·īx -ícis *f*

   embroider acū ping·ō -ere pīnxī píctus

   mend sárc·iō -íre sarsī sartus

   needle ac·ū -ūs *f*

   sew su·ō -ere -ī sūtus

secretary āmanuéns·is -is *mf;* ā manū *mf*

sheriff geraéf·a -ae *m*

shipbuilder naupég·us -ī *m*

   shipyard nāvál·ia -ium *npl*

shoemaker sūt·or -óris *m*

   shoe cálce·us -ī *m*

   shoemaker's shop sūtrín·a -ae *f*

singer cantát·or -óris *m,* cantátr·īx -ícis *f*

   sing canō canere cécinī cantus, cantáre

   song cant·us -ūs *m,* cántic·um -ī *n*

soldier mīl·es -itis *mf (see chapter on War and Peace)*

surgeon chīrúrg·us -ī *m* (·a -ae *f*)

   operate on sec·ō -áre -uī -tus

   operation sécti·ō -ónis *f*

   surgery chīrúrgi·a -ae *f*

tailor *(making clothes)* vestífic·us -ī *m* (·a -ae *f*); *(altering clothes)* sarcinát·or -óris *m (see seamstress)*

   tailor shop officín·a -ae *f* vestium

tax collector exáct·or -óris *m* (·rīx -rícis *f*), públicán·us -ī *m*

   collect taxes vectīgália éxig·ō -ere exégī exáctus

   tax vectíg·al -ális *n*

teacher magís·ter -trī *m,* magístr·a -ae *f (see the chapter on* **school***)*

travel agent itínerum prōcūrát·or -óris *m* (·rīx -rícis *f*)

typist dactylógraph·us -ī *m,* (·a -ae *f*)

   type dactylográphiō scrīb·ō -ere scrīpsī scrīptus

   typewriter dactylográphi·um -ī *n,* machínul·a -ae *f* scrīptória

   typing dactylográphica ar·s -tis *f*

undertaker pollínct·or -óris *m*

coffin cápul·us -ī *m*

corpse cadáv·er -eris *n*

funeral fūn·us -eris *n;* **to attend a funeral** in fūnus vén·iō *(of several* convén·iō*)* -íre vēnī

waiter miníst·er -rī *m*

    serve *(food)* appŏ́n·ō -ere appŏ́suī appŏ́situs

    wait on ministrā́re *(+ dat)*

waitress minístr·a -ae *f*

wholesaler magnā́ri·us -ī *m*

    wholesale *adj* magnā́ri·us -a -um

wine merchant vīnā́ri·us -ī *m,* oenopŏ́l·ēs -ae *m*

    barrel cūp·a -ae *f*

    wine vīn·um -ī *n*

    wine shop oenopŏ́li·um -ī *n*

wrestler luctā́t·or -ŏ́ris *m*

    wrestle luct·or -ā́rī -ā́tus sum

    wrestling, wrestling match luctā́ti·ō -ŏ́nis *f*

writer scrīpt·or -ŏ́ris *m,* scrīptr·īx -ícis *f)*

Chapter XIX: The City and Public Buildings

CONVERSATIONS

LEVEL I **Discussing the merits of city life.**

Anna

Dīc mihi, Guáltere, cūr praefers in urbe habitắre quam rūrī.

Anna: Tell me, Walter, why do you prefer living in the city rather than in the country?

Guálterus

Quia commódius est in urbe habitắre.

Walter: Because it is more convenient to live in the city.

Anna

Quid ita?

How so?

Guálterus

Pédibus īre possum ad scholam et ad váriās tabérnās.

I can go on foot to school and to the different shops.

Anna

Vīsitắsne umquam bibliothḗcam pū́blicam an pinacothḗcam an mūsḗum?

Do you ever visit the public library or art gallery or museum?

Guálterus

Rārṓ. Sed saepe eō ad stádium aut amphitheắtrum aut thermās aut gymnásium.

Rarely. But I often go to the stadium or the amphitheater or the baths or the gymnasium.

Anna

Nōnne commeắtus vehiculṓrum et strépitus viắrum turbaeque tibi moléstiae sunt?

Aren't the traffic and the noise of the streets and the crowds bothersome to you?

Guálterus

Estō! Intérdum istae rēs quidem moléstae sunt, sed ubi est vīta perfécta?

Granted! At times those things are bothersome all right, but where is life perfect?

Anna

Velḯsne in continéntibus habitắre?

Wouldn't you like to live in the suburbs?

Guálterus

Sānē in continéntibus sed rūrī numquam.

In the suburbs, yes, but never in the country.

Jennifer wants to go to town.

Iénnifer	Mārtíne, potésne mē addúcere in óppidum?	*Jennifer: Martin, can you take me into town?*
Mārtínus	Certē. Quid vīs fácere in óppidō?	*Martin: Sure. What do you want to do in town?*
Iénnifer	Multa. Prīmum volō īre in tabérnam chartáriam.	*Lots. First, I want to go to the stationery store.*
Mārtínus	Quid ibi émere vīs?	*What do you want to buy there?*
Iénnifer	Chartam scrīptóriam et librum coquinātórium.	*Writing paper and a cookbook.*
Mārtínus	At nōn vénditant librōs coquinātóriōs in tabérnā chartáriā sed in libráriā, ut putā, apud Sóssiōs Frātrēs.	*But they don't sell cookbooks in the stationery store but in a bookstore, for example at the Sossii Brothers.*
Iénnifer	Ubi terrárum est illa libráría?	*Where in the world is that bookstore?*
Mārtínus	Est in locō quod Argīlétum appellátur.	*It's in a place called the Argiletum.*
Iénnifer	Ubi ítaque est Argīlétum?	*Where then is the Argiletum?*
Mārtínus	Em, Argīlétum est in empóriō ínclutō Rōmae. Est exadvérsum macéllum.	*Well, the Argiletum is in Rome's famous business district. It's across the street from [lit: opposite] the market.*
Iénnifer	Eu! Sī tibi ótium sit, velim étiam in macéllum īre, nam obsónia mihi comparánda sunt.	*Great! If you have the time, I would also like to go to the market, since I have to get some groceries.*
Mārtínus	Ágedum, cito eámus. Mihi nōn est multum tempus subsicívum.	*Come on, let's go quickly. I don't have a lot of spare time.*

Asking for directions in the city.

Peregrínus	Ignósce mihi, bone vir. Mihi vídeor deërrāvísse. Quō mē vertam néscio.	*Foreigner: Pardon me, sir. I seem to have lost my way. I don't know which way to turn.*
Vigil	Quō vīs īre? Viam tibi libénter osténdam.	*Policeman: Where do you want to go? I'll gladly show you the way.*

Peregrínus	Ubi est stádium, quaesō?	*Where is the stadium, please?*
Vigil	Rēctā perge per trēs vīcōs ūsque ad theátrum; dein tē verte dextrórsum et prōcéde ūsque ad secúndum cómpitum. Stádium erit ad laevam.	*Go straight ahead for three blocks as far as the theater; then turn right and go on to the second intersection. The stadium will be on your left.*
Peregrínus	Et ubi est gymnásium?	*And where is the gymnasium?*
Vigil	Haud procul est ā stádiō. Ubi stádium praeteríeris, rēctā perge per duōs vīcōs; ibi stat templum in álterō ángulō et thermae in álterō ángulō. Tē verte sinistrórsum et ámbulā per trēs vīcōs. Cōnspíciēs dein gymnásium prope moénia urbis.	*It isn't far from the stadium. When you have passed the stadium, go straight ahead for two blocks; there a temple stands on the one corner and the baths on the other corner. Turn left and go three blocks. You will then see the gymnasium near the city walls.*
Peregrínus	Estne popína in eā vicíniā?	*Is there a restaurant in the vicinity?*
Vigil	Est popína in omnī ferē ángulō.	*There is a restaurant on practically every corner.*
Peregrínus	Grátiās multās!	*Thanks a lot.*
Vigil	Bene ámbulā!	*Have a good trip!*

TOPICAL VOCABULARY

alley angipórt·um -ī *n*

Argiletum Argīlét·um -ī *n (a district of Rome extending from the base of the Quirinal to the Capitoline and chiefly inhabited by booksellers and mechanics)*

amphitheater amphitheátr·um -ī *n*

apartment building ínsul·a -ae *f*

aqueduct aquaedúct·us -ūs *m*

art gallery pinacothéc·a -ae *f*

bakery pīstrín·a -ae *f*

bank argentári·a -ae *f*

barbershop tōnstrín·a -ae *f*

bath bálne·um -ī *n; (large bathing establishment)* therm·ae -árum *fpl*

blind alley fúndul·a -ae *f*

block vīc·us -ī *m*

bookstore librári·a -ae *f*

business district empóri·um -ī *n*

butcher shop lanién·a -ae *f*

church ecclḗsi·a -ae *f*

citadel ar·x -cis *f*

city urb·s -is *f*

clothing store tabérn·a -ae *f* vestiária

courthouse basílic·a -ae *f*

dead-end street fúndul·a -ae *f*

department store pantopóli·um -ī *n*

doctor's office medicín·a -ae *f*

drugstore medicāmentári·a -ae *f*

dry cleaner's fullónic·a -ae *f*

fire station státi·ō -ónis *f* vígilum

fish market for·um -ī *n* piscárium

flower shop tabérn·a -ae *f* flōrális

gas station státi·ō -ónis *f* benzīnária

grocery store macéll·um -ī *n*

gymnasium gymnási·um -ī *n*

hardware store tabérn·a -ae *f* ferrária

high school schol·a -ae *f* supérior

hospital valētūdinári·um -ī *n*

hotel hospíti·um -ī *n*, dēversóri·um -ī *n*

intersection cómpit·um -ī *n*, quadrívi·um -ī *n*

jewelry store gemmári·a -ae *f*

laundry fullónic·a -ae *f*

library bibliothéc·a -ae *f*

   bookshelf plúte·us -ī *m*

mall for·um -ī *n* subtēguláneum

museum mūsé·um -ī *n*

park hort·ī -órum *mpl*

pastry shop cuppedinári·a -ae *f*

perfume store tabérn·a -ae *f* unguentária

police station státi·ō -ōnis *f* vigilum

portico pórtic·us -ūs *f*

post office diribitóri·um -ī *n* cursuále

prison carc·er -eris *m*

race track hippódrom·us -ī *m*

restaurant caupón·a -ae *f*

saloon tabérn·a -ae *f* pōtória

school lūd·us -ī *m*, schol·a -ae *f*

savings bank argentári·a -ae *f* pecúliīs asservándīs

senate building cúri·a -ae *f*

shoemaker sūt·or -óris *m*

shoemaker's sūtrín·a -ae *f*

shop tabérn·a -ae *f; (workshop)* officín·a -ae *f*

side street dēvertícul·um -ī *n*

sidewalk crepíd·ō -inis *f*

square áre·a -ae *f*

stadium stádi·um -ī *n*

stationery store tabérn·a -ae *f* chartária

street vi·a -ae *f*, platé·a -ae *f;* **across the street from** exadvérsum (+ *acc*)

suburbs continént·ia -ium *npl*

synagogue synagóg·a -ae *f*

temple templ·um -ī *n*, aed·ēs -is *f*

theater theátr·um -ī *n*

tower turr·is -is *f*

town óppid·um -ī *n*

traffic comméát·us -ūs *m* vehiculórum

wall múr·us -ī *m;* **walls** moén·ia -ium *npl*

warehouse apothéc·a -ae *f*

zoo vīvári·um -ī *n*

Chapter XX: Government

CONVERSATIONS

┌──────── LEVEL I **A father explains to his son his involvement in politics.**

Fílius	Pater, cūr vīs cōnsul fíerī?	*Son: Father, why do you want to become a consul?*
Pater	Quia ego iam omnēs áliōs honṓrēs gessī.	*Father: Because I have already held all the other offices.*
Fílius	Quōs honṓrēs gessístī?	*What offices have you held?*
Pater	Prīmō quaestor eram, deínde aedílis, deínde praetor. Nunc cōnsulátum petō.	*First I was quaestor, then aedile, then praetor. Now I'm running for the consulship.*
Fílius	Suntne multī competītṓrēs?	*Are there many opponents?*
Pater	Sunt vērō.	*There are indeed.*
Fílius	Suntne eī omnēs patríciī dívitēs?	*Are they all rich patricians?*
Pater	Omnēs sunt virī magnae grátiae et dīvitiárum.	*All are men of great influence and wealth.*
Fílius	Potestne pauper creárī cōnsul?	*Can a poor man be elected consul?*
Pater	Fíerī potest sed difficíllimum est.	*It is possible, but it is very difficult.*
Fílius	Ubi comítia habēbúntur?	*Where will the elections be held?*
Pater	In Campō Mártiō, ut solent.	*In the Campus Martius as usual.*
Fílius	Quandō comítia habēbúntur?	*When will the elections be held?*
Pater	Hódiē post merídiem.	*This afternoon.*
Fílius	Tibi fēlíciter, pater!	*Good luck to you, Father.*
Pater	Grátiās, mī fīlī.	*Thank you, son.*

173

┌─────── LEVEL II   **A senator explains how government works.**

Senátor	Dā mihi togam praetéxtam et múlleōs.	*Senator: Give me my purple-bordered toga and senatorial shoes.*
Uxor	Quō abīs íterum?	*Wife: Where are you off to again?*
Senátor	Num ignórās mē hódiē prō rōstrīs orātiónem habitúrum esse?	*Don't you know that I am going to give a speech today from the rostrum?*
Uxor	Nōnne senátus hódiē convéniet?	*Isn't the senate meeting today?*
Senátor	Étiam. Legátī ē Graéciā dē vectīgálibus senátum adloquéntur.	*Yes. Ambassadors from Greece will address the senate about the taxes.*
Uxor	Querentúrne dē vectīgálibus an dē exāctóribus?	*Are they going to complain about the taxes or the tax collectors?*
Senátor	Dē utrísque. Ut scīs, Rōma novum vectígal istīs Graéculīs impósuit.	*About both. As you know, Rome imposed a new tax on those poor Greeks.*
Uxor	Quid praeses província Achaéae dē novō vectīgálī dīcit?	*What does the governor of the province of Achaea say about the new tax?*
Senátor	Praeses dīcit nōn sōlum vectígal sed étiam exāctórēs esse ádmodum iníquōs.	*The governor says that not only the tax but also the tax collectors are very unfair.*
Uxor	Cūr rēs pública vectīgália ex prōvínciīs nostrīs cōnstánter éxigit?	*Why does the government constantly collect taxes from our provinces?*
Senátor	Est simplex. Rōma mercédem tríbuit exāctóribus et conductóribus et ratiōcinātóribus et innúmerīs contubernálibus scrībísque.	*It is simple. Rome pays a salary to tax collectors, their employers, accountants, and innumerable staff members and clerks.*
Uxor	At sī vectīgália nōn impōneréntur et exigeréntur, nōn omnínō opus esset hīsce ómnibus mercédem tribúere.	*But if taxes were not imposed and collected, there would be no need at all to pay salaries to all these people.*
Senátor	Maniféstō tū rem públicam nōn intéllegis!	*Obviously you do not understand politics!*

┌────────── LᴇᴠᴇL III　**How the senate conducts business.**

Novus Homō	Nōnne senátus hódiē hábitus est?	***Freshman Senator:*** *A senate session was held today, wasn't it?*
Cōnsul	Hábitus est, sed nihil in senātū cōnféctum est.	***Consul:*** *It was, but nothing was accomplished in the senate.*
N. Homō	Quidnī? Dē quō disceptátum est?	*Why not? What was the debate about?*
Cōnsul	Crassus réttulit dē impériō Iúliī Caésaris, quī bellum Gallīs inférre vult.	*Crassus made a motion about the military command of Julius Caesar, who wants to go to war with the Gauls.*
N. Homō	Quíspiam in Crassī senténtiam dīcébat?	*Did anyone second Crassus' motion?*
Cōnsul	Pompéius vidēbátur assentírī Crassō, sed omnēs ferē optimátēs senténtiae Crassī obsistébant.	*Pompey seemed to go along with Crassus, but almost all the conservatives objected to Crassus' motion.*
N. Homō	Quid dixérunt Caesariánī?	*What did the members of Caesar's party say?*
Cōnsul	Cúriō, tribúnus plēbis, Caésaris causam magnō cum stúdiō ēgit.	*Curio, the tribune of the people, pleaded Caesar's cause with great enthusiasm.*
N. Homō	Et quid dē tē?	*And what about you?*
Cōnsul	Ego bréviter senténtiam dīxī, sed nóluī própalam assentírī Crassō.	*I expressed my opinion briefly, but I did not want to agree with Crassus openly.*
N. Homō	Num discéssiō facta est in Crassī senténtiam?	*Was a vote taken on Crassus' motion?*
Cōnsul	Nōn. Catō, homō équidem honéstus sed furiósus, senténtiae intercédere cōnátus est.	*No. Cato, a really respectable but mad man, tried to veto the motion.*
N. Homō	Praevalēbátne Catō? Senátūs cōnsúltum factum est?	*Did Cato win out? Was the senate decree passed?*
Cōnsul	Nōn factum est; senténtia tamen est perscrípta. Subínde, mē referénte, senátus dīmíssus est.	*It did not pass; however, the motion was put on record. After that, on my motion, the senate was dismissed.*

N. Homō   Quis in Crassī senténtiam īvit?   *Who supported Crassus'*
                                                proposal?

Cōnsul   Cúriō, tribúnus plēbis, et paucī   *Curio, the tribune of the people,*
              amícī Crassī.   *and only a few friends of*
                                                 Crassus.

N. Homō   Aestimásne Caésarem áliquid   *Do you think that Caesar will get*
              cōnsectúrum esse?   *anywhere?*

Cōnsul   Nullō modō. Hóminēs mox eius   *No way. People will soon forget*
              oblīvíscéntur. Numquam   *about him. He will never*
              exercítuī in Gálliā imperábit.   *command the army in Gaul.*

TOPICAL VOCABULARY

**according to the law, as the law
  prescribes** secúndum lēgem

administration administráti·ō -ónis *f*

aedile aedíl·is -is *m*

aedileship aedílit·ās -átis *f*

aristocracy nōbílit·ās -átis *f*, optimát·ēs
  -ium *mpl*

assembly concíli·um -ī *n*

ballot tabéll·a -ae *f*

ballot box suffrāgiórum cist·a -ae *f*

bill rogáti·ō -ónis *f*

bribery *(in politics)* ámbit·us -ūs *m*

bring to order in órdinem cōg·ō -ere
  coḗgī coáctus

bureau ministéri·um -ī *n*

bureaucracy graphēocráti·a -ae *f*

bureaucracy graphēócrat·es -ae *mf*

campaign petíti·ō -ónis *f*; **illegal
  campaign practices** ámbit·us -ūs *m*

campaign *intr* ámb·iō -íre -ívī *or* -iī
  -itum

candidate candidát·us -ī *m* (·a -ae *f*)

cast a vote suffrágium ferō ferre tulī
  lātus

censor cēns·or -óris *m*

city urb·s -is *f*, cívit·ās -átis *f*

citizen cīv·is -is *mf*; **private citizen**
  (who holds no political office)
  prīvát·us -ī *m* (·a -ae *f*)

city council decuriōn·ēs -um *mpl*

  council member decúri·ō -ónis *mf*

citizenship cívit·ās -átis *f*

civil cīvíl·is -is -e; **civil rights** iū·s -ris *n*
  cīvíle; **loss (taking away) of civil
  rights** dēminúti·ō -ónis *f* cápitis; **to
  deprive s.o. of civil rights** cápite
  alicūius dēmínu·ō -ere -ī

civilian *adj* togátus -a -um, prīvát·us -a
  -um

civilian *s* togát·us -ī *m; (opposite of
  soldier)* prīvát·us -ī *m*

command *(a legion, army)* praesíd·eō
  -ére praesédī (+ *dat*), imperáre (+
  dat)

committee concíli·um -ī *n*

community cívit·ās -átis *f*

congress congréss·us -ūs *m*

conservative *adj* cōnservātív·us -a -um

conservative *s* cōnservātív·us -ī *m* (·a
  -ae *f*); **conservatives** *(in ancient
  Rome)* optimát·ēs -ium *mpl*

constitution cōnstitū́t·a -ṓrum *npl*

consul cōnsul -is *m*

consulship cōnsulā́t·us -ūs *m*

debate *s* disceptā́ti·ō -ṓnis *f*

debate *tr* disceptā́re (dē + *abl*)

decide (to, not to) *(of the senate, also of supreme magistrates)* cḗns·eō -ḗre -uī (ut *or* ne + *subj*)

decree of the senate senā́tūs cōnsúlt·um -ī *n;* **to pass a decree of the senate** senā́tūs cōnsúltum fác·iō -ere fēcī factus

defeat repúls·a -ae *f;* **defeat at the polls** comítiīs repúlsa; **defeat in running for the consulship** repúlsa cōnsulā́tūs; **to suffer a defeat** repúlsam ferō ferre tulī lātus

democracy dēmocrā́ti·a -ae *f*

democrat dēmocrā́tic·us -ī *m* (·a -ae *f*)

democratic dēmocrā́tic·us -a -um

dictator dictā́t·or -ṓris *m*

dismiss *(the senate)* dīmítt·ō -ere dīmī́sī dīmíssus

edict ēdíct·um -ī *n*

elect creā́re; *(Roman senators)* coöptā́re

elections comíti·a -ṓrum *npl;* **to hold elections** comítia háb·eō -ḗre -uī -itus

emperor imperā́t·or -ṓris *m; (title chosen by Augustus)* prī́nc·eps -ipis *m*

faction fácti·ō -ṓnis *f*

fellow citizen cī́v·is -is *mf* suus (a)

get somewhere áliquid cṓnsequ·or -ī cōnsecū́tus sum

govern *(a province)* praesíd·eō -ḗre praesḗdī (+ *acc or dat*); **to govern the country** rem públicam gubernā́re

government rēs *f* pública *(gen:* reī públicae) *(also written as one word)*

governor praes·es -idis *mf,* gubernā́t·or -ṓris *m* (·rīx -rī́cis *f*); *(of a minor province)* prōcūrā́t·or -ṓris *m*

graft ámbit·us -ūs *m*

head of state rēct·or -ṓris *m* cīvitā́tis

hold *(an office)* ger·ō -ere gessī gestus

imperial imperiā́l·is -is -e

law lēx, lēgis *f; (divine law)* fas *n (indecl);* **in accordance with the law** lēge

leave *(office)* áb·eō -íre -iī (+ *abl*)

legally lēgítimē

legislator lēgislā́t·or -ṓris *m* (·rīx -rī́cis *f*) *(in Roman government, a proposer of a bill)*

lower class ōrd·ō -inis *m* īnférior

magistracy magistrā́t·us -ūs *m*

magistrate magistrā́t·us -ūs *m*

mayor praeféct·us -ī *m* urbī; mā́i·or -ṓris *mf*

motion senténti·a -ae *f;* **on my motion** mē referénte; **to approve a motion** senténtiam comprobā́re; **to make a motion regarding** réferō reférre réttulī relā́tus dē (+ *abl);* **to oppose a motion** senténtiae *(dat)* obsíst·ō -ere óbstitī

middle class ōrd·ō -inis *m* médius; *(in Rome)* équit·ēs -um *mpl*

municipality mūnicípi·um -ī *n*

neutral nullī́us partis (esse)

office hon·or -ṓris *m,* magistrā́t·us -ūs *m;* **to gain an office** magistrā́tum *(or* honṓrem) ádsequ·or -ī adsecū́tus sum

opponent adversā́ri·us -ī *m* (·a -ae *f); (for office)* competī́t·or -ṓris *m* (·rīx -rī́cis *f*)

party par·s -tis *f;* **to join a party** partī sē adiúng·ō -gere -xī

pass (a law) (rogātiṓnem *or* lēgem) pérferō perférre pértulī perlā́tus

patrician patríci·us -a -um

plebeian plēbéi·us -a -um

plebs plēbs, plēbis *f*

political cīvíl·is -is -e; **for political reasons** reī públicae causā; **political affairs** (*or* **matters**) rēs, rērum *fpl* cīvílēs

political career curs·us -ūs *m* honórum

politician vir, virī *m* cīvílis

politics rēs, reī *f* pública; rēs, reī *f* cīvílis (*also plural*); **to enter politics** rem públicam íneō ínīre inívī *or* íniī; **to take part in politics** in rē públicā vers·or -árī -átus sum

polling booth saept·um -ī *n*

polls saept·a -órum *npl*

praetor praet·or -óris *m*

praetorship praetúr·a -ae *f*

preside (over) praesíd·eō -ére praesédī (+ *dat*)

president praésid·ēns -éntis *m*

propose (a law) (lēgem) ferō ferre tulī lātus

province prōvínci·a -ae *f*

quaestor quaest·or -óris *m*

quaestorship quaestúr·a -ae *f*

ratify a bill lēgem iúb·eō -ére iussī iussus

recording secretary (*in the Roman senate*) librári·us -ī *m*

reject a bill lēgem (*or* rogātiónem) antīquáre

representative vīcári·us -ī *m* (·a -ae *f*)

republicans repúblicán·ī -órum *mpl* (·ae -árum *fpl*); (*in ancient Rome*) optimát·ēs -ium *mpl*

retire in ótium sē réferō reférre réttulī

rule *tr* reg·ō -ere rēxī rēctus

run for (*an office*) pet·ō -ere petívī petítus; **to run for office** pétere

senate building cúri·a -ae *f*

senate senát·us -ūs *m*

senate session senát·us -ūs *m;* **to call (hold) a senate session** senátum vocáre (háb·eō -ére -uī -itus)

senator senát·or -óris *mf*

senatorial senātóri·us -a -um

shake hands (*when campaigning*) manūs prēnsáre

shun publicity forum ac lūcem fúg·iō -ere fūgī fūgitúrus

spirit of the law volúnt·ās -átis *f* lēgis

squeeze the flesh (*when campaigning*) prēnsáre

state (*the state as a community*) cívit·ās -átis *f;* (*of the U.S.*) cívitās foederáta

statesman vir, virī *m* cīvílis

statute lēx, lēgis *f*

tariff portóri·um -ī *n*

tax vectíg·al -ális *n;* **to impose a tax on** vectígal impón·ō -ere impósuī impósitus (+ *dat*)

tax collector exáct·or -óris *m* (·rīx -rícis *f*)

term of office spáti·um -ī *n* (témporis) potestátis

town óppid·um -ī *n*

tribune of the people tribún·us -ī *m* plébis

tribunician power tribūnícia potést·ās -átis *f*

unanimously ūnā vóce

United States (of America) Ūnítī Statūs (Amerícae) (*gen:* Ūnītórum Státuum) *mpl;* Cīvītát·ēs -um *fpl* Foederátae Amerícae

upper class ōrd·ō -inis *m* supérior

upset (*at the polls*) offénsi·ō -ónis *f;* **to suffer an upset** offēnsiónem ferō ferre tulī lātus

veto *s* intercéssi•ō -ónis *f;* **to interpose a veto** intercéd•ō -ere intercéssī

veto *tr* intercéd•ō -ere intercéssī (+ *dat*)

vice president vice praésid•ēns -éntis *mf*

vote *s* suffrági•um -ī *n;* **a vote was taken on his motion** *(in the senate by moving to one side of the chamber)* discéssiō facta est in eius senténtiam; **to call for a vote** *(in the senate)* discessiónem fác•iō -ere fēcī factus

vote *intr* suffrágium ferō ferre tulī lātus; *(of a senator)* cēns•eō -ére -uī; **to vote for** suffrāgā́rī (+ *dat*)

voting booth saept•um -ī *n*

win *(office)* ádsequ•or -ī adsecútus sum, adipísc•or -ī adéptus sum

Chapter XXI: War and Peace

CONVERSATIONS

┌──────── LEVEL I   **Jenna finds that Dennis joined the army.**

Ienna   Salvē, Dennis. Ex quō témpore   *Jenna: Hello, Dennis. Since when*
             fuístī ōrnắtū mīlitắrī?   *have you been in military*
                                                  uniform?

Dennis   Abhinc quīnque ferē mēnsēs in   ***Dennis:*** *I went into the service*
             mīlítiam inī́vī.   *about five months ago.*

Ienna   Quandō rudīménta mīlitária   *When did you complete basic*
             cōnfēcístī?   *training?*

Dennis   Abhinc duōs mēnsēs. Nōn iam   *Two months ago. I am no longer*
             tīrō rudis sum!   *a raw recruit!*

Ienna   Quámdiū rudīménta mīlitária   *How long did basic training last?*
             dūrāvḗrunt?

Dennis   Dūrāvḗrunt quáttuor mēnsēs.   *It lasted four months. Now I am*
             Nunc domī sum in commeắtū.   *home on furlough.*

Ienna   Quámdiū iam domī es?   *How long have you been home?*

Dennis   Commeắtum trīgíntā diḗrum   *I got a thirty-day furlough.*
             impetrắvī.

Ienna   Quandō est commeắtūs diēs?   *When is your furlough up?*

Dennis   Crās profḗctō erit commeắtūs   *It'll be up tomorrow in fact.*
             diēs.

Ienna   Redībísne crās in castra?   *Will you return to camp*
                                                  tomorrow?

Dennis   Rēctē dīcis. Bene valē, Ienna.   *That's right. [lit: you speak*
                                                  correctly.] Bye-bye, Jenna.

┌─────── LEVEL II   **A grandson asks his grandfather about his military service.**

Cólinus	Erásne, tata, in mīlítiā inter Bellum Secúndum Mundánum?	**Colin:** *Granddad, were you in the service during the Second World War?*
Avus	Ita, mī nepōs. Ego et amícī omnēs in mīlítiam ívimus postquam bellum in Eurōpā exársit.	**Granddad:** *Yes, grandson. All my friends and I went into the service after war broke out in Europe.*
Cólinus	Erásne voluntárius an ēvocátus es?	*Were you a volunteer or were you called up?*
Avus	Ēvocátus sum. Dīléctus habēbátur, et ego dīléctum nōn subterfúgī.	*I was called up. They held a draft, and I did not dodge the draft.*
Cólinus	Meruistíne nauta an mīles?	*Did you serve as a sailor or a soldier?*
Avus	In exércitū méruī. Post rudīménta mīlitária, in Eurōpam ēvéctus sum. Advérsus Germániam pugnávī.	*I served in the army. After basic training, I was shipped out to Europe. I fought against Germany.*
Cólinus	Cūr advérsus Germánōs pugnāvístī?	*Why did you fight against the Germans?*
Avus	Quod Germánia foedus violáverat et cum fīnítimīs bellum íníverat.	*Because Germany had violated the treaty and had started a war with her neighbors.*
Cólinus	Cūr Germánia fīnítimīs bellum íntulit?	*Why did Germany go to war with her neighbors?*
Avus	Príncipēs enim Germániae tōtam Eurōpam superáre voluérunt.	*You see, the leaders of Germany wanted to conquer the whole of Europe.*
Cólinus	Quam diū in Eurōpā mīlitāvístī?	*How long did you serve as a soldier in Europe?*
Avus	Triénnium mīlítiam explévī ántequam nostrī sociíque coēgérunt Germánōs in dēditiónem veníre.	*I completed a three-year tour of duty before our men and our allies forced the Germans to surrender.*

| Cólinus | Gaúdeō, mī tata, tē salvum et sānum domum rediísse. | *I am glad, granddad, that you returned home safe and sound.* |
| Avus | Ego fēlīcíssimus eram. Nōn omnēs cḗterī tam fēlícēs erant. | *I was very lucky. Not all the others were so lucky.* |

LEVEL III   **Discussing the merits of alliances.**

Studēns	Mihi vidḗtur pátria nostra semper in bellīs extérnīs implicā́rī.	*Student: It seems to me that our country is always involved in foreign wars.*
Docēns	Ex foédere, pátria nostra amícīs sociísque in discrímine succúrrit.	*Instructor: According to the terms of the treaty, our country goes to the aid of its friends and allies in a crisis.*
Studēns	At América sē tam saepe bellīs extérnīs interpónit. Quī fit?	*But America so often interferes in foreign wars. How come?*
Docēns	América enim ubíque terrárum societā́tēs ad bellum dēfendéndum fēcit.	*You see, America formed defensive alliances all over the world.*
Studēns	Faciúntne adversā́riī nostrī societā́tēs ad bellum īnferéndum?	*Do our opponents form offensive alliances?*
Docēns	Utráque pars, ut opínor, facit societā́tēs ad bellum dēfendéndum. Sed áltera pars álterī partī nōn fídit. Inde armórum certámen fit.	*Each side, I suppose, forms defensive alliances. But one side does not trust the other, and that's why there's an arms race. [lit: hence an arms race comes about.]*
Studēns	Hīs condiciónibus, quemádmodum pāx inter gentēs cōnservā́rī potest?	*Under these conditions, how can peace be maintained between nations?*
Docēns	Simplex est. Utráque pars tantum apparā́tum bellī cómparat ut áltera pars álteram partem oppugnā́re nōn aúdeat.	*It is simple. Each side acquires such armaments of war that one side does not dare to attack the other.*

Studēns	At quid sī ūna cívitās ab utrā parte bellum ultrō ínferat?	*But what if one country on either side should become an aggressor in war?* [*lit: should bring on war unprovoked*]
Docēns	Tum sóciī omnēs ab álterā parte dēbent bellum indícere illī cīvitā́tī.	*Then all the allies on the other side have to declare war on that country.*
Studēns	At quidnī bellum compónunt?	*But why not terminate war by diplomacy?*
Docēns	Quod neutra pars vult imbecílla vidérī.	*Because neither side wants to seem weak.*
Studēns	Quae ígitur est solútiō?	*What then is the solution?*
Docēns	Suspíciō bonā fidē et mútuā observántiā substituénda est.	*Suspicion must be replaced by mutual trust and respect.*

Topical Vocabulary

absent without leave: to be absent without leave ad commeátūs diem nōn ad•sum -esse -fuī

active service: to be on active service stīpéndia fác•iō -ere fēcī factus

agreement foed•us -eris *n;* **according to the terms of the agreement** ex foédere

alliance foed•us -eris *n,* socíet•ās -átis *f;* **to conclude an alliance with** foedus īc•ō -ere -ī -tus cum (+ *abl*); **to form an alliance with** societátem fáciō -ere fēcī factus cum (+ *abl*)

airforce cōpi•ae -árum *fpl* áeriae

arm *tr* armáre

armaments apparát•us -ūs *m* bellī (*rarely pl of* apparátus)

armed armát•us -a -um; **to be armed** in armís esse

arms: arm•a -órum *npl;* **arms race** armórum certám•en -inis *n;* **by force of arms** vī et armís; **to be under arms** in armís esse; **to lay down**

arms ab armís discéd•ō -ere discéssī; **to take up arms** arma cáp•iō -ere cēpī captus

army exércit•us -ūs *m;* **to raise an army** exércitum comparáre

army buddy contubernál•is -is *mf*

artillery tormént•a -órum *npl*

barracks mílitum contubérni•um-ī *n*

basic training rudīménta *npl* mīlitária (*gen* rudīmentórum *npl* mīlitárium)

battle pugn•a -ae *f,* proéli•um -ī *n (in a country:* in (+ *abl*); *at or near a town* apud (+ *acc*), circā + *acc*); **in battle** proéliō; **naval battle off Tenedos** pugna nāvális ante Ténedum; **successful battle** proélium secúndum; **to fight a battle** proélium fác•iō -ere fēcī factus

battalion coh•ors -órtis *f*

battalion commander praeféctus -ī *m* cohórtis

battlefield áci•ēs -éī *f*

besiege (blockade) a town óppidum obsíd·ō -ere obsédī obséssus

bomb *s* bomb·a -ae *f;* **atomic bomb** bomba atómica; **nuclear bomb** bomba nucleáris

bomb *tr* bombīs oppugnáre

bomber āeróplan·um -ī *n* bombíferum

call up the troops ēvocáre cópiās

camp castr·a -órum *npl*

campaign expedíti·ō -ónis *f,* stīpéndi·um -ī *n*

cavalry equitát·us -ūs *m*

cease-fire indúti·ae -árum *fpl;* **the cease-fire is holding** indútiae dūrant; **to call for a cease-fire** indútiās posc·ō -ere popóscī

cohort coh·ors -órtis *f*

colonel tribún·us -ī *m* mílitum

combat proéli·um -ī *n,* pugn·a -ae *f;* **in hand-to-hand combat** cómminus *(adv)*

combatant proeliát·or -óris *m* (·rīx -rícis *f*)

command imperi·um -ī *n;* **to be in command (of)** prae·sum -esse -fuī (+ *dat*)

commander in chief imperát·or -óris *m;* **to be the commander in chief** impérii summam tén·eō -ére ténuī; impérii summae prae·sum -ésse -fuī

commence hostilities bellī inítium fác·iō -ere fécī factus

company centúri·a -ae *f*

company commander centúri·ō -ónis *m*

concentrate all the troops in one place cōg·ō -ere coégī coáctus omnēs cópiās in ūnum locum

conquer vinc·ō -ere vícī victus; **to conquer a country** terrā pót·ior -írī potítus sum

corporal decúri·ō -ónis *mf*

crack troops róbor·a -um *npl* péditum

critical: the situation is critical rēs est in summō discrímine

defeat *s* clád·ēs -is *f;* **to suffer a defeat** clādem accíp·iō -ere accépī accéptus

defeat *tr* superáre, vinc·ō -ere vícī victus

defensive and offensive alliance socíet·ās -átis *f* ad bellum dēfendéndum atque īnferéndum facta

defensive and offensive weapons tēl·a -órum *npl* ad tegéndum et ad nocéndum

disarm s.o. áliquem armīs éxu·ō -ere -ī -útus

dodge the draft mīlítiam subter·fúgiō -fúgere -fúgī

draft dīléct·us -ūs *m;* **to hold a draft** dīléctum háb·eō -ére -uī -itus

draft-dodger quī mīlítiam subtérfugit

drag out a war bellum trah·ō -ere traxī tractus

end fín·is -is *m;* **to put an end to a war** bellī fínem fác·iō -ere fécī factus

enemy host·ēs -ium *mpl*

enlist nōmen (*of several:* nómina) dō dare dedī

exchange prisoners captívōs permūtáre *or* commūtáre

exempt: to be exempt from military service mīlítiae vacātiónem háb·eō -ére -uī

exemption from military service mīlítiae vacáti·ō -ónis *f*

force: large force magnae cópiae *fpl;* **small force** exíguae cópiae

fort castéll·um -ī *n*

furlough commeát·us -ūs *m;* **end of the furlough** commeátūs di·ēs -éī *m;* **to get a furlough** commeátum impetráre

garrison praesídi·um -ī *n*

general dux, ducis *mf*

gun tormént·um -ī *n*

headquarters praetóri·um -ī *n*

helmet cass·is -idis *f*

hold out: the town held out for four months óppidum obsidiónem quáttuor mēnsēs sustínuit

home front: on the home front and on the front lines domī et mīlítiae *(or* in mīlítiā*)*

hostage obs·es -idis *mf*

infantry peditát·us -ūs *m*

infantryman ped·es -itis *m*

international law iūs, iūris *n* géntium

invade bellum ínferō īnférre íntulī illátus *(+ dat),* cum exércitū ingréd·ior -ī ingréssus sum

leave of absence commeát·us -ūs *m*

legion légi·ō -ónis *f*

lieutenant locumtén·ēns -éntis *mf*

march iter fác·iō -ere fēcī factus

marines classiári·ī -órum *mpl*

military mīlitár·is -is -e; **military age** aet·ās -átis *f* mīlitáris; **military service** mīlíti·a -ae *f;* **the military** mīlíti·a -ae *f;* **to enter military service** mīlítiam in·eō -íre -ívī *or* -iī; **to perform military service** mīlitáre

naval nāvál·is -is -e

navy cópi·ae -árum *fpl* nāválēs; **to have a powerful navy** nāvibus plúrimum posse

officer praeféct·us -ī *m;* **cavalry officer** praeféctus équitum

operations: to conduct military operations in the Gallic War rēs ger·ō -ere gessī Gállicō bellō

peace pāx, pācis *f;* **in peace and in war** domī et mīlítiae *(or* in mīlítiā*)*; **peace is concluded on condition that …** pāx cónvenit in eam condiciónem ut

… ; **to break the peace** pācem frang·ō -ere frēgī frāctus; **to bring about peace** pācem conciliáre; **to have peace negotiations with s.o.** ag·ō -ere ēgī āctus cum áliquō dē pāce; **to make peace with** pācem fác·iō -ere fēcī factus cum *(+ abl)*

prisoner of war captív·us -ī *m,* captív·a -ae *f;* **ransom prisoners** captívōs rédim·ō -ere redémī redémptus

private mīl·es -itis *mf* gregárius (-a)

promote prōmóv·eō -ére prōmóvī prōmótus; **to promote to higher rank** ad *(or* in*)* ampliórem gradum prōmovére

promotion prōmóti·ō -ónis *f*

raid excúrsi·ō -ónis *f*

raise the siege on the town óppidum obsidióne līberáre

rank grad·us -ūs *m*

raze a town to the ground óppidum solō aequáre

recruit tīr·ō -ónis *m;* **raw recruit** tīrō rudis

recruit troops dīléctum ag·ō -ere ēgī āctus

recruitment dīléct·us -ūs *m*

regiment légi·ō -ónis *f*

regimental commander legiónis legát·us -ī *m*

retake a town óppidum recíp·iō -ere recépī recéptus

review the army exércitum recéns·eō -ére -uī, lūstráre

rifle sclopét·um -ī *n*

sailor naut·a -ae *m* (·ria -riae *f*)

send relief to subsídium summítt·ō -ere summísī summíssus *(+ dat)*

sergeant opti·ō -ónis *mf*

serve stīpéndia fác·iō -ere fēcī factus, (stīpéndium) mér·eō -ére -uī; **to**

serve as a soldier or sailor (ut) mīles aut nauta merḗre

serviceman mīlitắr·is -is *m*

ship nāv·is -is *f*

shoot (*a person*) sclopétō trānsfǐg·ō -ere trānsfǐxī trānsfǐxus

soldier mǐl·es -itis *mf*

starve a town into surrender óppidum fāme dom·ō -ắre dómuī

storm a town óppidum oppugnắre

submarine nāv·is -is *f* submarǐna

success rēs, reī *f* fēlǐciter gesta, rēs bene gesta

supplies commeắt·us -ūs *m* (*used both as collective singular and in the plural*); **to cut off the enemy's supplies** inter·clǖdō -clǘdere -clǘsī hostēs commeắtibus

supply: to supply s.o. with men and arms álicui virōs et arma ministrắre

surrender *s* dēdíti·ō -ṓnis *f*

surrender *intr* sē dē·dō -dere -didī; **to force a people to surrender** pópulum in dēditiṓnem venǐre cōg·ō -ere coḗgī coáctus

swear in the soldiers mǐlitēs sacrāméntō ádig·ō -ere adḗgī adáctus

tactics: to change one's tactics ratiṓnem bellī geréndī mūtắre

tank autocúrr·us -ūs *m* armắtus

terms condiciṓn·ēs -um *fpl;* **on these terms** hīs condiciṓnibus; **to be on friendly terms with a country** in amīcítiā pópulī esse; **to stick by the terms** in condiciṓnibus mán·eō -ḗre mānsī

terms of peace pācis condiciṓn·ēs -um *fpl;* **to accept terms of peace** pācis condiciṓnēs accípi·ō -ere accḗpī (*opp:* repudiắre); **to dictate terms of peace to** pācis condiciṓnēs dīc·ō -ere dīxī (+ *dat*); **to propose terms of**

peace pācis condiciṓnēs ferō ferre tulī lātus

terrain nātǔr·a -ae *f* locī

theater of operations bellī sēd·ēs -is *f*

tour of duty mīlíti·a -ae *f;* **to complete a three-year tour of duty** triénnium mīlítiae éxpl·eō -ḗre -ḗvī -ḗtus

treaty foed·us -eris *n;* **according to the terms of the treaty** ex pactō, ex foédere; **to break a treaty** foedus frang·ō -ere frēgī frāctus; **to conclude a treaty with** foedus ǐcō ǐcere ǐcī ictus *or* fér·iō -ǐre cum (+ *abl*); **to violate a treaty** foedus violắre

truce indǘti·ae -ắrum *fpl;* **a six-years' truce** indǘtiae annṓrum sex; **to break a truce** indǘtiās violắre; **to make a truce** indǘtiās fácere

turn in weapons arma trād·ō -ere trắdidī trắditus

uniform ōrnắt·us -ūs *m* mīlitắris

veteran veterắn·us ī *m,* ēmérit·us -ī *m*

victory victṓri·a -ae *f;* **to gain** (*or* win) **a victory** victṓriam adipǐsc·or -ī adéptus sum; **to gain** (*or* win) **a victory over the enemy** victṓriam reportắre ab hoste; **to let a sure victory slip through one's fingers** victṓriam explōrắtam dīmítt·ō -ere dīmǐsī

volunteer voluntắri·us -ī *m* (·a -ae *f*)

war (against *or* **with)** bell·um -ī *n* (contrā *or* advérsus (+ *acc*) *or* cum (+ *abl*); **civil war** bellum cīvǐle *or* domésticum; **in war** bellō, bellī témpore; **foreign war** bellum extérnum; **guerilla war** bellum clandestǐnum; **in war and in peace** pāce bellṓque, domī bellṓque; **offensive war** (*of war yet to be begun*) bellum ultrō īnferéndum; (*of war already begun*) bellum ultrō illắtum; **to be involved in a war** bellō implicắrī; **to bring a war to a**

successful conclusion bellum cōnfíc·iō -ere cōnfḗcī cōnféctus; **to carry on war with** bellum ger·ō -ere gessī gestus cum (+ *abl*); **to cause a war** bellum móv·eō -ḗre mōvī mōtus; **to conduct a war** *(of a general)* bellum administrā́re; **to declare war on** bellum indī́c·ō -ere indī́xī indíctus (+ *dat*); **to drag out a war** bellum trah·ō -ere traxī tractus; **to end a war** bellum perfíc·iō -ere perfḗcī perféctus; **to fight a war with** bellum ger·ō -ere gessī gestus cum (+ *abl*); **to fight a war of aggression with** bellum *or* arma ultrō ī́nferō ī́nférre ī́ntulī illā́tus (+ *dat*); **to go off to war** proficī́sc·or -ī profḗctus sum ad bellum; **to go to war with** bellum ī́nferō ī́nférre ī́ntulī illā́tus (+ *dat*); **to prepare for war** bellum (com)parā́re; **to send to war** mitt·ō -ere mī́sī missus ad bellum; **to start a war with** bellum ín·eō -íre -ī́vī *or*

-íī cum (+ *abl*); **to stir up a war** bellum concitā́re *or* incitā́re; **to take part in a war** bellum capéss·ō -ere; **to terminate a war by diplomacy** bellum compṓn·ō -ere compósuī compósitus; **to wage war with** bellum ger·ō -ere gessī gestus cum (+ *abl*); **war against pirates** bellum pīrā́ticum; **war against slaves** bellum servī́le; **war is imminent** bellum ímminet *or* impḗndet *or* ī́nstat; **war of extermination** bellum internecī́num; **war breaks out** bellum exārdḗscit

warfare bell·um -ī *n*

weapons *(offensive)* tēl·a -ṓrum *npl*; *(defensive)* arm·a -ṓrum *npl*

win vinc·ō -ere vī́cī victus; **to win a battle** proéliō víncere

world war bellum mundā́num

years of service stīpéndi·a -ṓrum *npl*

Chapter XXII: Law and Criminal Justice

CONVERSATIONS _____

┌──────── LEVEL I   **News of an important trial.**

Rebécca	Salvē, Antṓnī. Unde venīs?	*Rebecca: Hello, Anthony. Where are you coming from?*
Antṓnius	Ā basílicā Iū́liā ā forō.	*Anthony: From the Julian courthouse in the forum.*
Rebécca	Quid ibi fiḗbat?	*What was going on there?*
Antṓnius	Iūdícium nōtum fiḗbat.	*A notorious trial was taking place.*
Rebécca	Quis iūs dīcḗbat?	*Who presided as judge?*
Antṓnius	Nésciō quis senā́tor.	*Some senator or other.*
Rebécca	Quis erat reus?	*Who was the defendant?*
Antṓnius	Negōtiā́tor. Em vḗrō pátruus meus.	*A businessman. Well, in fact, my uncle.*
Rebécca	Quis crī́mina in eum íntulit?	*Who brought charges against him?*
Antṓnius	Horténsius, amī́cus Cicerṓnis, erat accūsā́tor.	*Hortensius, Cicero's friend, was the prosecutor.*
Rebécca	Quis erat eius dēfḗnsor?	*Who was the defense lawyer?*
Antṓnius	Mū́cius Scaévola.	*Mucius Scaevola.*
Rebécca	Quae crī́mina in pátruum tuum íntulit?	*What charges did he bring against your uncle?*
Antṓnius	Horténsius eum míserum pecūlā́tūs accūsā́vit.	*Hortensius accused the poor guy of embezzlement.*
Rebécca	Prōdiḗrunt multī testḗs?	*Did many witnesses step forward?*
Antṓnius	Erant trēs tantúmmodo.	*There were only three.*

Rebécca	Quī?	*Who?*
Antṓnius	Duo sóciī eius et argentárius.	*Two associates of his and the banker.*

Rebécca	Estne absolū́tus an condemnā́tus?	*Was he acquitted or found guilty?*
Antṓnius	Absolū́tus est quidem ómnibus senténtiīs.	*Of course, he was acquitted unanimously.*

┌──────── LEVEL II   **The arrest of two hoodlums draws a crowd.**

Rīta	Quid reī est, praefécte? Cūr tanta turba hūc congregátur?	*Rita: What's up, Chief? Why is such a large crowd gathering here?*
Praeféctus vígilum	Modo apprehéndimus duōs nōtōs grassātṓrēs.	*Chief of Police: We just arrested two notorious hoodlums.*
Rīta	Quid áccidit?	*What happened?*
Praeféctus	Latrōcínium modo factum est.	*A robbery just took place.*
Rīta	Ubi?	*Where?*
Praeféctus	Istī latrṓnēs macéllum intrāvḗrunt et macellā́rium omnī argéntō eius spoliāvḗrunt.	*Those robbers entered the grocery store and robbed the grocer of all his money.*
Rīta	Latrōnḗsne macellā́riō vim attulḗrunt?	*Did the robbers assault the grocer?*
Praeféctus	Étiam. Istī macellā́rium fū́stibus concīdḗrunt.	*Yes, they beat the grocer up with clubs.*
Rīta	Effūgērúntne latrṓnēs?	*Did the robbers get away?*
Praeféctus	Nūllō modō! Vígilēs meī apprehendḗrunt istōs grassātṓrēs et mánicās eīs iniēcḗrunt.	*No way! My officers arrested those hoodlums and put handcuffs on them.*
Rīta	Ubi sunt istī latrṓnēs nunc?	*Where are those robbers now?*
Praeféctus	Vígilēs rapuḗrunt eōs in cárcerem.	*The police hauled them off to jail.*
Rīta	Nṓnne arguéntur dē latrōcíniō?	*They'll be charged with robbery, won't they?*
Praeféctus	Arguéntur dē vī et manū atque latrōcíniō.	*They'll be charged with assault and battery as well as with robbery.*

Rīta	Viae urbis nostrae nōn diútius tūtae sunt. Ego véreor nē per mē obsṓnem.	*The streets of our city are no longer safe. I am afraid to go shopping by myself.*
Praeféctus	Uxor mea idem dīcit.	*My wife says the same thing.*
Rīta	Spērō iúdicem summō iūre cum istīs āctū́rum esse.	*I hope the judge throws the book at them.*
Praeféctus	Adulēscéntula, ego hábeō máximam fidem nostrae ratiṓnī iūdiciā́lī.	*Young lady, I have the greatest confidence in our judicial system.*

┌─────────── LEVEL III   **A client gets himself a lawyer.**

Cliēns	Dēsī́derō iūriscōnsúltum. Potésne mihi succúrrere?	***Client:*** *I need a lawyer. Can you help me?*
Patrṓnus	Quid est? Estne causa prīvā́ta an causa pública?	***Patron:*** *What is it? Is it a civil or a criminal case?*
Cliēns	Est causa pública. Áliquis paríetem domūs meae perfṓdit.	*It's a criminal case. Someone broke into my home.*
Patrṓnus	Quandō effrāctū́ra facta est?	*When did the break-in take place?*
Cliēns	Médiā nocte, dum ego et família ábsumus.	*At midnight, while I and the family were away.*
Patrṓnus	Quid perfossṓrēs sustulḗrunt?	*What did the robbers steal?*
Cliēns	Pecúniam, pictū́rās, argéntea.	*Money, pictures, and silverware.*
Patrṓnus	Scīsne quis paríetēs perfṓderit?	*Do you know who broke into your home?*
Cliēns	Nésciō.	*No, I don't.*
Patrṓnus	Aderántne oculā́tī testēs?	*Were there any eyewitnesses?*
Cliēns	Ūnus ex vīcī́nīs meīs, nōmine Varrō.	*One of my neighbors, named Varro.*
Patrṓnus	Quid vīdit?	*What did he see?*
Cliēns	Vīdit et perfossṓrem et índicem eius.	*He saw the robber and his lookout man.*
Patrṓnus	Volḗtne testis prōdī́re?	*Will he be willing to step forward as a witness.*

Cliēns	Volet.	*Yes, he will.*
Patrốnus	Arcessīvistíne vígilēs?	*Did you call the police?*

Cliēns	Arcessívī. Vígilēs mīsérunt investīgātốrem ad mē. Investīgấtor iam coếgit nōnnúllōs suspéctōs.	*I did. The police sent an investigator to my home. The investigator has already rounded up several suspects.*
Patrốnus	Macte virtŭte estō! Ego suspéctōs quam prīmum in iūdícium addŭcam. Mihi crēde, mox in cárcere sedébunt.	*Good for you! I will take the suspects to court as soon as possible. Believe me, they will soon be sitting in jail.*

TOPICAL VOCABULARY

accusation accūsấti·ō -ốnis *f*

accuse accūsấre *(with acc of person and gen or* dē + *abl of the charge);* **to accuse s.o. of a capital offense** áliquem reī capitấlis re·um (-am) fácere

acquit (of) absólv·ō -ere -ī absolŭtus (dē + *abl; more rarely w. gen);* **to acquit s.o. of a capital crime** áliquem cápitis absólvere

acquittal absolŭti·ō -ốnis *f*

adjourn *tr* ampliấre

alimony alimốni·um -ī *n*

allegation: false allegation falsa īnsimulấti·ō -ốnis *f*

allege árgu·ō -ere -ī -ŭtus

appeal *s* appellấti·ō -ốnis *f;* **to allow an appeal** appellātiốnem admítt·ō -ere admī́sī admíssus; **to disallow an appeal** appellātiốnem improbấre

appeal *intr* **(to)** appellấre (ad + *acc)*

arrest apprehén·dō -dere -dī -sus

assault *s* vīs *f (acc:* vim; *abl:* vī); **to accuse s.o. of assault (and battery)** aliquem dē vī (et manū) accūsấre; **to commit assault against** vim fác·iō -ere fḗcī factus in (+ *acc)*

assault *tr* vim fác·iō -ere fḗcī factus in (+ *acc)*

attack *see* **assault**

attorney cógnit·or -ốris *m* (·rīx -rī́cis *f);* **to appoint an attorney to s.o.** cognitốrem álicui adscrī́b·ō -ere adscrī́psī adscrī́ptus

bar: to serve at the bar in iūdíciīs versấrī; in forō ag·ō -ere ḗgī

beat (with fists, clubs) (pugnīs, fŭstibus) caed·ō -ere cecī́dī caesus; **to beat up** concī́d·ō -ere -ī concī́sus

blame *s* culp·a -ae *f*

blame *tr* culpấre; **I am to blame** in culpā sum; **to blame s.o. for** áliquem culpấre ob (+ *acc)*

bludgeon *s* fŭst·is -is *m*

bludgeon *tr* fŭste *(or* fŭstibus) concī́d·ō -ere concī́dī concī́sus; **to bludgeon to death** fūstigấre

break into a home domūs paríetēs perfód·iō -ere perfốdī perfóssus

breaking and entering, break-in effrāctŭr·a -ae *f*

bribe *tr* corrúmp·ō -ere corrū́pī corrúptus

bribe *s* préti·um -ī *n*

bribery corruptél·a -ae *f;* **influenced by bribery** corrúpt·us -a -um

burglar effráct·or -óris *m* (·rīx -rícis *f*), perfóss·or -óris *m* (·trīx -trícis *f*); **to commit a burglary** paríetēs perfód·iō -ere perfódī perfóssus

burglary (domūs) latrōcíni·um -ī *n*

capital punishment supplíci·um -ī *n* cápitis; **to suffer capital punishment** supplíciō cápitis affícior áffícī afféctus sum

case caus·a -ae *f,* līs, lītis *f;* **civil case** causa prīváta; **criminal case** causa pública; **to lose a case** causam per·dō -dere -didī; **to plead a case** causam ag·ō -ere ēgī *or* dīc·ō -ere dīxī; **to settle a case (out of court)** lītem compón·ō -ere compósuī compósitus; **to win a case** causā (*or* iūdíciō) vinc·ō -ere vīcī victus

character witness advocát·us -ī *m* (·a -ae *f*)

charge *s* crīm·en -inis *n;* **capital charge** capitále crīmen; **false charge** calúmni·a -ae *f;* **to bring** *or* **file charges against s.o.** crímina álicui ínferō īnférre íntulī illátus

charge *tr* **to charge s.o. with a crime** áliquem crímine (*or* dē crímine *or* críminis) árgu·ō -ere -ī

chief of police praeféct·us -ī *m* vígilum

civil rights iūr·a -ium *npl* cīvília; **to deprive s.o. of civil rights** áliquem cápite dēmín·uō -úere -uī -útus

client cli·ēns -éntis *mf*

commit (a crime) (scelus) committ·ō -ere commísī commíssus

condemn condemnáre

convict convínc·ō -ere convícī convíctus (*w. acc. of the person and w. gen of the charge*); **convicted of** manifést·us -a (+ *gen*); **to convict s.o. on many counts of fraud** áliquem multīs crímínibus fraudis convíncere

conviction (for) condemnáti·ō -ónis *f* (+ *gen of the charge*)

counselor iūrisperít·us -ī *m* (·a -ae *f*)

count crīm·en -inis *n*

court iūdíci·um -ī *n;* **court of appeal** iūdícium appellātórium; **to hold court** iūs dīc·ō -ere dīxī dictus; **to take s.o. to court** áliquem in iūdícium addúc·ō -ere addúxī addúctus *or* vocáre

courthouse basílic·a -ae *f;* **Julian courthouse** basílica Iúlia (*begun by Julius Caesar in 54 B.C.*)

crime fácin·us -oris *n,* scel·us -eris *n,* crīm·en -inis *n* (*more often means merely the charge*)

custody custódi·a -ae *f;* **to be held in custody** in custódiā háb·eor -érī hábitus sum; **to take into custody** in custódiam trā·dō -dere -didī -ditus

death: to condemn s.o. to death áliquem cápitis damnáre; **to put s.o. to death** supplícium cápitis dē áliquō sūm·ō -ere sūmpsī sūmptus

death sentence: to receive the death sentence cápitis damnárī

death penalty supplíci·um -ī *n* cápitis

defend s.o. causam alicúius dēfénd·ō -ere -ī

defendant re·us -ī *m,* re·a -ae *f*

defense lawyer dēféns·or -óris *m* (·trīx -trícis *f*)

deprive: to deprive s.o. of áliquem prīváre (+ *abl*)

detective inquīsít·or -óris *m* (·rīx -rícis *f*)

divorce *tr* dīvórti·um fácere cum (+ *abl*)

divorce *s* dīvórti·um -ī *n;* **to seek a divorce** dīvórtium pet·ō -ere -ívī -ítus

embezzlement pecūlát·us -ūs *m*

enforce the law lēgem exérc•eō -ére -uī -itus

evidence testimṓni•um -ī *n;* **on what evidence will you convict me?** quō mē teste convíncēs?; **this evidence is not admissible** hoc testimṓnium nōn sūméndum est; **to give evidence against s.o.** testimṓnium dīc•ō -ere dīxī in áliquem; **to turn state's evidence** indícium profít•eor -ḗrī proféssus sum

extortion violénta exácti•ō -ṓnis *f* pecūniárum

eyewitness oculátus (a) test•is -is *mf*

fair aequ•us -a -um

falsely falsō

fault culp•a -ae *f;* **to be at fault** in culpā esse; **to not be at fault** extrā culpam esse

fine s.o. multáre áliquem (+ *abl of the fine)*

fraud frau•s -dis *f*

gang man•us -ūs *f*

gangster, gang member praed•ō -ṓnis *m* gregális

guard *s* custōdiári•us -ī *m* (•a -ae *f*)

guard *tr* custṓd•iō -íre -ívī *or* -iī -ītus

guilty re•us -a -um, sōn•s -tis; **guilty of** nóxi•us -a -um (+ *abl or gen);* **the guilty one** sōn•s -tis *mf;* **to be found guilty** nóxius iūdicárī; **to be guilty** in culpā esse; **to punish the guilty** poenam dē sóntibus éxig•ō -ere exḗgī exáctus

handcuff *tr* mánicās iníc•iō -ere iniḗcī iniéctus (+ *dat)*

handcuffs mánic•ae -árum *fpl*

haul off to prison ráp•iō -ere -uī -tus in cárcerem

hearing cogníti•ō -ṓnis *f;* **to hold a hearing** cognitiṓnem háb•eō -ére -uī -itus

homicide homicídi•um -ī *n*

hoodlum grassát•or -ṓris *m*

house arrest custṓdi•a -ae *f* líbera

hung jury: to be acquitted by a hung jury senténtiīs páribus absólv•or -ī absolútus sum

impartial incorrúpt•us -a -um et inte•ger -gra -grum

indict s.o. áliquem re•um (-am) fác•iō -ere fēcī factus

informant ind•ex -icis *mf*

innocent ínnoc•ēns -éntis

interrogate interrogáre

investigate investīgáre

investigator investīgát•or -ṓris *m* (•rīx -rícis *f*)

jail carc•er -eris *m*

jailer custōdiári•us -ī *m* (•a -ae *f*)

judge iūd•ex -icis *mf;* **to sit as judge (hold court)** iūs dīc•ō -ere dīxī

judicial iūdiciál•is -is -e; **judicial system** ráti•ō -ṓnis *f* iūdiciális

juror iūd•ex -icis *mf*

jury cōnsíli•um -ī *n;* iúdic•ēs -um *mpl*

just iūst•us -a -um

justice iūstíti•a -ae *f*

justly iūstē

law lēx, lēgis *f; (denoting the entire body of law)* iūs, iūris *n;* **against the law** contrā iūs; *(against a specific law)* contrā lēgem; **by law** lēge; **in accordance with the law** secúndum lēgem; **to break the law** lēgem violáre

lawsuit lī•s -tis *f;* **to bring** (*or* **file) a lawsuit against s.o.** lītem álicui inténd•ō -ere -ī

lawyer iūriscōnsúlt•us -ī *m* (•a -ae *f*); *(trial lawyer)* causídic•us -ī *m* (•a -ae *f*); *(for the defense)* advocát•us -ī *m* (•a -ae *f*)

legal lēgítim·us -a -um, secúndum
lēgem *or* lēgēs

legally lēgítimē, lēge

**life imprisonment: give s.o. life
imprisonment** áliquem damnáre
cárcerī quoad vīvat

lock up *(in prison)* in cárcerem
compíng·ō -ere -ī compēgī
compáctus

look-out ind·ex -icis *mf*

murder *s* nex, necis *f (passive in sense
while* caedēs *is active in sense); (by
hacking or striking)* caed·ēs -is *f,*
occísi·ō -ōnis *f*

murder *tr (by wicked and cruel means)*
necáre; *(violently and ruthlessly)*
trūcīdáre; *(by hacking or striking)*
caed·ō -ere cecídī caesus

murderer necát·or -ōris *m,* homicíd·a
-ae *mf; (of a father, mother, or near
relative)* parricíd·a -ae *mf*

murderess necátr·īx -ícis *f*

notorious nōt·us -a -um, īnfám·is -is -e

offenses dēlíct·a -ōrum *npl*

officer vig·il -ilis *mf*

pardon véni·a -ae *f; to grant s.o. a
pardon* véniam álicui dō dare dedī;
to obtain pardon véniam impetráre

penalty poen·a -ae *f; to pay the penalty*
poenās persólv·ō -ere -ī, poenās dō
dare dedī datus

perjure oneself pēieráre

perjury periŭri·um -ī *n; to commit
perjury* pēieráre

personal injury iniŭri·a -āe *f*

plaintiff petít·or -ōris *m (·rīx -rícis f)*

plead a case before the court causam
prō tribūnálī ag·ō -ere ēgī āctus

police officer vig·il -ilis *mf*

preside at a trial iūdíciō prae·sum -esse
-fuī, iūs dīc·ō -ere dīxī dictus

presiding judge quaesít·or -ōris *m (·rīx
-rícis f)*

prison carc·er -eris *m;* **to throw s.o.
into prison** áliquem in cárcerem
conníc·iō -ere coniécī coniéctus

prosecute s.o. áliquem iūdíciō
pérsequ·or -ī persecútus sum

prosecutor accūsát·or -ōris *m,*
accūsátr·īx -ícis *f*

punish pún·iō -íre -ívī -ítus; poenā
affíc·iō -ere affécī afféctus

punishment for crimes poen·a -ae *f*
facínorum

rape stupr·um -ī *n* per vim

rape *tr* per vim stupráre, stuprō violáre

rapist stuprát·or -ōris *m*

rebut dissólv·ō -ere -ī dissolútus

rebuttal dissolúti·ō -ōnis *f*

refute dissólv·ō -ere -ī dissolútus

rob ráp·iō -ere -uī -tus; **to rob s.o. of**
áliquem spoliáre *(+ abl)*

robber latr·ō -ōnis *m; (house breaker)*
perfóss·or -ōris *m*

robbery latrōcíni·um -ī *n*

safe (from) tūt·us -a -um (ab + *abl);*
safe and sound salv·us -a -um et
sān·us -a -um; **safe from danger**
tūtus ā perículō

scot-free: to get off scot-free
impunít·us (-a) dīmítt·or -ī dīmíss·us
(-a) sum

serve a summons on diem dare *(+ dat)*

steal fūr·or -árī -átus sum; clep·ō -ere -sī
-tus; toll·ō -ere sústulī sublátus

stool pigeon ind·ex -icis *mf*

sue s.o. lītem álicui ínferō īnférre íntulī
illátus

suffer punishment poenās ferō ferre
tulī lātus

suit ácti•ō -ónis *f;* **to bring a suit against s.o.** āctiónem álicui intén•dō -dere -dī

suspect suspéct•us -ī *m,* suspéct•a -ae *f*

theft fūrt•um -ī *n*

testify test•or -árī -átus sum

thief fūr, fúris *mf*

throw the book at s.o. summō iūre cum áliquō agō ágere ēgī āctus [*lit: to deal with s.o. with the utmost (rigor of the) law*]

treason prōdíti•ō -ónis *f*

trial quaésti•ō -ónis *f,* iūdíci•um -ī *n;* **to bring to trial** in iūdícium addúc•ō -ere addúxī addúctus; **to conduct a trial** quaestiónem exérc•eō -ére -uī -itus; **to be on trial for** iūdícium dē (+ *abl*) súb•eō -íre -ívī *or* -iī; **to be**

on trial for one's life iūdícium dē cápite subíre; **to go on trial** in iūs eō íre iī *or* īvī

trial lawyer āct•or -óris *m* (•rīx -rícis *f*) causárum, causídic•us -ī *m* (•a -ae *f*)

try: to try a case (of) causam cognósc•ō -ere cognóvī cógnitus (dē + *abl*)

verdict senténti•a -ae *f;* **to give a verdict of acquittal** absolūtóriam senténtiam ferō ferre tulī lātus; **to give a guilty verdict** condemnātóriam senténtiam ferre

unanimously ómnibus senténtiīs

witness test•is -is *mf* (**for** prō + *abl;* **against** in + *acc);* **to be called as a witness** contestárī; **to come** *or* **step forward as a witness** testis pródeō pródíre pródiī; **trustworthy witness** testis lócupl•ēs -étis

Chapter XXIII: Geography and Topography

CONVERSATIONS

Colin wants to migrate to the U.S.

Cólinus	Salvē, Gregórī. Ego in ánimō hábeō mox ex Hibérniā in Américam ēmigráre. Potésne nārráre mihi áliquid dē Américā?	*Colin: Hello, Gregory. I intend to emigrate from Ireland to America. Can you tell me something about America?*
Gregórius	Libénter. Prīmō, América est multō ámplior quam Hibérnia.	*Gregory: Gladly. First, America is much bigger than Ireland.*
Cólinus	Ítane est? Quae sunt mēnsúrae Cīvitátum Foederātárum Américae?	*Is that so? What are the dimensions of the United States?*
Gregórius	Ōra marítima orientális tantum abest ab ōrā occidentálī quantum Hibérnia abest ā Cīvitátibus Foederátīs Américae.	*The east coast is as far distant from the west coast as is Ireland from the United States.*
Cólinus	Incrēdíbile est! Estne Novum Eborácum caput Cīvitátum Foederātárum Américae?	*That's incredible. Is New York the capital of the United States?*
Gregórius	Novum Eborácum est urbs Américae amplíssima, sed, mīrábile dictū, nōn est caput.	*New York is the biggest city in America, but, strange to say, it is not the capital.*
Cólinus	Quae urbs est caput?	*What city is the capital?*
Gregórius	Vashintónia est caput Cīvitátum Foederātárum Américae.	*Washington is the capital of the United States.*
Cólinus	América ex quot cīvitátibus cōnstat?	*Of how many states does America consist?*
Gregórius	Sunt duodēquīnquāgíntā cīvitátēs in continénte, praeter Aláscam et Havaíōs.	*There are forty-eight states on the mainland, in addition to Alaska and Hawaii.*

Cólinus   Ubi est Alásca?   *Where is Alaska?*

Gregórius Est suprā Cánadam, quae attíngit   *It is north of Canada, which*
              Cīvitátēs Foederátās Américae ā   *borders the United States on the*
              septentriőne.   *north.*

Cólinus   Ubi sunt Havaíī?   *Where is Hawaii?*

Gregórius Havaíī sunt celébritās īnsulárum   *Hawaii is a cluster of islands a*
              longíssimē ante ōram   *very long way off the coast of*
              Califórniae.   *California.*

Cólinus   Quae est urbs óptima in quā ego   *What is the best city for me and*
              cum famíliā hábitem?   *family to live in?*

Gregórius Est difficíllimum dictū. Urbs enim   *That's very hard to say. Every*
              quaeque suās virtūtēs habet.   *city, you see, has its good*
                                                     points.

┌────────── LEVEL II   **Rene wants to learn about the Tiber..**

Renáta   Quis amnis ádluit Rōmam?   ***Rene:*** *Which river flows by*
                                                     Rome?

Magístra Tíberis, cuī vetus nōmen erat   ***Teacher:*** *The Tiber, whose old*
              Álbula.   *name was the Albula.*

Renáta   Unde óritur Tíberis flūmen?   *Where does the Tiber River rise?*

Magístra Fōns eius est in Apennínō monte   *Its source is in the Apennines*
              inter Etrúriam ab occidénte et   *between Etruria on the west*
              Úmbriam ab oriénte.   *side and Umbria on the east*
                                                     side.

Renáta   Estne Tíberis flūmen lātíssimum?   *Is the Tiber a very wide river?*

Magístra Lātitūdō eius scílicet vária est. Ut *Its width varies, of course. As it*
              ex Apennínō monte prófluit,   *flows down from the Apennines,*
              prīmō angústus est. Sed ut   *it is narrow at first. But as*
              flúviī in eum ínfluunt, Tíberis   *tributaries flow into it, the*
              lātitūdine augétur.   *Tiber increases in width.*

Renáta   Fertúrne Tíberis per dīrēctum?   *Does the Tiber flow in a straight*
                                                     line?

Magístra Mínimē. Ut scīs, Ītália intus est   *No. As you know, Italy is rugged*
              áspera et montána; ítaque   *and mountainous in the interior*
              Tíberis cursū meánte Rōmam   *and so the Tiber arrives at*
              pérvenit.   *Rome along a winding course.*

| **Renáta** | Erátne Tíberis flūmen nāvigábile aetáte Rōmánā? | *Was the Tiber a navigable river in Roman times?* |

Magístra Ita, sed suprā Rōmam rátibus tantum nāvigábilis erat. Inter Rōmam autem et óstium ómnibus nắvibus nāvigábilis erat.
Yes, but north of Rome it was navigable only to rafts. But between Rome and its mouth the Tiber was navigable to all ships.

Renáta Quā longitúdine est Tíberis?
What is the length of the Tiber?

Magístra Círciter centum quīnquāgíntā mília pássuum.
Around one hundred fifty miles.

Renáta Quantum abest Rōma ā Tíberis óstiō?
How far is Rome from the mouth of the Tiber?

Magístra Círciter quíndecim mília pássuum distat. Ibi in mare Tyrrhénum sē effúndit.
About fifteen miles. There it empties into the Tyrrhenian Sea.

Renáta Quae gēns suprā Tíberim habitábat?
What nation lived north of the Tiber?

Magístra Etrúscī, quórum prīnceps urbs erat Vēiī.
The Etruscans, whose chief city was Veii.

Renáta Estne Rōma clīvósa an plāna?
Is Rome hilly or flat?

Magístra Rōma est quidem clīvósa; compléctitur illōs ínclutōs septem montēs. Urbs appósita est fléxuī flúminis.
Rome is indeed hilly; it takes in the famous seven hills. The city is located at the bend in the river.

Renáta Quis mōns est próximus Tíberī?
Which hill is closest to the Tiber?

Magístra Mōns Aventínus est próximus; sed mōns Pālātínus est item prope flūmen.
The Aventine is closest; but the Palatine Hill is likewise close to the river.

Renáta Útinam aliquándō aspíciam Tíberim!
How I wish to see the Tiber someday!

Magístra Aspíciēs.
You will.

┌────────── LEVEL III   **Traveling from Rome to Greece.**

Gálfridus	Magíster, quā viā Rōmắnī antíquitus in Graéciam iter faciébant?	***Jeffrey:*** *Teacher, by what way did the Romans in antiquity travel to Greece?*
Magíster	In Ītáliā ipsā, via Áppia ā portā Capénā dūcit rēctā ad montem Albánum, deínde per palúdem Pomptīnam ad urbem Cápuam.	***Teacher:*** *In Italy itself, the Via Appia leads from the Porta Capena in a straight line to the Alban Mount, then through the Pomptine marshes to the city of Capua.*
Gálfridus	Estne Cápua in Látiō an in Campắniā?	*Is Capua in Latium or in Campania?*
Magíster	Cápua est proféctō prīnceps urbs Campắniae.	*Capua is, in fact, the principal city of Campania.*
Gálfridus	Quantum Rōma abest Cápuā?	*How far is Rome from Capua?*
Magíster	Abest paulō ámplius quam centum et vīgíntī mília pássuum, mēnsúrā cúrrente. Deínde via dūcit praeter Benevéntum in mediterrắneō trāns montem Apennínum ad portum apud Brundísium.	*It's a little more than a hundred and twenty miles, as the crow flies. Then the road leads past Beneventum in the interior across the Apennines to the harbor at Brindisi.*
Gálfridus	Tendítne mōns Apennínus ad merīdiắnās regiốnēs Ītáliae?	*Does the Apennine Range extend to the southern regions of Italy?*
Magíster	Ita. Mōns Apennínus, Ītáliae amplíssimus, tendit perpétuīs iugīs ab Álpibus ad Sículum frētum.	*Yes. The Apennines, the largest (mountains) of Italy, extend in an unbroken chain from the Alps to the Strait of Messina.*
Gálfridus	Nōnne fīnítur via Áppia ad portum?	*Does the Via Appia end at the harbor?*
Magíster	Ita. Etiámnum duae colúmnae altae ante portum índicant fīnem Viae Áppiae.	*Yes. Even today two high columns in front of the harbor mark the end of the Via Appia.*
Gálfridus	Nāvigābántne Rōmắnī per dīrḗctum ad sinum Corinthíacum?	*Did the Romans sail in a direct line to the Gulf of Corinth?*
Magíster	Nōn. Nam trắnsitus trāns Hadriắti- cum mare erat brevíssimus inter Brundísium et Apollốniam, quae in Illýricō est.	*No. You see, the passage across the Adriatic Sea was shortest between Brindisi and Apollonia in Illyria.*

Gálfridus	Viātṓrēs deínde terrḗnō itínere Athḗnās petḗbant?	*Did the travelers then head overland for Athens?*
Magíster	Prīmō nāvigábant in merídiem versus, secúndum ōram Illýricī; deínde intrábant sinum Corinthíacum. Postrḗmō vehēbántur terrḗnō itínere per isthmum in Átticam et Athḗnās.	*First they sailed southward close to the shore of Illyria; then they entered the Gulf of Corinth. Finally, they traveled overland along the isthmus to Attica and Athens.*

TOPICAL VOCABULARY

about *(approximately)* círciter, fermē

accommodations hospíti·um -ī *n*

across trāns (+ *acc*); **across from** ex advérsō (+ *gen*), exadvérsum (+ *acc*)

adjacent to contérmin·us -a -um (+ *dat*)

adjoin adiúng·or -ī adiúnctus sum (+ *dat*)

adjoining iūnct·us -a -um; **adjoining nations** iūnctae nātiṓnēs

Adriatic Hadriátic·us -a -um; **the Adriatic** Hadriáticum mar·e -is *n*

Africa Áfric·a -ae *f*

along per (+ *acc*), secúndum (+ *acc*)

Alps Alp·ēs -ium *fpl*

Alpine Alpín·us -a -um; **Alpine chain** Álpium iug·a -ṓrum *npl*

America Améric·a -ae *f;* **North America** América Septentriōnális; **South America** América Merīdiána

American Americán·us -a -um

Apennines, Apennine Range Apennínus mōn·s -tis *m*

Appian Way vi·a -ae *f* Áppia

area tract·us -ūs *m*

Asia Ási·a -ae *f*

at apud (+ *acc*)

Atlantic Atlántic·us -a -um; **Atlantic Ocean** Atlánticus ōcéan·us -ī *m*, Atlánticum mar·e -is *n*

Athens Athḗn·ae -árum *fpl*

Attica Áttic·a -ae *f*

bank rīp·a -ae *f;* **the Tiber having overflowed its banks** Tíberis super rīpās effúsus

bay sin·us -ūs *m*, recéss·us -ūs *m*

before *(in front of)* ante (+ *acc*)

begin at incíp·iō -ere incḗpī ab (+ *abl*)

Beneventum Benevént·um -ī *n*

big ampl·us -a -um

behind *(in the rear of)* ā tergō (+ *gen*)

bend *s (of a river)* flex·us -ūs *m*

bend *intr* sē flect·ō -ere flexī flexus

beyond ultrā (+ *acc*)

border on attíng·ō -ere (+ *acc*)

border fīn·is -is *m*, confíni·um -ī *n*

boundary fīn·is -is *m; (dividing line)* discrím·en -inis *n;* **at the boundary between Italy and Switzerland** ad discrímen Ītáliae et Helvétiae

bounded: on the east it is bounded by ... ab oriénte cláuditur (+ *abl*)

breadth lātitū́d·ō -inis *f;* **in breadth** lātitū́dine, in lātitū́dinem

Brindisi Brundísi·um -ī *n*

brook rívul·us -ī *m*

business district empóri·um -ī *n*

called dict·us, appellắt·us, vocitắt·us, vocắt·us, nuncupắt·us -a -um

Campania Campắni·a -ae *f*

canal foss·a -ae *f*

Capua Cápu·a -ae *f*

cape prōmontóri·um -ī *n*

capital cap·ut -itis *n*

cave spec·us -ūs *m*

cavern spēlúnc·a -ae *f*

causeway pedéstris trắnsit·us-ūs *m*

**chain: the Apennines extending in an unbroken chain from the Alps to … ** Apennínus mōns perpétuīs iugīs ab Álpibus tendēns ad (+ *acc*)

circumference circúit·us -ūs *m;* **its crater measures 500 feet in circumference** eius crātēr patet circúitū quīngéntōs pedēs

city urb·s -is *f*

climate cael·um -ī *n*

cluster *(of islands, etc.)* celébrit·ās -ắtis *f*

coast ōr·a -ae *f* (marítima); **on the coast** in ōrā (marítimā)

confluence cónflu·ēns -éntis *m;* **at the confluence of the Tiber and the Anio** inter cōnfluéntēs Tíberim et Aniónem

course curs·us -ūs *m;* **along a winding course** meánte cursū

continent par·s -tis *f* mundī (*or* orbis terrắrum)

Corinth Corínth·us -ī *f;* **gulf of Corinth** sin·us -ūs *m* Corinthíacus (*or* Corínthius)

crater crāt·ēr -éris *m*

creek rīv·us -ī *m*

crest *(of a hill)* iug·um -ī *n*

crossing *(passage)* trắnsit·us -ūs *m*

crow: as the crow flies mēnsū́rā currénte [*lit: in a running measurement*]

current flūm·en -inis *n* (*in the sense of "the flow"*); **against the current** advérsō flū́mine; **strong current** vīs *f* (*no gen; acc:* vim; *abl:* vī) flū́minis; **with the current** sēcúndō flū́mine

curve *(in a road, coast)* ānfrắct·us -ūs *m*

Danube river Danū́vius amn·is -is *m*

densely populated region rḗgiō ubérrimae multitū́dinis

desert dēsért·a -ṓrum *npl*

dimensions mēnsū́r·a -ae *f or* mēnsū́r·ae -ắrum *fpl*

directly rēctā, per dīréctum

distance spáti·um -ī *n;* **its distance from the sea is three miles** abest ā marī tria mília pássuum

distant longínqu·us -a -um; **to be distant from** abésse ab (+ *abl*), distắre ab (+ *abl*)

district tract·us -ūs *m*, ag·er -rī *m*

dotted: the river is dotted with towns on the right and left bank amnis accólitur (*or* frequentắtur) dextrā laevāque crēbrīs óppidīs

earthquake terrae mot·us -ūs *m*

east óri·ēns -éntis *m;* **on the east (side)** ab oriénte; **to the east** in oriéntem versus (versus *is an adverb*)

eastern orientắl·is -is -e

eastward in oriéntem versus (versus *is an adverb*)

empty (into) sē effúnd·ō -ere effū́dī effū́sus

end *s* fīn·is -is *m*

end *intr* dḗsin·ō -ere, fín·ior -írī

estuary aestuắri·um -ī *n*

Etruria Etrū́ri·a -ae *f*

Europe Eurṓp·a -ae *f*

European Eurōpaé·us -a -um

extend *(of land, body of water)* tend·ō -ere, prōténd·ō -ere, pát·eō -ḗre; **the region extends from ... to ...** régiō tendit ab (+ *abl*) ad (+ *acc*); **to extend over** *(to cover)* obtín·eō -ḗre

face spectā́re; **to face north (south, east, west)** spectā́re in *(or* ad*)* septentriṓnēs (merī́diem, oriéntem, occidéntem)

famous for ínclutus, nṓbilis (+ *abl*)

far longḗ; **farthest to the south** longíssimē in merī́diem; **(not) far from** (haud) procul ab (+ *abl*)

field ag·er -rī *m*

flat plān·us -a -um

flow flu·ō -ere flūxī flūxus; **to flow by** ádlu·ō, adlúere; **to flow down from** dēflúere dē (+ *abl*); **to flow into** īnflúere in (+ *acc*); **to flow out from** efflúere ab (+ *abl*); **to flow past** praeflúere (+ *acc*), praeterflúere (+ *acc*)

foot of a mountain rād·īx -ícis *m* montis; **at the foot of the mountain** rādī́ce montis

foothills rādī́c·ēs -um *mpl* montis

forest silv·a -ae *f*

formerly ánteā

front: in front of ante (+ *acc*)

frontier fīn·is -is *m*, términ·us -ī *m*

geography geōgráphi·a -ae *f*

Gibraltar Calp·ē -ēs *f;* **strait of Gibraltar** Gādītā́num frēt·um -ī *n*

Greece Graéci·a -ae *f*

gulf sin·us -ūs *m*

harbor port·us -ūs *m*

head for pet·ō -ere petī́vī petī́tus

hill coll·is -is *m*

hilly clīvṓs·us -a -um

how: how far is ... from quantum distat *(or* abest*)* ... ab (+ *abl*)

Illyria Illýric·um -ī *n*

increase *tr* aúg·eō -ḗre auxī auctus ‖ *intr* aúg·eor -ḗrī auctus sum

inland *adv* intus; **towns inland from Tarentum** óppida per continéntem ā Taréntō

inland *adj* intéri·or -or -us; **inland seas** már·ia -ium *npl* interiṓra

interior *s*: **in the interior** in mediterrā́neō, intus; **toward the interior** intus

interior *adj* intéri·or -or -us

Ireland Hibérni·a -ae *f*

island ínsul·a -ae *f;* **islands off the coast of Greece** ínsulae ante Graéciam

isthmus isthm·us -ī *m (f)*

Italy Ītáli·a -ae *f*

jut out *see* **project**

lagoon stāgn·um -ī *n*

lake lac·us -ūs *m*

land terr·a -ae *f*

lead *(of a road)* dūc·ō -ere dūxī ductus

left siníst·er -ra -rum, laev·us -a -um; **on the left** laevā, ā laevā; **(to the) left** sinistrṓrsum, laevṓrsum

length longitū́d·ō -inis *f;* **in length** longitū́dine, in longitū́dinem

lengthwise per longitū́dinem

lie iác·eō -ḗre -uī; **to lie in the direction of** verg·ō -ere ad (+ *acc*)

line līne·a -ae *f;* **in a straight line** per dīrḗctum

live *(dwell)* habitā́re; **to live near, *(in the case of a river)* to live on the banks of** áccol·ō -ere -uī accúltum

long long·us -a -um; **fifteen miles long** quíndecim mī́lia pássuum *(often written:* p.) in longitū́dinem *or* quíndecim mília pássuum in longitúdinem patēns

mainland cóntin·ēns -éntis *f*

map of the world orb·is -is *m* terrárum pīctus

meander meáre

measure pát·eō -ére, cóllig·ō -ere; **measuring ten miles in circumference** patēns (*or* cólligēns) decem mília pássuum circúitū

Mediterranean Sea Intérnum mar·e -is *n*, Tuscum mare, Tyrrhénum mare

mine metáll·um -ī *n;* **gold (lead, iron, copper, silver, tin) mine** metállum aurī (plumbī, ferrī, aeris, argéntī, plumbī albī)

moderate: of moderate size módic·us -a -um

mountain mōn·s -tis *m*

mountain chain mont·ēs -ium *mpl* perpétuī

mountainous montuós·us -a -um, montán·us -a -um

mouth (*of a river*) óst·ium -ī *n*

narrow angúst·us -a -um

nation gēn·s -tis *f*

navigable nāvigábi·lis -is -e

near vīcín·us -a -um (+ *dat*), prope (+ *acc*)

next *adv* próximē; **next comes, then ... then ... after that** unde ... dein ... dein ... inde ...

next to próxim·us -a -um (+ *dat*), iuxtā (+ *acc*)

north *adj* supér·ior -ior -ius, septentriōnál·is -is -e

north *adv* ad septentriónēs; **north of** suprā (+ *acc*), super (+ *acc*)

north *s* septéntri·ō -ónis *m or* septentrión·ēs -um *mpl;* **on the north**

ā septentrióne; **on the north (side)** látere septentriōnálī

northern septentriōnál·is -is -e

northward in septentriónēs versus (versus *is an adverb*)

ocean ōcéan·us -ī *m;* **the Atlantic Ocean** ōcéanus Atlánticus *or* mare Atlánticum

off (*said of an island*) ante (+ *acc*), apud (+ *acc*); **off (the coast of) Italy** ante Ītáliam

opposite *prep* versus (+ *acc*) (*often postpositive*), adversum (+ *acc*), contrā (+ *acc*); **opposite of** ex advérsō *or* exadvérsō (+ *gen*)

pass (*defile*) salt·us -ūs *m*

past praeter (+ *acc*)

peninsula paenínsul·a -ae *f*

plain camp·us -ī *m;* **open plains** campī paténtēs

Pomptine Marshes pal·ūs -údis *f* Pomptína

pond stāgn·um -ī *n*

pool stāgn·um -ī *n*

population multitúd·ō -inis *f;* **the total number of the population** númer·us -ī *m* omnis multitúdinis

port port·us -ūs *m*

previously ánteā

principal (*chief*) prínc·eps -ipis

productivity (*of fields, mines, etc.*) fertílit·ās -átis *f*

project (*of a promontory or cape*) excúrr·ō -ere; **to project far out into the sea** excúrrere longē in mare

race gēn·s -tis *f*

raft rat·is -is *f*

rapids vad·um -ī *n* cándicāns

reach (*arrive at*) pervén·iō -íre ad *or* in (+ *acc*)

region régi·ō -ónis *f*

ridge iug·um -ī *n*

right dexter -(e)ra -(e)rum; **on the right** dextrā, ā déxterā; **(to the) right** dextrórsum; **to turn right** dextrórsum sē vértere

rise *(of a mountain)* surg·ō -ere; *(of several mountains)* cōnsúrgere; *(of a river, have its source)* (ex)órior (ex)orírī; **the Tiber rising in the Apennines** Tíberis monte Apennínō (ex)óriēns

river flūm·en -inis *n*, amn·is -is *m (with no distinction as to size)*

river bed álve·us -ī *m*

Roman Rōmán·us -a -um

Rome Rōm·a -ae *f (often referred to simply as* urbs)

rugged asp·er -era -erum

sail nāvigáre, (nāve) vehor vehī vectus sum

sea mar·e -is *n*

seacoast ōr·a -ae *f* marítima, līt·us -oris *n*

seashore act·a -ae *f*

separate sēparáre, discérn·ō -ere, distíngu·ō -ere; **it is separated from Gaul by the Rhine River** discérnitur *(or* distínguitur *or* sēparátur) ā Gálliā amne Rhēnō

shallow tenu·is -is -e

short brev·is -is -e

side lat·us -eris *n;* **on the other side of** ultrā (+ *acc)*; **on the right (side) of** ā látere dextrō (+ *gen)*; **on this side of** cis *or* citrā (+ *acc)*

site sit·us -ūs *m*, loc·us -ī *m (pl:* loc·a -órum *npl)*

situated on, near appósit·us -a -um (+ *dat)*; **to be situated on a hill** īnsíd·ō -ere collem

size magnitúd·ō -inis *f*, amplitúd·ō -inis *f*

slope *s* clīv·us -ī *m;* **steep (gentle) slope** árduus (lēnis) clīvus

slope *intr* verg·ō -ere; **sloping toward the sea** vergēns ad mare

source fōn·s -tis *m*

south *adj* īnfér·ior -ior -ius, merīdián·us -a -um; **on the south side** látere merīdiánō

south *adv* ad merídiem; **south of** infrā (+ *acc)*

south *s* merídi·ēs -éī *m*, merīdián·um -ī *n;* **in the south** ā merídiē

southern *s* merīdián·us -a -um, īnfér·ior -ior -ius

southward in merídiem versus (versus *is an adverb)*

spring fōn·s -tis *m*

state stat·us -ūs *m*, cívit·ās -átis *f*

strait frēt·um -ī *n;* **Strait of Messina** frētum Sículum

stream rīv·us -ī *m*

stretch *see* **extend**

suburb subúrbi·um -ī *n;* **suburbs** continént·ia -ium *npl*

summit cacúm·en -inis *n*

swamp pal·ūs -údis *f*

then *(next)* dein, inde; *(at that time)* tum

Tiber Tíber·is -is *m; (acc:* Tíberim)

tide aest·us -ūs *m*

topography locórum dēscrípti·ō -ónis *f*

town óppid·um -ī *n;* **small town** oppídul·um -ī *n*

travel iter fác·iō -ere fēcī factus; *(by sea)* (nāve) veh·or -ī vectus sum

tributary flúvi·us -ī *m*

Tyrrhenian Sea Tyrrhénicum mar·e -is *n*, Tyrr(h)énum mare

Umbria Úmbri·a -ae *f*

United States (of America) Ūnītī Stat·ūs -uum *mpl* (Américae), Cīvitātēs Foederātae Americae *fpl*

universe ūnivérs·um -ī *n,* ūnivérsit·ās -átis *f*

valley vall·ēs -is *f*

Veii Vēi·ī -órum *mpl*

village vīc·us -ī *m*

west óccid·ēns -éntis *m;* **in the west** ab occidénte; **to the west** in occidéntem versus (versus *is an adverb*)

western occidentál·is -is -e

westward in occidéntem versus (versus *is an adverb*)

widen *intr (of a country)* sē pand·ō -ere

width lātitúd·ō -inis *f;* **in width** lātitúdine, in lātitúdinem

winding flexuós·us -a -um; **winding route** ámbit·us -ūs *m*

world mund·us -ī *m,* orb·is -is *m* terrárum

THE UNITED STATES OF AMERICA

Ūnītī Statūs Americae/Cīvitātēs Foederātae Americae

[**Note**—The name of each State is given, followed by the name of its capital *(cap)*, sometimes another large city or two, the adjective form and the substantive (s) for the inhabitant of the State.]

Alabama Alabám·a -ae *f; (cap)* **Montgomery** Mōn·s -tis *m* Goméricī; **Mobile** Móbil·is -is *f; adj* Alabāméns·is -is -e

Alabaman *s* Alabāméns·is -is *(gen pl:* -ium) *mf*

Alaska Alásc·a -ae *f; (cap)* **Juneau** Iunéll·um -ī *n;* **Anchorage** Ancorári·a -ae *f; adj* Alascán·us -a -um

Alaskan *s* Alascán·us -ī *m* (·a -ae *f*)

Arizona Arizón·a -ae *f; (cap)* **Phoenix** Phoen·ix -icis *f; adj* Arizōnéns·is -is -e

Arizonan *s* Arizōnéns·is -is *(gen pl:* -ium) *mf*

Arkansas Arcánsi·a -ae *f; (cap)* **Little Rock** Petrícul·a -ae *f; adj* Arcānsiéns·is -is -e

Arkansan *s* Arcānsiéns·is -is *(gen pl:* -ium) *mf*

California Califórni·a -ae *f; (cap)* **Sacramento** Sacrāmént·um -ī *n;* **Los Angeles** Angelópol·is -is *f;* **Hollywood** Ācrifōliórum Silv·a -ae *f;* **San Diego** Didacópol·is -is *f;* **San Francisco** Franciscópol·is -is *f; adj* Californiéns·is -is -e

Californian *s* Californiéns·is -is *(gen pl:* -ium) *mf*

Colorado Colōrát·um -ī *n; (cap)* **Denver** Denvéri·um -ī *n;* **Durango** Dūráng·um -ī *n; adj* Colōrāténs·is -is -e

Coloradan *s* Colōrāténs·is -is *(gen pl:* -ium) *mf*

Connecticut Connecticút·a -ae *f; (cap)* **Hartford** Hardifórdi·a -ae *f; adj* Connecticūténs·is -is -e; *s* Connecticūténs·is -is *(gen pl:* - ium) *mf*

Delaware Delevári·a -ae *f; (cap)* **Dover** Dubr·is -is *f; adj* Delavarián·us -a -um

Delawarean *s* Delevārián•us -ī *m* (•a -ae *f*)

Florida Flórid•a -ae *f; (cap)* **Tallahassee** Tellahássi•a -ae *f;* **Miami** Miámi•a -ae *f;* **Palm Beach** Ōr•a -ae *f* Palmária; *adj* Flōridián•us -a -um

Floridian *s* Flōridián•us -ī *m* (•a -ae *f*)

Georgia Geórgi•a -ae *f; (cap)* **Atlanta** Atlánt•a -ae *f;* **Athens** Athén•ae -árum *fpl;* **Savannah** Savánn•a -ae *f; adj* Georgián•us -a - um

Georgian *s* Georgián•us -ī *m* (•a -ae *f*)

Hawaii Havaí•ī -ṓrum *mpl; (cap)* **Honolulu** Honolúl•um -ī *n;* **Pearl Harbor** Port•us -ūs *m* Margarītárius

Hawaiian *adj* Havaián•us -a -um; *s* Havaián•us -ī *m* (•a -ae *f*)

Idaho Ídah•um -ī *n; (cap)* **Boise** Xylópol•is -is *f; adj* Idahḗns•is -is -e

Idahoan *s* Idahḗns•is -is *(gen pl:* -ium) *mf*

Illinois Illinoési•a -ae *f; (cap)* **Springfield** Cámpifōn•s -tis *m;* **Chicago** Chicág•um -ī *n; adj* Illinoesián•us -a -um

Illinois *s* Illinoesián•us -ī *m* (•a -ae *f*)

Indiana Indián•a -ae *f; (cap)* **Indianapolis** Indiānāpól•is -is *f; adj* Indiānḗns•is -is -e

Indianian *s* Indiānḗns•is -is *mf*

Iowa Íov•a -ae *f; (cap)* **Des Moines** Monachópol•is -is *f; adj* Iován•us -a -um

Iowan *s* Iován•us -ī *m* (•a -ae *f*)

Kansas Cánsi•a -ae *f; (cap)* **Topeka** Topéc•a -ae *f;* **Kansas City** Cānsiópol•is -is *f; adj* Cānsián•us -a -um

Kansan *s* Cānsián•us -ī *m* (•a -ae *f*)

Kentucky Kentúki•a -ae *f; (cap)* **Frankfort** Francofúrt•um -ī *n;*

Lexington Lexintóni•a -ae *f; adj* Kentukián•us -a -um

Kentuckian *s* Kentukián•us -ī *m* (•a -ae *f*)

Louisiana Ludovīcián•a -ae *f; (cap)* **Baton Rouge** Rubrobást•um -ī *n;* **New Orleans** Nov•a Auréli•a -ae *f; adj* Ludovīciānḗns•is -is -e

Louisianan *s* Ludovīciānḗns•is -is *mf*

Maine Cenománnic•a -ae *f; (cap)* **Augusta** Augúst•a -ae *f; adj* Cenománḗns•is -is -e

Mainer *s* Cenománnic•us -ī *m* (•a -ae *f*)

Maryland Terr•a -ae *f* Marḯae; *(cap)* **Annapolis** Annápol•is -is *f;* **Baltimore** Baltimōr•a -ae *f; adj (use genitive* Terrae Marḯae)

Massachusetts Massaciússet•a -ae *f; (cap)* **Boston** Bostóni•a -ae *f; adj* Massaciusetán•us -a -um; *s* Massaciussetán•us -ī *m* (•a -ae *f*)

Michigan Michigáni•a -ae *f; (cap)* **Lansing** Lánsing•a -ae *f;* **Detroit** Detroít•um ī *n; adj* Michiganḗns•is -is -e

Michigander Michiganḗns•īs -is *(gen pl:* -ium) *mf*

Minnesota Minnesṓt•a -ae *f; (cap)* **St. Paul** Paulópol•is -is *f;* **Minneapolis** Minneápol•is -is *f; adj* Minnesōtán•us -a -um

Minnesotan *s* Minnesōtán•us -ī *m* (•a -ae *f*)

Mississippi Mississíppi•a -ae *f; (cap)* **Jackson** Iacsṓni•a -ae *f; adj* Mississippián•us -a -um

Mississippian *s* Mississippián•us -ī *m* (•a -ae *f*)

Missouri Missū́ri•a -ae *f; (cap)* **Jefferson City** Ieffersṓni•a -ae *f; adj* Missūrián•us -a -um

Missourian *s* Missūrián•us -ī (•a -ae *f*)

Montana Montắn·a -ae *f; (cap)* **Helena**
Helenópol·is -is *f; adj* Montāniắn·us
-a -um

Montanan *s* Montāniắn·us -ī *m* (·a -ae *f*)

Nebraska Nebrásc·a -ae *f; (cap)*
Lincoln Lincólni·a -ae *f; adj*
Nebrascắn·us -a -um

Nebraskan *s* Nebrascắn·us -ī *m* (·a
-ae *f*)

Nevada Nivắt·a -ae *f; (cap)* **Carson
City** Carsóni·a -ae *f;* **Reno** Rēn·um -ī
n; adj Nivātḗns·is -is -e

Nevadan *s* Nivātḗns·is -is *(gen pl:*
-ium) *mf*

New Hampshire Nova Hantescír·a -ae
f; (cap) **Concord** Concórdi·a -ae *f;
adj* Novohantescirán·us -a -um; *s*
Novohantescirán·us -ī *m* (·a -ae *f*)

New Jersey Nova Caesarḗ·a -ae *f; (cap)*
Trenton Trentóni·a -ae *f;* **Newark**
Nov·a Arc·a -ae *f; adj*
Novocaesariḗns·is -is -e

New Jerseyite *s* Novocaesariḗns·is
-is *mf*

New Mexico Nov·um Méxic·um -ī *n;
(comp)* **Santa Fe** Fidépol·is -is *f; adj*
Novomexicắn·us -a -um

New Mexican *s* Novomexicắn·us -ī *m*
(·a -ae *f*)

New York *(state)* Nov·um Eborác·um -ī
n; (cap) **Albany** Álban·um -ī *n;*
Rochester Rúcup·ae -árum *fpl;*
Buffalo Búfal·um -ī *n; adj* Neo-
Eborācḗns·is -is -e

New York *(city)* Nov·um Eborác·um -ī
n; **Bronx** Brónxi·a -ae *f;* **Brooklyn**
Brúclin·um -ī *n;* **Long Island** Long·a
Ínsul·a -ae *f;* **Manhattan**
Manháttan·um -ī *n*

New Yorker *s* Neo-Eborācḗns·is -is *mf*

North Carolina Carolín·a -ae
Septentriōnắl·is -is *f; (cap)* **Raleigh**

Raléi·a -ae *f; adj* Carolīnḗns·is
Septentriōnắl·is -is -e

North Carolinian *s* Carolīnḗns·is -is *mf*
Septentriōnális

North Dakota Dacṓt·a -ae
Septentriōnắl·is -is *f; (cap)* **Bismark**
Bismarcópol·is -is *f*

North Dakotan Dacōtắn·us -ī *m* (·a -ae
f) Septentriōnális

Ohio Ohí·um -ī *n; (cap)* **Columbus**
Columbópol·is -is *f;* **Cincinnati**
Cincinnátópol·is -is *f; adj* Ohiḗns·is
-is -e

Ohioan *s* Ohiḗns·is -is *(gen pl:* -ium) *mf*

Oklahoma Oclahṓm·a -ae *f; (cap)*
Oklahoma City Oclahṓm·a -ae
Urb·s -is *f; adj* Oclahōmḗns·is -is -e

Oklahoman *s* Oclahōmḗns·is -is *(gen
pl:* -ium) *mf*

Oregon Oregóni·a -ae *f; (cap)* **Salem**
Salem *indecl n; adj* Oregōniḗns·is
-is -e

Oregonian *s* Oregōniḗns·is -is *(gen pl:*
-ium); *mf*

Pennsylvania Pennsilvắni·a -ae *f; (cap)*
Harrisburg Harrisbúrg·um -ī *n;*
Philadelphia Philadélphi·a -ae *f;*
Pittsburgh Pittsbúrg·um -ī *n; adj*
Pennsilvāniḗns·is -is -e

Pennsylvanian *s* Pennsilvāniḗns·is -is
(gen pl: -ium) *mf*

Rhode Island Rhodḗns·is -is Ínsul·a -ae
f; (cap) **Providence** Prōvidénti·a -ae
f; adj Rhodḗns·is -is

Rhode Islander *s* Rhodḗns·is -is *(gen
pl:* -ium) *mf*

South Carolina Carolín·a -ae
Merīdiōnắl·is -is *f; (cap)* **Columbia**
Colúmbi·a -ae *f; adj* Carolīnḗns·is
-is -e

South Carolinian *s* Carolīnḗns·is
-is *(gen pl:* -ium) *mf* Merīdiōnális

South Dakota Dacṓt·a -ae Merīdiōnắl·is -is *f; (cap)* **Pierre** Petrópol·is -is *f; adj* Dacōtān·us -a -um

South Dakotan *s* Dacōtắn·us -ī *m* (·a -ae *f*) Merīdiōnắl·is -is

Tennessee Tennési·a -ae *f; (cap)* **Nashville** Nasbúrg·um -ī *n; adj* Tennesiắn·us -a -um

Tennesseean *s* Tennesiắn·us -ī *m* (·a -ae *f*)

Texas Téxi·a -ae *f; (cap)* **Austin** Austinópol·is -is *f;* **Dallas** Dallási·um -ī *n;* **Houston** Hustópol·is -is *f; adj* Texiắn·us -a -um

Texan *s* Texiắn·us -ī *m* (·a -ae *f*)

Utah Ūta -ae *f; (cap)* **Salt Lake City** Urb·s -is *f* Lacūs Salsī; *adj* Ūtḗns·is -is -e

Utahan *s* Ūtḗns·is -is *m* (*gen pl* -ium) *mf*

Vermont Mōn·s -tis *m* Víridis *; (cap)* **Montpelier** Mōn·s -tis *m* Pessulắnus *adj* (use genitive Mōntis Víridis)

Virginia Virgíni·a -ae *f; (cap)* **Richmond** Ricmóndi·a -ae *f; adj* Virginiḗns·is -is -e

Virginian *s* Virginiḗns·is -is *(gen pl:* -ium) *mf*

Washington Vashintṓni·a -ae *f; (cap)* **Olýmpia** Olýmpi·a -ae *f; adj* Vashintōniḗns·is -is -e

Washingtonian Vashintōniḗns·is -is *(gen pl:* -ium) *mf*

West Virginia Virgíni·a -ae *f* Occidentắlis; *(cap)* **Charleston** Carolópol·is -is *f*

West Virginian Virginiḗns·is -is *(gen pl:* -ium) *mf* Occidentắl·is

Wisconsin Visconsíni·a -ae *f; (cap)* **Madison** Madisóni·a -āe *n; adj* Visconsiắn·us -a -um

Wisconsinite Visconsiắn·us -ī *m* (·a -ae *f*)

Wyoming Vyómin·a -ae *f;* **Casper** Caspéri·a -ae *f;* **Cheyenne** Cheyenn·a -ae *f; adj* Vyominắnus -a -um

Wyomingite Vyominắn·us -ī *m* (·a -ae *f*)

Chapter XXIV: Transportation

CONVERSATIONS

┌─────── LEVEL I   **At the New York train station.**

Diána   Salvē! Velim comparáre tésseram
itineráriam prīmae classis.

*Diane: Hello! I'd like to buy a
first-class ticket.*

Tesserárius Quō, quaesō?

Ticket agent: Where to, please?

Diána   In Califórniam.

To California.

Tesserárius Vīsne tésseram unĩus cursūs an
tésseram itũs reditũsque?

*Do you want a one-way ticket or
a round-trip ticket?*

Diána   Tésseram itũs reditũsque. Quotā
hōrā trāmen meum abscédit?

*A round-trip ticket. At what time
does the train depart?*

Tesserárius Hōrā ūndécimā.

At eleven o'clock.

Diána   Ā quotā crepídine trāmen
abscédit?

*From which platform does the
train depart?*

Tesserárius Ā crepídine quārtā, in órbitā
décimā.

From platform 4, on track 10.

Diána   Estne trāmen dīréctum?

Is it a through train?

Tesserárius Mínimē. Mūtábis trámina in
statióne Chicāgénsī. Quās
sárcinās tēcum habēs?

*No. You will change trains at the
Chicago station. What luggage
do you have with you?*

Diána   Ūnum riscum, ūnam bulgam,
ūnam pēram.

*One suitcase, a handbag, and a
shoulder bag.*

Tesserárius Cūrátiō sarcínārum est illíc, iuxtā
oecum praestōlātórium.

*The baggage check is over there
near the waiting room.*

Diána   Suntne báiulī in promptū?

Are there porters available?

Tesserárius Ita. Illī illīc stant prope scālās
móbilēs.

*Yes. They are standing there near
the escalator.*

Diána   Suntne currus cēnātórius et currus
dormītórius in hōc trámine?

*Are there a dining car and a
pullman car on this train?*

Tesserárius Certē.

Certainly.

Diána	Quam mox mihi licet trāmen ferriviárium īnscéndere?	*How soon may I board the train?*
Tesserárius	Vīgíntī aut summum trīgíntā minútīs. En, cape hoc hōrárium tráminum.	*In twenty or at most thirty minutes. Here, take this train schedule.*
Diána	Grátiās. Quantī cōnstat téssera itinerária?	*Thanks. How much is the ticket?*
Tesserárius	Centum octōgíntā quīnque dóllarīs.	*$185.00.*
Diána	Ecce vectúram.	*Here's the fare.*
Tesserárius	Grátiās. Bene ámbulā!	*Thanks. Have a good trip!*

┌─────────── LEVEL II   **At the airport.**

Rosa	Salvē! Velim tésseram itineráriam (ad urbem) Vindóbonam in Aústriam comparáre.	***Rose:*** *Hello! I'd like to buy a ticket to Vienna, Austria.*
Tesserárius	Habḗsne sēdem reservátam?	***Ticket agent:*** *Did you make a reservation?*
Rosa	Nōn hábeō.	*I have not.*
Tesserárius	Contíngit tibi ut áliquot sēdēs vácuae restent. Optásne sēdem prīmae classis an tūrísticae classis?	*Lucky for you, there are still some empty seats. Do you want a first-class or tourist-class seat?*
Rosa	Sēdem classis tūrísticae.	*A seat in the tourist class.*
Tesserárius	In quā parte āëróplanī vīs sedére? Inter fūmātórēs an inter nōn fūmātórēs?	*In what section of the plane do you want to sit, smoking or non-smoking?*
Rosa	Meā nīl ínterest. Volō autem prope éxitum sedére, sī fíerī potest.	*It makes no difference to me; but I want to sit near an exit if possible.*
Tesserárius	Probē. Hábeō forte vácuam sēdem in órdine décimō quartō.	*Fine. I happen to have an empty seat in row fourteen.*
Rosa	Praéferō sēdem fenestrálem.	*I prefer a window seat.*
Tesserárius	Bene hoc habet.	*That's fine.*

Rosa	Nōnne póterō volā́re rēctā in Aústriam?	*Can I fly directly to Austria?*
Tesserárius	Tibi volándum erit aut per Parī́siōs aut Francofórdiam.	*You will have to fly either by way of Paris or Frankfurt.*
Rosa	Mihi opus erit āëróplana mūtā́re?	*Will I have to change planes?*
Tesserárius	Ita, apud utrúmque āëropórtum.	*Yes, at either airport.*
Rosa	Apud quem āëropórtum est coniúnctiō mélior?	*At which airport is there the better connection?*
Tesserárius	Commorā́tiō apud āërpórtum Francofordiḗnsem est satis brevis: duās hōrās summum.	*The layover at the Frankfurt airport is fairly short: two hours at most.*
Rosa	Bene. Cápiam volā́tum per Francofórdiam.	*Good. I'll take the flight by way of Frankfurt.*
Tesserárius	Probē.	*Fine.*
Rosa	Licétne hanc sarcínulam manuā́lem mēcum in āëróplanum portā́re?	*May I take my hand luggage with me on the plane?*
Tesserárius	Licet tibi. Modo repṓne eam in retinā́culō sarcinā́lī suprā sēdem tuam.	*You may. Just put it in the luggage rack over your seat.*
Rosa	Quāntī cōnstat téssera?	*How much is the ticket?*
Tesserárius	Ecce tésseram tuam. Prétium est octingéntī trīgíntā dóllarī.	*Here's your ticket. The price is $830.00.*
Rosa	Praesentā́riam pecū́niam nōn hábeō. Ecce autem meam sýngrapham octingentṓrum trīgíntā dollarṓrum.	*I don't have the cash. But here's my check for $830.00.*
Tesserárius	Bene est. Grā́tiās. Bene valē!	*That's fine. Thanks. So long.*

┌──────── LEVEL III   **Getting ready to go by car.**

Uxor	Heus, tū, estne autocīnḗtum nostrum adhūc in officī́nā reparātṓriā? Ut satis scīs, mihi hódiē obsōnándum est.	*Wife: Hey, you, is our car still at the garage? As you well know, I have to go shopping today.*
Marítus	Mínimē. Ego id iam ex officī́nā reparātṓriā petī́vī.	*Husband: No. I've already fetched it from the garage.*

Uxor	Estne proínde iste currus tandem reparátus?	*That car, then, is finally repaired?*
Marítus	Ita, motórium rūrsus in bonō statū est.	*Yes, the motor is in good shape again.*
Uxor	Et quid dē cúmmeīs canthīs?	*And what about the tires?*
Marítus	Cúmmeī canthī iam ā mechánicō opífice mūtátae sunt.	*The mechanic has already changed the tires.*
Uxor	Quid autem de óleō mōtóriī?	*But what about the motor oil?*
Marítus	Óleum mōtóriī quidem mūtándum est, sed ipse id mūtātū́rus sum.	*The motor oil must be changed all right, but I am going to change it myself.*
Uxor	Habēmúsne áliquid óleī mōtóriī domī?	*Do we have any motor oil at home?*
Marítus	Ita. Sunt tria aut quáttuor váscula stánnea óleī mōtóriī in nostrō autocīnḗtī receptáculō.	*Yes, there are three or four cans of motor oil in our garage.*
Uxor	Dā óperam eīs rēbus contínuō! Nōn ūnivérsum diem hábeō quem absū́mam.	*See to those things immediately! I don't have all day to waste.*
Marítus	Dābō proféctō. Sed meméntō, necésse habébimus cōnsístere in statióne benzīnáriā ad benzī́num comparándum.	*I will all right. But remember that we will have to stop at the service station to get gas.*
Uxor	Rūrsus?	*Again?*
Marítus	Rūrsus quidem! Benzī́num enim iam déficit.	*Yes, again! The gas, you see, is running low.*
Uxor	Dī immortálēs! Ecquándō mihi erit locus obsōnā́ndī! Istuc autocīnḗtum est ingēns moléstia!	*Good heavens! When will I ever have a chance to shop? That car is a big pain in the neck!*
Marítus	*(Sḗcum)* Et sīc tū quoque!	*(To himself) And so are you!*

TOPICAL VOCABULARY

accelerator accelerátr·um -ī *n*

accident cās·us -ūs *m;* **an accident happened on the way** cāsus fortuítō ēvénit in itínere

airbag āérius foll·is -is *m*

airline trām·es -itis *m* āérius

airplane āëróplan·um -ī *n*

airport āëropórt·us -ūs *m*

air pressure préssi·ō -ónis *f* āéria

aisle *(of bus, plane, train)* ambulātiúncul·a -ae *f*

ambulance autoárcer·a -ae *f*

arrival advént·us -ūs *m*

arrival time temp·us -oris *n* adveniéndī

arrive advén·iō -íre advénī adventúrus; **arrive at** pervén·iō -íre pervénī ad *or* in (+ *acc*)

automobile autoréd·a -ae *f,* autocīnét·um -ī *n (used interchangeably)*

baggage cart chīramáxi·um -ī *n* sarcinárum

baggage check cūráti·ō -ónis *f* sarcinárum

board īnscénd·ō -ere -ī

bicycle bírot·a -ae *f*

brake *s* sufflám·en -inis *n;* **to apply the brake** rotās sufflāmináre

brake lights (autoraédae) lúminár·ia -ium *npl* postíca

bumper cont·us -ī *m* tūtórius

bus autoraéd·a -ae *f* longa, coenautocīnét·um -ī *n*

bypass circúit·us -ūs *m*

can váscul·um -ī *n* stánneum

car curr·us -ūs *m,* autoraéd·a -ae *f;* **to climb into a car** in currum *or* in autoraédam īnscénd·ō -ere -ī; **to drive a car** currum *or* autoraédam

gubernáre *or* agō ágere ēgī āctus; **to get (buy) a car** currum *or* autoraédam comparáre; **to get into a car** currum *or* autoraédam intrō·grédior -gredī -gréssus sum; **to get out of the car** dē currū *or* autoraédā ēgrédior égredī ēgréssus sum; **to go by** *(or* **in a) car** currū *or* autoraédā eō īre īvī *or* iī; **to go to town by car** autoraédā in urbem sē cónferō -ferre -tulī; **to head for someplace in a car** autóraedā áliquem locum pet·ō -ere -ívī -ítus; **to put the car into the garage** autoraédam in receptáculō collocáre; **to rent a car** autoraédam condúc·ō -ere condúxī condúctus; **to ride in a car** autoraédā vehor vehī vectus sum; **to stop the car** autoraédam sistō sistere stitī; **to take a ride in a car** gestātiónem autoraédā facere; **to take s.o. by car** áliquem autoraédā dūc·ō -ere dūxī ductus; **to take s.o. home in a car** áliquem domum autoraédā addúcere; **car door** autoraédae ōstíol·um -ī *n;* **car key** clav·is -is accēnsíva -ae *f*

carry *(luggage)* bāiuláre

car wash autocīnét·ī laváti·ō -ónis *f; (place)* autocīnétī lavātóri·um -ī *n*

change (buses, trains, planes) mūtáre (autoraédās longās, trámina, āëróplana)

check luggage sárcinās mandáre

class: first-class seat sēd·ēs -is *f* prīmae classis; **second-class seat** sēd·ēs -is *f* secúndae classis; **tourist-class seat** sēd·ēs -is *f* tūrísticae classis

clutch pedál·e -is *n* iūnctiónis *(or* cōpulātiónis)

cockpit céllul·a -ae *f* āëróplanī

collision collísi·ō -ónis *f*

concourse oec·us -ī *m* praestōlātórius

conductor *(of a train)* tráminis īnspect•or -óris *m*

connection coniúncti•ō -ónis *f*

depart abscéd•ō -ere abscéssī abscessúrus

departure abscéss•us -ūs *m*

detour flex•us -ūs *m*

diesel engine Dīseliánum mōtr•um -ī *n*

diesel fuel Dīseliánum benzín•um -ī *n*

dining car curr•us -ūs *m* cēnātórius

drive *(a car, truck, bus)* gubernáre, ag•ō -ere ēgī āctus; **to drive s.o. home** áliquem domum autocīnétō *(or* autoraédā) addúcere

driver autoraedári•us -ī *m* (•a -ae *f*), autocīnētíst•ēs *mf*

driver's license autoraedáriī diplóm•a -atis *n*

engine māchināmént•um -ī *n*, mōtr•um -ī *n*

escalator scāl•ae -árum *fpl* móbilēs

exhaust ēmissári•um -ī *n*

exhaust pipe tub•us -ī *m* ēmissárius

exit éxit•us -ūs *m*

express train trām•en -inis *n* rapidíssimum

fare vectúr•a -ae *f*

ferry nāv•is -is f trāiectória

fill it up, please! immissárium benzīnárium replē tótum, quaesō!

flight volát•us -ūs *m*

fly *tr* **fly a plane** āëróplanum gubernáre **‖** *intr* voláre; *(of a passenger)* āëróplanō vehor, vehī, vectus sum

fuel mātéri•a -ae *f* prōpulsória

gallon gall•on -ónis *m*

garage autocīnétī (autocīnētórum) receptácul•um -ī *n; (repair garage)* officín•a -ae *f* reparātória

gas benzín•um -ī *n;* **to step on the gas** acceleráre

gas pedal pedál•e -is *n* accelerātiónis

gas pump ántli•a -ae *f* benzīnária

gas station státi•ō -ónis *f* benzīnária

gas tank immissári•um -ī *n* benzīnárium

gate *(at airport)* ádit•us -ūs *m*

gearshift iúncti•ō -ónis *f* vēlōcitátum

get off *(a bus, plane, ship, train)* ēgrédior égredī ēgréssus sum dē (+ *abl)*

get on *(a bus, plane, ship, train)* īnscénd•ō -ere -ī in (+ *acc)*

grease úng•ō úngere ūnxī ūnctus

grease job úncti•ō -ónis *f*

handbag bulg•a -ae *f; (of leather and bigger than a* bulga) vídul•us -ī *m*

hand luggage sarcínul•ae -árum *fpl* manuálēs

hangar receptácul•um -ī *n* āëroplanórum

headlight autoraédae lūmináŕ•e -is *n;* **to turn on (turn off) the bright (dim) lights** lūmināria praecandéntia (candéntia) accénd•ō -ere -ī (exstíngu•ō -ere exstínxī)

helicopter helicópter•um -ī *n;* **to be taken by helicopter to** per helicópterum tráns•vehor -vehī -véctus sum; **to fly a helicopter** helicópterum gubernáre; **to fly in a helicopter** helicópterō vehor vehī vectus sum

highway vi•a -ae *f* autocīnética

hood plóxen•um -ī *n*

horn búcin•a -ae *f;* **to blow the horn** búcinā clang•ō -ere

hostess hóspit•a -ae *f* āéria

information īndíci•um -ī *n*

interchange coniúncti•ō -ónis *f* viárum

intersection cómpit•um -ī *n*

jet plane āёróplan·um -ī *n* pyraulocīnéticum

kilometer chīliómetr·um -ī *n*

land *(of a plane)* deórsum appéll·ō -ere áppulī, dēscénd·ō -ere -ī; *(of a ship)* ad terram appéllere; *(of a passenger on a ship)* in terram ēgrédior -ī ēgréssus sum

layover commoráti·ō -ṓnis *f*

lead: does this road lead to ... ? Dūcítne haec via ad (+ *acc)*?

license *(to drive)* diplṓm·a -atis *n* gubernātiṓnis

license plate notácul·um -ī *n* autocīnḗtī

liter lītr·a -ae *f*

locomotive curr·us -ūs *m* tractṓrius

lost: get lost aberrāre

lubrication úncti·ō -ṓnis f autocīnḗtī

luggage sárcin·ae -árum *fpl;* **piece of luggage** sárcin·a -ae *f; (small)* sarcínul·a -ae *f*

luggage rack retinácul·um -ī *n* sarcināle; **put up into the luggage rack** in retináculō repṓn·ō -ere repósuī

luggage tag pittáci·um -ī *n* sarcinále

mechanic mechánicus óp·ifex -íficis *m*

moped autobirótul·a -ae *f*

motel dēversṓri·um -ī *n* vehiculárium

motor mōtṓri·um -ī *n,* mōtr·um -ī *n*

motor boat scaph·a -ae *f* automatária

motorcycle autobírot·a -ae *f*

motorcyclist autobirotári·us -ī *m* (·a -ae *f*)

motorist autoraedári·us -ī *m* (·a -ae *f*), autocīnētíst·ēs -ae *mf*

motor oil óle·um -ī n mōtṓriī

no parking Cavē státuās vehículum!

no stopping Nē sístitō!

no passing Cavē praeveháris!

pack *(luggage)* cóllig·ō -ere collḗgī colléctus

park *tr* státu·ō -ere -uī **ǁ** *intr* autocīnḗtum statúere

parking fee tax·a -ae *f* statíva

parking lot áre·a -ae *f* statíva

parking-lot attendant cust·ōs -ṓdis *mf* áreae statívae

passenger vect·or -ṓris *m,* vectr·īx -ícis *f*

passenger train trām·en -inis *n* commū́ne

passing: No passing! Cavē praeveháris!

passport commeátūs diplṓm·a -atis *n*

pilot *s* gubernát·or -ṓris *m,* gubernátr·īx -ícis *f*

pilot *tr* gubernāre

plane āёróplan·um -ī *n*

platform *(in a train station)* crepíd·ō -inis *f*

porter báiul·us -ī *m*

pullman car curr·us -ūs *m* dormītṓrius

railroad ferrívi·a -ae *f*

railroad car curr·us -ūs *m* ferriviárius

railroad station státi·ō -ṓnis *f* ferriviária

reach *(arrive at)* pervén·iō -íre pervḗnī pervéntus ad *or* in (+ *acc)*

reservation reserváti·ō -ṓnis *f*

reserve reservāre

restaurant caupṓn·a -ae *f*

restroom loc·us -ī *m* sēcrétus

return réd·eō -íre -iī réditus

ride *(a car, plane, train)* vehor, vehī, vectus sum (autocīnḗtō, āёróplanō, trámine)

ride vécti·ō -ṓnis *f;* **to go for a ride** gestātiṓnem autocīnḗtō fácere

route certus curs·us -ūs *m*

row ōrd·ō -inis *m*

runway āeródrom·us -ī *m*

sail nāvigáre, nāve veh·or -ī vectus sum

schedule: bus schedule hōrári·um -ī *n* autoraedárum longárum; **flight schedule** hōrári·um -ī *n* āëroplanórum; **train schedule** hōrári·um -ī *n* tráminum

seat sēd·ēs -is *f;* **aisle seat** sēdēs andrōnális; **back seat** sēdēs postérior; **front seat** sēdēs antérior; **reserved seat** sēdēs reservāta; **window seat** sēdēs fenestrális

seatbelt cinctúr·a -ae *f* sēcūrītátis; **fasten (unfasten, take off) the seatbelt** cinctúram sēcūritátis adstríng·ō -ere adstríxī adstríctus (laxāre, leváre)

service station státi·ō -ónis *f* benzīnária

shoulder bag per·a -ae *f*

side street vi·a -ae *f* laterális

skycap báiul·us -ī *m*

sleeping car curr·us -ūs *m* dormītórius

slow down cursum réprimō reprímere représsī

spark plug candél·a -ae *f* accēnsíva

speed limit mod·us -ī *m* vēlōcitátis

steer gubernáre

steering wheel rot·a -ae *f* moderátrīx

steward hos·pes -itis *m* āérius

stewardess hóspit·a -ae *f* āéria

stop *(come to a stop)* cōnsist·ō -ere cōnstitī; **does the bus (train) stop in ...** subsistítne autoraéda longa (trámen) in (+ *abl*)?; **make a stop** *(of a bus, plane, train)* commór·or -árī -átus sum

stop-over commoráti·ō -ónis *f*

street *(paved)* strāt·a -ae *f*

streetcar curr·us -ūs *m* ēléctricus

street map tábul·a -ae *f* viária

subway ferrívi·a -ae *f* subterránea

suitcase vídul·us -ī *m,* risc·us -ī *m; (small one)* ríscul·us -ī *m*

taillight lūminár·e -is *n* postícum

take off *(of a plane)* sūrsum in áëra ascénd·ō -ere -ī

take-off *(of a plane)* āvoláti·ō -ónis *f*

taxi raed·a -ae *f* meritória

terminal státi·ō -ónis *f* terminális

ticket tésser·a -ae *f* (itinerária); **first-class (second-class) ticket** téssera prīmae (secúndae) classis; **one-way ticket** téssera ūnʒus cursūs; **punch the ticket** tésseram perforáre; **return ticket** téssera réditūs; **round-trip ticket** téssera itūs reditúsque

ticket agent tesserári·us -ī *m,* (·a -ae *f*)

ticket window ōstíol·um -ī *n* tesserárum

time table hōrári·um -ī *n*

tire cúmmeus canth·us -ī *m;* **to put air in the tire** cúmmeum canthum ínfláre

toll rotári·um -ī *n*

toll booth tabérn·a -ae *f* rotáris

toll road vi·a -ae *f* rotáris

tour peregrīnáti·ō -ónis *f*

tour bus coenautocīnét·um -ī *n* perigéticum

tour guide mystagóg·us -ī *m* (·a -ae *f*)

tourist peregrīná·tor -tóris *m* (·trīx -trícis *f*)

tourist class class·is -is *f* tūrística

track *(rail)* órbit·a -ae *f*

traffic celébrit·ās -átis *f* viae, vehiculórum frequénti·a -ae *f*

traffic cop vigil -is *mf* viatóri·us (-a)

traffic jam affluénti·a -ae *f* vehiculária

traffic light sēmáphor·um -ī *n* **(red rubrum; yellow** flāvum; **green** víride)

train trắm·en -inis *n;* **a through train** trāmen dīrḗctum

train schedule hōrắri·um -ī *n* ferriviále

train station státi·ō -ónis f ferriviária

train ticket tésser·a -ae *f* ferriviária

transfer to *(another train, etc.)* trānscénd·ō -ere -ī in (+ *acc*)

transportation vectŭr·a -ae *f,* commeắtūs vehícul·a -órum *npl*

travel iter fác·iō -ere fēcī factus, itinerắre; **travel by car (train, plane, ship)** autocīnḗtō (trắmine, āëróplanō, nāvī) vehor vehī vectus sum

travel agency sēd·ēs -is *f* periēgḗtica

travel agent itínerum prōcūrắ·tor -tóris *m* (·trīx -trícis *f*)

traveler viắt·or -óris *m,* viắtr·īx -ícis *f; (abroad)* peregrīnắ·tor -tóris *m* (·trīx -trícis *f*)

trip iter, itíneris *n;* **take a trip** iter fácere

trolley curr·us -ūs *m* ēléctricus

truck autocīnḗt·um -ī *n* onerárium, autocárr·um -ī *n*

truck driver, trucker autocīnḗtī onerárií gubernắt·or -óris *m*

trunk *(of a car)* receptắcul·um -ī *n* sarcinắrum; *(for clothes)* cist·a -ae *f*

tunnel *(for trains, cars)* spec·us -ūs *m* (ferriviắrius, autocīnḗticus)

turn *s (in the road)* flex·us -ūs *m* viae; **take a wrong turn** pérperam vert·or -ī versus sum

turn *intr* vert·or -ī versus sum; **turn around** convért·or -ī convérsus sum

turn-off dēvertícul·um -ī *n*

turnpike strāt·a -ae *f* autocīnḗtica quadripertíta

turn signal ind·ex -icis *m* dīrēctiónis

way vi·a -ae *f,* it·er -íneris *n;* **what is the quickest (best) way to … ?** Quae est via brevíssima (óptima) ad (+ *acc*)?

waiting room oec·us -ī *m* praestōlātórius

window *(of bus, car, etc.)* fenestéll·a -ae *f*

window seat sēd·ēs -is *f* fenestrális

windshield vitr·um -ī *n* antiāérium

windshield wiper vitritérgi·um -ū *n*

Chapter XXV: Grammar

CONVERSATIONS _____

[Note 1—In this chapter on teaching and learning Latin grammar in Latin, in place
of the usual model conversations, there will be questions by the teacher (**M**agistra,
Magister) and answers by the student (**S**tudēns). Using these exchanges as
models, Latin classes can be conducted in Latin. If some of the responses by the
student seem overly long, they may easily be reformulated into several shorter
questions. The grammatical terms and structures are based on the writings of the
Roman grammarians.

Note 2—It is possible to proceed directly to "The Parsing of Words" which follows
the section on principal parts, although it is better to at least read carefully the
discussion of the principal parts in order to become familiar with the grammatical
terminology before beginning to parse.]

┌────── Dē Pártibus Ōrātiónis   *The Parts of Speech*

Magist.	Partēs ōrātiónis quot sunt?	*How many parts of speech are there?*
Studēns	Octō.	*Eight.*
Magist.	Quae?	*Which (are they)?*
Studēns	Nōmen, prōnṓmen, verbum, adiectívum, advérbium, coniúnctiō, praepositiō, interiéctiō.	*Noun, pronoun, verb, adjective, adverb, conjunction, preposition, interjection.*

┌────── Dē Nómine   *The Noun*

[Note—When declining nouns, Roman grammarians used "hic, haec, hoc" as
definite articles, meaning "the," and not as demonstrative adjectives; they called
them "prōnōmina articulária praepositīva", that is, "prepositive pronouns serving
as articles." Therefore, they will be translated as "the" in the declensions.]

Magist.	Dīc [or dā] nōmen próprium.	*Give a proper noun.*
Studēns	Caesar.	*Caesar.*
Magist.	Dīc nōmen appellātívum.	*Give a common noun.*
Studēns	Puélla.	*Girl.*

Magist.	Dīc nōmen collectívum.	*Give a collective noun.*
Studēns	Pópulus.	*People.*
Magist.	Quārē "pópulus" dícitur nōmen collectívum?	*Why is "people" called a collective noun?*
Studēns	Quia "pópulus" est númerī singuláris at multitúdinem signíficāns.	*Because "people" is singular in number, but indicating plural.*
Magist.	Génera nóminum quot sunt?	*How many genders do nouns have?*
Studēns	Tria.	*Three.*
Magist.	Quae?	*Which (are they)?*
Studēns	Genus masculínum, ut "hic magíster"; genus fēminínum, ut "haec mātróna"; genus neutrum, ut "hoc dōnum."	*Masculine gender, for example, "the teacher"; feminine gender, for example, "the lady"; neuter gender, for example, "the gift."*
Magist.	Númerī nóminum quot sunt?	*How many numbers are there of nouns?*
Studēns	Duo.	*Two.*
Magist.	Quī?	*Which (are they)?*
Studēns	Singuláris, ut "hic magíster"; plūrális, ut "hī magístrī."	*Singular, for example, "the teacher"; plural, for example, "the teachers."*
Magist.	Cāsūs nóminum quot sunt?	*How many cases of nouns are there?*
Studēns	Sex.	*Six.*
Magist.	Quī?	*What (are they)?*
Studēns	Nōminātívus, ut "hic magíster"; genitívus, ut "hūius magístrī"; datívus, ut "huic magístrō"; accūsātívus, ut "hunc magístrum"; vocātívus, ut "ō magíster"; ablātívus, ut "ab hōc magístrō."	*Nominative, for example, "the teacher"; genitive, for example, "of the teacher"; dative, for example, "to the teacher"; accusative, for example, "the teacher"; vocative, for example, "oh teacher"; ablative, for example, "from the teacher."*

Magist.	Dā dēclīnātiṓnem nṓminis, géneris fēminī́nī, númerī singulā́ris.	*Give the declension of a noun of the feminine gender, singular number.*
Studēns	Nōminātī́vō cāsū: "haec puélla"; genitī́vō cāsū: "hūius puéllae"; datī́vō cāsū: "huic puéllae"; accūsātī́vō cāsū: "hanc puéllam"; vocātī́vō cāsū: "ō puélla"; ablātī́vō cāsū: "ab hāc puéllā."	*In the nominative case: "the girl"; in the genitive case: "of the girl"; in the dative case: "to the girl"; in the accusative case: "the girl"; in the vocative case: "oh girl"; in the ablative case: "from the girl."*
Magist.	Quae partēs ōrātiṓnis eṓdem modō dēclīnántur?	*What parts of speech are declined in the same way?*
Studēns	Nṓmina, prōnṓmina, adiectī́va, particípia, gerúndia.	*Nouns, pronouns, adjectives, participles, and gerunds.*
Magist.	Dēclīnātiṓnēs nṓminum quot sunt?	*How many declensions of nouns are there?*
Studēns	Quīnque.	*Five.*
Magist.	Prīma quae est?	*What is the first (declension)?*
Studēns	Prīma dēclīnā́tiō est nṓminis, cūius genitī́vus singulā́ris in "ae" diphthṓngō termirā́tur.	*The first declension is of a noun whose genitive singular ends in the diphthong "ae."*
Magist.	Dā exémplum.	*Give an example.*
Studēns	haec puélla hūius puéllae	*the girl* *of the girl*
Magist.	Secúnda dēclīnā́tiō quae est?	*What is the second declension?*
Studēns	Secúnda dēclīnā́tiō est nṓminis, cūius genitī́vus singulā́ris in "ī" longā termirā́tur.	*The second declension is of a noun whose genitive singular ends in a long "ī."*
Magist.	Dā exémplum.	*Give an example.*
Studēns	hic magíster hūius magístrī vel hoc dōnum hūius dōnī	*the teacher* *of the teacher* *or the gift* *of the gift*
Magist.	Tértia dēclīnā́tiō quae est?	*What is the third declension?*
Studēns	Tértia dēclīnā́tiō est nṓminis, cūius genitī́vus singulā́ris in "is" brevī termirā́tur, ut "hic pater", "hūius patris."	*The third declension is of a noun whose genitive singular ends in a short "is," for example, "the father," "of the father."*

Magist.	Quārta dēclīnātiō quae est?	*What is the fourth declension?*
Studēns	Quārta dēclīnātiō est nóminis, cūius genitívus singuláris in "ūs" longā terminátur, ut "hīc exércitus," "hūius exércitūs."	*The fourth declension is of a noun whose genitive singular ends in a long "ūs," for example, "the army," "of the army."*

Magist.	Quīnta dēclīnátiō quae est?	*What is the fifth declension?*
Studēns	Quīnta dēclīnátiō est nóminis, cūius genitívus singuláris terminátur in "ēī" dīvísīs, ut "hīc diēs," "hūius diéī."	*The fifth declension is of a noun whose genitive singular ends in "ēī" as separate letters, for example, "the day," "of the day."*

Magist.	Dēscríbe proprietátēs "magíster" nóminis.	*Parse the noun "teacher."*
Studēns	"Magíster" est nōmen appellātívum, masculínī géneris, númerī singuláris, cāsū nōminātívō.	*"Teacher" is a common noun, masculine gender, singular number, in the nominative case.*

Dē Prōnómine

The Pronoun

Magist.	Prōnómen quid est?	*What is a pronoun?*
Studēns	Pars ōrātiónis quae prō nómine pónitur.	*A part of speech which is used in place of a noun.*

Magist.	Númerī prōnóminum quot sunt?	*How many numbers do pronouns have?*
Studēns	Duo.	*Two.*

Magist.	Quī?	*Which (are they)?*
Studēns	Singuláris, ut "ille"; plurális, ut "illī."	*Singular, for example, "that one"; plural, for example, "those."*

Magist.	Génera prōnóminum quot sunt?	*How many genders do pronouns have?*
Studēns	Tria.	*Three.*

Magist.	Quae?	*Which (are they)?*
Studēns	Genus masculínum, fēminínum, neutrum.	*Masculine, feminine, and neuter gender.*

Magist.	Prōnṓmina sunt aut fīníta aut īnfīníta. Dā exémpla prōnṓminis fīnītī.	*Pronouns are either definite or indefinite. Give examples of a definite pronoun.*
Studēns	Ego, tū, ille.	*I, you, he.*
Magist.	Dā exémpla prōnṓminis īnfīnítī.	*Give examples of an indefinite pronoun.*
Studēns	Quī, áliquis.	*Who, someone.*
Magist.	Dā exémpla prōnṓminis dēmōnstrātívī.	*Give examples of a demonstrative pronoun.*
Studēns	Hic, ille.	*This one, that one.*
Magist.	Dā exémpla prōnṓminis relātívī.	*Give examples of a relative pronoun.*
Studēns	Quī, quae, quod.	*Who, who, which.*
Magist.	Dā exémpla prōnṓminis interrōgātívī.	*Give examples of an interrogative pronoun.*
Studēns	Quis, quid.	*Who, what.*
Magist.	Dā exémpla prōnṓminis intentiṓnis.	*Give examples of an intensive pronoun.*
Studēns	Ipse, ipsa, ipsum.	*Himself, herself, itself.*
Magist.	Dā exémpla prōnṓminis recíprocī.	*Give examples of a reflexive pronoun.*
Studēns	Sē, sibi.	*Himself (herself, itself), to himself (herself, itself).*
Magist.	Dā exémpla prōnṓminis persōnális.	*Give examples of a personal pronoun.*
Studēns	Ego, nōs, tū.	*I, we, you.*
Magist.	Prōnṓmen est aut simplex aut compósitum. Dā exémplum prōnṓminis símplicis.	*A pronoun is either simple or compound. Give an example of a simple pronoun.*
Studēns	Quis.	*Who.*
Magist.	Dā exémplum prōnṓminis compósitī.	*Give an example of a compound pronoun.*
Studēns	Quisnam.	*Just who.*

Magist.	Ex quibus "quisnam" compṓnitur?	*Of what is "just who" composed?*
Studēns	Ex "quis" prōnṓmine et ex "nam" partícula.	*Of the pronoun "who" and the particle "just."*

Magist.	Estne figū́ra "quisquis" prōnṓminis simplex an compósita?	*Is the form of the pronoun "whoever" simple or compound?*
Studēns	Est compósita.	*It is compound.*

Magist.	Dēscrī́be proprietā́tēs "ego" prōnṓminis.	*Parse the pronoun "I."*
Studēns	"Ego" est prōnṓmen fīnī́tum, géneris masculī́nī et fēminī́nī, persṓnae prīmae, númerī singulā́ris, cāsū nōminātī́vō.	*"I" is a definite pronoun, masculine and feminine, first person, singular, in the nominative case.*

Magist.	Dēscrī́be proprietā́tēs "quōrum" prōnṓminis.	*Parse the pronoun "of whom."*
Studēns	"Quōrum" est prōnṓmen relātī́vum aut interrōgātī́vum, persṓnae tértiae, númerī plūrā́lis, géneris masculī́nī et neutrī́us, cāsū genitī́vō.	*"Of whom" or "whose" is a relative or interrogative pronoun, third person, plural, masculine and neuter, in the genitive case.*

Dē Verbō   *The Verb*

[Note—Roman grammarians recognized five moods; modern Latin grammars recognize three: indicative, subjunctive, and imperative.]

Magist.	Verbum quid est?	*What is a verb?*
Studēns	Pars ōrātiṓnis cum témpore et persṓnā sine cāsū.	*A part of speech with tense and person, without case.*

Magist.	Modī quot sunt?	*How many moods are there?*
Studēns	Quīnque.	*Five.*

Magist.	Quī?	*Which (are they)?*
Studēns	Indicātī́vus, ut "legō"; subiūnctī́vus, ut "cum legam"; imperātī́vus, ut "lege"; īnfīnītī́vus, ut "légere"; impersōnā́lis, ut "légitur."	*Indicative, for example, "I read, am reading"; subjunctive, for example, "although I read"; imperative, for example, "read!"; infinitive, for example, "to read"; impersonal, for example, "people read."*

Magist.	Númerī verbórum quot sunt?	*How many numbers do verbs have?*
Studēns	Duo.	*Two.*
Magist.	Quī?	*Which (are they)?*
Studēns	Singuláris et plūrális.	*Singular and plural.*
Magist.	Persónae verbórum quot sunt?	*How many persons of verbs are there?*
Studēns	Trēs.	*Three.*
Magist.	Quae?	*Which (are they)?*
Studēns	Prīma, ut "legō"; secúnda, ut "legis"; tértia, ut "legit."	*First, for example, "I read, am reading"; second, for example, "you read, are reading"; third, for example, "he, she reads, is reading."*
Magist.	Témpora in dēclīnātióne verbórum quot sunt?	*How many tenses are there in the conjugation of verbs?*
Studēns	Sex.	*Six.*
Magist.	Quae?	*Which (are they)?*
Studēns	Praesēns, ut "legō"; praetéritum imperféctum, ut "legébam"; futúrum, ut "legam"; praetéritum perféctum, ut "lēgī"; praetéritum plūsquamperféctum, ut "légeram"; futúrum perféctum, ut "légerō."	*Present, for example, "I read, am reading"; imperfect, for example, "I was reading, used to read"; future, for example, "I shall read"; perfect, for example, "I read, have read"; pluperfect, for example, "I had read"; future perfect, for example, "I shall have read."*
Magist.	Coniugātiónēs verbórum quot sunt?	*How many conjugations are there?*
Studēns	Quáttuor.	*Four.*
Magist.	Quae?	*Which (are they)?*
Studēns	Prīma, secúnda, tértia, quārta.	*First, second, third, fourth.*

Magist.	Dēclínā verbum āctívum prīmae coniugātiónis, indicātívō modō, témpore praeséntī, númerō singulárī.	*Conjugate an active verb of the first conjugation, in the indicative mood, present tense, singular.*
Studēns	amō amās amat	*I love* *you love* *he or she loves*
Magist.	Dēclínā verbum āctívum secúndae coniugātiónis, indicātívō modō, témpore praetéritō imperféctō, plūráliter.	*Conjugate an active verb of the second conjugation, indicative mood, in the imperfect tense, in the plural.*
Studēns	docēbámus docēbátis docébant	*we were teaching* *you were teaching* *they were teaching*
Magist.	Dēclínā verbum āctívum tértiae coniugātiónis, indicātívō modō, témpore futúrō, númerō singulárī.	*Conjugate an active verb of the third conjugation, indicative mood, future, singular.*
Studēns	regam regēs reget	*I shall rule* *you will rule* *he or she will rule*
Magist.	Dēclínā verbum āctívum quártae coniugātiónis, indicātívō modō, témpore praetéritō plūsquamperféctō, plūráliter.	*Conjugate an active verb of the fourth conjugation, indicative mood, pluperfect tense, plural.*
Studēns	audīverámus audīverátis audíverant	*we had heard* *you had heard* *they had heard*

[**Note**—*genus* in connection with nouns means "gender"; in connection with verbs it means "voice."]

Magist.	Génera verbórum quot sunt?	*How many voices of verbs are there?*
Studēns	Quáttuor.	*Four.*
Magist.	Quae?	*Which (are they)?*
Studēns	Āctíva, passíva, neutra vel neutrália, dēpōnéntia.	*Active, passive, intransitive, deponent (verbs).*

Magist.	Dā exémpla verbī neutrális.	*Give (me some) examples of an intransitive verb.*
Studēns	Sédeō, stō, cubō.	*I sit, am sitting; I stand, am standing; I lie down, I am lying down.*
Magist.	Dā exémpla verbī dēpōnéntis.	*Give (me some) examples of a deponent verb.*
Studēns	Loquor, sequor, fruor.	*I speak, am speaking; I follow, am following; I enjoy, am enjoying.*
Magist.	Dā dēclīnātiónem verbī āctívī "legō" indicātívō modō, témpore praeséntī, singuláriter.	*Give the conjugation of the active verb "legō" in the indicative mood, present tense, in the singular.*
Studēns	Dēclīnátur: legō legis legit	*It is conjugated:* *I read, am reading* *you read, are reading* *he or she reads, is reading*
Magist.	Dēclínā idem verbum āctívum, témpore praetéritō imperféctō, plūráliter.	*Conjugate the same verb in the imperfect tense, in the plural.*
Studēns	Dēclīnátur: legēbámus legēbátis legébant	*It is conjugated:* *we were reading* *you were reading* *they were reading*
Magist.	Dā dēclīnātiónem eiusdem verbī āctívī, témpore praeséntī, modō subiūnctívō, singuláriter.	*Give the conjugation of the same active verb in the present tense, subjunctive, singular.*
Studēns	Dēclīnátur: legam legās legat	*It is conjugated:* *I may read* *you may read* *he or she may read*
Magist.	Dēclínā idem verbum āctívum témpore praetéritō plūsquamperféctō, modō subiūnctívō, plūráliter.	*Conjugate the same active verb in the pluperfect subjunctive plural.*
Studēns	Dēclīnátur: lēgissémus lēgissétis lēgíssent	*It is conjugated:* *we would have read* *you would have read* *they would have read*

| **Magist.** | Dīc imperātívum modum eiúsdem verbī, témpore praeséntī, singulāriter et plūráliter. | *Give the present imperative of the same verb in the singular and the plural.* |
| **Studēns** | "Lege!," "légite!" | *Read! (singular), read! (plural)* |

| **Magist.** | Dīc imperātívum eiúsdem verbī, témpore futū́rō, secúndā et tértiā persṓnā, singulā́riter et plūrā́liter. | *Give the future imperative of the same verb in the second and third person singular and plural.* |
| **Studēns** | Persṓnā secúndā: "légitō!," "legitṓte!"; persṓnā tértiā: "légitō!," "legúntō!" | *Second person: you will read! (singular); you will read! (plural); third person: let him or her read!; let them read!* |

| **Magist.** | Dīc participium hūius verbī, praesénтī témpore. | *Give the present participle of this verb.* |
| **Studēns** | Legēns. | *Reading.* |

| **Magist.** | Dīc participium hūius verbī, futū́rō témpore. | *Give the future participle of this verb.* |
| **Studēns** | Lēctū́rus. | *About to read.* |

| **Magist.** | Dīc participium hūius verbī, praetéritō perféctō témpore. | *Give the perfect participle of this verb.* |
| **Studēns** | Lēctus. | *Having been read.* |

| **Magist.** | Dīc īnfīnītívum āctívum hūius verbī, praeséntī témpore. | *Give the present active infinitive of this verb.* |
| **Studēns** | Légere. | *To read.* |

| **Magist.** | Dīc īnfīnītívum passívum hūius verbī, praesénтī témpore. | *Give the present passive infinitive of this verb.* |
| **Studēns** | Legī. | *To be read.* |

| **Magist.** | Dīc īnfīnītívum āctívum hūius verbī, praetéritō perféctō témpore. | *Give the perfect active infinitive of this verb.* |
| **Studēns** | Lēgísse. | *To have read.* |

| **Magist.** | Dīc īnfīnītívum passívum hūius verbī, praetéritō perféctō témpore. | *Give the perfect passive infinitive of this verb.* |
| **Studēns** | Lēctus esse. | *To have been read.* |

| **Magist.** | Dēscrī́be proprietā́tēs "legō" verbī. | *Parse the verb "legō."* |

Studēns "Legō" est verbum āctī́vum indicātī́vī modī, prīmae persṓnae, númerī singulā́ris, témporis praesḗntis, tértiae coniugātiṓnis.

"Legō" is an active verb, used in the indicative mood, first person, singular, present tense, third conjugation.

Magist. Dā exémpla verbī inaequā́lis.

Give (me some) examples of an irregular verb.

Studēns Fiō, sóleō, ferō, gaúdeō, nōlō.

I become, I am wont, I bear, I am glad, I do not want.

Magist. Quārē inaequā́lia dīcúntur?

Why are they called irregular?

Studēns Quia dēclīnātiṓnēs extrā régulam sunt.

Because they are conjugated outside the (normal) pattern.

Magist. Dā exémpla verbī dēfectī́vī.

Give (some) examples of a defective verb.

Studēns Pudet, ōdī.

It shames, I hate.

Magist. Quārē dēfectī́va dīcúntur?

Why are they called defective?

Studēns Quia haec verba quibúsdam figū́rīs egent.

Because these verbs lack certain forms.

Magist. Quibus figū́rīs "pudet" eget?

What forms does "pudet" (it shames) lack?

Studēns Eget persṓnā prīmā et secúndā. Dī́citur étiam verbum impersōnā́le.

It lacks the first and second person. It is also called an impersonal verb.

Magist. Quibus figū́rīs "ōdī" eget?

What forms does "ōdī" (I hate) lack?

Studēns Habet neque tempus praesēns, neque praetéritum imperféctum neque futū́rum.

It doesn't have a present, imperfect, or future tense.

Magist. Dā partēs prīncipā́lēs "dóceō" verbī.

Give the principal parts of the verb "doceō."

Studēns Dóceō, docḗre, dócuī, doctus.

I teach, am teaching; to teach; I taught, have taught; taught, having been taught.

Dē Advérbiō

The Adverb

Magist.	Advérbium quid est?	*What is an adverb?*
Studēns	Pars ōrātiṓnis quae verbō adícitur et verbum explắnat atque implet.	*The part of speech which modifies the verb and explains and completes it.*
Magist.	Cui dictiṓnī advérbium adícitur?	*What word does an adverb modify?*
Studēns	Vel verbō vel advérbiō vel adiectī́vō adiícitur.	*It modifies a verb, an adverb, or an adjective.*
Magist.	Dā advérbia locī́.	*Give (some) adverbs of place.*
Studēns	Hī́c, ibi, intus, forī́s, illī́c, inde.	*Here, there, inside, outside, there, from there.*
Magist.	Dā advérbia témporis.	*Give (some) adverbs of time.*
Studēns	Hódiē, nūper, aliquándō, mox.	*Today, recently, sometime, soon.*
Magist.	Dā advérbia númerī́.	*Give (some) adverbs of number.*
Studēns	Semel, bis, ter, déciēs.	*Once, twice, three times, ten times.*
Magist.	Dā advérbium affirmándī́.	*Give an adverb of affirmation.*
Studēns	Étiam.	*Yes.*
Magist.	Dā advérbium negándī́.	*Give an adverb of negation.*
Studēns	Nōn.	*No.*
Magist.	Dā advérbia interrōgándī́.	*Give (some) interrogative adverbs.*
Studēns	Cūr, quāre, quámobrem.	*Why, why, why.*
Magist.	Dā advérbia ṓrdinis.	*Give (some) adverbs of a series.*
Studēns	Prī́mum, deínde, postrḗmō.	*First, then, finally.*
Magist.	Dā advérbia quantitắtis.	*Give (some) adverbs of quantity.*
Studēns	Multum, parum.	*Much, little.*
Magist.	Dā advérbia qualitắtis.	*Give (some) adverbs of quality.*
Studēns	Pulchrē, bene, male.	*Beautifully, well, badly.*

Magist.	Quot gradūs comparātiṓnis sunt advérbiīs?	*How many degrees of comparison do adverbs have?*
Studēns	Trēs.	*Three.*

| **Magist.** | Quī? | *What (are they)?* |
| **Studēns** | Positī́vus, ut "saepe"; comparātī́vus, ut "saépius"; superlātī́vus, ut "saepíssimē." | *The positive, for example, "often"; the comparative, for example, "more often"; the superlative, for example, "very often."* |

| **Magist.** | Suntne advérbia declīnābília an indēclīnābília? | *Are adverbs declinable or indeclinable?* |
| **Studēns** | Sunt indēclīnābília. | *They are indeclinable.* |

Dē Adjectī́vō
The Adjective

Magist.	Adiectī́vum quid est?	*What is an adjective?*
Studēns	Pars ōrātiṓnis est quae nṓminī adícitur.	*It is a part of speech that modifies a noun.*

| **Magist.** | Quot gradūs comparātiṓnis sunt adiectī́vīs? | *How many degrees of comparison do adjectives have?* |
| **Studēns** | Trēs gradūs comparātiṓnis. | *Three degrees of comparison.* |

| **Magist.** | Quī? | *Which (are they)?* |
| **Studēns** | Positī́vus, ut "doctus"; comparātī́vus, ut "dóctior"; superlātī́vus, ut "doctíssimus" | *The positive, for example, "learned"; the comparative, for example, "more learned"; the superlative, for example, "most learned."* |

| **Magist.** | Quot terminātiṓnēs sunt adiectī́vīs, gradūs positī́vī? | *How many endings do adjectives have in the positive degree?* |
| **Studēns** | Trēs. | *Three.* |

| **Magist.** | Quae? | *Which (are they)?* |
| **Studēns** | Masculī́na, ut "doctus"; fēminī́na, ut "docta"; neutra, ut "doctum." | *Masculine, for example, "learned"; feminine, for example, "learned"; neuter, for example, "learned."* |

Magist.	Quot terminātiónēs sunt adiectívīs, gradūs comparātívī?	*How many endings do adjectives have in the comparative degree?*
Studēns	Duae.	*Two.*
Magist.	Quae?	*Which (are they)?*
Studēns	Masculína et fēminína, ut "dóctior"; neutra, ut "dóctius."	*Masculine and feminine, for example, "more learned"; neuter, for example, "more learned."*
Magist.	Quot terminātiónēs sunt adiectívīs, gradūs superlātívī?	*How many endings do adjectives in the superlative degree have?*
Studēns	Trēs, sícut in gradū positívō.	*Three, just as in the positive degree.*
Magist.	Dīc adiectívum possessívum.	*Give a possessive adjective.*
Studēns	Meus.	*My.*
Magist.	Dīc adiectívum quālitátis.	*Give an adjective of quality.*
Studēns	Bonus.	*Good.*
Magist.	Dīc adiectíva quantitátis.	*Give (some) adjectives of quantity.*
Studēns	Magnus, parvus.	*Big, small.*
Magist.	Dīc adiectíva númerī.	*Give (some) adjectives of number.*
Studēns	Ūnus, duo, trēs.	*One, two, three.*
Magist.	Dīc adiectíva númerī ōrdinális.	*Give (some) adjectives of ordinal numbers.*
Studēns	Prīmus, secúndus, tértius.	*First, second, third.*

Dē Particípiō

The Participle

Magist.	Particípium quid est?	*What is a participle?*
Studēns	Pars ōrātiónis partem adiectívī cápiēns, partem verbī.	*A part of speech assuming the role of an adjective and the role of a verb.*

Magist.	Témpora participiórum quot sunt?	*How many tenses do participles have?*
Studēns	Praesēns, ut "legēns"; praetéritum, ut "lēctus"; futúrum, ut "lēctúrus."	*The present, for example, "reading"; the perfect, for example, "read, having been read"; the future, for example, "about to read."*
Magist.	Quot particípia ab āctívō verbō véniunt?	*How many participles come from the active verb?*
Studēns	Duo.	*Two.*
Magist.	Quae?	*Which (are they)?*
Studēns	Praesēns, ut "legēns" et futúrum ut "lēctúrus."	*The present, for example, "reading", and the future, for example, "about to read."*
Magist.	Quot particípia ā passívō verbō véniunt?	*How many participles come from the passive verb?*
Studēns	Ūnum.	*One.*
Magist.	Quod?	*Which one?*
Studēns	Praetéritum perféctum, ut "lēctus."	*The perfect, for example, "read, having been read."*

Dē Gerúndiō

The Gerund

Magist.	Gerúndium quid est?	*What is a gerund?*
Studēns	Est nōmen verbále.	*It is a verbal noun.*
Magist.	Quārē sīc vocátur?	*Why is it called that?*
Studēns	Quia partem nóminis capit, partem verbī.	*Because it assumes the role of a noun and the role of a verb.*
Magist.	Dā exémplum gerúndiī.	*Give an example of a gerund.*
Studēns	*Legéndī* librōs causā.	*For the sake of reading books.*
Magist.	Quómodo capit partem nóminis?	*How does it assume the role of a noun?*
Studēns	Eō quod habet cāsūs oblíquōs, perínde ut nómina.	*In that it has oblique cases, just as nouns do.*

Magist.	Quốmodo capit partem verbī?	*How does it assume the role of a verb?*
Studēns	Eō quod adiúngitur cấsuī accūsātấvō, perínde ut verba.	*In that it takes the accusative case, just as verbs do.*

Dē Gerundívō — *The Gerundive*

Magist.	Gerundívum quid est?	*What is a gerundive?*
Studēns	Est adiectívum verbále.	*It is a verbal adjective.*
Magist.	Quārē sīc vocấtur?	*Why is it called that?*
Studēns	Quia partem adiectívī capit, partem verbī.	*Because it assumes the role of an adjective and the role of a verb.*
Magist.	Dā exémplum gerundívī.	*Give an example of a gerundive.*
Studēns	*Legẹndốrum* librốrum causā.	*For the sake of reading books.*
Magist.	Quốmodo partem adiectívī capit?	*How does it assume the role of an adjective?*
Studēns	Eō quod "librōs" nốminī adícitur.	*In that it modifies the noun "books."*

Dē Conjūnctiốne — *The Conjunction*

Magist.	Coniúnctiō quid est?	*What is a conjunction?*
Studēns	Pars ōrātiốnis connéctēns ōrdinấnsque senténtiam.	*A part of speech connecting and arranging a sentence.*
Magist.	Dā coniūnctiốnēs copulātívās.	*Give (some) coordinate conjunctions.*
Studēns	Et, atque, ac.	*And, and, and.*
Magist.	Dā coniūnctiốnēs disiūnctívās.	*Give (some) disjunctive conjunctions.*
Studēns	Aut, -ve, vel.	*Or, or, or.*
Magist.	Dā coniūnctiốnēs adversātívās.	*Give (some) adversative conjunctions.*
Studēns	Sed, at.	*But, but.*

Magist.	Dā coniūnctiṓnēs concessī́vās.	*Give (some) concessive conjunctions.*
Studēns	Quamquam, quamvīs.	*Although, although.*
Magist.	Dā coniūnctiṓnēs temporā́lēs.	*Give (some) temporal conjunctions.*
Studēns	Cum, ántequam, postquam.	*When, before, after.*
Magist.	Dā coniūnctiṓnēs condiciōnā́lēs.	*Give (some) conditional conjunctions.*
Studēns	Sī, nisi.	*If, unless.*

Dē Praepositiṓne   *The Preposition*

Magist.	Praeposítiō quid est?	*What is a preposition?*
Studēns	Pars ōrātiṓnis quae, áliīs pártibus ōrātiṓnis praepósita, significātiṓnem eárum implet aut mūtat.	*A part of speech which, placed before other parts of speech, completes or changes their meaning.*
Magist.	Quibus cā́sibus praepositiṓnēs sérviunt?	*What cases do prepositions take?*
Studēns	Accūsātī́vō et ablātī́vō.	*The accusative and the ablative.*
Magist.	Dā praepositiṓnēs cāsūs accūsātī́vī.	*Give (some) prepositions taking the accusative.*
Studēns	Ad, apud, ante, advérsum, ergā.	*To, at, before, against, toward.*
Magist.	Dā praepositiṓnēs cāsūs ablātī́vī.	*Give (some) prepositions taking the ablative case.*
Studēns	Ab, cum, cōram, clam, dē, ex, prō.	*From, with, in the presence of, without the knowledge of, concerning, out of, for.*
Magist.	Dā praepositiṓnēs utrīúsque cāsūs.	*Give (some) prepositions taking both cases.*
Studēns	In, sub, super, subter.	*In(to), under, above, below.*
Magist.	"In" et "sub" quandō ablātī́vō sérviunt?	*When do "in" and "under" take the ablative case?*
Studēns	Quandō significā́mus quṓslibet aut quaélibet in locō esse.	*When we mean that someone or something is in a place.*

Magist.	"In" et "sub" quandō accūsātívō sérviunt?	*When do "in" and "under" take the accusative?*
Studēns	Quandō significámus quóslibet aut quaélibet in locum īre.	*When we mean that someone or something is going into a place.*
Magist.	"Super" quam vim habet?	*What is the sense of "super"?*
Studēns	Ubi locum signíficat, magis accūsātívō cásuī servit quam ablātívō locī; ubi mentiónem alicúius fácimus, ablātívō cásuī dumtáxat servit, ut "Multa super Príamō rógitāns."	*When it indicates place, it takes the accusative rather than the ablative of place; when we · make mention of someone or something, it takes only the ablative, for example: "Asking many questions about Priam."*

┌───── Dē Interjectióne   *The Interjection*

Magist.	Interiéctiō quid est?	*What is an interjection?*
Studēns	Pars ōrātiónis signíficāns mentis afféctum vōce incónditā.	*A part of speech indicating an emotion with inarticulate sound.*
Magist.	Interiéctiō quid significáre potest?	*What can an interjection indicate?*
Studēns	Vel laetítiam, ut "evax"; vel dolórem, ut "heu"; vel admīrātiónem, ut "papaé"; vel metum, ut "attát."	*Either joy, for example, "hurrah!"; or grief, for example, "oh no!"; or astonishment, for example, "wow!"; or fear, for example, "oh!"*

┌───── Dē Accéntū   *The Accent*

Magist.	In quā sýllabā accéntum pónimus?	*On which syllable do we place the accent?*
Studēns	Aut in antepaenúltimā aut in paenúltimā.	*On the antepenult or the penult.*
Magist.	Quandō accéntum in paenúltimā sýllabā pónimus?	*When do we place the accent on the penult?*
Studēns	Quandō paenúltima sýllaba est longa, ut "amámus."	*When the penult is long, for example, "amāmus" (we love).*

Magist.	In quā sýllabā accéntum pónimus sī paenúltima sýllaba est brevis?	*On which syllable do we place the accent if the penult is short?*
Studēns	In antepaenúltimā sýllabā.	*On the antepenult.*
Magist.	Quandō accéntus pónitur in últimā sýllabā?	*When is the accent placed on the last syllable?*
Studēns	Numquam aut útique rāríssimō.	*Never or, in any event, very rarely.*

⎯⎯⎯ Dē Proprietátibus Dictiónum Dēscrībéndīs   *The Parsing of Words*

[Note—The genitive of quality, or better, of description, is generally used in parsing words, for example; "Cújus generis est 'puella'? (Of) what gender is "girl"? "Fēminīnī generis" (of the) feminine gender. But when indicating the case of a noun or adjective, the ablative is generally used, e.g., "homine" quō cāsū est? (In) what case is "the man"? "Ablātīvō." (In) the ablative case. The Romans also reverse our order of apposition, for example, "sī ultima syllaba in 'a' litterā terminātur . . . ." (if the last syllable ends in the letter "a").]

Magist.	Dēscrībámus nunc proprietátēs dictiónum in hāc senténtiā: **Ego arma virúmque canō, quī ōlim ā Trōiae ōrīs longínquīs vēnit.** "*Ego*" quae pars ōrātiónis est?	*Let's now parse the words of this sentence:* **I sing of war and a hero who once upon a time came from the distant shores of Troy.** *What part of speech is "I"?*
Studēns	Prōnómen.	*A pronoun.*
Magist.	Cūius est númerī?	*What number is it?*
Studēns	Númerī singuláris.	*Singular.*
Magist.	Cūius est géneris in hōc locō?	*What gender is it in this passage?*
Studēns	Masculínī.	*Masculine.*
Magist.	Cūius est persónae?	*What person is it?*
Studēns	Prīmae persónae.	*First person.*
Magist.	Quō est cāsū?	*In what case?*
Studēns	Cāsū nōminātīvō.	*In the nominative case.*
Magist.	Estne prōnómen fīnítum an infīnítum?	*Is it a definite or indefinite pronoun?*
Studēns	Prōnómen fīnítum.	*A definite pronoun.*

Magist.	*"Arma"* quae pars ōrātiónis est?	*What part of speech is "arms"?*
Studēns	Nōmen.	*A noun.*
Magist.	Quāle? Nōmen próprium an appellātívum?	*What kind? Proper or common?*
Studēns	Nōmen appellātívum.	*A common noun.*
Magist.	Cūius est géneris?	*What gender is it?*
Studēns	Neutríus.	*Neuter.*
Magist.	Cūius est númerī?	*What number is it?*
Studēns	Plūrális.	*Plural.*
Magist.	Quō cāsū est in hōc lōcō?	*What case is it in this passage?*
Studēns	Accūsātívō.	*Accusative.*
Magist.	Unde hoc certum est?	*How is that certain?*
Studēns	Ā syntáxe; "canō" enim verbum accūsātívō adiúngitur.	*From the syntax; for the verb "canō" takes the accusative case.*
Magist.	Quotae dēclīnātiónis est "arma"?	*What declension is "arms"?*
Studēns	Secúndae.	*Second.*
Magist.	Pōnitúrne "arma" própriē an figūrátē?	*Is "arms" used literally or figuratively?*
Studēns	Figūrátē.	*Figuratively.*
Magist.	Quārē?	*Why?*
Studēns	Quia prō "bellō" pónitur.	*Because it is used for "war."*
Magist.	*"Virum"* quae pars ōrātiónis est?	*What part of speech is "hero"?*
Studēns	Nōmen.	*A noun.*
Magist.	Cūius est géneris?	*What gender is it?*
Studēns	Masculínī.	*Masculine.*
Magist.	Cūius est númerī?	*What number is it?*
Studēns	Singulāris.	*Singular.*
Magist.	Quō cāsū est?	*What case is it?*
Studēns	Accūsātívō.	*Accusative.*

| **Magist.** | Dīc cāsum nōminātívum. | *Give the nominative case.* |
| **Studēns** | Vir. | *Vir (hero).* |

| **Magist.** | Quotae dēclīnātiốnis est "virum"? | *What declension is "the hero"?* |
| **Studēns** | Secúndae. | *Second.* |

| **Magist.** | Cūius est númerī? | *What number is it?* |
| **Studēns** | Singulấris. | *Singular.* |

| **Magist.** | Quāle? Próprium an appellātívum? | *What kind? Proper or common (noun)?* |
| **Studēns** | Nōmen appellātívum. | *Common (noun).* |

| **Magist.** | "*Que*" quae pars ōrātiốnis est? | *What part of speech is "and"?* |
| **Studēns** | Cōniứnctiō. | *A conjunction.* |

| **Magist.** | Cūius est potestấtis? Copulātívae an disiūnctívae? | *(Of) what function is it? Coordinate or disjunctive?* |
| **Studēns** | Copulātívae. | *Coordinate.* |

| **Magist.** | Cūius ốrdinis? Praepositívī an postpositívī? | *What is its word order? Prepositive or postpositive?* |
| **Studēns** | Postpositívī; ítaque dícitur enclíticum. | *It is postpositive; and so it is called an enclitic.* |

| **Magist.** | Fac compósitum ab eō quod est "que." | *Form a compound from "que."* |
| **Studēns** | Ítaque, neque, quoque. | *And so, neither, too.* |

| **Magist.** | "*Canō*" quae pars ōrātiốnis est? | *What part of speech is "sing"?* |
| **Studēns** | Verbum. | *A verb.* |

| **Magist.** | Cūius modī est? | *In what mood is it?* |
| **Studēns** | Indicātívī. | *The indicative.* |

| **Magist.** | Cūius persốnae est? | *What person is it?* |
| **Studēns** | Prīmae. | *First (person).* |

| **Magist.** | Dīc tertiam persốnam. | *Give the third person.* |
| **Studēns** | Canit. | *He or she sings, is singing.* |

Magist.	Cūius númerī est?	*What number is it?*
Studēns	Singuláris.	*Singular.*
Magist.	Dīc plūrálem prīmae persṓnae.	*Give the first person plural.*
Studēns	Cánimus.	*We sing.*
Magist.	Cūius géneris est? Āctī́vī an passī́vī?	*What voice is it? Active or passive?*
Studēns	Āctī́vī.	*Active.*
Magist.	Dīc passī́vum.	*Give the passive.*
Studēns	Canor.	*I am sung of.*
Magist.	Cūius témporis est?	*What tense is it?*
Studēns	Praeséntis.	*The present.*
Magist.	Dīc praetéritum imperféctum.	*Give the imperfect.*
Studēns	Canḗbam.	*I was singing, used to sing.*
Magist.	Dīc praetéritum perféctum.	*Give the perfect.*
Studēns	Cécinī.	*I sang, have sung.*
Magist.	Dīc particípium praesēns.	*Give the present participle.*
Studēns	Canēns.	*Singing.*
Magist.	Dīc particípium futū́rum.	*Give the future participle.*
Studēns	Cantū́rus.	*About to sing, going to sing.*
Magist.	Dīc īnfīnītī́vum āctī́vum.	*Give the active infinitive.*
Studēns	Cánere.	*To sing.*
Magist.	Dīc gerúndium.	*Give the gerund.*
Studēns	Canéndī.	*Of singing.*
Magist.	Dīc gerúndium cāsū nōminātī́vō.	*Give the gerund in the nominative case.*
Studēns	Gerúndium eget cāsū nōminātī́vō.	*The gerund lacks a nominative case.*
Magist.	"*Quī*" quae pars ōrātiónis est?	*What part of speech is "who"?*
Studēns	Prōnṓmen.	*A pronoun.*

Magist.	Quāle prōnṓmen?	*What kind of pronoun?*
Studēns	Relātī́vum prōnṓmen.	*A relative pronoun.*
Magist.	Quid est eius nōmen antecḗdēns?	*What is its antecedent?*
Studēns	Virum.	*A hero.*
Magist.	"Quī" cūius est géneris?	*What gender is "who"?*
Studēns	Masculī́nī.	*Masculine.*
Magist.	Cūius númerī est?	*What number is it?*
Studēns	Singulā́ris.	*Singular.*
Magist.	Quārē númerus singulā́ris pṓnitur?	*Why is the singular number used?*
Studēns	Quia nōmen antecḗdēns est númerī singulā́ris.	*Because the antecedent is singular.*
Magist.	Quō cāsū est "quī"?	*In what case is "who"?*
Studēns	Cāsū nōminātī́vō.	*In the nominative case.*
Magist.	Cūius poténtiae est?	*What is its function?*
Studēns	Est subiéctum "vēnit" verbī́.	*It is the subject of the verb "came".*
Magist.	"Ōlim" quae pars ōrātiṓnis est?	*What part of speech is "once upon a time"?*
Studēns	Advérbium.	*An adverb.*
Magist.	Cui dictiṓnī "ōlim" adícitur?	*Which word does "once upon a time" modify?*
Studēns	"Vēnit" verbō.	*The verb "came".*
Magist.	Estne advérbium locī́ an témporis an qualitā́tis an quantitā́tis?	*Is it an adverb of place or time or quality or quantity?*
Studēns	Témporis.	*Of time.*
Magist.	"Ā" quae pars ōrātiṓnis est?	*What part of speech is "from"?*
Studēns	Praepositíō.	*A preposition.*
Magist.	Cui cā́suī servit?	*What case does it take [lit: serve]?*
Studēns	Cā́suī ablātī́vō.	*The ablative case.*

Magist.	Cui nốminī adiúngitur?	*What noun is its object?*
Studēns	"Ōrīs" nốminī.	*The noun "shores".*

Magist.	"*Trōiae*" quae pars ōrātiốnis est?	*What part of speech is "Troy's"?*
Studēns	Nōmen.	*A noun.*

Magist.	Quāle? Prốprium an appellātī́vum?	*What kind? Proper or common?*
Studēns	Prốprium.	*Proper.*

Magist.	Cūius est géneris?	*What gender is it?*
Studēns	Fēminī́nī.	*Feminine.*

Magist.	Cūius est númerī?	*What number is it?*
Studēns	Singulā́ris.	*Singular.*

Magist.	Quō est cāsū?	*In what case is it?*
Studēns	Genitī́vō.	*The genitive.*

Magist.	"*Ōrīs*" quae pars ōrātiốnis est?	*What part of speech is "shores"?*
Studēns	Nōmen.	*A noun.*

Magist.	Quāle? Prốprium an appellātī́vum?	*What kind? Proper or common?*
Studēns	Appellātī́vum.	*Common.*

Magist.	Cūius géneris est?	*What gender is it?*
Studēns	Fēminī́nī.	*Feminine.*

Magist.	Quō cāsū est?	*What case is it?*
Studēns	Ablātī́vō plūrā́lī.	*Ablative plural.*

Magist.	Dīc cāsum nōminātī́vum singulā́rem.	*Give the nominative singular.*
Studēns	Ōra.	*"Shore."*

Magist.	"*Longínquīs*" quae pars ōrātiốnis est?	*What part of speech is "distant"?*
Studēns	Adiectī́vum.	*Adjective.*

Magist.	Quō est cāsū?	*In what case is it?*
Studēns	Ablātī́vō.	*The ablative.*

| **Magist.** | Cūius est géneris? | *What gender is it?* |
| **Studēns** | Fēminínī. | *Feminine.* |

| **Magist.** | Cūius est númerī? | *What number is it?* |
| **Studēns** | Plūrális. | *The plural.* |

| **Magist.** | Cui dictiónī adícitur? | *What noun does it modify?* |
| **Studēns** | "Ōrīs." | *"Shores."* |

| **Magist.** | Cūius gradūs comparātiónis est? | *What degree of comparison is it?* |
| **Studēns** | Positívī. | *The positive.* |

| **Magist.** | Dā gradum superlātívum. | *Give the superlative degree.* |
| **Studēns** | "Longinquíssim·us -a -um." | *"Most distant."* |

| **Magist.** | *"Vēnit"* quae pars ōrātiónis est? | *What part of speech is "came"?* |
| **Studēns** | Verbum. | *A verb.* |

| **Magist.** | Cūius est témporis? | *What tense is it?* |
| **Studēns** | Temporis praetéritī perféctī. | *The perfect.* |

| **Magist.** | Cūius persónae est? | *What person is it?* |
| **Studēns** | Tértiae. | *Third (person).* |

| **Magist.** | Dīc persónam prīmam. | *Give the first person.* |
| **Studēns** | Vēnī. | *"I came, have come".* |

| **Magist.** | Cūius númerī est? | *What number is it?* |
| **Studēns** | Singuláris. | *The singular.* |

| **Magist.** | Cūius modī est? | *What mood is it?* |
| **Studēns** | Indicātívī. | *Indicative.* |

| **Magist.** | Cūius géneris est? | *What voice is it?* |
| **Studēns** | Neutrális. | *Intransitive.* |

| **Magist.** | Cūius coniugātiónis est? | *What conjugation is it?* |
| **Studēns** | Quārtae. | *The fourth.* |

Magist.	Dīc partēs prīncipālēs "canō" verbī.	*Give the principal parts of the verb "sing".*
Studēns	Canō, cánere, cécinī, cantus.	*I sing, am singing; to sing; I sang, have sung; sung, having been sung.*

TOPICAL VOCABULARY

abbreviate *tr* breviáre

abbreviation *s* not·a -ae *f* compendiária

ablative *adj* ablātív·us -a -um; **ablative case** cās·us -ūs *m* ablātívus, ablātív·us -ī *m;* **in the ablative case** cāsū ablātívō

abstract noun *s* appelláti·ō -ốnis *f* (ut "bónitās" **goodness**)

accent *s* accént·us -ūs *m;* **to place the accent on a syllable** accéntum in sýllabā pốnere

active *adj* āctív·us -a -um; **active verb** verbum agéndī *or* agēns *or* āctívum; **active voice** gen·us -eris *n* āctívum

adjectival *adj* adiectīvál·is -is -e

adjective *s* adiectív·um -ī *n*

adverb *s* advérbi·um -ī *n*

adverbial *adj* adverbiál·is -is -e

alphabet *s* alphabét·um -ī *n*, prīmae lítter·ae -árum *fpl*

antecedent *s* nōm·en -inis *n* antecếdēns

antepenult *s* antepaenúltima sýllab·a -ae *f*

article *s* artícul·us -ī *m* (hic haec hoc, *normally demonstrative, serve as articles only in declensions*)

as *adv* sícut, ut; **as for instance** ut putā

capital letter *s* lítter·a -ae *f* grandis *(opp:* líttera minúta)

case *s* cās·us -ūs *m;* **a noun in the genitive case** nōmen genitívō cāsū; *or more rarely* nōmen cāsūs genitívī

clause *s* membr·um -ī *n;* **main clause** ōráti·ō -ốnis *f* [**Note**—ōrátiō *can be a complete sentence or a main clause*]

collective *adj* collectí·vus -a -um

combination *s* comprehếnsi·ō -ốnis *f;* **a syllable is a combination of letters** sýllaba est comprehếnsiō litterárum

combine *tr* compốn·ō -ere compốsuī compósitus; **prepositions can be combined with verbs** praepositiốnēs cum verbīs compốnī possunt

come *intr* (**from**) vén·iō -íre vēnī ventum (ab + *abl*), dērīvárī (ab + *abl*)

comma *s* comm·a -atis *n*

common noun *s* nōm·en -inis *n* appellātívum

comparative *adj* comparātív·us -a -um; **comparative degree** grad·us -ūs *m* comparātívus; **in the comparative** comparātívē, in comparātiốne

comparison *s* comparáti·ō -ốnis *f*

compound *adj* compósit·us -a -um (ut "indóctus" **uneducated**) *(opp:* simplex, ut "doctus")

concrete noun *s* vocábul·um -ī *n (opp:* appellátiō)

conjugate *tr* dēclīnáre

conjugation *s* dēclīnáti·ō -ốnis *f (more commonly used);* coniugáti·ō -ốnis *f*

conjunction *s* coniûncti·ō -ốnis *f*

consist of cōnst·ō -áre cốnstitī ex (+ *abl*)

consonant *s* cốnson·āns -ántis *f*

construction *s* cōnstrū́cti·ō -ṓnis *f*

coordinate conjunction *s* coniū́ncti·ō -ṓnis *f* cōpulātī́va

correlative *adj* relātī́vus -a -um (ut "tālis . . . quālis" **such . . . as**)

correct *adj* rēct·us -a -um, ēmendā́t·us -a -um

correct *tr* ēmendā́re

correction *s* ēmendā́ti·ō -ṓnis *f*

correctly *adv* rēctē, ēmendā́tē (*opp:* vitiṓsē)

dative *adj* datī́v·us -a -um

dative *s* datī́v·us -ī *m,* cās·us -ūs *m* datī́vus

declension *s* dēclīnā́ti·ō -ṓnis *f*

decline *tr* dēclīnā́re

defective *adj* dēfectī́v·us -a -um

define *tr* dēfī́n·iō -ī́re -ī́vī -ī́tus

definite *adj* fīnī́t·us -a -um (*opp:* īnfīnī́tus)

degree *s* grad·us -ūs *m;* **positive degree** gradus positī́vus; **comparative degree** gradus comparātī́vus; **superlative degree** gradus superlātī́vus

demonstrative *adj* dēmōnstrātī́v·us -a -um

deponent *s* dēpṓn·ēns -éntis *n,* verb·um -ī *n* dēpṓnēns

derive *tr* (**from**) dērivā́re (ab + *abl*)

diminutive *s* dēminutī́vum nōm·en -inis *n,* dēminūtī́v·um -ī *n*

diphthong *s* diphthóng·us -ī *f*

double *adj* gemi nā́t·us -a -um: **double "i" as in "armāriī"** "i" líttera gemi nā́ta, ut armā́riī

enclitic *s* enclī́tic·um -ī *n* (ut "-que," "-ve" **and, or**)

end *intr* (**in**) términ·or -ā́rī -ā́tus sum (in + *acc or abl*)

ending *adj* (**in**) terminā́t·us -a -um (in + *acc*)

ending *s* terminā́ti·ō -ṓnis *f*

error *s* víti·um -ī *n,* mend·um -ī *n*

explain *tr* explānā́re, explicā́re

express *tr* éxprimō exprímere expréssī expréssus

feminine *adj* fēminī́nus -a -um

figurative *adj* trānslātī́v·us -a -um

figuratively *adv* figūrā́tē, trānslātī́vē

final *adj* fīnā́l·is -is -e

form *tr* fác·iō -ere fēcī factus; **form the imperative of the verb "venīre"** fac imperātī́vum "venīre" verbī

form *s* figū́r·a -ae *f;* **the form is either simple, like "doctus," or compound, like "indoctus"** figū́ra est aut simplex, ut "doctus," aut compósita, ut "indóctus"

function *s* poténti·a -ae *f*

future *s* temp·us -oris *n* futū́rum

gender *s* gen·us -eris *n*

genitive *s* genitī́v·us -ī *m,* cās·us -ūs *m* genitī́vus

gerund *s* gerúndi·um -ī *n*

gerundive *s* gerundī́v·um -ī *n*

give *tr* dō dare dedī datus; dīc·ō -ere dīxī dictus; **give the plural form of gaudium** dā (*or* dīc) figū́ram plūrā́lem "gaúdium" nṓminis

grammar *s* grammátic·a -ae *f,* ar·s -tis *f* grammática

imperative *adj* imperātī́v·us -a -um; **imperative mood** mod·us -ī *m* imperātī́vus

imperfect tense *s* témp·us -ŏris *n* praetéritum imperféctum

impersonal *adj* impersōnā́l·is -is -e

incorrect *adj* vitiṓs·us -a -um

incorrectly *adv* vitiṓsē

indeclinable *adj* indēclīnábil·is -is -e

indefinite *adj* īnfīnít·us -a -um *(opp:* fīnítus)

indicate *tr* significáre

indicative *adj* indicātív·us -a -um *;* **in the indicative mood** modō indicātívō

infinitive *adj* īnfīnītív·us -a -um; **infinitive mood** mod·us -ī *m* īnfīnītívus

infinitive *s* īnfīnītív·um -ī *n*

inflect *tr* dēclīnáre

inflection *s* dēclīnáti·ō -ónis *f*

intensive pronoun *s* prōnóm·en -inis *n* intentiónis (ut "ipse" **himself**)

interjection *s* interiécti·ō -ónis *f* (ut "heus tū!" **hey you!**)

intransitive *adj* intrānsitív·us -a -um (ut "sédeō," "surgō" **I sit, I get up**)

irregular *adj* inaequál·is -is -e; **an irregular verb** inaequále verbum (ut "volō," "nōlō," "fīō" **I want, I do not want, I become**)

irregularly *adv* inaequáliter; **"duo" is irregularly declined** "duo" inaequáliter dēclīnátur

last *adj* últim·us -a -um

lengthen *tr* prōdúc·ō -ere prōdúxī prōdúctus *(opp:* corrípere)

letter *s* lítter·a -ae *f;* **letters form syllables** lítterae fáciunt sýllabās

literal *adj* própri·us -a -um *(opp:* trānslātívus)

literally *adv* próprie, ad verbum *(opp:* figūrátē)

long *adj* long·us -a -um, prōdúct·us -a -um *(opp:* brevis, corréptus); **a vowel is long by nature or by position** vocális est longa nātúrā aut positióne

mark *s* not·a -ae *f* (ut "nota longa," "nota brevis" **long mark, short mark**)

masculine *adj* masculín·us -a -um

mean *tr* significáre

meaning *s* significáti·ō -ónis *f*

meter *s* metr·um -ī *n*

mistake *s* víti·um -ī *n;* **to make a mistake** vítium fácere

modify *tr* adícior ádicī adiéctus sum (+ *dat*); **which noun does "bonus" modify?** cui nóminī "bonus" adícitur?

modifying *adj* adiéct·us -a -um (+ *dat*)

monosyllable *s* monosýllab·a -ae *f*

mood *s* mod·us -ī *m;* **imperative mood, e.g., "read!"** modus imperātívus, ut "lege!"; **indicative mood, e.g., "I read"** modus indicātívus, ut "legō"; **subjunctive mood, e.g., "although I read"** modus subiūnctívus, ut "cum legam"

neuter *adj* neu·ter -tra -trum, neutrál·is -is -e; **in the —** neutráliter

nominative *adj* nōminātív·us -a -um

noun *s* nōm·en -inis *n;* *(of an inanimate object)* vocábul·um -ī *n*

number *s* númer·us -ī *m*

numeral *s* nōm·en -inis *n* numerále (ut "ūnus," "duo," " trēs" **one, two three**)

object *s* *expressed by the verb* adiúngī, *for example,* **"the man" is the object of the verb** "hic homō" verbō adiúngitur [Note—Roman grammarians never used the word "obiectum" in connection with a verb or preposition. Whereas we would say, for example, "*man* is the object of the verb" the Romans would say "*man* is joined to the verb." See also the definition of "modify" above.]

ordinal *adj* ōrdinál·is -is -e (ut "prīmus", "secúndus" **first, second**)

parse *tr* proprietátēs (+ *gen*) dēscríbere

part of speech *s* par•s -tis *f* ōrātiōnis

participle *s* particípi•um -ī *n; past or* **perfect participle** praetéritī témporis particípium; **present participle** praeséntis témporis particípium

particle *s* partícul•a -ae *f (namely, the four parts of speech that are indeclinable: adverb, preposition, conjunction, interjection)*

passive *adj* passív•us -a -um

past *s* praetérit•um temp•us -ŏris *n*

pattern *s* régul•a -ae *f*

penult *s* paenúltima sýllab•a -ae *f*

perfect tense *s* temp•us -ŏris *n* praetéritum perféctum

period *s* pūnct•um -ī *n*

person *s* persón•a -ae *f*

personal *adj* persōnál•is -is -e

phrase *s* locúti•ō -ónis *f (also used of a single word)*

pluperfect tense *s* temp•us -ŏris *n* plūsquamperféctum

plural *adj* plūrál•is -is -e; **in the plural** plūráliter

plural *s* multitúd•ō -inis *f; signifying a plural* multitúdinem significāns

positive *s* grad•us -ūs *m* positívus

possessive *adj* possessív•us -a -um

prefix *s* praeposíti•ō -ónis *f* per compositiónem

preposition *s* praeposíti•ō -ónis *f* (per appositiónem); **prepositions take** *(lit:* **serve) either the accusative or the ablative case** praepositiónēs aut accūsātívō aut ablātívō cásuī sérviunt

present *adj* praes•ēns -éntis; **present tense** praesēns temp•us -ŏris *n*

principal parts part•ēs -ium *fpl* prīncipálēs

pronoun *s* prōnóm•en -inis *n*

pronounce *tr* prōnūntiáre; **to pronounce a vowel short or long** vocálem corréptē aut prōdúctē prōnūntiáre

proper noun *s* próprium nōm•en -inis *n* (ut "Hector" **Hector**) *(opp:* appellātívum nōmen (ut "homō" **man**)

punctuation *s* interpúncti•ō -ónis *f*

punctuation mark *s* interpúnct•um -ī *n*, pūnct•um -ī *n*

relative *adj* relātív•us -a -um

repeat *tr* répet•ō -ere -ívī -ítus

rule *s* régul•a -ae *f;* **to follow (observe) the rule** régulam serváre

sentence *s* senténti•a -ae *f*, ōráti•ō -ónis *f*

short *adj* brev•is -is -e, corrépt•us -a -um

singular *adj* singulár•is -is -e *(opp:* plūrál•is -is -e); **in the singular** singuláriter

sound *s* son•us -ī *m*

speak *tr & intr* loquor loquī locútus sum; **to speak Latin, to speak correct Latin** Latínē loquī

spell *tr* scrīb•ō -ere scrīpsī scríptus; **to spell correctly** rēctē scríbere; **to spell with** scríbere per (+ *acc);* **some spell "cum" with a "q" if it signifies time** quídam scrībunt "cum" per "q" lítteram, sī tempus significat

spelling *s* orthográphi•a -ae *f*, scrīptúr•a -ae *f*

subject *n (gram)* subiéct•um -ī *n; (topic studied)* gen•us -eris *n* studiórum, doctrín•a -ae *f*

subjunctive *adj* subiūnctív•us -a -um; **subjunctive mood** subiūnctívus mod•us -ī *m*

subjunctive *s* subiūnctív•us -ī *m*

subordinate conjunction *s* subiūnctíva coniūncti·ō -ṓnis *f*

superlative *adj* superlātív·us -a -um

superlative *s* grad·us -ūs *m* superlātívus; **in the superlative** superlātívē; **give me "laetus" in the superlative** dīc "laetus" superlātívē

supine *s* supín·um -ī *n*

syllable *s* sýllab·a -ae *f;* **syllables form words** sýllabae fáciunt dictiṓnēs

syntax *s (pure Latin)* ōrdináti·ō -ṓnis *f;* syntáx·is -is *f*

take *tr* accíp·iō -ere accḗpī accḗptus, recíp·iō -ere recḗpī recḗptus; **names of cities don't take prepositions, for instance, "I'm going to Rome"** nṓmina cīvitátum nōn accípiunt praepositiṓnēs, ut "Rōmam vādō"; **the preposition "ad" takes the accusative case** "ad" praepósitiō cásuī accūsātívō servit; **this verb takes the accusative case** hoc verbum coniúngitur *(or* adiúngitur*)* cásuī accūsātívō

tense *s* temp·us -ŏris *n*

transitive trānsitív·us -a -um

translate *tr* convért·ō -ere -ī convérsus, tránsferō trānsférre tránstulī trānslátus; **to translate from Latin to English** ex Latínō in Ánglicum convértere

translation *s* trānsláti·ō -ṓnis *f*

understood *tr* **it is understood** subaudítur; **"ego" is understood if I should say, "Sum philósophus."** subaudítur "ego" sī dīcam "sum philósophus."

use *tr* pōnō pṓnere pósuī pósitus; **Use "legō" in a sentence.** Pōne "legō" in senténtiā.

utter *tr* prṓferō prōférre prṓtulī prōlátus

verb *s* verb·um -ī *n*

verbal *adj* verbál·is -is -e

vocative *s* vocātívus -ī *m,* cās·us -ūs *m* vocātívus

voice *s* vōx, vōcis *f; (of a verb)* gen·us -eris *n;* **What voice is "audímur"? Passive.** Cūius géneris est "audítur"? Passívī. [**Note**—"genus," *in connection with nouns and adjectives means "gender", and in connection with verbs means "voice."*]

vowel *s* vocál·is -is *f*

word *s (gram)* dícti·ō -ṓnis *f;* **syllables form words** sýllabae fáciunt dictiṓnēs; **word for word** verbum prō verbō [**Note**—*In Roman grammars, "verbum" is used only for "verb"; Quintilian says: "Verbum, of course, has two meanings; in one sense, "verbum" covers all parts of which language is composed; in another sense, it is restricted to the part of speech such as "legō" and "scrībō". To avoid this ambiguity, some have preferred to say "vōcēs," "locūtiṓnēs," "dictiṓnēs."*]

write *tr* scrībō scríbere scrīpsī scrīptus; **to write Latin** Latínē scríbere

wrong *adj* vitiós·us -a -um; *adv* pérperam

Appendix I: Yes and No in Latin

It may strike you as strange, but the Romans did not have a single word for Yes and No. (We, too, can say "yes" or "O.K." or, informally, "yeah" or "yep" or, even more informally, "uhuh.") There are single Latin adverbs that mean "yes": **étiam, ita, sīc, sānē, máximē, ádmodum, óppidō, certē, plānē, plāníssimē.** These are not perfect synonyms. For example, **ita** and **sīc** mean "it is so"; **plāníssimē** means "yes, exactly so"; **certē** means "certainly"; **ádmodum** and **óppidō** both means "yes" or "quite so," but **óppidō** is slightly more emphatic, carrying the sense of "precisely so." Cicero indicates the most direct and simple response when he says: **aut "étiam" aut "nōn" respóndē** (answer either "yes" or "no.")

Probably the most frequent way of saying "yes" in Latin is to repeat the word on which the emphasis rests in the question:

Erus eam véndidit?
  Véndidit.

The master sold her?
  Yes.

Ad patrémne eam dūcis?
  Ad eum ipsum.

Are you taking her to her father?
  Yes.

An nōn dīxī hoc esse futúrum?
  Dīxístī.

Didn't I say that this was going to happen?
  Yes.

Aiō. Nēgās.
I say yes. You say no.

You can safely use any of the adverbs for "yes." When you get up your confidence, you can try to answer by repeating the emphatic word in the question. But then be sure to provide the correct form, as in the third example above.

As indicated above, the most direct negative particle is **nōn** (more frequently with the verb supplied from the question, or when something is immediately added). **Mínimē** is more emphatic, meaning "no, indeed" or "not in the least," strengthened by **vērō: mínimē vērō** = "no, certainly not" or the informal **mínimē géntium** "absolutely not."**Immō** or **īmō** is used especially where a correction of something in the question is given. These expressions are in turn made more emphatic by appeals to deities such as **ēcástor** "by Castor," **pol** or **édepol** "by Pollux," **hércule** or **mehércule** "by Hercules," **prō Iúppiter** "by Jupiter," **prō dī immortálēs** "by the immortal gods" and similar expressions. When refusing an offer with "no, thank you," the Romans simply said: **benígnē** or **rēctē.**

Appendix II: Colors

amber ēléctric•us -a -um

black: dull black ā•ter -tra -trum;
glossy black ni•ger -gra -grum;
pitch-black píce•us -a -um

beige flávid•us -a -um

blond flāv•us -a -um

blue: azure blue vénet•us -a -um; **dark
blue** cȳáne•us -a -um; **leaden blue**
lívid•us -a -um; **sky-blue** caerúle•us
-a -um *(esp. of eyes)*

bluish subcaerúle•us -a -um

bluish gray caési•us -a -um *(often
referred by the Romans to blue eyes)*

brown fulv•us -a -um *(ranging from
dull yellow to reddish brown;
applied to hair, wine, sand, gold,
stars, jasper);* **bright brown**
spādíce•us -a -um; **dark brown**
fusc•us -a -um [**Note:** brúnne•us -a
-um *is of Germanic origin.*]

chartreuse chlōrín•us -a -um

chestnut spād•íx -ícis; bádi•us -a -um
(applied to horses only)

color col•or -óris *m;* **to color** colōrāre

cream-colored ebúrne•us -a -um

crimson coccíne•us -a -um

dark colored pull•us -a -um

dun-colored gilv•us -a -um *(ranging
from almost neutral brownish gray
to dull grayish brown, applied to
horses)*

flame-colored flámme•us -a -um

flesh-colored cárne•us -a -um

golden auréol•us -a -um; aúre•us -a -um
(applied to hair)

gray: ash-gray cinére•us -a -um; **dark
gray** pull•us -a -um; **light gray**
cān•us -a -um *(esp. hair);* **to be gray**
cáneō -ére -uī; **to become gray**
cānésc•ō -ere; **to be gray-haired**
cānō cápite esse

grayish cānésc•ēns -éntis

green vírid•is -is -e *(most common term;*
vir•ēns -éntis, virídul•us -a -um, *are
shades of this);* **bright grass green**
prásin•us -a -um; **emerald green**
smarágdin•us -a -um; **grass green**
herbáce•us -a -um; **olive green**
oleváce•us -a -um; **(deep) sea green**
vénet•us -a -um; **(light) sea green**
glauc•us -a -um *(a dull green,
passing into graying blue);* **very
green** pervírid•is -is -e; **to be green**
(of green foliage) vír•eō -ére -uī; *(of
things growing)* vir•ēns -éntis,
vírid•ēns -éntis; **to become green**
virésc•ō -ere

greenish subvírid•is -is -e

hazel *(light to strong brown)* fulv•us -a
-um; *(strong brown)* spād•íx -ícis

lavander lavanduláce•us -a -um; *(pale
blue, with a slight mixture of gray)*
caési•us -a -um

mauve violáce•us -a -um

ochre sīláce•us -a -im

orange auránti•us -a -um, lúte•us -a -um;
dull orange armeníac•us -a -um
(apricot-color)

pink róse•us -a -um, pūníce•us -a -um

pinkish subróse•us -a -um

**purple (dull red with a slight dash of
blue)** purpúre•us -a -um [*purpura
was orignally the name of the shell
fish itself; later the name of the dye.*

This varied according to the shellfish used and the processing applied. The epithet purpúreus *came to cover various red colors; now it embraces colors between red and violet: purple, scarlet, crimson, rosy red)*

red rūf•us -a -um *(all shades);* ru•ber -bra -brum *(common term for any pure red);* **blood red** sanguíne•us -a -um; **bright red** rútil•us -a -um; **cardinal-red** cardinál•is -is -e; **dark red** rúbid•us -a -um; **cherry-red** cerásin•us -a -um; **deep red** coccíne•us -a -um; **pure lively red** phoeníce•us -a -um, pūníce•us -a -um

reddish súbru•ber -bra -brum, rubéll•us -a -um; subrúf•us -a -um, rúful•us -a -um *(of hair);* rubicúnd•us -a -um *(of the skin: flushed)*

rust-colored rubiginṓs•us -a -um

sandy *(hair)* fulv•us -a -um

scarlet miniát•us -a -um; **dull scarlet** phoeníce•us -a -um

silvery argénte•us -a -um

snow-white *see* **white**

strawberry-blond fulv•us -a -um

tan fulv•us -a -um

tawny fulv•us -a -um *(dull yellow, with a mixture of gray and brown);* cervín•us -a -um *(is a darker shade of it)*

turquoise túric•us -a -um

vermilion coccíne•us -a -um, miniát•us -a -um

violet violáce•us -a -um

white: dead white alb•us -a -um; **dull white** crētáce•us -a -um; **shiny white** cándid•us -a -um; **snow-white** níve•us -a -um *(the purest white)*

whitish subálb•us -a -um, álbul•us -a -um, subálbid•us -a -um

yellow flāv•us -a -um *(commonest term, a pale yellow);* **deep yellow** *(like egg yolk)* lúte•us -a -um *or* vitellín•us -a -um; **golden yellow** aúre•us -a -um; **lemon yellow** cítre•us -a -um *(purest yellow, without any brightness);* **pale yellow** gilv•us *or* gilb•us -a -um, lūtéol•us -a -um

yellowish flávidus -a -um; subfláv•us -a -um *(of hair, approaching blond)*

yellowish gray rāv•us -a -um

yellowish orange gilv•us -a -um

[**Note**—The prefix sub- means "somewhat", "almost" and can often be rendered by the English suffix "-ish." Thus, **albus** means "white" and **subálbus** means "whitish."

The vagueness of Latin color terms is due to the origin of colors out of dyestuff and pigments. The colors of minerals vary, and dyes produce different effects according to the mode of preparation and the materials dyed. Their applications have to be guessed from literary sources, which for the most part are incidental and vague. Color names used by poets tend to be applied metaphorically or indefinitely.

To get a better idea of how the Romans applied color terms, it is necessary to cite the objects to which colors were attached. For example, when Horace describes Augustus as being transformed into a god, he speaks of the lips of the deified Augustus as **purpúreus**, indicating his health. **Purpúreus,** at least there, is crimson, not purple.]

When asking what color something is, the Romans used either the genitive or ablative of description; e.g.

What color is the house? Quō colóre est domus tua?
or Cuius colóris est domus tua?

It is white. Est alba.

Appendix III: Numbers

	CARDINAL	ORDINAL	
1	ūnus, ūna, ūnum	prīmus	I
2	duo, duae, duo	secúndus	II
3	trēs, tria	tertius	III
4	quattuor	quārtus	IV
5	quīnque	quīntus	V
6	sex	sextus	VI
7	septem	séptimus	VII
8	octō	octávus	VIII
9	novem	nōnus	IX
10	decem	décimus	X
11	úndecim	ūndécimus	XI
12	duódecim	duodécimus	XII
13	trédecim	tērtius décimus	XIII
14	quattuórdecim	quārtus décimus	XIV
15	quíndecim	quīntus décimus	XV
16	sédecim	sextus décimus	XVI
17	septéndecim	séptimus décimus	XVII
18	duodēvīgíntī	duodēvīcésimus	XVIII
19	ūndēvīgíntī	ūndēvīcésimus	XIX
20	vīgíntī	vīcésimus	XX
21	vīgíntī ūnus	vīcésimus prīmus	XXI
	ūnus et vīgíntī		
22	vīgíntī duo	vīcésimus secúndus	XXII
	duo et vīgíntī		
30	trīgíntā	trīcésimus	XXX
40	quadrāgíntā	quadrāgésimus	XL
50	quīnquāgíntā	quīnquāgésimus	L
60	sexāgíntā	sexāgésimus	LX
70	septuāgíntā	septuāgésimus	LXX
80	octōgíntā	octōgésimus	LXXX
90	nōnāgíntā	nōnāgésimus	XC
100	centum	centésimus	C
101	centum ūnus	centésimus prīmus	CI
	centum et ūnus		
200	ducéntī, -ae, -a	ducentésimus	CC
300	trecéntī, -ae, -a	trecentésimus	CCC
400	quadringéntī, -ae, -a	quadringentésimus	CCCC
500	quīngéntī, -ae, -a	quīngentésimus	D
600	sescéntī, -ae, -a	sescentésimus	DC
700	septingéntī, -ae, -a	septingentésimus	DCC
800	octingéntī, -ae, -a	octingentésimus	DCCC
900	nōngéntī, -ae, -a	nōngentésimus	DCCCC
1,000	mille	millésimus	M
2,000	duo mília	bis millésimus	MM
10,000	decem mília	déciēs millésimus	CCI/C/C
100,000	centum mília	céntiēs millésimus	CCCI/C/C/C

251

Appendix IV: Proverbs and Sayings

[Note—The proverbs are arranged in alphabetical order. If a proverb does not begin with a significant word, a key word from the proverb is placed at the beginning to help you find the proverb that you are looking for.]

advantage: To whose advantage? Cui bonō?

advantage: One advantage in exchange for another. Quid prō quō. [*Something for something.*]

All or nothing. Aut Caesar aut nūllus. [*Either Caesar or no one.*]

Anger is brief madness. Īra furor brevis est.

apple cart: Don't upset the apple cart. Nōlī plaustrum percéllere. [*Don't knock over the wagon.*]

attack: A personal attack. Argūméntum ad hóminem. [*An argument against a person (instead of against the issue).*]

bigger: The bigger they come, the harder they fall. Cāsus excélsīs multō facílius nocet. [*The fall from high places more readily causes harm.*]

Birds of a feather flock together. Parēs cum páribus facíllimē congregántur. [*Likes easily flock together with likes.*]

bite off: Don't bite off more than you can chew. Quī maióra cupit saepe minóra capit. [*He who desires bigger things often gets the smaller (ones).*]

bold front: You're just putting on a bold front. Audácia prō mūrō habétur. [*Boldness serves as a wall.*]

borrowed time: You're living on borrowed time. Dē lucrō vīvis. [*You're living on profits.*]

buyer: Let the buyer beware. Cáveat ēmptor.

castles: You're building castles in the air. In arḗnā aedíficās. [*You are building on sand.*]

Caught in the act (*or* caught red-handed). In flagrántī dēlíctō. [*In a flagrant crime.*]

changes: After making all necessary adjustments. Mūtátīs mūtándīs. [*Things having been changed that must be changed.*]

Charity begins at home. Prīma cáritās íncipit ā sē ipsō. [*Charity first begins with oneself.*]

Cheap gift, cheap thanks. Vīle dōnum, vīlis grátia.

chickens: Don't count your chickens before they are hatched. Adhūc tua messis in herbā est. [*Your harvest is still on the stalk.*]

childhood: The old are in second childhood. Bis púerī senēs. [*Old men are boys twice.*]

companion: A constant companion. (*e.g., a favorite book*) Vāde mēcum. [*Go with me.*]

Crying brings a certain pleasure. Est quaedam volúptās flēre. [*To cry is a certain pleasure.*]

dead: Say nothing but good about the dead. Dē mórtuīs nīl nisi bonum.

deaf: To preach to deaf ears. Ad surdās aurēs cantáre [*To sing to deaf ears.*]

die: The die is cast. Iacta est álea.

Do nothing in excess. Nē nímium. [*Not too much.*]

Do unto others as you would have done unto you. Ab áliō exspéctēs álterī quod fḗceris. [*You may expect from another what you have done to the other.*]

dogs: Let sleeping dogs lie. Nōlī irritấre leónēs. [*Do not provoke lions.*]

Don't worry about tomorrow. Quid sit futū́rum crās, fuge quaérere. [*Don't ask what tomorrow will be.*]

drinking buddy: I hate a drinking buddy with a (good) memory. Ōdī mémorem compōtórem.

drop: A drop hollows out stone. Gutta cavat lápidem.

education: No one can take your education from you. Homō doctus in sē dīvī́tiās semper habet. [*An educated person always has wealth within himself.*]

eggs: Don't put all your eggs in one basket. Nē commíttās ómnia ūnī nāvī. [*Don't entrust everything to one ship.*]

eleventh: At the eleventh hour. Inter caesa et porrḗcta. [*between the slaughtering and the offering*]

end: Look, the end is in sight! Fínis ecce labórum! [*Behold, the end of troubles.*]

Enjoy the moment. Carpe diem. [*Pluck the day.*]

err: To err is human, to forgive, divine. Errấre hūmánum est, ignóscere dīvī́num.

Everyone has his price. Vēnális pópulus, vēnális cū́ria patrum. [*The people are for sale, for sale is the senate.*]

Experience is the best teacher. Ūsus est óptimus magíster.

faith: In good faith. Bonā fidē.

Familiarity breeds contempt. Conversátiō parit contémptum. [*Close association produces contempt.*]

fates: Fate leads the willing; it drags the unwilling. Dūcunt voléntem fāta, nōléntem trahunt.

favor: To accept a favor is to sell one's freedom. Benefícium accípere, lībertátem est véndere.

Fight over nothing. Dē lānā caprī́nā rīxā́rī. [*To quarrel about goat's wool.*]

fire: Fight fire with fire. Simília simílibus cūrántur. [*Like things are taken care of by like.*]

First come, first served. Prior témpore, prior iūre. [*First in time, first by right.*]

foot: You put your foot in your mouth. Ō sī tacuísses, philósophus mānsísses. [*Oh, if you had remained silent, you would have remained a philosopher.*]

forward: Not to go forward is to go backward. Nōn prógredī est régredī.

friend: A friend in need is a friend indeed. Is est amícus quī in rē dúbiā rē iuvat. [*He is a friend who really helps in need.*]

give: He gives twice who gives quickly. Bis dat, quī dat cito.

glory: So passes away the glory of the world. Sīc trānsit glṓria mundī.

God willing Deō volénte.

God helps those that help themselves. Fortēs fortū́na ádiuvat. [*Fortune helps the brave.*]

God: If God (is) for us, who (can be) against us? Sī Deus prō nōbīs, quis contrā nōs?

golden: The golden mean. Áurea mediócritās.

grain: With a grain of salt. Cum grānō sālis.

greedy: The greedy man always feels need. Semper avárus eget.

grief: True grief is a private matter. Ille dolet vērē quī sine teste dolet. [*He truly grieves who grieves without a witness.*]

guard: Who will guard the guards? Quis custódēs custódiet?

hair: Even a single hair casts a shadow. Étiam capíllus ūnus habet umbram suam.

Hard work overcomes all. Labor vincit ómnia.

Harp on the same old theme. Eándem recóquere crambem. [*To recook the same cabbage.*]

Haste makes waste. Festīnátiō tarda est. [*Haste is slow.*]

hat: That's old hat. Crambē repetíta est. [*It's cabbage served up again.*]

heart: One speaks what's in one's heart. Ex abundántiā cordis ōs lóquitur. [*From the abundance of the heart the mouth speaks.*]

high road: I see the high road but take the low road. Vídeō melióra probóque; dēterióra sequor. [*I see and approve of the better; I follow the worse.*]

High offices change one's character. Honórēs mūtant mōrēs.

holy of holies. Sānctum Sānctórum.

horse: A fast-running horse needs no spurs. Equō currénti nōn opus calcáribus.

hovel: A great man can come from a hovel. Exíre magnus vir ex tugúriō potest.

I am what you will be; I was what you are. *(On a Roman tombstone)* Sum quod eris; fuī quod es.

imitator: Oh imitators, you servile herd. Ō imitātórēs, servum pecus.

impressions: First impressions are deceptive. Frōns prīma multōs décipit. [*The first appearance deceives many.*]

indispensable: An indispensable condition. Causa sine quā nōn.

It's not who you are but what you are that counts. Nōn quis sed quid. [*Not who but what.*]

It's a good omen. Ōmen faustum est.

Jack of all trades. Áliquis in ómnibus, nūllus in síngulīs. [*A somebody in general, a nobody in particular.*]

Jack of all trades. Homō omnis Minérvae. [*A person of all Minerva = goddess of handicrafts.*]

justice: Let justice be done though the heavens fall. Fiat iūstítia, ruat caelum.

Kill two birds with one stone. Duōs paríetes dē eádem fidéliā dealbáre. [*To whitewash two walls with one bucket.*]

Kindness begets kindness. Grátia grátiam parit.

law: No one is above the law. Caesar nōn suprā grammáticōs est. [*Caesar is not above grammarians.*]

Like father, like son. Cólubra restem nōn parit. [*A snake does not give birth to a rope.*]

like: He who says whatever he likes, must hear what he does not like. Quī quae vult dīcit, quae nōn vult aúdiet.

live: Don't live one way in private, another in public. Nōn vīvēs áliter in sōlitúdine, áliter in forō.

logical: That's not logical. Nōn séquitur. [*It doesn't follow.*]

lonely: He is absolutely lonely who is friendless. Sōlus omnínō est quī sine amícō est.

Love is blind. Nēmō in amóre videt. [*No one sees when in love.*]

love: You can't hide love or a cough. Amor tussísque nōn cēlántur. [*Love and a cough do not hide.*]

lucky: You're lucky to be alive. Dē lucrō vīvis. [*You're living on profits.*]

make mountains out of molehills Ē rīvō flúmina magna fácere

matter: The matter is still undecided. Adhūc sub iúdice līs est. [*The case is still before the judge.*]

mind: A sound mind in a sound body. Mēns sāna in córpore sānō.

Moderation in all things. Modus in ómnibus.

moon: To promise the moon. Montēs aurī pollicérī. [*To promise mountains of gold.*]

nail: You've hit the nail on the head. Acū rem tetigístī. [*You've touched the thing with a needle.*]

Necessity is the mother of invention. Ingeniósa rērum egéstās est. [*Need of things is ingenious.*]

Necessity takes no vacation. Necéssitās caret fériīs.

needle: To look for a needle in a haystack. Nōdum in scirpō quaérere. [*To look for a knot on a bulrush.*]

Nip the thing in the bud. Prīncípiīs obstáre. [*To block the beginnings.*]

No sooner said than done. Cítius factō. (*also:* Dictum factum.)

No one is obliged to do more than he can. Ultrā posse nēmō obligátur.

nose: To lead someone by the nose. Lábiīs áliquem ductáre. [*To lead somone by the lips.*]

Nothing new under the sun. Nīl dictum quod nōn prius dictum. [*Nothing said that has not been said before.*]

Nothing ventured, nothing gained. Bene est tentáre. [*It is good to try.*]

Now or never. Nunc aut numquam.

office: By virtue of his (her) office. Ex offíciō.

One of a kind. Suī géneris.

One quarrel leads to another. Līs lītem génerat. [*Strife begets strife.*]

opinion: There are as many opinions as there are people. Quot hóminēs, tot senténtiae. [*As many people, so many opinions.*]

own: To each his own. Suum cuique.

pair: They make a pair. Pār bene comparátum. [*A well matched pair.*]

Patience is a cure for all pain. Cuivīs dolórī remédium est patiéntia.

peas: As like as two peas in a pod. Tam símilis quam lacte láctī est. [*As similar as milk is to milk.*]

plans: The best laid plans often go awry. Bene cōgitáta saepe cecidérunt male. [*Well thought-out things have often turned out badly.*]

please: You can't please everbody. Frūstrā labórat quī ómnibus placére studet. [*He who tries to please everyone labors in vain.*]

point: Carrying a point to extremes. Redúctiō ad absúrdum.

Pour oil on the flame. Óleum áddere camínō. [*To add oil to the stove.*]

Practice makes perfect. Exercitátiō óptima magístra est. [*Practice is the best teacher.*]

public: For the public good. Prō bonō públicō.

punishment: Let the punishment fit the crime. Culpae (or nóxiae) poena pār estō.

Quality rather than quantity. Nōn multa sed multum. [*Not many things but much.*]

reap: You reap what you sow. Ut seméntem féceris, ita metēs. [*As you will have done the sowing, so you shall reap.*]

Repetition is the mother of studies. Repetítiō est māter studiórum.

right: By what right? Quō iūre?

right: Where there's a right, there's an obligation. Ubi iūs, ibi offícium.

road: The road to the stars is through the rough. Per áspera ad astra. [*Through the rough to the stars.*]

rock: Between a rock and a hard place. Inter sacrum saxúmque. [*Between the altar and the sacrificial knife.*]

Rome: When in Rome, do as the Romans do. Cōnsuetúdō locī observánda est. [*The custom of the place must be observed.*]

scratch: You scratch my back, and I'll scratch yours. Manus manum lavat. [*A hand washes a hand.*]

scratch: To start over from scratch. Ad cárcerēs ā calce revocárī. [*To be called back from the finish line to the starting gate.*]

secret: If you want another to keep your secret, keep it first yourself. Álium silére quod volēs, prīmus silē.

Seeing is believing. Vidē et crēde. [*See and believe.*]

Self-love is blind. Caecus est amor suī. [*Love of oneself is blind.*]

Shame on you! Prō pudor! [*For shame.*]

Silence is consent. Quī tacet, cōnséntit. [*He who is silent gives his consent.*]

smoke: Where there's smoke, there's fire. Flamma fūmō est próxima. [*A flame is next to smoke.*]

sore spot: You've hit a sore spot. Tangis ulcus. [*You are touching a sore.*]

Speaking of the devil. Lupus in fábulā (or in sermóne). [*Wolf in the story (or conversation).*]

stomach: You can't study well on a full stomach. Plēnus venter nōn studet libénter. [*A full stomach does not study well.*]

stomach: The stomach doesn't have ears. (i.e., don't preach to the hungry.) Venter nōn habet aurēs.

stone: A rolling stone gathers no moss. Lapis volútus haud mūscō obdúcitur. [*A rolling stone does not get covered with moss.*]

Strike the iron when it is hot. Ferrum, dum in igne candet, cūdéndum est. [*Iron must be struck while it glows in the fire.*]

surpised: Be surprised at nothing. Nīl mīráre.

taste: You can't argue about taste. Dē gústibus nōn disputándum est. [*There should be no dispute about tastes.*]

tears: Nothing dries faster than tears. Lácrimā nihil cítius āréscit.

tea pot: To stir up a tempest in a tea pot. Excitáre flūctūs in símpulō. [*To stir up waves in a ladle.*]

Thank God. Deō grátiās.

tiger: I have a tiger by the tail. Aúribus téneō lupum. [*I have a wolf by the ears.*]

tiger: A tiger never changes his stripes. Vulpēs pilum mūtat, nōn mōrēs. [*The fox changes his fur, not his character.*]

Time brings all to light. Tempus ómnia revélat.

Time flies. Tempus fugit.

Time will tell. Diēs vēritátem áperit. [*Time uncovers the truth.*]

Times change, and we change with them. Témpora mūtántur, nōs et mūtámur in illīs.

tip: It's on the tip of my tongue. Versátur mihi in prīmóribus labrīs. [*It's on the edge of my lips.*]

tit: To give tit for tat. Pār parī respondére. [*To render like for like.*]

tongue: To have tongue in cheek. Tácitō rīdére nāsō. [*To laugh with a quiet nose.*]

treasure: Where your treasure is there is also your heart. Ubi est thesaúrus tuus, ibi est et cor tuum.

Trust begets trust. Fidēs facit fidem.

tune: You're singing the same old tune. Cantilénam eándem canis. [*You're singing the same refrain.*]

waste: You are wasting your time. Láterem crūdum lavās. [*You are washing an unbaked brick.*]

wealth: Where there are friends, there are riches. Ubi amíci, ibi opēs.

welfare: The welfare of the people is the supreme law. Salūs pópulī suprḗma est lēx.

Well, the last of the Romans! Em, últimus Rōmānórum.

Where there's life there's hope. Dum ánima est, spēs est. [*As long as there is breath, there is hope.*]

Winning is everything. Víncere aut morī. [*To conquer or to die.*]

wise: A word to the wise is sufficient. Dictum sapiéntī sat est.

world: The world wants to be deceived. Mundus vult décipī.

words: They went from words to blows. Ā verbīs ad vérbera. [*From words to blows.*]

wrong: One wrong does not excuse another. Iniúria nōn excúsat iniúriam.

You're getting in over your head. Magnum mare ingréderis. [*You're entering the great sea.*]

Appendix V: Computer Terms

address īnscrī́pti·ō -ṓnis *f* ēlectrónica

address book lib·er -rī *m* īnscrīptiṓnum ēlectronicárum

attachment appendícul·a -ae *f*, document·um -ī *n* annexum

boot up iníti·ō -áre -ávī systḗma

booting-up initiā́ti·ō -ṓnis *f* systḗmatis

browse *(the Web)* nāvigā́re; *(text documents)* perlūstrā́re

browser *(Web viewer)* nāvigā́tr·um -ī *n;* *(viewer of text documents)* perlūstrā́tr·um -ī *n*

button plēctr·um -ī *n*

byte octḗt·us -ī *m*

carbon copy exémpl·ar -áris *n* carbṓneum

CD compáctus disc·us -ī *m*

CD-ROM compáctus disc·us -ī *m* ópticus

chip tal·us -ī *m*

click *tr* dḗprim·ō -ere dēpréssī; pulsā́re; **left-click** sinistrṓrsum dēprímere; **right-click** dextrṓrsum dēprímere; **double-click** bis dēprímere *or* bis pulsā́re

close conclū́d·ō -ere -ī conclūsus

command iuss·um -ī *n*

compact disk (CD) compáctus disc·us -ī *m*

computer *s* computā́tr·um -ī *n*, ōrdinā́tr·um -ī *n*

computer *adj* computātrā́l·is -is -e, ōrdinātrā́l·is -is -e

computer game lūs·us -ūs *m* computātrā́lis; **to play a computer**

game lūsū computātrā́lem lūd·ō -ere lūsī

connect cōnéct·ō -ere cōnéxuī cōnéxus

connection connéx·us -ūs *m*

copy *s* exémpl·ar -áris *n*

copy exémplar fácere

crash *intr* córru·ō -ere -ī

cursor curs·or -ṓris *m*

cut and paste sec·ō secā́re sécuī et glūtinā́re

cyberspace cyberspáti·um -ī *n*

data dat·a -ṓrum *npl*

database datṓrum repositṓri·um -ī *n*

DCD digitā́lis compáctus disc·us -ī *m*

delete dḗl·eō dēlḗre dēlḗvī dēlḗtus

desktop *(on the screen)* in quadrō

digital digitā́l·is -is -e

directory plicā́rum ind·ex -icis *m*

disk disc·us -ī *m;* **floppy disk** discus flexíbilis

disk drive discṓrum receptácul·um -ī *n*, īnstrūmént·um -ī *n* discīs legéndīs

diskette díscul·us -ī *m*

download ex rēte prehén·dō -dere -dī -sus *(or* éxprom·ō -ere -psī -tus*)*

drag trah·ō -ere traxī

edit ḗdō ḗdere ḗdidī ḗditus

electronic ēlectrónic·us -a -um

e-mail *s* lítter·ae -árum *fpl* ēlectrónicae; *(the system)* curs·us -ūs *m* ēlectrṓnicus

e-mail *tr* (ad áliquem) lítterās ēlectrónicās míttere

e-mail address īnscrípti•ō -ṓnis *f*
ēlectrónica

enter *tr* in computátrum réferō reférre
rétulī relátus

file documént•um -ī *n*

folder coöpércul•um -ī *n*

font typ•us -ī *m*

format *s* form•a -ae *f*

format *tr* (discum) cōnformáre

forward (*e-mail letter*) défer•ō dēférre
détulī dēlátus

hacker plagiári•us -ī *m* (•a -ae *f*)
ēlectrónic•us (-a), effrāctári•us -ī *m*
(•a -ae *f*) ēlectronic•us (-a)

hard drive dūra státi•ō -ṓnis *f*

hardware apparát•us -ūs *m*
computātrális

home page págin•a -ae *f* doméstica

hypertext *adj* hypertextuál•is -is -e

hypertext *s* hypertéxt•us -ūs *m*

icon īcōn, ícōnis *f*

input *s* ínit•us -ūs *m;* **input and output**
(datṓrum) ínitus exitúsque

install ínstru•ō īnstrúere īnstrúxī
īnstrúctus

internet *s* interrḗt•e -is *n*

internet *adj* interrētiál•is -is -e

joystick vect•is -is *m*, véctul•us -ī *m*

key malléol• us -ī *m*, plḗctr•um -ī *n*

keyboard plēctrológi•um -ī *n*, ōrd•ō
-inis *m* plēctrṓrum

laptop computátrul•um -ī *n* portábile

link *tr* cōnéct•ō -ere cōnéxuī cōnéxus

link *s* cōnéx•us -ūs *m*

linker cōnéctr•um -ī *n*

linking *s* cōnéxi•ō -ṓnis *f*

list (*mailing list*) grex, gregis *m*
(interrētiális)

list owner gregis moderá•tor -tṓris *m*
(•trīx -trícis *f*)

log in *intr* ín•eō -íre -ívī *or* -iī initúrus

log out *intr* éx•eō -íre -ívī *or* iī exitúrus

magnetic magnétic•us -a -um

mail lítter•ae -árum *fpl* ēlectrónicae,
epístul•a -ae *f* ēlectrónica

memory memóri•a -ae *f*

menu iussṓrum tabéll•a -ae *f*

message núnti•us -ī *m*

modem trānsmodulátr•um -ī *n*

monitor monitóri•um -ī *n*, caps•a -ae *f*
computātrális

mouse múscul•us -ī *m*, mūs, mūris *m*

mouse clicker mūris pulsábul•um -ī *n*

net rēt•e -is *n*

open apér•iō -íre -uī -tus

operating system systém•a -atis *n*
intérnum

output éxit•us -ūs *m*

password tésser•a -ae *f*

personal computer computátr•um -ī *n*
domésticum

pointer (mūris) ind•ex -icis *m*

port port•us -ūs *m*

print typīs ímprim•ō -ere impréssī
impréssus

printer máchin•a -ae *f* typográphica,
impressóri•um -ī *n*

processor ēditóri•um -ī *n*

program *s* prográmm•a -atis *n*

program *tr* prográmm•ō -áre -ávī -átus

programmer programmá•tor -tṓris *m*
(•trīx -ícis *f*)

prompt mónit•us -ūs *m*

RAM memóri•a -ae *f* volátilis

reply respónd•eō -ére -ī

ROM memóri•a -ae *f* fíxa

run *tr* **to run a program** prográmma administrắre **‖** *intr* óper‧or -ắrī -ắtus sum; **the program is running** prográmma operắtur

save servắre

scan scan‧dō -dere -dī -sus

scanner scānsốri‧um -ī *n*

screen quadr‧um -ī *n* vīsíficum

scroll down dēvólv‧ō -ere -ī

send mitt‧ō -ere mīsī missus

shut down claud‧ō -ere clausī clausus

software part‧ēs -ium *fpl* programmātiốnis

spam sagīnắti‧ō -ốnis

speaker megaphốni‧um -ī *n*

spread sheet chart‧a -ae *f* computātíva

string sér‧iēs -éī *f*

subdirectory plicắrum subínd‧ex -icis *m*

subscribe subscríb‧ō -ere subscrípsī

terminal terminắl‧e -is *n*

text text‧us -ūs *m*

thread séri‧ēs -éī *f* epistulắrum ēlectronicắrum

toolbar īnstrūmentốrum tabéll‧a -ae *f*

tools īnstrūment‧a -ốrum *npl*

turn off exstín‧guō -gere -xī -tus

turn on excitắre

type dactylographắre

unsubscribe cessắre

URL Ūniversắle Rērum Locắtr‧um -ī *n,* īnscrípti‧ō -ốnis interrētiắlis

web site sit‧us -ūs *m* interrētiắlis

window fenestéll‧a -ae *f*

word processor prográmm‧a -atis *n* ēditốrium

World Wide Web (WWW) Tēl‧a -ae *f* Tōtíus Terrae (TTT)

write compốn‧ō -ere compósuī compósitus; **to write a program** prográmma compốnere

General Vocabulary

N.B.

1. The illustrative phrases and sentences within the entries are in alphabetical order.

2. The principal parts of the following commonly occurring verbs are not provided in the vocabulary:

accípiō accípere accēpī accéptus
agō agere ēgī āctus
dō dare dedī datus
dīcō dícere dīxī dictus
dūcō dúcere dūxī ductus
fáciō fácere fēcī factus
hábeō habére hábuī hábitus
lūdō lúdere lūsī lūsus
sum esse fuī futúrus
véniō veníre vēnī ventum

A: she explained everything to me from A to Z ab áciā et acū mihi ómnia expósuit

abbreviate breviáre, immínu·ō -ere -ī imminútus

abbreviation not·a -ae *f* (compendiária)

ABC's prīm·ae lítter·ae -árum *fpl;* **know one's ABC's** lítterās sciō scīre scīvī

abdomen ven·ter -tris *m*

ability facúlt·ās -átis *f;* **ability to read and write** legéndī scrībendíque facúltās; **natural ability** ingéni·um -ī *n;* **speaking ability** dīcéndī facúltās; **to the best of my ability** prō meā parte

ablative *adj* ablātív·us -a -um; **ablative case** cās·us -ūs *m* ablātívus, ablātív·us -ī *m;* **in the ablative case** cāsū ablātívō

able: be able to possum posse pótuī (+ *inf*), queō quīre quīvī *or* quiī (+ *inf*)

abounding in abúnd·āns -ántis (+ *abl*)

about *(approximately)* círciter, ferē; *(concerning)* dē (+ *abl*)

above suprā (+ *acc*); **be above** *(e.g., bribery)* indígn·or -árī -átus sum (+ *acc*)

abroad: from abroad extrínsec·us -a -um; **go abroad, live abroad, travel abroad** peregrín·or -árī

absence: in my absence mē absénte

absent abs·ēns -éntis; **be absent** absum abésse áfuī āfutúrus; **be absent without leave** ad commeátūs diem nōn adsum adésse ádfuī

absentee abs·ēns -éntis *mf*

absolutely omnínō, prōrsus; **absolutely nothing** nihil prōrsus

abstract noun *s* appellátio -ōnis *f* (ut "bónitās" **goodness**)

absurd absúrd·us -a -um

abusive malédic·us -a -um

academy acadḗmi·a -ae *f*

accent *s* accént·us -ūs *m;* **place the accent on a syllable** accéntum in sýllabā pōn·ō -ere pósuī pósitus

accent mark ap·ex -icis *m*

accident cās·us -ūs *m;* calámit·ās -átis *f* (autocīnética)

accidentally cāsū, fortuítō

accommodations hospíti·um -ī *n*

accomplish cōnfíc·iō -ere cōnfḗcī cōnféctus

accomplished ērudítus -a -um

accordion harmónic·a -ae *f* dīdúctilis

according to secúndum (+ *acc*)

account ráti·ō -ốnis *f;* **audit accounts** ratiốnēs dispún·gō -gere -xī -ctus; **balance accounts** ratiốnēs cốnferō cōnférre cóntulī collắtus; **the account balances** rátiō cōnstat

accountant ratiōcinắt·or -ốris *m,* ratiōcinắtr·īx -ícis *f*

account books tábul·ae -ắrum *fpl* (accéptī et expḗnsī)

accounting cōnfécti·ō -ốnis *f* tabulắrum; **keep (accounting) books** tábulās cōnfíc·iō -ere cōnfḗcī cōnféctus

accusation accūsắti·ō -ốnis *f*

accuse accūsắre *(with acc of person and gen or* dē + *abl of the charge);* árgu·ō -ere -ī *(with acc of the person and gen of the charge);* **accuse s.o. of a capital offense** áliquem reī capitắlis re·um (-am) fácere

ache *s* dol·or -ốris *m;* **have a headache** ā cápite labōrắre; **have a toothache** ā dente labōrắre

ache *intr* dól·eō -ére -uī; **I ache all over** tōtus (-a) dóleō

acquit (of) absólv·ō -ere -ī absolútus (dē + *abl; more rarely w. gen);* **acquit s.o. of a capital crime** áliquem cápitis absólvere

acquittal absolúti·ō -ốnis *f*

acrobat petauristắri·us -ī *m* (·a -ae *f*)

across trāns (+ *acc);* **across from** ex advérsō (+ *gen),* exadvérsum (+ *acc*)

act *intr* ag·ō -ere ḗgī āctus; **act as a friend** amícum ágere; *(behave)* **act badly** sē túrpiter ger·ō -ere gessī

active ála·cer -cris -cre; *(gram)* āctív·us -a -um; **active service: be on active service** stīpéndia fácere; **active verb** verbum agéndī *or* agēns *or* āctívum; **active voice** gen·us -eris *n* āctívum; **be active in** vers·or -ắrī -ắtus sum in (+ *abl*)

actor hístri·ō -ốnis *m,* āct·or -ốris *m*

actress āctr·īx -ícis *f*

acute *(illness)* acút·us -a -um

ad praecốni·um -ī *n*

Adam's apple pōm·um -ī *n* Adắmī; nōd·us -ī *m* gútturis

add (to) adíc·iō -ere adiḗcī adiéctus (+ *dat*)

adding machine máchin·a -ae *f* additiōnális

addition: in addition accḗdit quod (+ *indic*)

address *s* īnscrípti·ō -ốnis *f* cursuális; *(comput)* īnscríptiō ēlectrónica

address *tr* ádloqu·or -ī adlocútus sum; *(a letter)* īnscríb·ō -ere īnscrípsī inscríptus; **a letter addressed to you** epístula tibi īnscrípta

address book *(comput)* lib·er -brī *m* īnscrīptiốnum (ēlectronicắrum)

adhesive glūt·en -inis *n;* **adhesive tape** taéni·a -ae *f* adhaesíva

adjacent to contérmin·us -a -um (+ *dat*)

adjectival *adj* adiectīvắl·is -is -e

adjective *s* adiectív·um -ī *n*

adjoin adiúng·or -ī adiúnctus sum (+ *dat*)

adjoining iúnct·us -a -um; **adjoining rooms** iūncta cubícula

adjourn ampliắre

administration administrắti·ō -ốnis *f*

admirable admīrắbil·is -is -e

admiration admīrắti·ō -ốnis *f*

admission ticket tésser·a -ae *f* aditiắlis

adopt adoptắre

adoptive daughter fĩli·a -ae *f* adoptíva

adoptive son fĩli·us -ĩ *m* adoptívus

adore adōrắre

Adriatic **Adriatic** Hadriắticum mar·e -is *n*

adult *adj* adúlt·us -a -um, grand·is -is -e

adult *s* adúltus hom·ō -inis *m; (not including aged persons)* pūb·ēs -is *mf*

advantage bon·um -ĩ *n;* **be of advantage (to)** prōsum prōdésse prófuĩ (+ *dat);* **derive great advantage from** multum cómmodum ex áliquā rē cápere; **take advantage of s.o.'s ignorance** alicúius ignorántiam sibi quaéstuĩ habére; **take advantage of the opportunity** occāsiốnem nancĩsc·or -ĩ nānctus sum; **to whose advantage was it (that …)?** cui bonō fuit (+ *acc w. inf)?*

adverb *s* advérbi·um -ĩ *n*

adverbial *adj* adverbiắl·is -is -e

advertise prōscrĩb·ō -ere prōscrĩpsĩ prōscrĩptus

advertisement praecốni·um -ĩ *n; (poster)* prōscrĩpti·ō -ốnis *f*

advice cōnsíli·um -ĩ *n;* **good advice** rēctum cōnsílium; **I will take your advice on the matter** cōnsílium tuum illĩus reĩ cápiam; **on your advice** tē auctốre; **sound advice** vērum cōnsílium

advise suắd·eō -ére suāsĩ (+ *dat)*

aedile aedĩl·is -is *m*

aedileship aedĩlit·ās -átis *f*

affable affábil·is -is -e

affair rēs, reĩ *f;* **have an affair with s.o.** cōnsuetúdinem cum áliquō habére

affected affectắt·us -a -um

affection am·or -ốris *m*

affectionate am·āns -ántis

afraid formĩdulốs·us -a -um; **afraid of** tímid·us -a -um (+ *gen);* **be afraid (of)** tím·eō -ére -uĩ (+ *acc),* métuō metúere métuĩ; **I am afraid that …** vér·eor -érĩ véritus sum nē … ; **what are you afraid of?** quid est quod métuis?

after *conj* postquam (+ *indic)*

after *prep* post (+ *acc); (immediately after)* ē *or* ex (+ *abl),* dē (+ *(abl);* **after all** rē vērā; **after this** post hāc; **after that** deínde, subínde; **be after s.o.** *(romantically)* áliquem pet·ō -ere -ĩvĩ; **immediately after** statim ā *or* ab (+ *abl)*

afternoon temp·us -oris *n* postmerĩdiánum; **in the afternoon** postmerĩdiē, post merĩdiem; **this afternoon** hódiē post merĩdiem

afterwards pósteā

again íterum, rūrsus; **again and again** idéntidem, étiam atque étiam

age aet·ās -átis *f;* **at age fifteen** décimum quĩntum annum ag·ēns -éntis; **he is under twenty years of age** minor vĩgíntĩ annốrum est; **she was ten years of age** erat decem annōs nāta

aged annốs·us -a -um, longaév·us -a -um

agile ágil·is -is -e

ago *(prepositive)* abhinc, *e.g.,* **ten years ago** abhinc decem annōs; **a short while ago** paulō ante; **how long ago?** quam prĩdem?; **long ago** iamdúdum, iamprĩdem; **not so long ago** haud ita prĩdem; **sometime ago** prĩdem dūdum

agree (with) cōnsént·iō -íre cōnsénsĩ cōnsénsus (cum + *abl)*

agreeable cómmod·us -a -um, grāt·us -a -um

agreement foed·us -eris *n;* **according to the terms of the agreement** ex foédere

aha! attát!

ahead: go ahead, tell me! Ágedum, dīc mihi!; **ahead of time** ante tempus

ail: what ails you? quid tibi est?

ailment mal·um -ī *n*

airbag āérius foll·is -is *m*

air conditioner īnstrúment·um -ī *n* áërī temperándō

aircraft carrier nāv·is -is *f* āëroplanígera

airline trām·es -itis *m* āérius

airplane āëróplan·um -ī *n*

airport āëropórt·us -ūs *m*

air pressure préssi·ō -ónis *f* āéria

alarm suscitábul·um -ī *n; (terror)* pav·or -óris *m;* **set the alarm for (six o'clock)** óbicem ad (hōram sextam) īnfíg·ō -ere īnfíxī īnfíxus; **the alarm went off** suscitábulum sónuit

alarm clock hōrológi·um -ī *n* suscitātórium

alcohol álcohol -is *n*

alcoholic alcohólic·us -a -um

alert ā·cer -cris -cre

alibi abséntiae argūmént·um -ī *n*

alimony alimóni·um -ī *n*

all omn·is -is -e; **all along: I knew all along** ūsque ab inítiō scīvī; **all but** propémodum: **I have all but given up hope** propémodum spem dēmísī; **all in all** prōrsus; **in all** omnínō; **all over the world** ubíque terrárum; **all right** quidem, licet; **all the same** *(anyhow)* níhilō sétius; **all's well** salva rēs est; **all the way from** ūsque

ab (*+ abl);* **it's all over!** āctum est!; **all there: are you quite all there?** satísne sānus (-a) es?

allegation īnsimuláti·ō -ónis *f*

allege árgu·ō -ere -ī argútus

alley angipórt·um -ī *n*

alliance foed·us -eris *n,* socíet·ās -átis *f;* **conclude an alliance with** foedus íc·ō -ere -ī -tus cum (*+ abl);* **form an alliance with** societátem fácere cum (*+ abl)*

alluring illecebrós·us -a -um

almond amýgdal·um -ī *n*

almost paene, ferē *(postpositive);* **almost like** paene quasi

alone sōl·us -a -um

along per (*+ acc),* secúndum (*+ acc);* **along with** ūnā cum (*+ abl);* **I knew all along** iam inde ā prīncípiō scīvī

aloud clārē; **read aloud** clārē leg·ō -ere lēgī lēctus

alphabet *s* alphabét·um -ī *n,* prīm·ae lítter·ae -árum *fpl,* elemént·a -órum *npl*

Alpine Alpín·us -a -um; **Alpine chain** Álpium iug·a -órum *npl*

Alps Alp·ēs -ium *fpl*

already iam

alright licet

also étiam

alternating current fluént·um -ī *n* altérnum

although quamquam (*+ indic);* quamvīs (*+ subj),* cum (*+ subj)*

always semper

ambassador legát·us -ī *m* (·a -ae *f)*

ambition ambíti·ō -ónis *f*

ambitious ambitiós·us -a -um

ambulance árcer·a -ae *f,* autoárcer·a -ae *f*

America Améric·a -ae *f;* **North America** América Septentriōnális; **South America** América Merídiǎna

American Americǎn·us -a -um

amount: it amounts to the same thing tantúndem est

amphitheater amphitheǎtr·um -ī *n*

amplifier amplificǎtr·um -ī *n*

amuse oblectǎre

amusement: for one's amusement ánimī causā

amusement park hort·ī -ṓrum *mpl* públicī oblectǎriī

anchor *(anchor person)* nūntiǎ·tor -tṓris *m* (·trīx -trícis *f*)

and et, atque; **and so** ítaque; **and so forth** et perínde, et cétera

anger īr·a -ae *f*

angry (at) īrǎt·us -a -um (+ *dat);* **be angry (at)** succéns·eō -ére -uī (+ *dat);* **get angry with** īrásc·or -ǎrī (+ *dat);* **he did nothing for you to be angry at** nihil fēcit quod succénseās

anguish ang·or -ṓris *m*

animal anim·al -ǎlis *n;* **wild animal** fer·a -ae *f*

ankle tal·us -ī *m*

ankle-length tālǎr·is -is -e

anklet períscel·is -idis *f*

anniversary fēstus di·ēs -éī *m* anniversǎrius

announcer annūntiǎ·tor -tṓris *m* (·trīx -ícis *f*)

annoy male habére; **this annoys me** hoc mē male habet

annoyance molésti·a -ae *f*

annoyed: be annoyed at moléstē ferō ferre tulī

answer *s* respóns·um -ī *n;* **give s.o. an answer** álicui respónsum red·dō -dere -didī -ditus

answer *tr (in both speaking and writing: with dat of person and* ad + *acc of the thing)* respón·deō -dére -dī -sum; **answer a question** ad interrogǎtum respondére; **I'll answer you point by point** tibi respondébō *(in writing:* rescríbam) ad síngula; **now I'll answer your questions** nunc respondébō ad ea quae rogāvístī; **that's not an answer to my question** áliud tē rogō

answering machine respónstr·um -ī *n* tēlephónicum

ant formíc·a -ae *f*

antagonistic īnfést·us -a -um

antecedent *s* nōm·en -inis *n* antecédēns

antelope búbul·us -ī *m,* tarándr·us -ī *m*

antepenult *s* antepaenúltima sýllab·a -ae *f*

anthropology anthrōpológi·a -ae *f*

anthropologist anthrōpólog·us -ī *m* (·a -ae *f*)

antiquity: in antiquity antíquitus [*adv*]

anxiety anxíet·ās -ǎtis *f;* **anxiety about** cūr·a -ae *f* (+ *gen*)

anxious ánxi·us -a -um

anxiously ánxiē

anyhow *(just the same)* nec eō sétius; *(in any event)* útique

anyone quíspiam *(gen:* cūiúspiam); **if anyone** sī quis

anything else áliquid ámplius, quicquam áliud

apartment diaét·a -ae *f,* cēnácul·um -ī *n;* **furnished apartment** diaéta omnī supelléctile īnstrúcta

apartment building ínsul·a -ae *f*

apathetic dēs·es -idis

ape sími·us -ī *m,* sími·a -ae *f*

Apennines, Apennine Range Apennínus mōn·s -tis *m*

apologize (for) sē excūsáre (dē + *abl);* **I apologize to you** mē tibi excúsō

apology: please accept my apologies quaesō, áccipe excūsātiónēs

apparently ut vidétur

appeal *s (attractiveness)* suávit·ās -átis *f; (legal)* appelláti·ō -ónis *f;* **allow an appeal** appellātiónem admítt·ō -ere admísī admíssus; **disallow an appeal** appellātiónem improbáre

appeal *tr* **(to)** appelláre (ad + *acc)*

appear appár·eō -ére -uī; *(seem)* víd·eor -érī vīsus sum

appendicitis appendicít·is -idis *f*

appendix *(of a book; of the body)* appénd·ix -icis *f*

appetite (cibī) appeténti·a -ae *f,* (cibī) appetíti·ō -ónis *f;* **lack of appetite** inédi·a -ae *f;* **give s.o. a good appetite** álicui (cibī) appeténtiam excitáre *or* fácere

appetizer gustáti·ō -ónis *f*

apple mál·um -ī *n*

applecart: upset the applecart plaustrum percéll·ō -ere pérculī

apple pie māla *npl* in crustō cocta

apple polisher adulát·or -óris *m,* adulátr·īx -ícis *f*

apply *(a remedy)* adhíb·eō -ére -uī -itus; **apply oneself to** sē cónfer·ō cōnférre cóntulī (+ *dat or* ad + *acc)*

appointment: have an appointment with cōnstitútum habére cum (+ *abl);* **keep an appointment** ad cōnstitútum veníre

appreciate: I appreciate your kindness benefícium tuum túeor tuérī túitus sum

apricot armeníac·um -ī *n*

April mēns·is -is *m* Apríl·is; **in April** mēnse Aprílī

apron súblig·ar -áris *n*

aqueduct aquaedúct·us -ūs *m*

archeologist archaeólog·us -ī *m* (·a -ae *f);* **the archeologists excavated this site** archaeólogī hunc situm excavérunt

archeology archaeológi·a -ae *f*

archery sagittáti·ō -ónis *f (see Chapter V)*

architect architéct·us -ī *m*

architecture architectúr·a -ae *f*

Ardea Árde·a -ae *f*

area tract·us -ūs *m*

area code (tēlephónicus) númer·us -ī *m* praelēctórius

arena arén·a -ae *f*

Argiletum Argīlét·um -ī *n (a district of Rome extending from the base of the Quirinal to the Capitoline and chiefly inhabited by booksellers and mechanics)*

argue argūmént·or -árī; *(to wrangle)* altérc·or -árī; **stop arguing!** désine *(pl:* dēsínite) altercárī!

argument altercáti·ō -ónis *f;* **get into an argument** in lītem ambíguam dēscénd·ō -ere -ī; **put up an argument** recūsáre

aristocracy nōbílit·ās -átis *f,* optimát·ēs -ium *mpl*

arm *s* brácchi•um -ī *n; (upper)* lacért•us -ī *m (see* **arms)**

arm *tr* armā́re

armaments apparā́t•us -ūs *m* bellī *(rarely pl of* apparā́tus)

armchair sell•a -ae *f* bracchiā́ta

armed armā́t•us -a -um; **be armed** in armīs esse

armpit āl•a -ae *f,* axíll•a -ae *f*

arms: arm•a -ṓrum *npl;* **arms race** armṓrum certā́m•en -inis *n;* **be under arms** in armīs esse; **by force of arms** vī et armīs; **lay down arms** ab armīs discḗd•ō -ere discéssī; **take up arms** arma cápere

army exércit•us -ūs *m;* **join the army** ad mīlítiam īre; **raise an army** exércitum comparā́re

around circā́, círciter *(+ acc),* dē *(+ abl);* **around midnight** dē médiā nocte; **around noon** círciter merī́diem

arouse *(feelings)* exagitā́re, suscitā́re; **arouse suspicion** suspiciṓnem móv•eō -ḗre mōvī mōtus; **arouse from sleep** ē somnō excitā́re

arrest *s* prehḗnsi•ō -ṓnis *f*

arrest *tr* prehén•dō -dere -dī -sus

arrival advént•us -ūs *m*

arrive advén•iō -īre advḗnī advéntum; **arrive at** pervén•iō -īre pervḗnī pervéntum (ad *or* in + *acc)*

arrogance arrogánti•a -ae *f*

arrogant árrog•āns -ántis

art gallery pinacothḗc•a -ae *f*

artery artḗri•a -ae *f*

arthritis arthrī́t•is -idis *f*

artichoke cínar•a -ae *f*

article *s (in newspaper or magazine)* commentāríol•us -ī *m,* commentā́ti•ō -ṓnis *f; (clause in a law, treaty)* cap•ut -itis *n; (gram)* artícul•us -ī *m* (hic haec hoc, *normally demonstrative, serve as articles only in declensions);* **definite (indefinite) article** fīnī́tus (īnfinī́tus) artículus

articulate *adj* disért•us -a -um

articulate *tr* articulā́re

artillery tormént•a -ṓrum *npl*

artist ártif•ex -icis *m*

as *adv* sīcut, ut; **as far as** *(up to)* ūsque ad (+ *acc);* **as far as** *(e.g. I am concerned)* quoad; **as far as I know** quod sciō; **as for instance** ut putā; **as long as** quámdiū; **as often as** quotiēscúmque; **as soon as** cum prīmum; **as soon as possible** quam prīmum; **as well as** atque; **as yet** adhūc

ashamed: I'm ashamed of it mē pudet eius; **I'm ashamed to say** mē pudet dícere

ask rogā́re, pet•ō -ere petī́vī petī́tus; *(for information)* quaerō quaérere quaesī́vī quaesī́tus; **ask about (someone, something)** dē (áliquō) rogā́re; **ask a few questions** pauca quaérere; **ask further questions** quaérere ultrā; **ask s.o. s.th.** áliquem áliquid rogā́re; **ask s.o. for s.th.** ab áliquō áliquid rogā́re; **ask the teacher (student) a question** docéntem (discéntem) interrogā́re; **ask the price of an item** mercis prétium inquī́r•ō -ere inquīsī́vī inquīsī́tus; **ask this question** hoc quaérere; **he asked me whether** quaesī́vit ā mē *(or* dē mē *or* ex mē) num; **he asked you a question** ille tē interrogā́vit; **I want to ask you this** hoc tē rogā́re volō; **why do you ask me that?** quid mē istud rogās?

asparagus aspárag•us -ī *m*

assault *s* vīs *f (acc:* vim; *abl:* vī); **accuse s.o. of assault (and battery)** áliquem dē vī (et manū) accūsắre; **commit assault against** vim fácere in (+ *acc)*

assault *tr* vim fácere in (+ *acc)*

assembly concíli·um -ī *n*

assign assignắre

assignment pēns·um -ī *n; (written)* praescrípt·um -ī *n;* **do the assignment** pēnsum *(or* praescríptum) pér·igō -ígere -ḗgī -áctum

assistant assíst·ēns -éntis *mf*

associate sóci·us -ī *m* (·a -ae *f)*

asthma asthm·a -atis *n*

astronaut astronaút·a -ae *m,* astronaútri·a -ae *f*

astute astút·us -a -um

at apud (+ *acc)*; **at all** prōrsum, omnī́nō: **you have no common sense at all.** Nōn cor omnī́nō habḗs; **at least** útique; **at most** summum; **at once** contínuō, moméntō; **at the house of** apud (+ *acc)*

Athens Athḗn·ae -ắrum *fpl*

athlete āthlḗt·a -ae *m,* āthlḗtri·a -ae *f;* **like an athlete** āthlḗticē

athletic āthlḗtic·us -a -um; **athletic competition** āthlētắrum certắm·en -inis *n*

athletics āthlḗtic·a -ae *f*

Atlantic Atlántic·us -a -um; **Atlantic Ocean** Atlánticus ōcéan·us -ī *m,* Atlánticum mar·e -is *n*

atrium átri·um -ī *n*

atrocious atr·ōx -ṓcis

attack *s (of illness)* ímpet·us -ūs *m,* accéssi·ō -ṓnis *f; (verbal)* petī́ti·ō -ṓnis *f; (mil)* oppugnắti·ō -ṓnis *f*

attack *tr* oppugnắre, adórior adorī́rī adórtus sum; *(verbally)* impugnắre; *(of a disease)* occupắre

attend *tr (to be present at)* intér·sum -ésse -fuī (+ *dat); (school)* frequentắre ‖ *intr* **attend to** óperam dare (+ *dat)*; **I'll certainly attend to it** dabō équidem óperam

attention (ánimī) atténti·ō -ṓnis *f;* **pay attention** ánimum attén·dō -dere -dī -tus; **pay attention!** atténde! *(pl:* atténdite!) *or* ánimum atténde! *(pl:* ánimōs atténdite!); **pay attention to what I am saying!** dictīs meīs atténde! *(pl:* atténdite!)

attentive attént·us -a -um, ērḗct·us -a -um

attic subtēgulắne·um -ī *n*

attitude gest·us -ūs *m;* **I don't like your attitude** gestus tuus mihi dísplicet

attorney cógnit·or -ṓris *m,* cógnitr·īx -ī́cis *f;* **appoint an attorney to s.o.** cognitṓrem álicui adscríb·ō -ere adscrī́psī adscrī́ptus

attract conciliắre, trah·ō -ere traxī tractus

attractive lépid·us -a -um; *(esp. in looks)* speciṓs·us -a -um, venúst·us -a -um

audiocasette phōnocasḗt·a -ae *f*

audiotape phōnotaéni·a -ae *f*

audiovisual aid audīvīsíficum subsídi·um -ī *n*

August mēns·is -is *m* Augústus; **in August** mēnse Augústō

aunt *(father's side)* ámit·a -ae *f; (mother's side)* mātérter·a -ae *f*

austere asp·er -era -erum, austḗr·us -a -um

author auct·or -ṓris *m,* auctr·īx -ī́cis *f*

automobile autoraéd·a -ae *f,* auto-
cīnḗt·um -ī *n* [*used interchangeably*]

available: be available praestō [*indecl*]
esse

avalance lābín·a -ae *f* nivális

average *s* **on the average** médiā hábitā
ratiṓne; peraéquē

average *adj* módic·us -a -um

aw, keep quiet! au, tacē!

awake: be awake vigilā́re; **be awake all
night** pervigilā́re

awful dīr·us -a -um

awkward inconcínn·us -a -um

aye yai yai! heu heu!

baby īnf·āns -ántis *mf*

baby carriage chīramáxi·um -ī *n*

back *s* terg·um -ī *n;* **back of the
classroom** postérior par·s -tis *f*
conclávis scholáris; **back of the head**
occipíti·um -ī *n;* **get off my back!**
ápage tē ā dorsō meō!

back *tr* fáv·eō -ḗre fāvī fautū́rus (+ *dat*)

back door postíc·um -ī *n*

backhand *(tennis)* īct·us -ūs *m* invérsus

backpack mántic·a -ae *f*

back seat sēd·ēs -is *f* postérior

backside *(anat)* clūn·ēs -ium *mpl,* nat·ēs
-ium *fpl; (facetiously)* postíc·um -ī *n*

backstroke natáti·ō -ṓnis *f* resupína

backward *(mentally)* lent·us -a -um

backwards retrō

bacon lard·um -ī *n*

bad mal·us -a -um, ímprob·us -a -um,
aliḗn·us -a -um; *(weather)* advérs·us
-a -um, grav·is -is -e; **feel (very) bad
about** (valdē) dól·eō -ḗre -uī dē (+
abl); **too bad about Edward** male

dē Eduárdō; **wine is bad for you**
vīnum est aliḗnum tibi

badminton lūd·us -ī *m* pilae pinnátae;
play badminton pilā pinnátā lū́dere
(see Chapter V)

bag sacc·us -ī *m; (small bag)* sáccul·us -ī
m; (handbag) bulg·a -ae *f*

bagpipes ūtriculā́ri·um -ī *n;* **play the
bagpipes** ūtriculā́riō lū́dere

baggage car curr·us -ī *m* sarcinárius

baggage cart chīramáxi·um -ī *n*
sarcinárum

baggage check cūráti·ō -ṓnis *f*
sarcinárum

bait esc·a -ae *f*

bake coqu·ō -ere coxī coctus; tórr·eō
-ḗre -uī tostus; in furnō cóquere

baker pīst·or -ṓris *m,* pīstr·īx -ícis *f,*
pánif·ex -icis *m,* pānífic·a -ae *f*

bakery pīstrín·a -ae *f,* furnā́ri·a -ae *f*

balance beam tign·um -ī *n* aequilíbriī

bald calv·us -a -um

bald head calvíti·um -ī *n*

ball *(dance)* saltáti·ō -ṓnis *f*

ball pil·a -ae *f; (inflated)* foll·is -is *m;*
catch the ball pilam *or* follem
excíp·iō -ere excḗpī excéptus; **kick
the ball** follem pede pulsā́re; **play
ball** pilā *or* folle lū́dere; **throw the
ball** pilam *or* follem coníc·iō -ere
coniḗcī

ball field camp·us -ī *m* lūsórius

ball game lūs·us -ūs *m* pilae (*or* follis)

ballot tabéll·a -ae *f,* suffrā́gi·um -ī *n;*
cast a ballot suffrā́gium ferō ferre
tulī lātus

ballot box suffrāgiṓrum cist·a -ae *f*

ballpoint pen stil·us -ī *m* sphaerátus

baloney fárcim·en -inis *n;* **baloney!** fábulae!

bamboozle verba dare (+ *dat);)* **you bamboozled me** mihi verba dēdístī

banana ariēn·a -ae *f,* banán·a -ae *f;* **he wants to be top banana** vult sē esse prīmum ómnium rērum

band symphṓni·a -ae *f,* concént·us -ūs *m* músicus

bandage *s* fásci·a -ae *f*

bandage *tr (an arm, etc.)* ligā́re, dēligā́re; *(a wound)* adstrín·gō -gere -xī adstríctus

bang *(noise)* strépit·us -ūs *m*

bangs *(of hair)* ánti·ae -ā́rum *fpl*

banish *(worries, cares)* éxim·ō -ere exḗmī exémptus; *(a person)* exterminā́re

banister adminícul·um -ī *n*

bank argentā́ri·a -ae *f,* tabérn·a -ae *f* argentā́ria; *(of a river)* rīp·a -ae *f;* **manage a bank** argentā́riam móder·or -ā́rī moderā́tus sum; **the Tiber overflowed its banks** Tíberis super rīpās effúsus est

bank account ráti·ō -ṓnis *f* argentā́ria

bank book libéll·us -ī *m* comparsṓrum, argentā́riae libéll·us -ī *m*

banker argentā́ri·us (·a -ae *f)*

banking business argentā́ri·a -ae *f;* **run a (big) banking business** argentā́riam (máximam) fácere

bank manager argentā́riae moderā́·tor -tṓris *m* (·trīx -trícis *f)*

bankrupt: go backrupt dēcóqu·ō -ere dēcóxī dēcóctum

bankruptcy dēcócti·ō -ṓnis *f;* **declare bankruptcy** bonam cṓpiam ēiūrā́re

bank teller argentā́ri·us -ī *m* (·a -ae *f)*

bank window ōstíol·um -ī *n* argentā́rium

bar oec·us -ī *m* pōtṓrius; *(of chocolate or soap)* quádrul·a -ae *f;* **serve at the bar** in iūdíciīs versā́rī; in forō ágere

barbecue *tr* in crātícula assā́re

barbecue grill crātícul·a -ae *f*

barber tōns·or -ṓris *m*

barber chair sell·a -ae *f* tōnsṓria

barber shop tōnstrín·a -ae *f*

barely vix

bargain préti·um -ī *n* speciā́le; **buy at a good bargain** bene em·ō -ere ḗmī ḗmptus

baritone cant·or -ṓris *m* vōcis gravis

bark *s* latrā́t·us -ūs *m*

bark *intr* latrā́re; **bark at** allatrā́re

barley hórde·um -ī *n*

barn hórre·um -ī *n*

barnyard coh·ors -órtis *f*

barometer barómetr·um -ī *n*

barracks mílitum contubérni·um -ī *n*

barrel *(of pottery or wood)* dóli·um -ī *n;* *(wooden)* cūp·a -ae *f*

bar stool sedíl·e -is *n* praeáltum, seliquástr·um -ī *n*

bartender ministrā́·tor -tṓris *m* (·trīx -trícis *f),* īnsérvit·or -ṓris *m*

barytone barytoníst·a -ae *m*

base bas·is -is *f;* **first (second, third, home) base** basis prīma (secúnda, tértia, summa); **play first (second, third) base** apud prīmam (secúndam, tértiam) basim lū́dere *(see Chapter V)*

baseball *(the ball itself)* basípil·a -ae *f;* *(the sport)* lū́d·us -ī *m* basípilae; **a baseball game** basípilae lūs·us -ūs *m,* basípilae certā́men -inis *n;* **play baseball** basípilā lū́dere

baseman (first, second, third) (prīmus, secúndus, tértius) basiári•us -ī *m* (•a -ae *f*)

basement hypogé•um -ī *n*

basics elément•a -órum *npl*

basic training rudīménta *npl* mīlitária

basin aquál•is -is *m(f)*

basket corb•is -is *m;* **make a basket** follem per corbem iác•iō -ere iēcī

basketball corbifóll•is -is *m;* **play basketball** corbifólle lúdere *(see Chapter V)*

bass viol contrābáss•um -ī *n*

bat *s (club)* clāv•a -ae *f* (lūsória); *(bird)* vespertíli•ō -ónis *m*

bat *tr & intr* clāvō pulsáre

bath bálne•um -ī *n;* **public bath** therm•ae -árum *fpl*

bathe *tr (a sore limb)* fóv•eō -ére fōvī; *(a person)* laváre ‖ *intr* lavárī

bathroom bálne•um -ī *n; (small)* balnéol•um -ī *n; (toilet)* lātrín•a -ae *f; (public toilet)* fóric•a -ae *f*

bathroom sink lābéll•um -ī *n*

bath towel gausápin•a -ae *f*

bathtub sóli•um -ī *n*, lābr•um -ī *n*

battalion cohors, cohórtis *f*

battalion commander praeféct•us -ī *m* cohórtis

batter clavát•or -óris *m*, clavátr•īx -ícis *f*, pulsát•or -óris *m*, pulsátr•īx -ícis *f*

battery accumulátr•um -ī *n*

battle pugn•a -ae *f*, proéli•um -ī *n;* **the battle of** *(at or near a town)* proélium apud *or* ad *or* circā (+ *acc);* **fight a battle** proélium fácere; **in battle** proéliō, áciē; **naval battle off Tenedos** pugna nāvális ante Ténedum; **successful battle** proélium secúndum

battlefield aci•ēs -éī *f*

bay sin•us -ūs *m*, recéss•us -ūs *m*

bay window prōiectúr•a -ae *f*

be sum esse fuī futúrus, exst•ō -áre; **be here, be present** ádsum adésse ádfuī; **be off to** ábeō -íre -iī -itum hinc ad (+ *acc);* **be fine** bene sē habére; vál•eō -ére -uī; **be up for sale** vén•eō -íre -iī; **be up in years** aetáte prōvéct•us -a -um esse; **be up to a task** óperī par esse

beach lít•us -oris *n*

beach chair sell•a -ae *f* lītorális *(or* cubitória)

beam trabs, trabis *f*

bean fab•a -ae *f; (kidney bean)* phasél•us -ī *mf*

beak rōstr•um -ī *n*

bear urs•us -ī *m*, urs•a -ae *f;* **bears grunt** ursī grúnniunt

bear *tr* fer•ō ferre tulī lātus; *(children, young)* pár•iō -ere péperī partus; *(to tolerate)* toleráre; **bear in mind** recordárī

bear cub ursae cátul•us -ī *m*

beard barb•a -ae *f*

beat *tr (with fists, clubs)* (pugnīs, fústibus) caed•ō -ere cecídī caesus; *(eggs)* coagitáre; **beat up** concíd•ō -ere -ī concísus; *(in combat, in competition)* vinc•ō -ere vīcī victus; **beat the daylights out of** pulchre percopoláre ‖ *intr* **beat around the bush** circumitióne út•or -ī ūsus sum

beautician ōrnátr•īx -ícis *f*

beautiful pulch•er -ra -rum, formós•us -a -um

beauty pulchritúd•ō -inis *f*

beaver fi•ber -brī *m*

because quod, quia, quóniam

become fīō fíerī factus sum

becoming dec·ēns -éntis

bed lect·us -ī *m; (small)* léctul·us -ī *m;* **bed of roses** rosắri·um -ī *n;* **be confined to bed** lectō tén·eor -ếrī tentus sum; **get out of bed** ē lectō sur·gō -gere -réxī; **go to bed** cúbitum īre; **make the bed** lectum *(or* léctulum) stern·ō -ere strāvī strātus

bedbug sciníph·is -is *m*

bed covers strágul·a -ốrum *npl*

bedding strágul·a -ốrum *npl*

bed frame spond·a -ae *f*

bed-ridden valētūdinári·us -a -um

bedroom dormītốrium cubícul·um -ī *n*

bedspread opertốri·um -ī *n,* peristrốm·a -atis *n*

bee ap·is -is *f;* **bees buzz** apēs bómbilant

beehive álve·us -ī *m*

beef bűbul·a -ae *f;* **roast beef** bűbula assa

beer cervísi·a -ae *f*

beer glass hýal·us -ī *m* cervisárius

beer mug úrce·us -ī *m* cervisárius

before *adv* ántea

before *conj* ántequam, priúsquam (+ *indic*)

before *prep* ante (+ *acc*); *(directly in front of)* prō (+ *abl*); **before daylight** ante lūcem; **before long** propédiem; **before now** ántehāc

begin incíp·iō -ere incépī incéptus; **begin at** incípere ab (+ *abl*); **begin to bloom** flōrếsc·ō -ere; **to begin with** prīmum enim

beginning príncípi·um -ī *n;* **at the beginning of the year** príncípiō annī; ineúnte annō; **from the very beginning** iam inde ā prīncípiō

behave *(to act)* sē ger·ō -ere gessī; **behave oneself** sē probē gérere

behind *prep* post (+ *acc*); *(with verbs of motion)* pōne (+ *acc*); *(in the rear of)* ā tergō (+ *gen*)

behind *s (anat)* postíc·um -ī *n*

believe crēd·ō -ere crédidī créditum (+ *dat*); **believe me** mihi crēde

bell campắn·a -ae *f; (small bell)* tintinnắbul·um -ī *n*

bellow *(or* **low**) bōáre; műg·iō -íre -ívī *or* -iī -ítum

bell tower campāníl·e -is *n*

belly alv·us -ī *f*

belt cíngul·um -ī *n;* zōn·a -ae *f (wide belt, usu. of cloth, used by men and women with a tunic; often used as money belt)*

bench scabéll·um -ī *n,* scámn·um -ī *n*

bend *s (of a river)* flex·us -ūs *m*

bend *intr* sē flect·ō -ere flexī; **bend down** *(or* **over**) *(stoop)* sē inclīnáre

berry bacc·a -ae *f*

besides *adv* porrō, praetéreā

besides *prep* praeter (+ *acc*)

besiege (blockade) a town óppidum obsíd·ō -ere obsédī obséssus

best *adj* óptim·us -a -um; *(friend)* summ·us -a -um; **it is best to** óptimum est (+ *inf*)

best *adv* máximē; *(especially)* potíssimum

best *s* **do one's best** prō virílī parte; **make the best of it** aequō ánimō ferō ferre tulī lātus; **to the best of one's abilty** prō víribus

bet *s* spốnsi·ō -ốnis *f; (the stake)* pign·us -oris *n*

bet *tr* **I bet he has taken off** pōnō eum abívísse; **I bet you he doesn't win** tē spōnsiṓne prṓvocō illum nōn esse victū́rum

better *adv* mélius

better *adj* **it's better to** commódius est (+ *inf*); **there, that's better!** em istuc réctius!; **where is your better half?** úbinam est tua áltera?

better *s* **it's for the better** in mélius est

beyond ultrā (+ *acc*)

bicycle bírot·a -ae *f;* **ride a bicycle** bírotā veh·or -ī vectus sum

bicycle handlebars manúbri·um -ī *n*

bicycle pedal pedál·e -is *n*

bicycle seat sessíbul·um -ī *n*

bicylist birotári·us -ī *m,* birotári·a -ae *f*

big magn·us -a -um; ampl·us -a -um; **talk big** ampullárī

big-hearted magnánim·us -a -um

big-mouth: big-mouth! ōs dūrum!; **he was always a big-mouth** semper dūrae buccae fuit

big toe poll·ex -icis *m*

bile bīl·is -is *f*

bill *(parl)* rogáti·ō -ónis *f; (of money owed)* ráti·ō -ónis *f* débitī; *(paper money)* numm·us -ī *m* chartáreus, schedinúmm·us -ī *m;* **ten-dollar bill** nummus chartáreus decem dollarórum

biographer vītae (alicūius) scríp·tor -tóris *m* (·trīx -trícis *m,* biógraph·us -ī *m* (·a -ae *f*)

biographical biográphic·us -a -um

biography vīt·a -ae *f,* biográphi·a -ae *f*

biological biológic·us -a -um; **biolgical warfare** bell·um -ī *n* biológicum

biologist biólog·us -ī *m* (·a -ae *f*)

biology biológi·a -ae *f*

bird av·is -is *f*

egg ōv·um -ī *n*

feather penn·a -ae *f*

flap the wings ālīs plaud·ō -ere plausī plausum

flight volát·us -ūs *m*

fly voláre; **fly away** āvoláre

land (on) īnsíd·ō -ere īnsḗdī (+ *dat*)

nest nīd·us -ī *m;* **build a nest** nīdificáre

sing can·ō -ere cécinī cantum

song cant·us -ūs *m*

tail caud·a -ae *f*

wing āl·a -ae *f*

birth nātívit·ās -átis *f*

birthday di·ēs -ḗī *m* nātális *(or simply* nātál·is -is *m);* **Happy Birthday!** Fēlícem Nātálem (tibi exóptō)

birthday cake līb·um -ī *n* nātalícium

birthday party nātālíci·a -ae *f;* **give (throw) a birthday party** nātālíciam dare (agitáre)

birthday present nātālíci·um -ī *n*

birth place nātális loc·us -ī *m*

bishop epíscop·us -ī *m*

bite mors·us -ūs *m; (of a snake, insect)* ict·us -ūs *m;* **a bite to eat** gústul·us -ī *m*

bite *tr* mórd·eō -ére momórdī morsus; *(of a snake, insect)* īc·ō -ere -ī ictus

bitter acérb·us -a -um; *(in taste)* amár·us -a -um

bitterly: complain bitterly gráviter queror querī questus sum; **cry bitterly** gráviter lacrimáre, ūbértim fleō flḗre flḗvī

bitterness acérbit·ās -átis *f; (esp. of taste)* amāritū́d·ō -inis *f*

black āt·er -ra -rum; *(shiny black)* nig·er -ra -rum

black and blue līvid·us -a -um; **black and blue mark** līv·or -óris *m*

blackbird mérul·a -ae *f (see* **bird)**

blackboard tábul·a -ae *f* ātra, tábul·a -ae *f* scrīptória

bladder vēsíc·a -ae *f*

blade lámin·a -ae *f*

blame *s* culp·a -ae *f;* **push the blame on** culpam in (+ *acc)* cónferō cōnférre cóntulī collátus

blame *tr* culpáre, incūsáre; **blame s.o. for** áliquem culpáre ob (+ *acc);* **I am to blame** in culpā sum; **I don't blame you** tibi nōn impróperō

bland lēn·is -is -e

blanket lōd·īx -ícis *f;* **blanket of snow** tégim·en -inis *n* níveum

blast flāt·us -ūs *m*

bleachers for·ī -órum *mpl*

bleat *(of sheep, rams)* bāláre

blender máchin·a -ae *f* concīsória

bless *(eccles.)* bene·díc·ō -dícere -díxī; **bless you!** dī tē ament!; *(after s.o. has sneezed)* salvē! *or* salútem!

blind caec·us -a -um

blind alley fúndul·a -ae *f*

blindness caécit·ās -átis *f*

blinds *(on window)* trānsénn·a -ae *f* volúbilis; **close (open) the blinds** trānsénnam apériō -íre -uī (dēmítt·ō -ere dēmísī dēmíssus)

block *(of a city)* vīc·us -ī *m; s (sports)* obstrúcti·ō -ónis *f*

block *tr & intr (sports)* obstō obstáre óbstitī *(+ dat),* óbstru·ō -ere obstrúxī obstrúctus

blockhead *(slang)* caud·ex -icis *m*

blond flāv·us -a -um

blood sangu·is -inis *m; (outside the body)* cru·or -óris *m*

blood pressure pressúr·a -ae *f* sánguinis; **high blood pressure** hypertóni·a -ae *f*

bloodshot: he has bloodshot eyes óculī eius sánguine suffúsī sunt

blouse pēlúsi·a -ae *f,* blūs·a -ae *f*

blow flāre; **blow hard** perfláre

bludgeon *s* fūst·is -is *m*

bludgeon *tr* fūste *(or* fústibus) concíd·ō -ere concídī concísus; **bludgeon to death** fūstigáre

blunt *(not sharp)* heb·es -etis; *(abrupt)* inurbán·us -a -um

bluntly lībérius

blurt out effút·iō -íre

blush ērubésc·ō -ere ērúbuī

bluster *(boasting)* iactáti·ō -ónis *f*

blustery ventós·us -a -um

boar ap·er -rī *m;* **boars grunt** aprī grúnniunt

board *(of wood)* tábul·a -ae *f; (food)* vict·us -ūs *m; (council)* cōnsíli·um -ī *n;* **room and board** mánsi·ō -ónis *f* et vict·us -ūs *m*

board *tr (a ship, vehicle, airplane)* īnscénd·ō -ere -ī in (+ *acc)*

boarding school oecotrophḗ·um -ī *n*

boardwalk ambulácr·um -ī *n* in lítore

boastful iact·āns -ántis

body corp·us -oris *n*

bodyguard satellít·ēs -um *mpl*

boil *tr* fervefác·iō -ere fervefḗcī fervefáctus; **boil thoroughly** ēlixáre ‖ *intr* bulláre férv·eō -ére férbuī; **it makes my blood boil** facit ut sanguis ab īrā fervéscit

boiled ēlíx·us -a -um

bold aud·āx -ácis

boldness audáci·a -ae *f*

bolt *s (on a door)* ser·a -ae *f,* péssul·us -ī *m;* **bolt of lightning** ict·us -ūs *m* fúlminis

bolt *tr* **bolt the door** óstium obseráre

bomb *s* míssil·e -is *n* dirúmpēns, bomb·a -ae *f;* **atomic bomb** bomba atómica; **nuclear bomb** bomba nucleáris

bomb *tr* missílibus dirumpéntibus concút·iō -ere concússī concússus

bombastic bullát·us -a -um

bomber āeróplan·um -ī *n* bombíferum

bond *(on the stockmarket)* chrēmató-graph·um -ī *n*

bone os, ossis *n*

book li·ber -brī *m*

book bag mántic·a -ae *f* librária

book binder glūtinát·or -óris *m*

bookcase bibliothéc·a -ae *f;* **built-in bookcase** bibliothéca paríetī īnsérta

book cover tegimént·um -ī *n* librī

bookkeeper actuári·us -ī *m (·a -ae f)*

bookseller bibliopṓl·a -ae *mf*

bookshelf plúte·us -ī *m,* pegm·a -atis *n* librárium

bookstore librári·a -ae *f*

boorish agrést·is -is -e

boot pēr·ō -ónis *m (of rawhide, reaching up to the calf, worn by peasants, shepherds, soldiers);* cálig·a -ae *f (worn by soldiers of lower rank)*

boot up *(comput)* initiáre systéma

booting up *(comput)* initiáti·ō -ónis *f* systématis

booze tēmét·um -ī *n*

border fīn·is -is *m,* cōnfíni·um -ī *n*

border on attíng·ō -ere (+ *acc*)

bore *s* molést·us -ī *m (·a -ae f);* **don't be a bore** nē sīs odiṓsus (-a)

bore *tr* obtúnd·ō -ere óbtudī obtū́sus

boring taediṓsus -a -um

born: be born nāsc·or -ī nātus (-a) sum

borrow mútu·or -ā́rī -ā́tus sum; **borrow money at interest** pecúniam faénorī mūtuā́rī

bosom sin·us -ūs *m; (of a female)* mamíll·ae -ā́rum *fpl*

boss *(owner)* dómin·us -ī *m; (coll)* ípsim·us -ī *m,* ípsim·a -ae *f*

both utérque útraque utrúmque; **both of us** [*lit:, "each" of us*] utérque nostrum

bother *(annoy)* exérc·eō -ére -uī -itus; **don't bother** nōlī tē *(pl:* nōlī́te vōs) movére; **don't bother me** nē mihi moléstus (-a) sīs

bothered exercitát·us -a -um

bothersome molést·us -a -um

boundary fīn·is -is *m; (dividing line)* discrím·en -inis *n;* **at the boundary between Italy and Switzerland** ad discrímen Itáliae et Helvétiae

bounded: on the east it is bounded by ... ab oriénte claúditur (+ *abl*)

bowels alv·us -ī *f*

bowl *s* crāt·ēr -éris *m,* lanx, lancis *f; (large with handles)* catín·us -ī *m; (smaller)* catíll·us -ī *m*

bowl *intr* globum volutáre, cōnīs lúdere; **bowl a strike** omnēs cōnōs (simul) prōstérn·ō -ere prōstrávī; **go bowling** īre lūsum cōnṓrum

bowling cōnṓrum lūs·us -ūs *m,* cōnilū́di·um -ī *n (see Chapter V)*

bowling alley cōnṓrum vi·a -ae *f; (the room)* oec·us -ī *m* cōnṓrum lūsūs;

(the building) aedifíci•um -ī *n* cōnṓrum lūsūs

bowling ball glob•us -ī *m* lūsṓrius; globus *m* cōnṓrum

bowling lane vi•a -ae *f* cōnária

bowling pin cōn•us -ī *m* (lūsṓrius)

box pugi(l)láre

boxer pugil, púgil•is *m*

boxing pugilát•us -ūs *m,* pugiláti•ō -ṓnis *f (see Chapter V)*

boxing champion púgilum rēx, rēgis *m*

boxing glove caest•us -ūs *m*

boxing match pugilātṓrium certám•en -inis *n*

boxing ring suggést•us -ūs *m* pugilātṓrius

boyfriend (*or* **girlfriend**) am•āns -ántis *mf*

boyhood pueríti•a -ae *f,* aet•ās -átis *f* puerílis; **from boyhood on** ā puerō

bra stróphi•um -ī *n,* mamillár•e -is *n*

bracelet armíll•a -ae *f (worn on the upper arm by the Romans)*

brag sē iactáre; **brag about** iactáre; **he brags too much about his money** pecúniam nimis iactat

brain cérebr•um -ī *n;* **brains** corcíll•um -ī *n,* cor, cordis *n;* **she's got brains** corcíllum habet

brake *s* suffflám•en -inis *n;* **apply the brake** rotās sufflāmináre

brake pedal pedál•e -is *n* suffláminis

brake lights (autoraédae) lúmin•a -um *npl* postíca

brandy vīnī spírit•us -ūs *m*

bray (*of a mule*) rud•ō -ere -ívī -ítum

brat proc•āx -ácis púsi•ō -ṓnis *m,* frust•um -ī *n* púerī (*or* puéllae)

bread pān•is -is *m;* **loaf of bread** pānis

breadcrumb mīc•a -ae *f* pānis

breaded salígne•us -a -um

breadth lātitúd•ō -inis *f;* **in breadth** in lātitúdinem

break *tr (arm, dish, law, treaty, one's word)* frang•ō -ere frēgī frāctus; *(a law)* violáre; *(silence, law)* rump•ō -ere rūpī ruptus; **break one's word** fidem frángere ‖ *intr* **break into a home** domūs paríetēs perfód•iō -ere perfṓdī perfóssus

breakfast ientácul•um -ī *n;* **eat breakfast** ientáre; ientáculum sūm•ō -ere -psī -ptus

breaking and entering, break-in effrāctúr•a -ae *f*

breast (*of a female*) mamm•a -ae *f,* mammíll•a -ae *f*

breast stroke natáti•ō -ṓnis *f* prōna

breath: catch one's breath respiráre; anhélitum recípere

breathe spīráre; **breathe in** īnspīráre; **breathe out** exspīráre

breeze véntul•us -ī *m,* aur•a -ae *f*

brew *tr* **brew beer** cerevísiam cóqu•ō -ere coxī coctus ‖ *intr* **there is some trouble brewing** nésciō quid malī concinnátur

brewery (*of beer*) bracín•a -ae *f*

bribe *s* préti•um -ī *n*

bribe *tr* corrúmp•ō -ere corrúpī corrúptus

bribery corruptél•a -ae *f;* (*in politics*) ámbit•us -ūs *m;* **influenced by bribery** corrúpt•us -a -um

brick *s* lat•er -eris *m* (coctílis = **baked**); **lay bricks** láterēs stru•ō -ere struxī structus

brick *adj* lateríci•us -a -um

bricklayer láterum strūct·or -ṓris *m*

bride nūpt·a -ae *f*

bridegroom marít·us -ī *m*

brief brev·is -is -e; **make it brief!** in pauca cōnfer!

briefly bréviter, summátim, paucīs (verbīs); **to put it briefly** ut bréviter dīcam

bright *(person)* argút·us -a -um; *(day, sky)* serḗn·us -a -um; **bright eyes** végetī óculī

brilliant! sophos!; doctē!; **absolutely brilliant!** immō doctē!

bring (along) áfferō afférre áttulī allátus; **bring about** effíc·iō -ere effḗcī efféctus, cōnfíciō; **bring oneself to** *(do s.th.)* ánimum indúc·ō -ere indúxī ut (+ *subj); **bring to order** in ṓrdinem cōg·ō -ere coḗgī coáctus

broad lāt·us -a -um

broadcast *s* ēmíssi·ō -ṓnis *f*

broadcast *tr* ēmítt·ō -ere ēmḗsī ēmíssus

broadcast station ēmístr·um -ī *n*

brocade séric·um -ī *n* aurō *(or* argéntō) intéxtum *(or* intertéxtum)

broil tórr·eō -ēre -uī tostus

broke: be broke solvéndō nōn esse

brooch fíbul·a -ae *f*

brook rívul·us -ī *m*

broom scōp·ae -árum *fpl*

broth iūs, iūris *n*, iúscul·um -ī *n*

brother frā·ter -tris *m*

brown fusc·us -a -um

brother-in-law *(sister's husband)* marít·us -ī *m* soṓris; *(husband's brother)* lē·vir -virī *m*

browse *(comput) (the Web)* nāvigáre; *(text documents)* perlūstráre

brouser *(comput) (Web viewer)* nāvigátr·um -ī *n; (viewer of text documents)* perlūstrátr·um -ī *n*

bruise *s* contúsi·ō -ṓnis *f*

bruise *tr* contúnd·ō -ere cóntudī contúsus

brunette fusc·us -a -um

brush *s* pēnícul·us -ī *m*

brush *tr* verr·ō -ere -ī; **brush the teeth** dentēs purgáre

buckle up sē accíng·ō -ere accínxī; **buckle up!** tē accínge *(pl:* vōs accíngite)

bucket sítul·a -ae *f;* **come down in buckets** ūrceátim cad·it -ere cécidit cāsū́rus; **rain buckets** ūrceátim plúere; **kick the bucket** ánimam ēbúll·iō -íre -ívī

buffalo ūr·us -ī *m*

bug cīm·ex -icis *m*

buggy císi·um -ī *n;* **ride in a buggy** císiō veh·or -ī vectus sum

build éxstru·ō -ere exstrúxī exstrúctus, aedificáre

builder struct·or -ṓris *m,* aedificát·or -ṓris *m*

building aedifíci·um -ī *n;* **put up a building** aedifícium éxstru·ō -ere exstrúxī exstrúctus

building material aedificándī matéri·a -ae *f*

bull taur·us -ī *m; (slang)* fábul·āe -árum *fpl;* **sling the bull** *(slang)* cōnfábul·or -árī -átus sum

bullet glāns, glandis *f* plúmbea

bulletin libéll·us -ī *m; (message)* núnti·us -ī *m*

bulletin board tábul·a -ae *f* pública

bull's eye scop·us -ī *m* médius

bump: bump against offénd·ō -ere -ī;
  bump into s.o. *(meet accidentally)*
  álicui occúrr·ō -ere -ī

bumper cont·us -ī *m* tūtórius

bun collýr·is -idis *f*

bundle up *(against the cold)* sē bene
  opér·iō -íre -uī

bunker *(golf)* obstácul·um -ī *n; (mil)*
  subterráneum castéll·um -ī *n*

bureau ministéri·um -ī *n; (chest)*
  armári·um -ī *n*

burglar effráct·or -óris *m,* (paríetum)
  perfóss·or -óris *m*

burglary (domūs) latrōcíni·um -ī *n;*
  commit a burglary paríetēs
  perfód·iō -ere perfódī perfóssus

burn *tr* ur·ō -ere ūssī ūstus; *(burn to
  ashes)* cremáre; **burn down** dēúrere
  ‖ *intr* árd·eō -ére -uī

burner disc·us -ī *m* coctórius

burst out laughing rīsum effúnd·ō -ere
  effúdī

bury the hatchet *(fig)* simultátem
  dēpón·ō -ere dēpósuī

bus raéd·a -ae *f* longa, coenautocīnét·um
  -ī *n*

bus driver autoraedári·us -ī *m* (·a -ae *f*)

bush: don't beat around the bush nōlī
  (pl: nōlíte) schēmās loquī; **he didn't
  beat around the bush** nīl
  circumitióne ūsus est

bushel medímn·us -ī *m*

business *s* negóti·um -ī *n;* **be engaged
  in business** in negótiō vers·or -árī
  -átus sum; **do** *(or* **carry on) business**
  negóti·or -árī -átus sum; **I always
  mind my own business** negótium
  agō semper meum; **it's my (your,**
  etc.) **business to see what's going on**
  meum (tuum, *etc.)* est vidére quid
  agátur; **run a business** negótium

exérc·eō -ére -uī -itus; **put s.o. out of
  business** áliquem dē negótiō dēíc·iō
  -ere dēiécī dēiéctus; **transact
  business with s.o.** negótium cum
  áliquō tráns·igō -ígere -égī -áctus;
  that's none of your business nihil
  ad tē áttinet; **what business is it of
  yours?** quid id ad tē áttinet?

business *adj* negōtiál·is -is -e

business card chártul·a -ae *f* negōtiális

business district empóri·um -ī *n*

business establishment *(with its
  premises)* negōtiáti·ō -ónis *f*

business letter epístul·a -ae *f* negōtiális

businessman negōtiát·or -óris *m*

businesswoman negōtiátr·īx -ícis *f*

bust imág·ō -inis *f*

busy: busy oneself with vers·or -árī
  versátus sum in (+ *abl)*

busy occupát·us -a -um, negōtiós·us -a
  -um; **be busy** sát·agō -ágere -égī

busybody ardéli·ō -ónis *m*

but sed, vērum; *(when objecting to or
  correcting a previous statement)* at

butcher láni·us -ī *m (see chapter on
  food)*

butcher shop laniéna -ae *f*

butter būtýr·um -ī *n*

butter *tr* būtýrum adhibére ad (+ *acc)*

butterfly pāpíli·ō -ónis *m*

button *s* glóbul·us -ī *m; (comput)*
  plēctr·um -ī *n*

button *tr* glóbulīs string·ō -ere strīnxī
  stríctus

buttonhole s.o. áliquem prehēnsáre

buy em·ō -ere émī émptus; paráre **(from
  s.o.** dē aliquō); **buy at a bargain**
  bene émere

buyer émpt·or -óris *m,* ēmptr·īx -ícis *f*

buzz *(of a bee, horsefly)* bombiláre

by *(a certain time, not later than)* ad (+ *acc*); **by January** ad mēnsem Iānuárium; **by myself** per mē; **by now** iam; **by the way** óbiter

bye-bye bene valē *(pl:* valéte)

bypass circúit·us -ūs *m*

bystander persón·a -ae *f* mūta; **among the bystanders** in circumstántibus

byte *(comput)* octét·us -ī *m*

cabbage brássic·a -ae *f,* cramb·ē -ēs *f*

cabinet *(of advisors)* summum cōnsíli·um -ī *n; (furniture)* zothécul·a -ae *f*

cabinet member cōnsiliári·us -ī *m*

cafe café·um -ī *n*

cafeteria refectóri·um -ī *n*

cage cáve·a -ae *f*

cahoots: be in cahoots with s.o. cum áliquō collú·dō -dere -sī

cake placént·a -ae *f; (esp. for birthdays)* líb·um -ī *n*

calf vítul·us -ī *m,* vítul·a -ae *f; (anat)* sūr·a -ae *f*

cackle *(of geese)* gríng·iō -íre; *(of hens)* gracilláre

calculator máchínul·a -ae *f* calculātória

calendar calendári·um -ī *n; (in the Roman period)* fast·ī -órum *mpl*

call *(name)* nōmináre, vocáre, appelláre, dícere, nuncupáre; *(summon)* ad sē vocáre; arcéss·ō -ere -ívī -ítus; **call roll** nómina citáre; **call up the troops** ēvocáre cópiās

callous dūr·us -a -um

callousness dūríti·a -ae *f*

calm *s* tranquíllit·ās -átis *f* ventī, maláci·a -ae *f*

calm *adj* plácid·us -a -um

calmly aequō ánimō

camel camél·us -ī *m;* **camel's hump** gibb·er -eris *m*

camera phōtomáchin·a -ae *f,* máchínul·a -ae *f* phōtográphica

camp castr·a -órum *npl*

campaign *s* expedíti·ō -ónis *f; (pol)* petíti·ō -ónis *f*

campaign *intr (pol)* ámb·iō -íre -ívī *or* -iī -itum

camp ground camp·us -ī *m* tentórius

can *s* váscul·um -ī *n* stánneum

can *aux. v.* possum posse potuī, queō quíre quīvī *or* quiī

canal foss·a -ae *f*

canary fringíll·a -ae *f* Canária *(see* **bird**)

cancer can·cer -crī *m*

candid cándid·us -a -um, apért·us -a -um

candidate candidát·us -ī *m* (·a -ae *f),* petí·tor -tóris *m* (·trīx -trícis *f*)

candy cuppédi·ae -árum *fpl;* **piece of candy** dulcíol·um -ī *n*

canvas téxtil·e -is *n;* **a painting on canvas** pīctúra in téxtilī

cap píll·eus -ī *m*

cape prōmontóri·um -ī *n; (clothing)* humerál·e -is *n*

capital cap·ut -itis *n*

capital letter *s* lítter·a -ae *f* grandis *(opp:* líttera minúta); líttera māiúscula *(opp:* minúscula)

capital punishment supplíci·um -ī *n* cápitis; **suffer capital punishment** supplíciō cápitis affícior áffícī afféctus sum

captain *(of a ship)* naúarch·us -ī *m*

car autocínét·um -ī *n,* (auto)raéd·a -ae *f* *(used interchangeably);* **drive a car** raedam gubernáre *or* ágere; **get (buy)**

a car raedam comparáre; **go by** *(or in a)* **car** raedā eō īre īvī *or* iī; **put the car into the garage** raedam in receptáculō collocáre; **ride in a car** raedā vehor vehī vectus sum; **stop the car** raedam sistō sístere stitī; **take** *(or* **go for) a ride in a car** gestātiónem raedā fácere; **take s.o. by car** áliquem raedā dúcere

carbon copy exémpl·ar -áris *n* carbóneum

car door raedae ōstíol·um -ī *n*

car key clāvis -is *f* accēnsíva

car wash raedae laváti·ō -ónis *f; (place)* raedae lavātóri·um -ī *n*

card chártul·a -ae *f; (playing card)* chártul·a -ae *f* lūsória; **(ace** bíni·ō -ōnis *m;* **jack** pedísequ·us -ī *m;* **joker** chártul·a -ae *f* fortūnāns; **king** rēx, rēgis *m;* **queen** rēgín·a -ae *f;* **club** crux, crucis *(gen pl:* crucum) *f;* **diamond** rūt·a -ae *f;* **heart** cor, cord·is *n;* **spade** pāl·a -ae *f);* **card game** chartulárum (lūsōriárum) lūs·us -ūs *m;* **play cards** chártulīs (lūsóriīs) lúdere; **shuffle (cut, deal) the cards** chártulās mísc·eō -ére -uī mīxtus (sēpón·ō -ere sēpósuī sēpósitus, distríbu·ō -ere -uī); **suit** col·or -óris *m;* **trick** vicēs *fpl* (ūnae, bīnae, trīnae, quatérnae); **trump** col·or -óris *m* praelátus; *intr* chártulās fér·iō -íre

care cūr·a -ae *f; (diligence)* dīligénti·a -ae *f;* **take good care of your health!** cūrā dīligénter valētúdinem tuam!

care for *(like)* cūráre; **for all I care** meā causā; **I don't care about such things** ista nōn cūrō; **I don't care for her** ea meō cordī nōn cāra est; **I don't care to say more** nōn libet plūra dícere; **I don't really care as long as ...** meā nīl rēfert dum (+ *indic);* **take care of** *(treat)* cūráre;

take care of yourself cūrā ut váleās *(pl:* cūráte ut valeátis); **what do I care!** quid meā!

carefree sēcúr·us -a -um

careful dílig·ēns -éntis

careless incūriós·us -a -um

carelessness incúri·a -ae *f*

carpenter fa·ber -brī *m* tignárius

carpet tapét·um -ī *n*

carrot carót·a -ae *f*

carry gerō gérere gessī gestus; *(luggage)* bāiuláre; **don't get carried away with enthusiasm** nōlī *(pl:* nōlíte) stúdiō efférrī.

cartilage cartilág·ō -inis *f*

carve sculp·ō -ere -sī -tus

case *(container)* thēc·a -ae *f; (gram)* cās·us -ūs *m; (leg)* caus·a -ae *f,* līs, lītis *f;* **a noun in the genitive case** nōmen genitívō cāsū, *(or more rarely)* nōmen cāsūs genitívī; **civil case** causa prīváta; **criminal case** causa pública; **in that case** eō cāsū; ígitur; **get off my case!** nē mihi moléstus (-a) sīs!; **if that's the case** sī rēs sīc habet; **in any case** utcúmque; **in case you have not ...** sī minus ... ; **in no case** haudquáquam; **in that case** ígitur; eō cāsū; **lose a case** causam per·dō -dere -didī; **plead a case** causam ag·ō -ere ēgī; **settle a case (out of court)** lītem compón·ō -ere compósuī compósitus; **win a case** causā *(or* iudíciō) vinc·ō -ere vīcī victus; **since that's the case** quae cum ita sint; **that's not the case** nōn ita rēs est

cash argént·um -ī *n* presentárium; **I need cold cash** opus mihi est nummīs cálidīs; **pay $10 in cash for** dēnumeráre decem dóllarōs praesentáriōs prō (+ *abl)*

cashier arcári·us -ī *m*, arcári·a -ae *f*

casino aleātóri·um -ī *n*

casserole coctóri·um -ī *n*

cassette casét·a -ae *f; (for video)* caséta magnētoscópica

cassette recorder casētophón·um -ī *n*

cast a vote suffrágium ferō ferre tulī lātus

cat fēl·is *or* fēl·ēs -is *f*, catt·a -ae *f*, catt·us -ī *m;* **cats meow** fēlēs féliunt; **cats purr** fēlēs múrmurant

catch *s* **there's a catch to it** enim istaec cáptiō est; **what's the catch?** quid est cáptiō?

catch *tr (fish)* captáre; *(baseball)* excíp·iō -ere excépī excéptus; *(what one has said)* exaúd·iō -íre -ívī; **catch a cold** gravédine afflíg·or -ī afflíctus sum; **catch hell** convícium habére; **catch red-handed** flagrántī dēlíctō dēprehén·dō -dere -dī -sus; **catch sight of** cōnspíc·iō -ere cōnspéxī; **catch up with** cón·sequor -sequī -secútus sum; **I didn't quite catch what you said** nōn satis exaudiébam dicta tua; **let me catch my breath, please** sine respírem, quaesō

catcher except·or -óris *m*, excéptr·īx -ícis *f*

caterpillar ērúc·a -ae *f; (machine)* vehícul·um -ī *n* ērūcátum

catsup *see* **ketchup**

cattle bov·ēs -um *mpl (dat & abl pl:* bōbus *or* būbus); *(collective)* pec·us -oris *n;* **cattle bellow (or low)** bovēs múgiunt; **head of cattle** pec·us -oris *n*

cauliflower brássic·a -ae *f* Pompēiána

cause *tr* fác·iō -ere fēcī factus; *(pain, swelling, war)* móveō movére mōvī mōtus; *(stir up)* excitáre; **what**

caused him to leave? quid fēcit ut abíret?

causeway agger, ággeris *m* viae

caution caúti·ō -ónis *f;* **exercise caution** cáv·eō -ére cāvī cautum

cautious caut·us -a -um

cavalry equitát·us -ūs *m*

cave spec·us -ūs *m*

cavern spēlúnc·a -ae *f*

CD compáctus disc·us -ī *m*

CD player discophón·um -ī *n*

CD-ROM orbícul·us -ī *m* ópticus

CD-ROM drive īnstrūment·um -ī *n* orbículīs legéndīs

cease-fire indúti·ae -árum *fpl;* **call for a cease-fire** indútiās posc·ō -ere popóscī; **the cease-fire is holding.** indútiae dūrant .

ceiling tēct·um -ī *n; (arched or vaulted)* cámer·a -ae *f; (paneled)* lacún·ar -áris *n*

celebrate celebráre

celery helēoselín·um -ī *n*

cellar cellári·um -ī *n* subterráneum; hypogé·um -ī *n*

cello violoncéll·um -ī *n*

cell phone tēlephónul·um -ī *n* portábile

cement caemént·um -ī *n*

cemetery coemētéri·um -ī *n*

censor cēns·or -óris *m*

census pópulī recéns·us -ūs *m*

cent centésim·a -ae *f;* **I don't owe anyone a red cent** assem aerárium néminī débeō

central médi·us -a -um

central heating calefácti·ō -ónis *f* centrális

century saécul·um -ī *n*

cereal cereál·is -is *m*

certain cert·us -a -um; **a certain person** quīdam, quaedam; **I don't know for certain** nōn certō (*or* certum) sciō; **I take it as certain** prō certō hábeō

certainly certē, proféctō; (*in replies to denote emphatic agreement*) sānē

chain catén·a -ae *f;* (*small chain, esp. used for ornament*) catéll·a -ae *f;* **the Apennines extending in an unbroken chain from the Alps to ...** Apennínus mōns perpétuīs iugīs ab Álpibus tendēns ad (+ *acc*)

chair (*normally without back or arm-rests*) sell·a -ae *f;* (*w. rounded back*) arcisélli·um -ī *n;* **arm of a chair** anc·ō -ṓnis *m;* **back of a chair** arc·us -ūs *m* sellae

chairlift tēlephéric·a -ae *f* selláris

chairman magís·ter -trī *m*

chalk crēt·a -ae *f*

chance (*opportunity*) potést·ās -ātis *f;* **by chance** forte, cāsū; **he didn't give me a chance to answer** mihi nōn potestátem dedit responéndī

chancellor cancellári·us -ī *m* (·a -ae *f*)

chandelier lámpadum corýmb·us -ī *m*

change *s* mūtáti·ō -ṓnis *f;* (*coins*) numm·ī -ṓrum *mpl* minórēs, númmulī *mpl;* **change of heart** ánimī mūtátiō; **for a change** varietátis causā

change *tr* mūtáre; **(buses, trains, planes)** mūtáre (autoraédās longās, trámina, āëróplana); **change one's mind** senténtiam mūtáre ‖ *intr* mūtárī; **the wind changed** ventus sē vertit

changing (*weather*) vári·us -a -um

channel canál·is -is *m,* canālícul·us -ī *m;* (*arm of the sea*) frēt·um -ī *n*

chapter cap·ut -itis *n*

character mōr·ēs -um *mpl,* índol·ēs -is *f*

character witness advocát·us -ī *m* (·a -ae *f*)

charge *s* crím·en -inis *n;* **capital charge** capitále crīmen; **false charge** calúmni·a -ae *f;* **bring** *or* **file charges against s.o.** crímina álicui ínferō ínférre íntulī illátus

charge *tr* (*rush against*) incúrr·ō -ere -ī; **charge a price for** prétium cōnstítu·ō -ere -ī (+ *dat*); **charge s.o. with a crime** áliquem crímine (*or* dē crímine *or* críminis) árgu·ō -ere -ī argútus

charm amoénit·ās -átis *f,* lep·us -óris *m;* (*jewelry*) amulét·um -ī *n*

charming (*esp. to the eye*) amoén·us -a -um; (*cute*) bell·us -a -um; (*beautiful*) venúst·us -a -um; (*in manner*) lépid·us -a -um

chartreuse chlorín·us -a -um

chaste cast·us -a -um, pudíc·us -a -um

chat *s* **have a chat with** cōnfābulárī cum (+ *abl*)

chat *intr* fábul·or -árī -átus sum

chatter balbút·iō -íre; **my teeth are chattering** déntibus crépitō

chauffeur autoraedári·us -ī *m* (·a -ae *f*)

cheap vīl·is -is -e; **be dirt cheap** prō lutō esse

cheaply parvō *or* vīlī prétiō; **more cheaply** minóris prétiī

cheat fraudáre; (*in school*) fūrtim exscríb·ō -ere exscrípsī; **cheat someone out of his money** áliquem argéntō fraudáre

check *s* sýngraph·a -ae *f;* (*bill*) ráti·ō -ṓnis *f* nummária; **cash a check** arcáriō sýngrapham praéb·eō -ére -uī solvéndam; **write a check** sýngrapham perscríb·ō -ere perscrípsī

check *tr (investigate)* scrŭt·or -ắrī -ắtus sum, investīgắre; *(mark with a check mark)* annotắre; **check luggage** sárcinās mandắre; **check off** *(make a check mark at)* notắre; **check out** *(inquire into)* inquír·ō -ere inquīsívī inquīsítus in (+ *acc*)

checker latrúncul·us -ī *m;* **checkers** *(game)* latrunculórum lūd·us -ī *m;* **play checkers** latrúnculīs lúdere; **jump** *(an opponent's checker)* trānsíl·iō -íre -uī; **king** rēx, rēgis *m*

checkers latrúncul·ī -órum *mpl;* **play checkers** latrúnculīs lúdere

cheek gen·a -ae *f*

cheer *s* clām·or -óris *m;* **cheers!** prōsit!

cheer *intr* acclāmáre

cheer up *tr* (ex)hilaráre, laetificáre ‖ *intr* **cheer up!** habē *(pl:* habéte) ánimum bonum!

cheerful hílar·us -a -um

cheerfulness hilaritúd·ō -inis *f*

cheese cáse·us -ī *m*

cheese cake savíll·um -ī *n*

chef archimagír·us -ī *m* (·a -ae *f*)

chemical *adj* chémic·us -a -um

chemical *s* chémic·um -ī *n*

chemist chémic·us -ī *m* (·a -ae *f*)

chemistry chémi·a -ae *f,* chémic·ē -ēs *f*

cherry céras·um -ī *n*

cherry pie cérasa *npl* in crūstō cocta

chess lūd·us -ī *m* scācórum, scācilúdi·um -ī *n;* **castle** *s* turr·is -is *f; tr* adroccáre; **checkmate** rēgem tén·eō -ére -uī; **checkmate!** cavē rēgī!; **chessboard** scācári·um -ī *n;* **play chess** scācīs lúdere *(see Chapter V)*

chest *(anat)* pect·us -oris *n; (box)* armári·um -ī *n; (for clothes)* vestiári·um -ī *n*

chestnut *adj (of horse only)* bádius

chestnut *s* castáne·a -ae *f*

chew out *(scold)* pilāre; **chew s.o.'s ears off with tall stories** alicúius aurēs fábulīs ērādīcáre

chewing gum cumm·is -is *f* masticábilis

chick pull·us -ī *m*

chicken gallín·a -ae *f,* (gallīnáceus) pull·us -ī *m; (as food)* gallīnáce·a -ae *f*

chicken coop gallīnári·um -ī *n*

chicken-hearted mūrícid·us -a -um

chief *(principal)* prínc·eps -ipis

chief of police praeféct·us -ī *m* vígilum

children líber·ī -órum *mpl*

chilly frīgídul·us -a -um; **it's getting chilly** aër frīgéscit

chimney fūmári·um -ī *n*

chin ment·um -ī *n*

China fictília Sinénsium vās·a -órum *npl*

chirp *(birds)* pīpiláre, pīpáre; *(grasshoppers)* fritínn·iō -íre

chisel *s* scalpr·um -ī *n*

chisel *tr* scalprō caed·ō -ere cecídī caesus; **chisel s.o. out of** *(cheat)* áliquem ēmún·gō -gere -xī -ctus (+ *abl*)

chives porr·um -ī *n* sectívum

chocolate socolát·a -ae *f; (drink)* pōt·us -ūs *m* socolátae

chocolate bar tabéll·a -ae *f* socolátae

chocolate pudding érne·um -ī *n* socoláteum

choice *adj* exquisít·us -a -um, éléct·us -a -um

choice *s* ópti·ō -ónis *f;* **the choice is yours** óptiō tua est

choir chor·us -ī *m*

choir director chorī magís·ter -trī *m*
(·tra -ae *f*)

choir loft aps·is -idis *f*

chore pēns·um -ī *n;* **do chores** pēnsa
fácere

Christmas fēst·um -ī *n* nātivitátis
Chrīstī; **celebrate Christmas**
nātálem Chrīstī diem celebrắre;
Merry Christmas! faustum ac
fēlícem Chrīstī nātálem (tibi
exóptō)!; fausta festa nātālícia Chrīstī
(tibi exóptō)!

Christmas Eve prídiē nātálem Chrīstī

Christmas gift nātālícium mūnúscul·um
-ī *n (or* dōn·um -ī *n);* **give
(exchange, receive, wrap)
Christmas gifts** offérre (inter sē
dare, accípere, invólvere) nātālícia
mūnúscula

Christmas holidays fēri·ae -árum *fpl*
nātālíciae; **spend the Christmas
holidays (vacation)** fériās nātālíciās
ágere

Christmas tree arb·or -oris *f* nātālícia;
**decorate the Christmas tree with
lights, balls, and tinsel** árborem
nātālíciam īgnículīs et glóbulīs et
láminīs ornáre

chronic long·us -a -um

chronological order órd·ō -inis *m*
témporis; **in chronological order**
servátō témporis órdine

chubby corpulént·us -a -um

chum sodál·is -is *mf*

church ecclési·a -ae *f*

cider vīn·um -ī *n* mālínum

cigar sígar·um -ī *n*

cigarette sigaréll·um -ī *n;* **pack of
cigarettes** capséll·a -ae *f*
sigarellórum; **smoke a cigarette**
fūmum sigaréllī sūg·ō -ere sūxī

cigarette lighter ignitábul·um -ī *n*

circulate circuláre; *(of rumor, reports)*
percrēbréc·ō -ere precrébuī

circulation *(of blood)* circuláti·ō -ónis *f;*
be in circulation *(of books)* in
mánibus esse

circumference circúit·us -ūs *m;* **the
crater measures 500 feet in
circumference** crātēr patet circúitū
quīngéntōs pedēs

cistern cistérn·a -ae *f*

citadel ar·x -cis *f*

citizen cīv·is -is *mf;* **my fellow citizens**
cīvēs meī; **private citizen** *(who holds
no political office)* prīvát·us -ī *m*

citizenship cívit·ās -átis *f*

city *(physical entity)* urb·s -is *f;* cívit·ās
-átis *f*

city council decurión·ēs -um *mpl*

civil cīvíl·is -is -e; **civil rights** iū·s -ris *n*
cīvíle; **deprive s.o. of civil rights**
áliquem cápite dēmínu·ō -ere -ī; **loss
(taking away) of civil rights**
dēminúti·ō -ónis *f* cápitis

civilian *adj* togát·us -a -um, prīvát·us -a
-um

civilian *s* togát·us -ī *m,* prīvāt·us -ī *m*

civilized hūmán·us -a -um

claim *(say)* praedicáre; *(demand)*
postuláre; **claim as one's own**
vindicáre

clam my·ax -acis *m*

clam shell mýacis test·a -ae *f*

clamp cōnfíbul·a -ae *f*

clamp down on *(fig)* compésc·ō -ere

clam shell mýacis test·a -ae *f*

clarinet tíbi·a -ae *f* clarísona; **play the
clarinet** tíbiā clarísonā can·ō -ere
cécinī

clasp fíbul•a -ae *f*

class *(in school)* class•is -is *f; (social)* ōrd•ō -inis *m;* **be at the head of the class** classem dúcere; **first-class seat** sēd•ēs -is *f* prīmae classis; **lower class** ōrdō īnférior; **middle class** ōrdō médius; **second-class seat** sēdēs secúndae classis; **tourist-class seat** sēdēs turística; **upper class** ōrdō supérior; **working class** ōrd•ō -inis *m* operárius

classical clássic•us -a -um; **classical author** scrīpt•or -óris *m* vetus et probus

classics auctōr•ēs -um *mpl* utrīúsque linguae clāríssimī

classroom conclāv•e -is *n* scholáre

clause *s* membr•um -ī *n;* **main clause** ōráti•ō -ōnis *f* [*note:* ōrátiō *can be a main clause or a complete sentence*]

clean *(the house, etc.)* pūrgáre

cleaning rag drapp•us -ī *m*

clear clār•us -a -um; *(unclouded)* serén•us -a -um, sūd•us -a -um; *(conscience)* rēct•us -a -um

clear *tr* **clear the table** mundáre mēnsam; **clear out of here!** hinc ápage!; **clear $1000 in the first year** prīmō annō mille dóllarōs dētérg•eō -ére dētérsī dētersus; **clear up** *(difficulties)* expéd•iō -īre -īvī -ītus ‖ *intr* **clear up** disserēnáre

clerk scrīb•a -ae *mf; (in a shop)* tabernári•us -ī *m* (•a -ae *f*)

clever cállid•us -a -um; **very clever!** *(well said!)* facétē dictum!

cleverness callídit•ās -átis *f*

click *tr* déprim•ō -ere dēpréssī; pulsáre; **left-click** sinistrórsum dēprímere; **right-click** dextrórsum dēprímere; **double-click** bis dēprímere *or* bis pulsáre

client cli•ēns -éntis *mf*

climate cael•um -ī *n;* **hot (cold, temperate, warm) climate** fervēns (frígidum, temperátum, tépidum) cael•um -ī *n;* **mild climate** tempéri•ēs -éī *f*

climb ascénd•ō -ere -ī, ēscéndere; **climb a tree** in árborem ēscéndere; **climb the stairs** per scalās ascéndere

clippers māchínul•a -ae *f* capíllīs resecándīs

cloak pálli•um -ī *n (Greek item)*

clock hōrológi•um -ī *n;* **the clock keeps good time** hōrológium rēctē métitur; **look at the clock** hōrológium īnspíc•iō -ere īnspéxī; **set the clock** hōrológium temperáre; **wall clock** hōrológium parietárium; **wind the clock** hōrológium intén•dō -dere -dī inténsus

clogs sóle•ae -árum *fpl* lígneae

close *(comput)* conclúd•ō -ere -ī conclúsus

closet vestiári•um -ī *n* paríetī īnsértum

cloth *(as a fabric)* text•um -ī *n; (a piece of cloth)* pann•us -ī *m*

cloth-bound book lib•er -rī *m* līnō contéctus

clothe vést•iō -íre -ívī *or* -iī -ítus

clothes vestīmént•a -órum *npl;* hábit•us -ūs *m (outfit of a particular class or occasion)*

clothes closet vestiári•um -ī *n* (paríetī īnsértum)

clothes hanger fúlcim•en -inis *n* vestiárium

clothes hook unc•us -ī *m* vestiárius

clothing vestít•us -ūs *m,* vestīmént•a -órum *npl*

clothing store tabérn•a vestiári•a -ae *f*

cloud nūb·ēs -is *f*

cloudy nūbilṓs·us -a -um; **become cloudy** nūbilā́re

clown scurr·a -ae *mf*

club fūst·is -is *m; (social club)* sodālíci·um -ī *n*

cluck glṓc·iō -íre

clumsy incompósit·us -a -um

cluster *(of islands, etc.)* celébrit·ās -átis *f; (of grapes)* ūv·a -ae *f*

clutch pedál·e -is *n* iūnctiṓnis *(or* cōpulātiṓnis)

coach *s (sports)* exercitá·tor -tṓris *m* (·trīx -trícis *f*)

coach *tr* exercitáre

coast ōr·a -ae *f* (marítima); **off the coast of** ante (+ *acc); on the coast* in ṓrā (marítimā)

coal lap·is gag·as *(gen:* lapis gágatis) *m,* carb·ō -ṓnis *m*

coalmine fodī́n·a -ae *f* carbōnária

coat amícul·a -ae *f*

coat hook véstium unc·us -ī *m*

coat rack sustentácul·um -ī *n* véstium

cobweb arā́ne·a -ae *f*

Coca-Cola Cocacṓl·a -ae *f*

cockpit cell·a -ae *f* āëróplanī

cockroach blatt·a -ae *f*

cocktail própoma, propómatis *n,* cinn·is -is *m*

cocoa cṓco·a -ae *f*

coffee cáffe·a -ae *f*

coffee break cáffeae paus·a -ae *f*

coffee cup pōcíll·um -ī *n* caffeárium

coffee maker mā́chin·a -ae *f* caffeária

coffee pot hírnul·a -ae *f* cáffeae

coffee set sýnthes·is -is *f* caffeária

coffin cápul·us -ī *m*

cohort coh·ors -órtis *f*

coin numm·us -ī *m*

cold *adj (the most general word, applied to all degrees from pleasant coolness to severe cold; also, dispassionate)* frígid·us -a -um; gélid·us -a -um; **be or feel cold** álgeō algére alsī, frī́g·eō -ére; **get cold** algésc·ō -ere, frīgésc·ō -ere; **my hands and feet are cold** manūs pedésque frígent; **turn cold** frīgésc·ō -ere; **very cold** perfrígidus

cold *s* frī́g·us -oris *n,* gel·ū -ūs *n; (med)* gravéd·ō -inis *f;* **catch a cold:** gravédinem cón·trahō -tráhere -tráxī -tráctus; **have a cold** gravédine labōráre; **liable to catch cold** alsiṓs·us -a -um

coldcuts concī́s·a -órum *npl*

cold spell frī́gor·a -um *npl*

cold weather gel·u -ūs *n,* tempest·ās -átis *f* frígida *or* gélida

collar collár·e -is *n*

collective *adj* collēctī́v·us -a -um

college collḗgi·um -ī *n*

collision collī́si·ō -ónis *f*

colonel tribū́n·us -ī *m* mī́litum

color *s* col·or -óris *m*

color *tr (the hair, etc.)* colōráre, ting·ō -ere tīnxī tīnctus

colt ecúle·us -ī *m*

column colúmn·a -ae *f; (marching)* agm·en -inis *n*

comb *s* pect·en -inis *m*

comb *tr* pect·ō -ere pexī pexus; **comb back** repéctere; **comb the hair** capillum *(or* capíllōs *or* crīnēs *or* comam) péctere; **comb out** expéctere

combat proéli·um -ī *n,* pugn·a -ae *f;* **in hand-to-hand combat** cómminus [*adv*]

combatant proeliát·or -óris *m*

combination *s* comprehḗnsi·ō -ónis *f;* **a syllable is a combination of letters** sýllaba est comprehḗnsiō litterárum

combine *tr* compṓn·ō -ere compósuī compósitus; **prepositions can be combined with verbs** praepositiónēs cum verbīs compónī possunt

come vén·iō -íre vēnī ventum; **come about** ēveníre; **come back soon** redī (*pl:* redíte) cito; **come down with an illness** morbō corríp·ior -ī corréptus sum; **come from** veníre ab (+ *abl*), dērīvárī ab (+ *abl*); **come here this minute!** concéde hūc āctútum!; **come on!** ágedum!; **come what may, we'll take it philosophically** quod fors feret, ferḗmus aequō ánimō

comfort *s* leváti·ō -ónis *f*

comfort *tr* alleváre

comfortable cómmod·us -a -um; **make yourselves comfortable** rogō ut vōbīs suáviter sit

comics libéll·ī -órum *mpl* pīctográphicī

coming: he's got what's coming to him habet quod sibi dēbḗtur

comma *s* comm·a -atis *n*

command *s (comput)* iuss·um -ī *n*

command *tr (a legion, army)* imperáre (+ *dat*)

commander in chief imperát·or -óris *m;* **be the commander in chief** impériī summam tén·eō -ére ténuī

commence hostilities bellī inítium fácere

commerce commérci·um -ī *n*

commercial *(advertisement)* praecóni·um -ī *n*

commit (a crime) (scelus) commítt·ō -ere commísī commíssus

committee concíli·um -ī *n*

common noun *s* nōm·en -inis *n* appellātívum

common sense: have common sense cor habére

community cívit·ās -átis *f*

compact disk (CD) compáctus disc·us -ī *m*

company *(mil)* centúri·a -ae *f;* **keep each other company** inter sē col·o -ere -uī

company commander centúri·ō -ónis *m*

comparative (degree) grad·us -ūs *m* comparātívus; **in the comparative** comparātívē, in comparātióne

compare with comparáre cum (+ *abl*)

comparison *s* comparáti·ō -ónis *f*

compartment *(in a train, plane)* diaét·a -ae *f* (prīmae, secúndae classis)

compass pyx·is -idis *f* magnética

compassion clēménti·a -ae *f*

compassionate clēm·ēns -éntis

compile compṓn·ō -ere compósuī compósitus

complain about quer·or -ī questus sum dē (+ *abl*)

complete cōnfíc·iō -ere cōnfécī cōnféctus; *(a year)* expl·eō -ére -évī -étus

complexion col·or -óris *m;* **having a healthy complexion** colōrát·us -a -um

composition scrīptúr·a -ae *f,* composíti·ō -ónis *f*

compound *adj* compósit·us -a -um (ut "indóctus" **uneducated**) (*opp:* simplex, ut "doctus")

computer *s* computắtr•um -ī *n,* ōrdinắtr•um -ī *n*

computer *adj* computātrắl•is -is -e, ōrdinātrắl•is -is -e

computer engineer māchinắ•tor -tŏris *m* (•trīx -trĩcis *f*) computātrắlis

computer game lūs•us -ūs *m* computātrắlis; **play a computer game** lūsum computātrắlem lŭdere

con *tr* verba dare (+ *dat*)

concentrate all the troops in one place cōg•ō -ere coḗgī coắctus omnēs cŏpiās in ūnum locum; **concentrate on something** ánimum in áliquid dēfīg•ō -ere dēfīxī

concentration inténti•ō -ŏnis *f* ánimī

concern *s* cūr•a -ae *f*

concern *tr (to worry)* sollicitắre; **as far as I'm concerned** per mē; **how does that concern you?** quid id ad tē áttinet?; **it concerns me (you)** meā (tuā) rēfert; **it does not concern me (you)** meā (tuā) mínimē rēfert

concerned about (for) sollícit•us -a -um dē (prō) (+ *abl);* **I'm not terribly concerned about ...** labŏrō nōn valdē dē (+ *abl*)

concert concént•us -ūs *m;* **attend a concert** concéntuī adesse

concise brev•is -is -e

concrete *s* concrḗt•um -ī *n*

concrete noun *s* vocắbul•um -ī *n (opp:* appellắtiō)

condemn condemnắre

condition stat•us -ūs *m; (term of an agreement)* condíci•ō -ŏnis *f;* **in excellent condition** habitíssim•us -a -um; **in good (bad) condition** bene (male) hắbit•us -a -um; **on condition that** eā lēge ut (+ *subj);* **physical condition** córporis hắbit•us -ūs *m*

conductor *(of an orchestra)* symphoniacŏrum magís•ter -trī *m; (of a train)* trắminis cūrắt•or -ŏris *m*

conference congréss•us -ūs *m*

confide in cōnfīd•ō -ere cōnfĩsus sum (+ *dat*)

confidence fid•ēs -eī *f,* fĩdúci•a -ae *f; (esp. over-confidence, self-confidence)* cōnfīdénti•a -ae *f;* **have confidence in** fidem habḗre (+ *dat*)

confident cōnfĩd•ēns -éntis; **be confident** cōnfīd•ō -ere cōnfĩsus sum

confluence cŏnflu•ēns -éntis *m;* **at the confluence of the Tiber and the Anio** inter cōnfluéntēs Tíberim et Aniŏnem

congratulate grắtul•or -ắrī -ắtus sum (+ *dat*)

congratulations! macte virtŭte estō!

congress congréss•us -ūs *m*

conjugate *tr* dēclīnắre

conjugation *s* dēclīnắti•ō -ŏnis *f; (rarely occurs)* coniugắti•ō -ŏnis *f*

conjunction *s* coniúncti•ō -ŏnis *f*

connect *tr* cōnéct•ō -ere cōnéxuī cōnéxus

connection coniúncti•ō -ŏnis *f; (comput)* cōnéx•us -ūs *m*

conquer vinc•ō -ere vīcī victus; **conquer a country** terrā pót•ior -ĩrī potĩtus sum

conscience: bad conscience mala cōnsciénti•a -ae *f;* **good conscience** mēns *f* cŏnscia rēctī

consent: give one's consent permítt•ō -ere permĩsī (ut); **without my consent** mē invĩtō

conservative *adj* cōnservātĩv•us -a -um

conservative *s* cōnservātī́v·us -ī *m* (·a -ae *f); ***conservatives*** *(in ancient Rome)* optimā́t·ēs -ium *mpl*

consider: to consider it already done istuc iam prō factō habḗre

consist of cōnst·ō -ā́re cṓnstitī (+ *abl or* ex *or* dē + *abl)*

consonant *s* cṓnson·āns -ántis *f*

constant cṓnst·āns -ántis; *(incessant)* perpétu·us -a -um

constantly perpétuō

consternation cōnsternā́ti·ō -ṓnis *f*

constitution cōnstitū́t·a -ṓrum *npl*

construct *(with mechanical skill)* fabricā́re; *(buildings)* éxstru·ō -ere exstrúxī exstrúctus

construction *s* cōnstrúcti·ō -ṓnis *f*

consul cōnsul -is *m;* **elect a consul** cṓnsulem creā́re

consulship cōnsulā́t·us -ūs *m*

contempt contémpt·us -ūs *m*, dēspicā́ti·ō -ṓnis *f;* **feel contempt for** contémn·ō -ere -psī; **hold s.o. in contempt** áliquem dēspicā́tum habḗre

contemptuous (of) dēspíci·ēns -éntis (+ *gen)*

content (with) contént·us -a -um (+ *abl); ***to your heart's content*** arbitrā́tū tuō

contest *s* certā́m·en -inis *n*

continent par·s -tis *f* mundī [*not* cóntinēns, *which means "mainland"*]

continual contínu·us -a -um

continually contínuē

contract cóntrah·ō -ere contrā́xī contrā́ctus; **contract an illness** morbum *or* advérsam valētū́dinem contráhere

contradict contrā́dī́cere (+ *dat);* **contradict oneself** pugnántia loqu·or -ī locū́tus sum

control *s* *(restraint)* continénti·a -ae *f;* *(power)* potést·ās -ā́tis *f;* **out of control** effrēnā́t·us -a -um

control *tr* contín·eō -ére -uī; **control yourself!** tē cóntinē!

convalesce convalḗsc·ō -ere

convenience: at your convenience tuō cómmodō; **write me at your earliest convenience** scrībe ad mē cum commodíssimē póteris

convenient: when it will be convenient for you cum erit tuum cómmodum

conversation serm·ō -ṓnis *f,* collóqui·um -ī *n;* **engage in conversation with** sermṓnēs cum (+ *abl)* cṓnferō cōnférre cóntulī

convict convínc·ō -ere convī́cī convī́ctus *(w. acc. of the person and w. gen of the charge);* **convicted of** manifést·us -a (+ *gen);* **convict s.o. on many counts of fraud** áliquem multīs crī́minibus fraudis convíncere

conviction (for) condemnā́ti·ō -ṓnis *f* (+ *gen of the charge)*

convince persuā́d·eō -ére persuā́sī (+ *dat);* **I am firmly convinced that** plēnus (-a) persuāsiṓnis sum (+ *acc w. inf)*

coo *(of a pigeon)* gem·ō -ere -uī

cook *s* coqu·us -ī *m,* coqu·a -ae *f*

cook *tr* coqu·ō -ere coxī coctus; **cook up** *(fig)* excōgitā́re

cookie crū́stul·um -ī *n*

cooking pot ōll·a -ae *f*

cool frīgídul·us -a -um

cool off *tr* refrīgerā́re **ǁ** *intr* refrīgerā́rī

coolness *(indifference)* frīg·us -oris *n*

coop up inclū·dō -dere -sī -sus; **be cooped up in the house** in aédibus coartátus (-a) esse

coordinate conjunction s coniūncti·ō -ṓnis f cōpulātíva

cope with pār esse (+ dat); **unable to cope with** impār esse (+ dat)

copier polýgraph·um -ī n

copy s exémpl·um -ī n

copy tr exscríb·ō -ere exscrípsī (**from** ex + abl) (by cheating clandēstínō); (with printer) exémplum (+ gen) fácere

Corinth Corínth·us -ī f; **gulf of Corinth** sin·us -ūs m Corinthíacus (or Corínthius)

corkscrew extrácul·um -ī n

corn maízi·um -ī n; **corn on the cob** maízium -ī n in spícā

corner kick (soccer) ict·us -ūs m anguláris

corporal dēcúri·ō -ṓnis mf

corpse cadáv·er -eris n

correct adj rēct·us -a -um (opp: prāvus), ēmendát·us -a -um (free from faults), corréct·us -a -um (in the sense of "corrected")

correct tr (esp. mistakes in writing) ēmendáre; (a person or mistake) córrig·ō -ere corréxī corréctus

correction corrécti·ō -ṓnis f, ēmendáti·ō -ṓnis f

correctly rēctē (opp: prāvē), ēmendátē (opp: vitiṓsē); **speak (spell) correctly** rēctē loquī (scríbere)

correlative adj relātívus -a -um (ut "tālis ... quālis" such ... as)

correspond with epistolárum commércium habére cum (+ abl)

correspondence epistolárum commérci·um -ī n

corridor ambulácr·um -ī n

cost s impéns·a -ae f

cost intr cōnst·ō -áre cṓnstitī (+ gen or abl of price); **cost a lot (little, nothing, more, less)** multī (parvī, grātīs, plūris, minṓris) cōnstáre

couch léctul·us -ī m tōméntō fartus; (semicircular) stibádi·um -ī n

cough s tuss·is -is m; **have a cough** túss·iō -íre

cough intr túss·iō -íre

councilman decúri·ō -ṓnis m

counsel iūrisperít·us -ī m (·a -ae f)

count (leg) crīm·en -inis n

count tr numeráre; **count up** or **out** ēnumeráre; **you can count on me** potes nītī mē [abl]; **you can count on it that ...** erit tibi perspéctum (+ acc & inf); **you don't count** extrā númerum es mihi

country (as a political unit) rēs pública (gen: reī públicae) f; (as a community) cívit·ās -átis f; (native land) pátri·a -ae f; (as a physical entity) fīn·ēs -ium mpl; (as opposed to city) rūs, rūris n; **from the country** rūre; **in the country** rūrī; **to the country** rūs

country road vi·a -ae f regiōnális

courage fortitúd·ō -inis f

courageous fort·is -is -e

course curs·us -ūs m; (in school) curs·us -ūs m ācroásium; (of a meal) fércul·um -ī n; **along a winding course** meánte cursū; **be driven off course** cursū excút·ior -ī excússus sum; **in due course** mox; **in the course of** inter (+ acc); **in the course of time** prōcēdénte témpore; **of**

course proféctō, quidem, nempe, *(also sarcastically)* scīlicet

court iūdíci•um -ī *n; (of a king)* aul•a -ae *f;* **court of appeal** iūdícium appellātōrium; **hold court** iūs dīcere; **take s.o. to court** áliquem in iūdícium vocāre *(or* addūcere)

courteous cōm•is -is -e

courteously cōmiter

courtesy cōmit•ās -ātis *f*

courtesy call offíci•um -ī *n*

courthouse basílic•a -ae *f*

courtroom iūdíci•um -ī *n*

courtyard áre•a -ae *f; (in a Roman house)* peristȳli•um -ī *n*

cousin *(brother's child)* patruél•is -is *mf; (sister's daughter)* cōnsōbrīn•a -ae *f; (sister's son)* cōnsōbrīn•us -ī *m*

cover tegimént•um -ī *n; (lid)* opércul•um -ī *n; (shelter)* suffúgi•um -ī *n;* **take cover** suf•fúgiō -fúgere -fūgī; **under cover of darkness** nocte adiuvánte

cover up *(against the cold)* opér•iō -íre -uī -tus

cow vacc•a -ae *f;* **cows moo** *(or* **low)** vaccae mūgiunt

cozy cómmod•us -a -um

crab *(shellfish)* can•cer -crī *m; (person)* morōs•us -ī *m* (•a -ae *f)*

crabbiness morōsit•ās -ātis *f*

crabby morōs•us -a -um

crack *s* rīm•a -ae *f*

crack *tr* find•ō -ere fīdī fissus; *(nuts)* perfríng•ō -ere perfrēgī perfráctus ‖ *intr* rīmās ágere

cracked *(crazy)* cerrīt•us -a -um

crack troops rōbor•a -um *npl* péditum, cōpi•ae -árum *fpl* ēlectíssimae

cradle cūn•ae -árum *fpl*

craft artifíci•um -ī *n*

craftsman fa•ber -brī *m,* ártifex, artíficis *m*

craftsmanship artifíci•um -ī *n*

cramp convúlsi•ō -ōnis *f*

crane grūs, gruis *mf (see* **bird**); *(machine)* tolénn•ō -ōnis *m*

crash *(comput)* córr•uit corrúere córruit

crater crāt•ēr -ēris *m*

craving for appetīti•ō -ōnis *f (+ gen)*

crawl rēp•ō -ere rēpsī rēptum; *(esp. of snakes)* serp•ō -ere -sī

crazy dēlīr•us -a -um; **he's crazy about her** eam dēperit; **he's crazy about sports** morbōsus est in lūdōs

cream crēm•um -ī *n*

credible crēdíbil•is -is -e; **be credible** fīdem habére

credit *(com)* fid•ēs -eī *f;* **academic credit** insígn•e -is *n* acadēmicum; **buy on credit** fīdē suā émere; pecūniā haud praesentāriā émere; **get academic credit for this course** insígne acadēmicum merēre prō hōc cursū (ācroāsium); **have good credit** bonā fīdē esse

credit hour hōr•a -ae *f* acadēmica

creek rīv•us -ī *m*

creep *(term of contempt)* larv•a -ae *f;* **you give me the creeps** facis ut hórream

creep: it makes my skin creep facit ut hórream

crest *(of a hill)* iug•um -ī *n; (of animals, helmet)* crist•a -ae *f*

cricket gryll•us -ī *m; (game)* lūd•us -ī *m* báculī et pilae; **crickets chirp** gryllī strīdent

crime fácin·us -oris *n,* scel·us -eris *n;* crīm·en -inis *n (more often means merely the charge)*

criminal *adj* facinorṓs·us -a -um

criminal *s* sōns, sontis *mf,* crīminṓs·us -ī *m (·a -ae f)*

crisis discrī́m·en -inis *n*

critical: the situation is critical rēs est in summō discrī́mine

criticize reprehén·dō -dere -dī -sus

crocodile crocodī́l·us -ī *m*

crook *(thief)* fur, furis *m*

crooked curvắt·us -a -um; *(morally)* prắv·us -a -um; *(crafty)* dolṓs·us -a -um

crop up exsíst·ō -ere éxstitī; **unless something new crops up** nisi álquid novī exstíterit

crops *(standing grain)* seg·es -etis *f; (field produce)* frūg·ēs -um *fpl*

cross one's path álicui óbviam venī́re

cross-eyed strab·us -a -um

crossing *(passage)* trắnsit·us -ūs *m*

crossroads cómpit·um -ī *n*

crow *s* corn·ī́x -ī́cis *f;* **as the crow flies** mēnsū́rā curréntē [*lit:* in a running measurement]; **crows caw** cornī́cēs crṓcitant *(see* **bird)**

crow *intr (of roosters)* cūcū́r·iō -ī́re; can·ō -ere cécinī

crowd turb·a -ae *f*

cruel crūdḗl·is -is -e

cruelty crūdḗlit·ās -ắtis *f*

cry fleō flḗre flḗvī; *(of a baby)* vág·iō -ī́re; **cry out to** clāmắre (+ *dat);* **cry over** flḗre

cucumber cúcumis, cucúmeris *m*

cue verb·um -ī *n* monitṓrium

culture hūmắnit·ās -ắtis *f*

cunning collubrī́n·us -a -um

cup pócul·um -ī *n,* pōcíll·um -ī *n;* **cup of coffee (of tea)** pocíll·um -ī *n* cáffeae (theae)

cupboard armắri·um -ī *n* paríetī īnsértum

curable sānắbil·is -is -e

curb crepī́d·ō -inis *f* viária

cure *tr* sānắre

cure *s* remḗdi·um -ī *n*

curiosity cūriṓsit·ās -ắtis *f*

curl cirr·us -ī *m,* cincínnul·us -ī *m*

curl crīspắre

curler calamístr·um -ī *n*

curly crīsp·us -a -um, cirrắt·us -a -um, cincínnul·us -a -um; **have curly hair** cincínnulō capíllō esse

current *adj (in general use)* ūsitắt·us -a -um; *(opinion)* vulgắr·is -is -e

current *s* flūm·en -inis *n (in the sense of "the flow"); (electrical)* ēléctricum fluént·um -ī *n;* **against the current** advérsō flū́mine; **with the current** sēcúndō flū́mine

curriculum studiṓrum currícul·um -ī *n*

cursor *(comput)* curs·or -ṓris *m*

curtain *(on a window or shower)* vēl·um -ī *n; (in a theater)* aulaé·a -ṓrum *npl;* **draw the curtains** vēla obdū́cere

curve *(in a road, coast)* ānfrắct·us -ūs *m*

custody custṓdi·a -ae *f;* **be held in custody** in custṓdiā háb·eor -ḗrī hábitus sum; **take into custody** in custṓdiam trā·dō -dere -didī -ditus

custom mōs, mṓris *m*

customer ḗmp·tor -tṓris *m (·trīx -trī́cis f)*

cut *(hair)* tónd·eō -ḗre totóndī tōnsus; **cut and paste** *(comput)* secắre et

glūtinā́re; **cut it out!** dḗsinās! *(pl:*
dēsinā́tis!*)*; *(more emphatic)* dēsíste!
(pl: dēsístite!*)*; **cut that out right
now!** supersédē istīs rēbus iam; **cut
the talk!** sḗgregā sermṓnem!

cute bell·us -a -um, béllul·us -a -um

cutlery īnstrūmént·a -ṓrum *npl*
escā́riacyberspace cyberspáti·um -ī *n*

dad, daddy tat·a -ae *m*

daily *adj* cōtīdiā́n·us -a -um

daily *adv* cōtī́diē

dainty dēlicā́t·us -a -um

daisy bell·is -idis *f*

dance *s* saltā́ti·ō -ṓnis *f*

dance *intr* saltā́re

dance band symphōníac·ī -ṓrum *mpl*
saltātiṓnis

dancer saltā́·tor -tṓris *m* (·trīx -trī́cis *f*)

dangerous perīculṓs·us -a -um

Danube river Danū́vius amn·is -is *m*

dare aúd·eō -ḗre ausus sum *(semi-
deponent)*

daring aud·ēns -éntis, aud·āx -ā́cis

dark *adj* obscū́r·us -a -um; **as soon as it
got dark** prīmīs ténebrīs

dark *s* **after dark** dē nocte; **in the dark**
per obscū́rum; **I'm in the dark** *(fig)*
mihi ténebrae sunt

darkness ténebr·ae -ā́rum *fpl;* **darkness
fell** ténebrae factae sunt

darling *(terms of endearment)* anímul·us
-ī *m* (·a -ae *f*), océll·us -ī *m*, volúpt·ās
-ā́tis *f;* **my darling** *(in address)* mī
océlle

**darn: I don't give a darn about that
(him, them)** id (eum, eōs) nōn fáciō
floccī

darned: I'll be darned if ... male mī
sit, sī ...

dashboard tábul·a -ae *f* indicātṓria

data dat·a -ṓrum *npl*

database *(comput)* datṓrum
repositṓri·um -ī *n*

date di·ēs -ḗī *f;* **by what date?** quam ad
diem? **have a date with s.o.**
cōnstitū́tum cum áliquō habḗre; **to
date** adhūc

dative *adj* datī́v·us -a -um

dative *s* datī́v·us -ī *m*, cās·us -ūs *m*
datī́vus

daughter fī́li·a -ae *f*

daughter-in-law nur·us -ūs *f*

dawn dīlū́cul·um -ī *n;* **at dawn** prīmā
lūce; **before dawn** antelū́culō

day: di·ēs -ḗī *mf;* a day, *e.g.,* **twice a
day** bis (in) diē; **any day now**
propédiem; **by day** intérdiū; **day
after day** diem dē diē, in síngulōs
diēs; **day and night** et diēs et noctēs;
every day cōtī́diē, in síngulōs diēs;
from day to day in diēs; **from that
day on** ex eō diē; **just the other day**
nū́per quidem; **one day** *(on a certain
day in the past)* quōdam diē; **on the
day before he departed** prī́diē quam
abī́ret; **on the day before the Ides**
prī́diē Īdūs; **(on) the following day**
pósterō diē; **on the third day before
the Calends of March** ante diem
quārtum Kaléndās Mā́rtiās; **the day
after** postrī́diē; **the day after that**
postrī́diē eius diḗī; **the day after
tomorrow** peréndiē; **the day before**
prī́diē; **the day before yesterday**
nudiustértius [*adv*]; **till late in the
day** ad multum diem; **two days after
that** post diem tértium eius diḗī;
these days hīs tempóribus

daybreak dīlū́cul·um -ī *n;* **at daybreak**
prīmā lūce; **till daybreak** in prīmam
lūcem

daycare center nēpiagṓgi·um -ī *n*

daylight lūx, lūcis *f,* diēs, diḗī *m;* **let in the daylight** diem admítt•ō -ere admī́sī

dead-end street fúndul•a -ae *f*

dead: I'm dead! intériī! *or* périī!

deaf surd•us -a -um; **you're preaching to deaf ears** ad surdās aurēs cantās

deal *s (pact)* pácti•ō -ṓnis *f;* **a good deal of** aliquántum (+ *gen);* **it's a deal** pactam rem habḗtō *(pl:* habētṓte); **let's make a deal** pactiṓnem faciámus

deal *intr* **with** *(topic)* tractā́re, ágere dē (+ *abl); (a person)* ágere cum (+ *abl);* **I will deal with you later** tēcum mihi rēs erit sḗrius

dealer merc•ā́ns -ántis *mf,* mercā́•tor -tṓris *m* (•trīx -trī́cis *f*)

dean decā́n•us -ī *m* (•a -ae *f*)

dear cār•us -a -um

death mor•s -tis *f;* **condemn s.o. to death** áliquem cápitis damnā́re; **put s.o. to death** supplícium dē áliquō sūm•ō -ere sūmpsī sūmptus

death penalty supplíci•um -ī *n* cápitis

death sentence: receive the death sentence cápitis damnā́rī

debate *s* disceptā́ti•ō -ṓnis *f*

debate *tr* disceptā́re dē (+ *abl)*

debt aes, aeris *n* aliḗnum; **be in debt** in aere aliḗno esse; **this has put me in debt** hoc mihi aes aliḗnum áttulit

DCD digitā́lis compáctus disc•us -ī *m*

decathlon decā́thl•um -ī *n*

deceitful fall•āx -ā́cis

December mēns•is -is *m* Decémber; **in December** mēnse Decémbrī

decency decénti•a -ae *f*

decent dec•ēns -éntis; **do the decent thing** frūgem fácere

decide cōnstítu•ō -ere -ī cōnstitū́tus; **decide to** *or* **not to** *(of the senate, also of supreme magistrates)* cḗns•eō -ḗre -uī (ut *or* ne + *subj)*

decision *(a win in sports)* praevālénti•a -ae *f* pūnctṓrum; **make a (wise) decision** (sapiénter) dēcérn•ō -ere dēcrḗvī dēcrḗtus

deck chair sell•a -ae *f* cubitṓria

decked out exōrnā́t•us -a -um; **why are you all decked out?** quam ob rem sīc subōrnā́t•us (-a) es?

declaration dēnūntiā́ti•ō -ṓnis

declarative dēclārātī́v•us -a -um

declension *s* dēclīnā́ti•ō -ṓnis *f*

decline *tr* dēclīnā́re

decree of the senate senā́tūs cōnsúlt•um -ī *n;* **pass a decree of the senate** senā́tūs cōnsúltum fácere

deepfreezer arc•a -ae *f* gelātṓria

deep red coccíne•us -a -um

deep-seated ī́nsit•us -a -um

deer cerv•us -ī *m,* cerv•a -ae *f*

defeat *s (mil)* clād•ēs -is *f; (pol)* repúls•a -ae *f;* **a defeat at the polls** comítiīs repúlsa; **defeat in running for the consulship** repúlsa cōnsulā́tūs; **suffer a defeat** *(pol)* repúlsam ferō ferre tulī lātus; *(mil)* clādem accípere

defeat *tr* superā́re, vinc•ō -ere vīcī victus

defective *adj* vitiṓs•us -a -um; *(gram)* dēfectī́v•us -a -um

defend dēfénd•ō -ere -ī dēfénsus

defendant re•us -ī *m,* re•a -ae *f*

defender *(sports)* dēfḗns•or -ṓris *m,* dēfḗnstr•īx -ī́cis *f*

defense lawyer dēfḗns•or -ṓris *m,* dēfḗnstr•īx -ī́cis *f*

defensive and offensive alliance
soçíet·ās -átis *f* ad bellum
dēfendéndum atque īnferéndum facta

defensive and offensive weapons tēl·a
-órum *npl* ad tēgéndum et ad
nocéndum

define *tr* dēfín·iō -íre -ívī -ítus

definite *adj* fīnít·us -a -um *(opp:*
īnfīnítus)

degree *s* grad·us -ūs *m; (diploma)*
studiórum diplōm·a -atis *n;* **positive
degree** gradus positívus;
comparative degree gradus
comparātívus; **superlative degree**
gradus superlātívus

dejected dēmíss·us -a -um

delete *(comput)* dél·eō -ére -évī -étus

delicate dēlicát·us -a -um

delight dēlectáre

deliver *(mail)* red·dō -dere -didī -itus;
**the mailman delivered the letter
yesterday** tabellárius lítterās herī
réddidit

demanding: be demanding multa éxigō
exígere exēgī

demented dēm·ēns -éntis

democracy dēmocráti·a -ae *f*

democrat dēmócrat·a -ae *m,*
dēmocrátri·a -ae *f*

democratic dēmocrátic·us -a -um

demonstration prōtestáti·ō -ónis *f*
populáris

demonstrative *adj* dēmōnstrātív·us -a
-um

denarius dēnári·us -í *m (worth about
one dollar)*

dense dēns·us -a -um

densely populated region régiō
ubérrimae multitúdinis

dentist médic·us -í *m* dentárius, médic·a
-ae *f* dentária

denture prósthes·is -is *f* dentális

deny īnfíti·or -árī -átus sum

depart abs·cédō -cédere -céssī -céssum

department *(academic)* facúlt·ās -átis *f;*
department of classics litterárum
classicárum facúltās

department store pantopóli·um -í *n*

departure abscéss·us -ūs *m*

depend: it (all) depends on you tōtum
in tē pósitum est; **it depends a lot on
whether ...** plúrimum rēfert num ...

deponent *s* dēpón·ēns -éntis *n,* verb·um
-í *n* dēpónēns

deposit money in a bank pecúniam in
argentáriā dēpón·ō -ere dēpósuī
dēpósitus

depressed abiéct·us -a -um; **be
depressed** abiéctō ánimō esse

depression abiécti·ō -ónis *f* ánimī

deprive: deprive s.o. of áliquem prīváre
(+ *abl*)

deranged *(mind)* commót·us -a -um;
(person) mente capt·us -a

derive *tr* (**from**) dērīváre (ab + *abl*)

desert dēsért·a -órum *npl*

deserving (of) dign·us -a -um (+ *abl*)

desire cupídit·ās -átis *f*

desk mēns·a -ae *f* scrīptória; *(teacher's
desk)* púlpit·um -í *n*

desktop *(comput) (on the screen)* in
quadrō

despair *s* dēspēráti·ō -ónis *f*

despair *intr* (**of**) dēspēráre (dē + *abl*)

desperate dēspērát·us -a -um

desperation dēspēráti·ō -ónis *f*

despicable dēspicát·us -a -um

despise dēspíc•iō -ere dēspéxī dēspéctus

dessert bellári•a -ṓrum *npl,* secúnda mēns•a -ae *f*

destination loc•us -ī *m* dēstinátus

destructive exitiṓs•us -a -um

detail: go into a matter in detail rem per síngula ín•eō -íre -iī *or* -ívī; **in detail** per síngula, singulátim

detective inquīsí•tor -tṓris *m* (•trīx -trícis *f*), indāgá•tor -tṓris *m* (•trīx -trícis *f*)

detergent lōmént•um -ī *n*

detour circúit•us -ūs *m;* **take a detour** viam flect•ō -ere flexī

develop *(character, mind)* cōnfirmáre; *(improve)* éxcol•ō -ere excóluī excúltus

dew rōs, rōris *m*

dial *s (of a clock)* tábul•a -ae *f* hōrária; *(of a telephone)* tábul•a -ae *f* sēlēctṓria

dial *tr* sélig•ō -ere sēlḗgī sēléctus ‖ *intr* númerum sēlígere

diaphragm praecórdi•a -ṓrum *npl*

dictophone dictophṓn•um -ī *n*

dictate dictáre

dictation dictáti•ō -ṓnis *f;* **take dictation** dictáta exscríb•ō -ere exscrípsī

dictator dictát•or -ṓris *m*

dictionary dictiōnár•ium -ī *n,* léxic•on -ī *n*

die mór•ior -ī mórtuus sum

diesel Dīseliấn•us -a -um

diet *s* victūs ráti•ō -ṓnis *f*

diet *intr* victūs ratiṓnem observáre

difference differénti•a -ae *f;* **difference of opinion** dissénsi•ō -ṓnis *f;* **how much difference does it make?** quantum ínterest?; **it makes no (a lot of) difference to me (you,** *etc.)*

whether ... or nīl (multum) meā (tuā, *etc.)* ínterest (*or* rēfert) utrum ... an (+ *subj*); **what's the difference anyhow!** quid útique ínterest! *or* quid útique rēfert?

difficult difficíl•is -is -e

dig *(a garden, well)* fód•iō -ere fōdī fóssus; **dig a hole through** perfódere (+ *acc*); **dig up s.th. about** quicquam éru•ō -ere -ī dē (+ *abl*)

digest cón•coquō -cóquere -cóxī -cóctus

digestion concócti•ō -ṓnis *f*

digital digitál•is -is -e

digital clock hōrológi•um -ī *n* digitále

dignified grav•is -is -e

dignity grávit•ās -átis *f,* dígnit•ās -átis *f*

diligence dīligénti•a -ae *f*

diligent dílig•ēns -éntis

dimensions mēnsū́r•a -ae *f or* mēnsū́r•ae -árum *fpl*

diminutive *s* dēminūtív•um -ī *n*

dine cēnáre; **dine out** forīs cēnáre

dining car curr•us -ūs *m* cēnātṓrius

dining couch lect•us -ī *m*

dining room trīclíni•um -ī *n; (informal)* cēnáti•ō -ṓnis *f*

dining table mēns•a -ae *f* escária

dinner cēn•a -ae *f;* **eat dinner** cēnáre, cēnam sūm•ō -ere -psī -ptus; **have a roast for dinner** assum in cēnā habḗre; **over dinner** per cēnam; **what are you having for dinner?** quid in cēnā habḗbis?

dinner clothes cēnātṓri•a -ṓrum *npl,* sýnthes•is -is *f*

dinnertime hōr•a -ae *f* cēnándī

dinosaur dinosaúr•us -ī *m*

diocese dioecḗs•is -is *f*

diphthong *s* diphthóng•us -ī *f*

diploma studiórum diplóm•a -atis *n;* **get a diploma** studiórum diplóma mér•eō -ére -uī

directly rēctā, per dīréctum

directory *(comput)* plicárum ind•ex -icis *m*

dirt cheap prō lutō

dirty *(clothes, shoes)* immúnd•us -a -um; **give s.o. a dirty look** respíc•iō -ere respéxī áliquem minus familiárī vultū

disagree: I strongly disagree with you veheménter ā tē disséntiō

disappear ēvanésc•ō -ere ēvánuī; **disappear from sight** ē cōnspéctū aúferor auférrī ablátus sum

disappoint frustr•or -árī -átus sum; **I'll not disappoint you** nōn fallam opīniónem tuam

disappointment *(act)* dēstitúti•ō -ónis *f;* *(result)* incómmod•um -ī *n*

disarm s.o. áliquem armīs éxu•ō -ere -ī -útus

discharge *(mil)* míssi•ō -ónis *f;* **honorable (dishonorable) discharge** míssiō honésta (ignōminiósa) míssiō

discipline disciplín•a -ae *f*

disciplinarian: a strict disciplinarian exác•tor -tóris *m* (•trīx -trícis *f*) gravíssimus (-a) disciplínae

discotheque discothéc•a -ae *f*

discount remíssi•ō -ónis *f;* **five- (ten- twenty-) percent discount** quinárum (dēnárum, vicēsimárum) centēsimárum remíssiō

discuss disputáre dē (+ *abl*)

discussion disputáti•ō -ónis *f*

disease morb•us -ī *m*

disgrace dédec•us -oris *n,* ignómini•a -ae *f;* **be a disgrace to** dēdécorī esse (+

dat); **that's a darn disgrace!** édepol fácinus ímprobum est!

disgraceful dēdecór•us -a -um, ignōminiós•us -a -um

dish catíll•us -ī *m;* *(open and flat)* pátin•a -ae *f;* *(large)* lān•x -cis *f;* **dishes** *(including pots and pans)* vās•a -órum *npl;* **wash the dishes** vāsa (coquinātória) élu•ō -ere -ī ēlútus

dishonorable dēdecór•us -a -um

dishwasher máchin•a -ae *f* ēlūtória

disk *(comput)* disc•us -ī *m;* **floppy disk** discus flexíbilis

disk drive *(comput)* īnstrūmént•um -ī *n* dísculīs legéndīs

diskette *(comput)* díscul•us -ī *m*

dismay cōnsternáti•ō -ónis *f*

dismiss dīmítt•ō -ere dīmísī dīmíssus

disposition afféct•us -ūs *m* (ánimī)

distance spáti•um -ī *n;* **its distance from the sea is three miles** abest ā marī tria mília pássuum

distant longínqu•us -a -um; **be distant from** abésse ab (+ *abl*), distáre ab (+ *abl*)

distinguished illústr•is -is -e

distress dol•or -óris *m;* *(difficulty)* angústi•ae -árum *fpl*

district tract•us -ūs *m,* ag•er -rī *m*

distrust *s* (**of**) diffīdénti•a -ae *f* (+ *gen*)

distrust *tr* diffíd•ō -ere diffīsus sum *(semi-deponent)* (+ *dat*)

dive *(of a swimmer)* praeceps dēsíl•iō -íre -uī; *(to submerge)* ūrín•or -árī -átus sum

diver ūrīná•tor -tóris *m* (•trīx -trícis *f*)

diving board tábul•a -ae *f* dēsultória

divorce *s* dīvórti•um -ī *n*

divorce *tr* dīvórti‧um fácere cum (+ *abl*)

diziness vertíg‧ō -inis *f*

dizzy vertīginṓs‧us -a -um

do fácere, ágere; *(the hair)* cōm‧ō -ere cōmpsī cōmptus; **do in: he has done me in** pérdidit mē; **do one's best** óperam dō dare dedī; **do good: it will do you (a lot of, no) good** prṓderit (multum, nihil) tibi; **do right well** rēctē valére; **I don't know what to do** quid fáciam nésciō; **it won't do to** (+ *inf*) nōn satis est (+ *inf*); **what else can I do?** quid áliud fáciam?; **what more can I do?** quid fáciam ámplius?; **will this do?** sátin(e) est?

doctor médic‧us -ī *m* (‧a -ae *f*); *(as an academic title)* doct‧or -ṓris *m*, doctr‧īx -īcis *f*

doctorate doctōrắt‧us -ūs *m*

doctor's degree doctṓris grad‧us -ūs *m*

documentary documentári‧um -ī *n*

dodge the draft mīlítiam subter‧fúgiō -fúgere -fúgī

doing: what's doing? quid ágitur?

doll pūp‧a -ae *f*

dollar dóllar‧us -ī *m*, dollári‧um -ī *n*

dolphin delphín‧us -ī *m*

done for: I'm done for! nūllus sum! *or* périī!

donkey ásin‧us -ī *m*

dormitory hospíti‧um -ī *n* (discipulṓrum *or* discipulắrum)

door iánu‧a -ae *f*, ṓsti‧um -ī *n;* **double doors** for‧ēs -ium *fpl;* **folding doors** valv‧ae -ắrum *fpl;* **out of doors** forīs

doorbell ṓstiī tintinábul‧um -ī *n;* **ring the doorbell** pulsábulum cómprim‧ō -ere compréssī; **the doorbell is ringing** ṓstiī tintinábulum tinnit

doorknob iánuae manúbri‧um -ī *n*

door lock claustr‧um -ī *n*

doorpost post‧is -is *m*

doorstep līm‧en -inis *n*

doorway ṓsti‧um -ī *n*

dorsal fin pinn‧a -ae *f* dorsális

dose pórti‧ō -ṓnis *f;* **small dose** portiúncul‧a -ae *f*

double *adj* geminất‧us -a -um: **double "i" as in "armāriī"** "i" líttera gemináta, ut armắriī

double *s* **on the double** currículō; **doubles** *(in tennis)* lūd‧us -ī *m* bis bīnṓrum

double home dom‧us -ūs *f* duplex

double room conclắve -is *n* duṓrum lectṓrum

doubt *s* **I have no doubt that …** nōn mihi dúbium est quīn (+ *subj*)

doubt *tr* & *intr* dubitắre

dove palúmb‧ēs -is *f (see* **bird***)*

downcast dēiéct‧us -a -um; dēmíss‧us -a -um; **be downcast** iác‧eō -ére -uī; **with downcast eyes** dēiéctus óculōs

downhearted dēmíss‧us -a -um; **be downhearted** ánimō percúlsō esse

downhill *adj* dēclív‧is -is -e, prōclív‧is -is -e; **it was all downhill after that** prōclívia ómnia erant postílla

downhill *adv* per dēclíve; **things are going downhill** inclīnắta rēs est

downhill racing dēcúrsi‧ō -ṓnis *f* simplex

download *(comput)* ex rēte prehén‧dō -dere -dī -sus, ex rēte éxprom‧ō -ere -psī -ptus

down pat: you have the whole thing down pat órdine omnem rem tenēs

down payment árrab‧ō -ṓnis *f;* **make a down payment of $20** *(or* **pay $20 down)** vīgíntī dóllarōs arrabṓnī dare

downstairs *(direction)* deórsum; *(position)* in īmō tabulátō; **go downstairs** per scālās dēscénd•ō -ere -ī; **he is downstairs** in īmō tabulátō est

draft *s (mil)* dīléct•us -ūs *m;* **hold a draft** dīléctum habére

draft cōnscríb•ō -ere cōnscrípsī cōnscríptus

draft-dodger quī mīlítiam subtérfugit

drag *tr (comput)* trah•ō -ere trāxī tractus; **drag out (a war)** (bellum) tráhere *or* prōdúc•ō -ere ‖ *intr* **drag on** trah•or -ī

draw (water) (aquam) haúr•iō -íre hausī haustus; **(lines)** (líneās) dúcere

drawbridge pōns, pontis *m* sublevábilis

drawer lócul•us -ī *m,* fórul•us -ī *m* recíprocus

dread formīdáre

dreadful dīr•us -a -um

dress *s* vest•is -is *f* mulíebris; *(anklelength)* vestis tāláris; *(Roman)* stol•a -ae *f*

dress *tr* índuō indúere índuī indútus, vést•iō -íre -ívī *or* -iī -ítus; **dress oneself, get dressed** sē indúere, sē vestíre ‖ *intr* **dress up** sē exōrnáre

dressing *(on a salad)* embámm•a -atis *n*

dressing table mēns•a -ae *f* cōmātória

dressmaker vestífic•a -ae *f*

dress shoes socc•ī -órum *mpl,* sóccul•ī -órum *mpl (for women, of different colors and often decorated with gems)*

dribble *tr (a basketball)* repercutitáre

dribbling repercúti•ō -ónis *f*

drifter larífug•a -ae *m*

drill *s (tool)* térebr•a -ae *f; (in school)* exercíti•um -ī *n; (mil)* exercitáti•ō -ónis *f*

drill *tr* terebráre; *(students)* īnstítu•ō -ere -ī īnstitútus; *(mil)* exérc•eō -ére -uī -itus

drink *s* póti•ō -ónis *f;* **drinks** pōtión•ēs -um *fpl,* pōtulént•a -órum *npl*

drink *tr* pōtáre

drive *s (enthusiasm)* stúdi•um -ī *n; (in a vehicle)* gestáti•ō -ónis *f*

drive *tr (a car, truck, bus)* gubernáre, ágere; **drive s.o. home** áliquem domum autocīnétō *(or* autoraédā) addúcere; **drive s.o. mad** áliquem dēméntem fácere

driver autoraedári•us -ī *m* (•a -ae *f*), autocīnētíst•ēs -is *mf*

driver's license autoraedáriī diplóm•a -atis *n*

drizzle *s* plúvi•a -ae *f* rāra et minúta

drizzle *intr* **it is drizzling** léniter pluit

drop *s (e.g., of rain)* gutt•a -ae *f*

drop in on *(to visit)* invís•ō -ere -ī; **drop it!** *(no more of that!)* missa istaec fac!; **drop it, please!** mittē, amábō!; **drop off to sleep** obdormísc•ō -ere; **let's drop the subject** missa haec faciámus

drug medicám•en -inis *n; (narcotic)* medicāmént•um -ī *n* psychotrópicum

druggist medicāmentári•us -ī *m* (•a -ae *f*), pharmacopól•a -ae *m* (•ria -riae *f*)

drugstore medicāmentári•a -ae *f*

drum týmpan•um -ī *n;* **play the drum** týmpanum pulsáre

drummer tympaníst•a -ae *m* (•ria -riae *f*)

drunk ébri•us -a -um

drunkenness ēbríet•ās -átis *f; (habitual drunkenness)* ēbriósit•ās -átis *f*

dry cleaner full·ō -ṓnis *m*

dry cleaner's *(establishment)* fullṓnic·a -ae *f*

dryer *(for hair; for clothes)* īnstrūmént·um -ī *n* siccātṓrium (capillṓrum; véstium)

duck *s* an·as -atis *f; (as food)* anatín·a -ae *f;* **ducks quack** ánatēs tetrínniunt

duck *tr (in the water)* dḗprim·ō -ere dēprḗssī dēprḗssus; **duck the issue** rem ēvītáre ‖ *intr* caput inclināre

dull heb·es -etis

dummy *(slang)* frut·ex -icis *m,* bār·ō -ṓnis *m*

dumpling off·a -ae *f*

duped: you've been duped good and proper tibi ōs est súblitum plánē et probē

during inter (+ *acc*)

dust *tr* **dust the furniture** supelléctilem dētér·geō -gḗre -sī -sus

dustpan vatíll·um -ī *n*

DVD digitális díscul·us -ī *m* magnētoscópicus

dye ting·ō -ere tīnxī tīnctus

dying to know: I am dying to know how you are doing valdē áveō scīre, quid agās

each quisque quaeque quodque

eager (for) cúpid·us -a -um (+ *gen*)

eagle áquil·a -ae *f;* **eagles screech** áquilae strīdent

ear aur·is -is *f; (outer)* aurícul·a -ae *f*

earlobe lann·a -ae *f*

early *(at an early period)* mātūrē; **early in the morning** bene māne; *(too soon)* praemātūrē

earrings inaúr·ēs -ium *fpl*

earthquake terrae mōt·us -ūs *m*

earthworm lumbríc·us -ī *m*

east óri·ēns -éntis *m;* **on the east (side)** ab oriénte; **to the east** in oriéntem versus [versus *is an adverb*]

Easter *adj* Paschál·is -is -e

Easter *s* Pasch·a -ae *f,* Pasch·a -átis *n*

eastern orientál·is -is -e

eastward in oriéntem versus [versus *is an adverb*]

easy chair arcisélli·um -ī *n* tōméntō fartum

easy-going fácil·is -is -e

eat edō ésse *or* édere ēdī ēsus; *(breakfast, lunch, dinner)* sūm·ō -ere sūmpsī sūmptus; **eat out** forīs cēnāre

edict ēdíct·um -ī *n*

edit ēdō édere édidī éditus

edition ēdíti·ō -ṓnis *f*

editor redáct·or -ṓris *m,* redáctr·īx -ícis *f; (of a newspaper, magazine)* édit·or tóris *m* (tríx -trícis *f*); **editor in chief** redáctor prínceps *m,* redáctrīx prínceps *f*

educate īnstít·uō -úere -uī -útus, ērúd·iō -íre -iī -ítus

educated ērudít·us -a -um

education īnstitúti·ō -ṓnis *f,* ērudíti·ō -ṓnis *f (Note that ēdūcátiō refers to "raising, bringing up" and can apply to the raising of children as well as livestock and crops, the training of the body, etc.)*

eel anguíll·a -ae *f*

effeminate effēmināt·us -a -um

efficient hábil·is -is -e

efficiency habílit·ās -átis *f*

effort: it's (not) worth the effort prétium óperae (nōn) est; **make an effort to be on time** dā óperam ut tempestívē adsīs; **you've wasted all your effort** omnem óperam perdidístī

egg ōv·um -ī *n* (**fried** frīctum; **hard-boiled** dūrum; **soft-boiled** ápalum; **scrambled** permíxtum)

egg on concitắre

egg white albúm·en -inis *n*

eggplant melongén·a -ae *f*

either ... or aut ... aut

elbow cúbit·um -ī *n*

elect creắre; *(Roman senators)* coöptắre

elections comíti·a -ốrum *npl;* **hold elections** comítia habére

electric(al) ēléctric·us -a -um

electrical appliances ēléctrica īnstrūmént·a -ốrum *npl*

electrical outlet cápsul·a -ae *f* contáctūs ēléctricī

electric cord fūnícul·us -ī *m* ēléctricus

electric current fluént·um -ī *n* ēléctricum

electric fan máchin·a -ae *f* ventígena

electrician ēléctridis ártif·ex -icis *m*

electricity ēléctr·is -idis *f*

electric light lūm·en -inis *n* ēléctricum; **turn off (turn off) the light** lūmen accénd·ō -ere -ī accēnsus (exstíngu·ō -ere extínxī extínctus)

electric shaver rāsốri·um -ī *n* ēléctricum

electric stove fócul·us -ī *m* ēléctricus

electric wire fīl·um -ī *n* ēléctricum

electronic ēlectrónic·us -a -um

elegance ēlegánti·a -ae *f*

elegant éleg·āns -ántis

elementary school litterárius lūd·us -ī *m*

elephant elephánt·us -ī *m;* **elephants trumpet** elephántī bárriunt

elevator céllul·a -ae *f* scānsốria

eloquent éloqu·ēns -éntis

else: anyone else quīvīs álius; **anything else?** áliquid ámplius? **no one else** nēmō álius; **nothing else** nihil áliud; **who else is more deserving?** quis alter est dígnior homō?

elsewhere álibī

e-mail *s* lítter·ae -árum *fpl* ēlectrónicae; *(the system)* curs·us -ūs *m* ēlectrónicus

e-mail *tr* lítterās ēlectrónicās míttere ad (+ *acc*)

e-mail address īnscrípti·ō -ốnis *f* ēlectrónica

embarrass perturbắre

embarrassed: I am embarrassed by sum perturbắtus cum (+ *abl*)

embezzle ēvért·ō -ere -ī ēvérsus

embezzlement pecūlắt·us -ūs *m*

embroider acū ping·ō -ere pīnxī pīctus

embroidered *(with colors)* pīct·us -a -um

emerald *s* smarágd·us -ī *m*

emerald *adj* smarágdin·us -a -um

emigrate ēmigrắre

emotion ánimī mōt·us -ūs *m;* **express emotions** ánimī mōtūs éxprim·ō -ere expréssī expréssus

emperor imperắt·or -ốris *m; (title chosen by Augustus)* prínc·eps -ipis *m*

employ *(to use)* ūt·or -ī ūsus sum (+ *abl*); *(to hire)* condúcere

employee condúct·us -ī *m* (·a -ae *f*), mercēnári·us -ī *m* (·a -ae *f*)

employer (óperae) condúc·tor -tốris *m* (·trīx -trícis *f*)

employment *(act)* ūs·us -ūs *m; (occupation)* quaest·us -ūs *m*

empty (into) sē effúnd·ō -ere effūdī effūsus (in + *acc*)

enclitic *s* enclític·um -ī *n* (ut "-que," "-ve" **and, or**)

encourage adhórt·or -árī -átus sum

encouragement hortát·us -ūs *m*, hortám·en -inis *n*

end *s* fín·is -is *m;* **in the end** ab extrémō; **put an end to a war** bellī fīnem fácere; **toward the end of his life** témpore extrémō; **that's the end of me** āctum est dē mē

end fín·iō -íre -ívī -ítus ‖ *intr* désin·ō -ere, fín·ior -írī finítus sum; *(gram)* **(in)** términ·or -árī -átus sum (in + *acc or abl*)

ending *adj (gram)* **(in)** minát·us -a -um (in + *acc*)

ending *s (gram)* termináti·ō -ónis *f*

enemy host·ēs -ium *mpl; (personal enemy)* inimíc·us -ī *m* (·a -ae *f*)

energetic náv·us -a -um

enforce the law lēgem exérc·eō -ére -uī -itus

engine māchināmént·um -ī *n*, mótr·um -ī *n*

engineer māchiná·tor -tóris *m* (·trīx -trícis *f*

engineering māchinális sciénti·a -ae *f*

enjoy *(good health, company, etc.)* ūtor ūtī ūsus sum (+ *abl*)

enlist nōmen *(of several:* nómina) dare

enough satis; **enough and more than enough** satis supérque; **enough of this!** haec háctenus!

enter intráre; *(comput)* in computátrum réferō referre rétulī relátus

enthusiasm stúdi·um -ī *n*

enthusiastic *(about)* studiós·us -a -um (+ *gen)*

entrance *(entering)* intróit·us -ūs *m; (approach)* ádit·us -ūs *m; (doorway)* ósti·um -ī *n*

envelope involúcr·um -ī *n* epistuláre

envious ínvid·us -a -um; **be envious of** invíd·eō -ére invídī (+ *dat)*

environment coniéct·a -órum *npl*

envy *s* invídi·a -ae *f*

envy *tr* invíd·eō -ére invídī invísum (+ *dat)*

epilepsy morb·us -ī *m* comitiális

equally aequē

erase ērád·ō -ere -ī ērásus

eraser *(for a blackboard)* dētersóri·um -ī *n; (on a pencil)* cumm·is -is *f* dēlétilis

erasure litúr·a -ae *f*

error err·or -óris *m; (in writing)* mend·um -ī *n*, mend·a -ae *f*, víti·um -ī *n*; **commit (make) an error** mendum admítt·ō -ere admísī admíssus

escalator scál·ae -árum *fpl* móbilēs *(or* volúbilēs)

escape *s* effúgi·um -ī *n*

escape *tr* **escape the notice of** fall·ō -ere feféllī ‖ *intr* effúg·iō -ere effúgī

esophagus gul·a -ae *f*

especially potíssimum, praecípuē

essay tractát·us -ūs *m*

espresso cáffe·a -ae *f* expréssa

esteem *s* aestimáti·ō -ónis *f;* **hold s.o. in high (highest) esteem** áliquem magnī (máximī) fácere

esteem *tr* aestimáre

estranged: become estranged from s.o. áliquem ā sē aliēnáre

estuary aestuári·um -ī *n*

Etruria Etrúri·a -ae *f*

Europe Európ·a -ae *f*

European Eurōpaé•us -a -um

evasive ambígu•us -a -um

even étiam; **even today** etiámnum; **not even** ne . . . quidem; **get even with s.o.** áliquem ulcísc•or -ī ultus sum

evening vesp•er -erī *m,* vésper•a -ae *f;* **all evening** tōtā vésperā; **early in the evening** prīmō vésperī; **in the evening** vésperī, véspere; **last evening** herī vésperī; **on Saturday evening** diē Sātúrnī vésperī; **this evening** hódiē vésperī; **toward evening** sub vésperum; **very late in the evening** pervésperī; **yesterday evening** herī vésperī

evening wear cēnātóri•a -ốrum *npl*

ever umquam

every omn•is -is -e; **every day** cōtídiē; **every month** quot ménsibus; **every night** per síngulās noctēs; **every now and then** intérdum; **every year** quotánnīs

evidence testimốni•um -ī *n;* **give evidence against s.o.** testimốnium dícere in áliquem; **on what evidence will you convict me?** quō mē teste convíncēs?; **this evidence is not admissible** hoc testimốnium nōn sūméndum est; **turn state's evidence** indícium profít•eor -ếrī proféssus sum

evidently maniféstē

exact accūrắt•us -a -um, exáct•us -a -um

exaggerate: don't exaggerate everything! nōlī *(pl:* nōlíte) omnia in māius extóllere!

exam exắm•en -inis *n,* probắti•ō -ốnis *f;* **flunk an exam** cad•ō -ere cécidī cāsúrus in exámine; **pass an exam** exámen sustín•eō -ếre -uī; **take an exam** exámen ób•eō -íre -iī; **tough exam** exámen rigōrốsum

examine exāminắre

example exémpl•um -ī *n;* **set a good example** bonum exémplum praéb•eō -ếre -uī

excavator máchin•a -ae *f* fōssốria

except praeter (+ *acc*); **except that** nisi quod (+ *indic*)

excessive (in) immódic•us -a -um (+ *gen or abl*)

exchange permūtắre; **exchange greetings** cōnsalūtắre; **exchange prisoners** captívōs inter sē permūtắre

excite excitắre

excited commốt•us -a -um, excitắt•us -a -um

excitement ánimī commốti•ō -ốnis *f;* **feel excitement** éxcit•or -ắrī excitắtus sum

exclamation exclāmắti•ō -ốnis *f*

exclamation point sign•um -ī *n* exclāmātiốnis

excuse *(pardon)* ignốsc•ō -ere ignốvī (+ *dat*); **excuse me** ignốsce mihi; **please excuse me** óbsecrō, mihi ignốscās; **excuse oneself** sē excūsắre

exempt: be exempt from military service mīlítiae vacātiốnem habếre

exemption from military service mīlítiae vacắti•ō -ốnis *f*

exercise *s (written)* exercíti•um -ī *n;* *(practice)* exercitắti•ō -ốnis *f*

exercise *intr* sē exérc•eō -ếre -uī

exhale exspīrắre

exhaust ēmissắri•um -ī *n*

expect exspectắre; **what do you expect?** quid vīs fíerī?

expense impếns•a -ae *f,* sūmpt•us -ūs *m;* **at my expense** meō sūmptū; **at your own expense** prīvắtō sūmptū

expensive cār•us -a -um, pretiốs•us -a -um

experience experiénti·a -ae *f,* ūs·us -ūs *m*

experienced (in) perít·us -a -um (+ *gen*)

expert in gnār·us -a -um (+ *gen*)

expert *s* expért·us -ī *m* (·a -ae *f*)

explain explānáre, explicáre

explanation explānáti·ō -ónis *f,* explicáti·ō -ónis *f*

express éxprim·ō -ere expréssī expréssus

expression vult·us -ūs *m;* **change one's expression** vultum flect·ō -ere flexī flexus

expressive *(eyes)* argút·us -a -um

express train trām·en -inis *n* rapidíssimum

extend *intr (of land, body of water)* tend·ō -ere, prōténd·ō -ere, pát·eō -ére; **the region extends from ... to ...** regiō tendit *(or* patet) ab (+ *abl*) ad (+ *acc*); **extend over** *(to cover)* obtín·eō -ére

extortion violénta exácti·ō -ónis *f* pecūniárum

extracurricular extraōrdināri·us -a -um

eye ócul·us -ī *m;* **keep an eye on that guy** adsérvā *(pl:* adserváte) istum; **keep your eyes open** cavē circumspíciās; **look me in the eye** aspícedum contrā mē; **with eyes wide open** hiántibus óculīs

eyeball orb·is -is *m* óculī

eyebrow supercíli·um -ī *n*

eye doctor médic·us -ī *m* oculárius, médic·a -ae *f* oculária

eyeglasses perspicíll·a -órum *npl,* vitr·a -órum *npl* oculária; **wear eyeglasses** perspicíllīs ūt·or -ī ūsus sum

eyelash pálpebrae pil·us -ī *m;* **eyelashes** palpebrárum pil·ī -órum *mpl*

eyelid pálpebr·a -ae *f*

eyewitness oculátus (-a) test·is -is *mf*

fabric *(pattern of weaving)* text·us -ūs *m* (**coarse** crassus; **sheer, thin** ténuis; **thick** pinguis)

face *s* fáci·ēs -éī *f;* **be face to face with you** praesēns praeséntī tibi esse; **make a face** ōs dúcere; **on the face of it** prīmā fáciē; **we can discuss that face to face** cōram id ágere póssumus

face *tr* spectáre; *(to withstand, e.g., danger)* óbviam īre (+ *dat*); **face north (south, east, west)** spectáre in *(or* ad) septentriónēs (merídiem, oriéntem, occidéntem)

fact: as a matter of fact enimvérō; **in fact** proféctō, vērō, quidem; **the fact that ...** quod (+ *indic*); **the facts speak for themselves** rēs ipsa índicat *or* rēs prō sē lóquitur

faction fácti·ō -ónis *f*

factory fábric·a -ae *f*

faculty ōrd·ō -inis *m* professórum

fail *tr* **fail an exam (test, quizz)** in exámine (probātióne, probātiúnculā) cad·ō -ere cecidī; **words fail me** quid dīcam nōn invéniō

fair aequ·us -a -um; *(complexion)* candid·us -a -um; *(weather)* serén·us -a -um, sūd·us -a -um; **fair and square** sine fūcō ac falláciīs; **I think that's fair** id aequī fáciō; **that's not fair of you** nōn aequum facis

fairly *(in a fair way)* aequē; *(somewhat)* aliquántulum; *(moderately)* mediócriter

fairground(s) prāt·um -ī *n* fēstívum

fair-minded aequ·us -a -um

fairness áequit·ās -átis *f*

fairy dīv·a -ae *f*

faith fid·ēs -eī *f;* **in bad faith** dē fidē malā; **in good faith** (ex) bonā fidē

faithful fidél·is -is -e

fake simulā́re

faker simulā́·tor -tóris *m* (·trīx -trī́cis *f*)

falcon falc·ō -ṓnis *m (see* **bird**)

fall *s* autúmn·us -ī *m*

fall *adj* autumnā́l·is -is -e

fall *intr* cadō cádere cécidī cāsū́rus; **fall asleep** obdormísc·ō -ere; **fall (desperately) in love with** (pérditē) amā́re coep·ī -isse; **fall flat** *(of a speech, etc.)* frī́geō frīgére; **fall for** *(a trick)* fall·or -ī (+ *abl*); **fall in love at first sight** ūnō aspéctū in amṓrem íncid·ō -ere -ī; **fall sick** in morbum incídere

false fals·us -a -um

falsely falsō

family famíli·a -ae *f;* **come from a good family** honéstō locō nāt·us -a esse

family name gentī́le nōm·en -inis *n*

family tree stirp·s -is *f*

famous praeclā́r·us -a -um; **famous for** ínclutus *(+ abl)*, nṓbilis *(+ abl)*

fan *s* flabéll·um -ī *n; (admirer)* faut·or -ṓris *m,* fautr·īx -ī́cis *f;* **electric fan** māchínul·a -ae *f* ventígena

fan *tr* ventilā́re

fantastic mīrífic·us -a -um

far *(by far)* longē; **as far as I'm concerned** per mē; **by far** longē, multō; **far be it from me to say** équidem dī́cere nōlim; **far from** procul ab (+ *abl*); **how far?** quoad, quoúsque?; **(not) far from here** (haud) procul hinc; **far from it!** mínimē!; **farthest to the south** longíssimē in merídiem; **so far so good** bellē adhūc; **so far, thus far** háctenus

faraway *(distant)* longínqu·us -a -um

far-fetched idea conquisī́tum cōnsíli·um -ī *n*

fare vectū́r·a -ae *f*

farewell valē (*pl:* valḗte)

farm fund·us -ī *m,* rūs, rūris *n;* **on the farm** rūrī

farm animals pec·us -oris *n or* pécor·a -um *npl*

farmer agrícol·a -ae *m*

farm house vīll·a -ae *f* rū́stica

farsighted prṓvid·us -a -um

fashion cultūs mod·us -ī *m;* **be in fashion** more fíerī; **come into fashion** in morem vén·iō -íre vénī; **go out of fashion** obsolḗsc·ō -ere obsolḗvī obsolḗtum

fast cel·er -eris -ere; **be fast asleep** artē dórm·iō -íre -ívī

fat obḗs·us -a -um *(opp:* grácil·is -is -e)

fathead *(slang)* fátu·us -ī *m* (·a -ae *f)*

father pa·ter -tris *m;* **father of the family** paterfamíliās (*gen:* patrisfamíliās) *m*

father-in-law soc·er -erī *m*

fatigue fatigā́ti·ō -ṓnis *f*

fatigued fess·us -a -um

faucet epitóni·um -ī *n;* **turn on (off) the faucet** epitónium versā́re (reversā́re)

fault culp·a -ae *f;* **be at fault** in culpā esse; **not be at fault** extrā culpam esse

faultless ēmendā́t·us -a -um

favor benefíci·um -ī *n,* grā́ti·a -ae *f,* grāt·um -ī *n;* **accept and return a favor** benefícium accípere et réddere; **ask s.o. for a favor** grā́tiam ab áliquō pet·ō -ere petī́vī; **do s.o. a favor** grātum álicui fácere; **do s.o. a big favor** gratíssimum álicui fácere;

return s.o. a favor grátiam álicui
réferō reférre rétulī; **please do me
this favor!** amábō tē, fac (*or for a
previous favor:* refer) hanc grátiam
mihi

favorable (*auspices, circumstances,
gods, wind*) secúnd•us -a -um

fax tēlecópi•a -ae *f*

fax machine tēlecōpiátr•um -ī *n*

fear *s* met•us -ūs *m;* **he put the fear of
God into them** cūrávit ut illīs
Iúppiter īrátus esset

fear *tr* métu•ō -ere -ī

fearful (*terrible*) dīr•us -a -um; **fearful
of** tímid•us -a -um (+ *gen*)

fearless impávid•us -a -um

feather penn•a -ae *f;* (*soft, downy*)
plūm•a -ae *f*

February mēns•is -is *m* Februárius; **in
February** mēnse Februáriō

feeble imbēcíll•us -a -um

feebleness imbēcíllit•ās -átis *f*

feed pāsc•ō -ere pāvī pāstus

feel *tr* (*with the hands*) tentáre; (*hunger,
pain, cold, etc.*) sent•iō -íre sēnsī
sēnsus; **feel one's way** viam tentáre;
(*fig*) cautē et cogitátē rem tractáre;
feel pain dolóre afficior áfficī
affectus sum ‖ *intr* **because I felt
like it** quia mihi líbitum est; **I wasn't
feeling well** ego mē nōn bellē
habébam; **feel annoyed** grav•or -árī
-átus sum; **feel bad (good)**
(*physically*) sē male (bene) habére;
feel better (*physically*) mélius sē
habére; mélius vál•eō -ére -uī; **feel
down and out** īnfráctum ánimum
ger•ō -ere gessī; **feel fine** sē bene
habére; **feel glad** laet•or -árī laetátus
sum; **feel happy** gaúd•eō -ére gāvísus
sum; **feel really bad about** valdē

dól•eō -ére -uī dē (+ *abl*); **feel sad**
maest•us -a -um esse

feelers: put out feelers to tentáre

feeling sēns•us -ūs *m,* afféct•us -ūs *m;*
(*feelings esp. with reference to
anger*) ánim•us -ī *m;* **hurt s.o.'s
feelings** áliquem offénd•ō -ere -ī

fellow citizen cīv•is -is *mf* su•us (-a)

fellow passenger convéct•or -óris *m,*
convéctr•īx -ícis *f*

fellow soldier conmílit•ō -ónis *m*

fellow student condiscípul•us -ī *m* (•a
-ae *f*)

fellow worker sóci•us -ī *m* (•a -ae *f*)
óperis

felon scelést•us -ī *m* (•a -ae *f*)

felony scel•us -eris *n*

feminine fēminín•us -a -um

fence saepíment•um -ī *n*

fender luticípul•um -ī *n*

ferry nāv•is -is *f* trāiectória (*or* vectória)

fetch petō pétere petívī (*or* pétiī) petítus

fever febr•is -is *f;* **constant fever**
contínua febris; **high fever** magna *or*
ārdēns febris; **run a fever** febricitáre;
slight fever febrécul•a -ae *f*

few: a few pauc•ī -ae -a

fiction fābulósa narráti•ō -ónis *f*

fiddle fidícul•a -ae *f;* **play the fiddle**
fidículā can•ō -ere cécinī

fiddlesticks! nūgae!

fidelity fidélit•ās -átis *f*

field ag•er -rī *m;* (*untilled*) camp•us -ī *m;*
(*of study*) disciplín•a -ae *f*

fierce fer•ōx -ócis

figurative trānslát•us -a -um

figuratively per trānslātiónem, trānslátīs
verbīs

figure: female figure mulíebris form·a -ae *f;* **figure of speech** figúr·a -ae *f* ōrātiónis

figure on *(rely on)* nīt·or -ī nīxus sum *or* nīsus sum (+ *abl*)

figure out excōgitáre

figure skating patináti·ō -ónis *f* artificiósa

file *(tool)* līm·a -ae *f; (for receiving papers)* scap·us -ī *m; (comput)* documént·um -ī *n;* **files** documént·a -órum *npl,* āct·a -órum *npl*

fill ímpl·eō -ére -évī -étus; **fill it up, please!** quaesō, immissárium benzínárium replē tótum!

film taeníol·a -ae *f,* pellícul·a -ae *f;* **documentary film** taeníol·a -ae *f* documentária; **movie film** taeníola cīnēmatográphica; **photographic film** pellícula phōtográphica; **show a film** taeníolam (cīnēmatográphicam) exhíb·eō -ére -uī -itus

filter filtr·um -ī *n*

fin pinn·a -ae *f*

final últim·us -a -um, extrém·us -a -um

finally tandem; *(at last)* ad extrémum

find repér·iō -íre répperī repértus

fine *adj (outstanding)* prae·stāns -stántis; *(weather)* serén·us -a -um; **everything's fine** rēctē est; **fine!** probē!; **fine arts** art·ēs -ium *fpl* ēlegantiórēs; **fine weather** serénit·ās -átis *f;* **that's fine** bene hoc habet; **you did fine** fēcístī probē

fine *tr* **fine s.o.** multáre áliquem (+ *abl* of the fine)

finger *s* dígit·us -ī *m;* **index finger** ind·ex -icis dígitus *m;* **little finger** dígitus mínimus; **middle finger** dígitus médius; *(as an obscene gesture)* dígitus inpudícus; **not lift a finger** pressīs mánibus séd·eō -ére

sēdī; **point the finger at s.o.** dígitum ad áliquem inténd·ō -ere -ī; **ring finger** dígitus ānuláris; **snap the fingers** dígitīs cóncrep·ō -áre -uī

finger *tr (to handle)* attrectáre; *(to inform on)* déferō dēférre détulī

fingernail ungu·is -is *m*

finger tip dígitus -ī *m* primóris

finish cōnfíc·iō -ere cōnfécī cōnféctus; **finish off** *(to destroy)* per·dō -dere -didī; *(to kill)* occíd·ō -ere -ī occísus; **finish writing** *(a book, etc.)* absólv·ō -ere -ī absolútus; **put the finishing touch to** últimam manum áfferō afférre áttulī (+ *dat*)

finish line *(sports)* calx, calcis *f,* crēt·a -ae *f*

fire *s* incéndi·um -ī *n;* **be on fire** árd·eō -ére -uī; **catch fire** ignem concíp·iō -ere concépī; **put out a fire** incéndium exstíngu·ō -ere exstínxī exstínctus; **set on fire** incénd·ō -ere -ī incénsus

fire *tr (to dismiss)* āmóv·eō -ére āmóvī āmótus

fire alarm sign·um -ī *n* monitórium incéndiī

fire chief praeféct·us -ī *m* vígilum

fire engine síph·ō -ónis *m*

firefighter vig·il -ilis *m;* síphōnári·us -ī *m* (·a -ae *f*)

fireplace foc·us -ī *m*

fire station státi·ō -ónis *f* vígilum

fireworks spectácul·um -ī *n* pyrotéchnicum

firm *adj* firm·us -a -um

firm *s* sóciet·ās -átis *f*

first *(in a series, followed by* deínde, postrémō) primum; **at first** (ā) primō, inítiō; **first of all** primum ómnium, in primīs; **for the first time** primum; **he**

was the first to enter prīmus introī́vit

first-class *(masterly)* gráphic•us -a -um; **first-class seat** sēd•ēs -is *f* prīmae classis

fish *s* pisc•is -is *m; (as food)* piscát•us -ūs *m;* **catch fish** piscēs captā́re; **teeming with fish** piscṓs•us -a -um

fish *intr* pisc•or -ā́rī -ā́tus sum; **go fishing** piscā́tum eō īre īvī *or* iī

fisherman piscát•or -ṓris *m*

fish food ēsc•a -ae *f* piscā́ria

fish hook hām•us -ī *m*

fishing bait ēsc•a -ae *f*

fishing line lī́ne•a -ae *f* (piscātṓria)

fishing net rēt•e -is *n* (piscātṓrium)

fishing pole harúnd•ō -inis *f*

fishing rod cálam•us -ī *m* (piscātṓrius)

fishing tackle īnstrūmént•um -ī *n* piscātṓrium

fish market for•um -ī *n* piscā́rium

fish pond piscī́n•a -ae *f*

fishy *(smell)* pisculént•us -a -um; *(fig)* suspiciṓs•us -a -um

fix *s* **be in a fix** in angústiīs vers•or -ā́rī -ā́tus sum

fix *tr (to repair)* refíc•iō -ere refḗcī reféctus; *(time, place, limits)* státu•ō -ere -uī statū́tus

flabbergast conturbā́re

flabbergasted: we were absolutely flabbergasted nōs omnīnō conturbābā́mur

flag *s* vexíll•um -ī *n*

flag *tr* signō indicā́re

flame *(of fire; sweetheart)* flámm•a -ae *f*

flap the wings ālīs plaud•ō -ere plausī plausus

flash of lightning fulg•ur -uris *n*

flashlight īnstrūmént•um -ī *n* micāns

flashy speciṓs•us -a -um

flat *(level)* plān•us -a -um; *(dull, stale, e.g., joke)* frī́gid•us -a -um; **fall flat** *(of a speech)* frīgḗre

flatter blánd•ior -ī́rī -ī́tus sum (+ *dat*)

flattering blánd•us -a -um

flattery blandíti•a -ae *f* ·

flatware īnstrūmént•a -ṓrum *npl* escā́ria

flea pūl•ex -icis *m*

flea market for•um -ī *n* rērum vēnā́lium

flesh car•ō -nis *f*

flight volā́t•us -ūs *m*

flirt *s* dēsúlt•or -ṓris *m*, vaga puéll•a -ae *f*

flirt with subblánd•ior -ī́rī (+ *dat*)

flock *(of birds, sheep, goats)* grex, gregis *m*

floor *(paved)* pavīmént•um -ī *n*, sol•um -ī *n; (story)* tabulā́t•um -ī *n*, contignā́ti•ō -ṓnis *f;* **ground floor** pedeplā́n•a -ṓrum *npl;* **marble floor** pavīméntum *(or* solum) marmóreum; **mosaic floor** pavīméntum *(or* solum) tesselā́tum; **wooden floor** tabulā́t•um -ī *n*

floppy disk *(comput)* dískul•us -ī *m* flexíbilis

flounder *s (fish)* pass•er -eris *m*

flounder *intr* vólut•or -ā́rī -ā́tus sum; *(in speech)* haesitā́re

flour farī́n•a -ae *f*

flow flu•ō -ere flūxī flūxus; **flow by** ádlu•ō, adlúere; **flow down from** dēflúere dē (+ *abl);* **flow into** īnflúere in (+ *acc);* **flow out from** efflúere ab (+ *abl);* **flow past** praeterflúere (+ *acc)*

flower *(lit & fig)* flō•s -ris *m*

flower shop tabérn·a -ae *f* flōrǽlis

fluent prṓflu·ēns -éntis

flunk: flunk a test cad·ō -ere cécidī cāsū́rus in probātiṓne

fluorescent light túbul·us -ī *m* lūcífluus

flute tībi·a -ae *f*

fly *s* musc·a -ae *f;* **a fly buzzes** musca bómbilat

fly *tr* **fly a plane** āëróplanum gubernáre **‖** *intr* voláre; *(of a passenger)* āëróplanō vehor, vehī, vectus sum; **fly away** āvoláre; **fly off the handle** cito férv·eō -ére férbuī

fog nébul·a -ae *f*

foggy nebulṓs·us -a -um

fold plicáre; **fold up** complicáre

folder integūmént·um -ī *n* astrictṓrium; *(comput)* coöpércul·um -ī *n*

fond: fond of cúpid·us -a -um (+ *gen);* **be fond of** dī́lig·ō -ere dīléxī dīléctus, amáre

font typ·us -ī *m*

fondness am·or -ṓris *m*

food cib·us -ī *m*

food processor máchin·a -ae *f* conquīnária

fool stult·us -ī *m,* stult·a -ae *f;* **make a fool of** lūdificáre; **make a fool of oneself** inépt·iō -íre

foolhardy temerári·us -a -um

foolish dēsípi·ēns -éntis

foolishly: act foolishly inépt·iō -íre

foolishness dēsipiénti·a -ae *f*

foot pēs, pedis *m;* **foot of a mountain** rād·īx -ícis *m* montis; **at the foot of the mountain** rādíce montis

football *(ball)* pedifóll·is -is *m; (game)* pedifólli·um -ī *n,* pedilū́di·um -ī *n;* **kick the (foot)ball** pedifóllem

pulsáre; **pass the (foot)ball to** pedifóllem trānsmíttere ad (+ *acc);* **play football** pedifólle lū́dere; **play in the first (second) half** in parte priṓre (álterā) certáminis lūdere *(see Chapter V)*

football player pedilū́s·or -ṓris *m*

foothills rādíc·ēs -um *mpl* montis

footnote adnotáti·ō -ṓnis *f* īmae páginae

for *(during a certain period, expressed by acc),* e.g., **for ten days** decem diēs; *(to denote the appointment of definite time)* in (+ *acc),* e.g., **he invited her to dinner for the following day** eam ad cēnam vocávit in pósterum diem; *(because of)* ob (+ *acc); (on behalf of)* prō (+ *abl); (since)* nam; **as for** quod áttinet ad (+ *acc);* **for all that** nec eō sétius *or* níhilō sétius; **for nothing** grātīs, grātuī́tō; *(in vain)* frustrā; **for that matter** ádeō; **for the last three months** in ternōs novíssimōs mēnsēs; **for the rest of the year** in réliquum annī tempus; **for these reasons** hīs dē causīs; **to be for** *(to be in favor of)* fáv·eō -ére fāvī (+ *dat)*

force *s* vīs *f;* **by force** vī; **large force** magnae cṓpiae *fpl;* **small force** exíguae cṓpiae; **be in force** *(of laws)* vál·eō -ére -uī; **use force** vim adhíb·eō -ére -uī -itus

force *tr* cōg·ō -ere coḗgī coáctus

forearm uln·a -ae *f*

forecast praenūntiáti·ō -ṓnis *f* (tempestátis)

forefathers átav·ī -ṓrum *mpl*

forehand *(in tennis)* īct·us -ūs *m* dīréctus

forehead frōns, frontis *f*

foreign *(of another country)* extérn·us -a -um; *(coming from abroad)* peregrī́n·us -a -um

foreigner peregrín•us -ī *m* (•a -ae *f*)

forelady prōcūrátr•īx -ícis *f*

foreman prōcūrát•or -óris *m*

forest silv•a -ae *f*

forget (about) oblīvíscor -ī oblítus sum (+ *gen);* **forget about it!** éiece id ex ánimō!

fork furcíll•a -ae *f,* fuscínul•a -ae *f*

form *s* form•a -ae *f; (of a word)* figúr•a -ae *f;* **the form is either simple, like "doctus," or compound, like "indoctus"** figúra est aut simplex, ut "doctus," aut compósita, ut "indóctus"

form *tr* fác•iō -ere fēcī factus; *(a plan, partnership, alliance)* ín•eō -íre -iī *or* -ívī -itus; **form an opinion** iūdícium fácere; **form the imperative of the verb "venire"** fac imperātívum "veníre" verbī

format *s (comput)* form•a -ae *f*

format *tr* (discum) cōnformáre

formerly ánteā

fort castéll•um -ī *n*

fortunate fortūnát•us -a -um

fortune: tell fortunes haríol•or -árī -átus sum

fortuneteller haríol•us -ī *m,* haríol•a -ae *f*

forum for•um -ī *n*

forward *(sports)* oppugná•tor -tóris *m* (•trīx -trícis *f*)

forward *(mail, e-mail)* déferō dēférre détulī dēlátus

foul: commit a foul *(sports)* poenáliter ag•ō -ere ēgī

fountain pen gráphi•um -ī *n* replébile

fox vulp•ēs -is *f;* **foxes yelp** vulpēs gánniunt

frame of mind ánim•us -ī *m;* **be in a good frame of mind** bonō ánimō esse

frank apért•us -a -um, cándid•us -a -um

frankly apértē, cándidē

fraud frau•s -dis *f*

fraternity sodálit•ās -átis *f* alumnórum

free líb•er -era -erum; **free time** temp•us -oris *n* líberum; **if you are free** sī vacábis

free-style swimming natáti•ō -ónis *f* líbera

freeze *tr* geláre ‖ *intr* gelárī

freezer caps•a -ae *f* frīgorífica

freezing gélid•us -a -um

freezing, freezing mark pūnct•um -ī *n* glaciále; **three degrees above freezing** trēs gradūs suprā pūnctum glaciále

freight train trām•en -inis *n* onerárium

French Gallofránc•us -a -um

French fries pōm•a -órum *npl* (terréstria) frīcta

fresh rec•ēns -éntis

freshman tīr•ō -ónis *mf*

Friday di•ēs -éī *m* Véneris

friend amíc•us -ī *m,* amíc•a -ae *f;* **she's my best friend** amíca summa mea est

friendly amíc•us -a -um; **in a friendly way** amícē

friendship amīcíti•a -ae *f*

frighten térr•eō -ére -uī -itus

fringe fímbri•a -ae *f*

frivolous frívol•us -a -um

frog rān•a -ae *f;* **frogs croak** rānae coáxant

from *prep* ab *or* dē *or* ex (+ *abl*); **from a to z** ab áciā et acū; **from here** hinc; **from there** illinc; **from where** unde

front *adj* prī•or -or -us; *(teeth, feet)* prīm•us -a -um

front *s* frōn•s -tis *f*; **in front** ā fronte; **in front of** *(position)* ante (+ *acc*), prō (+ *abl*); *(in the presence of)* coram (+ *abl*); **front of the classroom** prior par•s -tis *f* conclávis scholáris; **front of the house** frōns aédium

front door antíc•um -ī *n*

front hall vēstíbul•um -ī *n*

frontier fīn•is -is *m*, términ•us -ī *m*

front seat sēd•ēs -is *f* antérior

frost pruín•a -ae *f*

frosty pruīnṓs•us -a -um

frozen rig•ēns -éntis

fruit pōm•a -ṓrum *npl*

fuit juice sūc•us -ī *m* pōmárius

frustrate frūstr•or -árī -átus sum

frustration frūstráti•ō -ṓnis *f*

fry frīg•ō -ere frīxī frīctus

frying pan sartág•ō -inis *f*

fuel mātéri•a -ae *f* prṓpulsória

full (of) plēn•us -a -um (+ *abl or gen*); **full moon** plēnilū́ni•um -ī *n*, plēna lū́n•a -ae *f*

full-grown adúlt•us -a -um

full-length *(dress)* tālár•is -is -e

fully *adv* fúnditus

fun ioc•us -ī *m*; **he always makes fun of me** *(or* **pokes fun at me)** iste mē semper ēlū́dit *(or* inrídet); **she said it for fun** id per iocum dīxit; **it's no fun if you …** nōn iūcúndum est sī tū … ; **it was pure fun** hilária mera erat; **have fun** sē oblectáre

function *s (gram)* poténti•a -ae *f*

funeral fūn•us -eris *n*; **attend** *(or* **go to) a funeral** in fūnus veníre

funnel īnfundíbul•um -ī *n*

funny iocṓs•us -a -um, rīdícul•us -a -um; *(humorous)* fēstív•us -a -um

fur coat amícul•um -ī *n* pellícium

fur jacket iacc•a -ae *f* pellícia

furlough comméāt•us -ūs *m*; **be on furlough** in comméātū esse; **end of the furlough** comméātūs di•ēs -éī *m*; **get a furlough** comméātum impetráre

furnish a home (an apartment) domum (diaétam) supelléctile ínstru•ō -ere īnstrúxī īnstrúctus

furniture supéll•ex -éctilis *f*; **piece of furniture** supelléctilis par•s -tis *f*

future futū́r•a -ṓrum *npl*, temp•us -oris *n* futū́rum; **for the future** in pósterum; **in the future** posthāc

gale procéll•a -ae *f*

gallon gall•on -ṓnis *m*

gallop curs•us -ūs *m* citátus

gallop *intr* quadrupedáre

gamble *tr* **gamble away** in áleā per•dō -dere -didī -ditus ‖ *intr* áleā lū́dere

gambler lū́s•or -ṓris *m*, aleá•tor -tṓris *m*, aleátr•īx -ícis *f*

game *(play)* lūd•us -ī *m*, lūs•us -ūs *m*; *(prey)* praed•a -ae *f*, vēnáti•ō -ṓnis *f*

game show spectácul•um -ī *n* lūsṓrium

gang man•us -ūs *f*, grex, gregis *m*

gangster, gang member praed•ō -ṓnis *m* gregális

garage autocīnḗtī (autocīnētṓrum) receptácul•um -ī *n*; *(repair garage)* officín•a -ae *f* reparātṓria

garden hort•us -ī *m* rū́sticus; **vegetable garden** hortus (h)olitṓrius

garden hose túbul•us -ī *m* hórticus

gardner hortulắn•us -ī *m* (•a -ae *f)*

garlic ắli•um -ī *n,* ắlli•um -ī *n*

garrison praesídi•um -ī *n*

garter períscelis, periscélidis *f*

gas benzín•um -ī *n,* gási•um -ī *n;* **step on the gas** pedále benzīnárium déprim•ō -ere dēpréssī; **step on the gas!** *(fig)* matūrā *(pl:* matūráte)

gas pedal pedắl•e -is *n* benzīnárium

gas pump ántli•a -ae *f* benzīnária

gas station státi•ō -ốnis *f* benzīnária

gas stove fócul•us -ī *m* gáseus

gas tank immissári•um -ī *n* benzīnárium

gate port•a -ae *f; (at airport)* ắdit•us -ūs *m*

gather *tr* cog•ō -ere coḗgī coáctus ‖ *intr* cóngreg•or -ắrī -átus sum, conveníre

gearshift iúncti•ō -ốnis *f* vēlōcitátum

gee! hercle! *or* édepol!

geez! eu édepol! *or* eu hércle!

gender *s* gen•us -eris *n*

general dux, ducis *m,* imperất•or -ốris *m*

general: in general ferē, vulgō

generally plērúmque

general store pantopốli•um -ī *n*

generosity līberálit•ās -átis *f*

generous benéfic•us -a -um, līberál•is -is -e

genitals genitắl•ia -ium *npl; (female)* muliébr•ia -ium *npl*

genitive *s* genitív•us -ī *m,* cās•us -ūs *m* genitívus

gentle clēm•ēns -éntis, mīt•is -is -e

geography geōgráphi•a -ae *f*

German *s* Germắn•us -ī *m,* Germắn•a -ae *f*

German *adj* Germắnic•us -a -um; *(ling.)* Theodísc•us -a -um

Germany Germắni•a -ae *f*

gerund *s* gerúndi•um -ī *n*

gerundive *s* gerundív•um -ī *n*

get *tr (to acquire)* nancísc•or -ī nanctus sum; *(to receive)* accipere; *(by asking)* impetrắre; *(by purchase)* parắre, comparắre; *(understand)* tén•eō -ḗre -uī; **get back** répet•ō -ere -ívī -ítus; recíp•iō -ere recḗpī recéptus; **get out** *(bring forth)* prōm•ō -ere -psī -ptus; **get (the business) over and done with** (negótium) absólv•ō -ere -ī absolútus; **I can't get him to talk** nōn queō ōrắre ut loquắtur; **now get this** nunc cognôsce rem ‖ *intr* **get along with** concórditer cóngru•ō -ere -uī cum (+ *abl*); **get along well with each other** *(or* **one another)** concórditer inter sē congrúere; **I get along well with them** bene mihi cónvenit cum illīs; **get away** *(escape)* effúg•iō -ere effúgī effūgitắrus; **get anywhere** *(accomplish s.th.)* ắliquid cônsequ•or -ī cōnsecútus sum; **get carried away by** *or* with éfferor efférrī ēlắtus sum (+ *abl*); **get even with s.o. for** ulcísc•or -ī ultus sum ắliquem quod (+ *indic*); **get off** *(a bus, plane, ship, train)* ēgrédior ēgredī ēgréssus sum dē (+ *abl*); **get on** *(a bus, plane, ship, train)* īnscénd•ō -ere -ī in (+ *acc*); **get out of my way!** dē viā meā dēcéde *(pl:* dēcédite)!; **get over** *(grief, anger, etc.)* superắre; **get rid of: I want to get rid of that pest** istum moléstum āmolírī volō; **get somewhere** ắliquid cônsequ•or -ī cōnsecútus sum; **get to** *(a place)* pervén•iō -íre pervénī pervéntum ad *or* in (+ *acc*); **get up** *(rise)* surg•ō -ere surréxī; *(said of several)* cōnsúrgere

Gibraltar Calp·ē -ēs *f;* **strait of Gibraltar** Gādītānum frēt·um -ī *n*

gift dōn·um -ī *n,* mūn·us -eris *n,* mūnúscul·um -ī *n;* **natural gift** dōs, dōtis *m* (nātúrae)

gifted ingeniós·us -a -um

gills bránchi·ae -árum *fpl*

gin vīn·um -ī *n* iūníperum

gingerbread līb·um -ī *n* mellítum

giraffe camēlopárdal·is -is *f*

girdle stropp·ī -órum *mpl*

girlfriend amícul·a -ae *f*

gist: the gist of what he said was this: ... hanc in senténtiam dīxit: ...

give *tr* dō dare dedī datus; *(as a gift)* dōnáre; **give it here!** cedo *(pl:* cette)! [*an old imperative; can take a direct object*]; **give it to 'em!** ádhibē! *(pl:* adhíbite!);* **give the plural form of gaudium** dā *(or* dīc) figúram plūrálem "gaúdium" nóminis

glad laet·us -a -um; **be glad** laet·or -árī -átus sum

gladly libénter

glass *(for drinking)* pócul·um -ī *n* vítreum; hýal·us -ī *m;* **glasses** *(eyeglasses)* perspicíll·a -órum *npl;* **wear glasses** perspicíllīs ūt·or -ī úsus sum; **wine glass** hýalus vīnárius

glider anemóplan·um -ī *n,* vélvol·um -ī *n*

glisten nít·eō -ére -uī

gloat over exsultáre (+ *abl*)

globe glob·us -ī *m* terrárum

gloom maestíti·a -ae *f*

gloomy maést·us -a -um

glove digitábul·um -ī *n*

glue glūt·en -inis *n*

glue glūtináre; **glue together** conglūtináre

glued: I'm glued to my books in librīs haér·eō -ére haesī

glum maest·us -a -um, trist·is -is -e; **why so glum?** quid tū es tam tristis?

glutton héllu·ō -ónis *m;* **be a glutton** héllu·or -árī

gluttonous ed·āx -ácis

gluttony edácit·ās -átis *f*

gnat cul·ex -icis *m*

go eō īre ívī *or* iī itum, sē ágere; **go and see whether he has come home or not** abī, vīse redierítne an nōndum domum; **go around** *(of a rumor)* pervagárī; **go by** *(to pass)* praetér·eō -íre -ívī; *(the rules)* serváre; **go down** *(fever)* conquiéscit -ere conquiévit; *(swelling)* sē summíttit -ere summísit; *(prices)* laxárī; *(sun)* occídere; *(ship)* merg·or -ī mersus sum; **go for** *(fetch a person)* addúc·ō -ere addúxī addúctus; *(fetch a thing)* ádferō adférre áttulī; **at what price do these items go for?** quibus prétiīs hae mercēs véneunt?; **I don't go for** *(don't like)* nīl mor·or -árī -átus sum (+ *acc);* **I don't go in for sports** lūdīs [*dat*] nōn stúd·eō -ére -uī; **go into a matter** rem íneō ínfre ínii *or* inívī; **go on** prōcéd·ō -ere prōcéssī; **go on!** perge *(pl:*pérgite) porrō!; **go to bed** dormítum *(or* cúbitum) [*supine*] eō íre iī *or* ívī itum; **go to see** vīs·ō -ere -ī; **go to the aid of** succúrr·ō -ere -ī (+ *dat);* **go on: what's going on?** quid negótī est? *or* quid ágitur?; **what's going on here?** quid reī hīc est?; **go well: things are going fairly well** ágitur satis; **please, let me go!** mitte mē sīs!

goal port·a -ae *f;* **score a goal** *(in soccer)* follem in portam pede pulsáre

goal keeper portári·us -ī *m,* portári·a -ae *f*

goal line calx, calcis *f,* crēt·a -ae *f*

goal post pāl·us -ī *m* portae

goat cap·er -rī *m,* capr·a -ae *f;* **goats bleat** caprī bālant

God bless you! tibi dī bene fáciant; *(to s.o. sneezing)* salvē! *or* salū́tem!

going: good going! bene factum!

gold, golden aúre·us -a -um

goldfish híppur·us -ī *m*

goldmine aurīfodī́n·a -ae *f*

golf pilamálle·us -ī *m;* **play golf** pilamálleō lū́dere *(see Chapter V)*

golf club clāv·a -ae *f; (driver)* clāva agitātṓria; *(iron)* clāva férrea

golf course pilamálleī camp·us -ī *m*

golfer pilamálleī lūs·or -ṓris *m,* lūstr·īx -ícis *f*

golf green áre·a -ae *f* víridis

golf hole scrobícul·us -ī *m*

golf tee grū́mul·us -ī *m*

goner: geez, I'm a goner périī hercle; hercle, nullus (-a) sum

good *adj (also morally)* bon·us -a -um; *(esp. moral)* prob·us -a -um; *(advice)* rēct·us -a -um; *(weather)* serḗn·us -a -um; **be good for** prōsum prōdésse prófuī prōfutū́rus (+ *dat);* **good for you!** *(said in praise)* macte virtū́te estō!; **good, good!** euge, euge!; **good job!** bene *(or* rēctē*)* factum!; **good Lord!** O dī bonī!; **good luck to you!** tibi fēlíciter!; **good thinking!** bene putās!; **how long is that good for?** quam diū valḗbit?; **you're a good fellow** frūgī *[indecl]* es

good *s:* **do s.o. good** álicui prōsum prōdésse prófuī prōfutū́rus

good and proper plānē et probē

goodbye valē *(pl:* valḗte); bene valē *(pl:* bene valḗte); **goodbye and good luck** bene valē et bene tibi sit

good-for-nothing *adj* nēquam *[indecl]*

good-for-nothing *s:* **be a good-for-nothing** nihil hóminis esse

good-hearted benévol·ēns -éntis, benévol·us -a -um

good-natured fácil·is -is -e

goodness *(integrity, good behavior)* bónit·ās -átis *f*

goodwill benevolénti·a -ae *f*

goose ans·er -eris *m;* **geese cackle** ánserēs gíngriunt *(see* **bird)**

gossip *s (talk)* rūm·or -ṓris *m (esp. pl.); (person)* fāmigerā́·tor -tṓris *m (·trīx -trícis f)*

gossip *intr* gárr·iō -íre

govern *(a province)* praesíd·eō -ére praesḗdī *(+ acc or dat);* **govern the country** rem pū́blicam gubernáre

government régim·en -inis *n;* rēs *f* pū́blica *(gen:* reī pū́blicae) *[also written as one word]*

governor praes·es -idis *mf,* gubernā́·tor -tṓris *m (·trīx -trícis f); (of a minor Roman province)* prōcūrā́t·or -ṓris *m*

gown tāláris vest·is -is *f; (Roman)* stol·a -ae *f*

grade *s* grad·us -ūs *m,* class·is -is *f; (mark or letter for performance)* not·a -ae *f*

grade *tr (papers)* notā́re; *(evaluate student's work)* aestimā́re

graduate *s* graduā́t·us -ī *m (·a -ae f)*

graduate *intr* diplṓma adipísc·or -ī adéptus sum, gradūs suscíp·iō -ere suscḗpī

graft ámbit·us -ūs *m*

grain frūmént·um -ī *n; (a grain)* grān·um -ī *n;* **with a grain of salt** cum grānō salis

grammar *s* grammátic·a -ae *f,* ar·s -tis *f* grammática; *(book)* ars, artis *f*

grandchild nep·ōs -ốtis *m,* nept·is -is *f*

granddaughter nept·is -is *f*

grandfather av·us -ī *m*

grandmother ávi·a -ae *f*

grand piano clāvīcórdi·um -ī *n* ālifórme

grandson nep·ōs -ốtis *m*

granted estō; **granted, he himself is nothing** estō, ipse nihil est

grape ūv·a -ae *f; a bunch of grapes* ūva

grapevine vīt·is -is *f*

grasshopper grill·us -ī *m;* **grasshoppers chirp** grillī fritínniunt

grateful: I am deeply grateful to you tibi grátiam hábeō maxímam

gratis grātīs

grave *adj* grav·is -is -e

grave *s* sepúlcr·um -ī *n*

gravy iūs, iūris *n*

gravy bowl váscul·um -ī *n* iūris

grease job ūncti·ō -ốnis *f* autocīnḗtī

grease ung·ō (unguō) úngere ūnxī ūnctus

great magn·us -a -um; **that's great!** bene hercle factum!

great! Eu!; papae! *(expression of surprise and delight)*

great-grandfather próav·us -ī *m*

great-grandmother proávi·a -ae *f*

greater māi·or -or -us

greatest máxim·us -a -um

Greece Graéci·a -ae *f*

greed avāríti·a -ae *f*

greedy avắrus -a -um; **greedy for** avắrus *(+ gen)*

Greek *adj* Graec·us -a -um

Greek *s* Graec·us -ī *m* (·a -ae *f*); **know (speak, write) Greek** Graecē scīre (loquī, scríbere)

green vírid·is -is -e; *(unripe)* crūd·us -a -um

green pepper piperít·is -idis *f*

gregarious *(sociable)* congregábil·is -is -e

grief maer·or -ốris *m;* **feel grief** condolḗsc·ō -ere condóluī

grill *s* crātícul·a -ae *f*

grill *tr* super crātículam assắre

groan gem·ō -ere -uī -itum

groan gémit·us -ūs *m*

grocer macellári·us -ī *m* (·a -ae *f*)

groceries obsốni·a -ốrum *npl, (or)* obsốni·um -ī *n*

grocery store macéll·um -ī *n,* tabérn·a -ae *f* alimentária

groin ingu·en -inis *n*

ground floor pedeplán·a -ốrum *npl*

ground beef búbul·a -ae *f* concísa

growl *(of a dog)* ring·or -ī rictus sum

grow old senḗsc·ō -ere sénuī; **grow up** iuvenḗsc·ō -ere iúvenī

grown-up *adj* adúlt·us -a -um

grumble increpắre

grumbling increpáti·ō -ốnis *f*

grunt *s (of a pig, bear)* grunnít·us -ūs *m*

grunt *intr (of a pig, bear)* grúnn·iō -íre -ívī *or* -iī -ítum

guard *s* cust·ōs -ốdis *mf*

guard *tr* custốd·iō -íre -ívī *or* -iī -ítus

guest hosp·ēs -itis *mf*

guest room hospíti·um -ī *n*

guidance counselor cōnsiliát·or -óris *m* acadḗmicus, cōnsiliátr·īx -ícis *f* acadḗmica

guide *s* dux, ducis *mf*

guide *tr* dūc·ō -ere dūxī ductus

guidebook lib·er -rī *m* periēgḗticus

guilty re·us -a -um, sōn·s -tis; **be found guilty** nóxius dīiūdicárī; **be guilty** in culpā esse; **guilty of** nóxi·us -a -um (+ *abl or gen*); **punish the guilty** poenam dē sóntibus éxig·ō -ere exḗgī exáctus; **the guilty one** sōn·s -tis *mf*

guitar cíthar·a -ae *f* Hispánica

gulf sin·us -ūs *m*

gullible crédul·us -a -um

gum *(of the mouth)* gingív·a -ae *f;* *(chewing gum)* cumm·is -is *f* masticábilis

gun sclopét·um -ī *n;* **fire a gun** sclopētáre

gym gymnási·um -ī *n (see Chapter V)*

gym instructor exercitát·or -óris *m,* exercitátr·īx -ícis *f*

gymnasium gymnási·um -ī *n*

gymnastic gymnástic·us -a -um

gym shoes cálce·ī -órum *mpl* gýmnicī

ha-ha-ha! hahahae!

habit cōnsuetúd·ō -inis *f*

hacker plagiári·us -ī *(or* effrāctári·us -ī) *m* ēlectrónicus

haddock gad·us -ī *m*

hail *s* grand·ō -inis *f*

hail *impers v* grándin·at -áre

hailstorm grándin·ēs -um *fpl*

hair *(a single hair or hair collectively)* capíll·us -ī *m;* *(hair in locks)* crīn·is -is *m*; com·a ae *f; (long, flowing hair)* caesári·ēs -ēī *f;* **layer the hair** comam in gradūs frang·ō -ere frēgī frāctus; **long hair** *(left uncut)* capíllī prōmíssī; **split hairs** cavillárī

haircut tōns·us -ūs *m,* tōnsúr·a -ae *f;* **get a haircut** fácere ut capillus tondeátur

hairbrush pēnícul·us -ī *m* comātórius

hairdo cōmpt·us -ūs *m*

hairdresser ōrnátr·īx -ícis *f,* tónstr·īx -ícis *f*

hair drier favóni·us -ī *m*

hairpin ac·us -ūs *f* comātória

hair style cōmpt·us -ūs *m*

hale and hardy salv·us et válid·us -a -um

half-time *(sports)* dīmídium temp·us -oris *n*

hall *(large room)* oec·us -ī *m*

hallway ambulácr·um -ī *n*

halter capístr·um -ī *n*

ham pern·a -ae *f;* **smoked ham** perna fūmósa

hamburger búbul·a -ae *f* concísa

hammer málle·us -ī *m*

ham sandwich pastíll·um -ī *n* pernā fartum

hamstring popl·es -itis *m*

hand *s* man·us -ūs *f; (of a clock)* ind·ex -icis *m;* **have one's hands full** sátag·ō -ere satégī; **sit on one's hands** *(doing nothing)* compréssīs mánibus séd·eō -ére sēdī

hand *tr* **hand in** trā·dō -dere -didī -ditus; **hand me that food** pórrige mihi illum cibum; **hand it over!** cedo *(pl:* cette)! [*an old imperative; can take a direct object*]

handbag bulg·a -ae *f; (of leather)* pérul·a -ae *f* coriácea

hand brake sufflắm·en -inis *n* manuále

handcuff *tr* mánicās iníc·iō -ere iniécī iniéctus (+ *dat*)

handcuffs *spl* mánic·ae -árum *fpl*

handkerchief mūcínni·um -ī *n*, lintéol·um -ī *n*

handle *s* manúbri·um -ī *n*

handle *tr* tractáre

handlebars manúbri·um -ī *n*

hand luggage sarcínul·ae -árum *fpl* manuálēs

handsome pulch·er -ra -rum, speciós·us -a -um

handwriting chīrógraph·um -ī *n*

hang: hang around with frequēns adésse ūnā cum (+ *abl*); **hang down** dēpénd·eō -ére -ī; **you can just go and hang yourself!** ī dīrécte in máximam malam crúcem!

hangar receptácul·um -ī *n* āёróplanī

happen fīō fíerī factus sum, áccid·ō -ere -ī; **happen to** contíng·ō -ere cóntigī (+ *dat*); **I just happened to spot him** forte eum cōnspéxī; **what happened?** quid factum est?

happiness beātitúd·ō -inis *f*

happy beát·us -a -um, laet·us -a -um

harbor port·us -ūs *m*

hard *(to the touch)* dūr·us -a -um; *(difficult)* diffícil·is -is -e *(with abl of the supine)*; **hard on** inimíc·us -a -um (+ *dat*), dūr·us -a -um in (+ *acc*); **hard work** op·us -eris *n* árduum; **hard to please** diffícil·is -is -e; **he was hard on me** in mē dūrus erat; **it's hard to do, but I'll try just the same** diffícile factū est, sed conábor níhilō sétius; **take this hard** hoc dūrum accípere, hoc aegrē ferō ferre tulī

hardback *or* **hardcover book** lib·er -rī *m* līnō contéctus

hard drive *(comput)* dūra státi·ō -ónis *f*

hardware ferrāmént·a -órum *npl*; *(comput)* apparát·us -ūs *m* computātrális

hardware store tabérn·a -ae *f* ferrária

hard-working labōriós·us -a -um

harmonica harmónic·a -ae *f* īnflátil·is

harp harp·a -ae *f*; **play the harp** harpā lúdere

harp on the same theme cantilénam eándem can·ō -ere cécinī

harsh sevér·us -a -um; **harsh toward** dūr·us -a -um in (+ *acc*)

harshness dūríti·a -ae *f*

harvest *s* *(reaping)* mess·is -is *f*; *(the crops themselves)* próvént·us -ūs *m*

harvest *tr* démet·ō -ere dēmessuī dēméssus

hat pétas·us -ī *m* *(with broad brim)*

hate *s* ódi·um -ī *n*

hate *tr* ōdī ōdísse *(defect v)*

hateful ōdiós·us -a -um

hatred (of, toward) ódi·um -ī *n* (in + *acc*)

haughty ēlát·us -a -um, supérb·us -a -um

haul off to prison ráp·iō -ere -uī -tus in cárcerem

have *(possess)* háb·eō -ére -uī -itus; *(e.g., dinner)* sūm·ō -ere -psī -ptus; *(a sickness)* labōráre (+ *abl*); **have a tough time of it** valdē labōráre; **have it in for s.o.** álicui perículum dēnuntiáre; **have it your way!** estō ut lubet!; **have to do: what do you have to do with her?** quid reī tibi est cum illā?; **have to say: this I have to say** haec hábeō dícere.

hawk accípi·ter -tris *m;* **hawks caw** accípitrēs crócitant *(see* **bird)**

hay fēn·um -ī *n;* **make hay** fēnum sec·ō -áre -uī -tus; **make hay while the sun shines!** occāsiónem ampléctere!; carpe diem!

hayloft fēnī́l·ia -ium *npl*

hazelnut avellán·a -ae *f*

head *s* cap·ut -itis *n;* **back of the head** occipíti·um -ī *n;* **be a head taller than** tōtō vértice suprā (+ *acc)* esse; **come into one's head** in buccam veníre [*lit: come into one's cheek*]; **from head to foot** ā cápite ūsque ad calcem; **head of state** rēct·or -óris *m* cīvitátis; **put heads together** cápita cónferō cōnférre cóntulī; **top of the head** vert·ex -icis *m*

head *tr (a committee, etc.)* prae·sum -ésse -fuī (+ *dat)* ‖ *intr* **head east** ad oriéntem tend·ō -ere teténdī; **head for** pet·ō -ere -ī́vī -ī́tus

head-first prae·ceps -cípitis

heading capítul·um -ī *n*

headlight (autocīnḗtī) luminár·e -is *n;* **turn on (turn off) the bright (dim) lights** lūminária praecandéntia (candéntia) accénd·ō -ere -ī (exstíngu·ō -ere exstínxī)

headmaster scholae rēct·or -óris *m*

headmistress scholae rēctr·īx -ī́cis *f*

headquarters *(mil)* praetóri·um -ī *n; (of a business)* sēd·ēs -is *f*

headway: make headway prōfíc·iō -ere prōfḗcī; **make no headway** nihil prōfícere; **we are making some headway, I hope** ut spērō, prōfícimus aliquántum

heal *tr* sānáre ‖ *intr* sānḗsc·ō -ere

health *(good or bad)* valētū́d·ō -inis *f;* **bad health** advérsa *(or* mala, gravis, īnfírma) valētū́dō; **bad health**

suddenly hit me mala valētū́dō mē repéntē invásit; **for reasons of bad health** valētū́dinis causā; **good health** bona *(or* firma, cómmoda, próspera) valētū́dō; **here's to your health!** tibi salútem propī́nō!; bene tibi!; **in sound health** válid·us -a -um

healthy sān·us -a -um, salv·us -a -um

hear aúd·iō -ī́re -ī́vī *or* -iī -ī́tus; *(to find out about)* cognṓsc·ō -ere cognṓvī cógnitus

hearing *(sense)* audī́t·us -ūs *m; (legal)* cogníti·ō -ónis *f;* **hold a hearing** cognitiónem habḗre

heart cor, cordis *n;* **from the heart** ex ánimō; **heart and soul** tōtō péctore; **my heart was in my throat** ánima mihi in nā́sō erat [*lit: my breath was in my nose*]; **take to heart** familiáriter ferō ferre tulī lātus

heartache cūr·a -ae *f,* cordóli·um -ī *n*

heaven: for heaven's sake obsécrō [*lit: I pray*]; **heavens!** édepol! **heavens above!** O dī immortálēs!; **heaven forbid!** dī mélius faxint!; **I'm in seventh heaven** dígitō caelum attíngō; **in heaven's name!** per fortū́nās!

heck: give s.o. heck áliquem verbīs malīs obiūrgáre; **heck no!** mínimē vērō hercle!; **who the heck are they?** quī, malum, istī sunt?

heehaw *s* rudī́t·us -ūs *m*

heehaw *intr* rud·ō -ere -ī́vī -ī́tum

heel cal·x -cis *f; (of a shoe)* fulmént·um -ī *n; (slang)* nequam hom·ō -inis *mf;* **take to one's heels** sē conícere in pedēs

heifer iuvénc·us -ī *m* (·a -ae *f)*

helicopter helicópter·um -ī *n;* **be taken by helicopter to** per helicópterum tráns·vehor -vehī -véctus sum; **fly a**

helicopter helicópterum gubernáre; **fly in a helicopter** helicópterō vehor vehī vectus sum

hell: go to hell! ī *(pl:* īte) in malam crucem!; **I'm going to catch hell** habébō convícium.

hello! salvē! *(pl:* salvéte)!; salvus (-a) sīs! *(pl:* salvī (-ae) sītis)!; **hello there!** eho istinc!; **Terentia says hello to you** Terentia tibi salútem dīcit

helmet *(of leather)* gále·a -ae *f; (of metal)* cass·is -idis *f*

help *s* auxíli·um -ī *n*

help *tr* iuv·ō -áre iūvī iūtus, succúrr·ō -ere -ī succúrsum (+ *dat)*

helpless in·ops -opis

helplessness inópi·a -ae *f*

hem limb·us -ī *m*

hen gallín·a -ae *f (see* **bird)**

henpecked uxórius

herd *(of cattle, swine)* grex, gregis *m; (of oxen and large animals)* armént·um -ī *n*

here hīc; **here and now** dēpraesentiárum [*adv]*; **here I am!** Ecce mē! **here with it!** cedo! *(pl:* cette!) *(can take an accusative object, e.g.:* **Here with that book!** cedo istum librum!)

heroin heroín·um -ī *n;* **use heroin** heroínō ūtor ūtī ūsus sum

hey heus!; **hey you, I'm talking to you!** heus tū, tibi ego dīcō!

hi! salvē *(pl:* salvéte)

hide *s* córi·um -ī *n;* **be after s.o.'s hide** córium alicúius pet·ō -ere petívī; **risk one's own hide** coriō suō lúdere; **save one's own hide** córium serváre

high *adj* alt·us -a -um; *(rank)* ampl·us -a -um; *(opinion, price)* magn·us -a -um; *(fever)* ārd·ēns -éntis; *(note)*

acút·us -a -um ; *(on alchohol, drugs)* ébri·us -a -um; **be high on drugs** ā medicāméntīs psychotrópicīs inebriáre; **high blood pressure** hypertóni·a -ae *f*

high *adv* **to aim high** magnās rēs áppet·ō -ere -ívī

highjacking abdúcti·ō -ónis *f* āéria

high jump salt·us -ūs *m* in altum

highrise (building) multizóni·um -ī *n*

high school schol·a -ae *f* supérior

highway strāt·a -ae *f* autocīnética

hike *s* ambuláti·ō -ónis *f*

hike *intr* ambuláre

hill coll·is -is *m*

hilly clīvós·us -a -um

hip cox·a -ae *f,* coxénd·ix -icis *f*

hippie anticōnformíst·a -ae *m (·ria -riae f)*

hippopotamus hippopótam·us -ī *m*

hiss *s* síbil·us -ī *m*

hiss *intr* sībiláre

history história -ae *f*

historian históric·us -ī *m (·a -ae f)*

hit *s (in baseball)* puls·us -ūs *m*

hit *tr (to strike)* īc·ō -ere -ī ictus; *(a baseball)* pulsáre; **did you hit it off with them?** concordābásne cum illīs?; **hit s.o. for a loan** feríre áliquem mútuō argéntō

hmmm *interj* hem

hoarse rauc·us -a -um

hockey lūd·us -ī *m* hoccéius, alsūlégi·a -ae *f;* **field hockey** lūdus hoccéius campéstris; **ice hockey** lūdus hoccéius glaciális; **play hockey** hoccéiō *(or* alsūlégiā) lúdere *(see Chapter V)*

hockey player alsūlegắri·us -ī *m* (·a -ae *f*)

hockey stick ped·um -ī *n,* férul·a -ae *f* repánda

hockey puck disc·us -ī *m*

hog sūs, suis *mf;* **hogs oink** sūēs grúnniunt

hogwash: that's hogwash! quisquíliae!

hold *tr* tén·eō -ếre -uī -tus; *(contain)* cáp·iō -ere cēpī; *(an office)* ger·ō -ere gessī gestus; *(a meeting)* habére; **hold it!** *(stop!)* astā!; **hold it please!** manē obsécrō!; **hold s.o. in high (highest) esteem** áliquem magnī (máximī) fácere; **hold up** *(detain)* dētín·eō -ếre -uī, impéd·iō -íre -ívī -ítus; **what held you up?** quid tē impedívit? ‖ *intr* **hold out** dūrắre

hole in the wall *(shabby lodgings)* stábul·um -ī *n*

holiday fếri·ae -ắrum *fpl; (from school)* di·ēs -ếī *m* fēriắtus; **today is a holiday** hódiē fếriās ágimus

holiness sắnctit·ās -ấtis *f*

holy sānct·us -a -um

home dom·us -ūs *f; (direction)* domum; **at home** domī; **at your home** domī tuae, apud tē; **from home** domō; **to my home** ad mē

home appliance īnstrūmént·um -ī *n* domésticum ēléctricum; **home appliances** ēléctrica domūs ūtēnsíl·ia -ium *npl*

home front: on the home front and on the war front domī et mīlítiae

home plate bas·is -is *f* summa *(or* doméstica)

homely īnspeciốs·us -a -um

home page *(comput)* págin·a -ae *f* doméstica

home run circúit·us -ūs *m* básium; **hit a home run** circúitum básium fácere

homesick: be homesick ex dēsīdériō labōrắre; **I am homesick for** mē dēsīdérium tenet (+ *gen*)

homework pēns·um -ī *n* domésticum; *(written)* praescrípt·um -ī *n* domésticum

homicide homicídi·um -ī *n*

honest prob·us -a -um; *(speaking the truth)* vēr·āx -ắcis; **honest to God** prō deum fidem

honestly: tell me honestly dīc bonā fide

honey mel, mellis *n; (terms of endearment)* melíll·a -ae *f,* mel *n,* mélcul·um -ī *n*

honor honōrắre

honorable honést·us -a -um

honorably honéstē

hood plóxen·um -ī *n*

hoodlum grassắt·or -ốris *m*

hoof úngul·a -ae *f*

hooky: play hooky ínsciīs paréntibus ā scholā abesse

hoot *s* **I don't give a hoot about him** eum floccī nōn fáciō

hoot *intr (of owls)* būbilắre

hope *s* spēs, speī *f;* **give up hope** dēspērắre

hope *intr* spērắre; **hope that** spērắre (+ *acc* & *inf*)

hopeless dēspērắt·us -a -um

hopper lābéll·um -ī *n* íntimum, sell·a -ae *f* familiắrica

horizontal bar ferr·um -ī *n* trānsvérsum

hormone hormốn·um -ī *n*

horn bűcin·a -ae *f;* **blow the horn** bűcinā clang·ō -ere

hornet crābr•ō -ónis *m*

horrible horríbil•is -is -e

horse equ•us -ī *m*

horsefly tabán•us -ī *m;* **horseflies buzz** tabánī bómbilant

hose *(for watering)* túbul•us -ī *m*

hospital valētūdinári•um -ī *n*

hostage obs•es -idis *mf*

hostess hóspit•a -ae *f* āéria

hot *(of a person, sun, water, bath, day)* cálid•us -a -um *(opp:* frígid•us -a -um); *(boiling hot)* férvid•us -a -um; *(sultry)* aestuós•us -a -um; *(spicey)* acer, acris, acre; **be hot** cál•eō -ére -uī; **become hot** calésc•ō -ere; **be uncomfortably hot** aestuáre; **hot weather** aest•us -ūs *m;* **it is hot today** hódiē calétur

hot dog hill•a -ae calēns *(gen:* hillae caléntis) *f*

hot pants brevíssimae brā•cae -árum *fpl* fēminínae

hotplate disc•us -ī *m* coctórius

hot-tempered īrācúnd•us -a -um

hotel dēversóri•um -ī *n;* **stay at a hotel** in dēversóriō mor•or -árī -átus sum

hotel manager dēversóriī dīréc•tor -tóris *m* (•trīx -trícis *f*)

hour hōr•a -ae *f;* **a half hour** sēmihór•a -ae *f;* **an hour and a half** sēsquihór•a -ae *f;* **a quarter of an hour** quadr•āns -ántis *m* hōrae; **every hour** síngulīs hōrīs; **from hour to hour** in hōrās; **three quarters of an hour** dōdr•āns -ántis *m* hōrae

hourly in hōrās

house dom•us -ūs *f*, aed•ēs -ium *fpl*

house arrest custódi•a -ae *f* líbera

how *(in what way)* quómodo, quō pactō; *(chiefly after verbs of hearing,* *telling, etc.)* ut (+ *subj); (to what degree)* quam; **how are you? (how are you doing?)** quid agis? *(pl:* quid ágitis?); ut valēs? *(pl:* ut valétis?); **how come?** quī fit? *or* quī istuc? **how far** quoúsque; **how far is ... from** quantum distat *(or* abest) ... ab (+ *abl);* **how goes it?** quid fit?; **how long** quámdiū, quoúsque; **how long ago?** quam prídem? *or* quam dūdum?; **how many** quot [*indecl*]; **how many times** quótiēns, quótiēs; **how much** quant•us -a -um; **how much did you sell it for?** quantī hoc vēnit?; **how much is this?** quantī hoc cōnstat?; **how much does it cost?** id quantī cōnstat?; **how often** quótiēns; **how old are you?** quot annōs nāt•us (-a) es?; **how so?** quid ita?; *(whatever made you say that?)* quídum?; **how soon?** quam mox?; **how's that?** *(What did you say?)* quídum? *or* quid iam?

however autem

hug compléct•or -ī compléxus sum; **hug each other** inter sē compléctī

hum *s* murm•ur -uris *m; (of bees)* bomb•us -ī *m*

hum *intr* murmuráre; *(of bees)* bombiláre

human being hom•ō -inis *mf*

humane hūmán•us -a -um

humid úmid•us -a -um

humor *s* fēstívit•ās -átis *f*

humor *tr* **humor s.o.** álicui mōrem gerō gérere gessī

humorous fēstív•us -a -um

humorously fēstívē

hump gibb•er -eris *m*

hung jury: be acquitted by a hung jury senténtiīs páribus absólv•or -ī absolútus sum

hunger fam·ēs -is *f*

hunt *(also* **go hunting)** vēn·or -ắrī -ắtus sum *(see Chapter V)*

hunting vēnắt·us -ūs *m*

hunting dog can·is -is *m* vēnắticus

hunting gear īnstrūmént·um -ī *n* vēnātórium

hurray! euax!

hurricane tȳph·ōn -ốnis *m*

hurry *s:* **be in a hurry** properắre, festīnắre; **but I'm in a hurry** at próperō; **what's your hurry?** Quid festīnās?**hurry** *intr* properắre; **hurry!** mātūrắ! *(pl:* mātūrắte!)

hurt *tr* nóc·eō -ếre -uī (+ *dat)* ‖ *intr* dól·eō -ếre -uī; **hurt a lot** veheménter dolếre

husband marīt·us -ī *m*

hygiene hygiến·ē -ēs *f;* **practice hygyiene** hygiếnēn exérc·eō -ếre -uī -itus

hygienic hygiếnic·us -a -um

hypertext *s* hypertéxt·us -ūs *m*

hypertext *adj* hypertextuắl·is -is -e

hypocrite simulắt·or -ốris *m,* simulắtr·īx -ícis *f*

hypocritical coắct·us -a -um, simulắt·us -a -um

ice glắci·ēs -ếī *f;* **turn to ice** glaciắrī

ice cream gélidum crēm·um -ī *n*

ice hockey *(see* **hockey)**

ice rink stắdi·ōn -ī *n* glaciále

ice-skate *s* pátin·us -ī *m*

ice-skate *intr* patinắre

ice-skater patinắt·or -ốris *m,* patinắtr·īx -ícis *f*

ice-skating patinắti·ō -ốnis *f (see* Chapter V)

icicle stíri·a -ae *f*

icon *(comput)* īcōn, íconis *f*

icy glaciắl·is -is -e

idea cōnsíli·um -ī *n,* cogníti·ō -ốnis *f;* **you're full of ideas** plēnus (-a) cōnsíliī es

ideal exémpl·ar -ắris *n*

identical idéntic·us -a -um, īdem et pār

identification identificắti·ō -ốnis *f*

identify identificắre

identity idéntit·ās -ắtis *f*

idiom figứr·a -ae *f,* propríet·ās -ắtis *f* linguae (Latínae *or* Ánglicae)

idiomatic expressions quae linguae Latínae *(or* Ánglicae) própria sunt

idiot fátu·us -ī *m* (·a -ae *f)*

if sī; **if only** útinam (+ *subj)*

iffy *(slang)* dúbi·us -a -um

ignoramus nesápi·us -ī *m,* nesápi·a -ae *f*

ignorance īnsciénti·a -ae *f*

ignorant īnscít·us -a -um; *(unlearned)* indóct·us -a -um

ill *(used of body and mind)* ae·ger -gra -rum; *(used of body only)* aegrốt·us -a -um; **be ill** aegrōtắre; **fall ill** in morbum íncid·ō incídere íncidī

ill health (advérsa) valētúd·ō -inis *f;* **for reasons of ill health** valētúdinis causā

ill-mannered male mōrắt·us -a -um

illiterate analphabét·us -a -um

illness morb·us -ī *m,* (mala) valētúd·ō -inis *f;* **serious illness** gravis valētúdō

illogical absúrd·us -a -um

ills mal·a -ốrum *npl*

imagine imắgin·or -ắrī -ắtus sum

immature immātứr·us -a -um

immaturity immātū́rit·ās -ā́tis *f*

immediately statim, contínuō, extémplō

immoderate immódic·us -a -um

immodest impudíc·us -a -um

impartial aequ·us -a -um, incorrúpt·us -a -um et ínte·ger -gra -grum

impatient: be impatient with iníquō ánimō ferō ferre tulī (+ *acc)*

impatiently iníquō ánimō

imperative *adj* imperātív·us -a -um; **imperative mood** mod·us -ī *m* imperātívus

imperfect tense *s* temp·us -oris *n* praetéritum imperféctum

imperial imperiál·is -is -e

impersonal *adj* impersōnál·is -is -e

impetuous férvid·us -a -um

impolite inurbán·us -a -um

importance: it is of the greatest importance to me that ... permágnī meā ínterest (+ *acc & inf)*

important magn·us -a -um; **it is (very) important to me (you) that** magnī (máximē) meā (tuā) ínterest (+ *acc & inf); it's not all that important** tantī nōn est

impress commóv·eō -ére commóvī commótus

impression: make a deep impression on máximē commóv·eō -ére commóvī (+ *acc)*

improper índec·ēns -éntis

improve *tr* ēmendáre **‖** *intr* mel·ior -ior -ius fíō fíerī factus sum; *(in studies)* prōfíc·iō -ere prōfécī

improvement prōféct·us -ūs *m*

imprudent imprúd·ēns -éntis

impulse ánimī ímpet·us -ūs *m*

in *prep* in (+ *abl); (in the writings of)* apud (+ *acc); in all** ex tōtō

in *adv (motion)* intrō; *(rest or motion)* intus; **is your father in?** estne pater intus?

inappropriate inépt·us -a -um

incisors dentēs *mpl* prīmṓrēs

include contín·eō -ére -uī

incorrect vitiós·us -a -um

incorrectly vitiósē

increase *tr* aúg·eō -ére auxī auctus **‖** *intr* crēsc·ō -ere crēvī

incredible incrēdíbil·is -is -e

indecent índec·ēns -éntis

indecisive ambígu·us -a -um

indeclinable indēclīnábil·is -is -e

indeed proféctō, quidem, vērō

indefinite īnfīnít·us -a -um *(opp:* fīnítus*)*

indicate *tr* significáre

indicative indicātív·us -a -um; **in the indicative mood** modō indicātívō

indict s.o. áliquem re·um (-am) fácere

indifference frīg·us -oris *n*

indigestion crúdit·ās -átis *f*

indignant indignābúnd·us -a -um

inept inépt·us -a -um

inexpensive vīl·is -is -e

inexperienced (in) inexpért·us -a -um (ab + *abl or* in + *acc or* advérsus + *acc)*

infamous īnfám·is -is -e

infancy īnfánti·a -ae *f*

infant īnfāns, īnfántis *mf*

infantry peditát·us -ūs *m*

infantryman ped·es -itis *m*

infatuated: be infatuated with s.o. áliquem efflíctim amáre

**infer: I infer from what you say that
... ex** verbīs tuīs cólligō (+ *acc &
inf*)

infinitive *s* īnfīnītī́v•um -ī *n*

infirmary valētūdinā́ri•um -ī *n*

inflame īnflammā́re

inflammation īnflammā́ti•ō -ṓnis *f*

inflect *tr* dēclīnā́re

inflection *s* dēclīnā́ti•ō -ṓnis *f*

influence grā́ti•a -ae *f;* **have a lot of
(more, little, no) influence on**
multum (plus, paulum, nihil) posse
apud (+ *acc*)

influential grātiṓs•us -a -um

inform: inform s.o. about áliquem
certiṓrem fácere dē (+ *abl*)

informant ind•ex -icis *mf*

information indíci•um -ī *n*

ingenious artificiṓs•us -a -um

initiative: on my own initiative meā
sponte

injustice iniūstíti•a -ae *f*

ink ātrāmént•um -ī *n*

inland *adj* intéri•or -or -us; **inland seas**
már•ia -ium *npl* interiṓra

inland *adv* intus; **towns inland from
Tarentum** óppida per continéntem ā
Taréntō

in-law affín•is -is *mf*

inn caupṓn•a -ae *f*

inning *(of baseball)* miss•us -ūs *m*

innkeeper caup•ō -ṓnis *m*

innocence innocénti•a -ae *f*

innocent (of) ínnoc•ēns -éntis (+ *gen*)

innumerable innúmer•us -a -um

input *(comput)* (datṓrum) ínit•us -ūs *m;*
input and output (datṓrum) ínitus
exitúsque

inquisitive cūriṓs•us -a -um

insane īnsā́n•us -a -um

insanity īnsā́nit•ās -ā́tis *f*

insect īnséct•um -ī *n*

insensitive dūr•us -a -um

insensitivity dūríti•a -ae *f*

inside: go inside! ī *(pl:* īte) intus!

insincere īnsincḗr•us -a -um

install *(comput)* ínstru•ō -ere īnstrúxī
īnstrúctus

installment pḗnsi•ō -ṓnis *f;* **pay in five
installments** quīnque pēnsiṓnibus
solv•ō -ere -ī solū́tus

instruct īnstítu•ō -ere -ī īnstitū́tus;
instruct s.o. in s.th. īnstrúere
áliquem áliquō

instruction *(teaching)* īnstitū́ti•ō -ṓnis *f;*
instructions praecépt•a -ṓrum *npl;*
(orders to do something) mandā́t•a
-ṓrum *npl*

instructor praecépt•or -ṓris *m,*
praecéptr•īx -ī́cis *f*

insurance caútí•ō -ṓnis *f,* assēcūrā́ti•ō
-ṓnis *f;* **car insurance** assēcūrā́tiō
vehiculā́ria; **casuality insurance**
assēcūrā́tiō indemnitā́tis; **health
insurance** assēcūrā́tiō valētudinā́ria;
insurance company socíet•ās -ā́tis *f*
vītae cautiṓnī exercendae; **life
insurance** prō vītā caútiō, vītae
assēcūrā́tiō

integrity intégrit•ās -ā́tis *f*

intellect intelléct•us -ūs *m*

intelligence intellegénti•a -ae *f*

intelligent intélleg•ēns -éntis

intend dēstinā́re; in ánimō esse (+ *dat of
the subject);* **I intended to set out
straight for home** erat mihi in ánimō
rēctā proficī́scī domum

intense *(emotions)* grand•is -is -e

intensive pronoun *s* prōnṓm·en -inis *n* intentiṓnis (ut "ipse" **himself**)

intentions: with the best intentions óptimō ánimō ūtēns

interchange coniúncti·ō -ṓnis *f* viárum

interest *s* **interest (in)** stúdi·um -ī *n* (+ *gen*); *(fin)* faen·us -oris *n*, ūsū́r·a -ae *f*; **compound interest** anatocísm·us -ī *m*; **lend money at interest** pecúniam faénorī dare; **rate of interest** ūsū́r·ae -árum *fpl*; **3 percent (4 percent, 5 percent, 6 percent, 12 percent) interest per annum** quadrántēs (triéntēs, quīncúncēs, sēmíssēs) centésimae ūsū́rae; **simple interest** perpétuum faen·us; **take an interest in something** stúdiō alicū́ius tenḗrī

interest *tr* tén·eō -ḗre -uī; **sports don't interest me** lūdī mē nōn tenent

interested: I am interested in music mū́sicae [*dat*] stúdeō; **I am interested in that** id mihi cū́rae est; **I am not the least bit interested in the races** circḗnsibus nē levíssimē quidem téneor

interesting *(in appearance)* speciṓs·us -a -um; **that book is interesting** ille liber mē tenet

interfere in sē interpṓn·ō -ere interpósuī (+ *dat*)

interior *adj* intéri·or -or -us

interior *s*: **in the interior** in mediterrā́neō, intus; **toward the interior** intus

interjection *s* interiécti·ō -ṓnis *f* (ut "heus tū!" **hey you!**)

international law iūs, iūris *n* géntium

internet *s* interrḗt·e -is *n*

internet *adj* interrētiál·is -is -e

interrogate interrogáre

interrupt interpelláre; **don't interrupt me!** nōlī *(pl:* nōlī́te) mē interpelláre! *(or* mihi óbloquī!)

intersection cómpit·um -ī *n*, quadrívi·um -ī *n*

interview collóqui·um -ī *n* interrogātṓrium

interviewer interrogā́·tor -tṓris *m* (·trīx -trícis *f*)

intestines intestī́n·a -ṓrum *npl*

intransitive *adj* intrānsitī́v·us -a -um

introduce *(e.g., a custom)* introdúcere; *(a person)* **(to)** trād·ō -ere -idī -itus (+ *dat*)

introductory intrōductṓri·us -a -um

invade invā́d·ō -ere invā́sī invā́sus in (+ *acc*), cum exércitū ingréd·ior -ī ingréssus sum

invest collocáre

investigate investigáre

investigator investigā́·tor -tṓris *m* (·trīx -trícis *f*)

investment pecúniae collocáti·ō -ṓnis *f*

invite invītáre; *(esp. to dinner)* vocáre

involve implicáre; **be involved in** vers·or -ā́rī -ā́tus sum in (+ *abl*)

Ireland Hibérni·a -ae *f*

Irish *adj* Hibérnic·us -a -um

iron *tr* prem·ō -ere pressī pressus, (ferrō) lēvigáre

irregular *adj* inaequā́l·is -is -e; **an irregular verb** inaequā́le verbum (ut "volō," **I want**)

irregularly *adv* inaequā́liter; **"duo" is irregularly declined** "duo" inaequā́liter dēclī́nātur

irresponsible inofficiṓs·us -a -um

irritable īrācúnd·us -a -um

irritate exasperáre

is est; **is that so?** ítane est?

island ínsul·a -ae *f*

isthmus ísthm·us -ī *m (f)*

it id, eius

Italy Itáli·a -ae *f*

itch *intr* prūr·iō -íre; *(fig)* gést·iō -íre; **I'm just itching to** géstiō quidem (+ *inf)*

item of merchandise merx, mercis *f*

its eius

jacket iacc·a -ae *f; (of leather)* iacc·a -ae *f* scórtea

jail carc·er -eris *m*

jailer custōdiári·us -ī *m* (·a -ae *f)*

jam baccárum condītúr·a -ae *f;* **be in a jam** in angústiīs vers·or -árī -átus sum

January mēns·is -is *m* Iānuárius; **in January** mēnse Iānuáriō

jaw mal·ae -árum *fpl*

jawbone maxíll·a -ae *f*

jealous ínvid·us -a -um; **be jealous of** invíd·eō -ére invídī (+ *dat)*

jealousy invídi·a -ae *f*

jeans brāc·ae -árum *f* Genuénsēs

jello sorbíll·um -ī *n* concrétum

jelly cil·on *(also* quil·on) -ī *n*

jet plane āërópl an·um -ī *n* pyraulocīnéticum

jewel gemm·a -ae *f*

jeweler aúrif·ex -icis *m*

jewelry store gemmári·a -ae *f*

jitters scrúpul·us -ī *m;* **give s.o. the jitters** álicui scrúpulum iníc·iō -ere iniécī

job *(piece of work)* op·us -eris *n; (as a means of livelihood)* quaest·us -ūs *m;* **good job!** rēctē factum!; **it's a big**

job but ... magnum opus est sed tamen ...

jog tolútim cursitáre

joint artícul·us -ī *m*

joke *s* ioc·us -ī *m;* **as a joke** per iocum

joke *intr* ioc·or -árī -átus sum; **all joking aside** iocō remótō; **now you're joking** iocáris nunc tū

jokingly per iocum *or* inter iocum

jot down annotáre, dēnotáre

journal commentári·ī -órum *mpl* periódicī

journalist diurnári·us -ī *m* (·a -ae *f)*

journalism diurnária ar·s -tis *f*

joy gaúdi·um -ī *n;* **feel joy** gaúd·eō -ére gāvísus sum

joystick *(comput)* véctul·us -ī *m*

juice succ·us -ī *m*

judge iūd·ex -icis *m;* **sit as judge (hold court)** iūs dícere

judgment iūdíci·um -ī *n;* **against my better judgment** adversum ingénium meum; **in my judgment** meō iūdíciō

judicial iūdiciál·is -is -e; **judicial system** ráti·ō -ónis *f* iūdiciális

judo luct·a -ae *f* iūdóica

July mēns·is -is *m* Iúlius; **in July** mēnse Iúliō

jump sál·iō -íre -uī *or* -iī; **jump down** dēsilíre; **jump for joy** exsultáre; **jump rope** ad fūnem salíre

June mēns·is -is *m* Iúnius; **in June** mēnse Iúniō

junior iúni·or -óris *m*

juror iūd·ex -icis *m*

jury cōnsíli·um -ī *n;* iúdic·ēs -um *mpl*

just *adv* modo; **just about** *(pretty well, virtually)* propémodum; **just a**

moment ago modo; **just as** cum máximē: **just as I was writing that** cum haec máximē scríberem; **just before** *(an event)* sub *(+ acc);* **just in time** témporī; **just now** modo; **just then** tunc máxime; **just the other day** modo; **just the same** *(anyhow)* tamen *or* níhilō sétius; **just when** cum máximē; **just what?** quidnam?; **just who?** quisnam?

just *adj* iūst·us -a -um

justice iūstíti·a -ae *f*

justly iūstē

jut out *see* **project**

kangaroo halmatúr·us -ī *m*

karate luct·a -ae *f* carática

keen-scented sagācíssim·us -a -um

keep *(retain)* tén·eō -ére -uī -tus; *(confine)* contín·eō -ére -uī conténtus; **am I keeping you?** num dētíneō tē?; **keep a stiff upper lip!** fac ut ánimō fortī sīs!; **keep this to yourself** haec tū tēcum habétō; **keep your cool!** compésce mentem!; **what kept you?** quid ténuit quō minus venírēs?

ketchup kétsup·um -ī *n*

key clāv·is -is *m; (of a typewriter or computer)* plēctr·um -ī *n*, malléol·us -ī *m;* **room key** clāv·is -is *f* conclávis

keyboard *(of a typewriter or computer)* plēctrológi·um -ī *n*, ōrd·ō -inis *m* plēctrórum; *(of a piano or organ)* clāviatúr·a -ae *f*

kick *tr (a ball)* pede pulsáre; **kick the bucket** ánimam búll·iō -íre -iī

kid *s (coll)* fust·um -ī *n* púerī *or* puéllae

kid *tr* lúdere, lūdificáre; **don't kid me** nē mē lūdās; **you're kidding!** lūdis mē!

kidney rēn, rēnis *m*

kidney bean phasél·us -ī *m(f)*

kill occíd·ō -ere -ī occísus, necáre; **kill time** tempus fall·ō -ere feféllī; **you're killing me!** mē énicās!

kilometer chīliómetr·um -ī *n*

kind *adj* **(to, toward)** benévol·us -a -um (ergā + *acc*)

kind *s (type)* gen·us -eris *n;* **what kind of person is ... ?** quālis homō est ...?

kindergarten paedotrophé·um -ī *n*

kind-hearted benévol·us -a -um, benígn·us -a -um

kindness benevoléntia -ae *f; (kind deed)* benefíci·um -ī *n;* **show kindness to s.o.** benevoléntiam álicui praest·ō -áre praéstitī

kiss *s* óscul·um -ī *n*, suávi·um -ī *n; (passionate)* bási·um -ī *n*

kiss *tr* ōsculárī, suāviárī, suávium dare (+ *dat*), bāsiáre

kitchen culín·a -ae *f*

kitchen knife cul·ter -trī *m* coquīnáris

kitchen utensils īnstrūmént·a -órum *npl* coquinātória

knapsack saccipéri·um -ī *n* dorsuále

knee gen·ū -ūs *n*

kneecap patéll·a -ae *f*

knife cult·er -rī *m; (small knife)* cultéll·us -ī *m*

knock down déic·iō -ere dēiécī dēiéctus; *(in boxing)* stern·ō -ere strāvī strātus; **knock out** cōnstérnere

knock it off! parce! *(pl:* párcite!)

know sciō scīre scīvī scītus; *(to be familiar with a person or place)* nōv·ī -isse *(defective verb);* **get to know** nōsc·ō -ere nōvī nōtus; **he thinks he knows better than I do** cēnset sē plūs sápere quam mē; **I'm dying to know how you are doing** quid agās, valdē áveō scīre; **know for sure** certum (or certō) scīre; **know how to** scīre (+ inf); **let me know what you are doing** mē velim certiṓrem fáciās, quid agās; **let me know where you are** fácitō ut sciam ubi sīs; **not know** nésc·iō -íre

knowledge sciénti·a -ae f; (acquisition of knowledge) cogníti·ō -ṓnis f; **without the knowledge of** clam (+ abl); **without your knowledge** clam vōbīs

known nōt·us -a -um; **make known** palam fácere; **well known** nōtíssim·us -a -um

knuckle artícul·us -ī m dígitī

knucklehead bār·ō -ṓnis m

laborer operári·us -ī m, operári·a -ae f

lacrosse lūd·us -ī m lacrossénsis; **play lacrosse** lūdō lacrossḗnsī lū́dere

lacrosse stick (or **crosse**) cróci·a -ae f; **cradle the stick** cróciam agitáre

ladle trūll·a -ae f

lagoon stāgn·um -ī n

lake lac·us -ūs m

lamb agn·us -ī m, agn·a -ae f; (as food) agnī́n·a -ae f; **lambs bleat** agnī bālant

lamp lucérn·a -ae f

land s terr·a -ae f; (a piece of land) ag·er -rī m

land intr (of a ship) (ad terram) appéll·ō -ere áppulī; (of a passenger on a ship) in terram ēgrédior -ī ēgréssus sum; (of a plane) deórsum appéllere; (of a bird) (on) īnsī́d·ō -ere īnsḗdī (+ dat)

landing (of a plane) appúls·us -ūs m; (on stairs) scālári·um -ī n

landscape regiṓnis form·a -ae f

language lingu·a -ae f, serm·ō -ṓnis m; **the Latin language** lingua Latína, sermō Latínus

language lab officī́n·a -ae f loquēláris

lap grémi·um -ī n

laptop (comput) computátrul·um -ī n portábile

lark alaúd·a -ae f (see **bird**)

last adj últim·us -a -um; (in line) novíssim·us -a -um; (immediately preceding) próxim·us -a -um; (adj used where English uses an adv) novíssim·us -a -um, e.g., **Cicero spoke last** Cícerō novíssimus locū́tus est; **at last** dēmum; **last night** herī vésperī, próximā nocte; **the night before last** superiṓre nocte

last intr dūráre, perdūráre

late adj sēr·us -a -um

late adv sērō; **all too late** immō iam sērō; **too late** sérius; **very late** sēríssimē

lately nūper

later pósteā; **a little later** pósteā aliquántō; **postpone till later** díf·ferō -férre dístulī dīlátus in áliud tempus

latest: at latest summum; **perhaps tomorrow, at latest the day after that** fortásse crās, summum peréndiē

Latin (to know, read, teach, speak, understand, write) Latī́nē; **are you learning Latin?** discísne Latī́nē?; **did you forget Latin?** esne oblítus (-a) Lātī́nē?; **do you know Latin?** nōstíne Latī́nē?; **do you know how to speak Latin?** scīsne Latī́nē lóquī?; **do you read Latin easily?** legísne Latī́nē fácile?; **do you speak Latin (fluently)?** loquerísne Latī́nē (prōfluénter)?; **do you teach Latin?** docḗsne Latī́nē?; **do you understand Latin?** intellegísne Latī́nē?; **first-year Latin** prīmus Latīnitátis ann·us -ī m; **since when have you been learning Latin?** ex quō témpore Latī́nē didicístī?; **where did you**

study Latin? ubi Latíne studuístī?; **who is able to write Latin?** quis Latíne scríbere potest?

Latin teacher Latīnitátis magístr•a -ae *f or* magíst•er -rī *m*

Latium Láti•um -ī *n (district in which Rome lies)*

laugh ríd•eō -ére rīsī; **I laughed till I cried** rīsī ūsque ad lácrimās; **laugh at** rīdére

laundry fullónic•a -ae *f,* officín•a -ae *f* lavātória; *(dirty clothes)* lavandári•a -órum *npl*

lavender lavanduláce•us -a -um

law lēx, lēgis *f; (divine law)* fas *n (indecl); (denoting the entire body of law)* iūs, iūris *n;* **against the law** contrā iūs; *(against a specific law)* contrā lēgem; **by law** lēge; **break the law** lēgem violáre; **in accordance with the law** lēge

lawfully legítimē

lawn prátul•um -ī *n;* **mow the lawn** prátulum resecáre

lawnmower herbiséctr•um -ī *n*

lawsuit lī•s -tis *f;* **bring** *(or* **file) a lawsuit against s.o.** lītem álicui inténd•ō -ere -ī

lawyer iūriscōnsúlt•us -ī *m (•a -ae f); (trial lawyer)* causídic•us -ī *m (•a -ae f) (for the defense)* advocát•us -ī *m (•a -ae f)*

lay *(to place)* pōn•ō -ere pósuī pósitus; *(bricks)* stru•ō -ere -xī -ctus; *(eggs)* pár•iō -ere péperī; **lay a finger on s.o.** áliquem ūnō dígitō attíng•ō -ere áttigī; **lay off!** désine *(pl:* désínite) tandem!

layer the hair comam in gradūs fráng•ō -ere frēgī frāctus

layover commoráti•ō -ónis *f*

laziness ignávi•a -ae *f*

lazy ignáv•us -a -um, pi•ger -gra -grum

lead dūc•ō -ere dūxī ductus; **all roads lead to Rome** omnēs viae Rōmam dūcunt

lead pencil stil•us -ī *m* plumbátus, gráphi•um -ī *n*

leader prínc•eps -ipis *m*

learn disc•ō -ere dídicī; **learn by heart** ēdíscere; **learn thoroughly** perdíscere

learned doct•us -a -um, ērudít•us -a -um

learner disc•ēns -éntis *mf*

leash *s* cíngul•um -ī *n*

leash *tr* **(a dog)** (canem) cíngulō alligáre

least mínimē; **at least** útique, saltem

leather *s* córi•um -ī *n*

leather *adj* ex córiō; *(for weatherproofing)* scórte•us -a -um; **leather raincoat** scórte•a paénul•a -ae *f*

leave *(depart)* discéd•ō -ere discéssī discessúrus; *(office)* áb•eō -íre -iī (+ *abl);* **leave it up to s.o. to ...** álicui mandáre ut (+ *subj);* **leave me alone!** omítte *(pl:* omíttite) mē!; **leave no stone unturned** nullō locō dēsum dēésse défuī

leave of absence commeát•us -ūs *m*

lecherous libīdinós•us -a -um

lecture ācroás•is -is *f; (explicating an author)* praelécti•ō -ónis *f;* **give a lecture** ācroásin fácere, sermónem habére

lecture hall audītóri•um -ī *n*

left siníst•er -ra -rum, laev•us -a -um; **on the left** ā sinístrā; **(to the) left** sinistrórsum

leg crūs, crūris *n*

legal lēgítim•us -a -um, secúndum lēgem *or* lēgēs

legally lēgítimē, lēge *or* lḗgibus

legislation lēgisláti•ō -ṓnis *f*

legislator lēgislát•or -ṓris *m (in Roman government, a proposer of a bill)*

leisure time ṓti•um -ī *n*

lemon cítre•um -ī *n*

lemonade līmonắt•a -ae *f*

length longitū́d•ō -inis *f;* **in length** in longitū́dinem

lengthen *tr* prōdū́c•ō -ere prōdū́xī prōdū́ctus *(opp:* corrípere)

lengthwise per longitū́dinem

lens lēns, lentis *f* óptica

lentil lēn•s -tis *f*

leopard pard•us -ī *m*

lesson lḗcti•ō -ṓnis *f,* praecépt•um -ī *n*

let permítt•ō -ere permī́sī permíssus; **let fall:** dēmítt•ō -ere dēmī́sī dēmíssus; **let fly** ēmítt•ō -ere ēmī́sī ēmíssus; **let me go!** mitte *(pl:* míttite) mē!; **let me know** fac *(pl:* fácite) ut sciam; **let me see** licet (ut) videam; **let s.o. down** álicui dēsum dēésse dḗfuī; **let's go** eámus; **let up** *(of rain, snow)* dētumḗscit -ere

letter *s* epístul•a -ae *f,* lítter•ae -árum *(of the alphabet)* lítter•a -ae *f;* **letters form syllables** lítterae fáciunt sýllabās

letter opener ēnsícul•us -ī *m* epistuláris

lettuce lactū́c•a -ae *f*

leukemia leukaémi•a -ae *f*

level *s (instrument)* lībr•a -ae *f* (aquária); **be on a level with s.o.** par esse álicuī

lever vect•is -is *m*

librarian bibliothēcári•us *m* (•a -ae *f)*

library bibliothḗc•a -ae *f*

license *(to drive)* diplṓm•a -atis *n* gubernātiṓnis

license plate notácul•um -ī *n* autocīnḗtī

lie *s* fals•um -ī *n,* mendáci•um -ī *n;* **tell a lie** mendácium dī́cere

lie *intr (be lying down)* iác•eō -ēre -uī; *(in bed)* cub•ō -áre -uī; *(be situated)* sit•us -a -um esse; *(tell a lie)* mént•ior -ī́rī mentī́tus sum; **lie down** *(to rest)* dēcúmb•ō -ere dēcúbuī; **lie in the direction of** verg•ō -ere ad (+ *acc)*

lieutenant locumten•ēns -éntis *mf*

life vīt•a -ae *f;* **but such is life** sed vīta fert; **it's not a question of life or death** nōn cápitis rēs ágitur; **lead the life of Riley** vītam Chiam ger•ō -ere gessī; **on my life!** ita vīvam!

life imprisonment: give s.o. life imprisonment áliquem damnáre cárcerī quoad vīvat

lift weights librāménta toll•ō -ere sústulī sublátus

ligament ligám•en -inis *n*

light *s* lūm•en -inis (ēléctricum) *n;* **turn on (off) the light** lūmen accénd•ō -ere -ī accénsus (expéd•iō -íre -ī́vī)

light *adj* **make light of** in levī habḗre

light bulb glóbul•us -ī *m* ēléctricus

lighter ignitábul•um -ī *n*

lightning *s* fulm•en -inis *n;* **be struck by lightning** fúlmine *(or* ē caelō) īcor īcī ictus sum

lightning *intr* **it is lightning** fulget fulgḗre fulsit, fulguráre

lightning bug musc•a -ae *f* ignífera

like *adj* símil•is -is -e (+ *gen or, more rarely, dat);* **he said something like this** haec ferē dīxit; **that's more like it** propémodum est

like *tr (care for)* cūráre; **I'd like to** velim (+ *inf);* **I'd like you to come**

velim (ut) vénias; **I like s.th. (best)** áliquid mihi (potíssimum) placet; **I like summer** aestās mihi placet; **I like the city** urbs mē déléctat; **I like this** hoc mihi placet; **I like to do this** mē iuvat hoc fácere; **I like to watch the races** libénter circénsēs spectō

likely vērīsímil·is -is -e; **it is more likely that ...** vērīsimílius est *(acc + inf);* **most likely she will come** próximum est ut véniat *(or* vērīsímllimē est eam ventûram esse)*

line líne·a -ae *f; (of prose or poetry)* vers·us -ūs *m;* **draw a line with a ruler** líneam per régulam dûcere; **drop me a line when you have time** scrībe áliquid litterárum quandō vacās; **form a long line** longum agmen fácere; **in a straight line** per dīréctum, rēctā; **he's feeding you a line** verba tibi iste dat; **lay it on the line** dīréctum loquor loquī locútus sum

linen *adj* líne·us -a -um; **linen cloth** sában·um -ī *n*

linen *s* línteum -ī *n,* līn·um -ī *n*

linesman *(sports)* iūd·ex -icis *m* līneárius

link *s (comput)* cōnéx·us -ūs *m*

link *tr (comput)* cōnéct·ō -ere cōnéxuī cōnéxus

linker *(comput)* cōnéctr·um -ī *n*

linking *(comput)* cōnéxi·ō -ónis *f*

lion le·ō -ónis *m,* leaén·a -ae *f;* **lions roar** leónēs rúgiunt

lip labr·um -ī *n;* **lower lip** labrum ínférius; **upper lip** labrum supérius; **keep a stiff upper lip** fac, ut ánimō fortī sīs

list númer·us -ī *m; (e-mail list)* grex, gregis *m* (interrētiális)

listless dēs·es -idis

list owner *(comput)* gregis moderá·tor -tóris *m* (·trīx -trícis *f*)

liter lītr·a -ae *f*

literal *adj* própri·us -a -um *(opp:* trānslātívus)

literally *adv* próprie, ad verbum *(opp:* figūrátē)

litter lectíc·a -ae *f*

little *adj* parv·us -a -um; **for a little while** paulísper; **little brother** frátércul·us -ī *m;* **little sister** sorórcul·a -ae *f*

little *adv* paulum; **a little** paúlulum; **a little bigger** paulō ámplior

live *(be alive)* vīv·ō -ere vīxī víctum; *(reside)* habitáre; **live it up** victitáre volup; **live near,** *(in the case of a river)* **live on the banks of** áccol·ō -ere -uī accúltum; **live on** *(e.g., a venison)* vesc·or -ī *(+ abl);* **you're living on borrowed time** dē lucrō vīvis *(pl:* vívitis)

live *adj* vīv·us -a -um

liveliness alácrit·ās -átis *f*

lively ála·cer -cris -cre

liver iec·ur -oris *n*

livestock pec·us -oris *n*

living *s* **make a living** quaestum fácere *or* vīctum quaeritáre

living room sessóri·um -ī *n,* synoéci·um -ī *n*

lizard lacért·us -ī *m,* lacért·a -ae *f*

loaded *(with money)* cōpiós·us -a -um; *(drunk)* mádid·us -a -um

loaf *intr* cessáre

loaf of bread pān·is -is *m*

loan argént·um ī *n* mútuum; **may I hit you for a loan?** licetne tē mútuō feríre?

lobster ástac·us -ī *m*

local number númer·us -ī *m* locális

local train trām·en -inis *n* commúne

located sit·us -a -um

lock up occlú·dō -dere -sī -sus; *(in prison)* in cárcerem compíng·ō -ere -ī compégī compáctus

locket *(worn by boys, of leather, silver or gold)* bull·a -ae *f;* **wearing a locket** bullát·us -a -um

locust lōcúst·a -ae *f;* **locusts chirp** lōcústae strīdent

log in *intr (comput)* ín·eō -íre -ívī *or* -iī

log out *intr (comput)* éx·eō -íre -ívī *or* -iī

loneliness sōlitúd·ō -inis *f*

lonely sōl·us -a -um

long *adj* long·us -a -um, prōdúct·us -a -um *(opp:* brevis, corréptus); **a vowel is long by nature or by position** vocális est longa nātúrā aut positióne; **fifteen miles long** quíndecim mília pássuum *(often written:* p.) in longitúdinem *or* quíndecim mília pássuum in longitúdinem patēns

long *adv* diū; **(for a) long time now** iamdúdum; **how long** quam diū; **how much longer** quámdiū étiam; **it would take too long to ...** longum erat *(+ inf);* **long ago** prídem; **long after (before)** multō post (ante); **longer** diútius; **too long** diútius, nímium diū

long-distance number númer·us -ī *m* longínquus

long for dēsīderáre

longing (for) dēsīdéri·um -ī *n (+ gen)*

long jump *(sports)* salt·us -ūs *m* in longum

long-sleeved manicát·us -a -um

look aspíc·iō -ere aspéxī aspéctus; *(appear, seem)* vídeor vidérī vīsus sum; **it looks that way to me** ita mihi vidétur; **look!** ecce!; **look after** cūráre; **look around** circumspícere; **look at** īnspíc·iō -ere īnspéxī īnspéctus; **look down on** *(despise)* dēspectáre; **look for** qaer·ō -ere quaesívī quaesítus: **aha, the very person I was looking for!** attat, quem quaerébam!; **look forward to** exspectáre; **look here, you!** eho tū!; **look into** īnspícere; *(examine)* perscrūtárī; **look like** víd·eor -érī vīsus sum similis (+ *dat or gen*); **I don't know what he** *(or she)* **looks like** quā sit fácie, nésciō; **look out of the window** ex fenéstrā prōspícere; **look over** *(someone)* contempláre; *(a book, essay)* perlég·ō -ere perlégī; **look someone in the eye** áliquem rēctīs óculīs intú·eor -érī intúitus sum; **look up** *(a reference)* inquír·ō -ere inquīsívī inquiīsítus in (+ *acc);* **look up at** suspícere; **look up to** *(out of respect)* suspícere

look-out: keep a careful look-out ómnia circumspectáre

look-out man ind·ex -icis *m*

loose *(not tight)* lax·us -a -um; *(morally)* dissolút·us -a -um

loose-leaf folder collēctóri·um -ī *n*

loose-leaf tablet cōdicíll·us ī *m* chartárum

lose *(mostly unintentionally)* āmítt·ō -ere āmísī āmíssus; *(mostly blamably)* per·dō -dere -didī -ditus

lop-sided inaequál·is -is -e

loud *adj* magn·us -a -um, clār·us -a -um

loud *adv* magnā voce, clārē

loudmouth clāmát·or -óris *m,* clāmátr·īx -ícis *f*

loudspeaker megaphón·um -ī *n*

louse pēdícul·us -ī *m*

lousy foed·us -a -um; *(weather)* spurc·us -a -um; **feel lousy** sē male habére

lovable amábil·is -is -e

love *s* am·or -óris *m (followed by* erga *or* in + *acc, or by gen, if the object is not a person);* **fall in love at first sight** ūnō aspéctū in amórem íncid·ō -ere -ī

love *tr* amáre

lover amát·or -óris *m,* amátr·īx -ícis *f*

love seat bisélli·um -ī *n* (tōméntō fartum)

loving am·āns -ántis

low *intr (of cattle)* múg·iō -íre -ívī *or* -iī

low: I am low on *(e.g., paper)* (charta) mihi dēest; **in a low voice** summíssā vōce; **run low** dēfíc·iō -ere dēfécī

low-born ignóbil·is -is -e

lower jaw mandíbul·a -ae *f*

loyal fidél·is -is -e, fíd·us -a -um; **remain loyal** in fidē mán·eō -ére mānsī

loyalty fidélit·ās -átis *f*

lub job, lubrication úncti·ō -ónis *f* autocīnétī

luck fortún·a -ae *f;* **good luck!** fēlíciter!

luckily fēlíciter

lucky fēl·íx -ícis, fortūnát·us -a -um

luggage vās·a -órum *npl;* sárcin·ae -árum *fpl;* **piece of luggage** sárcin·a -ae *f; (small)* sarcínul·a -ae *f*

luggage rack retinácul·um -ī *n* sarcinále

luggage tag pittáci·um -ī *n* sarcinále

lump *s* tūbércul·um -ī *n*

lump *tr* **lump s.o. together with** áliquem accúd·ō -ere (+ *dat)*

lunch prándi·um -ī *n;* **eat lunch** pránd·eō -ére prandī; **have lunch** prándium súm·ō -ere sūmpsī sūmptus

lung pulm·ō -ónis *m*

lust cupídit·ās -átis *f; (sexual desire)* libíd·ō -inis *f*

lying falsíloqu·us -a -um

lyre lyr·a -ae *f*

macaroni past·a -ae *f* tubuláta

machine máchin·a -ae *f*

machinery māchinále īnstrūmént·um -ī *n*

machinist māchinát·or -óris *m*

mackerel scomb·er -rī *m*

mad *(insane)* īnsán·us -a -um; *(angry)* īrát·us -a -um; **be mad about** *(be madly in love with)* dēpér·iō -íre -iī (+ *acc);* **go mad** mente aliēnárī; **I'm mad at you** tibi suscénseō *or* ego tibi īrátus sum

magazine commentári·ī -órum *mpl* periódicī imāgíneī

magic *s* mágica ar·s -tis *f;* **practice magic** mágicās artēs exérc·eō -ére -uī

magic, magical *adj* mágic·us -a -um; **do magic tricks** praestígi·or -árī

magician mag·us -ī *m,* mag·a -ae *f*

magistracy magistrát·us -ūs *m*

magistrate magistrát·us -ūs *m*

magnetic magnétic·us -a -um

maid ancíll·a -ae *f,* fámul·a -ae *f*

mail *s* epístul·ae -árum *fpl,* rēs (rērum) *fpl* cursuálēs; *(postal system)* curs·us -ūs *m* públicus; *(comput)* lítter·ae -árum *fpl* ēlectrónicae, epístul·a -ae *f* ēlectrónica; **deliver mail** rēs cursuálēs red·dō -dere -didī -ditus; **forward mail** rēs cursuálēs déferō dēférre détulī dēlátus; **stack of mail** multíiugae lítterae *fpl*

mail *tr* dō dare dedī datus; **I mailed the letter yesterday** lítterās herī dedī

mailbox cápsul·a -ae *f* tabellária

mailman tabellári·us -ī *m*

mainland cóntin·ēns -éntis *f*

main road vi·a -ae *f* prīncipális

major in óperam prīmáriam (cuidam disciplínae) dare

make believe that adsimuláre quasi (+ *subj*), simuláre (+ *acc w. inf*)

malaria malári·a -ae *f*

mall for·um -ī *n* subtēguláneum

man vir, virī *m*

manage cūráre; *(e.g., a bank)* móder·or -árī -átus sum; *(esp. on a large scale)* administráre; **if you can manage it** sī id cōnfícere póteris

manager moderát·or -óris *m,* moderátr·īx -ícis *f*

mane iūb·a -ae *f*

manuscript manuscrípt·um -ī *n*

many mult·ī -ae -a

map chart·a -ae *f* geográphica; **map of the world** orb·is -is *m* terrárum pīctus

March *s* mēns·is -is *m* Mártius; **in March** mēnse Mártiō

march *intr* iter fácere

margarine margarín·um -ī *n*

marine míl·es -itis *m* clássicus; **the marines** classiári·ī -órum *mpl*

mark *tr (draw or make a mark on anything)* notáre; *(set down mentally)* dēsignáre; **mark my words** ánimum inténde *(pl:* inténdite*)* in dicta mea

mashed potatoes pultícul·a -ae *f* ex solánīs

mason fa·ber -brī *m* lapidárius

mast māl·us -ī *m*

master's degree grad·us -ūs *m* magistrális

match rāmént·um -ī *n* flammíferum; *(sports)* certám·en -inis *n*

mathematics mathemátic·a -ae *f*

matter *s* rēs, reī *f;* **for that matter** ádeō; **no matter how…** quamvīs (+ *subj*); **what on earth's the matter?** quidnam est?; **what's the matter with you?** quid est tēcum? *or* quid istuc est reī?

matter *intr* **it doesn't matter to me** nihil ad mē pértinet; **what does that matter to me (you, us)?** quid id meā (tuā, nōbīs) rēfert?

mattress cúlcit·a -ae *f;* **air mattress** cúlcita īnflátilis

may: I (you, *etc.*) **may** mihi (tibi, *etc.*) licet; **may I leave?** licétne mihi abíre *or* licétne mihi (ut) ábeam? *(Note: in short phrases the* ut *is often omitted)*

May mēns·is -is *m* Māius; **in May** mēnse Māiō

maybe fortásse

mayonnaise liquám·en -inis *n* Magónicum

mayor urbis magís·ter -trī *m,* (·tra -trae *f*)

meadow prāt·um -ī *n*

meal cib·us -ī *m*

mean *tr* significáre; *(intend)* volō velle voluī; **do you know whom I mean?** scīsne quem dīcam?; **do you mean me?** mēne vīs? **yes, you** tē; **do you really mean it?** Aisne vērō? **Yes, I do** aiō; **how do you mean that?** quī istuc vīs?; **now you know what I mean** scīs iam quid loquar; **what does this mean?** quid hoc sibi vult?; **what do you mean?** quid tibi vīs?; **what do you mean by that?** quid istuc est verbī?; **what I mean is** *(in correcting a misunderstanding)* at enim

meaning s significắti·ō -ốnis f

means: by all means! mắximē!, immo!;
by fair means rēctē; **by means of**
render by abl or per (+ acc); **by no
means** haudquắquam

meanwhile ínterim

measles morbíli·i -ốrum mpl

measure intr pắt·eō -ḗre -uī, cốllig·ō
-ere collḗgī; **measuring ten miles in
circumference** patēns (or cốlligēns)
decem mília pássuum circúitū

meat car·ō -nis f

meatball glốbul·us -ī m cárneus

meat grinder mắchin·a -ae f carnária

meat tray carnắri·um -ī n

mechanic mechắnicus ốpif·ex -icis m

medal nomísm·a -atis n; **gold (silver,
bronze) medal** nomísma aúreum
(argénteum, aéreum)

medical practice medicín·a -ae f

medication medicāmént·um -ī n

medicine medicín·a -ae f, medicắm·en
-inis n; **practice medicine**
medicínam exérc·eō -ḗre -uī

Mediterranean Sea intérnum mar·e -is
n, Tuscum mare, Tyrrhḗnum mare

meet tr & intr con·véniō -veníre -vḗnī
-véntus

meeting congréss·us -ūs m

megaphone megaphṓn(i)·um -ī n

melt tr dissól·vō -vere -vī -útus **‖** intr
liquḗsc·ō -ere

member (of the body) membr·um -ī n;
(of an organization) sodắl·is -is mf

memorize ēdísc·ō -ere ēdídicī

memory memóri·a -ae f; **commit to
memory** memóriae mandắre; **have a
good memory** bonā memóriā esse; **if
my memory serves me right** sī ego

satis comméminī; **in memory of** in
memóriam (+ gen)

mend (clothes) sárc·iō -íre sarsī sartus

mention s ménti·ō -ốnis f; **since
mention has been made of money**
quóniam nummốrum méntiō facta est

mention tr **I don't want to mention
him by name** eum nōlō nōminắre;
not to mention ut nōn (or nihil)
dīcam dē (+ abl); **not to mention the
fact that** ... ut mittam quod (+ indic)

menu cibốrum ind·ex -icis m, cibốrum
tabéll·a -ae f; (comput) iussốrum
tabéll·a -ae f

merchandise vēnālíci·a -ốrum npl,
merc·ēs -ium fpl

merchant mercắt·or -ốris m; (in a
market) macellắri·us -ī m (·a -ae f)

mermaid nymph·a -ae f marína

merrily hílarē, fēstívē

merry hílar·is -is -e, hílar·us -a -um;
Merry Christmas! Faustum ac
Fēlícem Chrīstī Nātắlem (tibi
exóptō)! Fausta Fēsta Nātālícia
Chrīstī (tibi exóptō)!

merry-go-round circumvectắbul·um -ī n

mess (dirt) squāl·or -ốris m; (confusion)
turb·a -ae f; **geez, what a mess!** eu
édepol rēs turbuléntās!; **make a mess
of it** turbās concí·eō -ḗre concívī
concítus

message núnti·us -ī m

metal metáll·um -ī n

meter (unit of measure, verse) metr·um
-ī n

meticulous accūrắt·us -a -um

microphone microphốn·um -ī n

microscope microscópi·um -ī n

microwave oven furn·us -ī m undắrum
brévium

middle class ōrd•ō -inis *m* médius; *(in Rome)* équit•ēs -um *mpl*

middle school schol•a -ae *f* média

midget nān•us -ī *m,* nān•a -ae *f*

midnight média no•x, -ctis *f;* **around midnight** médiā círciter nocte; **at midnight** (dē) médiā nocte; **before midnight** ante médiam noctem

midwife obstétr•īx -ícis *f*

migraine hēmicráni•a -ae *f;* **have a migraine headache** dól•eō -ére -uī ab hēmicrániā

mild clém•ēns -éntis, mīt•is -is -e

mile mille pass•ūs -uum *mpl;* **two miles** duo mília *npl* pássuum

military mīlitár•is -is -e; **military age** aet•ās -ātis *f* mīlitáris; **military service** mīlíti•a -ae *f;* **enter military service** mīlítiam infre; **perform military service** mīlitáre; **the military** mīlíti•a -ae *f*

milk *s* lac lactis *n*

milk *tr* múl•geō -gére -sī -sus *or* -ctus

mince: without mincing words sine fūcō ac falláciīs

mind *s* mēn•s -tis *f,* ánim•us -ī *m;* **be in one's right mind** apud sē esse; **change one's mind** mentem mūtáre; **come to mind** in mentem veníre; **enter my mind** mihi in mentem veníre; **have in mind to** in ánimō habére (+ *inf*); **he's out of his mind** aliēnátus est ā sē; **I made up my mind to leave** constítuī hinc abíre *or* certum est mihi hinc abíre; **I was out of my mind when ...** dēsipiébam mentis cum ... ; **it slipped my mind to write to you** fūgit mē ad tē scríbere; **of sound mind** comp•os -otis mentis; **set your mind at ease** habē ánimum lēnem et tranquíllum;

what's on your mind? quid tibi in ánimō est?

mind *tr (look after)* cūráre, tú•eor -érī túitus sum; *(regard)* respíc•iō -ere respéxī respéctus; *(object to)* aegrē *(or* moléstē) ferō ferre tulī lātus; **I don't mind if you stay** nōn labórō sī manēs; **if you don't mind** sī tibi moléstum nōn est; sī tibi vidétur; **mind my words** auscúltā *(pl:* auscultáte) dictīs meīs!; **mind one's own business** negótium suum agō ágere ēgī; **never mind!** sine! *(pl:* sínite!); **never mind what he says** mitte *(pl:* míttite) quod dīcit

mine *s* metáll•um -ī *n,* fodín•a -ae *f;* **coal mine** fodín•a -ae *f* carbōnária; **gold mine** aurifodín•a -ae *f;* **gold (lead, iron, copper, silver, tin) mine** metállum aurī (plumbī, ferrī, cuprī, argéntī, plumbī albī)

mine *tr* effód•iō -ere effódī effóssus

miner metallári•us -ī *m,* fōss•or -óris *m*

mineral water aqu•a -ae *f* minerális

mine shaft fodínae púte•us -ī *m*

miniskirt cástul•a -ae *f* brevíssima *(or* dēcurtáta)

minister *(eccl)* minís•ter -trī *m* (•tra -trae *f),* pāst•or -óris *m*

minute minút•a, -ae *f;* **in a minute** mōméntō témporis; **the minute I saw you** extémplō ubi ego tē vīdī; **this minute** *(right now)* iam; *(immediately)* āctútum; **wait a minute** manē dum

mirror spécul•um -ī *n;* **look at oneself in the mirror** sē in spéculō intú•eor -érī; **look into the mirror** in spéculum īnspíc•iō -ere īnspéxī īnspéctus

misbehave sē male *(or* indecórē) ger•ō -ere gessī

miserable mis·er -era -erum

misery miséri·a -ae *f*

misquote: you are misquoting me mē aliīs verbīs pōnis

miss *(feel the want of)* dēsīderáre; *(pass by without noticing)* praeter·míttō -míttere -mísī; **miss the mark** dēstinátō aberráre

missile missíl·e -is *n*

mist nébul·a -ae *f*

mistake err·or -óris *m*, errát·um -ī *n; (esp. in writing)* mend·um -ī *n;* **by mistake** imprúdēns, pérperam; **make a mistake** erráre; **you're making a big mistake** errās pervérsē *or* veheménter errās

mistaken *(idea)* fáls·us -a -um; **unless I am mistaken** nisi fallor

misty nebulós·us -a -um

mixed salad commíxta acētári·a -órum *npl*

mixer máchin·a -ae *f* mīxtória

mobile home domúncul·a -ae *f* subrotáta; *(trailer home)* habitácul·um -ī *n* remulcátum

model exémpl·ar -áris *n; (of clothes)* vestimentórum mōnstátr·īx -ícis *f (or* mōnstrát·or -óris *m)*

modem *(comput)* trānsmodulátr·um -ī *n*

moderate *(of persons)* moderát·us -a -um; *(of things)* módic·us -a -um; **of moderate size** módic·us -a -um

modest modést·us -a -um

modesty modésti·a -ae *f*

modify *tr* adícior ádicī adiéctus sum (+ *dat);* **which noun does "bonus" modify?** cui nómini "bonus" adícitur?

modifying *adj* adiéct·us -a -um (+ *dat)*

mole talp·a -ae *f*

molars dentēs *mpl* māxillárēs

mom mamm·a -ae *f*

moment mómént·um -ī *n* témporis; **at any moment** ómnibus moméntīs; **at the very moment** ipsō témpore; **at the very same moment** pūnctō témporis eódem; **for a moment** paulísper; **in a moment** *(i.e., presently)* statim; **just a moment ago** modo

Monday di·ēs -éī *m* Lūnae

money argént·um -ī *n*, pecúni·a -ae *f*, numm·ī -órum *mpl; (of paper)* monét·a -ae *f* chartácea

money belt ventrál·e -is *n; (of cloth)* zōn·a -ae *f*

money order (nummárium) mandát·um -ī *n* cursuále

monitor *(comput)* monitóri·um -ī *n*, caps·a -ae *f* computātrális

monkey sími·us -ī *m*, sími·a -ae *f;* **monkeys chatter** símiī strīdent

monopoly monopóli·um -ī *n;* **play monopoly** monopóliō lúdere

monosyllable *s* monosýllab·a -ae *f*

month mēns·is -is *m*

monument monumént·um -ī *n*

moo múg·iō -íre -ívī *or* -iī

mood afféct·us -ūs *m* ánimī, ánim·us -ī *m; (gram)* mod·us -ī *m;* **be in a good mood** bonum ánimum habére; **get over one's mood** ánimum superáre; **imperative mood,** *e.g.,* **"read!"** modus imperātívus, ut "lege!"; **indicative mood,** *e.g.,* **"I read"** modus indicātívus, ut "legō"; **subjunctive mood,** *e.g.,* **"although I read"** modus subiūnctívus, ut "cum legam"

moose alc·ēs -is *f*

moped autobirótul·a -ae *f*

more *adj* plūs, plūris *n;* plūr•ēs -ium *mf pl; (denoting greater extent of space or time; also number)* ámplius; **more (things)** plūr•a -ium *npl;* **but more of this another time** sed dē hōc áliās plū́ribus; **more money, strength, power** plūs pecū́niae, vírium, poténtiae

more *adv* magis; **more or less** magis minúsve; **more than** magis quam; **more (less) than ... years old** māior (minor) ... annōs nāt•us -a -um

moreover praetérea

morning mātūtī́n•um -ī *n,* temp•us -oris *n* mātūtī́num; **early in the morning** bene māne, multō māne; **from morning till evening** ā māne ūsque ad vésperam; **good morning!** salvē!; **in the morning** māne; **sleep all morning** tōtum māne dormíre; **the next morning** māne postrī́diē; **this morning** hódiē māne

mortar harēnā́t•um -ī *n*

mortgage *s* hypothḗc•a -ae *f;* **pay off a mortgage** hypothḗcam līberā́re; **take out a mortgage** hypothḗcam obligā́re

mortgage *tr* hypothḗcā obligā́re

mosquito cul•ex -icis *m*

most *adj* plerī́que, pleraéque, pléraque; **most people** plerī́que *or* plerī́que hóminēs

most *adv (with verbs)* máximē; *(with adjs and advs, expressed by the superlative degree); (in the case of an adj in -ius máximē + positive)*

mostly *(for the most part, principally)* máximam partem; *(generally)* plērúmque

motel dēversṓri•um -ī *n* vehiculā́rium

moth blatt•a -ae *f*

mother mā•ter -tris *f*

mother-in-law socr•us -ūs *f*

motherless mātre orb•us -a -um

motherly mātérn•us -a -um

motion mōt•us -ūs *m; (parl)* senténti•a -ae *f;* **approve a motion** senténtiam comprobā́re; **make a motion regarding** réferō reférre réttulī relā́tus dē (+ *abl);* **on my motion** mē referénte; **oppose a motion** senténtiae [*dat*] obsíst•ō -ere óbstitī

motivate concitā́re

motivation (for) rátiō -ṓnis *f* (+ *gen*)

motive caus•a -ae *f,* rátiō -ṓnis *f;* **what was his motive in coming?** Cuius reī causā vénerat?; **he had a strong motive** magna rátiō eī erat

motor mōtṓri•um -ī *n,* mōtr•um -ī *n*

motor boat scaph•a -ae *f* automatā́ria

motorcycle autobírot•a -ae *f*

motorcylist autobirotā́ri•us -ī *m* (•a -ae *f*)

motorist autoraedā́ri•us -ī *m* (•a -ae *f*), autocīnētíst•ēs -ae *mf*

motor oil óle•um -ī *n* mōtṓriī

mountain mōn•s -tis *m*

mountain chain mont•ēs -ium *mpl* perpétuī

mountain climbing ascénsi•ō -ṓnis *f* móntium *(see Chapter V)*

mountainous montuṓs•us -a -um, montā́n•us -a -um

mourn *tr & intr* lū́g•eō -ḗre lūxī lūctus

mourning maer•or -ṓris *m; (outward expression of grief)* lūct•us -ūs *m*

mouse *(animal)* mūs, mūris *m); (comput)* mūs, mūris *m,* mū́scul•us -ī *m;* **mice squeak** mūrēs míntriunt

mouse clicker *(comput)* mūris pulsā́bul•um -ī *n*

mouth ōs, ōris *n; (of a river)* ṓsti•um -ī *n;* **I had better keep my mouth shut**

táceam óptimum est; **shut your mouth!** óbserā ōs tuum!

move *tr* móv·eō -ḗre mōvī mōtus **‖** *intr* movḗrī, sē movḗre; *(to change residence)* migrā́re

movie taeníol·a -ae *f* cīnēmatográphica, fắbul·a -ae *f* cīnēmatográphica; **go to see (watch) a movie** taeníolam cīnēmatográphicam vīs·ō -ere -ī; **show a movie** taeníolam cīnēmatográphicam exhíb·eō -ḗre -uī -itus *(see Chapter V)*

movie camera māchínul·a -ae *f* cīnēmatográphica

movie projector prōiectṓri·um -ī *n* cīnēmatográphicum

movie screen línte·um -ī *n* lātē exténtum

movie theater cīnēmatḗ·um -ī *n;* **go the movie theater** *(or* **to the movies)** in cīnēmatḗum eō īre īvī

movies imágin·ēs -um *fpl* movéntēs

mow the lawn grāmen *(or* prátulum) résecō -ā́re -uī -tus

muffin scriblī́t·a -ae *f*

mug *s (cup)* pócul·um -ī *n*

mug *tr* mulcā́re

mugger percúss·or -ṓris *m*

muggy aestuṓs·us -a -um

mulberry mōr·um -ī *n*

mule mūl·us -ī *m,* mūl·a -ae *f;* **mules bray** mūlī rudunt

mull over aestuā́re in (+ *abl*)

mumps parōtī́t·is -idis *f*

municipality mūnicípi·um -ī *n*

murder *s* nex, necis *f (passive in sense while* caedēs *is active in sense); (by hacking or striking)* caed·ēs -is *f,* occī́si·ō -ṓnis *f*

murder *tr (by wicked and cruel means)* necā́re; *(violently and ruthlessly)*

trūcīdā́re; *(by hacking or striking)* caed·ō -ere cecī́dī caesus

murderer necā́t·or -ṓris *m,* homicī́d·a -ae *mf; (of a father, mother, or near relative)* parricī́d·a -ae *mf*

murderess necā́tr·īx -ī́cis *f*

muscle mū́scul·us -ī *m;* **pull a muscle** mū́sculum distórqu·eō -ḗre distórsī distórtus

muscle-bound mū́sculīs cōntríct·us -a -um

muscular mūsculṓs·us -a -um

museum mūsḗ·um -ī *n*

mushroom fung·us -ī *m; (a choice kind)* bōlḗt·us -ī *m*

music mū́sic·a -ae *f*

musical mū́sic·us -a -um; **musical instrument** īnstrūmént·um -ī *n* mū́sicum; **musical note** not·a -ae *f* mūsicā́lis

musician mū́sic·us -ī *m* (·a -ae *f*)

must: I (you) must go mihi (tibi) eúndum est

mustache súbi·um -ī *n*

mustard sinā́p·is -is *f*

mutter mussā́re

mutual mū́tu·us -a -um

myth mȳth·os -ī *m*

mythological mȳthólógic·us -a -um

mythology mȳthológi·a -ae *f*

my me·us -a -um

my oh my! vae míserō (-ae) mihi!

nag *tr* obiurgitā́re

nail clav·us -ī *m; (of a finger, toe)* ungu·is -is *m;* **cut the nails** unguēs résec·ō -ā́re -uī -tus; **drive in a nail** clāvum fīg·ō -ere fīxī fīxus; **you hit the nail on the head** tū rem acū tetigístī

nail *tr* **(to)** clāvō *(or* clāvīs) cōnfīg·ō -ere cōnfīxī cōnfīctus (+ *dat of that to which);* **to nail (boards) together** (tábulās) inter sē clāvīs cōnfīgere

name *s* nōm·en -inis *n;* **Varrō by name** nómine Varrō

name *tr* nōmināˊre; *(enumerate)* nuncupāˊre

nap brevis somn·us ī *m;* **take a nap** brevem somnum cápere

napkin mapp·a -ae *f,* máppul·a -ae *f*

narcotic medicāmént·um -ī *n* psychotrópium

narrow angúst·us -a -um, ténu·is -is -e

narrow-minded angúst·us -a -um; **be narrow-minded** angústī ánimī esse

narrow-mindedness angústi·ae -āˊrum *fpl* (péctoris)

nasty *(foul)* foed·us -a -um; *(mean)* turpis -is -e

nation gēn·s -tis *f*

natural secúndum nātúram; *(unaffected)* incompósit·us -a -um, simpl·ex -icis

naturally nātūrāˊliter; *(of course)* nempe, útpote; *(unaffectedly)* simplíciter

nature nātúr·a -ae *f; (physical world)* nātúra rērum; *(of a person)* ingéni·um -ī *n*

naughty ímprob·us -a -um; *(saucy)* pétul·āns -ántis

naval nāvāˊl·is -is -e

navel umbílic·us -ī *m*

navigable nāvigāˊbi·lis -is -e

navy cópi·ae -āˊrum *fpl* nāvāˊlēs; **have a powerful navy** nāˊvibus plúrimum posse

near *prep* prope (+ *acc)*

near *adj (not distant in place or time)* propínqu·us -a -um; *(neighboring)* vīcín·us -a -um (+ *dat),* prope (+ *acc)*

nearby in próximō

nearsighted my·ōps -ōˊpis

nearsightedness myóp·ia -ae *f*

neat *(clean; elegant)* mund·us -a -um; **neat!** óptimē!

necessary necessāˊri·us -a -um; **if it is necessary for you to stay on** sī opus est tē commorāˊrī; **if it is necessary for your health** sī opus est ad tuam valētúdinem; **it is necessary** necésse est

neck coll·um -ī *n,* cerv·īx -ˊīcis *f (usually used in the plural)*

necklace tórqu·ēs -is *m,* monīˊl·e -is *n; (of precious stones)* monīˊle gemmāˊtum

necktie fōcāˊl·e -is *n*

need dēsīderāˊre; ég·eō -ˊēre -uī (+ *abl, more rarely* + *gen);* **I (you, we) need money** opus est mihi (tibi, nōbīs) argéntō [*abl*]

needle ac·us -ūs *f*

needless to say quid quaeris?

needy in·ops -opis

negligence negligénti·a -ae *f,* incúri·a -ae *f*

negligent néglig·ēns -éntis

neigh *s* hinnīˊt·us -ūs *m*

neigh *intr* hínn·iō -ˊīre -iī; **neigh at** adhinnīˊre

neighbor *(on the border)* fīnítim·us -ī *m* (·a -ae *f); (nearby or next door)* próxim·us -ī *m* (·a -ae *f); (one in the neighborhood)* vīcín·us -ī *m* (·a -ae *f)*

neighborhood vīcíni·a -ae *f*

neither neu·ter -tra -trum; **that's neither here nor there** *(a matter of indifference)* susque dēque est

nephew fīˊli·us -ī *m* sorōˊris; fīˊlius frātris

nerd umbrátic·us -ī *m* (·a -ae *f)*

nerve nerv·us -ī *m;* **what nerve!** O audắciam!

nervous inténtus -a -um, trépid·us -a -um

nervousness trepidắti·ō -ốnis *f,* ánim·us -ī *m* trépidus

nest nīd·us -ī *m;* **build a nest** nīdificắre

net *(also comput)* rēt·e -is *n*

neuter *adj* neu·ter -tra -trum, neutrắl·is -is -e; **in the neuter** neutrắliter

neutral nullī́us partis (esse)

never numquam; **never yet** nōndum

nevertheless tamen, nihilōsḗtius

new nov·us -a -um

news *(esp. brought by a messenger)* nū́nti·us -ī *m;* **I just got news that** modo mihi nūntiắtum est (+ *acc w. inf);* **if you happen to have any news about ...** sī quid forte novī habēs dē (+ *abl);* **if you have no news about ...** sī nihil novī habēs dē (+ *abl);* **I'll tell you when I have any news** narrắbō, cum áliquid habḗbō novī; **is there any news?** numquid novī? **no other news** nihil praetéreā novī

news broadcast nū́ntiī -ốrum *mpl* (radiophốnicī, tēlevīsī́ficī)

newscast tēlediắri·um -ī *n*

newspaper āct·a -ốrum *npl* diúrna, diắri·um -ī *n;* **morning (evening) newspaper** diắrium matutī́num (vespertī́num); **newspaper article** commentắti·ō -ốnis *f;* **weekly newspaper** ācta hebdomadắlia

newsstand diāriốrum tabérnul·a -ae *f*

next *adj* próxim·us -a -um; **next to** próxim·us -a -um (+ *dat),* iuxtā (+ *acc)*

next *adv* próximē; **next comes, then ... then ... after that** unde ... dein ... dein ... inde ...

nice *(courteous)* cóncinn·us -a; *(in personality)* lépid·us -a; *(cute)* bell·us -a -um; **nice weather** caelum serḗnum; **it was nice of you to invite me, but no, thank you** bene vocās, sed tam grắtia est; **it wasn't nice of you to say that** nōn bellē fēcī́stī quī id dī́xeris

nick: you've come in the nick of time in ipsō artículo témporis ádvenīs

nickname agnốm·en -inis *n*

niece fī́li·a -ae *f* sorốris; fī́li·a -ae *f* frātris

night nox, noctis *f;* **at night** noctū, dē nocte; **at this time of night** hōc noctis; **by night** noctū, dē nocte; **day and night** *(continually)* per diēs et noctēs, diem noctémque; **every night** per sī́ngulās noctēs; **from morning till night** ā māne ad noctem ū́sque; **good night** *(greeting)* bene vắleās et quiḗscās; **last night** próximā nocte; **late at night** multā dē nocte; **night after night** per sī́ngulās noctēs; **night and day** *(continually)* noctēs et diēs; **one night** quādem nocte; **on the following night** próximā *(or* īnsequénte nocte; **(on) the night before last** superiốre nocte; **spend the night** pernoctắre; **till late at night** ad multam noctem

nightclub discothéc·a -ae *f*

nightfall: at nightfall sub noctem; **till nightfall** ū́sque ad noctem

nightgown camī́si·a -ae *f* noctúrna

nightmare sómni·um -ī turbuléntum; **have a nightmare** sómnium turbuléntum pát·ior -ī passus sum

night owl *(person)* noctis av·is -is *f;* *(bird)* nóctu·a -ae *f*

night table mḗnsul·a -ae *f* cubiculắris

nipple papíll·a -ae *f*

nitwit bárcal·a -ae *mf*

no *adj* núll·us -a -um; **no one** nēm·ō -inis *m*; **no parking** cavē státuās vehículum!; **no passing** cavē praeveháris!; **no stopping** nē sistitō!; **no way!** nūllō modō! *or* nēquáquam!

no *adv* nōn, mínimē; **no longer** nōn iam, nōn diútius

noble *(sentiments)* grand·is -is -e

nominative *adj* nōminatív·us -a -um

nonsense! nūgās! *(acc is frequent with exclamations)*

nonsense nūg·ae -árum *fpl*; **cut out the nonsense!** omítte *(pl:* omíttite) nūgās! **no nonsense!** nē nūgáre! **that's a lot of nonsense** nūgae sunt istae magnae; **you are talking nonsense** nūgās garris; nūgáris

noodle collýr·a -ae *f*

noodle soup iū·s -ris *n* collýricum

noon merídi·ēs -éī *m*; **at noon** merídiē; **before noon** antemerídiē

north *adj* septentriōnál·is -is -e

north *adv* ad septentriónēs; **north of** suprā (+ *acc*)

north *s* septentrión·ēs -um *mpl*; **on the north** ā septentriónibus

northern septentriōnál·is -is -e

northward in septentriónēs versus [versus *is an adverb*]

north wind Áquil·ō -ónis *m*

nose nās·us -ī *m*; **have a good nose for these things** haec fēstívē odōrárī; **under his very nose** ante óculōs

nosey cūriós·us -a -um; **I don't want to be nosey but ...** nōn libet cūriósus (-a) esse sed ...

nostrils nār·ēs -ium *fpl*

not nōn; haud *(more emphatic than* nōn, *and used chiefly before adjs and advs); (softened negative)* parum; **and not** nec, neque; **not at all** nōn omnínō; **not bad** nōn male; **not even** nē ... quidem; **not only ... but also** nōn sōlum ... sed étiam; **not that** nōn quod (+ *subj); **not yet** nōndum

note *s* not·a -ae *f; (short letter)* codicíll·ī -órum *mpl*; **musical note** nota música; **notes** annotātión·ēs -um *fpl*; **take notes** ēnotáre

note *tr* notáre; **note down** ēnotáre

notebook libéll·us -ī *m*, pugillár·ēs -ium *mpl*

note pad pugillár·ēs -ium *mpl*

nothing nihil

notice notáre

notorious nōt·us -a -um, īnfám·is -is -e

noun *s* nōm·en -inis *n; (of an inanimate object)* vocábul·um -ī *n*

November mēns·is -is *m* Novémber; **in November** mēnse Novémbrī

novel op·us -eris *n* fabulósum

now nunc; *(denoting emphasis and urgency)* iam; *(transitional, never in first place)* autem; **even now** étiam nunc; **just now** *(a moment ago)* modo; **now and then** subínde; **now at last** nunc tandem; **now here's the point** nunc cognósce rem; **now ... now** modo ... modo; **now that** posteáquam (+ *indic); **now what?** quid nunc?; **right now** *(immediately)* iam iam; **ten years from now** ad decem annōs

nowadays hódiē, nunc

nowhere nusquam

nuclear nucleár·is -is -e; **nuclear power** vīs *f* nucleáris

nudge fodicáre

number *s* númer·us -ī *m*

numeral *s* nōm·en -inis *n* numerále (ut "ūnus," "duo," " trēs" **one, two, three**)

nurse nosócom·a -ae *f; (male)* nosócom·us -ī *m*

nursery concláv·e -is *n* īnfántium

nursing home nosocómi·um -ī *n*

nut nux, nucis *f;* **be nuts about someone** (amóre) dēpér·eō -íre -iī áliquem; **he's nuts** aliēnátus est ā sē; **you're nuts** dēlírās

nymph nymph·a -ae *f* marína

oak *adj* rōbóre·us -a -um

oak rōb·ur -uris *n,* querc·us -ūs *f*

oats avén·a -ae *f*

obedient (to) oboédiēns -éntis *(dat)*

object *s (gram) expressed by the verb* adiungī, *for example,* **"the man" is the object of the verb** "hic homō" verbō adiúngitur **[Note:** *Roman grammarians never used the word "obiéctum" in connection with a verb or preposition. Whereas we would say, for example, "man is the object of the verb" the Romans would say "man is joined to the verb." See also the definition of "modify" above.*]

object (to) obsíst·ō -ere óbstitī (+ *dat*)

objection: I have no objection per mē licet; **if you have no objection** sī per tē licet

object lesson document·um -ī *n*

obliged: I'm much obliged to you for sending me your book fēcístī mihi pergrátum quod librum ad mē mīsístī

obliging cómmod·us -a -um

obscurity ignōbílit·ās -átis *f*

obviously maniféstō

occasion: for the occasion in tempus; **if occasion should arise** sī fúerit occásiō

occasionally per occāsiónem, subínde

occupation *(means of livelihood)* quaest·us -ūs *m;* **what is your occupation?** quem quaestum facis?

occupy *(take possession of)* occupáre; *(take by force)* cáp·iō -ere cēpī captus; **be occupied with something** in áliquā rē versárī

occur *(take place)* íncid·ō -ere -ī; *(come up)* obvén·iō -íre; **that had never occurred to me** mihi istuc numquam in mentem vénerat.

ocean ōcéan·us -ī *m;* **the Atlantic Ocean** ōcéanus Atlánticus *or* mare Atlánticum

ochre sīláce·us -a -um

o'clock: at two o'clock *(8:00 A.M.)* hōrā diéī secúndā *(see end of Chapter IX)*

October mēns·is -is *m* Octóber; **in October** mēnse Octóbrī

odd *(strange)* īnsólit·us -a -um, mīr·us -a -um; *(number)* impār, ímparis; **how odd!** rīdículum!

off *(said of an island)* ante (+ *acc*); **off (the coast of) Italy** ante Itáliam ; **be far off** procul esse; **be a long way off** longē abésse; **be off to** hinc áb·eō -íre -ívī *or* -iī ad (+ *acc*); **be well off** loculēs esse; **I'm off to the forum** ego hinc mē ad forum (agō); **where are you off to?** quō tē agis?

offenses dēlíct·a -órum *npl*

office hon·or -óris *m,* magistrát·us -ūs *m;* *(work place)* officín·a -ae *f;* *(teacher's)* studíol·um -ī *n;* **gain an office** magistrátum *(or* honórem) ádsequ·or -ī adsecútus sum

officer praeféct•us -ī *m;* **cavalry officer** praeféctus équitum; *(police)* vig•il -ilis *mf*

offside: be offside seórsum stō stāre stetī

often saepe, nōnnúmquam

oh boy! eu!

oh my! vae mihi

oho! eho!

O.K. fiat *or* licet; **if it's O.K. with you** sī tibi vidétur; **we're O.K.** bene habémus

old vet•us -eris *(single-ending adj),* vétul•us -a -um; **be ... years old ...** annōs nāt•us -a -um esse; **older** māior nātū; **oldest** máxim•us -a nātū

old age senéct•ūs -útis *f,* senéct•a -ae *f*

old-age home gerontocómi•um -ī *n*

old lady an•us -ūs *f;* **little old lady** anícul•a -ae *f*

old man sen•ex -is *m*

oldster sen•ex -is *m*

old woman an•us -ūs *f*

olive olív•a -ae *f*

olive oil óle•um -ī *n*

omelet lágan•um -ī *n* ex ōvīs

once *(on a certain occasion)* quōdam diē; *(one time)* semel; **once I get started, I can't stop** quandō incípiō, dēsínere nōn queō; **at once** *(immediately)* ílicō, statim; *(simultaneously)* simul; **once and for all** semel in perpétuum; **once or twice** semel atque íterum; **once upon a time** ōlim

one ūn•us -a -um; **at one time** *(formerly)* ōlim; **one another** inter sē: **they embraced one another** inter sē ampléxī sunt; **one and the same** ūnus et īdem; **one house** ūnae aed•ēs -ium *fpl;* **one ... the other** alter ... alter; **one would think** créderēs; **we can discuss that one on one** dē eō cōram disputáre póssumus

one-way street vi•a -ae *f* ūníus cursūs

onion caep•a -ae *f*

only sōlum, tantúmmodo *(usu. after the word it emphasizes)*

open *adj (not shut)* apért•us -a -um; *(candid)* cándid•us -a -um; **in the open (air)** sub dīvō

open *tr* apér•iō -íre apéruī apértus

openly própalam

opera melodrám•a -atis *n;* **go to see an opera** melodráma vīs•ō -ere -ī

opera house theátr•um -ī *n* melodrāmáticum

operate on sec•ō -áre -uī -tus

operating system *(comput)* systém•a -atis *n* intérnum

operation operáti•ō -ónis *f; (surgical)* sécti•ō -ónis *f (or* operátio) médica; **conduct military operations** rēs ger•ō -ere gessī

operetta melodrāmáti•um -ī *n*

opinion senténti•a -ae *f;* **express an opinion** senténtiam dícere; **in my opinion** meā senténtiā, meō iūdíciō; **what is your opinion about ... ?** quid opīnáris dē (+ *abl*)?

opinion poll interrogáti•ō -ónis *f* (política)

opponent adversári•us -ī *m* (•a -ae *f*); *(for office)* competí•tor -tóris *m* (•tríx -trícis *f*)

opposite *prep* versus (+ *acc*) *(often postpositive),* advérsum (+ *acc*), contrā + *acc*); **opposite of** ex advérsō *or* exadvérsō (+ *gen*)

optician fa•ber -brī *m* ópticus

or aut, vel; *(in double questions)* an

orange *adj (color)* auránti•us -a -um, lúte•us -a -um

orange māl•um -ī *n* aurántium; *(color)* col•or -ốris *m* lūteus

orangeade mālī aurántiī pốti•ō -ốnis *f*

orange juice aurántiī succ•us -ī *m*

orbit órbit•a -ae *f*

orchard pōmắri•um -ī *n*

orchestra symphốni•a -ae *f*, symphōníac•ī -ốrum *mpl*

ordinal *adj* ōrdinál•is -is -e (ut "prīmus" **first**)

organ *(anat)* vīsc•us -eris *n; (musical instrument)* órgan•um -ī *n* músicum; **pipe organ** órganum fístulīs fabricắtum

ostrich strūthiocamếl•us -ī *m (see* **bird)**

other áli•us -a -ud

ouch! au!, ei!

ought dếb•eō -ếre -uī -itus**ounce** únci•a -ae *f*

our nost•er -ra -rum

out: out of doors forīs; **out of place: if it is not out of place** nisi aliếnum est; **out of fear** propter metum; **out of wood** dē lignō; **out with it!** *(tell me!)* cedo! *(pl:* cette!) [*an old imperative*]; **the book is not yet out** liber ē prēlō nōndum éxiit

outdo superắre

outdoors forīs

outfielder extérn•us cust•ōs -ốdis *mf*

outfit hábit•us -ūs *m*, sýnthes•is -is *f*

outlet *(electrical)* ēléctrica cápsul•a -ae *f* contáctūs

outline dēlīneắti•ō -ốnis *f*

outline *tr* dēlīneắre

output *(comput)* éxit•us -ūs *m*

outside *(direction)* forās; *(position)* forīs

outspoken lībéri•or *(gen:* -ốris)

outstanding praest•āns -ántis

oven furn•us -ī *m*

over *(above) (with motion)* super (+ *acc); (in position)* suprā (+ *acc);* **it's all over!** āctum est!; **over sixty years old** māior (quam) annōs sexāgíntā nāt•us -a; **when the battle was over** cōnféctō proéliō

overalls encombốm•a -atis *n*

overcast nūbilốs•us -a -um, nűbil•us -a -um; **become overcast** nūbilắre

overcoat superindūmént•um -ī *n*

over-confident nimis cōnfíd•ēns -éntis

overhead projector prōiectốri•um -ī *n* superācapitắle

overtime *(in a game)* additícium temp•us -oris *n*

overture exốrdi•um -ī *n* (melodrắmatis)

overwhelmed: be overwhelmed with work óbru•or -ī óbrutus sum, tamquam flūctū, sīc ópere

owl būb•ō -ốnis *m;* **owls hoot** būbốnēs búbilant *(see* **bird)**

ox bōs, bovis *m;* **oxen bellow** bovēs boant

oyster óstre•a -ae *f*

oyster bed ostreắri•um -ī *n*

oyster shell óstreae test•a -ae *f*

pack *s (of cigarettes)* capséll•a -ae *f; (throng)* turb•a -ae *f*

pack *(e.g., a theater)* stipắre; **pack up the luggage** sárcinās *(or* sarcínulās *or* vāsa) cóllig•ō -ere collḗgī colléctus

package, packet fascícul•us -ī *m*

page págin•a -ae *f;* **at the bottom (top) of the page** in īmā (summā) páginā

pain dol·or -óris *m;* **be a big pain in the neck** molestíssim·us -a -um esse; **feel pain** dolóre affíc·ior -ī afféctus sum; **be in pain** dól·eō -ére -uī; **severe pain** ingēns *or* véhemēns dolor; **stop being a pain in the neck** moléstus (-a) nē sīs; **take pains to** óperam dare ut (+ *subj)*

painstaking operós·us -a -um

paint *s* pigmént·um -ī *n*

paint *tr & intr* ping·ō -ere pīnxī pictus

paint brush pēnicíll·us -ī *m*

painter pict·or -óris *m,* pictr·īx -ícis *f; (house painter)* dealbát·or -óris *m*

painting *(the art; picture)* pictúr·a -ae *f; (painting on a board)* tábul·a -ae *f* (picta) *(see Chapter V)*

pair pār paris *n*

pajamas sýnthes·is -is *f* dormītória

palate palát·um -ī *n*

pale pállid·us -a -um

palm *(of the hand)* palm·a -ae *f*

pancake artolágan·um -ī *n*

panther panthér·a -ae *f*

pantry cell·a -ae *f* pēnária

pants brāc·ae -árum *fpl;* **hot pants** pérbrevēs brācae fēmíneae

pantyhose tībiál·ia -ium *npl* brācária

paper chart·a -ae *f*

paperback lib·er -rī *m* chartā contéctus

paper clip fībícul·a -ae *f* chartárum

paperhanger tapētári·us -ī *m*

paprika cápsic·um -ī *n*

parachute dēcidícul·um -ī *n*

paragraph parágraph·us -ī *m*

parakeet psittácul·us -ī *m*

parallel bars hast·ae -árum *fpl* parallélae

parcel fasc·is -is *m (or* fascícul·us -ī *m)* cursuális

pardon *s* véni·a -ae *f;* **grant s.o. a pardon** véniam álicui dare; **obtain pardon** véniam impetráre

pardon *tr* ignósc·ō -ere ignóvī (+ *dat);* **pardon me for what I said** ignósce mihi, quod díxerō

parent parēns -éntis *mf*

parentage gen·us -eris *n*

park *s* hort·ī -órum *mpl,* viridári·um -ī *n*

park *tr (the car)* státu·ō -ere -uī -útus (autocīnétum)

parking: no parking! cavē státuās vehículum

parking fee tax·a -ae *f* statíva

parking lot áre·a -ae *f* statíva

parking-lot attendant cust·ōs -ódis *mf* áreae statívae

parking meter statímetr·um -ī *n;* **put a coin into the parking meter** nummum in statímetrum immítt·ō -ere immísī immíssus

parliament parlāmént·um -ī *n;* **member of parliament** parlāmentári·us -ī *m* (·a -ae *f)*

parrot psíttac·us -ī *m*

parse *tr* proprietátēs (+ *gen)* dēscríb·ō -ere dēscrípsī

parsley petroselín·um -ī *n*

part *s* par·s -tis *f; (in the hair)* discrím·en -inis *n*

part *tr (the hair)* discrimináre

part of speech par·s -tis *f* ōrātiónis

participle particípi·um -ī *n;* **past** *or* **perfect participle** praetéritī témporis particípium; **present participle** praeséntis témporis particípium

particle partícul·a -ae *f (namely, the four parts of speech that are indeclinable:*

adverb, preposition, conjunction, interjection)

particular particulár·is -is -e; **in particular** potíssimum

partridge perd·īx -ícis *mf (see* **bird)**

party *(side)* par·s -tis *f,* fácti·ō -ónis *f; (celebration)* convívi·um -ī *n;* **give a party** convívium dare; **throw a party** convívium agitáre; **join a party** partī sē adiún·gō -gere -xī

pass *s (defile)* salt·us -ūs *m; (basketball)* corbifóll·is -is *m* trānsmíssus; *(football)* pedifóll·is -is *m* trānsmíssus

pass *tr (go by)* praetér·eō -íre -iī -itus; *(ride by)* praetér·vehor -vehī -véctus sum; *(the time, life)* ter·ō -ere trīvī trītus; *(basketball, football, lacrosse)* trāns·míttō -míttere -mīsī -míssus; **pass a law** (rogātiónem *or* lēgem) pérferō perférre pértulī perlátus; **pass a test** probātiónem sustín·eō -ére -uī; **pass out** distríbu·ō -ere -uī -tus; **pass sentence** dēcérn·ō -ere dēcrévī dēcrétus; **pass the bread, please!** pórrige pānem quaesō ‖ *intr (of time)* trānsíre; **pass away** *(die)* dēcéd·ō -ere dēcéssī; **it came to pass** factum est; **pass by** *(go or ride by)* praeteríre, praetérvehī; **pass for** *(appear to be)* probáre prō (+ *abl); pass out (faint)* colláb·or -ī collápsus sum

passage *(in a text)* loc·us -ī *m; (across water)* trânsit·us -ūs *m*

passbook *(bank book)* argentáriae libéll·us -ī *m*

passenger vect·or -óris *m,* vectr·īx -ícis *f*

passenger train trām·en -inis *n* commúne

passing: no passing! cavē praeveháris!

passion cupídit·ās -átis *f; (lust)* libíd·ō -inis *f*

passionate ārd·ēns -éntis

passionately efflíctim

passive *adj* passív·us -a -um

Passover Pascha *n [indecl],* Pasch·a -atis *n*

passport commeátūs diplóm·a -atis *n*

password *(also comput)* tésser·a -ae *f*

past *prep* praeter (+ *acc)*

past *s* praetérit·um temp·us -oris *n;* **in the past** ántehāc

pasta collýr·a -ae *f*

pastries cuppédi·a -órum *npl*

pastry baker cuppēdinári·us -ī *m (·a -ae f)*

pastry shop cuppedinári·a -ae *f*

pasture páscu·um -ī *n*

pathetic ēlāmentábil·is -is -e

patience patiénti·a -ae *f*

patient *adj* páti·ēns -éntis

patient *s* ae·ger -grī *m,* ae·gra -grae *f*

patiently aequō ánimō

patrician patríci·us -a -um

patriot amá·tor -tóris *m (·trīx -trícis) f* pátriae

patriotic am·āns -ántis pátriae

patriotism am·or -óris *m* pátriae

pattern *s* régul·a -ae *f; (of weaving)* text·us -ūs *m*

pauper paup·er -eris *mf*

pave: pave the way to viam fácere ad (+ *acc)*

pavement pavīmént·um -ī *n*

paw pēs, pedis *m*

pay *s* merc·ēs -édis *f; (in the military)* stīpéndi·um -ī *n (see* **wages)**

pay *tr* solv·ō -ere -ī solútus; **pay off** persólvere, exsólvere; **pay off a debt**

débitum persólvere; **pay on time** ad tempus *or* ad diem dictam sólvere; **pay out (money) to** dēnumerāre (nummōs) (+ *dat*); **pay s.o. $20 for** dēnumerāre álicui vīgíntī dóllarōs prō (+ *abl*); **pay s.o. a visit** áliquem invīs·ō -ere -ī ‖ *intr* **it pays to listen** prétium óperae est auscultāre

pay phone tēlephṓn·um -ī *n* nummārium

payment solū́ti·ō -ṓnis *f* (pecū́niae)

pea pīs·um -ī *n*

peace pāx, pācis *f;* **break the peace** pācem frang·ō -ere frēgī frāctus; **bring about peace** pācem conciliāre; **have peace negotiations with s.o.** ágere cum áliquō dē pāce; **in peace and in war** domī et mīlítiae *(or* in mīlítiā*);* **peace was concluded on condition that ...** pāx convḗnit in eam condiciṓnem ut ... ; **make peace with** pācem fácere cum (+ *abl*)

peach pérsic·um -ī *n*

peacock pāv·ō -ṓnis *m*, pāv·a -ae *f (see* **bird)**

peanut aráchis, aráchidis *f* hypogḗa

peanut butter būtȳr·um -ī *n* ex arachídibus; **put peanut butter on bread** būtȳrum ex arachídibus pānī adhibḗre

pear pir·um -ī *n*

pearl margarī́t·a -ae *f*

pearl earrings margarī́tae -ā́rum *fpl* dēpendéntēs

pearl necklace monī́l·e -is *n* baccátum

pea soup iūs, iū́ris *n* ex pīsī́s

pedal pedā́l·e -is *n*

pedestrian ped·es -itis *mf*

pedestrian crossing trā́nsit·us -ūs *m* péditum

pee ming·ō -ere mī́nxī mī́ctum

peel *s* cut·is -is *f; (rind, thick skin)* córi·um -ī *n*, cort·ex -icis *m;* **apple peel** mālī cut·is -is *f;* **orange peel** córium mālī aurántiī

peel *tr* resecā́re cutem (+ *gen*)

pelican onocrótal·us -ī *m (see* **bird)**

pen penn·a -ae *f*, cálam·us -ī *m* scrīptṓrius

penalty poen·a -ae *f;* **pay the penalty** poenās persólv·ō -ere -ī, poenās dare

penalty kick *(from 11 meters)* ict·us -ūs *m* úndecim metrṓrum; *(from 7 meters)* ictus septem metrṓrum

pencil gráphi·um -ī *n*, stil·us -ī *m* plúmbeus

pencil sharpener īnstrūmḗnt·um -ī *n* cuspidárium

pendulum perpendícul·um -ī *n*

peninsula paenī́nsul·a -ae *f*

pentathlon pentáthl·um -ī *n;* **win the pentathlon** pentáthlō vinc·ō -ere vīcī

penult *s* paenúltima sýllab·a -ae *f*

people hómin·ēs -um *mpl;* **people who speak Latin** quī Latḗnē loquúntur

pepper pip·er -eris *n*

pepper shaker piperī́n·um -ī *n*

percent centḗsim·a -ae *f*

perch *(fish)* perc·a -ae *f; (for birds)* pértic·a -ae *f*

perch *intr* **(on)** īnsī́dō -ere īnsḗdī (+ *dat*)

perfect perféct·us -a -um

perfectly *(totally)* plānē

perfect tense *s* temp·us -oris *n* praetéritum perféctum

perform *(duty)* praest·ō -áre praéstitī, fung·or -ī functus sum (+ *abl*)

perfume unguént·um -ī *n*

perfume shop tabérn·a -ae *f* unguentária

perhaps fortásse

period *(punctuation mark)* pūnct•um -ī *n; (span of time)* spáti•um -ī *n;* **I'll not give in. period!** nōn concḗdam. dīxī!; **period of life** aet•ās -ātis *f* vītae

periodical periódic•um -ī *n*

peristyle peristýli•um -ī *n*

perjure oneself periūrắre

perjury periúri•um -ī *n;* **commit perjury** pēriūrắre

persistence assidúit•ās -ắtis *f*

persistent assídu•us -a -um

person hom•ō -inis *mf*

personal *adj* persōnắl•is -is -e; **personal finances** rēs, reī *f* familiáris; **personal injury** iniúri•a -āe *f;* **personal computer** computátr•um -ī *n* do/mésticum

personally *adv expressed by* ipse, per mē, per tē, *etc.*

personality índol•ēs -is *f*

pessimistic īnfḗl•īx -ícis

pester moléstiās áf•ferō -férre áttulī (+ *dat)*

pet dēlíci•ae -ắrum *fpl*

pet *tr (stroke)* permúlc•eō -ére permúlsī; *(fondle)* subigitắre **‖** *intr* inter sē subigitắre

pharmacist *(see* **druggist***)*

pheasant phāsián•a -ae *f (see* **bird***)*

phew *interj* fī!; **phew! what's that stench?** fī! quidnam est iste fētor?

phlegm pītuít•a -ae *f*

phobia phóbi•a -ae *f*

phone *(see* **telephone***)*

phoney affectắt•us -a -um

photo *(see* **photograph***)*

photocopier máchin•a -ae *f* phōtotýpica

photocopy *s* exémpl•ar -ắris *n* phōtotýpicum

photocopy *tr* phōtotýpicē dēscrībere

photograph *s* imắg•ō -inis *f* phōtográphica; **take photographs** imáginēs lūce exprímere

photograph *tr* phōtográphicē redd•ō -ere réddidī rédditus

photographer phōtógraph•us -ī *m* (•a -ae *f)*

photographic film taeníol•a -ae *f* phōtográphica

photography phōtográphi•a -ae *f*

photo shop officín•a -ae *f* phōtográphica

phrase *s* locúti•ō -ṓnis *f*

physical condition córporis hábit•us -ūs *m*

physical therapist iātralípt•ēs -ae *m*

physical therapy iātralíptic•ē -ēs *f*

pianist clávic•en -inis *mf*

piano clāvicórdi•um -ī *n;* **play the piano** clāvicórdiō lūdere

pick *(pluck)* carp•ō -ere -sī -tus; *(gather)* leg•ō -ere lēgī lēctus; **pick (out)** *(select)* ḗlig•ō -ere ēlḗgī ēléctus; **pick pockets** manticulắrī **‖** *intr* **pick on** *(someone)* cárpere; **pick up a language** linguam pérbibō perbībere pérbibī

pickle sálgam•um -ī *n;* **be in a pickle** in angústiīs vers•or -ắrī -ắtus sum

pickpocket sacculắri•us -ī *m* (•a -ae *f)*

picnic cḗnul•a -ae *f* subdiắlis; **go on a picnic** excursiṓnem ad cḗnulam subdiắlem sūméndam fácere

picnic basket pānắri•um -ī *n*

picture pictū́r•a -ae *f,* imắg•ō -inis *f*

picture tube tub•us -ī *m* tēlevīsíficus

pie crūst•um -ī *n;* **cherry pie** cérasa *npl* in crūstō cocta

piece frūst•um -ī *n; (often not expressed by any separate word, the substantive denoting the piece, e.g.,* pānis **a piece of bread;** cáseus **a piece of cheese;** charta, chártula **a piece of paper); break in pieces** cōnfríng•ō -ere cōnfrḗgī cōnfráctus

pig porc•us -ī *m;* **pigs oink** porcī grúnniunt

pigeon colúmb•a -ae *f,* colúmb•us -ī *m;* **piegeons coo** colúmbae gemunt *(see bird)*

pigeon coop columbā́ri•um -ī *n*

pigsty suī́l•e -is *n*

pill pílul•a -ae *f*

pillow cervī́c•al -ális *n*

pillow case cervīcā́lis tégim•en -inis *n*

pilot *s* gubernā́•tor -tóris *m* (•trīx -trī́cis *f*)

pilot *tr* gubernā́re

pin ac•us -ūs *f*

pinch *s* **a pinch of salt** mēnsū́r•a -ae *f* salis duórum *(or* trium) digitórum; **in a pinch** *(fig)* in angústiīs; *(in a doubtful situation)* in rē dúbiā

pinch *tr* vellicā́re **‖** *intr* **if the shoe pinches** sī cálceus ūrit

pineapple māl•um -ī *n* pī́neum

Ping-Pong mēnsuā́lis pilae lūs•us -ūs *m;* **play Ping-Pong** mēnsuā́lī pilā lū́dere

pink róse•us -a -um

pipe fī́stul•a -ae *f* aquā́ria; *(of an organ)* órganī fī́stula

pitcher úrce•us -ī *m; (in baseball)* coniéc•tor -tóris *m* (•trīx -trī́cis *f*)

pitcher's mound coniectóris (coniectrī́cis) grūm•us -ī *m*

pitiful flḗbil•is-is -e; *(contemptible)* abiéct•us -a -um

pity *s* misericórdi•a -ae *f;* **feel pity for** commiserḗsc•ō -ere (+ *gen*)

pity *tr* misér•eor -ḗrī -itus sum (+ *gen);* **I pity you** miséreor tuī *(pl:* vestrī)

pizza pitt•a -ae *f*

place loc•us -ī *m (pl* loc•a -órum *npl);* **in the first place** prīmum; **in the same place** íbidem; **from that place** illinc; **in place of a parent** in locum paréntis; **out of place** aliḗn•us -a -um; **take place** *(occur)* fiō fī́erī factus sum; **take s.o.'s place** locum alicū́ius ūsurpā́re; **to that place** eō; **this is not the place to ...** nōn est hic locus ut (+ *subj);* **to the same place** eódem

plain camp•us -ī *m;* **open plains** campī paténtēs

plaintiff petī́t•or -óris *m,* petī́tr•īx -ī́cis *f*

plan *s* cōnsíli•um -ī *n;* **form a plan** cōnsílium ín•eō -íre -iī -tus; **make plans for the trip** cōnsílium cápere dē itínere

plan *tr* in ánimō habḗre, intén•dō -dere -dī -tus

plane āḕróplan•um -ī *n; (carpenter's tool)* runcī́n•a -ae *f*

plane *tr (e.g., a board)* runcīnā́re

plant *s* plant•a -ae *f*

plant *tr* ser•ō -ere sēvī sátus; **plant a field** agrum cōnsérere

plaster *s* tēctóri•um -ī *n*

plaster *tr* **(a wall)** tēctórium (paríetī) indū́cere

plasterer tḗct•or -óris *m*

plate pátin•a -ae *f,* catī́n•us -ī *m; (smaller size)* patéll•a -ae *f,* catíll•us -ī *m*

platform suggést•us -ūs *m; (in a train station)* crepī́d•ō -inis *f* (ferriviā́ria)

play *s (fun)* lūd•us -ī *m; (in a theater)* fábul•a -ae *f*

play *tr & intr* lúdere; *(an instrument)*
cán•ō -ere cécinī cantus (+ *abl of the
instrument*); *(records, tapes)* impéll•ō
-ere ímpulī impúlsus; **play a game**
lūdum lúdere; **play a good game**
bene lúdere; **play a trick on**
lūdífic•or -ắrī -ấtus sum (+ *acc*); **play
ball** pilā lúdere; **play checkers**
latrúnculīs lúdere; **play sports**
dispórtibus lúdere; **play the drum**
týmpanum pulsắre; **play the flute**
tībiā cánere; **play the guitar** cítherā
Hispắnicā cánere; **play the organ**
órganō cánere; **play the lead role**
prīmās partēs ágere; **play the role of
a general** imperātṓrem ágere; **play
the trumpet** tūbā cánere; **play the
piano** clāvicórdiō cánere ‖ *intr*
lúdere; **play up to s.o.** áliquem col•ō
-ere cóluī; **stop playing games**
dēsíste lūdōs fácere

player lūs•or -ṓris *m,* lūs•rīx -ícis *f*

playground ắre•a -ae *f* lūsṓria

playing card chártul•a -ae *f* lūsṓria

playing field camp•us -ī *m* lūsṓrius

playwright fābulārum scrīp•tor -tṓris *m*
(•trīx -trícis *f*)

plead a case before the court causam
prō tribūnắlī ágere

pleasant amoén•us -a -um, iūcúnd•us -a
-um

pleasantness iūcúndit•ās -ắtis *f*

please *(in making an appeal)* quaesō, sīs
(= sī vīs); *(informally)* amắbō tē;
whenever I please quotiēscúmque
(mihi) libet

pleased to meet you! mihi pergrắtum est
tē convenīre!

pleasing grắt•us -a -um

pleasure volúpt•ās -ắtis *f;* **at their own
pleasure** suō arbítriō; **derive great
pleasure from** magnam voluptắtem

cắpere ex (+ *abl*); **with pleasure**
libénter

pleated undulắt•us -a -um

plebeian plēbéi•us -a -um

plebs plēbs, plēbis *f*

pliers for•ceps -cipis *m*

plight: oh, what a sorry plight! O rem
míseram!

plow *s* arắtr•um -ī *n*

plow *tr* arắre

plug *(electrical)* spin•a -ae *f* contắctūs
ēléctricī

plug in adnéct•ō -ere adnéxuī adnéxus

plum prūn•um -ī *n*

plumber fab•er -rī *m* plumbắrius

plummet perpendícul•um -ī *n*

pluperfect tense *s* temp•us -oris *n*
plūsquamperféctum

plural *adj* plūrắl•is -is -e; **in the plural**
plūrắliter

plural *s* multitúd•ō -inis *f;* **signifying a
plural** multitúdinem signíficāns

plus: consider it a plus id dḗputā esse
in lucrō; **2 plus 2 are 4** duo et duo
sunt *(or* fiunt) quattuor

plus sign crucícul•a -ae *f*

pocket lócul•us -ī *m*

pocketbook *(purse)* crumḗn•a -ae *f;*
(small book) lib•er -rī *m* pugillắris

pocketknife cultéll•us -ī *m* plicắbilis

poem poḗm•a -atis *n;* **write a poem**
poḗma fácere, con•dō -dere -didī
-ditus

poet poḗt•a -ae *m*

poetess poḗtri•a -ae *f*

poetry poḗs•is -is *f*

poinsettia euphórbi•a -ae *f*

pointer *(comput)* (mūris) ind·ex -icis *m*

point out indicáre, mōnstráre

point *(sharp end)* acúm·en -inis *n; (of a spear)* cusp·is -idis *f; (gram, sports)* pūnct·um -ī *n;* **at this point** hīc; hōc locō; **be on the point of ...** in eō esse ut (+ *subj);* **beside the point** nihil ad rem; **but to return to the point ...** sed ad prōpósitum ... ; **get the point?** tenésne *(pl:* tenētísne) rem?; **get to the point!** venī ad rem!**; good point** vírt·ūs -útis *f;* **it got to the point where** eō dēcúrsum est ut (+ *subj);* **main point** summ·a -ae *f;* **now here's the point** nunc cognósce rem; **on that point** hāc dē rē; **score a point** pūnctum ferō ferre tulī lātus; **that's the main point** caput est; **the point is that I no longer care about such things** quod caput est, iam ista nōn cūrō; **up to this point** háctenus; **what was the point of your writing to me?** quid rétulit tē míttere ad mē lítterās?; **what's the point of that?** quam ad rem istud rēfert?; **what's your point?** *(what are you driving at?)* quō ēvádis?; **you miss the point** nihil ad rem pértinet

pole vaulting salt·us -ūs *m* perticárius *(see Chapter V)*

police officer vig·il -ilis *mf*

policy ráti·ō -ónis *f*

polish *s (for shoes)* cérōm·a -atis *n*

polish shoes cálceōs pól·iō -íre -ívī -ítus

polite (to) cōm·is -is -e (+ *dat or* ergā *or* in + *acc)*

politeness cómit·ās -átis *f*

political cīvíl·is -is -e; **for political reasons** reī públicae causā; **political affairs** *(or* **matters)** rēs, rērum *fpl* cīvílēs; **political career** curs·us -ūs *m* honórum; **political science** sciénti·a -ae *f* cīvílis

politician vir -ī *m* cīvílis, fémina -ae *f* cīvílis

politics rēs público *(gen:* reī públicae) *f,* res cīvílis *(also plural);* **enter politics** rem públicam íneō infre infvī *or* íniī; **take part in politics** in rē públicā vers·or -árī -átus sum

polka saltáti·ō -ónis *f* Bohémica; **dance the polka** Bohémicē saltáre

polling booth saept·um -ī *n*

polls saept·a -órum *npl*

polo alsūlégi·a -ae *f* equéstris

polo shirt subúcul·a -ae *f* cum curtīs mánicīs

pomegrante māl·um -ī *n* grānátum

pompous glōriós·us -a -um

pond stāgn·um -ī *n*

pony mann·us -ī *m*

pool stāgn·um -ī *n; (for swimming)* piscín·a -ae *f; (billiards)* lūd·us -ī *m* tudiculáris; **shoot pool** glóbulōs ebúrneōs clāvā tudiculárī super mēnsam impéll·ō -ere ímpulī

poor *(pitiful)* mis·er -era -erum; *(impoverished)* paup·er -eris [*single-ending adj*]; **poor guy** mis·er -erī *m*

poppy papáv·er -eris *n*

popular grātiós·us -a -um; **be popular with s.o.** grātiósus (-a) esse apud áliquem

pop tat·a -ae *m*

pop music músic·a -ae *f* populáris

popularity gráti·a -ae *f;* **enjoy popularity among** grátiam háb·eō -ére -uī -itus apud (+ *acc)*

population multitúd·ō -inis *f;* **the total number of the population** númer·us -ī *m* omnis multitúdinis

porch pérgul·a -ae *f*

porcupine hystr·ix -icis *f*

pork porcín·a -ae *f*

pork chop off·a -ae *f* porcína

port *(also comput)* port·us -ūs *m*

porter báiul·us -ī *m*

portico pórtic·us -ūs *f*

position loc·us -ī *m;* **what position do you play?** quō locō lūdis?

positive *s (gram)* grad·us -ūs *m* positívus

possessive *adj (gram)* possessív·us -a -um

possible possíbil·is -is -e; **if (it is) possible** sī fíerī potest; **is it really possible that ... ?** numquid ... ?; **is it really possible that you are telling the truth?** numquid vēra dícis?

postage vectúr·a -ae *f* (litterárum); **pay the postage** prō vectúrā epístulae solv·ō -ere -ī

postage stamp pittáci·um -ī *n* cursuále

postal delivery perláti·ō -ónis *f* cursuális

postcard chártul·a -ae *f* cursuális; *(with a picture)* phōtochártul·a -ae *f* cursuális

poster fóli·um -ī *n* mūrále

postman tabellári·us -ī *m*

post office diribitóri·um -ī *n* cursuále

post office window ostíol·um -ī *n* cursuále

potato sólan·um -ī *n* tuberósum; póm·um -ī *n* terréstre

potato chips lámin·ae *fpl* solanórum

pot *(of clay)* oll·a -ae *f; (of metal)* a(h)én·um -ī *n;* **go to pot** pessum eō íre iī; **pots and pans** vās·a -órum *npl* coquīnária

pot belly vent·er -ris *m* obésus

potter fígul·us -ī *m*

potter's wheel rot·a -ae *f* figuláris

pottery fictíl·ia -ium *npl*

poultry av·ēs -ium *fpl* cohortálēs

pound líbr·a -ae *f;* **per pound** in líbrās

power drill térebr·a -ae *f* māchinális

power saw serr·a -ae *f* māchinális

practically ferē

practice *tr (patience, medicine)* exérc·eō -ére -uī ‖ *intr* sē exercére

practice *s* exercitáti·ō -ónis *f*

praetor praet·or -óris *m*

praetorship praetúr·a -ae *f*

precise exáct·us -a -um

prefer mālō malle máluī; praé·ferō -férre -tulī -látus

prefix *s* praepósiti·ō -ónis *f* per compositiónem

prepare *(make ready)* paráre; *(make ready beforehand)* praeparáre

preposition *s* praepósiti·ō -ónis *f* (per appositiónem); **prepositions take** *(lit:* serve) **either the accusative or the ablative case** praepositiónēs aut accūsātívō aut ablātívō cásuī sérviunt

prescription praecépt·um -ī *n* médicum

present *adj* praes·ēns -éntis; **at the present time** praeséntī témpore, in praeséntī; **be present (at)** adsum adésse ádfuī adfutúrus (+ *dat);* **for the present time** in praesēns tempus; **present tense** praesēns temp·us -oris *n*

preside (over) praesíd·eō -ére praesédī (+ *dat);* **preside at a trial** iūdíciō praeésse, iūs dícere

president praésid·ēns -éntis *mf*

presiding judge quaesít·or -óris *m,* quaesítr·īx -ícis *f*

press *s (for printing)* prél·um -ī *n; (journalists)* diurnári·ī -órum *mpl; (printed matter)* scrípta *npl* typīs édita; **come off the press** prēlō éx•eō -íre -iī; **send (a work) to the press** (opus) prēlō subíc•iō -ere subiḗcī subiéctus

press *tr* prem•ō -ere pressī pressus; *(clothes)* lēvigắre; *(a typewriter key)* dēprímere **II** *intr* **press on** instắre; **press on and finish the job!** instā, pérfice!

press conference convént•us -ūs *m* diurnắriīs docéndīs

prestige auctốrit•ās -ắtis *f*

presumptuous cōnfíd•ēns -éntis

pretend: I'll pretend I don't know him dissimulắbō mē eum nōvísse; **I'll pretend I'm leaving** assimulắbō quasi ábeam.

pretext praetéxt•um -ī *n;* **a pretext for war** praetéxtum bellī; **he left under the pretext that ...** hinc ábiit quasi (+ *subj*)

pretty bell•us -a -um, béllul•us -a -um

pretty well *(just about)* propémodum

pretzel pretíol•a -ae *f,* líxul•a -ae *f;* **soft pretzel** pretíola mollis

previously ánteā, ántehāc, prius

prey praed•a -ae *f*

price préti•um -ī *n;* **at a high (low, very low, exorbitant) price** magnō (parvō, mínimō, nímiō); **higher price** prétium ámplius; **set a price** prétium fácere; **the price for it is 10 denarii per pound** prétium eī in librās est decem dēnắriīs

pride glốri•a -ae *f;* **source of pride** glốri•a -ae *f;* **take pride in** glốri•or -ắrī dē *or* in (+ *abl*)

priest sacérd•ōs -ốtis *mf*

priesthood sacerdốti•um -ī *n*

prime minister minís•ter -trī *m* prīmắrius

principal *s (of a school)* scholae rēct•or -ốris *m,* rēctr•íx -ícis *f; (fin)* cap•ut -itis *n,* sors, sortis *f;* **deduct the interest from the principal** dē cápite ūsúrās dēdúcere

principal parts part•ēs -ium *fpl* prīncipắlēs

print *s (printed dress)* vest•is -is *f* imāgínibus impréssa

print *tr (with type)* typīs ímprimō imprímere impréssī impréssus

printer *(person)* typốgraph•us -ī *m; (mechanical device)* mắchin•a -ae *f* typográphica, impressốri•um -ī *n*

printer's typographḗ•um -ī *n*

printing *(abstract)* typográphi•a -ae *f*

printing office officín•a -ae *f* typográphica

printing press prēl•um -ī *n* typográphicum, typographḗ•um -ī *n*

print shop officín•a -ae *f* typográphica

prison carc•er -eris *m;* **throw s.o. into prison** áliquem in cárcerem coníc•iō -ere coniḗcī coniéctus

prisoner of war captív•us -ī *m* (•a -ae *f);* **ransom prisoners** captívōs rédim•ō -ere redḗmī redḗmptus

private *adj* prīvắt•us -a -um; **in private** in prīvắtō

private *s (mil)* mīl•es -itis *mf;* gregắrius (•a)

privately clam, sēcrḗtō; **I want to speak with you privately** velim tēcum loquī secrḗtō

prize praémi•um -ī *n;* **first prize** prīmắri•um -ī *n;* **second prize** secundắri•um -ī *n;* **win a prize** praémium aúferō, auférre ábstulī ablắtus

problem quaésti•ō -ốnis *f; (math)* problḗm•a -atis *n;* **have stomach (heart, back) problems** stómachō (corde, tergō) dól·eō -ére -uī; **the problem is …** quaéritur … ; **what's the problem?** quid est negótī?

processor *(comput)* ēditóri·um -ī *n*

producer chorág·us -ī *m*

productivity *(of fields, mines, etc.)* fertílit·ās -átis *f*

profession *(learned occupation)* proféssi·ō -ónis *f*

professor proféss·or -óris *m*, proféstr·īx -ícis *f*

profit lūcr·um -ī *n;* **make profit** lūcrum fácere

program *s (also comput)* prográmm·a -atis *n*

program *tr (comput)* programmáre

programmer *(comput)* programmá·tor -tóris *m*, (·trīx -trícis *f*)

progress prōféct·us -ūs *m;* **make progress** prōfíc·iō -ere prōfécī prōféctum

projector proiectóri·um -ī *n;* **overhead projector** proiectórium suprācapitále

promise *s* prōmíss·um -ī *n;* **break promises** prōmissa frang·ō -ere frēgī frāctus; **I am not making any definite promise** nihil certī pollíceor; **keep promises** prōmíssa serváre; **make many promises** multa prōmíttere

promise *tr* prōmítt·ō -ere prōmísī prōmíssus

promote prōmóv·eō -ére prōmóvī prōmótus; *(the arts, etc.)* fóv·eō -ére fōvī fōtus; *(in school)* ad superiórem classem prōmovére; **promote to higher rank** ad *(or* in) ampliórem gradum prōmovére

promotion prōmóti·ō -ónis *f*

prompt *(comput)* mónit·us -ūs *m*

pronoun prōnóm·en -inis *n*

pronounce *tr* prōnūntiáre; **pronounce a vowel short or long** vocálem corréptē aut prōdúctē prōnūntiáre

proof documént·um -ī *n; (esp. of guilt)* indíci·um -ī *n*

proofread leg·ō -ere lēgī lēctus et ēmendáre

proper dec·ēns -éntis, decór·us -a -um

proper noun *s* próprium nóm·en -inis *n* (ut "Hector" **Hector**) *(opp:* appellātívum nōmen (ut "homō" **man**)

property bon·a -órum *npl*

propose (a law) (lēgem) ferō ferre tulī lātus

prose prōs·a -ae *f*

prosecute iūdíciō pérsequ·or -ī persecútus sum

prosecutor accūsá·tor -tóris *m* (·trīx -trícis *f*)

prostitute méretr·īx -ícis *f*, prōstitū́t·a -ae *f;* **be a prostitute** prōst·ō -áre próstitī

proud glōriós·us-a -um; *(haughty)* supérb·us -a -um; **be proud of** glóri·or -árī (+ *acc or* dē *or* in + *abl*)

prove *(by evidence, argument)* probáre; **this proves that …** documéntō est (+ *acc & inf*)

province prōvínci·a -ae *f*

prune prūn·um -ī *n* condítum

psychiatric psȳchīátric·us -a -um

psychiatrist psȳchīát·er -rī *m* (·ria -riae *f*)

psychiatry psȳchīātrí·a -ae *f*

psychic psýchic·us -a -um

psychoanalysis psȳchoanálys·is -is *f*

psychoanlyst psȳchoanalýst·a -ae *m* (·ria -riae *f*)

psychologist psȳchólog•us -ī *m* (•a -ae *f*)

pyschopath psȳchopáthic•us -ī *m* (•a -ae *f*)

public públic•us -a -um; **in public** in públicō; *(opp. domī)* forīs; **appear in public** pród•eō -íre -iī in públicum

publish ēd•ō -ere édidī éditus, publicáre

publisher ēdit•or -óris *m; (publishing house)* dom•us -ūs *f* ēditória

pudding érne•um -ī *n*

pull trah•ō -ere traxī tractus; **pull a fast one on s.o.** ōs álicui súb•linō -línere -lévī; **pull oneself together** sē cóllig•ō -ere collégī; **pull the wool over s.o.'s eyes** súbdol•us (-a) esse advérsus áliquem

pullman car curr•us -ūs *m* dormītórius

pulse vēnárum puls•us -ūs *m;* **(fast** vegétior; **weak** languídior); **feel s.o.'s pulse** vēnās *or* pulsum vēnárum alicúius tentáre

pumpkin cucúrbit•a -ae *f*

punch *s* pugno *(or* pugn•us -ī *m;* **give s.o. a punch** *(or* **land a punch on s.o.)** pugnum álicui dúcere

punch *tr* pugnō *or* pugnīs caed•ō -ere cecídī

punching bag córyc•us -ī *m,* foll•is -is *m* pugilātórius

punctual díllig•ēns -éntis, prompt•us -a -um

punctually témporī, ad tempus

punctuate inter•púngō -púngere -púnxī -púnctus

punctuation *s* interpúncti•ō -ónis *f*

punctuation mark *s* interpúnct•um -ī *n,* púnct•um -ī *n*

punish pún•iō -íre -ívī *or* -iī -ítus; poenā affíc•iō -ere afféci afféctus

punishment for crimes poen•a -ae *f* facínorum

puny pusíll•us -a -um

pup cátul•us -ī *m;* **pups whimper** cátulī gánniunt

pupil discípul•us -ī *m* (•a -ae *f*); *(of the eye)* pūpíll•a -ae *f*

puppet neuropást•um -ī *n*

puppy cátul•us -ī *m;* catéll•us -ī *m,* catéll•a -ae *f*

purchase *s* ēmpt•um -ī *n*

purchase *tr* merc•or -árī -átus sum; comparáre

purchasing émpti•ō -ónis *f*

purr *s (of a cat)* murm•ur -uris *n*

purr *intr (of a cat)* murmuráre

purse crumén•a -ae *f,* marsúpi•um -ī *n*

put pōn•ō -ere pósuī pósitus; **put an end to** fīnem impónere (+ *dat); **put away** sēpónere; **put down** dēpónere; **put off: let's put this off to another time** hanc rem in áliud tempus differámus; **put on** *(clothes)* índu•ō -ere -ī -útus *(opp: exúere)*; **put s.o. in prison** áliquem in custódiam trā•dō -dere -didī -ditus; **put up for sale** vēnum dare; **put up with with s.o.** áliquem perpét•ior -ī perpéssus sum; **put words into s.o. mouth** verba in ore alicúius pónere; **put yourself in my place** fac quī ego sum, esse tē; **you're putting it on a little thick** es pūtidiúculus (-a)

puzzle aenígm•a -atis *n*

pyjamas sýnthes•is -is *f* dormītória

quaestor quaest•or -óris *m*

quaestorship quaestúr•a -ae *f*

quail cotúrn•īx -ícis *f (see* **bird**)

quarrel rīx•a -ae *f*

quarrel *intr* (with s.o. about) altercárī *or* rīxárī (cum + *abl*, dē + *abl*)

question rogát·um -ī *n*, interrogát·um -ī *n;* **ask a question** interrogáre; **ask a loaded question** captiṓsē interrogáre; **ask many questions** multa interrogáre; **answer the question** ad rogátum (*or* interrogátum) respónd·eō -ére -ī; **call into question** in dúbium vocáre; **I ask you this question** tē hoc rogō; **many questions are raised** multa quaerúntur; **no question, he's at fault** nempe in culpā est; **that's a loaded question** captiṓsum interrogátum est; **why do you ask such questions?** cūr ista quaeris?; **without question** sine dúbiō

question mark sign·um -ī *n* interrogátī

quick cel·er -eris -ere; (*mentally*) astū́t·us -a -um

quickly cito

quiet quiét·us -a -um; (*silent*) tácit·us -a -um; (*taciturn*) tacitúrn·us -a -um; **quiet!** fac (*pl:* fácite) siléntium!, tacḗ! (*pl:* tacḗte)!; **why don't you keep quiet?** quīn tū tacēs?

quite ádmodum; **not quite** parum

quiz probātiúncul·a -ae *f* (*see* **exam**)

rabbi rabbín·us -ī *m*

rabbit cuníc̆ul·us -ī *m*

race (*lineage*) gen·us -eris *n*; (*foot race*) certám·en -inis *n* cursū́s; (*horse race*) curs·us -ūs *m* equṓrum; (*of chariots*) currícul·um -ī *n*; (*of cars*) certám·en -inis *n* autocīnētṓrum

race car, racing car autocīnēt·um -ī *n* currīle

race track currícul·um -ī *n*, stádi·um -ī *n*; (*for horses*) hippódrom·us -ī *m*

racket (*noise*) strepit·us -ūs *m*; (*shouting*) clám·or -óris *m*; (*tennis*) rētícul·um -ī *n*; **raise a racket** clāmṓrem toll·ō -ere sústulī sublátus

radiator calṓris radiátr·um -ī *n*

radio radiophón·um -ī *n*; **turn on (turn off) the radio** radiophónum excitáre *or* accénd·ō -ere -ī (expéd·iō -íre -ívī -ítus); **turn down (turn up) the radio** vim radiophṓnī remítt·ō -ere remísī (amplificáre)

radio broadcast ēmíssi·ō -ṓnis *f* radiophṓnica

radio station státi·ō -ṓnis *f* radiophṓnica

radish rādícul·a -ae *f*, ráphan·us -ī *m*

raft rat·is -is *f*

rage fur·or -óris *m*; **fly into a rage** īrā éfferor efférrī ēlátus sum

raid excúrsi·ō -ṓnis *f*

railroad ferrívi·a -ae *f*

railroad car curr·us -ūs *m* ferriviárius

railroad station státi·ō -ṓnis *f* ferriviária

rain *s* plúvi·a -ae *f*; (*heavy and stormy*) im·ber -bris *m*; **heavy, steady rain** magnī et adsíduī imbrēs; **the rain is letting up** *or* **is tapering off** imber dētūmḗscit

rain *impers v* pluit plúere pluit; **rain buckets** urceátim plúere; **rain cats and dogs** cattīs canibúsque plúere; **rain hard** veheménter (*or* multum) plúere

rain basin (*in the atrium*) implúvi·um -ī *n*

rainbow plúvius arc·us -ūs *m*

rain cloud nimb·us -ī *m*

raincoat scórte·a -ae *f*; (*hooded*) paénul·a -ae *f*; (*open mantle, fastened at the shoulder*) lacérn·a -ae *f*

rainy plúvi·us -a -um

raise *(children, crops, animals)* ēducā́re; *(lift up)* toll•ō -ere sústulī sublā́tus; *(prices)* aúg•eō -ḗre auxī auctus

raisin (ūva) pass•a -ae *f*

rake rastéll•us -ī *m*

rake rastéllō ērā́•dō -dere -sī -sum

ram ari•ḗs -etis *m;* **rams bleat** aríetēs bā́lant

RAM *(comput)* memóri•a -ae *f* volā́tilis

rank grad•us -ūs *m*

rape stupr•um -ī *n* per vim

rape *tr* per vim stuprā́re, stuprō violā́re

rapids vad•um -ī *n* cándicāns

rapist stuprā́t•or -ṓris *m*

rare sēmicóct•us -a -um *(opp:* percóctus)

rarely rā́rō

raspberry mōr•um -ī *n* Ī́daéum

rat mū•s -ris *m,* ratt•us -ī *m; (pej)* hom•ō -inis *m* nequam [*indecl*]; **I smell a rat** áliquid mihi súbolet; **like drowned rats** tamquam mūrēs ūdī; **rats squeak** rattī míntriunt

rat on s.o. áliquem dḗferō dēférre dḗtulī

rate: at any rate útique

rather pótius; *(somewhat)* aliquántō, paulō; **do you know this fellow?** huncne nōvístī? **rather!** fácile!

ratify a bill lēgem iúb•eō -ḗre iussī iussus

rattle off cito volv•ō -ere -ī

raven corv•us -ī *m;* **ravens croak** corvī crṓcitant *(see* **bird)**

raze to the ground solō aequā́re

razor novā́cul•a -ae *f;* **electric razor** rāsṓri•um -ī *n* ēléctricum

reach *s* **out of reach** extrā ictum; **within my reach** sub meō ictū

reach *tr (arrive at)* pervén•iō -ī́re ad *or* in (+ *acc);* **reach out the hand** manum pórrig•ō -ēre porrḗxī

read leg•ō légere lēgī lēctus

readily *(willingly)* libénter

reading lḗcti•ō -ṓnis *f*

reading lamp lamp•as -adis *f* lēctṓria

reading room oec•us -ī *m* lēctṓrius

ready parā́t•us -a -um, prompt•us -a -um

real estate rēs *fpl* solī; **piece of real estate** praédi•um -ī *n*

real estate broker praediā́•tor -tṓris *m,* (•trīx -trícis *f*)

really quidem, vērō

reap met•ō -ere méssuī messus

reaper mess•or -ṓris *m*

rear (end) *(coll)* postíc•um -ī *n*

reason *(faculty, reasonable ground)* rā́ti•ō -ṓnis *f; (cause)* caus•a -ae *f;* **for that reason** hāc dē causā; **for various reasons** multīs dē causīs; **what's the reason why ...** quid est enim, cūr ...

rebut dissólv•ō -ere -ī dissolū́tus

rebuttal dissolū́ti•ō -ṓnis *f*

recall revocā́re; *(to memory)* memóriā répet•ō -ere -ī́vī -ī́tus; **as I recall** ut mea memória est

receipt ápoch•a -ae *f*

receiver *(of a telephone)* auscultā́bul•um -ī *n*

recent rec•ḗns -éntis

recently nūper, recénter

recess paus•a -ae *f*

recitation recitā́ti•ō -ṓnis *f*

recite recitā́re

record orb•is -is *m* phōnográphicus; phōnodísc•us -ī *m;* **play (listen to)**

records orbēs phōnográphicōs exhíb·eō -ére -uī (aúd·iō -íre -ívī)

record player māchínul·a -ae *f* phōnográphica; discophón·um -ī *n*

recording secretary *(in the Roman senate)* librári·us -ī *m*

recover *tr* recípere suam valētúdinem (bonam) **‖** *intr (recuperate)* revalésc·ō -ere, suam valētúdinem recípere; **recover from a serious illness** ē gravī morbō recreárī

recruit *s* tīr·ō -ốnis *m;* **raw recruit** tīrō rudis

recruit *tr* **recruit troops** dīléctum ágere

recruitment dīléct·us -ūs *m*

rectum ān·us -ī *m*

red ru·ber -bra -brum; **be red** rúb·eō -ére

red cent: I don't owe anyone a red cent assem aerárium nếminī débeō; **I haven't a red cent** assem aerárium hábeō nūllum

redhead rūf·us -ī *m,* rứtil·us -ī *m;* rūf·a -ae *f,* rứtil·a -ae *f*

referee árbi·ter -trī *m* (·tra -trae *f*)

refined hūmán·us -a -um

reform ēmendáre

refrigerator frīgidár·ium -ī *n*

regards: give him (her) my best regards dícitō eī multam meīs verbīs salútem

regiment légi·ō -ốnis *f*

regimental commander legiốnis legát·us -ī *m*

region régi·ō -ốnis *f*

regret *s* paeniténti·a -ae *f*

regret *tr* **I regret** mē paénitet (+ *gen*)

regularly assíduē

reindeer tarándr·us -ī *m*

reject a bill lēgem (*or* rogātiốnem) antīquáre

relative *adj* relatív·us -a -um

relative *s* cognát·us -ī *m* (·a -ae *f*)

relax sē remíttō -ere remísī

relentless dīr·us -a -um

relief: be a relief levāméntō esse

relieve leváre

rely on cōnfíd·ō -ere cōnfísus sum (+ *dat*); **relying on** frēt·us -a -um (+ *dat or abl*)

remain mán·eō -ére mānsī mānsúrus; **it remains to** restat ut (+ *subj*)

remedy remédi·um -ī *n;* **apply a remedy** remédium adhibére

remember commemoráre; mémin·ī -ísse (+ *gen or acc*); memóriā tén·eō -ére -uī; **if I remember right** sī bene méminī

reminder: as a reminder memóriae causā

remote control moderátr·um -ī *n* remótum

renown fām·a -ae *f*

repeat répet·ō -ere -ívī -ítus, iteráre; **repeat after me** eísdem verbīs mihi redde (*pl:* réddite)

repeatedly idéntidem

repetition repetíti·ō -ốnis *f*

reporter diurnári·us -ī *m* (·a -ae *f*)

representative vīcári·us -ī *m* (·a -ae *f*)

repress *(emotions)* cohíb·eō -ére -uī -itus

repression continénti·a -ae *f*

republican rēpúblic·us -a -um

republicans optimát·ēs -ium *mpl*

reputation fām·a -ae *f;* **bad reputation** īnfámi·a -ae *f;* **good reputation** honést·ās -átis *f*

rescue ēríp·iō -ere -uī ēréptus

research s investīgắti·ō -ốnis f, indāgắti·ō -ốnis f

research tr investīgắre, indāgắre

resentful īrācúnd·us -a -um

resentment īrācúndi·a -ae f

reservation reservắti·ō -ốnis f

reserve reservắre

resolute cōnfirmắt·us -a -um

respect s observánti·a -ae f; **show repect to** observắre

respect tr observắre

respectability honést·ās -ắtis f

respectable honést·us -a -um

respected honōrắt·us -a -um

respectful obsérv·āns -ántis

respectfully honōríficē, reverénter

responsibility for cūr·a -ae f (+ gen); **it is my responsibility to** ... est mihi cūrae (+ inf)

rest: the rest of the cếter·ī -ae -a

restaurant caupốn·a -ae f

restless inquiét·us -a -um

restroom loc·us -ī m sēcrḗtus

retailer propốl·a -ae m

retake (e.g., a town) recíp·iō -ere recḗpī recéptus

retire (from a job) in ốtium veníre

retirement ốti·um -ī n; **go into retirement** in ốtium veníre

return tr (give back) redd·ō -ere -idī -itus ‖ intr (go back) réd·eō -íre -iī or -ívī -itum

review s (e.g., of a lesson) retractắti·ō -ốnis f

review tr (e.g., a lesson) retractắre; **review the army** exércitum recḗns·eō -ḗre -uī, lūstrắre

rhinoceros rhīnócer·ōs -ốtis m

rib cost·a -ae f

ribbon taéni·a -ae f

rice orýz·a -ae f

rich dīv·es -itis

rich buck (slang) sacc·ō -ốnis m

riches dīvíti·ae -ắrum fpl

rid: get rid of (worries) dílu·ō -ere -ī; (persons) āmốl·ior -írī āmōlítus sum

ride s vécti·ō -ốnis f; **go for a ride** gestātiốnem autocīnḗtō fácere

ride tr (in a car, plane, train) vehor, vehī, vectus sum (autocīnḗtō, āёróplanō, trắmine)

rider vect·or -ốris m, vectr·īx -ícis f

ridge iug·um -ī n

ridiculous rīdícul·us -a -um

rifle sclopét·um -ī n; **automatic rifle** sclopétum automắtum; **fire a rifle** sclopētắre

rifleman sclopētắt·or -ốris m

right adj (opp. of left) dext·er -(e)ra -(e)rum; (correct, proper) rḗct·us -a -um; **do the right thing** frūgem fácere; **on the right** ab dextrā, ā déxterā; **(to the) right** dextrốrsum; **that's right** sīc est; **you're right** probē dīcis [literally, you say correctly], bene dīxístī or vḗra dīcis.

right adv (correctly) rḗctē; **right away** statim, contínuō; **right from the start** in prīncípiō ílicō; **right now** nunciam; **turn right** dextrốrsum sē vértere

right s iūs, iūris n; **civil rights** iūs cīvíle; **you have every right to** ...

omne fās tibi est (+ *inf*); **waive one's rights** dēcéd·ō -ere dēcéssī iūre suō

rim *(of a wheel)* vit·us -ūs *f*

rind *(thick skin of fruit)* córi·um -ī *n*

ring ánul·us -ī *m*; *(for boxing)* suggést·us -ūs *m* pugilātórius; **take off a ring** ánulum détrah·ō -ere dētráxī; **wear a ring** ánulum gestáre

rise *(of a person, mountain)* surg·ō -ere surréxī; *(of several persons, mountains)* cōnsúrgere; *(out of respect)* adsúrgere; *(of heavenly bodies)* ór·ior -írī ortus sum; *(of a river, have its source)* (ex)órior (ex)orírī; **the Tiber rising in the Apennines** Tíberis monte Apennínō (ex)óriēns

risk: at your own risk tuō perículō; **run the risk** perículum fácere; **take a risk** perículum ád·eō -íre -ívī

risky anceps, ancípitis

river flūm·en -inis *n*, amn·is -is *m* *(with no distinction as to size)*

river bed álve·us -ī *m*

roar *(of a lion)* rúg·iō -íre -iī

roast *s* ass·um -ī *n*

roast *tr* assáre

roast beef búbul·a -ae *f* assa

roast pork porcín·a -ae *f* assa

roast veal vitulín·a -ae *f* assa

rob ráp·iō -ere -uī -tus; **rob s.o. of** áliquem spoliáre (+ *abl*)

robber latr·ō -ónis *m*; *(home invader)* perfóss·or -óris *m*

robbery latrōcíni·um -ī *n*

robe vest·is -is *f*

robin rubécul·a -ae *f*; **robins chirp** rubéculae pīpant *(see* **bird***)*

rocket rochét·a -ae *f*

rocking chair sell·a -ae *f* ōscilláris

role model exémpl·ar -áris *n*

roll pānícul·us -ī *m*, pānicéll·us -ī *m*; **call roll** nómina recitáre

roll call nóminum recitáti·ō -ónis *f*; **take roll call** nómina recitáre

rollerblade, rollerskate *intr* pedírotīs lābor lābī lāpsus sum *(see Chapter V)*

rollerblades pedírot·ae -árum *fpl*

rollerskate *s* cálce·us -ī *m* subrotátus, pátin·us -ī *m* rotális

rollerskate *intr* rótulīs patináre

rollerskating patináti·ō -ónis *f* rotális *(see Chapter V)*

rolling pin fístul·a -ae *f*

ROM *(comput)* memóri·a -ae *f* fīxa

Roman Rōmán·us -a -um

Rome Rōm·a -ae *f* *(often referred to simply as* urbs*)*

roof tēct·um -ī *n*

roof tile tégul·a -ae *f*

room conclāv·e -is *n*, cubícul·um -ī *n*; *(small room)* cell·a -ae *f*; **room with bath** cubícul·um -ī *n* bálneō *or* lavácrō (pluviō) īnstrúctum

room key clāv·is -is *f* cubiculáris

roommate sóci·us -ī *m* (·a -ae *f*) cubiculáris

rooster gall·us -ī *m*; **roosters crow** gallī cūcúriunt, canunt *(see* **bird***)*

rose ros·a -ae *f*

round *(in boxing)* congréss·us -ūs *m*

rouge purpuríss·um -ī *n*, fūc·us -ī *m*

rough asp·er -era -erum; *(weather)* túrbid·us -a -um; **rough guess** īnformáta cogitáti·ō -ónis *f*

round up cōg·ō -ere coégī coáctus

route certus curs·us -ūs *m*

row ōrd•ō -inis *m*

row *tr* rēmigā́re *(see Chapter V)*

rowboat scaph•a -ae *f* rēmígera

row home aed•ēs -ium *fpl* seriā́lēs

rowing rēmigā́ti•ō -ṓnis *f*

rubbish! quisquíliae!

ruckus: why are you raising such a ruckus? quid istum clāmṓrem tollis *(pl:* tóllitis)?

rude *(character)* asp•er -era -erum

rug tapḗt•e -is *n*

rugby harpást•um -ī *n;* **play rugby** harpástō lū́dere

rugged asp•er -era -erum

rule *s* rḗgul•a -ae *f;* **break the rule** rḗgulam frang•ō -ere frḗgī frāctus; **follow (observe) the rule** rḗgulam servā́re

rule *tr* reg•ō -ére rēxī rēctus

ruler *(instrument)* rḗgul•a -ae *f* *(sovereign)* rēct•or -ṓris *m*

rum vīn•um -ī *n* Índicum

rumor rūm•or -ṓris *m;* **there's a rumor going around** rūmor pervagā́tur

run *tr* *(a business, shop)* (negṓtium, tabérnam) exérc•eō -ére -uī -itus; *(comput)* **run a program** prográmma administrā́re; **run up bills** aes aliḗnum cōnflā́re ∥ *intr* curr•ō -ere cucúrrī cursum; **run around** cursā́re; **run into s.o. on the street** áliquem offénd•ō -ere -ī in platéā; **run for** *(an office)* pet•ō -ere petī́vī petítus; **run low** dēfíc•iō -ere dēfḗcī; **run out** *(of time)* exī́re; **run up and down** modo hūc modo illūc cursā́re; *(comput)* **the program is running** prográmma operā́tur

running cursū́r•a -ae *f*

runny nose distillāti̇́ón•ēs -um *fpl*

runway āérdrom•us -ī *m*

Sabbath sábbat•a -ṓrum *npl*

saber ēns•is -is *m* falcā́tus

sad trist•is -is -e; *(showing grief one one's face)* maest•us -a -um

saddle sessóbul•um -ī *n*

sadness tristíti•a -ae *f,* maestíti•a -ae *f*

safe *(from)* tūt•us -a -um (ab + *abl);* **safe and sound** salv•us -a -um et sān•us -a -um; **safe from danger** tūtus ā perículō

safe-deposit box dēpositṓri•um -ī *n* syngraphā́rum

safety pin fī́bul•a -ae *f*

sail *s* vēl•um -ī *n*

sail *intr* nāvigā́re, nāve vehor vehī vectus sum

sail boat scaph•a -ae *f* vēlífera

sailing vēlificā́ti•ō -ṓnis *f (see Chapter V)*

sailor naut•a -ae *m,* naútri•a -ae *f*

sake: for heaven's sake obsécrō *(lit: I pray);* **for the sake of** causā (+ *gen) (following the dependent genitive);* **for your sake** tuā *(pl:* vestrā) causā

salad acētā́ri•a -ṓrum *npl*

salary merc•ēs -ḗdis *f;* **pay s.o. a fair salary** aequam mercḗdem álicui solv•ō -ere -ī solū́tus

sale vēndíti•ō -ṓnis *f;* **for sale, on sale** vēnālíci•us -a -um, vēnál•is -is -e; **put up for sale** vēnum dare; **this house is for sale** hae aedēs sunt vēnálēs

saleslady *(in a shop)* tabernā́ri•a -ae *f; (in a clothing store)* vestiā́ri•a -ae *f*

salesman *(in a shop)* tabernā́ri•us -ī *m;* **traveling salesman** ínstit•or -ṓris *m*

saliva salív•a -ae *f*

salmon salm•ō -ṓnis *m*

saloon tabérn·a -ae *f* pōtṓria

salt sāl, salis *n*

salt shaker salín·um -ī *n*

same īdem éadem idem (*gen:* eiúsdem *for all genders*); **it's all the same to me** meā nihil ínterest; **the same thing** idem

sandal (*w. covered toes*) sandáli·um -ī *n;* (*simplest form of sandal, with the sole fastened to feet with thongs*) sóle·a -ae *f;* (*with thick leather sole, tied with straps, characteristically worn by Greeks*) crépid·a -ae *f*

sand trap (*golf*) harēnári·a -ae *f*

sandwich pastíll·um -ī *n* fartum; **ham sandwich** pastíllum pernā fartum

sarcasm dicácit·ās -átis *f*

sarcastic dicácul·us -a -um, dic·āx -ácis

sardine sard·a -ae *f*

sash zōn·a -ae *f*

satisfaction: to your satisfaction ex tuā senténtiā

satisfied contént·us -a -um

satisfy satis fácere (+ *dat*); (*hunger, thirst*) expl·eō -ére -évī -étus; **you can't satisfy everyone** nōn potes ómnibus satis fácere

Saturday di·ēs -éī *m* Sātúrnī

sauce iūs, iūris *n;* (*a dressing, esp. one made with vinegar*) embámm·a -atis *n*

saucer páter·a -ae *f*

sauna sūdātóri·um -ī *n*

sausage farcím·en -inis *n*

save (*also comput*) serváre

savings account cómput·us -ī *m* conditórius

savings bank argentári·a -ae *f* pecúliīs asservándīs

saw *s* serr·a -ae *f*

saw *tr* serrā sec·ō -áre -uī -tus ‖ *intr* serram dúcere

saxophone saxophón·um -ī *n*

say dīc·ō -ere dīxī dictus; **say hello to Rose** iubē (*pl* iubéte) Rosam salvére; **so they say** ita aiunt

scale *s* (*of a fish*) squām·a -ae *f;* (*for weighing*) trútin·a -ae *f*

scale *tr* (*a fish*) dēsquāmáre

scaly squāmós·us -a -um

scan (*poetry, also comput*) *tr* scand·ō -ere -ī scānsus; (*read over quickly*) cito perlégere

scanner (*comput*) scānsóri·um -ī *n*

scandalous flāgitiós·us -a -um

scare térr·eō -ére -uī -itus

scared térrit·us -a -um; **I am scared to death** exanimátus (-a) metū sum

scarf amictóri·um -ī *n* (colláre)

scenery scēn·a -ae *f*

schedule hōrári·um -ī *n;* **bus schedule** hōrárium autoraedárum longárum; **flight schedule** hōrárium āëroplanórum; **train schedule** hōrárium tráminum

scholar érudít·us -ī *m* (·a -ae *f*)

scholarly érudít·us -a -um

school *adj* (*of or at a school*) scholár·is -is -e

school lūd·us -ī *m;* (*advanced*) schol·a -ae *f;* **attend school** scholam frequentáre; **go to school** scholam óbeō obíre óbiī *or* obívī; **skip school** ínsciīs paréntibus ā scholā abésse

school book lib·er -rī *m* scholáris

schoolboy discípul·us -ī *m*

school building aedíffci·um -ī *n* scholáre

schoolgirl discípul·a -ae *f*

schoolmate condiscípul·us -ī *m* (·a -ae *f*)

school supplies īnstrúment·um -ī *n* scholáre

scissors forf·ex -icis *f*

scold obiurgáre

scolding obiurgáti·ō -ónis *f;* **get a scolding** obiurgárī

score *s* stat·us -ūs *m,* summ·a -ae *f* pūnctórum; *(in golf)* summa íctuum; **final score** status fīnális; **he doesn't know what the score is** *(fig)* nescit quid agátur; **keep score** ratiónem notáre; **the score is tied** summae pūnctórum sunt parēs

score a goal *(soccer)* follem pede pulsáre *(lacrosse)* pilam per portam iáci·ō -ere iēcī iactus; **score a point** pūnctum ferō ferre tulī lātus; **score a touchdown** calcem *(or* crétam) attíng·ō -ere áttigī attáctus

scorn contémpti·ō -ónis *f*

scorpion scórpi·ō -ónis *m;* **scorpions sting** scropiónēs īcunt

scot-free: get off scot-free impunít·us (-a) dīmítt·or -ī dīmíss·us (-a) sum

scram! ápage!

scrape: scrape together the money argéntum con·rádō -rádere -rásī -rásus

screen *(on television or computer)* quadr·um -ī *n* vīsíficum; *(movie screen)* línte·um -ī *n* cīnēmato-gráphicum

screenplay scrīpt·um -ī *n* scaenárium

screw cóchle·a -ae *f*

screw *(cheat)* dēfraudáre; *(sexually)* dēbattuáre

screwdriver cochleatórstr·um -ī *n*

scribble cōnscrībilláre

scroll down *(comput)* dēvólv·ō -ere -ī

scrub térg·eō -ére tersī tersus

sculptor sculpt·or -óris *m*

sculptress sculptr·īx -ícis *f*

sculpture sculptúr·a -ae *f*

sea mar·e -is *n*

seacoast ōr·a -ae *f* marítima

sea gull gávi·a -ae *f*

seal sign·um -ī *n; (of the sea)* phōc·a -ae *f*

seal *(an envelope)* conglūtináre

seam sūtúr·a -ae *f*

seamstress *(making clothes)* vestífic·a -ae *f; (altering clothes)* sarcinátr·īx -ícis *f*

searchlight lūminár·e -is *n*

seashore act·a -ae *f*

season *s* temp·us -oris *n* annī; **in season** tempestív·us -a -um

season *tr* cónd·iō -íre -ívī *or* -iī -ítus

seasoning condīmént·um -ī *n*

seat sēd·ēs -is *f; (on a fixed bench or chair)* sedíl·e -is *n; (in school)* subsélli·um -ī *n* (scholáre); **back seat** sedēs postérior; **front seat** sedēs antérior; **reserved seat** sedēs reserváta

seatbelt cinctúr·a -ae *f* sēcūritátis; **fasten** *(or* **put on) one's seatbelt** cinctúram accín·gō -gere -xī -ctus; **unfasten one's seatbelt** cinctúram sēcūritátis laxáre

second *adj* secúnd·us -a -um

second *s (of time)* secúnd·a -ae *f*

secretary sēcrētári·us -ī *m* (·a -ae *f);* **corresponding secretary** ab epístulīs

secretary of agriculture adminíst·er -rī *m* agricultúrae prōvehendae

secretary of education adminíst·er -rī *m* ērudītiónis

secretary of state adminíst·er -rī *m* rērum externárum

secretary of the interior adminíst·er -rī *m* rērum internárum

secretary of the treasury adminíst·er -rī *m* fiscális

section *(of a city)* régi·ō -ónis

seductive illecebrós·us -a -um

see vídeō vidére vīdī vīsus; *(look at)* aspíc·iō -ere aspéxī aspéctus; **I see** *(I understand)* iam téneō; **see again** revidére; **see to it that** cūrā *(pl:* cūráte) ut *(+ subj)*; **you see** *[parenthetical]* enim

seem víd·eor -érī vīsus sum

self: he was not his usual self nōn fuit cūius modī solet

self-confidence fīdúci·a -ae *f*

self-confident cōnfíd·ēns -éntis; **be self-confident** sibi cōnfíd·ō -ere cōnfísus sum

self-control abstinénti·a -ae *f*

self-controlled comp·os -otis suī

self-respect dígnit·ās -átis *f*

sell vénd·ō -ere véndidī vénditus; *(of a merchant)* vēnditáre

seller véndit·or -óris *m*, vénditr·īx -ícis *f*

semester seméstr·e -is *n*

seminar sēmínári·um -ī *n* acadēmicum

senate senát·us -ūs *m*

senate building cúri·a -ae *f*

senate session senát·us -ūs *m;* **call (hold) a senate session** senátum vocáre (habére)

senator senát·or -óris *mf*

senatorial senātóri·us -a -um

senior séni·or -óris *mf*

sense of duty, of responsibility píet·ās -átis *f*

sensible prúd·ēns -éntis; **be sensible** sáp·iō -ere

sentence *s (gram)* senténti·a -ae *f*, ōráti·ō -ónis *f; (leg)* iūdíci·um -ī *n;* **pass sentence on** iūdícium fácere dē (+ *abl)*

separate sēparáre

September mēns·is -is *m* Septémber; **in September** mēnsē Septémbrī

sergeant ópti·ō -ónis *mf*

serious grav·is -is -e; **are you serious?** sēriône dīcis tū?

seriousness grávit·ās -átis *f*

sermon homíli·a -ae *f;* **give a sermon** homíliam habére

serpent serp·ēns -éntis *m;* **serpents bite (crawl, hiss)** serpéntēs īcunt (serpent, síbilant)

serve *s (tennis)* dēiéct·us -ūs *m*

serve *tr (a person)* sérv·iō -íre -iī (+ *dat); (food)* appón·ō -ere appósuī appósitus; *(mil)* stīpéndia fácere, (stīpéndium) mér·eō -ére -uī; **serve a summons on** diem dare (+ *dat);* **serve as a soldier or sailor** (ut) mīles aut nauta merére; **serve one's country** dē rē públicā merére ‖ *intr (tennis)* dēíc·iō -ere dēiécī

service station státi·ō -ónis *f* benzīnária

service: be at s.o.'s service álicui praestō esse; **be of service to s.o.** álicui prōsum prōdésse prófuī

serviceman mīlitár·is -is *m*

set *s (e.g., of tools)* īnstrūmént·um -ī *n*

set *tr (to put)* pōn·ō -ere posuī pósitus; **set a price** prétium fácere *or* státu·ō -ere -ī statútus; **set aside** pónere; **set on fire** incénd·ō -ere -ī incénsus; **set the table** mēnsam pónere ‖ *intr (of* *the sun)* óccid·it -ere -it; **set out** profícísc·ōr -ī proféctus sum

seventh heaven: be in seventh heaven in caelō esse

sew su·ō -ere -ī sūtus

sewing machine máchin·a -ae *f* sūtória

sex *(gender)* sex·us -ūs *m; (act)* stupr·um -ī *n;* **have sex with** stuprum fácere cum (+ *abl)*

sh-h-h-h! st, st!

shabby sórdid·us -a -um

shake hands dextrae iúngere dextram *or* dextram iúngere (cum áliquō); *(when campaigning)* manūs prēnsáre

shake up commóv·eō -ére commóvī commótus, perturbáre

shallow ténu·is -is -e

shame ignōmíni·a -ae *f;* **shame on you!** prō pudor!; **that's a darn shame** édepol fácinus ímprobum; **what a shame!** fácinus indígnum!; O rem indígnam!

shameful ignōminiós·us -a -um

shameless ímprob·us -a -um

shampoo lōmént·um -ī *n* capilláre

shape fōrm·a -ae *f;* **be in bad (good) shape** malī (bonī) hábitūs esse, in malō (bonō) hábitū esse

share *(stock)* ácti·a -ae *f*

shark pistr·is -is *m;* **a shark's dorsal fin** pistris pinn·a -ae *f* dorsális

shave *s* rāsúr·a -ae *f*

shave *tr* rād·ō -ere rāsī rāsus; **shave every day** fáciem cōtídiē rāsitáre

sheep ov·is -is *f*

sheer *(fabrics)* rall·us -a -um

sheet *(of paper)* sched·a -ae *f,* fóli·um -ī *n* chartáceum; *(for the bed)* strágul·um -ī *n* línteum

shell *(of clam, oyster)* test·a -ae *f; (of turtle)* testúd·ō -inis *f; (of peanut)* putám·en -inis *n*

shepherd pāst·or -óris *m*

sheriff geraéf·a -ae *m*

shifting *(wind, weather)* vári·us -a -um

shifty móbil·is -is -e; **shifty like the wind** ventós·us -a -um

shinbone tíbi·a -ae *f*

shine lúc·eō -ére lūxī; **shine on** illūcére (+ *dat)*

ship *s* nāv·is -is *f*

ship *tr* déveh·ō -ere dēvéxī dēvéctus

shipyard nāvál·ia -ium *npl*

shirt indúsi·um -ī *n,* camísi·a -ae *f*

shiver *s* trem·or -óris *m; (severe)* membrórum quassáti·ō -ónis *f*

shiver *intr* trem·ō -ere -uī

shock ēlétricus íct·us -ūs *m*

shock *(emotionally)* átton·ō -áre -uī -itus

shoe *(worn with toga)* cálce·us -ī *m; (oxfords)* cálceus subtāláris; *(fancy low shoe, of different colors, gold, yellow, decorated with pearls, etc.)* socc·us -ī *m,* sóccul·us -ī *m; (red shoes of senator)* cálceus múlleus

shoelace corrígi·a -ae *f*

shoemaker sūt·or -óris *m*

shoemaker's shop sūtrín·a -ae *f*

shoe polish cēróm·a -atis *n* sūtórium

shoe store tabérn·a -ae *f* sūtrína

shook: all shook up veheménter perturbát·us -a -um

shoot *(a person)* sclopétō trānsfíg·ō -ere trānsfíxī trānsfíxus

shop *s* tabérn·a -ae *f; (workshop)* officín·a -ae *f*

shop *intr* (*at a grocery store*) obsōnâre; **go shopping** ēmptum eō īre īvī; **I shopped for clothes** per tabērnās lustrâvī ut vestēs émerem

shopkeeper tabernâri·us -ī *m* (·a -ae *f*)

shopper ēmpt·or -ôris *m*, ēmptr·īx -ícis *f*; (*for groceries*) obsōnât·or -ôris *m*, obsōnâtr·īx -ícis *f*

shopping ēmpti·ō -ônis *f*; (*for groceries*) obsōnât·us -ūs *m*

shop window fenéstr·a -ae *f* mercātôria

shore ōr·a -ae *f* marítima

short *adj* brev·is -is -e; (*vowel*) corrépt·us -a -um

short *s* **in short** in summā, ad summam

shorts subligâcul·um -ī *n*; (*street wear*) dēcurtâtae brāc·ae -ârum *fpl*

shortstop intermédius basiâri·us -ī *m*, intermédia basiâri·a -ae *f*

shorty brevícul·us -ī *m* (·a -ae *f*), pūmíli·ō -ônis *mf*

shoulder (h)úmer·us -ī *m*; **shrug the shoulders** úmerōs allevâre

shoulder bag pēr·a -ae *f*

shoulder blade scápul·a -ae *f*

shotgun focíl·e -is *n* (bifistulâtum)

shovel pāl·a -ae *f*

show mōnstrâre, ostén·dō -dere -dī -sus *or* -tus; **show off** sē iactâre; **show up** appâr·eō -ére -uī; **this shows that …** indíciō est (+ *acc & inf*)

shower balnéol·um -ī *n* plúvium; (*rain*) im·ber -bris *m*; **take a shower** balnéolō plúviō ūtor ūtī ūsus sum

shrewd astût·us -a -um, cállid·us -a -um

shrimp squill·a -ae *f*; (*a little guy*) pūmíli·ō -ônis *mf*

shrine sacrâri·um -ī *n*

shrub frût·ex -icis *m*

shuffle (*cards*) mísc·eō -ére -uī mīxtus

shun publicity forum ac lūcem fúg·iō -ere fūgī

shut claud·ō -ere clausī clausus; **shut down** (*comput*) claúdere; **shut up!** óbserā ōs tuum!; **why don't you just shut up?** quīn tū tacēs modo?

shutter forícul·a -ae *f*

shy tímid·us -a -um

sick (*of body or mind*) ae·ger -gra -grum; (*of body*) aegrôt·us -a -um; **get sick** in morbum íncid·ō -ere -ī; **I am sick and tired of hearing the same thing over and over** (mē) valdē pertaédet iam audîre éadem idéntidem; **I am sick and tired of the business** mē negôtī valdē pertaédet

sickly male válid·us -a -um

sickness morb·us -ī *m*

side *s* (*of a body, hill, camp, ship, etc.*) lat·us -eris *n*; (*quarter, direction*) par·s -tis *f*; (*faction*) part·ēs -ium *fpl*; (*party*) par·s -tis *f* (*mostly plural*); **be on the side of** stāre ab (+ *abl*), sént·iō -îre sēnsī cum (+ *abl*); **from** (*or* **on**) **all sides** úndique; **on both sides** utrímque; **on his mother's side** mātérnō génere; **on the other side of** ultrā (+ *acc*); **on the right side of** ā lâtere dextrō (+ *gen*); **on this side of** cis *or* citrā (+ *acc*)

side *intr* **side with** stāre ab (+ *abl*), partēs (+ *gen*) sequ·or -ī secútus sum

sideline (*sports*) lín>e·a -ae *f* laterâlis

side street dēvertícul·um -ī *n*, vi·a -ae *f* laterâlis, via secundâria

sidewalk crepíd·ō -inis *f* viâria

sieve crībr·um -ī *n*

sigh *s* gémit·us -ūs *m*

sigh *intr* gem·ō -ere -uī -itum; **sigh over** gémere

sight *(sense)* vīs•us -ūs *m;* **at first sight** *(on the first appearance of a person or thing)* prīmā spéciē; *(view subjectively)* prīmō aspéctū; **catch sight of** cōnspíc•iō -ere cōnspéxī; **lose sight of** ē cōnspéctū āmítt•ō -ere āmīsī

sign *(a document)* subscrīb•ō -ere subscrípsī subscríptus

silence silénti•um -ī *n;* **call for silence** siléntium fácere

silent tácit•us -a -um; **become** *(or* **fall) silent** conticḗsc•ō -ere; **be silent** tác•eō -ére -uī; **keep s.th. silent** áliquid tacére

silk *adj* séric•us -a -um; **silk clothes** séric•a -ōrum *npl*

silk *s* séric•um -ī *n*

silliness inépti•a -ae *f*

silly dēsípi•ēns -éntis; **be silly** dēsíp•iō -ere, inépt•iō -īre; **don't be silly** nōlī ineptíre

silverware argénte•a -ōrum *npl*

simple simpl•ex -icis [*single-ending adj*]

simply *(in a simple manner; merely)* simplíciter; *(only)* tantúmmodo; **I simply don't know what he is thinking of** iam plānē quid cōgitet nésciō; **simply not** nōn omnínō

since *prep* ex (+ *abl*), ab (+ *abl*); **ever since** ūsque ab (+ *abl*), ex quō témpore

since *conj (because)* quia, quóniam, cum; **since** *(temporal)* ut (+ *indic*), postquam (+ *indic*), ex quō témpore (+ *indic*)

sincere sincḗr•us -a -um

sing canō cánere cécinī cantus, cantáre

singer cantát•or -ōris *m,* cantátr•īx -ícis *f*

single sōl•us -a -um; *(unmarried male)* caeleb•s -is; *(unmarried female)* innúpta

single room conclāv•e -is *n* ūníus lectī

singular *adj* singulár•is -is -e *(opp:* plūrál•is -is -e);* **in the singular** singuláriter

sink *(in a bathroom)* labéll•um -ī *n; (in a kitchen)* fusóri•um -ī *n*

sip sorbilláre

sir! bone vir!

sister sor•or -óris *f;* **little sister** sorórcul•a -ae *f*

sister-in-law glos, glōris *f; (sister of husband)* soror -óris *f* marítī; *(wife of brother)* ux•or -óris *f* frātris

sit séd•eō -ére sēdī sessúrus; **sit down** cōnsíd•ō -ere cōnsédī; **sit up!** rēctē sedē *(pl:* sedéte)!

site sit•us -ūs *m,* loc•us -ī *m (pl:* loc•a -ōrum *npl)*

sitting room exédr•a -ae *f,* sessóri•um -ī *n*

situated sit•us -a -um; **situated on, near** appósit•us -a -um (+ *dat*)

situation: that's the situation here in Rome hīc Rōmae rēs sē sīc habent; **you see what the situation is** vidēs quō in locō haec rēs sit

situps: do situps idéntidem resíd•eō -ére resḗdī

size magnitúd•ō -inis *f,* amplitúd•ō -inis *f*

skate *s* cálce•us -ī *m* subrotátus *(see Chapter V)*

skate *intr* (rótulīs) patináre

skateboard tábul•a -ae *f* subrotáta

skater patinát•or -óris *m,* patinátr•īx -ícis *f*

skating *s* patináti•ō -ónis *f*

ski *s* nart·a -ae *f;* **put on skis** nartās pédibus aptáre, nartās adstrín·gō -gere -xī; **take off the skis** nartās dēstríngere; **wax the skis** nartās inceráre *(see Chapter V)*

ski *intr* nartáre

ski boot cálig·a -ae *f* nartātória

skier nartát·or -óris *m,* nartátr·īx -ícis *f*

skiing *s* nartáti·ō -ónis *f*

ski instructor nartándī magís·ter -trī *m* (·tra -trae *f*)

ski jump suggést·us -ūs *m* dēsultórius

ski jumping dēsultúr·a -ae *f* nartātória

ski lift anabáthr·um -ī *n* nartātórium

skill artifíci·um -ī *n*

skilled cállid·us -a -um

skillful artificiós·us -a -um; **skillful in** scīt·us -a -um (+ *gen*)

skillfulness callídit·ās -átis *f*

ski lodge cas·a -ae *f* nartātórum

skin cut·is -is *f* (**pale** pállida; **dry** árida; **soft** móllis; **tough** dúra; **wrinkled** rūgósa)

ski pole bácul·um -ī *n* nartātórium

skirt gunn·a -ae *f,* cástul·a -ae *f*

ski run currícul·um -ī *n* nartātórium

ski slope clīv·us -ī *m* nartātórius, nartātória dēcúrsi·ō -ónis *f*

skull calvári·a -ae *f;* **I'll break your skull** dímínuam ego tibi caput

skunk vivérr·a -ae *f* pútida; *(slang)* hom·ō -inis *mf* pútid·us (-a)

sky cael·um -ī *n*

skycap *(at airport)* báiul·us -ī *m*

skylight complúvi·um -ī *n*

slalom dēcúrsi·ō -ónis *f* flexuósa

slam dunk tuxtax-immíssi·ō -ónis *f*

slap *s* álap·a -ae *f*

slap *tr* álapam dare (+ *dat*)

sled tráhe·a -ae *f,* sclódi·a -ae *f* (lūsória)

sledgehammer marc·us -ī *m*

sleep *s* somn·us -ī *m;* **deep sleep** sop·or -óris *m*

sleep *intr* dórm·iō -íre -ívī *or* -iī -ítum; **go to sleep** dormítum eō īre iī *or* īvī; *(doze off)* obdormísc·ō -ere, obdormívī; **put to sleep** in sumnum collocáre

sleeping bag sacc·us -ī *m* dormītórius

sleeping car curr·us -ūs *m* dormītórius

sleepy somniculós·us -a -um

sleet im·ber -bris *m* grándine mīxtus

sleeve *(reaching to the hand)* mánic·a -ae *f;* **with long sleeves** manicát·us -a -um

sleeveless sine mánicīs

sleigh tráhe·a -ae *f;* **go sleigh riding** tráheā veh·or -ī vectus sum

slice segmént·um -ī *n*

slide *s* imág·ō -inis *f* trānslúcida; **show slides** imáginēs trānslúcidās exhíb·eō -ére -uī -itus

slide *intr* lāb·or -ī lāpsus sum

slide projector prōiectóri·um -ī *n* imáginum trānslūcidárum

slim grácil·is -is -e *(opp: obésus)*

slip *s (clothing)* indúcul·a -ae *f* īnférior, hypozóni·um -ī *n; (of paper)* schédul·a -ae *f; (error)* peccát·um -ī *n;* **a slip of the tongue** laps·us -ūs *m* linguae

slip *tr (give furtively)* fúrtim dare; **it slipped my mind** ē memóriā éxcidit; **it slipped my mind to …** fúgit mē (+ *inf*) ‖ *intr* lāb·or -ī lápsus sum; *(leave furtively)* **slip out** sē subdúcere

slipper socc·us -ī *m; (of felt)* ūd·ō -ónis *m*

slippery lúbric•us -a -um

slope *s* clīv•us -ī *m*; **steep (gentle) slope** árduus (lēnis) clīvus

slope *intr* verg•ō -ere; **sloping toward the sea** vergēns ad mare

sloppy *(weather)* spurc•us -a -um; *(person)* néglig•ēns -éntis; *(road)* lutulént•us -a -um

slow *adj (physically, mentally)* lent•us -a -um; **slow to learn** segn•is -is -e

slow down cursum réprim•ō reprímere représsī

sluggish heb•es -etis; **be sluggish** héb•eō -ére

sly astūt•us -a -um; **on the sly** clam

small parv•us -a -um; párvul•us -a -um

smaller min•or -or -us

small-mindedness humílit•ās -átis *f*

smallpox varíol•ae -árum *fpl;* **have smallpox** varíolīs labōráre; **smallpox vaccination** variolárum vaccináti•ō -ónis *f*

smart *(clever)* cállid•us -a -um; *(talented)* ingeniós•us -a -um; *(impertinent)* ínsol•ēns -éntis; **don't talk smart to me** nōlī male mihi dícere; **she is smart** ingeniósa est

smell *(sense)* odōrát•us -ūs *m; (odor)* od•or -óris *m*

smell *tr* olfác•iō -ere olfécī ‖ *intr (good, bad)* (bene, male) ól•eō -ére -uī; *(stink)* obolére

smile subríd•eō -ére subrísī

smoke fumáre; *(tobacco)* tabáco ūtor ūtī ūsus sum

smoker fūmá•tor -tóris *m* (•trīx -ícis *f*)

smooth-talking blandíloqu•us -a -um

smug cōnfíd•ēns -éntis

smugness cōnfídénti•a -ae *f*

snack merénd•a -ae *f;* **have a snack** meréndam cápere

snack bar vorātrín•a -ae *f*

snail cóchle•a -ae *f*

snake angu•is -is *mf*

snarl *(of an animal)* gánn•iō -íre

sneak off clánculum áb•eō -íre ábiī

sneakers cálce•ī -órum *mpl* gýmnicī

sneeze *s* sternūmént•um -ī *n*

sneeze *intr* stérnu•ō -ere -ī

snobbish fastīdiós•us -a -um

snore ronc•or -árī -átus sum

snow *s* nix, nivis *f*

snow *impers v* ningit níngere nīnxit

snowball pil•a -ae *f* nívis

snowdrift agg•er -eris *m* níveus

snowed: I am snowed under with óbru•or -ī óbrutus, tamquam fluctū, sīc ego (+ *abl*)

snowfall nivis cās•us -ūs *m*

snowstorm ning•or -óris *m*

snowy nivós•us -a -um, nivál•is -is -e

so *(with adj or adv)* tam, ita; *(with verb)* ádeō, sīc; **and so** ítaque; **how so?** quid ita?; **is it really so?** ítane vērō?; **is that so?** ítane?; **so far so good** bellē adhūc; **so many** tot; **so much** tant•us -a -um; **so much for that** eátenus; **so so** *(tolerably well)* ita tenúiter; **so to speak** ut ita dícam; **that's not so!** haud ita est!

soak made•fáciō -fácere -fécī -fáctus

soaking rain largus im•ber -bris *m*

soap sap•ō -ónis *m;* **bar of soap** sapónis quádrul•a -ae *f;* **liquid soap** sapō liquidus

sober *(not drunk)* sóbri•us -a -um *(opp:* ébrius)

soccer pedifólli·um -ī *n,* pedilūdi·um -ī *n;* **play soccer** pedifólle lúdere *(see Chapter V)*

soccer ball pedifóll·is -is *m*

soccer player lūs·or -ốris *m,* lūstr·īx -ícis *f* pedifólliī

soccer field camp·us -ī *m* pedifóliī, campus lūsốrius

soccer shoes calceāmént·a -ốrum *npl* pedifóliī

soccer stadium stádi·um -ī *n* pedifólliī

socks impíli·a -ốrum *npl*

sociable sociábil·is -is -e

social security assēcūrắti·ō -ốnis *f* sociális

socket contáct·um -ī *n* (ēléctricum)

soda aqu·a -ae *f* Selterắna

sofa tor·us -ī *m* tōméntō fartus

soft moll·is -is -e

softly *(in a low voice)* summíssā voce

software *(comput)* part·ēs -ium *fpl* programmatiốnis

soldier mīl·es -itis *mf (see chapter on War and Peace)*

sole *(of shoe or foot)* sol·um -ī *n,* plant·a -ae *f*

solution solúti·ō -ốnis *f*

some *adj* áliquī áliqua áliquod *(pl:* áliquī áliquae áliqua);* **some** *(a number of)* áliquot *(indecl);* **some (amount of)** áliquid *(+ gen);* **some meat** áliquid carnis; **some ... or other** nésciō quī, nésciō quae, nésciō quod; **some senator or other** nésciō quī senátor

someday *(in indef fut)* aliquándō, áliquā diē

someone áliquis, alicúius

sometime (or other) aliquándō; **sometime ago** dūdum, prídem

sometimes nōnnúmquam; intérdum; **sometimes ... sometimes** modo ... modo, intérdum ... intérdum

somewhat *adv* aliquántō; **feel somewhat better** *(of a patient)* meliúscul·us -a -um esse

son fíli·us -ī *m*

song cant·us -ūs *m,* cántic·um -ī *n*

son-in-law gen·er -erī *m*

soon mox; *(in a minute)* iam; *(at any moment)* iam iam; **as soon as** cum prímum; **as soon as possible** quam prímum; **soon thereafter** mox deínde; **how soon?** quam mox?; **too soon** nímium cito; **very soon** pérbrevī témpore

sooner: no sooner said than done dictō cítius *or* dictum factum; **sooner or later** sérius ócius

sophomore sophomốr·us -ī *m* (·a -ae *f*)

soprano suprāníst·a -ae *f*

sore throat exasperátae fauc·ēs -ium *fpl*

sorority sodálit·ās -átis *f* alumnárum

sorry: I feel sorry for the others mē míseret aliốrum; **I'm (you're) sorry** mē (tē) paénitet

sound *adj* ínte·ger -gra -grum

sound *s* son·us -ī *m*

soup iúscul·um -ī *n,* sorbíti·ō -ốnis *f*

soup bowl mágid·a -ae *f*

soup spoon cóchle·ar -áris *m* capácius

source fōn·s -tis *m,* cap·ut -itis *n*

south *adj* ínfér·ior -ior -ius, merīdiắn·us -a -um; **on the south side** látere merīdiắnō; **south of** infrā (+ *acc*)

south *adv* ad merídiem

south *s* merīdi·ēs -éī *m,* merīdiắn·um -ī *n;* **in the south** ā merídiē

southern merīdiōnál·is -is -e, merīdián·us -a -um, īnfér·ior -ior -ius

southward in merídiem versus [versus *is an adverb*]

south wind Aus·ter -trī *m*

sow porc·a -ae *f,* sū·s -is *f;* **sows oink** sūēs grúnniunt

spacious ampl·us -a -um

Spain Hispáni·a -ae *f*

spaghetti spacéll·ī -órum *mpl*

spam (*comput*) saginắti·ō -ónis *f*

spark plug candél·a -ae *f* accēnsíva

spare time temp·us -oris *n* subsicívum

sparrow pass·er -eris *m* (*see* **bird**)

spasm spasm·us -ī *m;* **have a muscle spasm** ā músculī spasmō labōrắre

speak *tr & intr* loqu·or -ī locútus sum; dīc·ō -ere dīxī dictus; **speak Latin, speak correct Latin** Latínē loquī; **so to speak** ut ita dīcam; **speak! I'm listening** lóquere! áudiō; **speak of the devil** lupus in fábulā; **well, speak up!** quīn tū ēlóquere!

speaker megaphṓn(i)·um -ī *n*

special delivery letter epístul·a -ae *f* accelerắta

speech ōrắti·ō -ónis *f;* **make a speech** ōrātiónem habére

speed limit vēlōcitắtis mod·us -ī *m*

spell *tr* scrīb·ō -ere scrīpsī scrīptus; **spell correctly** rēctē scríbere; **spell with** scríbere per (+ *acc*); **some spell "cum" with a "q" if it signifies time** quīdam scríbunt "cum" per "q" lítteram, sī tempus signíficat

spelling *s* orthográphi·a -ae *f*

spend (*time*) agō ágere ēgī áctus, cōnsúm·ō -ere -psī -ptus; **spend the night** pernoctấre; **spend time (effort, money) on** tempus (óperam,

pecúniam) impénd·ō -ere -ī impénsus (in + *acc*)

spicy ácer ācris ācre

spider aráne·us -ī *m* (·a -ae *f*)

spider web aráne·a -ae *f*

spill *tr* effúnd·ō -ere effúdī effúsus **‖** *intr* effúndor effúndī effúsus sum

spinach spináci·a -ae *f*

spine (*anat*) spīn·a -ae *f* dorsī

spirit: spirit of the law volúnt·ās -ắtis *f* lēgis; **that's the right spirit now** nunc tū frūgī bonae es

spit *s* spūt·um -ī *n*

spit *tr & intr* spu·ō -ere -ī spūtus; (*frequentative*) sputáre

splendid: absolutely splendid! nimis factum bene!; **splendid!** euge!

split one's sides laughing ília sua rīsū dissólv·ō -ere -ī

spoon cóchle·ar -ắris *n*

sport āthlētic·a -ae *f,* dispórt·us -ūs *m*

sport shirt camísi·a -ae *f* campéstris

sportswear vest·is -is *f* campéstris

spouse con·iūnx -iugis *mf*

sprain *s* luxātúr·a -ae *f*

sprain *tr* luxáre

spread sheet (*comput*) chart·a -ae *f* computātíva

spring fōn·s -tis *m;* (*season*) vēr, vēris *n*

spring break féri·ae -ắrum *fpl* vernae; **spend the spring break** fériās vernās agō ágere ēgī āctus

sprint curs·us -ūs *m* brevis

spunk alácrit·ās -ắtis *f*

spunky ála·cer -cris -cre

squabble *s* rīx·a -ae *f*

squabble *intr* rīx·or -ắrī -ắtus sum

square *s* quadrắt·um -ī *n; (rectangular space surrounded by buildings or streets)* ắre·a -ae *f; (carpenter's tool)* norm·a -ae *f*

square *intr* **this simply doesn't square** nōn sānē quadrat

squeak *(of mice, rats)* míntr·iō -íre

squeeze the flesh *(when campaigning)* prēnsắre

squirrel sciŭr·us -ī *m*

stability fírmit·ās -átis *f*

stable *adj* firm·us -a -um

stable *s* stábul·um -ī *n; (for horses)* equíl·e -is *n; (for cows)* bovíl·e -is *n; (for sheep)* ovíl·e -is *n; (for pigs)* suíl·e -is *n*

stadium stádi·um -ī *n*

staff member, staff officer contubernál·is -is *mf*

stag cerv·us -ī *m*

stage scēn·a -ae *f*, proscéni·um -ī *n; (step in progress)* grad·us -ūs *m;* **go on the stage** in scēnam prṓd·eō -íre -iī; **stage of life** aetátis grad·us -ūs *m*

stair well scālári·um -ī *n*

staircase scál·ae -árum *fpl*

stairs scál·ae -árum *fpl;* **climb the stairs** per scālās ascénd·ō -ere -ī

stamp pittáci·um -ī *n* cursuále

stand *tr* **I can't stand him** istum ferre nōn queō; **I can't stand the cold** frígoris impátiēns sum ‖ *intr* stō stāre stetī; **I'd like to know how matters stand** velim scīre quō modō rēs sē hábeant

standing ovation: give s.o. a standing ovation álicui stantēs plau·dō -dere -sī

stands *(bleachers)* for·ī -ṓrum *mpl*

staple úncul·us -ī *m*, uncín·us -ī *m*, cōnfíbul·a -ae *f*

stapler uncīnátr·um -ī *n*, cōnfībulátr·um -ī *n*

starling sturn·us -ī *m (see* **bird)**

start iníti·um -ī *n;* **at the start of the year** annō ineúnte; **you've made a good start** bene hábent tibi prīncípia

starter *(on a car)* incitátr·um -ī *n;* **for starters** prīncipiō

starvation fam·ēs -is *f*

starve *tr* fāme cōn·fíciō -fícere -fḗcī -féctus ‖ *intr* fāme cṓnficī; **I'm starved** fame ēnéctus sum

state *(the state as a community)* cívit·ās -átis *f;* **state of mind** affécti·ō -ṓnis *f* ánimī

statesman vir, virī *m* cīvílis

stationery chart·a *f* epistuláris

stationery store tabérn·a -ae *f* chartária

statue státu·a -ae *f*, sign·um -ī *n*

status stat·us -ūs *m*

statute lēx, lēgis *f*

stay mán·eō -ére -sī -súrus; *(temporarily)* mor·or -ắrī -átus sum

steak frūst·um -ī *n* búbulae

steal fūr·or -ắrī -átus sum; clep·ō -ere -sī -tus; toll·ō -ere sústulī sublátus

steeple turr·is -is *f* campānária

steer *s* iuvénc·us -ī *m*

steer *tr* gubernáre

steering wheel rot·a -ae *f* moderátrīx

step *s* grad·us -ūs *m;* **step by step** gradátim; **steps** *(of stairs)* grad·ūs -uum *mpl;* **take steps** *(take measures)* ratiṓnem infre

step grádi·or -ī gressus sum; **step on it!** mātúrā! *(pl:* mātūráte!)*

stepbrother *(on father's side)* vītricī fíli·us -ī *m; (on mother's side)* novércae fílius

stepdaughter prīvígn·a -ae *f*

stepfather vítric·us -ī *m*

stepmother novérc·a -ae *f*

stepsister *(on father's side)* vītricī fíli·a -āe *f; (on mother's side)* novércae fília

stepson prīvígn·us -ī *m*

stereo stereophóni·um -ī *n*

stern asp·er -era -erum

stew *tr* lentō igne coqu·ō -ere coxī coctus ‖ *intr* aestuáre; **I stewed over it for a long time** in eō aestuávī diū

steward hosp·es -itis *m* āérius

stewardess hóspit·a -ae *f* āéria

stewed *(drunk)* ēlíx·us -a -um

stick to one's guns in senténtiā stō stāre stetī; **stick to the truth** in vēritáte mán·eō -ére mānsī

still *(till now)* adhūc

sting *s (on a bee)* acúle·us -ī *m; (bite)* ict·us -ūs *m*

sting *tr* īc·ō -ere īcī ictus

stingy sórdid·us -a -um

stink foét·eō -ére

stinky foétid·us -a -um

stock ácti·a -ae *f*

stock exchange burs·a -ae *f*

stock broker chrēmatíst·a -ae *m* (·ria -riae *f*)

stocking tībiál·e -is *n; (of felt and covering part of the legs)* impíli·um -ī *n*

stock market chrēmatistéri·um -ī *n*, burs·a -ae *f*

stomach stómach·us -ī *m*, ven·ter -tris *m*

stomach ache dol·or -óris *m* stómachī

stone: I will leave no stone unturned nihil praetermíttam

stoned *(drunk)* ēlíx·us -a um

stool scabéll·um -ī *n; (for sitting or mounting)* scamn·um -ī *n*

stool pigeon ind·ex -icis *mf*

stop *(come to a stop)* sist·ō -ere stitī; *(desist from)* désin·ō -ere dēsívī *or* désiī (+ *inf);* **does the bus (train) stop in ...** subsístitne autoraéda longa (trāmen) in (+ *abl)?;* **stop!** astā!; **stop off at** dēversárī apud (+ *acc);* **stop off at s.o.'s house** dēvért·ō -ere -ī ad áliquem; **stop right there!** stā ílicō!; **stop talking!** désine (*pl:* dēsínite) loquī! **they finally stopped talking** fínem loquéndī dēmum fēcérunt

stop-over commoráti·ō -ónis *f;* **make a stop-over** commór·or -árī -átus sum

stop sign sign·um -ī *n* subsisténdī

stop watch chronoscópi·um -ī *n*

store tabérn·a -ae *f; (supply)* cópi·a -ae *f*

storeroom cell·a -ae *f*

stork cicóni·a -ae *f (see* **bird***)*

storm tempést·ās -átis *f;* procéll·a -ae *f;* **a storm arose** tempéstās coórta est

stormy procellós·us -a -um, turbulént·us -a -um

story *(tale)* fábul·a -ae *f; (rumor)* fām·a -ae *f; (floor)* tabulát·um -ī *n*, contignáti·ō -ónis *f;* **to make a long story short** nē longus sim *or* nē longam fáciam

stove foc·us -ī *m*, fócul·us -ī *m;* **electric (gas) stove** focus ēléctricus (gáseus)

straight dīréct·us -a -um; **go straight home!** ī (*pl:* īte) rēctā domum!

straighten out a matter rem explicáre

strait frēt·um -ī *n;* **Strait of Messina** frētum Sículum

strange mīr·us -a -um; **strange to say** mīrắbile dictū

strap lōr·um -ī *n;* *(for shoe or sandal, sometimes decorated with gems)* obstrắgul·um -ī *n*

straw strāmént·um -ī *n;* *(for drinking)* sīph·ō -ónis *m*

strawberry frāg·um -ī *n*

stream rīv·us -ī *m*

street vi·a -ae *f;* *(with houses)* platế·a -ae *f;* *(paved)* strāt·a -ae *f;* **across the street from** exadvérsum (+ *acc*)

street clothes forếns·ia -ium *npl*

street map tábul·a -ae *f* viária

streetcar curr·us -ūs *m* ēléctricus

stretch *see* **extend**

stretch spáti·um -ī *n*

strict sevếr·us -a -um; *(person in authority)* acérb·us -a -um

strictly speaking próprie

strike *(work stoppage)* operistíti·um -ī *n;* **be** *or* **go on strike** opus inter·míttō -míttere -mísī; **make a strike** *(in bowling)* omnēs cōnōs simul prōstérn·ō -ere prōstrắvī

string chord·a -ae *f,* fīl·um -ī *n;* *(comput)* seri·ēs -éī *f*

strip *(e.g., of bacon)* segmént·um -ī *n*

stroke of luck lūs·us -ūs *m* fortúnae

stroll *s* **would you like to take a stroll?** velísne spatiárī?

stroll *intr* spáti·or -árī -átus sum, dēambulāre

strong válid·us -a -um *(opp:* imbecíll·us -a -um)

stubborn obstināt·us -a -um

stuck: he is stuck on some girl or other in amóre haeret apud nésciō quam vírginem; **I'm stuck** *(out of ideas)* haéreō

stuck-up: be stuck-up fastíd·iō -íre; **see how stuck-up he is!** vide ut fastídit!

student discípul·us -ī *m* (·a -ae *f*), stud·ēns -éntis *m,* studentíss·a -ae *f*

studies stúdi·a -órum *npl*

study *(a room)* studíol·um -ī *n*

study stúd·eō -ére -uī (+ *dat*) ‖ *intr* studére

study period spáti·um -ī *n* studiósum

stuff *(junk)* nūg·ae -árum *fpl*

stumble over new words nova verba offénd·ō -ere -ī

style mod·us -ī *m;* **go out of style** exolésc·ō -ere exolévī

subdirectory *(comput)* plicárum subínd·ex -icis *m*

subject *(e.g., history, math, etc.)* disciplín·a -ae *f;* *(topic)* argúment·um -ī *n;* *(gram)* subiéct·um -ī *n ;* *(topic studied)* gen·us -eris *n* studiórum, doctrín·a -ae *f*

subject matter mātéri·a -ae *f*

subjunctive *adj* subiūnctív·us -a -um; **subjunctive mood** subiūnctívus mod·us -ī *m*

subjunctive *s* subiūnctív·us -ī *m*

submarine nāv·is -is *f* submarína

subordinate conjunction *s* subiūnctíva coniúncti·ō -ónis *f*

subscribe subscríb·ō -ere subscrípsī

substitute *adj* vicári·us -a [*not neuter*]

substitute *s* succēdáne·us -ī *m* (·a -ae *f*)

substitute *tr* (**for**) substítu·ō -ere -ī -tus (prō + *abl*)

subtract détrah·ō -ere dētráxī dētráctus

suburb subúrbi•um -ī *n;* **suburbs** continént•ia -ium *npl*

subway ferrívi•a -ae *f* subterránea

success rēs, reī *f* fēlíciter gesta, rēs bene gesta

success succéss•us -ūs *m*

such a tāl•is -is -e; **such a big** tant•us -a -um; **such is the case** rēs sē ita habet

sucker *(fool)* bárcal•a -ae *mf;* **take s.o. for a sucker** álicui ōs súblinō sublínere sublévī

suddenly statim, súbitō, repénte

sue s.o. lītem álicui ínferō īnférre íntulī illátus

suffer *tr* ferō ferre tulī lātus; **suffer punishment** poenam dare ‖ *intr* pát•ior -ī passus sum; **suffer from** dól•eō -ēre -uī (+ *abl of ailment or affected part);* **suffering from** oppréss•us -a -um (+ *abl*)

suffer punishment poenās ferō ferre tulī lātus

sugar sácchar•um -ī *n;* **cube of sugar** cub•us -ī *m* sáccharī

sugar bowl váscul•um -ī *n* sáccharī

suggest sub•íciō -ícere -iécī -iéctus; **as you suggest** quemádmodum suádēs

suggestion: at your suggestion tē auctóre

suit sýnthes•is -is *f; (leg)* ácti•ō -ónis *f;* **bring a suit against s.o.** āctiónem álicui intén•dō -dere -dī

suitcase risc•us -ī *m; (small suitcase)* ríscul•us -ī *m*

suite *(of rooms)* diaét•a -ae *f*

sultry aestuós•us -a -um

sum: to sum up ad summam *or* in summam *or* in summā

summary summári•um -ī *n,* breviári•um -ī *n*

summer *adj* aestív•us -a -um

summer *s* aest•ās -átis *f*

summer vacation fériae aestívae; **spend the summer vacation** fériās aestívās ágere

summit cacúm•en -inis *n*

sun sōl, sōlis *m;* **full sun** plúrimus sōl

sunbathe apríc•or -árī

sunbathing aprīcáti•ō -ónis *f*

Sunday di•ēs -éī *m* Sōlis; *(eccles)* Domínica *f*

sun glasses perspicíll•a -órum *n* sōlária *(or* īnfuscáta)

sunny apríc•us -a -um

sunrise ort•us -ūs *m* sōlis; **at sunrise** sōle ortō

sunset occás•us -ūs *m* sōlis

sunshine sōl, sōlis *m*

suntan adústus col•or -óris *m;* **get a suntan** colōráre

suntanned adúst•us -a -um

superintendent superinténd•ēns -éntis *mf*

superlative *adj* superlatív•us -a -um

superlative *s* grad•us -ūs *m* superlatívus; **in the superlative** superlatívē; **give me "laetus" in the superlative** dīc "laetus" superlatívē

supermarket superīnstitóri•um -ī *n*

supine *s* supín•um -ī *n*

supper cēn•a -ae *f;* **for supper** in cēnam

supplies commeát•us -ūs *m (used both as collective singular and in the plural);* **cut off the enemy's supplies** inter•clúdō -clúdere -clúsī hostēs commeátibus

supply: supply s.o. with men and arms álicui virōs et arma ministráre

suppose opín·or -árī -átus sum; **I suppose** [*parenthetical*] ut opínor

sure *adj* cert·us -a -um; **be sure to come** fácitō (*or* fac) modo ut véniās; **for sure** prō certō; **I am sure that** certus (-a) sum (+ *acc & inf*); **know for sure** certum (*or* prō certō) sciō scīre scīvī scītus; **to be sure** nempe

surely certē, quidem, sānē

surf *intr* tábulā flūctívagā per summās undās prōláb·or -ī prōlápsus sum

surfboard tábul·a -ae *f* flūctívaga

surgeon chīrúrg·us -ī *m* (·a -ae *f*); **the surgeon operated on her** chīrúrgus eam sécuit

surgery (*the art*) chīrúgi·a -ae *f;* (*practice*) man·us -ūs *f;* **use surgery** manum adhibére

surly morós·us -a um et difficil·is -is -e

surrender *s* dēdíti·ō -ónis *f*

surrender *intr* sē dē·dō -dere -didī; **force a people to surrender** pópulum in dēditiónem veníre cōg·ō -ere coégī coáctus

suspect *s* suspéct·us -ī *m* (·a -ae *f*)

suspect *tr* suspíc·iō -ere suspéxī suspéctus

suspense: be in suspense ánimī péndeō pendére pepéndī; **not to keep you any longer in suspense** nē diútius in suspénsō péndeās

suspicion suspíci·ō -ónis *f;* **come under suspicion** in suspiciónem veníre

suspicious súspic·āx -ācis; (*suspected*) suspéct·us -a -um

swallow hirúnd·ō -inis *f* (*see* **bird**)

swamp pal·ūs -údis *f*

swan cycn·us -ī *m* (*see* **bird**)

swarm (*of bees, wasps, locusts*) exám·en -inis *n*

swear in the soldiers mílitēs sacrāméntō ádig·ō -ere adégī adáctus

sweat *s* sūd·or -óris *m;* **break a sweat** īnsūdáre; **no sweat!** nōn labórō!

sweat *intr* sūdáre

sweater thōr·āx -ácis *m* lánius

sweat suit vest·is -is *f* gýmnica

sweep the floor pavīméntum verr·ō -ere -ī versus

sweeper (*soccer*) lūs·or -óris *m* líber, lūsr·īx -ícis *f* líbera

sweet dulc·is -is -e

sweetheart: my sweetheart volúptās mea; óculus meus, océllus meus; (*in address*) mea volúptās, mī ócule, mī océlle

swell (up) (*of limbs*) túrg·eō -ére tursī, sē attóll·ō -ere (*opp:* sē summíttere)

sweltering aestuós·us -a -um

swim natáre

swimming *s* natáti·ō -ónis *f* (*see Chapter V*)

swimming instructor natándī magís·ter -trī *m* (·tra -trae *f*)

swimming meet certám·en -inis *n* natātórium

swimming pool piscín·a -ae *f*

swimsuit vest·is -is *f* balneáris

swim trunks subligácul·um -ī *n* balneáre

swing *s* oscíll·um -ī *n*

swing *intr* oscilláre

swipe (*steal*) surr·ípiō -rípere -rípuī -réptus

Swiss Helvéti·us -a -um

switch (*electrical*) mūtátr·um -ī *n*

Switzerland Helvéti·a -ae *f*

swollen túmid·us -a -um

swivel chair sell·a -ae *f* versátilis

syllable *s* sýllab·a -ae *f;* **syllables form words** sýllabae fáciunt dictiónēs

sympathy: show sympathy for commíser·or -árī -átus sum (+ *acc*)

symphony symphóni·a -ae *f*

symptom not·a -ae *f,* indíci·um -ī *n*

synagogue synagóg·a -ae *f*

syntax *s* sýntax·is -is *f*

table mēns·a -ae *f;* **set the table** mēnsam pōn·ō -ere pósuī; **sit down at the table** mēnsae ad·sídō -sídere -sḗdī; **wipe off the table** mēnsam pertérg·ō -ere pertérsī

tablecloth mantél·e -is *n*

table tennis (*see* **Ping-pong**)

tablet (*for writing*) tábul·a -ae *f; (of medication*) pastíll·us -ī *m*

tableware īnstrūmént·a -órum *npl* escária

tactics: change one's tactics ratiónem bellī geréndī mūtáre

tail caud·a -ae *f*

taillight lūm·en -inis *n* postícum

tailor (*making clothes*) vestífic·us -ī *m* (·a -ae *f*); (*altering clothes*) sarcinát·or -óris *m*

tailor shop vestificín·a -ae *f*

take *tr* (*accept*) accíp·iō -ere accépī accéptus; (*to a person or place*) áfferō afférre áttulī allátus; (*to escort, lead*) dūc·ō -ere dūxī ductus; **here, take it** em, áccipe; **I can't take it anymore** patī néqueō ámplius; **I take it** (*parenthetical*) ut opínor; **take away** (*hope, freedom, sleep, life*) ádim·ō -ere adḗmī adémptus; **take down** (*notes, lecture*) excípere; (*unfasten*) refíg·ō -ere refíxī; **take for** (*regard as*) habére; **take** (*a dog*) **for a walk** dúcere; **take in s.o.** (*con s.o.*) álicui verba dare; **take into**

consideration respíc·iō -ere respéxī; **take it easy!** parce! (*pl:* párcite!); **take it hard that** gráviter ferō ferre tulī (+ *acc & inf*); **take off** (*clothes*) éxuō exúere éxuī exútus; (*clothes, shoes, ring*) détrahō détráhere détráxī; **take pains to** in magnō negótiō habére (+ *inf*); **take place** fíō fíerī factus sum; **take pleasure in** cápere laetítiam ex (+ *abl*); **take upon oneself (to)** in sē conférre (+ *inf*); **the preposition "ad" takes the accusative case** "ad" praeposítiō cásuī accūsātívō servit; **they know that they were taken in** sciunt sibi data esse verba; **this verb takes the accusative case** hoc verbum coniúngitur (*or* adiúngitur) cásuī accūsātívō ǁ *intr* **take after** símilis esse (+ *gen*); **take off** (*lit: go away*) áb·eō -íre -ívī *or* -iī; (*coll*) apoculáre; (*of a plane*) avoláre

take-off (*of a plane*) āvoláti·ō -ónis *f*

talent ingéni·um -ī *n*

talented ingeniós·us -a -um

talk *s* serm·ō -ónis *m;* **(childish, silly, everyday) talk** (puerílis, stultus, quotidiánus) sermō; **small talk** sermúncul·us -ī *m;* **give a talk** sermónem habére; **have a talk with s.o.** cum áliquō dīligénter cólloqu·or -ī collocútus sum; **that's mere talk** verba istaec sunt

talk *tr & intr* loqu·or -ī locútus sum; **talk s.th. over with s.o.** áliquid cum áliquō communicáre

talk show spectácul·um -ī *n* disputatívum; (*on radio*) disputáti·ō -ónis *f* radiophónica

talkative loqu·āx -ácis

tall prōcér·us -a -um; **be a head taller than** tōtō vértice esse suprā (+ *acc*); **he is tall** statúrā prōcérā est

tank lac·us -ūs *m; (mil)* autocúrr·us -ūs *m* armátus

tape *s (adhesive)* taéni·a -ae *f* adhaesíva; *(audiotape)* phōnotaeníol·a -ae *f; (audiocasette)* phōnocasét·a -ae *f;* **make a tape** phōnotaeníolam cōnfícere

tape *tr* in phōnotaeníolā ímprim·ō imprímere impréssī impréssus

tape recorder magnētophón·um -ī *n,* casētophón·um -ī *n*

target scōp·us -ī *m*

tariff portóri·um -ī *n*

task op·us -eris *n,* pēns·um -ī *n*

taste *s (sense)* gustát·us -ūs *m; (flavor)* sap·or -óris *m; (foretaste, sample)* gust·us -ūs *m;* **lack of good taste** dēfórmit·ās -átis *f;* **this is not to my taste** hoc nōn meī stómachī est

taste *tr & intr* sáp·iō -ere -ívī *or* -iī; **taste like** sápere (+ *acc*)

tax vectíg·al -ális *n;* **collect taxes** vectīgália éxig·ō -ere exégī exáctus; **impose a tax on** vectígal impón·ō -ere impósuī impósitus (+ *dat*); **pay taxes** vectīgália pēnsitáre

tax collector exáct·or -óris *m,* pūblicán·us -ī *m*

taxi raéd·a -ae *f* meritória

tea the·a -ae *f*

teach *(w. double acc)* dóc·eō -ére -uī -tus; **teach Latin** Latínē docére

teacher magís·ter -trī *m* (·tra -trae *f*)

teachers' room oec·us -ī *n* magistrórum *(or* magistrárum)

teaching method docéndī ráti·ō -ónis *f*

teacup pocíll·um -ī *n* theánum

team turm·a -ae *f*

teapot hírni·a -ae *(or* hirníol·a -ae) *f* theána

tear *s* lácrim·a -ae *f;* **shed tears** lácrimās profúnd·ō -ere profúdī profúsus

tear *tr* scind·ō -ere scidī scissus; **I can't tear myself away from my books** in librīs haér·eō -ére haesī; **tear down** *(building)* díru·ō -ere -ī dirútus; **tear to bits** *or* **pieces** laniáre, dīlaceráre; **tear up** *(paper)* discíndere ‖ *intr (to rush)* ru·ō -ere -ī; *(of clothes, etc.)* scind·or -ī scissus sum; **tear along the road** viam voráre

tease taxáre

teaspoon parvum cóchle·ār -áris *n*

telephone *adj* tēlephónic·us -a -um

telephone *s* tēlephón·um -ī *n;* **by telephone** tēlephónicē; **call s.o. on the telephone** áliquem per tēlephónum vocáre; **dial a number** númerum (tēlephónicum) sélig·ō -ere sēlégī sēléctus; **dial the area code** númerum praesēlēctórium sēlígere; **speak with s.o. on the telephone** cum áliquō tēlephónicē cólloquor cólloquī collocútus sum; **the telephone is ringing** tēlephónum tinnit; **use a pay phone** tēlephónō monētálī ūtor ūtī ūsus sum

telephone *tr* per tēlephónum vocáre

telephone book tēlephónicus ind·ex -icis *m;* **look in the telephone book** tēlephónicum índicem īnspíc·iō -ere īnspéxī

telephone booth cell·a -ae *f* tēlephónica

telephone call (local, long-distance) tēlephōném·a -atis *n* (locále, longínquum)

telephone conversation tyēlephōném·a -atis *n*

telephone line cōnéxi·ō -ónis *f* tēlephónica

telephone number númer·us -ī *m* tēlephónicus

telephone receiver auscultắbul·um -ī *n;*
pick up the receiver auscultắbulum
toll·ō -ere sústulī

telephone ring tinnī́t·us -ūs *m*
tēlephṓnicus

telescope tēlescópi·um -ī *n*

television tēlevī́si·ō -ṓnis *f; (set)*
tēlevīsṓri·um -ī *n;* **turn on (turn off)
the television** tēlevīsṓrium excitấre
(exstíngu·ō -ere exstī́nxī exstī́nctus);
turn down (up) the television vim
tēlevīsṓriī remítt·ō -ere remī́sī
(áúg·eō -ére auxī); **watch television**
tēlevīsiṓnem spectấre

television audience tēlevīsṓr·ēs -um *mpl*

television broadcast ēmíssi·ō -ṓnis *f*
tēlevīsífica

television channel tēlevīsṓrius canắl·is
-is *m*

television news tēlediúrn·a -ṓrum *npl*

television program prográmm·a -atis *n*
tēlevīsíficum

television screen quadr·um -ī *n*
tēlevī́sicum

television series séri·ēs -éī *f* tēlevīsífica

television set tēlevīsṓri·um -ī *n*

television viewer tēlevī́s·or -ṓris *m* (·trīx
-trī́cis *f*)

tell nārrấre; **tell about** nārrấre dē (+
abl); **tell a lie** mendắcium dī́cere; **tell
a secret** sēcrḗtum ḗloqu·or -ī ēlocū́tus
sum; **tell the truth** vērum dī́cere

temper īrācúndi·a -ae *f;* **have a bad
temper** summā īrācúndiā esse; **keep
one's temper** īrācúndiam cohíb·eō
-ére -uī; **lose one's temper** īrācúndā
éfferor efférrī ēlấtus sum

temperature temperātū́r·a -ae *f;* **the
temperature fell below thirty-two
degrees** temperātū́ra lāpsa est subter
duōs et trīgíntā gradūs; **the**

**temperature is two degrees above
freezing** temperātū́ra est ad duōs
gradūs suprā pūnctum glaciắle; **what
is the temperature?** quō gradū stat
temperātū́ra?

temple templ·um -ī *n,* aed·ēs -is *f; (anat)*
temp·us -oris *n*

ten decem [*indecl*]; **ten times** déciēs

tendon tend·ō -inis *m,* nerv·us -ī *m;* **torn
tendon** tendō sēparátus

tennis tenilū́di·um -ī *n,* tenísi·a -ae *f;*
play tennis tenísiā lū́dere *(see
Chapter V)*

tennis ball pil·a -ae *f* tenísiae

tennis court camp·us -ī *m* tenilū́diī

tennis doubles lūd·us -ī *m* bis bīnṓrum

tennis match certắm·en -inis *n* tenilū́diī

tennis net rēt·e -is *n* tenísiae

tennis player tenilū́di·us -ī *m* (·a -ae *f)*

tennis racket rētícul·um -ī *n*
(manubriắtum)

tenor cant·or -ṓris *m* vṓcis médiae

tense *adj* inténtus -a -um

tense *s (gram)* temp·us -oris *n*

tension conténti·ō -ṓnis *f*

tent tentṓri·um -ī *n*

tenterhooks: be on tenterhooks ánimī
pénd·eō -ére pepéndī

term *(expression)* verb·um -ī *n;*
(semester) studiṓrum spáti·um -ī *n,*
sēmḗstr·e -is *n;* **term of office**
spáti·um -ī *n* (témporis) magistrátūs

terminal státi·ō -ṓnis *f* termināális;
(comput) termināl·e -is *n*

terms condiciṓn·ēs -um *fpl;* **be on
friendly terms with a country** in
amīcítiā pópulī esse; **I'm on good
terms with** in grátiā sum cum (+
abl); mihi cum (+ *abl)* magna
necessitū́dō est; **on these terms** hīs

condiciónibus, hīs légibus; **stick by the terms** in condiciónibus mán·eō -ére mānsī

terms of peace pācis condición·ēs -um *fpl;* **accept terms of peace** pācis condiciónēs accípere *(opp: repudiáre);* **dictate terms of peace to** pācis condiciónēs dícere *(+ dat);* **propose terms of peace** pācis condiciónēs ferō ferre tulī lātus

terrace xyst·us -ī *m*

terrain nātúr·a -ae *f* locī

terrible terríbil·is -is -e

terrific exími·us -a -um; **terrific!** euge!

terrify terrificáre, térr·eō -ére -uī -itus

terror terr·or -óris *m*

test probáti·ō -ónis *f;* **flunk a test** cad·ō -ere cécidī in probātióne; **pass a test** probātiónem sustín·eō -ére -uī

testicle testícul·us -ī *m*

testy īrācúnd·us -a -um

text *(comput)* text·us -ūs *m*

textbook li·ber -brī *m* scholáris

than *(in comparisons)* quam

thank grátiās ágere *(+ dat);* **no, thank you** benígnē; **no, thank you just the same** tam grátia est; **thank heaven!** sit dīs grátia!; **thank you** *(familiar form) (for a future favor)* amábō tē; *(for a favor done)* amō tē; **thank you for** tibi grátiās ágere quod *(+ indic);* **thank you for helping me** grátiās tibi agō quod mē iūvistī

thankful: I am thankful to you grátiam tibi hábeō; **you ought to be thankful to me** grátiam hábeās mihi

thanks grátiās!; **thanks a lot!** multās grátiās!; **thanks a lot for** tē multum amō quod *(+ indic);* **thanks a million!** sescéntās grátiās!; **thanks for your gifts** grátiās tibi dē dōnīs

tuīs; **thanks to me (you,** *etc.)* meā (tuā, *etc.)* óperā

that ill·e -a -ud; *(sometimes pej)* ist·e -a -ud; **is that so?** ítane est?; **that'll do** sat est; **that's it!** *(enough!)* tantum est!; **that's right** *(in response to a question)* sīc est; **that's so** ita est

thaw *tr* dissólv·ō -ere -ī **||** *intr* tabésc·ō -ere tábuī

theater theátr·um -ī *n;* **theater of war** bellī sēd·ēs -is *f*

theft fūrt·um -ī *n*

theme *(topic)* mātéri·a -ae *f,* argūmént·um -ī *n; (essay)* tractát·us -ūs *m;* **write a theme** tractátum cōnscríbere

then *(and so)* ítaque; *(at that time)* tum; *(in that case)* ígitur; *(next)* deínde, deínceps; *(therefore)* ergō; **just then** tunc máximē; **then and there** ílicō, ibi contínuō

therapist therapeút·a -ae *m* (·ria -riae *f)*

therapy therapí·a -ae *f;* **therapy treatment** cūráti·ō -ónis *f* therapeútica

there *(position)* ibi; *(direction)* illūc

therefore ergō

thermometer thermómetr·um -ī *n*

thick dēns·us -a -um

thief fūr, fūris *mf*

thigh fem·ur -oris *n*

thimble digitál·e -īs *n*

think putáre, céns·eō -ére -uī, aestimáre; **I don't think so** ego nōn putō; **I think so** id opínor; **think s.th. over** áliquid sēcum reputáre; **that is exactly what I think** ita prórsus exístimō; **what do you think?** quid cēnsēs?

thirty trīgíntā

this hic haec hoc

thought: on second thought cum ego recógitō

thread fīl·um -ī *n; (comput)* sér·iēs -éī *f* epistulárum ēlectronicárum; **hang by a thread** *(fig)* fīlō pénd·eō -ére pepéndī

thrifty frūgál·is -is -e, frūgī [*indecl*]

throat fauc·ēs -ium *fpl*

throw coníc·iō -ere coniécī coniéctus; **throw out of the game** ā campō relegáre; **throw the book at s.o.** *(fig)* summō iūre cum áliquō ágere

throw-in *(soccer)* iniéct·us -ūs *m* (laterális)

thrush turd·us -ī *m (see* **bird**)

thumb tack cuspidíol·a -ae *f* graphiária

thunder *s* tónitr·us -ūs *m*

thunder *impers v* tonat tonáre tónuit

thunderbolt fulm·en -inis *n*

Thursday di·ēs -éī *m* Iovis

Tiber Tíber·is -is *(acc:* Tíberim) *m*

ticket tésser·a -ae *f* (itinerária); **first-class (second-class) ticket** téssera prīmae (secúndae) classis; **one-way ticket** téssera ūníus cursūs; **return ticket** téssera réditūs; **round-trip ticket** téssera itūs reditúsque

ticket agent tesserári·us -ī *m* (·a -ae *f*)

ticket window ōstíol·um -ī *n* tesserárium

tide aest·us -ūs *m;* **high tide** aestūs accéss·us -ūs *m;* **low tide** aestūs recéss·us -ūs *m*

tidy up ōrdináre

tie *(necktie)* fōcál·e -is *n*

tie *adj (in a game)* **be tie** parēs esse

tie *tr* ligáre, alligáre; *(in a knot)* nodáre; **be tied up** *(e.g., with business)* impéd·ior -írī -ítus sum; **my money**

is tied up argéntum occupátum est; **tie back** revínc·iō -íre revínxī, revínctus; **tie up** *(in work, etc.)* impéd·iō -íre -ívī -ítus

tie-up *(on the highway)* affluénti·a -ae *f* vehiculária

tiger tigr·is -is *or* -idis *m;* **tigers growl** tigrēs fremunt

tight *(knot, clothes)* strict·us -a -um; *(shoe)* restríct·us -a -um; *(stingy)* sórdid·us -a -um

tight-fisted astríct·us -a -um

tile lámin·a -ae *f* fíctilis

till *tr (the soil)* col·ō -ere -uī cultus

till *prep* ūsque ad (+ *acc*), in (+ *acc*); **till late at night** ad multam noctem; **till late in the day** ad multum diem; **till the month of July** in mēnsem Iúlium

time temp·us -oris *n; (leisure)* óti·um -ī *n; (age, period)* aet·ās -átis *f; (of day)* hōr·a -ae *f;* **ahead of time** ante tempus; **a long time already** (+ *present temse*) iam dūdum, e.g., **I've been here a long time already** iam dūdum adsum; **around the time of** sub tempus (+ *gen);* **ask the time** quaérere hōrās; **ask what time it is** hōrās inquírere; **at about the same time** sub idem tempus; **at another time** áliās; **at one time ... at another** áliās ... áliās; **at that time** ad id témporis, tum; **at the right time** tempestívē; **at the time when** quā tempestáte; **at the wrong time** intempestívē; **at times** intérdum; **a very short time ago** modo; **before time** *(prematurely)* ante tempus; **for a long time** iam diū; **for a short time** brevī témpore; **for some time** aliquámdiū; **for the first time** prīmum; **for the last time** extrémum; **for the time being** in tempus, prō témpore; **from that time on** ex eō; **from time to time** subínde; **he's**

having a good time by himself eī
bene est sōlī; **I always have time for**
semper vacō (+ *dat*); **I haven't the
time** haud mihi ṓtium est; **I'm
having a good (lousy) time** mihi
bene (male) est; **in my spare time**
cum tempus subsicívum mihi est; **in
Roman times** aetā́te Rōmā́nā; **I have
no time** tempus nōn est mihi; **in a
short time** in brevī spátiō; **in good
time, in plenty of time** mātū́rē; **in
(the course of) time** témpore,
prōcēdénte témpore; **it is high time
for you to** tempus máximē est ut tū
(+ *subj*); **make up for lost time**
cessā́ta témpora córrig·ō -ere corréxī;
not to have the time to ṓtium nōn
habḗre *(w. dat ger)*; **once upon a
time** ōlim; **one time** *(once)* semel; **on
time** témperī; **postpone to another
time** différre in áliud tempus; **see
what time it is** hōrās ī́nspícere;
spend time tempus sū́mere *(or* ágere
or agitā́re); **some time ago** dū́dum,
prī́dem; **there is no time to study**
nōn vacat studḗre; **there is no time
to waste** matūrā́tō opus est; **there
was a time when** (tempus) fuit cum;
waste time tempus per·dō -dere
-didī; **what time is it?** quota hōra
est? *or* quot hōrae sunt? **while away
the time** tempus fall·ō -ere feféllī

times *(use numeral adverbs) e.g.,* **ten
times** décies; **no more than three
times** ter nec ámplius

timetable hōrā́ri·um -ī *n*

tin plumb·um -ī *n* album, stann·um -ī *n*

tip ap·ex -icis *m; (money)* corollā́ri·um -ī
n, stip·s -is *f*; **it was on the tip of the
tongue** erat in labrīs prīmṓribus

tire cúmmeus canth·us -ī *m; put air in
the tire* cúmmeum canthum īnflā́re

tired fess·us -a -um

tireless assídu·us -a -um

tissue mūcínni·um -ī *n* chárteum

title *(of a book)* īnscrī́pti·ō -ṓnis *f; (of a
person)* appellā́ti·ō -ṓnis *f*

title page frontispíci·um -ī *n*

toad būf·ō -ṓnis *m*

toast *s* pān·is -is *m* tostus; *(in drinking)*
propīnā́ti·ō -ṓnis *f*; **drink a toast to**
propīnā́re (+ *dat*); **here's to you!** *(as
a toast)* bene tē! *(pl:* bene vōs)!

toast *tr (bread)* tórr·eō -ḗre -uī tostus;
(drink to) propīnā́re (+ *dat*)

toaster tostr·um -ī *n*

toboggan sclṓdi·a -ae *f*

toboggan run dēcúrs·us -ūs *m* sclṓdiae

today hódiē; **before today** ante hunc
diem; **starting today** ex hōc diē

toe dígit·us -ī *m* pedis; **big toe** poll·ex
-icis *m*

toenail ungu·is -is *m* pedis

toga tog·a -ae *f; (bright-white toga,
worn by candidates)* toga candidā́ta;
*(worn by men and boys after the age
of about fifteen)* toga virī́lis *or* pūra;
*(toga with purple border, worn by
curule magistrates, by boys up to the
age of manhood, and by girls until
marriage)* toga praetéxta; *(toga
embroidered with silver stars)* toga
pī́cta; *(toga of smooth cloth)* toga
rāsa; **receive the toga of manhood**
togam virī́lem sūm·ō -ere -psī -tus

toilet latrī́n·a -ae *f; (public)* fóric·a -ae *f*;
I must go to the toilet mihi eúndum
est in latrī́nam; **may I go to the
toilet?** licetne īre in latrī́nam?; **sit on
the toilet (hopper)** in sellā
familiā́ricā sedḗre

toilet bowl lābéll·um -ī *n* íntimum

toilet paper chártul·a -ae *f* hygiḗnica

toilet seat sell·a -ae *f* familiā́rica

toll *(highway fee)* vectíg·al -ális *n* rotáre

toll booth tabérn·a -ae *f* vectīgális rotáris

toll call tēlephōném·a -atis *n* longínquum

toll road vi·a -ae *f* vectīgális rotáris

tomato lycopérsic·um -ī *n*

tomorrow crās, di·ēs -éī *m* crástinus;
day after tomorrow peréndiē;
tomorrow morning crās māne;
tomorrow night crās nocte; **until tomorrow** in crástinum

tongue lingu·a -ae *f*

tonight hāc nocte

tonsils tonsíll·ae -árum *fpl*

too *(excessively)* nimis; *(also)* quoque *(comes after the word it emphasizes);*
too bad about male (mehércule) dē (+ *abl);* **too bad about Marcus!** male dē Márcō!

tool īnstrūmént·um -ī *n;* **tools** *(comput)* īnstrūmént·a -órum *npl*

toolbar īnstrūmentórum tabell·a -ae *f*

tooth dēns, dentis *m;* **tooth and nail** *(fig)* tōtō córpore et ómnibus úngulīs

toothache dol·or -óris *m* déntium

toothbrush pénícul·us -ī *m* dentárius

toothpaste past·a -ae *f* dentária

top *tr* superáre; **to top it off** in summō

top *adj* summ·us -a -um

top *s* ap·ex -icis *m;* *(of house)* fastígi·um -ī *n;* *(of tree)* cacúm·en -inis *n;* **at the top of one's voice** summā vōce; **at the top of the page** ab summā páginā; **on (the) top** suprā; **on top of that** quīn et, ínsuper; **top of the mountain** summus mōn·s -tis *m*

top *tr (surpass)* superáre; **to top it off** in summō

topaz topázi·us -a -um

topcoat superindūmént·um -ī *n*

topic mātéri·a -ae *f,* rēs, reī *f*

topography locórum dēscrípti·ō -ónis *f*

topsy-turvy: everything was topsy-turvy ómnia erant sūrsum deórsum; **turn everything topsy-turvy** ómnia sūrsum deórsum versáre

tornado turb·ō -inis *m*

touch *(sense)* tāct·us -ūs *m;* **put the final touches to** últimam (*or* summam) manum impón·ō -ere impósuī impósitus (+ *dat)*

touch *tr* tang·ō -ere tétigī tāctus; *(to stir)* móv·eō -ére mōvī mōtus; **touch deeply** commovére

touchdown: make a touchdown calcem (*or* crētam) attíng·ō -ere áttigī attáctus

tough dūr·us -a -um

tour *s (in a foreign country)* peregrīnáti·ō -ónis *f; (e.g., of a factory)* iter, itíneris *n;* **complete a three-year tour of duty** triénnium mīlítiae éxpl·eō -ére -évī -étus; **tour of duty** mīlíti·a -ae *f*

tour bus coenautocīnét·um -ī *n* perigéticum

tour guide mystagóg·us -ī *m,* dux, ducis *mf* itinerári·us (-a)

tourist peregrīná·tor -tóris *m* (·trīx -trícis *f)*

tourist class class·is -is *f* tūrística

towel gausapín·um -ī *n;* **bath towel** gausapínum balneárium; **hand towel** manutérgi·um -ī *n*

tower turr·is -is *f*

town óppid·um -ī *n; (in Italy, subject to Rome, but self-governed)* mūnicípi·um -ī *n;* **small town** oppídul·um -ī *n*

town hall cúri·a -ae *f* mūnicipális

tow truck carr·us -ī *m* remulcándī

toy lūdíbri·um -ī *n*

trace *s* vestígi·um -ī *n*

trace *tr* indāgáre; *(outline)* dēlīneáre; **trace back** répet·ō -ere -īvī -ītus

track vestígi·um -ī *n; (wheel-track, rut)* órbit·a -ae *f; (path)* sémit·a -ae *f; (the sport)* cursûr·a -ae *f; (course laid out for runners)* currícul·um -ī *n (see Chapter V) (of a railroad)* órbit·a -ae *f* ferriviária

track indāgáre; **track down s.th.** áliquid indāgáre

tractor tractr·um -ī *n*

trade mercātûr·a -ae *f; (profession)* artifíci·um -ī *n*

trade union syndicát·us -ūs *m*

traffic commeát·us -ūs *m* vehiculórum; **heavy traffic** celébrit·ās -átis *f* viae *(or* viárum)

traffic cop vigil -is *mf* viātóri·us (-a)

traffic jam affluénti·a -ae *f* vehiculária

traffic light sēmáphor·um -ī *n* (**red** rubrum; **yellow** flāvum; **green** víride)

train *s* trām·en -inis *n* (ferriviárium); **a through train** trāmen dīréctum

train *tr (for physical proficiency)* exercitáre ‖ *intr* sē exercitáre

trainer *(of athletes)* exércit·or -óris *m,* exércitr·īx -ícis *f*

train schedule hōrári·um -ī *n* tráminum

train station státi·ō -ónis *f* ferriviária

train ticket tésser·a -ae *f* ferriviária

tramp larífug·a -ae *m*

trampoline dēsultóri·um -ī *n*

transfer to *(another train, etc.)* trānscénd·ō -ere -ī in (+ *acc)*

transitive trānsitív·us -a -um

translate *tr* (con)vért·ō -ere -ī (con)vérsus, trấnsferō trānsférre trấnstulī trānslátus; **translate from Latin to English** ex Latínō in Ánglicum (con)vértere

translation *s* trānsláti·ō -ónis *f*

transparency págin·a -ae *f* pellúcida

transportation vectûr·a -ae *f*

travel iter fácere; **travel by car (train, plane, ship)** autocīnétō (trámine, āëróplanō, návī) vehor vehī vectus sum

travel agency sēd·ēs -is *f* periēgética

travel agent itínerum prōcūrấ·tor -tóris *m* (·trīx -trícis *f)*

traveler viát·or -óris *m,* viátr·īx -ícis *f; (abroad)* peregrīnất·or -óris *m,* pregrīnátr·īx -ícis *f*

tray fércul·um -ī *n*

treason prōdíti·ō -ónis *f*

treat *(person, subject)* tractáre; *(medically)* cūráre

treatment tractáti·ō -ónis *f;* **(for)** cūráti·ō -ónis *f* (+ *gen of illness)*

treaty foed·us -eris *n; according to the terms of the treaty* ex pactō, ex foédere; **break a treaty** foedus frang·ō -ere frēgī frāctus; **conclude a treaty with** foedus īcō ícere īcī ictus *or* fér·iō -íre cum (+ *abl); **violate a treaty** foedus violáre

tree arb·or -oris *f*

treetop cacúm·en -inis *n*

tremble trem·ō -ere -uī; **tremble all over** cóntrem·ō -ere -uī

trend inclīnáti·ō -ónis *f*

trial quaésti·ō -ónis *f,* iūdíci·um -ī *n;* **be on trial for** iūdícium dē (+ *abl)* súb·eō -íre -īvī *or* -iī; **be on trial for one's life** iūdícium dē cápite subíre; **conduct a trial** quaestiónem exérc·eō

-ére -uī -itus; **go on trial** in iūs eō īre iī *or* īvī

trial lawyer causídic·us -ī *m* (·a -ae *f*)

tribune of the people tribún·us -ī *m* plēbis

tribunician power tribūnícia potést·ās -átis *f*

tributary flúvi·us -ī *m;* **the Allia is a tributary of the Tiber** Állia Tíberim ínfluit

trick dol·us -ī *m;* **be up to some tricks** lascív·us -a -um esse; **is this a trick?** num hoc est cáptiō?; **play tricks on** lūdōs fácere (+ *dat*)

tricky dolós·us -a -um

tricycle trírot·a -ae *f*

trip iter, itíneris *n;* **take a trip** iter fácere

tripod trip·ēs -edis *m* phōtográphicus

trolley curr·us -ūs *m* ēléctricus

trombone tub·a -ae *f* dúctilis

trouble sollicitáre; **I don't want to trouble you** nōlō tibi moléstus (-a) esse

trouble *s (annoyance)* molésti·a -ae *f,* mal·um -ī *n; (when the idea of difficulty predominates)* lab·or -óris *m; (effort, pains)* óper·a -ae *f;* **be in trouble** labōráre; **cause s.o. big trouble** moléstiam gravem álicui adhíb·eō -ére -uī *or* exhíbeō; **have stomach trouble** stómachō labōráre; **get s.o. into trouble** in áliquem aerúmnam óbser·ō -ere obsévī; **if it is no trouble** sī grave nōn erit; **I'm expecting some big trouble** nésciō quod magnum malum exspéctō; **it's not worth the trouble** nōn est prétium óperae; **make big trouble for s.o.** dare magnum malum álicui; **more trouble** ámplius negótī; **what's**

the trouble? quid illuc malī est? *or* quid est negótī?

troubled exercitát·us -a -um

trousers brāc·ae -árum *fpl*

trout truct·us -ī *m,* truct·a -ae *f*

trowel trull·a -ae *f*

truce indúti·ae -árum *fpl;* **a six-years' truce** indútiae annórum sex; **break a truce** indútiās violáre; **make a truce** indútiās fácere

truck autocīnét·um -ī *n* onerárium, autocárr·um -ī *n*

truck driver, trucker autocīnétī onerárii gubernát·or -óris *m*

true vēr·us -a -um; **that's true** rēs ita est *or* ita proféctō est

trumpet *(musical instrument)* tub·a -ae *f; (of an elephant)* barrít·us -ūs *m*

trumpet *intr (of an elephant)* bárr·iō -íre

trunk *(of a tree)* trunc·us -ī *m; (of a car)* receptácul·um -ī *n* sarcinárum; *(for clothes)* cist·a -ae *f; (of an elephant)* man·us -ūs *f*

trust *s* fid·ēs -éī *f,* bona fid·ēs -éī *f;* **put one's trust in** (cōn)fídere (+ *dat*)

trust *tr* fīd·ō -ere fīsus sum *(semi-deponent)* (+ *dat or abl*)

trusting cōnfíd·ēns -éntis

trustworthiness fidúci·a -ae *f*

trustworthy lócupl·ēs -étis

trusty fíd·us -a -um, firm·us -a -um

truth vēr·um -ī *n;* **to tell the truth** ut vēra *(or* vērum) dícam *(or* loquar)

truthful vērídic·us -a -um

try temptáre, con·or -árī -átus sum; **try a case (of)** causam cognósc·ō -ere cognóvī cógnitus (dē + *abl*); **try on** *(clothes)* induéndō probáre; **try one's best to (not to)** óperam dō dare dedī

ut (nē) (+ *subj); **try one's patience**
patiéntiā abŭt·or -ī abŭsus sum

trying *(tough)* exercitắt·us -a -um;
(annoying) molést·us -a -um

T-shirt tunícul·a -ae *f*

tuberculosis phíthis·is -is *f*

tuck up succíng·ō -ere succínxī
succínctus

Tuesday di·ēs -ḗī *m* Mārtis

tuna thunn·us -ī *m*

tunnel *(for trains, cars)* spec·us -ūs *m*
(ferriviắrius, autocīnḗticus)

turkey gallopắv·ō -ónis *m;* **talk turkey
with** Latínē loqu·or -ī locútus sum
cum (+ *abl*)

turn *s (in the road)* flex·us -ūs *m* viae; **a
good turn** benefíci·um -ī *n;* **in turn**
ínvicem; **out of turn** extrā ōrdinem;
take a turn for the worse in dētérius
inclīnárī; **take turns driving** ínvicem
(or per vicēs, in vicēs) gubernáre

turn *tr* (con)vért·ō -ere -ī; **turn in
weapons** arma trád·ō -ere trádidī
tráditus; **turn off** *(a light, computer)*
exstíngu·ō -ere exstínxī exstínctus;
turn on *(a light)* accénd·ō -ere -ī; *(a
computer)* excitáre; **turn upside
down** subvértere **‖** *intr* vert·or -ī
versus sum; **turn around** convertī;
turn into mūtắrī in (+ *acc);* **turn out
fine** bellē cadō -ere cécidī cāsúrus;
something will turn up, I hope fiet
áliquid, spérō

turn-off dēvertícul·um -ī *n*

turnpike autocīnḗtica vi·a -ae *f*
quadripertíta

turn signal ind·ex -icis *m* dīrēctiónis

turquoise túrcic·us -a -um

turtle testúd·ō -inis *f*

tutor *s* domésticus praecépt·or -óris *m,*
doméstica praecéptr·īx -ícis *f*

tutor *tr* prīvắtim īnstítu·ō -ere -ī -tus

TV *(see* **television)**

TV room conclắv·e -is *n* tēlevīsṓriō
īnstrúctum

tweezers volséll·a -ae *f*

twilight crepúscul·um -ī *n*

two duo, duae, duo; **two each** bīn·ī
-ae -a

two-faced dupl·ex -icis, bilíngu·is -is -e

two-time fraudáre

two-timer īnfidél·is -is *mf*

type *s* gen·us -eris *n; (print)* typ·us -ī *m;*
that type of person istíus géneris
homō

type *tr* dactylographáre

typesetter typóthet·a -ae *m*

typewriter dactylográphi·um -ī *n*

typewriter key malléol·us -ī *m;* **press a
key** malléolum dḗprim·ō -ere
dēpressī *(or* pulsáre)

trypewriter ribbon taéni·a -ae *f*
dactylográfica

typing dactylográphica ar·s -tis *f*

typist dactylógraph·us -ī *m* (·a -ae *f)*

udder ūb·er -eris *n*

ugliness dēfórmit·ās -átis *f*

ugly dēfórm·is -is -e, turp·is -is -e

ugh! vah!

uh-oh! *(when taken by surprise)* attat!;
áttatae!

umbrella umbréll·a -ae *f*

umpire árbit·er -rī *m* (·ra -rae *f)*

unanimous ūnánim·is -is -e

unanimously ūnā vōce, ómnibus
senténtiīs

unattractive invenúst·us -a -um

uncle *(father's brother)* pátru•us -ī *m;* *(mother's brother)* avúncul•us -ī *m*

uncontrolled effrēnắt•us -a -um

uncouth hórrid•us -a -um

underbrush dūmḗt•a -ốrum *npl*

underpants brāc•ae -árum *fpl* interiốrēs

underpass viaedúct•us -ūs *m*

undershirt *(worn by both sexes)* subū́cul•a -ae *f*

understand intélleg•ō -ere intelléxī intelléctus; **do you understand now?** iam tenēs?; **I don't quite understand** nōn satis intéllegō; **"ego" is understood if I should say, "sum philósophus"** subaudítur "ego" sī dīcam "sum philósophus"

undertaker pollínct•or -ốris *m* (•rīx -rīcis *f*)

undress éxuō exúere éxuī exū́tus; **get undressed** sē exúere, vestiménta exúere

uneducated inērudī́t•us -a -um, indóct•us -a -um

unfair iníqu•us -a -um

unfairly iníquē

unfaithful īnfidḗl•is -is -e

unfriendly inimíc•us -a -um

unhappiness īnfēlī́cit•ās -átis *f*

unhappy īnfḗl•īx -ī́cis [*single-ending adj*]

uniform hábit•us -ūs *m;* **in uniform** subōrnắt•us -a -um; **military uniform** ōrnắt•us -ūs *m* mīlitáris

United States (of America) Ūnī́tī Statū́s (Américae) *(gen:* Ūnītốrum Státuum) *mpl;* Cīvītắt•ēs -um *fpl* Foederắtae Américae

universe ūnivérs•um -ī *n,* ūnivérsit•ās -átis *f*

university (studiốrum) ūnivérsit•ās -átis *f*

unpleasant iniūcúnd•us -a -um

unprovoked ultrō

unrestrained effrēnắt•us -a -um, effū́s•us -a -um

unstable īnstábil•is -is -e

unsteady *(tottering)* cadū́c•us -a -um

unsubscribe *(comput)* cessắre

until *conj* dōnec

until *prep* ūsque ad (+ *acc*)

untrustworthy īnfī́d•us -a -um

up sūrsum; **up in the air** *(in uncertainty)* in médiō relíct•us -a -um; **be up in the air** *(to be undecided)* péndeō pendḗre pepéndī; **up till now** ántehāc

uphill *adj* acclī́v•is -is -e; **have an uphill struggle** clīvō labōrắre

uphill *adv* advérsus clīvum -is -e

uproar tumúlt•us -ūs *m;* **cause an uproar** tumultuắrī

upbringing ēducắti•ō -ốnis *f*

upholstery tōmént•um -ī *n*

ups and downs: he has his ups and downs eī modo bene, modo male est; **there are ups and downs** est modo sīc, modo sīc

upset *s* *(at the polls)* offénsi•ō -ốnis *f;* **suffer an upset** offēnsiốnem ferō ferre tulī lātus

upset *adj* commốt•us -a -um; **don't be upset** nōlī *(pl:* nōlī́te) perturbắrī

upset *tr* commóv•eō -ḗre commố vī commốtus, perturbắre

upsetting: that was more upsetting to me than to you illud mihi māiốrī stómachō erat quam tibi

upside down: everything was upside down ómnia erant sūrsum deórsum; **turn upside down** sūrsum deórsum versáre

upstairs *(direction)* sūrsum; *(position)* in superióre tabuláto; **go upstairs** scālīs *(or* per scālās) ascénd•ō -ere -ī; **the upstairs** dom•us -ūs *f* supérior

upstairs bedroom cubícul•um -ī *n* supérius

urge *s* ánimī ímpet•us -ūs *m*

urge *tr* úrg•eō -ére ursī

URL Ūniversále Rērum Locátr•um -ī *n,* īnscrípti•ō -ónis *f* interrētiális

use *s* **it's no use** ílicet; **what's the use?** quid opus est?

use *tr* ūtor ūtī ūsus sum (+ *abl); (e.g. a word in a sentence)* pónō pónere pósuī pósitus; **use "legō" in a sentence** pōne "legō" in senténtiā.

usual *adj* sólit•us -a -um; **you were wrong as usual** errábās ut solébās *(or* ex cōnsuetúdine tuā)

usually plērúmque

utter *adj* tōt•us -a -um

utter *tr* emítt•ō -ere ēmísī ēmissus, próferō próférre prótulī prōlátus; **she never uttered a word** nullum verbum ēmísit.

vacation vacáti•ō -ónis *f,* féri•ae -árum *fpl;* **at the end of vacation** fériīs peráctīs; **spend the vacation** fériās ágere; **summer vacation** fériae aestívae, vacátiō aestíva

vaccinate vaccīnáre

vaccination vaccīnáti•ō -ónis *f*

vaccine vaccín•um -ī *n*

vacuum cleaner púlveris haurītóri•um -ī *n*

valley vall•ēs *(or* vall•is) -is *f*

valuable pretiós•us -a -um; **be valuable** prétium habére

vampire sanguisúg•a -ae *m*

various vári•us -a -um

vary variáre

VCR videoexceptóri•um -ī *n*

veal vitulín•a -ae *f*

vegetable hol•us -eris *n* [*also collective for vegetables*]

vegetable garden hort•us -ī *m* holitórius

Veii Vēi•ī -órum *mpl*

veil vēl•um -ī *n*

vein vēn•a -ae *f;* **in a similar vein** ad símilem senténtiam

Venetian blinds trānsénn•a -ae *f* volúbilis; **open (close, let down, raise** aperíre, claúdere, dēmíttere, subvólvere)

venison vēnáti•ō -ónis *f*

verb *s* verb•um -ī *n*

verbal verbál•is -is -e

verdict senténti•a -ae *f;* **give a guilty verdict** condemnátóriam senténtiam ferō ferre tulī lātus; **give a verdict of acquittal** absolútóriam senténtiam ferre

vertebra vértebr•a -ae *f*

very ádmodum, valdē; **very good** óptim•us -a -um; **very good!** óptimē!; **very well!** *(in agreement)* fiat!

vestibule vēstíbul•um -ī *n*

veteran veterán•us -ī *m* (•a -ae *f),* ēmérit•us -ī *m* (•a -ae *f)*

veterinarian veterinári•us -ī *m* (•a -ae *f)*

veto *s* intercéssi•ō -ónis *f;* **interpose a veto** intercéd•ō -ere intercéssī

veto *tr* intercéd•ō -ere intercéssī (+ *dat)*

vice víti•um -ī *n,* prắvit•ās -ấtis *f; (tool)* retinắcul•um -ī n

victorious víct•or -ốris *m,* victr•īx -ícis *f;* **be victorious** vinc•ō -ere vīcī

victory victốri•a -ae *f;* **gain** (*or* **win**) **a victory** victốriam adipísc•or -ī adéptus sum; **gain** (*or* **win**) **a victory over the enemy** victốriam reportắre ab hoste

video cassette casét•a -ae *f* magnētoscópica; **listen to (play) a video cassette** aúd•iō -íre -ívī *or* -iī -ítus (ēvólv•ō -ere -ī) casétam magnētoscópiam

video cassette recorder (VCR) magnētoscópi•um -ī *n*

video game lūs•us -ūs *m* magnētoscópicus; **play video games** lūsūs magnētocópicōs lúdere

videotape taeníol•a -ae *f* magnētoscópica

vigorous álac•er -ris -re

villa vīll•a -ae *f*

village vīc•us -ī *m*

vinegar acét•um -ī *n*

vinegar bottle acētắbul•um -ī *n*

violence violénti•a -ae *f*

violent violént•us -a -um

violin fīdícul•a -ae *f,* violín•a -ae *f;* **play the violin** violínā canō cánere cécinī

violinist violīníst•a -ae *m* (•ria -riae *f*)

virtually propémodum

visit vīs•ō -ere -ī -us, vīsitắre; **go to visit, pay a visit to** vīsere

vitamin vitamín•um -ī *n*

vocabulary vocắbul•a -ốrum *npl,* cốpi•a -ae *f* verbốrum

vocative *s* vocātívus -ī *m,* cās•us -ūs *m* vocātívus

voice *s* vōx, vōcis *f; (of a verb)* gen•us -eris *n;* **what voice is "audímur"? passive** cúius géneris est "audímur"? passívī [NOTE—"genus," *in connection with nouns and adjectives means "gender," and in connection with verbs means "voice"*]

volleyball foll•is -is *m* volắtilis; *(game)* lūs•us -ūs *m* follis volắtilis; **play volleyball** folle volắtilī lúdere *(see Chapter V)*

volt vốlti•um -ī *n*

volunteer *s* voluntắri•us -ī *m* (•a -ae *f*); *(mil)* mīl•ēs -itis *mf* voluntắri•us (-a)

volunteer *intr (mil)* sponte nōmen dare; **volunteer to do s.th.** áliquid ultrō fácere

vomit vom•ō -ere -uī vómitum

vote *s* suffrắgi•um -ī *n;* **a vote was taken on his motion** *(in the senate by moving to one side of the chamber)* discéssiō facta est in eius senténtiam; **call for a vote** *(in the senate)* discessiốnem fácere; **cast a vote** suffrắgium ferō ferre tulī lātus; **give s.o. a vote of confidence** álicui cálculum album ferō ferre tulī lātus

vote *intr* suffrắgium ferō ferre tulī lātus; *(of a senator)* cḗns•eō -ére -uī; **vote for** suffrāgắrī (+ *dat);* **vote for s.o.'s motion** *(of an individual senator)* in alicúius senténtiam eō īre iī *or* īvī

voter suffrāgắ•tor -tốris *m* (•trīx -trícis *f*)

voting booth saept•um -ī *n*

vowel vocắl•is -is *f*

vulture vult•ur -uris *m*

waffle vāfl•um -ī *n*

wages merc•ēs -ḗdis *f;* **receive (fair, good, low, poor, unfair) wages** (aequam, magnam, parvam, iníquam) mercḗdem accípere; **pay wages** mercḗdem tríbu•ō -ere -ī

wagon carr·us -ī *m; (for agricultural purposes)* plaustr·um -ī *n*

wait exspectáre; **wait a minute, please!** manē, manē dum, quaesō!; **wait for** exspectáre (+ *acc*); **wait on** ministráre (+ *dat*)

waiter miníst·er -rī *m*

waiting room oec·us -ī *m* praestōlātórius

waitress minístr·a -ae *f*

wake up *tr* (ē somnō) excitáre ‖ *intr* expergísc·or -ī experréctus sum; ēvigiláre

walk *s (act)* dēambuláti·ō -ónis *f; (place)* ambulácr·um -ī *n;* **go for a walk** dēambuláre, dēambulátum eō īre īvī

walk *intr* ambuláre; **walk up and down** dēambuláre

wall mūr·us -ī *m; (inner or outer wall of a house)* páriēs, paríetis *m;* **walls** *(of a town)* moén·ia -ium *npl*

wall clock hōrológi·um -ī *n* parietárium

wallet pēr·a -ae *f*

wallop *(coll)* percolopáre

wallow volút·or -árī -átus sum

walnut iūgl·āns -ándis *f*

waltz *s* saltáti·ō -ónis *f* in gyrum

waltz *intr* saltáre in gyrum

want cúp·iō -ere cupívī cupítus; volō velle vóluī; **now what do you want?** quid nunc tibi vīs?

war (against *or* **with)** bell·um -ī *n* (contrā *or* advérsus (+ *acc*) *or* cum (+ *abl*); **be involved in a war** bellō implicárī; **bring a war to a successful conclusion** bellum cōnfíc·iō -ere cōnfécī cōnféctus; **carry on war with** bellum ger·ō -ere gessī gestus cum (+ *abl*); **cause a war** bellum móv·eō -ére mōvī mōtus; **civil war** bellum cīvíle *or* domésticum; **conduct a war** *(of a*

general) bellum administráre; **declare war on** bellum indíc·ō -ere indíxī indíctus (+ *dat*); **drag out a war** bellum trah·ō -ere traxī tractus; **end a war** bellum perfíc·iō -ere perfécī perféctus; **fight a war with** bellum ger·ō -ere gessī gestus cum (+ *abl*); **fight a war of aggression with** bellum *or* arma ultrō ínferō ínférre íntulī illátus (+ *dat*); **foreign war** bellum extérnum; **go off to war** proficísc·or -ī proféctus sum ad bellum; **go to war with** bellum ínferō ínférre íntulī illátus (+ *dat*); **guerilla war** bellum clandestínum; **in war** bellō, bellī témpore; **in war and in peace** páce bellóque; **offensive war** *(of war yet to be begun)* bellum ultrō ínferéndum; *(of war already begun)* bellum ultrō illátum; **prepare for war** bellum (com)paráre; **start a war with** bellum ín·eō -íre -ívī *or* -iī cum (+ *abl*); **stir up a war** bellum incitáre; **take part in a war** bellum capéss·ō -ere; **terminate a war by diplomacy** bellum compón·ō -ere compósuī compósitus; **wage war with** bellum ger·ō -ere gessī gestus cum (+ *abl*); **war against pirates** bellum pīráticum; **war against slaves** bellum servíle; **war is imminent** bellum ímminet *or* impéndet *or* ínstat; **war of extermination** bellum internecínum; **war breaks out** bellum exārdéscit

wardrobe *(place to keep clothes)* vestiári·um -ī *n; (clothes)* vestimént·a -órum *npl*

warehouse apothéc·a -ae *f*

wares merc·ēs -ium *fpl*

warfare bell·um -ī *n,* mīlíti·a -ae *f*

warship nāv·is -is *f* béllica

warm *adj (quite warm)* cálid·us -a -um; *(lukewarm)* tépid·us -a -um; *(fig)*

férvid•us -a -um; **it is getting warm**
tepéscit

warm *tr* calefácere, tepefácere

warm-hearted am•āns -ántis

warmly dressed spissīs véstibus
involút•us -a -um

warm-up exercitáti•ō -ónis *f*

wash *s* línte•a -órum *npl* lavánda

wash *tr* lav•ō -áre lāvī lautus **‖** *intr*
lavárī, sē laváre

washcloth drapp•us -ī *m* lavātórius

washer, washmachine máchin•a -ae *f*
lavātória

wasp vesp•a -ae *f*

waste *s (of time, money)* iactúr•a -ae *f*

waste *tr (time, effort)* perd•ō -ere pérdidī
pérditus; **I'm wasting my time**
frustrā tempus cónterō; **waste one's
breath** *(fig)* óperam pérdere; **waste
time and effort** labórem ac témpora
pérdere

waste basket scirpícul•us -ī *m* chartárius

watch *s* hōrológi•um -ī *n*

watch *tr (guard)* custód•iō -íre -ívī -ítus;
(observe) spectáre, observáre; **hey
you, watch out!** heus tū, cavē!

water *s* aqu•a -ae *f*

water *tr (flowers, etc.)* irrigáre

waterfall cataráct•a -ae *f*

watering can nassitérn•a -ae *f*

water pipe fístul•a -ae *f* aquária

water-ski *s* nart•a -ae *f* aquática *(see
Chapter V)*

water-ski *intr* per summās undās nartáre

watermelon pep•ō -ónis *m*

watt vátti•um -ī *n*

wax cēr•a -ae *f*

wax *tr* inceráre

wax paper chart•a -ae *f* cēráta

way *(road)* vi•a -ae *f; (route)* iter,
itíneris *n; (manner)* mod•us -ī *m;* **all
the way from** ūsque ab (+ *abl*)*;* **all
the way to** ūsque ad (+ *acc*)*;* **be a
long way off** longē distáre; **be in the
way** óbvi•us -a -um esse; *(to hinder)*
ob•stō -stáre -stetī; **be on the way to**
iter habére ad (+ *acc*)*;* **by the way**
óbiter; **by way of** viā (+ *gen*)*;* **get
out of the way!** Ápage!; **have it
your way!** estō ut lubet!; **have one's
own way** rēs prō arbítriō ger•ō -ere
gessī; **he must always have his own
way** semper faciéndum est quod vult;
**if it's not too much out of the way
for you** sī tibi nōn sānē dévium erit;
I'm in a bad way mihi male est; **in
the same way** eódem modō; **is that
the way you help me?** istócine pactō
mē ádiuvās?; **no way!** nullō modō;
on one's way inter viās; **what is the
quickest (best) way to ... ?** quae est
via brevíssima (óptima) ad (+ *acc*)?

weak īnfírm•us -a -um, imbecíll•us -a
-um, inválid•us -a -um; **weak
constitution** ténuis valetúd•ō -inis *f;*
weak voice exílis vōx, vōcis *f*

wealth dīvíti•ae -árum *fpl*

wealthy dív•es -itis

weapons *(offensive)* tēl•a -órum *npl;*
(defensive) arm•a -órum *npl*

wear ger•ō -ere gessī gestus, gestáre;
(wear regularly) ūtor ūtī ūsus sum (+
abl)*;* **wearing a belt** zōnā incínct•us
-a -um; **wear out** *(clothes, a person)*
cónter•ō -ere contrívī contrítus

weasel mustél•a -ae *f*

weather *s (good or bad)* tempést•ās -átis
f, cael•um -ī *n;* **kinds of weather**
tempestátēs; **owing to changes in the
weather** propter caelī varietátēs;
**beautiful (clear, cloudless, cloudy,
fine, foul, lousy, rainy) weather**

egrégia (clāra, sūda, nebulốsa serếna, foeda, spurca, pluviốsa) tempéstās

weather *tr* **weather the storm** procéllam dūrấre; *(fig)* rēs advérsās superấre

weather conditions tempestất·ēs -um *fpl*

weather forecast praenūntiấti·ō -ốnis *f* tempestấtis, praesấgi·um -ī *n* tempestấtis

weather report renūntiấti·ō -ốnis *f* tempestấtis

web rēt·e -is *n*

website sit·us -ūs *m* interrētiấlis

wedding *s* nū́pti·ae -ấrum *fpl*

wedding *adj* nūptiấl·is -is -e; **wedding day** di·ēs -ếī *m* nūptiấrum; **wedding gown** vest·is -is *m* nūptiấlis; **wedding present** nūptiấle dōn·um -ī *n;* **wedding reception** convī́vi·um -ī *n* nūptiấle

Wednesday di·ēs -ếī *m* Mercúriī

week hébdom·as, hebdốmadis *f,* septimấn·a -ae *f*

weekday di·ēs -ếī *m* prōfếstus

weekend fīn·is -is *m* hebdốmadis; **on the weekend** exeúnte hebdốmade

weekly hebdomadấl·is -s -e; **weekly newspaper** diấri·um -ī *n* hebdomadấle; **weekly wages** mer·cēs -cếdis *f* per síngulās hebdốmadēs solū́ta

weekly *adv (every week)* síngulīs hebdomádibus

weight lifting sublấti·ō -ốnis *f* pónderis

welcome grāt·us -a -um; **welcome!** advéntus tuus grātíssimus est! *or* salvē!

well *adv* bene, rēctē; **I am doing well** mihi bene est; **well done!** factum óptimē!; **well said!** facếtē dictum!

well *interj* em, immō, quīn; *(be it so)* estō; **well, well** enim vērō

well *adj* salv·us -a -um; **get well again** convalếsc·ō -ere convắluī

well-born honést·us -a -um

well-heeled bene aerất·us -a -um

well-mannered bene mōrất·us -a -um

well-off bene aerấtus -a -um

west óccid·ēns -éntis *m;* **in the west** ab occidénte; **to the west** in occidéntem versus [versus *is an adverb*]

west wind Zéphyr·us -ī *m*

western occidentấl·is -is -e

westward in occidéntem versus [versus *is an adverb*]

whack *(coll)* percolopấre

whale balaén·a -ae *f*

what quid, cū́ius; **what about me?** quid dē mē?; **what about the dough (money)?** quid dē argéntō?; **what a mess!** eu édepol rēs turbuléntās!; **what do you take me for? for a fool?** prō quō mē habēs? prō stultō?; **what else** quid ámplius; quid áliud; **what else can I do for you?** quid est quod tibi effícere possum ámplius?; **what for?** quam ob rem? *or* quā causā? **what is it?** *(what's the probem?)* quid est negốtī?; **what is it? out with it!** quid id est? cedo!; **what (is the trouble) now?** quid iam?; **what kind of** quấl·is -is -e; **what next?** quid deínde? **what sort of** quāl·is -is -e; **what's it to me how you ...** quid istuc ad mē áttinet, quōmodo tū (+ *subj)*?; **what's that?** *(what did you say?)* quid id est?; **what's that to you?** quid ad tē áttinet?; **what's the matter?** quid est?; **what's the reason why ...** quid est quod (+ *indic); **what's up?** quid reī est?; **what's wrong?** quid est?

whatever quidquid; **whatever!** quidvīs!

wheat trític·um -ī *n*

wheel rot·a -ae *f*

wheelbarrow pab·ō -ốnis *m*

wheelchair sell·a -ae *f* rotális

when *conj* cum, quandō, ubi, ut; *(interrog)* quandō?

whenever quandōcúmque, utcúmque, quótiēns, quotiēscúmque

where *(direction)* quō; *(position)* ubi; **from where** unde; **where are you from?** unde es?; **where on earth** ubi terrárum; úbinam géntium

while *s* **after a little while** paulō post; **a little while before** paulō ante; **a short while ago** paulō ante

while *conj* dum *(with pres indic to indicate an action going on in the past)*

while *tr* **while away the time** fall·ō -ere feféllī tempus

whimper *(of pups)* gánn·iō -íre

whip *s* flagéll·um -ī *n*

whip *tr* flagelláre; **whip out** ēríp·iō -ere -uī ēréptus

whipped cream crēm·um -ī *n* battútum

whipping: get a whipping vapuláre

whiskers vibríss·ae -árum *fpl*

whisky víschi·um -ī *n*

whisper *s* susúrr·us -ī *m*

whisper *tr & intr* sussuráre

whistle *s (sound)* síbil·us -ī *m; (pipe)* fístul·a -ae *f;* **blow the whistle** fístulā sibiláre; **final (starting) whistle** fīnális (initiális) síbilus *(see Chapter V)*

whistle *tr* **whistle a tune** fistulátō ōre can·ō -ere cécinī ‖ *intr* sibiláre; *(of the wind)* stríd·eō -ére -ī

white alb·us -a -um; *(shiny white)* cándid·us -a -um; **white bread** pān·is -is *m* cándidus

who quis, cūius; **who are you?** quis tū homō es?; **who is he (she)?** quis homō est?; **who is it? it's I.** quis homō est? ego sum; **who says so?** quis hoc dīcit factum?; **who the devil** quis malum

whoa! eho!

whole tōt·us -a -um, cūnct·us -a -um; **taken as a whole** in summam

wholesale magnári·us -a -um

wholesaler magnári·us -ī *m* (·a -ae *f*)

whole-wheat bread autopýr·us -ī *m*

why *(interj)* quīn; **why, this very day** quīn hódiē

why *(interrog)* cūr, quam ob rem, quā causā, quārē; **why is it that ...** quid est quod (+ *indic*); **why not?** *(challenging what has been said)* quid ita nōn? *(as an expression of assent: of course)* quíppinī? *or* quidnī?; **why say more?** quid plūra?; **why so? because ...** quid ita? quia ... ; **why the devil** cūr malum

wicked ímprob·us -a -um

wickedness impróbit·ās -átis *f*

wide lāt·us -a -um

widen *tr* dīlatáre ‖ *intr (of a country)* sē pand·ō -ere

width lātitúd·ō -inis *f;* **in width** in lātitúdinem

wife ux·or -óris *f*

wiff *s (slight smell)* od·or -óris *m; **get a wiff of** suból·eō -ére -uī

wig capillámént·um -ī *n*

wild *(animal)* fer·us -a -um; *(growing in the wild)* agrést·is -is -e; *(uncontrolled)* efferát·us -a -um

willing: be willing vol·ō velle vóluī

willy-nilly nōlēns volēns

wily dolṓs·us -a -um, súbdol·us -a -um, va·fer -fra -frum

win *s* victṓri·a -ae *f;* **a win on points** praevalénti·a -ae *f* pūnctṓrum

win *tr* vinc·ō -ere vīcī victus; *(office)* ádsequ·or -ī adsecū́tus sum, adipī́sc·or -ī adéptus sum; **win a battle** proéliō víncere; **win a bet** sponsiṓne víncere; **win a case in court** iudíciō víncere; **win over** (sibi) conciliā́re ‖ *intr* víncere; **win out** *(prevail)* paevál·eō -ḗre -uī

wind *(a clock, watch)* intén·dō -dere -dī -tus *or* -sus

wind vent·us -ī *m;* **head wind** ventus advérsus; **tail wind** ventus secúndus; **wind storm** procéll·a -ae *f;* **I got wind of it long ago** iam prīdem id mihi subolḗbat

winding flexuṓs·us -a -um; **winding route** ámbit·us -ūs *m*

window *(an opening for light and air, closed by shutters)* fenéstr·a -ae *f;* *(glass window)* fenéstra vítrea; *(comput)* fenestéll·a -ae *f*

window pane vitr·um -ī *n* fenéstrae, quadr·um -ī *n* vítreum

window seat sēd·ēs -is *f* fenestrális

windpipe artḗri·a -ae *f* áspera

windshield vitr·um -ī *n* antiāérium

windshield wiper vitritérgi·um -ī *n*

windy ventṓs·us -a -um

wine vīn·um -ī *n* (**dry** austérum; **sweet** dulce; **red** sanguíneum; **light** ténue; **white** album)

wine cellar cellári·um -ī *n* vīnárium

wine glass hýal·us -ī *m* vīnárius

wing *(of a bird, of an army)* āl·a -ae *f;* *(of a building)* lat·us -eris *n*

wink nictā́re; **wink at** nictā́re (+ *dat*)

winter *adj* hībérn·us -a -um

winter *s* hiem·s -is *f;* **at the beginning of winter** híeme ineúnte; **at the end of winter** híeme exeúnte; **because of the severity of the winter** propter híemis magnitū́dinem; **spend the winter** hiemā́re; **winter time** temp·us -oris *n* hiemā́le

wire fīl·um -ī *n*

wise guy! ímpudēns! **don't be a wise guy!** nē sīs ímpudēns!

wish *s* *(act of wishing)* optā́ti·ō -ṓnis *f;* *(object wished)* optā́t·um -ī *n;* **according to your wishes** secúndum voluntā́tem tuam; **I give you three wishes** trēs optātiṓnēs tibi dō

wish cúp·iō -ere -ī́vī -ī́tus, optā́re; **wish earnestly** exoptā́re

witch ságan·a -ae *f*, strig·a -ae *f*

witchcraft ar·s -tis *f* mágica

without sine (+ *abl*)

witness test·is -is *mf* (**for** prō + *abl;* **against** in + *acc*); **be called as a witness** contést·or -ā́rī -ā́tus sum; **trustworthy witness** testis lócuplēs *(gen:* testis locuplḗtis*) m*

wolf lup·us -ī *m*, lup·a -ae *f;* **wolves howl** lupī úlulant

wolf cub lupae cátul·us -ī *m*

woman múli·er -eris *f;* **old woman** an·us -ūs *f;* **young woman** muliércul·a -ae *f*

womb úter·us -ī *m;* *(belly)* ven·ter -tris *m*

wonder *s* **and no wonder** nec mīrum; **seven wonders of the world** septem mīrácula mundī

wonder *tr* mīr·or -ā́rī -ā́tus sum; **I wonder what's up** mīror, quid hoc sit negṓtī; **I wonder where he is** ubi sit dēmī́ror

wonderful (ad)mīrā́bil·is -is -e

wooden spoon cócle·ar -ā́ris *n* coquinā́rium

woodpecker pī́c·us -ī *m (see* **bird)**

woods silv·a -ae *f*

wool lān·a -ae *f*

woollen lā́ne·us -a -um

word *s* verb·um -ī *n; (gram)* dícti·ō -ṓnis *f;* [*Note*—In Roman grammars, "verbum" *is used only for "verb"*]; **break one's word** fidem frang·ō -ere, frḗgī; **give one's word** fidem dare; **in a word** bréviter, ad summam; **I want a word with you** paucīs tē volō; **keep one's word** fidem servā́re; **syllables form words** sýllabae fáciunt dictiṓnēs; **why should I take your word for it?** cūr tibi crḗdam?; **word for word** verbum prō verbō; **word of honor** fid·ēs -eī *f;* **words fail me** mihi verba dḗsunt; **you took the words right out of my mouth** tū quidem ex ōre ōrātiṓnem mihi ēripuístī

word processor *(comput)* prográmm·a -atis *n* ēditṓrium

wordy verbṓs·us -a -um

work lab·or -ṓris *m,* óper·a -ae *f; (piece of work, literary work)* op·us -eris *n*

work *tr (to exercise)* exérc·eō -ére -uī -itus; *(the soil)* col·ō -ere -uī cultus; *(a machine)* administrā́re ‖ *intr* labōrā́re, operā́rī; *(to function)* fung·or -ī fū́nctus sum

worker operā́ri·us *m (·*a -ae *f)*

workshop officī́n·a -ae *f*

world mund·us -ī *m; (earth)* orb·is -is *m* terrā́rum; **where in the world?** ubi terrā́rum?; **where in the world are we?** úbinam géntium sumus?; **worst**

poet in the world péssimus poḗta ómnium

world war bell·um -ī *n* mundā́num

World Wide Web (WWW) Tēl·a -ae *f* Tōtī́us Terrae (TTT)

worm verm·is -is *m; (earth worm)* lumbrī́c·us -ī *m*

worn out *(person)* fatigā́t·us -a -um; *(clothes)* trīt·us -a -um

worry cūr·a -ae *f,* sollicitū́d·ō -inis *f*

worry *tr* sollicitā́re ‖ *intr* sollicitā́rī; **don't worry!** nōlī *(pl:* nōlī́te) sollicitā́rī!

worse pēi·or -or -us; dētéri·or -or -us; *(more severe)* grávi·or -or -ius; **get worse** ingravésc·ō -ere; **make matters worse** rēs exasperā́re; **turn out for the worse** in pēiṓrem partem vertor vertī versus sum

worth: he's worth a lot of money dīvítiās máximās habet; **he's worth nothing** nihil est; **it isn't worth it** nōn est óperae prétium; **it's not worth all that** tantī nōn est

worthless inū́til·is -is -e; *(containing nothing of value)* inā́n·is -is -e; *(person)* nequam [*indecl*]

worthlessness inā́nit·ās -ā́tis *f*

worthwhile: it is worthwhile óperae prétium est

worthy (of) dign·us -a -um (+ *abl*)

wow! *(in shocked surprise)* vāh!; hui!; *(in astonishment)* papae!

wrap *s* amíct·us -ūs *m*

wrap *tr* invólv·ō -ere -ī involū́tus; **wrap up** obvólvere

wrapper involū́cr·um -ī *n*

wreath corṓn·a -ae *f*

wrestle luct·or -ā́rī -ā́tus sum *(see Chapter V)*

wrestler luctắt·or -ṓris *m*

wrestling luctắti·ō -ṓnis *f*

wrestling match certắm·en -inis *n* luctātiṓnis

wrinkle rūg·a -ae *f*

wrinkled rūgṓs·us -a -um

wrist prīmṓris man·us -ūs *f; ***sleeves reaching all the way to the wrists** mánicae prōlíxae ūsque in primṓrēs manūs

wrist bone carp·us -ī *m*

wrist watch hōrológi·um -ī *n* armillắre

write *tr* scrībō scríbere scrīpsī scrīptus; **write a program** *(comput)* prográmma compṓn·ō -ere compósuī compósitus; **write Latin** Latīnē scríbere

writer scrīpt·or -ṓris *m,* scrīptr·īx -ícis *f*

writing *(act)* scrípti·ō -ṓnis *f; (result)* scrīpt·um -ī *n,* scrīptū́r·a -ae *f;* **writings** scrīpt·a -ṓrum *npl*

writing paper chart·a -ae *f* epistulắris

wrong *adj (incorrect, mistaken)* fals·us -a -um; *(faulty)* vitiṓs·us -a -um; *(unfair)* iníqu·us -a -um; *(morally)* nefas *indecl;* **be wrong** errắre; **if I have done anything wrong, I'm sorry** sī quid pérperam fēcī, mē paénitet; **what's wrong with you?** quid est tibi? *or* quid est tēcum?

wrong *adv* pérperam

yard ắre·a -ae *f* domūs; *(measure)* uln·a -ae *f;* **back yard** ắrea postíca

yawn ōscitắre, hiắre

year: annus -ī *m; ***a hundred years from now** ad centum annōs; **at the beginning of the year** ineúnte annō, prīncípiō annī; **at the end of the year** exeúnte annō; **a year from now** ad annum; **every year** quotánnīs; **for a year** in annum; **in my twenty-first**

year annum prīmum et vīcésimum ag·ēns -éntis ego … ; **I wish you a happy New Year** Novum Annum laetum tibi exóptō; **last year** annō superiṓre; **the following year** próximus annus; **the previous year** supérior annus; **twice a year** bis (in) annō; **up in years** aetắte prōvéct·us -a -um

yearn for dēsīderắre

yell *s* ululắt·us -ūs *m; (in pain)* ēiulắti·ō -ṓnis *f*

yell *intr* ululắre; *(in pain)* ēiulắre

yellow flāv·us -a -um; **deep yellow** fulv·us -a -um; **pale yellow** lū́rid·us -a -um, gilv·us -a -um

yellowish subflắv·us -a -um

yes étiam, sānē, ita, immō; **I say yes; you say no** ego aiō; tū negās *(see Appendix I)*

yesterday herī; **the day before yesterday** núdius tértius [*adv, also written as one word*]

yokel rū́stic·us -ī *m* (·a -ae *f*)

you tū; *(pl:* vōs)

you see *(parenthetical)* enim, nam

young parv·us -a -um (nātū), párvul·us -a -um (nātū); **younger** iúni·or -or -us; min·or -or -us (nātū); **youngest** mínim·us -a -um (nātū)

young daughter fīlíol·a -ae *f*

young lady adulḗsc·ēns -éntis *f,* adulēscéntul·a -ae *f,* muliércul·a -ae *f*

young man adulḗsc·ēns -éntis *m; (between approximately the ages of 20 and 40)* iúven·is -is *m*

young son fīlíol·us -ī *m*

youngster adulēscéntul·us -ī *m* (·a -ae *f*)

your tu·us -a -um, vest·er -ra -rum

youth *(age)* adulēscénti·a -ae *f (between* puer *and* iúvenis, *between 15 and 30 years and even beyond); (young men collectively)* iuvént·ūs -ū́tis *f; (young person)* iúven·is -is *mf*

youthful iuveníl·is -is -e; íuven·is -is -e

zeal stúdi·um -ī *n*

zealous studiṓs·us -a -um

zero zer·um -ī *n*

zip code númer·us -ī *m* cursuắlis *(or* dīrēctṓrius)

zig-zag tortuṓs·us -a -um; **zig-zag streets** anfráct·ūs -uum *mpl* viắrum

zipper clausū́r·a -ae *f* tráctilis

zoo vīvắri·um -ī *n*